Clinical Textbook of Addictive Disorders
Second Edition

Clinical Textbook of Addictive Disorders

Second Edition

Edited by
RICHARD J. FRANCES
AND
SHELDON I. MILLER

THE GUILFORD PRESS
New York London

© 1998 The Guilford Press
A Division of Guilford Publications, Inc.
72 Spring Street, New York, NY 10012
http://www.guilford.com

Printed in the United States of America

This book is printed on acid-free paper.

Last digit is print number: 9 8 7 6 5 4 3 2 1

Library of Congress Cataloging-in-Publication Data

Clinical textbook of addictive disorders / edited by Richard J.
  Frances and Sheldon I. Miller.—2nd ed.
    p. cm.
  Includes bibliographical references and index.
  ISBN 1-57230-383-2 (hardcover : alk. paper)
  1. Substance abuse. 2. Alcoholism. I. Frances, Richard J.
II. Miller, Sheldon I.
  [DNLM: 1. Substance-Related Disorders—diagnosis. 2. Substance-
Related Disorders—therapy. WM 270C6416 1998]
RC564.C55 1998
616.86—dc21
DNLM/DLC
for Library of Congress   98-28510
                                                               CIP

Marsha, Jenny, Avram, and David
Sarah, Lynne, and David
We love you!

Contributors

Robert C. Abrams, MD, Associate Professor of Clinical Psychiatry, The New York Hospital–Cornell University Medical Center, New York, New York

George S. Alexopoulos, MD, Associate Professor of Clinical Psychiatry, Cornell University Medical College–New York Hospital, Westchester Division, White Plains, New York

Arthur I. Alterman, PhD, Professor of Psychiatry, University of Pennsylvania School of Medicine, Philadelphia, Pennsylvania

Judith S. Beck, PhD, Clinical Assistant Professor of Psychology in Psychiatry, University of Pennsylvania, Philadelphia, Pennsylvania; Director, The Beck Institute for Cognitive Therapy and Research, Bala Cynwyd, Pennsylvania

Sheila B. Blume, MD, CAC, Medical Director, Alcoholism, Chemical Dependency and Compulsive Gambling Program, South Oaks Hospital, Amityville, New York; Clinical Professor of Psychiatry, State University of New York at Stony Brook, Stony Brook, New York

Betty J. Buchan, PhD, DABFT, President, Final Analysis, Inc., Forensic Toxicology Consultants, Tampa, Florida

Oscar G. Bukstein, MD, Associate Professor of Psychiatry, Western Psychiatric Institute and Clinic, Pittsburgh, Pennsylvania

Ricardo Castañeda, MD, Associate Clinical Professor of Psychiatry and Director, New York University Medical Center, New York, New York

Leslie Chernen, PhD, Research Associate/Clinical Faculty, Center for Alcohol and Addiction Studies, Brown University, Providence, Rhode Island

Lisa A. Darton, MD, Medical Director, Outpatient Behavioral Health Services, Denver, Colorado

Stephen L. Dilts, MD, PhD, Clinical Professor of Psychiatry, University of Colorado Health Sciences Center, Denver, Colorado; Medical Director, Colorado Physician Health Program, Denver, Colorado

Lance M. Dodes, MD, Assistant Clinical Professor of Psychiatry, Harvard Medical School, Boston, Massachusetts; Faculty, Boston Psychoanalytic Society and Institute, Boston, Massachusetts

Caroline M. DuPont, MD, Director of Clinical Research, Institute for Behavior and Health, Inc., Rockville, Maryland; Vice President, DuPont Associates, P.A., Rockville, Maryland

Robert L. DuPont, MD, President, Institute for Behavior and Health, Inc., Rockville, Maryland; Clinical Professor of Psychiatry, Georgetown University School of Medicine, Washington, DC; DuPont Associates, P.A., Rockville, Maryland

Richard J. Frances, MD, President and Medical Director, Silver Hill Hospital, New Canaan, Connecticut; Clinical Professor of Psychiatry, New York University Medical School, New York, New York; Adjunct Professor of Psychiatry, University of Medicine and Dentistry of New Jersey, New Jersey Medical School, Newark, New Jersey

Hugo Franco, MD, Medical Director, Pollak Mental Health Services, Monmouth Medical Center, Long Branch, New Jersey

John Franklin, MD, Associate Professor of Psychiatry and Director, Addiction Psychiatry, Northwestern University School of Medicine, Chicago, Illinois

Marc Galanter, MD, Professor of Psychiatry and Director, Division of Alcoholism and Drug Abuse, New York University Medical Center, New York, New York

Deborah L. Haller, PhD, Associate Professor of Psychiatry, Internal Medicine and Anesthesiology, Virginia Commonwealth University, Richmond, Virginia

Anthony W. Heath, PhD, Senior Consultant, Heath Consultation Services, Lisle, Illinois

James M. Hill, PhD, Assistant Professor of Clinical Psychiatry, University of Medicine and Dentistry of New Jersey, New Jersey Medical School, Newark, New Jersey

Norman Hymowitz, PhD, Professor of Psychiatry, University of Medicine and Dentistry of New Jersey, New Jersey Medical School, Newark, New Jersey

Yifrah Kaminer, MD, Associate Professor of Psychiatry, University of Connecticut Health Center, Alcohol Research Center, Farmington, Connecticut

Lori D. Karan, MD, Assistant Adjunct Professor of Psychiatry and Medicine, University of California, San Francisco, California

Cheryl Ann Kennedy, MD, Assistant Professor of Psychiatry and Preventive Medicine and Community Health, University of Medicine and Dentistry of New Jersey, New Jersey Medical School, Newark, New Jersey

Edward J. Khantzian, MD, Clinical Professor of Psychiatry, Harvard Medical School at The Cambridge Hospital, Cambridge, Massachusetts; Tewkesbury Hospital, Tewkesbury, Massachusetts

Thomas R. Kosten, MD, Professor of Psychiatry, Yale School of Medicine, New Haven, Connecticut; Chief of Psychiatry, VA Connecticut Healthcare System, West Haven, Connecticut

David C. Lewis, MD, Professor of Medicine and Community Health, Donald G. Millar Professor of Alcohol and Addiction Studies and Director, Center for Alcohol and Addiction Studies, Brown University, Providence, Rhode Island

Bruce S. Liese, PhD, Professor of Family Medicine and Psychiatry, University of KansasMedical Center, Kansas City, Kansas

Marylinn Markarian, MD, Assistant Professor of Psychiatry and Medical Director, Addiction Services, University of Illinois at Chicago, Chicago, Illinois

Elinore F. McCance-Katz, MD, PhD, Associate Professor of Psychiatry, Yale School of Medicine, New Haven, Connecticut; Medical Director, Opiate Treatment Program, VA Connecticut Healthcare System, West Haven, Connecticut

James R. McKay, PhD, Assistant Professor of Psychology in Psychiatry, University of Pennsylvania, School of Medicine, Philadelphia, Pennsylvania

A. Thomas McLellan, PhD, Professor of Psychiatry, University of Pennsylvania School of Medicine, Philadelphia, Pennsylvania; Psychologist, Substance Abuse Treatment Unit, Philadelphia Veterans Affairs Medical Center, Philadelphia, Pennsylvania

Norman S. Miller, MD, Director of Addiction Medicine Services, Departments of Psychiatry and Internal Medicine, College of Human Medicine, Michigan State University, East Lansing, Michigan

Sheldon I. Miller, MD, Lizzie Gilman Professor and Chairman, Department of Psychiatry and Behavioral Sciences, Northwestern University School of Medicine, Chicago, Illinois

Robert B. Millman, MD, Saul P. Steinberg Distinguished Professor of Psychiatry and Public Health, Cornell University Medical College, New York, New York

Steven M. Mirin, MD, Medical Director, American Psychiatric Association, Washington, DC; Professor of Psychiatry, Harvard Medical School, Boston, Massachusetts

Edgar P. Nace, MD, Medical Director, Charter Dallas Behavioral Health System, Plano, Texas; Clinical Professor of Clinical Psychiatry, Southwestern Medical School, Dallas, Texas

Lisa M. Najavits, PhD, Assistant Professor of Psychology in Psychiatry, Harvard Medical School, Boston, Massachusetts; Associate Psychologist, McLean Hospital, Belmont, Massachusetts

Alexander E. Obolsky, MD, Instructor of Psychiatry and Director, Division of Forensic Psychiatry, Department of Psychiatry and Behavioral Sciences, Northwestern University Medical School, Chicago, Illinois

Charles P. O'Brien, MD, PhD, Professor and Vice Chairman of Psychiatry, University of Pennsylvania School of Medicine, Philadelphia, Pennsylvania; Chief of Psychiatry, Philadelphia Veterans Affairs Medical Center, Philadelphia, Pennsylvania

Patricia I. Ordorica, MD, Associate Professor, University of South Florida, College of Medicine, Tampa, Florida; Chief of Staff, Mental Health and Behavioral Sciences, Psychiatry Service, James A. Haley Veterans Affairs Medical Center, Tampa, Florida

Peggy J. Ott, PhD, Director of Training and Education, Center for Education and Drug Abuse Research, Western Psychiatric Institute and Clinic, University of Pittsburgh Medical Center, Pittsburgh, Pennsylvania

Steven J. Schleifer, MD, Professor and Chairman, Department of Psychiatry, University of Medicine and Dentistry of New Jersey, New Jersey Medical School, Newark, New Jersey

Sidney H. Schnoll, MD, PhD, Chairman, Division of Substance Abuse Medicine and Professor of Internal Medicine and Psychiatry, Virginia Commonwealth University, Richmond, Virginia

M. Duncan Stanton, PhD, Dean, School of Professional Psychology and Social Work, Spalding University, Louisville, Kentucky

Ralph E. Tarter, PhD, Professor of Psychiatry and Neurology, University of Pittsburgh School of Medicine, Western Psychiatric Institute and Clinic, Pittsburgh, Pennsylvania

Carlton E. Turner, PhD, Sc, President, Carrington Laboratory, Irving, Texas

Karl Verebey, PhD, DABFT, President and Director, Leadtech Corporation, North Bergen, New Jersey; Associate Professor of Psychiatry, SUNY Health Science Center at Brooklyn, Brooklyn, New York

Carol J. Weiss, MD, Clinical Assistant Professor of Psychiatry and Public Health, Cornell University Medical College, New York, New York

Roger D. Weiss, MD, Clinical Director, Alcohol and Drug Abuse Program, McLean Hospital, Belmont, Massachusetts; Assistant Professor of Psychiatry, Harvard Medical School, Boston, Massachusetts

Joseph Westermeyer, MD, MPH, PhD, Chief of Psychiatry Service, Minneapolis Veterans Administration Medical Center; Professor of Psychiatry and Adjunct Professor of Anthropology, University of Minnesota, Minneapolis, Minnesota

Preface

In the decade since we began work on the first edition of the *Clinical Textbook of Addictive Disorders,* there has been an explosion of knowledge about the treatment and biology of addiction. There has also been a change in the delivery of health care in general and in addiction treatment specifically. If nicotine addiction is included, addictive disorders are clearly the nation's and possibly the world's number one public health problem.

Approximately a quarter of all deaths can be attributed to nicotine and other substance-related causes. Approximately 55% to 90% of individuals with other psychiatric disorders smoke, 30% of the general population of the United States smokes, and 18% have a lifetime incidence of substance-related disorders (American Psychiatric Association, 1994). The direct and indirect costs of addictive disorders nationally, including health care, job loss, and effects on families, approximate a staggering $300 billion annually (American Psychiatric Association, 1995). The last decade has seen major developments in the understanding of biological mechanisms of addictions. Alan Leshner, the director of the National Institute of Drug Abuse, has called addiction a brain disease that is not just a brain disease but has psychosocial and cultural components as well. Addiction to all substances is a chronic relapsing disease of the brain that has its roots in a single, deep brain pathway in the mesolimbic system with an important role extending from the central tegmentum to the nucleus accumbens in reward systems that lead to compulsive drug-taking behavior at the expense of important social obligations (Leshner, 1997). Common brain effects of addictive substances suggest common brain mechanisms that underlie all addictions. Treatment aims at reversing these changes through medications and behavioral treatment, which also alter brain function. Other advances include better understanding of receptor mechanisms, the effects of substances on biological membranes, and the development of new pharmacological tools, such as naltrexone, that seem to reduce craving for alcohol. Evidence has grown for the effectiveness of addiction treatment, and refinements have been made in cognitive, behavioral, and psychodynamic methodologies. These changes are the focus of this volume. The integration of treatment approaches for patients with comorbid psychiatric and substance-related disorders has also enhanced treatment effectiveness and is another focus (Khantzian, 1997). Direct brain imaging through PET (positron emission tomography) scanning of brain areas related to cocaine addiction has led to better understanding of pervasive brain effects. The role of specific neurotransmitters such as dopamine and γ-amniobutyric acid, and ultimately the development of a better understanding of mechanism and patterns of genetic transmission will, in the next decade, further our understanding of the biological basis of addictive disorders (Koob & Le Moal, 1997).

Medical and psychiatric comorbidity associated with substance-related disorders now is included in virtually all medical school curricula and should be a part of every health care worker's armamentarium. An American Psychiatric Association position statement calls for strengthening substance abuse training during psychiatric residency (American Psychiatric Association, 1996; Kick et al., 1997). Even though approximately 1,100 psychiatrists have received Added Qualifications in Addiction Psychiatry and more than 24 residencies (fellowships) in addiction psychiatry have been ACGME (American College of Graduate Medical Education) approved, there is a shortage of psychiatrists knowledgeable about addictions. Psychiatric generalists with an understanding of addictions and addiction specialists still need to be trained.

The economics of health care delivery in the United States has shifted remarkably, and in many ways managed care has had more of an impact on the way substance-related disorders are treated than on many other illnesses. The high cost of health care in the late 1980s and early 1990s, especially the rapid growth of inpatient services to adolescents for all psychiatric diagnoses and to adults for addiction services, is among the factors that led to a search for a more efficient and cost-effective means of health care delivery. Hundreds of inpatient beds have been closed across the nation, and there has been a shift to outpatient treatment of addictive disorders, including detoxification, wherever possible. The recovering community and the treatment field continue to rely on Twelve-Step and other self-help programs (Alterman et al., 1994). However, evaluation and treatment should be professionally guided, and the use of Twelve-Step approaches should be an adjunct to rather than a substitute for a professionally directed treatment plan. Treatment programs are emphasizing briefer, more direct forms of treatment, such as cognitive-behavioral psychotherapy. Emphasis continues to be placed on group treatment, early identification, and prevention of addictive disorders (Beck, Wright, Newman, & Liese, 1993). Community-based models of care delivery for severely mentally ill substance abusers are increasingly being developed. There has been a shift toward decreased societal tolerance for drug dealing and drug-related behavior and an increase nationally in the prison population. Unfortunately, there is not a concomitant increase in availability of drug-related treatment in prisons. With continuing deinstitutionalization, populations of psychiatric patients who were formerly placed in state hospitals are now housed in community settings. Many of these patients have developed comorbid addictive disorders with a high prevalence of alcoholism, cocaine addiction, marijuana use, and heroin addiction. Homelessness, intravenous drug use, and prostitution have resulted in high rates of tuberculosis and human immunodeficiency virus infection (Frances, 1996).

The chapter authors who contributed to the first edition of the *Clinical Textbook of Addictive Disorders* included many prestigious clinicians, educators, writers, and researchers in the addiction field. This second edition has again tapped the original pool of talent and has added chapters on women, ethnicity, primary care, and forensic issues. The new volume should offer a comprehensive view of the addiction psychiatry field and be a convenient source of useful information for all health care clinicians. Psychiatrists, primary care physicians, psychologists, social workers, nurses, certified addiction counselors, psychiatric residents, and medical, nursing, social work, and counseling students will find this a useful reference and guide to addiction treatment. The fourth edition of *Diagnostic and Statistical Manual of Mental Disorders* (American Psychiatric Association, 1994), as well as advances in diagnosis, has made it more likely for general psychiatrists to recognize the role of substance-related disorders as part of a full diagnostic workup. A deeper understanding of epidemiology, pathophysiology, complications, and treatment outcome studies has expanded treatment choices. The updated chapters incorporate the latest developments in treatment guidelines, diagnostic issues, and consensus approaches to treatment based on a careful review of the research literature. The authors clearly state their opinions, which are sometimes divergent and reflect a rapidly developing and controversial field. Public interest in the need to prevent, diagnose, and treat alcohol and drug addiction waxes and wanes. The availability of quality care for addicted patients remains mercurial, and currently only a minority of patients receive a proper diagnosis and treatment for their illness. As in the first edition, the authors in this edition focus on clinically relevant material in an effort to avoid extensively detailed presentations of research data. Chapters are practical and present guidelines on how to best treat patients. Efforts have been made to achieve consistency and reduce redundancy, and the authors review and summarize developments with clarity and authority. This volume is the product of many who worked long and hard to update what was already a strong textbook. We want to thank our scholarly authors who were diligent, accommodating, wise, and tolerant of our revisions. We are indebted to Seymour Weingarten, Editor-in-Chief of The Guilford Press, whose constructive suggestions and keen insights enriched the book and make it more pleasant to read.

We are grateful to Rochelle Morrow, Elizabeth Lopato, and Veronica Jefferson, whose editorial expertise has been instrumental in the preparation of the manuscript. Additional thanks go to Allen Frances, MD, Ishier Jacobson, Sultan Niazi, Joseph Scavetta, MD, and Sheila Cooperman, MD, for their advice and support. Dina Lokets-Beischrot helped with references and Cathy Rehnberg also assisted in copy editing. We are grateful to the members of AAAP, American Academy of Addiction Psychiatry, who form an important body of consensus opinion about quality treatment practices. Our wives,

Marsha and Sarah, have been patient and helpful. We hope that our children, Jenny, Avram, David, Lynne, and David, will enjoy reading the text and be able to use it in their work. Finally, this volume has been improved by the suggestions of those who used and critiqued the first edition. We have also benefited from the comments of reviewers, who made us realize that this book has already played a role in improving patient care by providing clinician readers the necessary skills, attitudes, and knowledge about addictions. We remain fascinated by patients with addictive disorders and find no population more interesting, challenging, or rewarding to work with, or currently more underdiagnosed and undertreated.

RICHARD J. FRANCES, MD
SHELDON I. MILLER, MD

REFERENCES

Alterman, A. I., McClellan, A. T., O'Brien, C. P., August, D. S., Snider, E. C., Droba, M., Cornish, J. W., Hall, C. P., Raphaelson, A. H., & Schrade, F. (1994). Effectiveness and costs of inpatient versus day hospital cocaine rehabilitation. *Journal of Nervous and Mental Disease, 182,* 157–163.

American Psychiatric Association. (1994). *Diagnostic and statistical manual of mental disorders* (4th ed.). Washington, DC: American Psychiatric Press.

American Psychiatric Association. (1995). Practice guideline for the treatment of patients with substance use disorders: Alcohol, cocaine, opioids. *American Journal of Psychiatry, 152*(Suppl.), 5–59.

American Psychiatric Association. (1996). Position on training needs in addiction psychiatry (official actions). *American Journal of Psychiatry, 153,* 852–855.

Beck, A. T., Wright, F. D., Newman, C. F., & Liese, B. S. (1993). *Cognitive therapy of substance abuse.* New York: Guilford Press.

Frances, R. J. (1996). Schizophrenia and substance abuse. *Psychiatric Annals, 265*(8), 523–527.

Khantzian, E. J. (1997). The self-medication hypothesis of substance use disorders: A reconsideration and recent applications. *Harvard Review of Psychiatry, 4,* 231–244, 1997.

Kick, S. D., Morrison, M., & Kathol, R. G. (1997, July). Medical training in psychiatric residency: A proposed curriculum. *General Hospital Psychiatry, 19*(4), 259–267.

Koob, G. O., & Le Moal, M. (1997). Frontiers in neuroscience: the science of substance abuse. Drug abuse: Hedonic homeostatic dysregulation. *Science, 278,* 52–57.

Leshner, A. I. (1997). Addiction is a brain disease, and it matters. *Science, 278,* 45–47.

Contents

Clinical Textbook of Addictive Disorders
Second Edition

Part I

Overview and Historical Context

1

□

Addiction Treatment
Overview

RICHARD J. FRANCES
SHELDON I. MILLER

INTRODUCTION

What makes the treatment of addictive disorders so challenging and rewarding? First we review the challenges. Patients with addictive disorders can be difficult to diagnose and treat for a variety of reasons. Tailoring the correct treatment or combination of treatments that best fits a patient's needs is a difficult task. Patients, families, and employers are likely to deny problems for unconscious and conscious reasons, sometimes to avoid the stigma or label.

A careful assessment of patients with substance abuse requires a skillful, knowledgeable therapist with a positive attitude. Helping to motivate a patient to follow a treatment plan can be equally challenging (Prochaska & DiClemente, 1992). It can be difficult to separate the effects of intoxication and withdrawal from the chronic effects of substances. The interaction of medical and psychiatric problems can be masked or can mask an addictive disorder. It is important to help patients move from their goal, which is often to gain control or reduce the harmful effects of substance use and help them attain abstinence, prevent or reduce relapses, and obtain optimal levels of functioning for as long as possible (Kaufman, 1994). Setting priorities, timing, and targeting limited treatment resources to maximally improve patient function requires knowledgeable, skillful clinicians. The purpose of this volume is to expand the knowledge base of clinicians ranging from beginners to those experienced in treating addicted patients.

Clinicians are faced with decisions of which treatment or treatment combination can be most effective for each patient, the level of care, staging of treatment, and techniques to use to help motivate the patient (American Psychiatric Association, 1995). To provide quality care at a reasonable cost, administrative and programmatic means of achieving these objectives must be well designed, well integrated, and seamless. Helping patients maximize their motivation for abstinence, rebuild a substance-free lifestyle, develop healthy substitutions for addiction, improve family and job function, improve medical and psychiatric health, address spiritual issues, reduce harmful social impact, and prevent relapses are rewarding for the provider of care and the patient. We are in an era in which providers must take into account the scarcity of resources in planning treatment. Cost–benefit calculations and time constraints have become a necessary part of treatment planning as waystations to achieving patient abstinence and a substance-free lifestyle. Patients may lapse or relapse or have comorbid conditions. The therapist must roll with the punches, provide support, and be flexible and at the same time know when to confront the patient and when to apply boundaries and control.

TRENDS IN DIAGNOSIS

In the fourth edition of the *Diagnostic and Statistical Manual of Mental Disorders* (DSM-IV; American Psychiatric Association, 1994), the term "substance-related disorders" broadens the idea of substance abuse to include the unintentional use of a substance and medication side effects. DSM-IV does not limit the definition of substances to chemicals used to alter mood or behavior. Medications that can alter behavior (e.g., anticholinergics, antihistamines, and steroids) are classified under a different (or unknown) substance-related category. There is a distinction between substance use disorders, which include abuse and dependence, and substance-induced disorders, which include intoxication, withdrawal, delirium, dementia, amnestic, psychotic, mood, sexual dysfunction, anxiety, and sleep disorders. The criteria for substance dependence have not been altered in major ways. Clinicians must specify whether physiological dependence (i.e., tolerance and withdrawal) is part of substance dependence. These criteria are grouped together.

Idiosyncratic alcohol intoxication, which was listed in DSM-III-R, has been eliminated in DSM-IV because of a lack of empirical evidence to support this diagnosis. The centrality of using tolerance and withdrawal as key criteria of dependence has survived a number of revisions of the diagnostic schema. Neither tolerance nor withdrawal alone is necessary or sufficient for the diagnosis of substance dependence. Some individuals show compulsive use without tolerance and withdrawal. A compulsive pattern of substance use can characterize dependence without physiological dependence.

In DSM-IV, some course specifiers go from full remission through early partial remission, sustained full remission, and sustained partial remission. In DSM-IV, disorders that were formerly in a "psychoactive substance-induced organic mental disorders" section, such as substance-induced delusional disorder and substance-induced mood disorders, have been moved to sections with which they overlap phenomenologically. For example, substance-induced mood disorder is placed in the mood disorder section, increasing the likelihood of clinicians correctly labeling a mood disorder as connected to a substance-related problem.

Specific substance-induced disorders have a three-part name (e.g., cocaine, intoxication mood disorder with manic features), including the name of the substance occurring with intoxication, withdrawal, or beyond and the phenomenological presentation. These are found in the substance-related section and in the mood disorder section. In DSM-IV, an effort is made to more clearly distinguish the boundaries between nonpathological substance use, abuse, and dependence. Specific terms are used which define substance abuse and the influence of cultural and situation-specific factors that have an impact on the definition. Criteria related to social difficulties and use in hazardous situations are important in making a diagnosis of substance abuse (Franklin & Frances, 1996; Hales, Yudofsky, & Talbott, 1996).

Compared with other chronic illnesses, addictions are highly treatable and addiction treatment is a worthwhile medical endeavor. It is necessary for physicians to change their attitudes about treatment of addictive disorders and see these disorders as a category along with other disorders that require long-term or lifelong treatment. In their review of the literature, O'Brien and McLellan (1996) find addiction treatment to be as successful as the treatment of disorders such as hypertension, diabetes, and asthma. They find a success rate for alcoholism of approximately 50% (range: 40–70%); opiate dependence, 60% (range: 50–80%); cocaine dependence, 55% (range: 50–60%); and nicotine dependence, 30% (range: 20–40%). Typically, patients who comply with recommended regimens of education and counseling have typically favorable outcomes during treatment and longer-lasting posttreatment benefits. Of course, frustration exists when patients do not comply. Newer approaches are coming on line to improve motivation. Patients are often persuaded to enter treatment against their will by their family, employer, or physician.

Often there are challenges in dealing with fiscal constraints and legal sanctions which may make it difficult to provide quality treatment. Factors associated with lack of treatment compliance and relapse include low socioeconomic status, familial alcoholism, comorbid psychiatric conditions, and lack of family or social supports for continued abstinence.

Compliance with taking medications that are useful in treating opiate and alcohol dependence is also an important factor. The use of methadone, LAAM (levo-α-acetyl methadol), buprenorphine, and naltrexone for opiate patients and naltrexone and disulfiram for alcoholism are pharmacological treatments that have been well tested and effective (O'Brien & McLellan, 1996).

Success rates for treatment of addictive disorders vary with the population treated. Physicians or nurses with opiate problems have a positive prognosis, whereas street-addicted intravenous drug users with antisocial personality have poor treatment outcomes. Studies in North America, including one in

California, found that the benefits of alcohol and other drug treatments outweigh the cost of treatment by fourfold to twelvefold depending on the type of drug and the type of treatment (O'Brien, 1997b; Holder & Blose, 1986).

Although substance problems are among the most commonly encountered clinical diagnoses and many studies report high treatment effectiveness and cost benefit, a fraction of addicted people are diagnosed and treated. Fewer than 10% of addicted patients either are in self-help groups or receive professional treatment, and very few receive psychiatric evaluation. The field's major challenge is helping substance abusers to become motivated and to continue treatment. Addicted patients in primary care offices, emergency rooms, and general hospitals and those seen in consultation by social workers, teachers, and probation officers are often not diagnosed, confronted, or treated. Patients who have comorbid psychiatric disorders and medical problems are also not properly evaluated and treated because often a substance-related disorder has not been addressed (Ziedonis & Brady, 1997).

The training of physicians, nurses, social workers, and psychologists has often not led to the development of clinical skills, attitudes, and knowledge that are adequate and essential for evaluating and treating patients with substance abuse. The stigma associated with substance-related disorders affects the public's willingness to make treatment resources available. It can also cause treating staff to develop attitudinal problems. These attitudes can be altered by updating their skills and knowledge. The battle continues between a moral model—viewing addicts as having defects in character which require punishment—versus a medical model, in which addiction is viewed as a treatable illness with a biopsychosocial etiology, morbidity, mortality, and a clinical course.

There have been significant advances in medical education, certification, and accreditation regarding substance-related disorders. The American Board of Psychiatry and Neurology has approved Added Qualifications in addiction psychiatry and the psychiatry Residency Review Committee had given ACGMG accreditation to 24 programs by December 1997. Approximately 1,100 addiction psychiatrists achieved added qualifications by January 1998. However, more needs to be done to adequately train physicians and those in related health care disciplines to recognize and treat substance-related disorders. Although the treatment of substance-related disorders is taught in most U.S. medical schools, almost one-half of the nation's residency training programs in primary care specialties do not offer formal instruction (Graham, Altpeter, Emmitt-Myers, Parvan, & Zyzanski, 1996). Often there is no integrated, organized clinical experience which is reinforced throughout an educational process and which includes supervision by those experienced in treatment. Payers and consumers of health care are demanding quality, affordable, integrated behavioral health care, including services for substance-related disorders, and that physicians and other health care providers be competent to diagnose and treat these patients (Sirica, 1995).

MAGNITUDE OF THE PROBLEM

The Institute of Medicine suggests that approximately 5.5 million individuals, or 2.7% of the population of the United States over 12 years of age, clearly need drug treatment. An additional 13 million probably need treatment for alcohol use disorders. Two-thirds of alcoholics are male and one-third have a concurrent substance use disorder involving a drug other than alcohol (Institute of Medicine, 1990a).

Addictive disorders pose a dangerous threat to our nation's health, play a major role in crime and corruption, and lead to enormous direct and indirect costs. Both cheap and highly available, alcohol, tobacco, and illegal drugs are used and abused and lead to dependence. The lifetime incidence of alcohol and drug abuse approaches one-fifth of the population and has devastating effects on families and significant others. Estimates of direct and indirect costs are in excess of $300 billion annually (Institute of Medicine, 1990b).

Victims of accidents, homicide, and family violence add to the numbers of those adversely affected by addictive disorders (Institute of Medicine, 1990a). Drug use by teenagers increased 33% between 1994 and 1995 and 105% from a 10-year low in 1992, with 10.9% of teens having used illegal drugs the month before being surveyed. Since 1992, the use of marijuana among 12-year-olds to 17-year-olds rose 141% and the use of LSD (D-lysergic acid diethylamide) and other hallucinogens increased 183%. Cocaine use rose 166% from 1994 to 1995 (Folsom & Judkins, 1997). Between 1992 and 1995, emergency room (ER) cases associated with marijuana use rose 96%. ER cases associated with heroin use rose 58% during the same period (Greenblatt, 1997).

The myths, misinformation, and misunderstandings regarding addicted patients lead to avoidance of important issues and to stigmatization, which further contributes to denial, neglect, fear, and suffering. Addicts' behavior is labeled as entirely willful rather than part of a treatable illness. The recent emphasis on strict laws increases the danger of using addicts as scapegoats for society's problems rather than stressing that any individual may one day have to be rescued from an addictive disorder.

The frustration with inadequate antidrug campaigns has led a growing group of well-intentioned political and professional leaders to debate drug legalization (MacCoun & Reuter, 1997). They believe that legalization will remove the profit motive for illegal drug sales. However, most clinicians in the addiction field oppose legalization and feel that availability, use, abuse, and dependence will increase and dangerously exacerbate the problem (Kleber, 1994). Similar consequences followed the end of Prohibition in the 1930s. Direct results of increased cocaine use, for example, are widespread psychiatric and medical complications of addiction and more babies born affected by their mothers' cocaine use. The corrupting effects of cocaine on personality are increased if drugs are legally available. With legalization, incentives for drug treatment would probably decline, and more individuals would be trapped in an addictive cycle. Addiction to stimulants and opiates would be more prevalent.

Fortunately, the United States is not ready for legalization of drugs—the idea is impractical on clinical, political, and moral grounds. Proponents of legalization have been successful in passing laws allowing for medical uses of marijuana. The issue of medical uses of marijuana warrants further study; unfortunately it has been used by some as a Trojan horse for general legalization.

Efforts to stop drugs from entering the country and the current means of substance abuse treatment and prevention are not sufficient to reduce the problem. Considerable attention should be paid to research to find new and more effective means of addressing prevention and treatment. The price of ignoring and forgetting the high social costs of addiction, which can come from an overzealous effort to cut treatment costs, can be a rise in substance abuse, particularly by youth.

GENERAL TREATMENT ISSUES

The phases of treatment for patients with substance-related disorders include comprehensive psychiatric and physical assessment, treatment of intoxication and withdrawal, and the formulation and implementation of an overall treatment strategy (Kaufman, 1994). Both drug-free and substitution strategies of treatment along with psychotherapy have been successfully applied to opiate addiction (Woody, McLellan, Luborsky, & O'Brien, 1995); however, the ultimate goal of abstinence only with regard to abusable drugs is recommended for all other substances of abuse. Along with psychosocial treatments, specific medications such as naltrexone for alcohol are used to reduce craving. Other psychotropic medications, most notably antidepressants and antipsychotic agents, are used in combination with psychosocial treatments to treat associated psychiatric and medical conditions. Treatment goals include abstinence, reduction and prevention of relapses with the aim of reducing the frequency and severity of relapse, and the improvement of psychological functioning (American Psychiatric Association, 1995).

In addition to assessing the patient's general and medical history and physical examination, the practitioner should evaluate the use of substances and evaluate their effects on physical and mental functioning. An essential part of the workup is evaluating old records and collateral sources of information, such as a family and social history which provide a history of prior psychiatric treatments and outcomes. The screening of blood, breath, hair, or urine for abused substances and other laboratory tests confirm the presence of comorbid conditions which are frequently associated with substance use disorders. It is necessary that the clinician establish and maintain the therapeutic alliance with regular visits to monitor the patient's clinical status. The physician must manage intoxication and withdrawal states, gain the patient's cooperation and motivation to follow the treatment plan, prevent relapses, reduce complications, and provide education about substance use disorders. A team approach integrating substance-related treatments with other treatments produces the best environment in which to provide services, especially to patients with comorbid psychiatric and physical problems. Frequently, specific pharmacological and psychosocial treatment approaches are used for intoxication, withdrawal, reduction of craving, and reduction of reinforcing effects of substances and unpleasant reactions. Psychosocial treatments often have cognitive–behavioral, behavioral, psychodynamic, and interpersonal components. Psychosocial treatments can be individual, group, family, and self-help oriented. The formulation of a treatment plan includes psychiatric management, setting of treatment goals (e.g., abstinence and prevention of relapses), efforts to increase motivation and improve functioning, and integrating treatment approaches for comorbid conditions (American Psychiatric Association, 1995).

TREATMENT SETTINGS

The past few years have seen a major shift to outpatient detoxification, organized outpatient treatment programs (both evening and day), office care, and referral to Twelve-Step self-help treatment (Alterman et al., 1994). Patients are seen in general hospitals, psychiatric hospitals, residential treatment facilities, partial hospitals, organized outpatient programs, and office practices. There is continuing debate about the criteria for the use of inpatient facilities. Depending on which set of criteria is used, different criteria and standards emerge. Many of the managed care companies use their own standards, and groups such as American Society of Addiction Medicine have created sets of criteria for determining treatment settings (American Society of Addiction Medicine, 1996). These criteria for hospitalization include the following:

- Drug overdose requiring inpatient treatment.
- Risk for severe or medically complicated withdrawal.
- Comorbid general medical conditions or psychiatric conditions, including high suicidality, that would impair the ability to participate, comply, or benefit from treatment or would require inpatient care.
- A history of not stopping use after being treated in a less intensive residential or outpatient setting.
- Use of substances and behavior considered to be an acute danger to the patient.
- The substance use disorder poses an ongoing threat to the patient's physical and mental health.

Many in the field feel that residential programs should be used when patients cannot maintain abstinence in an outpatient setting and when they do not meet the criteria for hospitalization. When they are capable of refraining from use of substances, outpatient detoxification and partial hospitalization are indicated. Partial hospitalization can be an alternative to hospitalization or can be used as aftercare for patients who have been hospitalized. Gradations from organized outpatient treatment to a partial hospital program are available, and a less intensive outpatient treatment is recommended for patients who do not require a more intensive level of care. Seamless integrated systems of care, where patients can move between levels with a minimal disruption of treatment, are optimal. The duration of treatment in a system varies from several days to weeks to months to several years.

Studies show that a majority of patients treated for substance dependence eventually abstain from using substances or experience brief substance use that does not progress to substance abuse or dependence (O'Brien, 1997a). Clearly, social support and other psychosocial and economic factors affect this statement. A minority of patients experience a pattern of chronic relapse requiring repetitive intervention (Leshner, 1997). Those who maintain abstinence for more than 2 years are highly likely to remain free for 10 years. Approximately one-third of hospitalized psychiatric patients manifest comorbid, nonnicotine substance abuse disorders (Kessler et al., 1997).

MAJOR TRENDS

Major trends in the field include the following:

1. Increased knowledge and information about etiology, pathophysiology, epidemiology, clinical course, and treatment outcome of addictive disorders.
2. Use of structured interviews, laboratory tests, and computer-based rating instruments that can better screen, diagnose, refer patients, and customize addiction treatment.
3. Putting greater knowledge in the hands of primary care specialists regarding screening, diagnosis, and treatment of addictive disorders.
4. Increasing the number of addiction experts who have completed fifth-year residencies and received added qualifications in addiction psychiatry.
5. Increased effort at quality improvement and providing integrated treatment approaches for patients with comorbid addiction, psychiatric, and medical comorbidity.
6. A widening distribution of knowledge shared by patients and their families.
7. Increased attention to cost-effectiveness.
8. Increased partnership among the medical community, lay advocacy groups, and Twelve-Step self-help programs.
9. Efforts to have "one-stop shopping" in outpatient and organized outpatient treatment programs to contain costs by limiting inpatient care.

10. More rapidly available information about changes in the epidemiology and patterns of use.
11. Greater efforts at prevention at the level of school, family, mass media, and medical screening programs.
12. Increased use of team and community outreach programs requiring close communication among disciplines.
13. An increase in managed and capitated forms of care, with cost containment.
14. An increase in basic and clinical research targeted at the development of new pharmacological approaches to counter the negative effects of drugs and reduce craving.
15. Increased peer review quality assurance efforts to remove abuses in the field.
16. An increase in the development of specific cognitive-behavioral approaches with measured clinical outcomes.

Perhaps the largest challenge to the treatment community and to the patients suffering from addictive disorders is the advent of managed care and its impact on the treatment system. As is often true with new payment approaches, there are those in the field who are ethical and interested not only in the economics of the treatment system but in the quality of care rendered to the patient. Unfortunately, there are great potential profits for the unscrupulous managed care companies that will maximize their profits without concern for the well-being of the patient. Ethics do not seem dependent on the size of the company and unethical companies appear from among the largest as well as the smallest companies. Responsible insurers similarly come from all parts of the size continuum.

The impact of the best of managed care has been viewed by some as a detriment to the field and by others as initiating changes that are long overdue (Schreter, Scharfstein, & Schreter, 1997). Clearly the changes have made us rethink the role of different settings in the care of the patient. We have been forced to ask hard questions (about the relative value of many of our treatments and to begin to measure in a routine way the outcomes of our treatment approaches. We have also become more sensitive to the consumer needs of patients and their families. Less intensive and less expensive settings for the care of patients are being used more often and there is reason to believe that this is occurring without a major decrease in the quality of care or in the long-term outcome for the patient. Much of this remains to be proven by outcome studies that are in progress. For the moment, however, it is clear that there is and will be a continuing need to keep costs under control and to carefully measure the effect of those treatments that we administer to people with substance use disorders. Managed care and health care reform in general are here to stay. The form and content may change and ideally there will be improved monitoring of the payers, but the fact of change is firm. The task for the future is to continue to improve treatment while maintaining a concern for the cost of that treatment and the way in which it is delivered. The pressures from the economy are for increasing efficiency and effectiveness with a growing tendency for payers to gravitate toward providers who are part of groups and who truly practice within a multidisciplinary and multidimensional format.

Although there is a tendency to mourn the loss of what was, we need instead to rise to the challenge of what is and what will be. There is a great opportunity to be innovative and to advance the treatment of addictive disorders. Data and not impression will become the rule of the day. Although the pressure may be coming from the economic side of care, the result may yet be beneficial for the patient and the provider.

REFERENCES

Alterman, A. I., McClellan, A. T., O'Brien, C. P., August, D. S., Snider, E. C., Droba, M., Cornish, J. W., Hall, C. P., Raphaelson, A. H., & Schrade, F. (1994). Effectiveness and costs of inpatient versus day hospital cocaine rehabilitation. *Journal of Nervous and Mental Disease, 182,* 157–163.

American Psychiatric Association. (1994). *Diagnostic and statistical manual of mental disorders* (4th ed.). Washington, DC: Author.

American Psychiatric Association. (1995). Practice guideline for the treatment of patients with substance use disorder: Alcohol, cocaine, opioids. *American Journal of Psychiatry, 152*(Suppl.), 5–59.

American Society of Addiction Medicine. (1996). *Patient placement criteria for the treatment of substance-related disorders* (2nd ed.). Chevy Chase, MD: Author.

Folsom, R. E., & Judkins, D. R. (1997). *Model based estimates from the 1991–1993 National Household Surveys on Drug Abuse: Methodology report.* Rockville, MD: Department of Health and Human Services, Substance Abuse and Mental Health Services Administration.

Franklin Jr., J. E., & Frances, R. J. (1996). Substance-related disorders. In J. R. Rundell & M. G. Wise (Eds.), *Textbook of consultation-liaison psychiatry* (pp. 428–429). Washington, DC: American Psychiatric Press.

Graham, A. V., Altpeter, M., Emmitt-Myers, S., Parran, N., & Zyzanski, S. (1996). Teaching faculty about substance abuse: Evaluating clinical competence and professional development. *Substance Abuse, 17*(3), 139–150.

Greenblatt, J. (1997). *Mid-year preliminary estimates from the 1996 drug abuse warning network/G.* Rockville, MD: Department of Health and Human Services, Substance Abuse and Mental Health Services Administration, Office of Applied Studies.

Hales, R. E., Yudofsky, S. C., & Talbott, J. A. (Eds.). (1996). *The American Psychiatric Press textbook of psychiatry* (2nd ed.). Washington, DC: American Psychiatric Press.

Holder, H. D. & Blose, J. O. (1986). Alcoholism treatment and total health care utilization and costs: A four-year longitudinal analysis of federal employees. *Journal of the American Medical Association, 256*(11), 1456–1460.

Institute of Medicine. (1990a). *Broadening the base of treatment for alcohol problems.* Washington, DC: National Academy Press.

Institute of Medicine. (1990b). A study of the evolution, effectiveness and financing of public and private drug treatment systems. In D. R. Gerstein & H. J. Harwood (Eds.), *Treating drug problems* (Vol. 1). Washington, DC: National Academy Press.

Kaufman, E. (1994). *Psychotherapy of addicted persons.* New York: Guilford Press.

Kessler, R. C., Crum, R. M., Warner, L. A., Nelson, C. R., Schulenberg, J., & Anthony, J. C. (1997). Lifetime co-occurrence of DSM-III-R alcohol abuse and dependence with other psychiatric disorders in the National Comorbidity Survey. *Archives of General Psychiatry, 54,* 313–321.

Kleber, H. (1994). Our current approach to drug abuse: Progress, problems, proposals. *New England Journal of Medicine, 330,* 361–365.

Leshner, A. I. (1997). Addiction is a brain disease, and it matters. *Science, 278,* 45–47.

MacCoun, R., & Reuter, P. (1997). Interpreting Dutch cannabis policy: Reasoning by analogy in the legalization debate, *Science, 2,* 78.

O'Brien, C. P. (1997a). Progress in the science of addiction. *American Journal of Psychiatry, 154,* 1195–1197.

O'Brien, C. P. (1997b). A range of research-based pharmacotherapies for addiction. *Science, 278,* 66–69.

O'Brien, C. P., & McLellan, A. T. (1996). Myths about the treatment of addiction. *Lancet, 347,* 237–240.

Prochaska, J. O., DiClemente, C. C., & Norcross, J. C. (1992). In search of how people change: Applications to addictive behavior. *American Psychologist, 47,* 1102–1114.

Schreter, R. K., Sharfstein, J. S., & Schreter, C. A. (1997). *Managing care not dollars.* Washington, DC: The Continuum of Mental Health Services, APPI Press.

Sirica, C. M. (1995). *Training about alcohol and substance for all primary care physicians.* New York: Josiah Macy, Jr., Foundation.

Woody, G. E., McLellan, A. T., Luborsky, L., & O'Brien, C. P. (1995). Psychotherapy in community methadone programs: A validation study. *American Journal of Psychiatry, 152,* 1302–1308.

Ziedonis, D., & Brady, K. (1997). Dual diagnosis in primary care: Detecting and treating both the addiction and the mental illness. In J. H. Samet, P. G. O'Connor, & M. D. Stein (Eds.), *The medical clinics of North America: Alcohol and other substance abuse* (Vol. 81, pp. 1017–1036). Philadelphia: Saunders.

2

Historical and Social Context of Psychoactive Substance Disorders

JOSEPH WESTERMEYER

INTRODUCTION

Historical and social factors are key to the understanding of addictive disorders. These factors affect the rates of addictive disorders in the community, the types of substances abused, the characteristics of abusers, the course of these disorders, and the efficacy of treatment. Knowledge of these background features helps in understanding the genesis of these disorders, their treatment outcome, and preventive approaches.

Psychoactive substances subserve several human functions that can enhance individual as well as social existence. On the individual level, desirable ends include the following: relief of adverse mental and emotional states (e.g., anticipatory anxiety before battle and social phobia at a party), relief of physical symptoms (e.g., pain and diarrhea), stimulation to function despite fatigue or boredom, and "time out" from day-to-day existence through altered states of consciousness. Socially, alcohol and drugs are used in numerous rituals and ceremonies, from alcohol in Jewish Passover rites and the Roman Catholic Mass, to peyote in the Native American Church and the serving of opium at certain Hindu marriages. To a certain extent, the history of human civilization parallels the development of psychoactive substances (Westermeyer, 1992).

Paradoxically, these substances that bless and benefit our existence can also torment and decivilize us. Individuals, societies, and cultures began learning this disturbing truth at least a few and possibly several millennia ago. We continue to rediscover this harsh reality today and tomorrow, as though each new generation must learn afresh for itself. As our societies become more complex, so too do our psychoactive substances, our means of consuming them, and the problems associated with them. Preventive and treatment efforts, also age-old and wrought at great cost, are our forebears' gifts to us for dealing with psychoactive substance use gone astray (Anawalt & Berdan, 1992).

HISTORY AND ORIGINS

Prehistory

Methods for the study of psychoactive substance use disorders through time and space include the archaeological record, anthropological studies of time, preliterate societies, and the historical record. Archaeological data document the importance of alcohol commerce in late prehistorical and early historical times, both in the Mediterranean (where wine vessels have been discovered in numerous shipwrecks) and in China (where wine vessels have been found in burial sites). Poppy seed caches have been recorded in a prehistoric site in northern Turkey. Incised poppy capsules have been noted in the prehistoric headdresses of Cretan goddesses or priestesses, indicating an early awareness of opium harvest methods. Availability of carbohydrate in excess of dietary needs, fostered by neolithic farming technology and animal husbandry, probably permitted sporadic cases of alcohol abuse (Westermeyer, 1992).

Anthropological studies of preliterate societies have shown the almost universal use of psychoactive substances. Tribal and peasant societies of North and South America focused on the development of stimulant drugs (e.g., coca leaf, tobacco leaf, and coffee bean) and numerous hallucinogenic drugs (e.g., peyote). Hallucinogens in particular were used for ritual purposes, and stimulant drugs were used for such secular purposes as hard labor or long hunts. New World peoples discovered diverse modes of administration, such as chewing, nasal insufflation or "snuffing," pulmonary inhalation or "smoking," and rectal clysis (DuToit, 1977). African and Middle Eastern ethnic groups produced a smaller number of stimulants, such as qat, and hallucinogens, such as cannabis (Kennedy, Teague, & Fairbanks, 1980). Groups across Africa and the Eurasian land mass specialized in obtaining alcohol from numerous sources, such as honey, grains, tubers, fruits, and mammalian milk. Certain drugs were also used across vast distances, such as opium across Asia and the stimulant sedative combination betel-areca across South Asia to Oceania. Of interest is the fact that Old World peoples primarily consumed drugs by ingestion prior to Columbus's travel to the New World; nasal insufflation, smoking, and clysis were not known (Westermeyer, 1991).

Early History

Historical records of alcohol, opium, and other psychoactive substances appear with the earliest Egyptian and Chinese writings. Opium was described as an ingested medication in these first documents, especially for medicinal purposes. Mayan, Aztec, and Incan statues and glyphs indicated drug use for ritual reasons (Furst & Coe, 1977; Anawalt & Berdan, 1992). Medieval accounts recorded traditional alcohol and drug use. Travelers of that era often viewed use patterns in other areas as unusual, aberrant, or problematic; examples include reports of Scandinavian "beserker" drinkers by the English and reports by Crusaders of Islamic military units or "assassins" intoxicated on cannabis. Along with animal sacrifice and the serving of meat, the provision of alcohol, betel, opium, tobacco, or other psychoactive substances came to represent hospitality or to have cultural, ritual, or religious symbolism (Smith, 1968). Affiliation with specific ethnic groups, social classes, sects, and castes came to be associated with consumption of specific psychoactive substances. For example, one group in India consumed alcohol but not cannabis, whereas an adjacent group consumed cannabis but not alcohol (Carstairs, 1954). Cultural change may be signaled by altered patterns of psychoactive usage (Caetano, 1987). Religious as well as ethnic identity may be tied to alcohol or drug consumption. For example, wine is a traditional aspect of Jewish, Catholic, and certain other Christian rituals and ceremonies, whereas Islam and fundamentalist Christian sects prohibit alcohol drinking. In addition to distinguishing people from one another, substance use may serve to maintain cooperation and communication across ethnic groups, as Heath (1971) observed in Bolivia.

Culture and Social Change

In recent centuries, political, commercial, and technical advances have modified the types, supply, cost, and availability of psychoactive substances, along with modes of administration (Westermeyer, 1992). International commerce, built on cheaper and more efficient transportation, and increasing income have fostered drug production and distribution. Increasing disposable income has resulted in greater recreational intoxication (Caetano, Suzman, Rosen, & Voorhees-Rosen, 1983). Development of parenteral injection for medical purposes was readily adapted to recreational drug self-administration in the mid-1800s, within several years of its invention. Purification and modification of plant compounds (e.g., cocaine from the coca leaf, morphine and heroin from opium, and hashish oil from the cannabis plant) produced substances that were both more potent and more easily smuggled and sold illicitly. Laboratory synthesis has led to new drugs (e.g., the stimulant amphetamines, the sedative barbiturates and benzodiazepines, the opioid fentanyl, and the hallucinogen phencyclidine) that are more potent and often cheaper than purified plant compounds.

Historical and cultural factors may theoretically affect the pharmacokinetics and pharmacodynamics of psychoactive substance, just as the pharmacology of these substances may affect their historical and traditional use. A case in point is the flushing reaction observed among a greater-than-expected number of Asians and Native Americans (but neither universal in these peoples, nor limited to them). Absence of alcohol among the northern Asian peoples who subsequently peopled much of East Asia and the Americas is a likely explanation, but the exact reason is unknown. Of interest to epidemiologists, the flushing reaction has been promulgated as a reason for two opposite phenomena:

1. The low rates of alcoholism among Asian peoples, who presumably find the reaction aversive and hence drink little—although rates are increasing across much of Asia (Johnson & Nagoshi, 1990).
2. The high rates of alcoholism among certain Native American groups, who presumably must "drink through" their flushing reaction to experience other alcohol effects (Becker, Wiggins, Key, & Samet, 1992; Gallagher, Fleming, Berger, & Sewell, 1992).

Flushing may also be more or less desirable, depending upon how the culture values this biological effect. Among many East and Southeast Asian peoples influenced by Buddhist precepts, flushing is viewed as the emergence of cupidity or rage and the loss of control. Native Americans do not have the same attitude toward flushing. Modal differences in alcohol metabolism have also been observed among ethnic groups, and these differences support arguments in favor of biological causation. However, the intraethnic differences in alcohol metabolism greatly exceed the interethnic differences (Fenna, Mix, Schaefer, & Gilbert, 1971). Large sample sizes can also lead to the so-called Meehl effect, in which small and unimportant but statistically significant differences frequently result. Despite some minimal pharmacokinetic differences among people of different races, the observed differences appear to be more due to pharmacodynamics. That is, the influence of people vis-à-vis the drug (i.e., their traditions, taboos, expectations, and patterns of use) appears to exert greater influence than the drug vis-à-vis the people (e.g., rates of absorption and catabolism and flushing reactions). It may be that both pharmacodynamic and pharmacokinetic factors are simultaneously in operation but in ways not yet well understood.

As psychoactive substance use phased into substance abuse in many advanced civilizations, social and cultural means evolved to control usage. One method was law and law enforcement. Aztecs utilized this method in pre-Columbian times to limit the frequency and amount of drinking (Anawalt & Berdan, 1992). Later, in the post-Columbian period, England countered its "gin plague" with a tax on imported alcohol-containing beverages (Thurn, 1978) and its later "opium epidemic" with prescribing laws (Kramer, 1979). Another method has been religious stricture. Early in the Buddhist religious movement, abstinence from alcohol was recommended as a means of quitting earthly bondage to achieve contentment in this life and eternal nirvana after death. Islam became the second great religion to adopt abstinence from alcohol, reportedly when a town was sacked as a result of a drunken nighttime guard. The gin plague in England spawned several abstinence-oriented Christian sects, despite the earlier status of wine as a Christian sacramental substance (Johnson & Westermeyer, in press). The Church of Jesus Christ of Latter-Day Saints (the group popularly known as the Mormans) forbids any use of psychoactive substances, including caffeine and nicotine.

In addition to religion as a preventive measure, religion has also served as a therapy for psychoactive substance abuse. Native Americans and Latin Americans, plagued with high rates of alcoholism, have joined fundamentalist Christian sects as a means of garnering social support while resisting peer pressures to drink (Mariz, 1991). Many Native Americans have joined the Native American Church, in which peyote is a sacramental substance but alcohol is proscribed (Albaugh & Anderson, 1974).

Patterns of Psychoactive Substance Use

Traditional patterns of psychoactive substance use in most societies were episodic, coming at times of personal celebrations (e.g., birth and marriage), rituals (e.g., arrivals, departures, and changes in status), and seasonal celebrations (e.g., harvest and New Year). Exceptions to this pattern were daily or at least occasional use of alcohol as a foodstuff and use of various stimulants (e.g., betel-areca, tea and coffee, and coca leaf) in association with long, hard labor (e.g., paddy rice or taro farming and silver mining). Daily beer or wine drinking was limited to Europe, especially the para-Mediterranean wine countries and central grain-beer countries. Such daily or "titer" use is not without its problems, even when socially sanctioned. Although binge-type alcohol problems (e.g., delirium tremens, fights, and falls) were and are rare, hepatic cirrhosis and other organ damage may result from daily use of more than 2 to 4 ounces of alcohol, depending on body weight (Baldwin, 1977). Daily use of stimulants, especially if heavy or addictive, can lead to biomedical or psychosocial problems, such as oral cancers in the case of betel-areca chewing (Ahluwalia & Ponnampalam, 1968) or psychobehavioral changes in the case of coca-leaf chewing (Negrete, 1978).

Socially sanctioned, episodic psychoactive substance use may involve even heavy use and marked intoxication or drunkenness (Bunzel, 1940). In a low-technology environment, this pattern caused few problems, although psychotomimetic drugs such as cannabis could cause toxic psychosis (Chopra & Smith, 1974). In a high-technology environment, with motor vehicles and industrial machinery, intoxication even at mild traditional levels is life-threatening (Stull, 1972).

Among other consequence of technology and advanced civilization are widespread substance abuse epidemics, or long-lasting endemics. In the pre-Columbian era, sporadic cases of acute and chronic substance abuse problems had been known for at least a millennium, and possibly two millennia. However, relatively sudden, massive substance abuse increases appeared early in the post-Columbian era. One of these was the English gin epidemic or gin plague (Thurn, 1978), which began in the late 1600s and continued for several decades. Transatlantic intercontinental trade and the beginnings of the Industrial Revolution were the immediate causes. At about the same time, opium epidemics broke out in several Asian countries. The origins of these epidemics were somewhat different. The post-Columbian spread of tobacco smoking to Asia introduced the inhabitants to inhalation as a new mode of drug administration. This new route of administration applied to an old drug, opium, produced a combination more addictive than the old opium-eating tradition. Governmental pressures against tobacco smoking (which was viewed as wasteful and associated with seditious elements) probably accelerated the popularity of opium smoking. Subsequently, European colonialism and international trade contributed to the import of Indian opium to several East Asian countries (Westermeyer, 1992). Opium epidemics also occurred in Europe and North America (Kramer, 1979). Although East Asia has largely controlled its opium problem, opiate endemics continue in Southeast and South Asia, the Middle East, most of Europe, and much of North America.

HISTORICAL MODELS OF SUBSTANCE USE

Although ceremonial alcohol use is widely appreciated, the ceremonial use of drugs is not so well-known. Peyote buttons are a sacramental substance in the Native American Church (Bergman, 1971). Hallucinogen use for religious purposes still occurs among many South American ethnic groups (DuToit, 1977). Supernatural sanctions, both prescribing use within certain bounds and proscribing use outside these bounds, inveigh against abuse of these substances by devotees. Thus, ceremonial or religious use tends to be relatively safe. Examples of abuse do occur, however, such as the occasional Catholic priest who becomes alcoholic beginning with abuse of sacramental wine.

Secular but social use of alcohol and drugs occurs in numerous quasi-ritual contexts. Drinking may occur at annual events, such as New Year or harvest ceremonies (e.g., Thanksgiving in the United States). Weddings, births, funerals, and other family rituals are occasions for alcohol or drug use in many cultures. Marking of friendships, business arrangements, or intergroup competitions can virtually require substance use in some groups. For example, the *dutsen* in German-speaking Central Europe is a brief ritual in which friends or associates agree to address each other by the informal *du* ("thou") rather than by the formal *Sie* ("you"). Participants, holding an alcoholic beverage in their right hands, link their right arms, toast each other, and drink with arms linked. The use of betel-areca, pulque or beer, coca leaf, and other intoxicants has accompanied group work tasks, such as harvests or community *corvée* obligations (e.g., maintaining roads, bridges, and irrigation ditches). Although substance use may be heavy at ceremonial events, even involving intoxication, the social control of the group over dosage and the brief duration of use augurs against chronic abuse (although problems related to acute abuse may occur). Problems can develop if the group's central rationale for existence rests on substance use (e.g., habitués of opium dens, cocktail lounges, and ethnic bars and street drinking groups). In these latter instances, group norms for alcohol or drug use may foster substance abuse rather than prevent it (Kahn et al., 1990; Keaulana & Whitney, 1990; Moncher, Holden, & Grimble, 1990).

Medicinal reasons for substance use have prevailed in one place or another with virtually all psychoactive substances, including alcohol, opium, cannabis, tobacco, the stimulants, and the hallucinogens (Hill, 1990). Insofar as substances are prescribed or administered solely by healers or physicians, abuse is rare or absent. For example, the prescribing of oral opium by Chinese physicians over many centuries had few or no adverse social consequences. On the other hand, self-prescribing for medicinal purposes carries risks. For example, certain Northern Europeans, Southeast Asians, and others use alcohol for insomnia, colds, pain, and other maladies—a practice that can and does lead to chronic alcohol abuse. Self-prescribing of opium by poppy farmers similarly antedates opium addiction in a majority of cases (Westermeyer, 1982). Thus, professional control over medicinal use has been relatively benign, whereas individual control over medicinal use of psychoactive compounds has often been problematic.

Dietary use of substances falls into two general categories: (1) the use of alcohol as a source of calories and (2) the use of cannabis and other herbal intoxicants to enhance taste. Fermentation of grains, tubers, and fruits into alcohol has been a convenient way of storing calories that would otherwise deteriorate. Unique tastes and eating experiences associated with beverage alcohol (e.g., various wines) have further fostered their use, especially at ritual, ceremonial, or social meals. Cannabis has also been used from the Middle East to the Malay Archipelago as a means of enhancing soups, teas, pastries, and other sweets. Opium and other substances have been served at South Asian ceremonies (e.g., weddings) as a postprandial "dessert."

Recreational use can presumably occur in either social or individual settings. Much substance use today occurs in recreational or "party" settings that have some psychosocial rationales (e.g., social "time out" and meeting friends), but minimal or no ritual or ceremonial aspects. So-called recreational substance use in these social contexts may in fact be quasi-medicinal (i.e., to reduce symptoms associated with social phobia, low self-esteem, boredom, or chronic dysphoria). Even solitary psychoactive substance use can be recreational (i.e., to enhance an enjoyable event) or medicinal (i.e., to relieve loneliness, insomnia, or pain).

Other purposes exist, but are not as widespread as those described above. In the 19th century, young European women took belladonna before social events in order to give themselves a ruddy, blushing complexion. A particular substance or pattern of use can represent a social or ethnic identity (Carstairs, 1954; Caetano, 1987). Children may inhale household or industrial solvents as a means of mimicking adult intoxication (Kaufman, 1975). Intoxication may simply serve as a means for continuing social behaviors, such as fights or homicide, that previously existed without intoxication (Levy & Kunitz, 1969). Particular patterns of alcohol/drug production or use may represent rebellion by disenfranchised groups (Connell, 1961; Lurie, 1970).

HISTORY OF SUBSTANCE ABUSE TREATMENT

Historical and literary accounts have long documented individual attempts to draw back from the abyss of alcohol and drug abuse. At various times autobiographical, biographical, journalistic, and anecdotal, these descriptions list centuries-old methods still employed today in lay and professional settings. Modalities include gradual decrease in dosage; symptomatic use of nonaddicting medications; isolation from the substance; relocation away from fellow users; religious conversion; group support; asylum in a supportive and non-demanding environment; and treatment with a variety of shamanistic, spiritual, dietary, herbal, and medicinal methods (Westermeyer, 1992).

Beginning with Galenic medicine, a key strategy has been to identify certain syndromes as having their etiology in alcohol and drug abuse. Once the etiology is determined, the specific treatment (i.e., cessation of substance abuse) can be prescribed. Examples of such substance-associated disorders include delirium tremens (i.e., alcohol and sedative withdrawal) and withdrawal seizures, morphinism (i.e., opioid withdrawal), cannabis-induced acute psychosis, stimulant psychosis, and various fetal effects, such as fetal alcohol syndrome. Thus, description of pathophysiological and psychopathological processes, together with diagnostic labeling, has been a crucial historical step in the development of modern assessment and treatment for substance use disorders (Rodin, 1981; Westermeyer, 1992).

Modern treatment approaches have their origins in methods developed by Benjamin Rush, a physician from the Revolutionary War era who is often credited as the father of American psychiatry. Rush developed a categorization of drinkers and alcoholics. He further prescribed treatment that consisted of a period of "asylum" from responsibilities and access to alcohol, to take place in a family-like setting, in a milieu of respect, consideration, and social support. As Rush's concepts were extrapolated to the growing American society, large state-supported institutions were developed—although some smaller, private asylums or sanitoria for alcoholics have persisted up to the current time (Johnson & Westermeyer, in press).

Medical treatments can interact with cultural factors. For example, disulfiram can act as an excuse for Native American alcoholics to resist peer pressures to drink (Savard, 1968). Ethnic similarity between patients and staff appears to be more critical to the treatment process than in other medical or psychiatric conditions (Shore & Von Fumetti, 1972). Strong ethnic affiliation may be associated with more optimal treatment outcomes, although ethnic affiliation may change as a result of treatment (Westermeyer & Neider, 1985).

On a federal level, treatment for drug abuse (largely opiate dependence) began with the Harrison Act of 1914, which outlawed nonmedical use of opiate drugs. For a time, heroin maintenance was prescribed and dispensed in several clinics around the country. Although research studies were not conducted, case reports from these clinics indicated that many patients were able to resume stable lives while receiving maintenance doses of heroin. These clinics were phased out, largely because of moral, political, and religious opposition. Two long-term prison-like hospitals for opiate addicts were established (one in Kentucky and one in Texas). Research in these institutions contributed greatly to our understanding of opiate addiction (and alcoholism, which was also studied), but the demonstrated inefficacy of prison treatment led to their demise as treatment facilities. These legal and medical approaches beginning in 1914 were effective in reducing opiate dependence in the societal mainstream. However, certain occupational, geographical, and ethnic groups continued to use drugs that were made illicit by the Harrison Act. These included seamen, musicians, certain minority groups, and inhabitants of coastal-border areas involved in smuggling (e.g., San Antonio, Texas; Louisiana seaports; San Francisco, California; and New York City).

Following World War II, medical and social leaders were more aware of widespread mental disabilities in the country, because of the high rate of psychiatric disorders among inductees and veterans. This led to the establishment of the National Institute of Mental Health (NIMH), which had divisions of alcoholism and drug abuse. By the 1970s, it became apparent that substance use disorders were widely prevalent. Numerous indices of alcohol abuse and alcoholism had been increasing since World War II, including hepatic cirrhosis and violence-related mortality. Endemic abuse of cocaine and opiates exploded into an epidemic in the late 1960s, followed by the appearance of stimulant and hallucinogen abuse. It was evident that neither the alcohol epidemic nor the drug epidemic was being adequately addressed by NIMH. This led to the formation of the National Institute on Alcohol Abuse and Alcoholism (NIAAA) and the National Institute on Drug Abuse (NIDA), both of which have equal status with NIMH under the Alcohol, Drug Abuse, and Mental Health Administration (ADAMHA). Located within the Department of Health and Human Services, ADAMHA has fostered the development of substance abuse research, training, clinical services, and prevention. Governmental support for these efforts has come largely from elected officials who have personally experienced psychoactive substance use disorders, either in themselves or in their families. For example, most of the last several presidents have had a spouse, parent, sibling, or offspring with a substance disorder.

SOCIAL AND SELF-HELP MOVEMENTS

Abstinence-oriented social movements first appeared among organized religions (Johnson & Westermeyer, in press). Certain South Asian sects, arising from early Persian religions and Hinduism, abstained from alcohol over 2 millennia ago. Buddhist clergy were forbidden to drink alcoholic beverages, and pious Buddhist laity were urged to refrain from drinking or at least to drink moderately. Early on, Moslems were urged not to drink; tradition has it that Mohammed himself established abstinence for his followers. Abstinence-oriented Christian sects evolved in England and then in Central Europe at about the time of the gin epidemic.

Religiomania has long served as a cure for dipsomania and narcotomania.

Opium addicts in Asia have gone to monasteries in the hope that worship, meditation, or clerical asceticism would cure them, which it sometimes did (Westermeyer, 1982). Many Latin Americans and Native Americans with high rates of alcoholism have abandoned Catholicism and Anglicanism in favor of abstinence-prescribing fundamentalist Christian sects and the Native American Church (Hippler, 1973; Albaugh & Anderson, 1974). Children raised in these sects are taught the importance of lifelong abstinence from alcohol and other drugs of abuse. Despite this childhood socialization, those leaving these sects as adults can develop substance use disorders. Thus, the anti-substance-disorder effects of various religions appear to persist only as long as one is actively affiliated with the group.

Abstinent societies not tied to specific religions began to appear in the 18th and 19th centuries. Examples include the Anti-Opium Society in China and the Women's Christian Temperance Union in the United States. These groups engaged in political action, public education, social pressure against addiction or alcoholism, and support for abstinence. These led eventually to "prohibition" movements that sought legal strictures against the production, sale, and/or consumption of psychoactive substances outside religious or medical contexts. In Asia, these movements began against tobacco (which was viewed in the 1600s and 1700s as a habit associated with political sedition) and then later changed to oppose primarily opium. In Northern Europe and the United States, prohibition laws first involved opiates and cannabis but later expanded to include alcohol. As Moslem peoples emerged from colonial regimes, their nations passed antialcohol legislation that ranged from mild strictures for Moslems alone, to harsh measures against all inhabitants of the country.

Numerous self-help groups in the United States were founded during the Depression era. Many more were begun after World War II. These groups involved individuals who banded together to meet their common financial, social, or personal needs (Lieberman & Borman, 1976). Movements of its era differed in several important aspects from earlier abstinence-oriented groups as follows:

- Individuals could remain in their homes, families, and jobs rather than joining a separate sect or going off to an asylum or special group.
- Considerable structure was involved, with specific meetings and phased "step" recovery activities.
- The concept of a recovery process over time was introduced, as distinct from a sudden cure or conversion; this had biological, psychological, social, and spiritual dimensions.
- Organization was kept predominantly atomistic (i.e., autonomous small groups) rather than hierarchical.
- Membership required self-identity as an alcoholic or addict (i.e., supportive or concerned persons were excluded).

Like earlier movements, these self-help groups also emphasized the importance of abstinence from psychoactive substance abuse (although tobacco and coffee are notably present at some AA meetings today), reliance on a superior spiritual force (the "Higher Power"), and social affiliation or "fellowship" for mutual support. Alcoholics Anonymous, perhaps the best known of these groups today, was first established in the United States. It has spread to many other parts of the world over the last 50 years and has served as a model for similar groups whose identity centers on other drugs and even other problems (i.e., Narcotics Anonymous, Cocaine Anonymous, Overeaters Anonymous, Gamblers Anonymous, and Emotions Anonymous [formerly Neurotics Anonymous]). Groups for those personally affected by alcoholism have also appeared, such as Alateen for the teenage offspring of alcoholic parents and Al-Anon for the spouses, parents, and other concerned associates of alcoholic persons. Over the last several years, the Adult Children of Alcoholics and Addicts (ACOAA) movement has also evolved to meet the needs of those distressed or maladaptive adults raised by alcoholic parents. Mothers Against Drunk Drivers (MADD) was originally formed to meet the support needs of parents whose children were killed by drunken auto drivers. MADD has since expanded its activities as a "watchdog" group that follows the records of legislators and judges in regard to alcohol-related legal offenses. The social and cultural composition of the self-help group appears to be an important factor in effecting therapeutic outcomes (Jilek-Aal, 1978).

FACTORS AFFECTING ALCOHOL–DRUG EPIDEMICS

Numerous factors contributed to the development of substance abuse "epidemics" or "plagues." One of the first of these, the gin epidemic (which involved other alcohol-containing beverages besides gin) in late 17th- and 18th-century England, was fostered by the following factors:

- English merchant ships returning empty from trips to its colonies loaded on gin, rum, and other alcohol-containing beverages as ballast before returning to England.
- Rum was derived from sugar cane grown with slave labor and gin from grains grown with indentured labor. With no import tax, calories of these alcohol-containing beverages were literally cheaper than calories of bread in London.
- The beginnings of the industrial revolution gave rise to repressive social conditions and a loss of traditional rural values, fostering widespread drunkenness with inexpensive beverage alcohol.
- Although traditions and social controls existed for the drinking of mead and ale, these traditions and controls did not extend to gin and rum drinking, with the result that daily excessive drinking appeared.

During this period, numerous sequelae of alcoholism were first recognized, including the description of the fetal alcohol syndrome (Rodin, 1981). The gin epidemic raged for several decades, perhaps as long as a century. It eventually receded under such pressures as an import tax on imported alcohol-containing beverages, antialcohol propaganda in the literature and art of the day, and evolution of abstinence-oriented Protestant sects for the working classes.

The opium epidemic in many countries of East and Southeast Asia began about the same time as the European alcohol epidemic. Several factors, some similar to the European situation but some different, contributed to the opium epidemic. These were as follows:

- Tobacco smoking was introduced to Asia from the New World; it became a popular pastime in smoking houses that were frequented by the artisans, artists, adventurists, and literati of the day.
- As European and New World concepts and artifacts flooded into Asia, tobacco–smoking houses were viewed as places of cultural change and even political sedition; they were gradually outlawed.
- Opium eating, primarily a medicinal activity, which had never been a significant social problem, was combined with this new technology (i.e., drug consumption by volatilization and inhalation); recreational opium smoking subsequently became widespread.
- Political corruption, government inefficiency, and absence of statecraft skills to deal with widespread drug abuse, abetted by the political and economic imperialism of Western colonial powers, led to centuries of widespread opium addiction among various Asian nations. Some countries have reversed the problem in this century (e.g., Japan, Korea, China, and Manchuria); others have not (e.g., Thailand, Laos, Burma, Pakistan, Afghanistan, Iran, and India).

TRENDS IN PROBLEMS ACROSS TIME AND SPACE

The appearance of new drugs (or reappearance of old ones in new forms) exposed social groups to agents against which they had no sociocultural protection or "immunity." That is, the community or nation had no tradition for problem-free or at least controlled use of the substance. Users themselves may not have perceived the actual risks associated with the new psychoactive substance. This situation also occurred when the group was familiar with the substance but in a different form. For example, traditions may exist for wine but not beer or distilled alcohol; pipe smoking may be subject to customs that do not extend to cigarette smoking.

Symbolic aspects of certain drugs or modes of drug administration may displace the issue from psychoactive substance use per se, to associated issues of ethnic identity, cultural change, political upheaval, class struggle, or intergenerational conflict (Robbins, 1973). Examples include the following: the use of cannabis by one caste or ethnic group and the use of alcohol by an adjacent but different group (Carstairs, 1954), cannabis and hallucinogen use as antiauthority symbols in the late 1960s and 1970s, alcohol abuse among indigenous peoples (Moncher et al., 1990; Thompson, 1992), and illicit raising of poppy as a cash crop and opium smuggling by ethnic minorities in Asia (Westermeyer, 1982).

As drug use has spread in the last few centuries, drug production and commerce have become important economic resources in many areas (Westermeyer, 1991). Early examples in the 1800s were the British trading companies in large areas of India, which depended for their wealth on opium sales to China. Numerous backward areas in the world today maintain their participation in national and world markets through their participation in illicit drug production and sales: Afghanistan, Burma, Laos, Mexico, Pakistan, and Thailand in opium and heroin; the Caribbean nations and Mexico in cannabis production and cocaine commerce; and several South and Central American countries in cocaine production and commerce. Several states in the United States count cannabis as a major, albeit illicit, cash crop: North Carolina, Tennessee, Kentucky, Kansas, Nebraska, New Mexico, California, and Hawaii (Culhane, 1989).

Government instability, corruption, or inefficiency can cause or result from drug production, export, and/or smuggling today. For example, Iran was largely free of illicit drug use and production until the political disruption and war of the last several years. Other unstable countries in South Asia, the Middle East, Africa, and Latin America have become producers, transshippers, or importers of illicit drugs. Breakdown of traditional Islam has led to increased alcohol abuse in some Moslem countries, contributing to a backlash of Islamic fundamentalism. Likewise, in the United States and Latin America, widespread alcoholism predates the shift to Christian fundamentalism.

Industrialization and technological advances have fostered a redefinition of substance abuse (Stull, 1972). An intoxicated or "hung-over" (withdrawing) ox-cart driver can effect limited damage, other than to cart, ox, and self. The alcohol- or drug-affected driver of a modern high-speed bus, captain of an oil supertanker, or pilot of a jet transport can kill scores of people and destroy equipment and material worth millions of dollars. Handicraft artisans under the influence of drugs or alcohol can do little damage, whereas workers in a factory can harm themselves or others as well as destroying expensive machinery and bringing production to a halt.

Since World War II, and especially since the 1960s, adolescent-onset substance abuse has escalated from rare sporadic cases to a high prevalence in many communities (Cameron, 1968; Dick, Manson, & Beals, 1993). Several factors appear to foster it: widespread parental substance abuse, societal neglect of adolescents, poverty, rapid social changes, and political upheaval. Whatever the cause, the consequences are remarkably similar: undermining of normal adolescent psychosocial development, poor socialization of children to assume adult roles, lack of job skills, emotional immaturity, increased rates of adolescent psychiatric morbidity, and increased adolescent mortality (i.e., suicide. accidents, and homicide) (Grossman, Milligan, & Deyo, 1991).

TRENDS IN TREATMENT AND PREVENTION

From the time of Benjamin Rush, two central treatment methods were established based on the psychiatric treatment methods of the late 1700s: (1) "asylum" in a supportive environment away from drink and companion drinkers and (2) "moral treatment," consisting of a civil, respectful consideration for the recovering person. Both methods persist today and remain as two standard treatment strategies (although neither has been validated by research). They were not and are not inevitably successful, however. Nor were these methods readily available to the increasing numbers of alcoholics and addicts generated in the 1800s and 1900s. Consequently, other methods were tried (Johnson & Westermeyer, in press).

One of these methods was the substitution of one drug for another. For example, laudanum (combined alcohol and opiates) was once prescribed for alcoholism. Morphine and later heroin were recommended for opium addiction during the mid-1800s. This approach is not extinct, as exemplified by the frequent recommendation in the 1970s that alcoholics substitute cannabis smoking for alcohol. Currently methadone is used for chronic opiate addicts who have failed attempts at drug-free treatment. Despite aversive selection factors, methadone maintenance patients tend to do well as long as they comply with treatment. Following the original method of Dole and Nyswander (1965), methadone maintenance should be accompanied by an active, well-staffed psychosocial treatment program that has both individual and group therapies.

Detoxification became prevalent in the mid-1900s. Public detoxification facilities, established first in Eastern Europe, spread throughout the world. For many patients, this resource offers an entree into recovery. For others, "revolving door" detoxification may actually produce lifelong institutionalization on the installment plan (Gallant et al., 1973). The problem of the treatment-resistant public inebriate exists today in all parts of the United States.

The so-called Minnesota model of treatment developed from several sources: a state hospital program (at Wilmar) and a later private program (at Hazelden), supplemented by the first day program for alcoholism (at the Minneapolis Veterans Administration Hospital). The characteristics of this "model" have varied over time as treatment has evolved and changed, and definitions still differ from one person to the next. However, characteristics often ascribed to the model include the following:

1. A period of residential or inpatient care, ranging from a few weeks to several months.
2. A focus on the psychoactive substance use disorder, with little or no consideration of associated psychiatric conditions or individual psychosocial factors.
3. Heavy emphasis on AA self-help concepts, resources, and precepts, such as the "Twelve Steps" of recovery.

4. Referral to AA or another self-help group on discharge from residential or inpatient care, with minimal or no ongoing professional treatment.
5. Minimal or no family therapy or counseling (although family orientation to AA principles and Al-Anon may take place).
6. Negative attitudes toward ongoing psychotherapies and pharmacotherapies for substance use disorder or associated psychiatric disorder.

At the time of its evolution in the 1950s and 1960s, this model served to bridge the formerly separate hospital programs and self-help groups—a laudable achievement. However, if it is applied rigidly in light of current knowledge, some patients (who might otherwise be helped) will fail in or drop out of treatment. Nowadays, many treatment programs employ aspects of the old "Minnesota model," integrating them flexibly with newer methods in a more individualized and patient-centered manner.

The workplace has been a locus of prevention, early recognition, referral for treatment, and rehabilitation. Following World War II, Hudolin and coworkers in Yugoslavia established factory-based and farm commune-based recovery groups, with ties to treatment facilities. Over the last two decades, alcoholism counselors have worked in similar "employee assistance programs" in the United States.

More sophisticated methods of pharmacotherapy have appeared recently, although these remain few by comparison with other areas of medicine. Safe detoxification is possible through increased basic and clinical appreciation of withdrawal syndromes. Disulfiram, naltrexone, and methadone may be selectively prescribed as maintenance drugs in the early difficult months and years of recovery. Other medications are currently being investigated for use in special circumstances.

Several new diagnostic and treatment methods are currently being tried in an attempt to improve clinical outcomes. One of these is the recognition of comorbid conditions accompanying substance abuse, in which concurrent or modified treatment may improve success. For example, concurrent treatment for affective disorders, anxiety disorders, eating disorders, and pathological gambling is being attempted. For chronic conditions—such as mild mental retardation, borderline intelligence, organic brain syndrome, or chronic schizophrenia—substance abuse treatment, rehabilitation, and self-help procedures may need to be modified. Intensive outpatient programs, conducted during the day, evening, or weekend, may assist certain patients to recover when other measures fail. These intensive outpatient programs are modeled after similar psychiatric programs. Much of the treatment time is spent in groups of various sizes, although individual and family sessions may occur as well. Staff is typically multidisciplinary, with counselors, nurses, occupational and recreational therapists, psychologists, psychiatrists, and social workers. Matching of patients to specific treatment modalities or therapists may be effective, but further research is needed to develop this approach. Monitoring of recovery in several contexts and by several sources (e.g., at work, by licensing agencies or unions, in the family, and with medical resources) appears to enhance outcome (Westermeyer, 1989).

Preventive techniques first applied to the gin epidemic are still useful today: control over hours and location of sales, taxes or duties to increase cost, changing of public attitudes via the mass media, education, and abstinence-oriented religion (Popham, Schmidt, & DeLint, 1975; Smart, 1982; Thompson, 1992). The prolonged Asian opium epidemic demonstrated that laws alone are ineffective unless accompanied by socially integrated treatment; recovery programs; compulsory abstinence in identified cases; police pressure against drug production, commerce, and consumption; and follow-up monitoring (Westermeyer, 1976). Experience with antialcohol prohibition laws in Europe and North America demonstrated the futility of outlawing substance use that was supported by many citizens. Adverse results from the Prohibition era in the United States included increased criminality associated with bootlegging alcohol, lack of quality control (e.g., methanol and lead contaminants), and development of unhealthy drinking patterns (e.g., surreptitious, rapid, without food, and in a deviant setting). Public-interest groups such as MADD may aid in reducing certain alcohol- and drug-related problems. Much work still remains to be done in this area. Despite expenditures of over $20 billion by the United States since 1970 to reduce the supply of and demand for drugs, the government is still unable to prevent the import and production of drugs. Mortality from hepatic cirrhosis, alcohol-related accidents, and suicide continue at an unprecedented level among young American males.

REFERENCES

Ahluwalia, H. S., & Ponnampalam, J. T. (1968). The socioeconomic aspects of betel-nut chewing. *Journal of Tropical Medical Hygiene, 71,* 48–50.

Albaugh, B. J., & Anderson, P. O. (1974). Peyote in the treatment of alcoholism among American Indians. *American Journal of Psychiatry, 131,* 1247–1256.

Anawalt, P. R., & Berdan, F. F. (1992, June). The Codex Mendoza. *Scientific American, 266,* 70–79.

Baldwin, A. D. (1977). Anstie's alcohol limit: Francis Edmund Anstie 1833–1874. *American Journal Public Health, 67*(7), 679–681.

Becker, T. M., Wiggins, C. L., Key, C. R., & Samet, J. N. (1992). Changing trends in mortality among New Mexico's American Indians, 1958–1987. *International Journal of Epidemiology, 21*(4), 690–700.

Bergman, R. L. (1971). Navaho peyote use: Its apparent safety. *American Journal of Psychiatry, 128,* 695–699.

Bunzel, R. (1940). The role of alcoholism in two Central American Cultures. *Psychiatry, 3,* 361–387.

Caetano, R. (1987). Acculturation and drinking patterns among U.S. Hispanics. *British Journal of Addiction, 82,* 789–799.

Caetano, R., Suzman, R. M., Rosen, D. H., & Vorhees-Rosen, D. J. (1983). The Shetland

Islands: Longitudinal changes in alcohol consumption in a changing environment. *British Journal of Addiction, 78,* 21–36.

Cameron, D. C. (1968). Youth and drugs: A world view. *Journal of the American Medical Association, 206,* 1267–1271.

Carstairs, G. M. (1954). *Daru* and *bhang*: Cultural factors in the choice of intoxicant. *Quarterly Journal of Studies on Alcohol, 15,* 220–237.

Chopra, G. S., & Smith, J. W. (1974). Psychotic reactions following cannabis use in East Indians. *Archives of General Psychiatry, 30,* 24–27.

Connell. K. H. (1961). Illicit distribution: An Irish peasant industry. *Historical Studies of Ireland, 3,* 58–91.

Culhane, C. (1989). Pot harvest gains across country. *United States Journal, 13*(8), 14.

Dick, R. W., Manson, S. M., & Beals, J. (1993). Alcohol use among male and female Native American adolescents: Patterns and correlates of student drinking in a boarding school. *Journal of Studies on Alcohol, 54,* 172–177.

Dole, V. P., & Nyswander, M. E. (1965). A medical treatment of diacetylmorphine (heroin) addiction. *Journal of the American Medical Association, 193,* 646–650.

DuToit, B. M. (1977). *Drugs, rituals and altered states of consciousness.* Rotterdam: Balkema.

Fenna, D. L., Mix, O., Schaefer, J., & Gilbert, A. L. (1971). Ethanol metabolism in various racial groups. *Canadian Medical Association Journal, 105,* 472–475.

Furst, P. T., & Coe, M. D. (1977). Ritual enemas. *Natural History, 86,* 88–89.

Gallagher, M. M., Fleming, D. W., Berger, L. R., & Sewell, C. M. (1992). Pedestrian and hypothermia deaths among Native Americans in New Mexico. *Journal of the American Medical Association, 267*(10), 1345–1348.

Gallant, D. M., Bishop, M. P., Mouledoux, A., Faulkner, M. A., Brisolara, A., & Swanson, W. A. (1973). The revolving door alcoholic. *Archives of General Psychiatry, 28,* 633–635.

Grossman, D. C., Milligan, B. C., & Deyo, R. A. (1991). Risk factors for suicide attempts among Navajo adolescents. *American Journal of Public Health, 81*(7), 870–874.

Heath, D. (1971). Peasants, revolution, and drinking: Interethnic drinking patterns in two Bolivian communities. *Human Organization, 30,* 179–186.

Hill, T. W. (1990). Peyotism and the control of heavy drinking: The Nebraska Winnebago in the early 1900s. *Human Organization, 49*(3), 255–265.

Hippler, A. E. (1973). Fundamentalist Christianity: An Alaskan Athabascan technique for overcoming alcohol abuse. *Transcultural Psychiatric Research Review, 10,* 173–179.

Jilek-Aal, L. (1978). Alcohol and the Indian–White relationship: A study of the function of Alcoholics Anonymous among Coast Salish Indians. *Confinia Psychiatrica, 21,* 195–233.

Johnson, D. R., & Westermeyer, J. (in press). Psychiatric therapies influenced by religious movements. In J. Boehnlein (Ed.), *Textbook on religion and psychiatry.* Washington, DC: American Psychiatric Press.

Johnson, R., & Nagoshi, C. (1990). Asians, Asian-Americans and alcohol. *Journal of Psychoactive Drugs, 22*(1), 45–52.

Kahn, M. W., Hunter, E., et al. (1990). Australian Aborigines and alcohol: A review. *Drug and Alcohol Review, 10*(4), 351–366.

Kaufman, A. (1975). Gasoline sniffing among children in a Pueblo Indian village. *Pediatrics, 51,* 1060–1063.

Keaulana, K. A., & Whitney, S. (1990, Summer). Ka wai kau mai o Maleka—Water from America: The intoxication of the Hawaiian people. *Contemporary Drug Problems,* 161–194.

Kennedy, J. G., Teague, J., & Fairbanks, L. (1980). Quat use in North Yemen and the problem of addiction: A study in medical anthropology. *Culture, Medicine and Psychiatry, 4,* 311–344.

Kramer, J. C. (1979). Opium rampant: Medical use, misuse and abuse in Britain and the west in the 17th and 18th centuries. *British Journal of Addiction, 74,* 377–389.

Levy, J. E., & Kunitz, S. J. (1969). Notes on some White Mountain Apache social pathologies. *Plateau, 42,* 11–19.

Lieberman, M. A., & Borman, L. D. (1976). Self-help groups. *Journal of Applied Behavioral Science, 12,* 261–403.

Lurie, N. O. (1970). The world's oldest on-going protest demonstration: North American Indian drinking patterns. *Pacific Historical Review, 40,* 311–332.

Mariz, C. L. (1991). Pentecostalism and alcoholism among the Brazilian poor. *Alcoholism Treatment Quarterly, 8*(2), 75–82.

Moncher, M. S., Holden, G. W. (1990). Substance use among Native-American youth. *Journal of Consulting and Clinical Psychology, 58*(4), 408–415.

Negrete, J. C. (1978). Coca leaf chewing: A public health assessment. *British Journal of Addiction, 73,* 283–290.

Popham, R. E., Schmidt, W., & DeLint, J. (1975). The prevention of alcoholism: Epidemiological studies of the effects of government control measures. *British Journal of Addiction, 70,* 125–144.

Robbins, R. H. (1973). Alcohol and the identity struggle: Some effects of economic change on interpersonal relations. *American Anthropologist, 75,* 99–122.

Rodin, A. E. (1981). Infants and gin mania in 18th-century London. *Journal of the American Medical Association, 245,* 1237–1239.

Savard, R. J. (1968). Effects of disulfiram therapy on relationships within the Navajo drinking group. *Quarterly Journal of Studies on Alcohol, 29,* 909–916.

Shore, J. H., & Von Fumetti, B. (1972). Three alcohol programs for American Indians. *American Journal of Psychiatry, 128,* 1450–1454.

Smart, R. G. (1982). The impact of prevention legislation: An examination of research findings. In A. K. Kaplan (Ed.), *Legislative approaches to prevention of alcohol-related problems.* Washington, DC: Institute of Medicine.

Smith, W. R. (1965). Sacrifice among the Seminites. In W. A. Lessa & E. Z. Vogt (Eds.), *Reader in comparative religion* (pp. 39–48). New York: Harper & Row.

Stull, D. D. (1972). Victims of modernization: Accident rates and Papago Indian adjustment. *Human Organization, 31,* 227–240.

Thompson, J. W. (1992). Alcohol policy considerations for Indian people. *American Indian and Alaska Native Mental Health Research, 4*(3), 112–119.

Thurn, R. J. (1978). The gin plague. *Minnesota Medicine, 61,* 241–243.

Westermeyer, J. (1976). The pro-heroin effects of anti-opium laws. *Archives of General Psychiatry, 33,* 1135–1139.

Westermeyer, J. (1982). *Poppies, pipes and people: Opium and its use in Laos.* Berkeley: University of California Press.

Westermeyer, J. (1989). Monitoring recovery from substance abuse: Rationales, methods and challenges. *Advances in Alcohol and Substance Abuse, 8,* 93–106.

Westermeyer, J. (1991). Historical and social context of psychoactive substance disorders. In R. J. Frances & S. I. Miller (Eds.), *Clinical textbook of addictive disorders* (pp. 23–40). New York: Guilford Press.

Westermeyer, J. (1992). The sociocultural environmental in the genesis and amelioration of opium dependence. In J. Pogge (Ed.), *Anthropological research: Process and application* (pp. 115–132). New York: State University of New York Press.

Westermeyer, J., & Neider, J. (1985). Cultural affiliation among American Indian alcoholics: Correlation and change over a ten year period. *Journal of Operational Psychiatry, 16*, 17–28.

Part II

Diagnostic Instruments

3

❑ _____

Comprehensive Substance Abuse Evaluation

PEGGY J. OTT
RALPH E. TARTER

INTRODUCTION

All psychometric procedures have one characteristic in common—they selectively evaluate cognitive, emotional, or behavioral processes. Over the past decade, the trend in psychometric assessment in substance abuse disorders is toward comprehensive rather that selective evaluation. Indeed, inherent in the diagnosis of substance abuse disorders is the assessment of the impact of the disorder on multiple areas of one's life. To be thorough, assessment then must encompass evaluating the far-reaching effects and impact of the disorder on various domains of interest. The importance of a comprehensive and uniform assessment has utility in both research settings and treatment environments. The psychometric instruments reviewed in this chapter meet the following criteria: (1) the multiple psychometric properties of the instrument have been established, (2) the instruments have well-established utility with individuals with substance abuse disorders, and (3) the instruments are feasible and efficient for use in both research and clinical settings.

In a recent overview of guidelines used to evaluate substance abuse disorders, Rounsaville (1993) emphasized the importance of using comparable measures in the assessment of substance abuse whether in clinical or in research settings. In his view, the use of heterogeneous measures in these settings prevents the development of a standardized battery of psychometric instruments that can be used nationally to evaluate temporal trends, changing populations, changing rates of frequency and severity of use, patterns of abuse, and so on. Moreover, the issue of comparative measures has become increasingly important to the systematic evaluation of prevention and treatment modalities. With the recent advance of managed health care with emphasis on cost-effectiveness, the importance of empirically establishing the efficacy of a particular treatment modality or technique cannot be neglected.

Inclusion of particular instruments in a comprehensive battery of tests to assess substance abuse must take into consideration two key factors. First, an evaluation of a substance abuse disorder is complicated by the multifactorial etiology of substance abuse. A comprehensive multivariate psychometric assessment protocol is necessary to fully characterize the individual. Second, beyond the complication of the multiple causes underlying addiction, an assessment of a substance abuse disorder is also complicated by the psychological ramifications of these disorders. That is, there are numerous psychological disturbances that either presage or are concomitant to or a consequence of substance abuse. A comprehensive psychometric assessment of substance abuse must shed light on both etiological factors as well as other psychological manifestations of addiction.

Inclusion of instrumentation in this review of psychometric tools to assess substance abuse is also determined by the extent to which the instrument taps into a key domain of functioning. The general domains of experience that guide this review include (1) alcohol and drug use history; (2) health status/medical history; (3) psychiatric status and history; (4) personality; (5) cognition (general cognitive functioning, neuropsychological deficits); (6) family functioning (cohesion, adaptability, communication); and (7) social adjustment (social support, social roles, peer affiliation, social skills, vocational adjustment, school adjustment, recreation/leisure).

This chapter is divided into three main sections. First, we discuss the scope of a comprehensive psychometric assessment. To familiarize the clinician with the purpose and context of a psychometric assessment, the first section of the chapter describes the attributes of such an assessment and briefly reviews the issues that, from a psychological perspective, are particularly pertinent to understanding substance abuse. We also delineate the psychometric requirements of a comprehensive assessment. Second, we describe the methods for conducting a psychometric assessment, clustered around seven circumscribed domains of experience. Finally, the third section presents a decision-tree format for conducting a psychometric evaluation so that the results link to specific modes of treatment.

SCOPE AND ATTRIBUTES
OF A COMPREHENSIVE ASSESSMENT

There are three broad categories of processes requiring psychometric evaluation in cases of known or suspected substance abuse—cognitive, psychological, and social. A disturbance in one category may or may not involve a disturbance in another. That is, these three categories of functioning are not necessarily causally related to each other. For instance, among individuals with an alcohol disorder some may be disturbed emotionally whereas others are more affected socially. Hence, within a given diagnostic category (e.g., substance abuse disorder) there is substantial heterogeneity in the population with respect to the component disturbances contributing to the overall psychological presentation. A major task, therefore, in the psychometric assessment is to ascertain what processes are disturbed. Once assessed, the task then becomes one of analyzing the causal interrelationships among these disturbances.

Moreover, characterizing the cognitive, psychological, and social spheres of functioning depends to a great extent on the type of facility in which the substance abuser is seeking treatment. For example, people with alcohol addiction who present for treatment at a liver unit or gastroenterology service typically manifest less severe emotional disorder and present with better social adjustment than do individuals with alcohol disorders who are admitted to psychiatric facilities (Ewusi-Mensah, Saunders, & Williams, 1984). In contrast, they may be more likely to manifest either an acute or low-grade hepatic encephalopathy compared to persons who are admitted to psychiatric facilities where adjustment problems precipitate their treatment rather than the disease effects from chronic alcoholism. Thus, clinicians must be cognizant of the general characteristics of the population from which their clients are drawn to focus and structure accordingly the psychometric examination. A point to be emphasized in this regard is that a diagnostic label alone conveys very little useful information. Rather, by understanding cognitive, psychological, and social processes within the individual, the comprehensive psychometric evaluation can substantially assist in clarifying the factors that are etiologically related to the abuse of alcohol and other drugs.

In summary, the products of a comprehensive psychometric evaluation are fourfold: (1) to acquire objective and quantitative information about current cognitive, psychological, and social functioning; (2) to understand the idiosyncratic and causal interrelationships among these three spheres of functioning; (3) to elucidate the etiology of the substance use disorder with respect to the origin and relative contribution of cognitive, psychological, or social disturbances; and (4) to accrue information which identifies the treatment needs of the client.

PSYCHOMETRIC REQUIREMENTS
OF A COMPREHENSIVE ASSESSMENT

The information acquired from the psychometric assessment must satisfy two basic requirements: validity and reliability.

Validity

The tests administered must have proven validity. This ensures that the findings are factual so that the clinician can have confidence in the information obtained. *Construct validity* means that the psychological processes claimed to be measured are, in fact, what are being assessed. For instance, for a given client, it is essential to know that poor performance on a neuropsychological test of memory capacity is due to a central nervous system (CNS) injury and is not the consequence of emotional problems or any other factor unrelated to neurological status. The point to be made is that the ultimate utility of any psychometric instrument (and therefore the safeguard against misinterpretation) depends on its capacity to evaluate accurately the processes intended to be measured.

In addition, clinicians should select psychometric instruments that have *predictive validity*. That is, the psychological processes sampled and measured by the test should yield scores that facilitate prediction of some aspect of the individual's behavior in the natural environment. For example, low scores on tests of educational aptitude should be associated with academic underachievement. High scores on tests of anxiety should be found in conjunction with avoidant social behavior. Thus, predictive validity enables the clinician to make inferences about how the individual is ordinarily functioning beyond the circumscribed context of the assessment. These predictions should be oriented to meaningful and specific domains of functioning, such as the person's potential to respond to a particular type of treatment, hold a certain type of job, or attend college. Although psychometric tests must be recognized as not being the absolute or even the only method for making predictions, they should nevertheless be administered to gather the type of information that can maximize the client's prognosis in multiple spheres of everyday functioning. Clearly, predictive validity is an essential ingredient in a comprehensive assessment because it yields information that can help guide the particular type of rehabilitation, which can then promote the best prognosis.

Finally, it should be noted that psychometric testing is warranted only when the obtained data have *incremental validity*. That is, the test should yield information beyond what can be acquired from informal interviewing or casual observation. It is pointless to measure depression if the self-report of symptoms and observed pathognomonic signs are readily obtained. Psychometric procedures are most prudently utilized in cases in which the objectivity of measurement and quantification of the process—against either population norms or criterion cutoff scores—yield information that is either too complex or too subtle to be obtained from casual observation. In this fashion, information accrued from psychometric tests increases the level of understanding to sophisticated intelligibility. Because it is both expensive and labor-intensive, clinicians should not request the psychometric evaluation merely to confirm clinical impressions.

Reliability

Of the various types of psychometric reliability, two need to be considered here: test–retest and interrater reliability. *Test–retest reliability* refers to the stability of the individual on the measured characteristic. The clinical meaningfulness of any set of test results is contingent upon their repeatability. Changes monitored in the individual using a particular instrument, therefore, should truly reflect a change in the person's status. Thus, for example, if the psychometric instrument has established test–retest reliability, the test can be use repeatedly to monitor any changes in status occurring between any two points in time during the course of treatment or aftercare.

The second type of reliability is *interrater reliability*. A test score obtained by one psychometrician should nearly equal the score obtained if the test is administered by another person. Confidence can then be placed in the results accrued as being an accurate description of the client and not the product of idiosyncratic interaction between the psychometrician and the client.

In summary, the data accrued from the psychometric evaluation must satisfy several fundamental requirements pertaining to validity and reliability. In essence, the scores obtained must consistently and accurately reflect the psychological process claimed to be measured, must have predictive value, must be stable over time, and should not be an artifact of the particular assessment context or assessor.

PROCESSES INTEGRAL TO SUBSTANCE ABUSE

Cognitive Processes

Cognitive processes encompass both cognitive style and cognitive capacity. Both aspects are relevant to understanding substance abuse. Cognitive style refers to the general strategy an individual uses to process information. For example, substantial evidence indicates that substance abusers are more inclined than the general population to analyze perceptual stimuli in a global, inarticulate manner (Sugerman & Schneider, 1976). This rather stable trait is referred to as "perceptual field dependency." Significantly, this cognitive style appears to be related to treatment prognosis (Karp, Kissin, & Hustmeyer, 1970). Another type of cognitive style commonly found among substance abusers is "stimulus augmentation"—the propensity to magnify sensory input (Buchsbaum & Ludwig, 1980). Stimulus augmentation is related to a motivational disposition characterized by impulsivity, behavioral disinhibition, and sensation or novelty seeking. Interestingly, this cognitive style is found primarily among persons with low platelet monoamine oxidase (MAO) activity (Schooler, Zahn, Murphy, & Buchsbaum, 1978). Low platelet MAO activity is particularly associated with alcoholism in cases in which there is a conjoint antisocial disorder (Von Knorring, Bohman, Von Knorring, & Oreland, 1985).

Understanding the person's cognitive style may thus assist in treatment planning and in formulating a differential diagnosis. Unfortunately, the techniques for assessing this aspect of cognition have not been inculcated into general psychometric assessment practice, although it is possible to make inferences about perceptual field dependency by using a simple test measuring flexibility of perceptual closure (Jacobson, Pisani, & Berenbaum, 1970) and stimulus augmenting by measuring sensation-seeking behavior (Zuckerman, Bone, Neary, Mangelsdorff, & Brastman, 1972).

Cognitive capacities are commonly impaired in people with alcohol disorders as a result of CNS injury either directly caused by alcohol neurotoxicity or indirectly mediated by organ/system damage (e.g., hepatic encephalopathy, obstructive pulmonary disease, and hypertension). Multiple sources typically compromise CNS functioning where cognitive deficits are found. In other words, besides the specific effects of drugs or alcohol on the brain, a neglectful lifestyle and trauma (e.g., head injuries from accidents and fights), as well as poor health status, contribute to the CNS disturbances. The psychometric evaluation must, therefore, not only be aimed at detecting and describing the pattern of disturbances in CNS functioning by means of validated neuropsychological tests but should additionally attempt to determine from other psychometric instruments (as well as from biomedical or laboratory tests) the possible etiological basis for the manifest disturbances.

Approximately 75% of individuals with alcohol addiction demonstrate some form of CNS disturbance as measured by neuropsychological tests (Tarter & Edwards, 1985). Emerging findings also suggest that other forms of substance abuse are frequently associated with deficits on neuropsycholocial tests (Grant, Mohns, Miller, & Reitan, 1976). Generally speaking, chronic alcohol abuse can cause both cognitive and physical damage to the brain especially expressed by visual–motor deficits with verbal ability remaining essentially intact (Mearns & Lees-Haley, 1993). Impairments are most frequently observed on tasks measuring abstract thinking and memory capacity as well as on tests measuring visuospatial processes (Tarter & Ryan, 1983). These deficits appear to be most pronounced in individuals who are in less than optimal health or who have experienced the cumulative effects of multiple CNS insults (Grant, Adams, & Reed, 1979). With respect to biomedical factors, a low-grade chronic hepatic encephalopathy may contribute substantially to the cognitive deficits found in cirrhotic alcoholics; this neuropsychiatric disturbance itself has a complex etiology. For example, the encephalopathy, revealed as poor performance on cognitive tests, may be produced by the liver's failure to catabolize circulating neurotoxins (Tarter, Edwards, & Van Thiel, 1986) in addition to the liver's failure to absorb and store vitamin E. Hence, neuronal membranes are injured because of the absence of vitamin E to protect them from oxidation by free radicals. Furthermore, it should be noted that an hepatic encephalopathy may have a variety of other etiological determinants (Tarter et al., 1986). The point is that the manifest cognitive deficits found in people with alcohol addiction have a multifactorial etiology.

Neuropsychological deficits associated with alcoholism are well documented. Indeed, two syndromes of cognitive disorder have been described. A dementia has been observed that is distinguishable according to both neuroanatomical and cognitive manifestations from the more florid amnestic or Korsakoff's syndrome (Wilkinson & Carlen, 1980). A number of other neurological conditions have also been described, although their neuropsychological manifestations have not yet been studied.

Less is known regarding the neuropsychological sequelae of other drugs having abuse liability. Evidence has been presented indicating that the chronic use of such drugs as phencyclidine (PCP), inhalants, benzodiazepines, heroin, cocaine, and amphetamines may be associated with neuropsychological impairments in some individuals (Grant & Judd, 1976; Parsons & Farr, 1981). One major methodological problem in this area of study is that it is not possible to ascertain the specific effects of a certain drug on CNS functioning because polydrug abuse is the typical pattern of consumption. Also the frequency and quantity of drug use are extremely variable; hence, determining dose–effect relationships vis-à-vis cognitive functioning is difficult if not impossible. These qualifications notwithstanding, the available evidence does indicate that as a group, substance abusers perform deficiently on certain neuropsychological tests indexing CNS integrity. As is the case among individuals with alcohol addiction, poor neuropsychological test performance probably has a multifactorial etiology. For instance, the poor performance may be reflective of multiple minor brain injuries, poor overall health, and premorbid neurodevelopmental disorder.

Neuropsychological tests are very sensitive indicators of cerebral integrity (Lezak, 1983). Their sensitivity surpasses that of either the clinical neurological examination or the electroencephalogram (EEG; Goldstein, Deysach, & Kleinknecht, 1973). Moreover, in the early stages of a dementing disease, psychometric procedures probably also exceed the diagnostic sensitivity of neuroradiological procedures, where gross morphological injury may not be present or detectable upon visual inspection. More important, perhaps, neuropsychological tests are especially informative for rehabilitation purposes because the data obtained describe functional cerebral integrity, and as such, they characterize the person according to commonly recognized cognitive processes (e.g., attention, memory, language, learning, and concentration) that are generally understood to be important for educational, vocational, and social adjustment. Indeed, it is the relationship between neurological status and these latter processes, rather than the test scores per se, that underscores the importance of the neuropsychological assessment.

Documenting cognitive capacity and efficiency via neuropsychological assessment is important for several reasons. During the drug withdrawal phase at the onset of rehabilitation, cognitive capacity may be too impaired for the person to achieve meaningful gains from didactic therapy or counseling. Assessment of the subjective effects of intoxication or withdrawal status from various substances of abuse have been developed by the Addiction Research Center (Haertzen, 1974). Handelsman et al. (1987) have developed other assessment instruments for intoxication and withdrawal. This latter group of researchers promote the use of these subjective measures in conjunction with objective evaluation, namely, a serum drug level.

A brief cognitive screening used on repeated occasions can determine the client's readiness for rehabilitation. Cognitively limited individuals may not be able to solve daily problems, develop broad strategic plans to restructure their lives, acquire insight into their problems, or benefit from vocational rehabilitation. Neuropsychological assessment can assist in the formulation of a treatment plan and aftercare program for individuals with these types of difficulties. For instance, most persons respond to didactic psychotherapy, whereas those whose thinking is concrete benefit best from structured interventions not requiring insight (Kissin, Platz, & Su, 1970). Furthermore, it is important to note that everyday activities such as driving a car, using power machinery, or performing tasks where there are safety risks may be impaired because of CNS damage from chronic substance abuse. Neuropsychological testing, particularly in the area of psychomotor capacities, may therefore assist in a determination of injury risk to self and/or others.

Neuropsychological assessment has also been increasingly utilized as part of forensic evaluation. In criminal cases, the objective, quantitative assessment capacities can contribute to a better understanding of behavior due to CNS injury. In this regard, the expertise of the neuropsychologist who understands the neurobehavioral mechanisms associated with alcohol or substance abuse disturbances (e.g., blackouts and anterograde amnesia) can provide important information about the severity of the addiction, its consequences for the functional capacities of the particular individual, and the impact of cognitive deficits on emotional and psychosocial processes.

The systematic delineation of cognitive strengths and weaknesses, particularly as they relate to the onset and pattern of substance use behavior, is important for several additional reasons. This type of evaluation may yield important information about etiology. For example, an attentional disorder or learning disability often precedes the onset of substance abuse (Tarter, Alterman, & Edwards, 1985). This has treatment implications because it may be possible to prevent or treat the substance use behavior for some individuals by ameliorating the problem that initially motivated drug use. In addition, the assessment of cognitive deficits has importance for understanding the person's everyday abilities, such as remembering appointments, following simple as well as complex directions, and learning new material. Demonstrating the presence of a deficit lends itself to implementing a treatment program that also encompasses cognitive rehabilitation. For example, cognitive retraining by either teaching the person compensatory strategies where there is an irreversible deficit or reestablishing a capacity that was not permanently impaired affords the opportunity to maximize social and vocational adjustment as part of multidisciplinary rehabilitation. It is noteworthy that cognitive rehabilitation as a subspecialty of clinical neuropsychology has been shown to be a useful adjunct to treatment of neurologically impaired individuals, although these procedures have yet to be applied to substance abusers.

Psychological Processes

The intensity of emotional experience and appropriate expression of emotion in adaptive behaviors are strongly associated with overall quality of psychological well-being. Conflicts over anger and guilt, or the display of intense emotional reactions such as rage or panic, have long been known to accompany substance use behavior in many individuals. These disruptive emotions may either presage substance abuse or emerge following drug use onset. Not uncommonly, the consumption of psychoactive substances is motivated by a need to ameliorate negative affective states. The inability to express emotions effectively in the social context, particularly negative feelings, is also frequently associated with drug abuse.

Emotional disturbance is often encompassed within psychopathology. Although not all drug or alcohol users demonstrate psychopathology, the range of manifest psychopathology includes the spectrum of neurotic, characterological, and psychotic disturbances. From the psychometric perspective, clinically significant psychopathology is present in cases in which the severity exceeds two standard deviations above the population mean (i.e., individuals who rank in excess of the 95th percentile in the population of a trait qualify for a diagnosis). Whether such psychopathological disturbance requires treatment can only be determined by integrating the findings obtained from the psychiatric and psychometric assessments. For example, a chronic state of tension or depression may be integral to substance abuse for an individual, even if it is not of sufficient severity to qualify for a diagnosis. Under these circumstances, the negative affective states may contribute directly to drug-seeking motivation. Khantzian (1985) described the association between negative affects and particular substances of abuse. And further, Dodes (1990) postulated that addiction modulates one's affective state, bringing the negative affective experiences of helplessness or powerlessness under one's control.

At the other extreme, it is important to be cognizant of the possibility that a psychopathological disorder, even if qualifying for a psychiatric diagnosis, may spontaneously remit following effective treatment for substance use. Indeed, it is not uncommon for psychopathological symptoms to dissipate in conjunction with sobriety or abstinence from drugs. Furthermore, it is essential to recognize that emotional distress (e.g., anger, helplessness, and guilt) can both precipitate and sustain a psychopathological disorder. Hence, characterizing the client's emotional status should enable the clinician to determine whether an emotional disturbance underlies the emergence of psychopathology or, alternatively, is a symptomatic correlate of the psychopathology. For example, intense unresolved anger can either provoke or be concomitant to a psychopathological disorder such as depression.

Psychometric tests measure traits or dimensions, in comparison to a psychiatric assessment, which is concerned with assigning the person to a diagnostic category. Traits are usually measured on a continuum that ranges from low to high. Structured psychiatric interviews (e.g., the Schedule for Affective Disorders and Schizophrenia, Diagnostic Interview Schedule, and

Structured Clinical Interview for DSM-III-R) characterize the person dichoto-mously according to the presence or absence of symptoms. The aggregate of symptoms determines the severity of the syndrome. Whether a categorical or dimensional approach is utilized, the most frequently observed psycho-pathological disturbances comorbid to alcohol or drug abuse are anxiety and depression. However, virtually every Axis I and Axis II disturbance has been observed concomitant to substance abuse (Dackis, Gold, Pottash, & Sweeney, 1985; Daley, Moss, & Campbell, 1987; Helzer & Pryzbeck, 1988; Peace & Mellsop, 1987; Weissman, 1988).

In addition to recognizing the importance of objectively evaluating emotion and affect in the context of both psychopathology and substance abuse, it is essential to emphasize the complexity of this task. Emotional disturbance as well as psychopathology can emerge at any time during the natural history of the substance use disorder and often has a complicated etiological basis. Disturbances, for example, may be manifested as the result of genetic predisposition or life stress or may appear as neuropsychiatric sequelae emanating from the drug's actions on the CNS. With respect to genetic predisposition, a careful and systematic evaluation of the first- and second-degree relatives of the client can help the clinician to ascertain whether the psychopathology or the substance abuse is the primary disorder. One objective of the psychometric assessment should be to determine the likely etiological basis for the observed disturbances through an examination of family psychiatric history, so that the most effective interventions can be applied.

Social Processes

The third component of a comprehensive psychometric assessment pertains to the degree to which substance use relates to social performance and interpersonal adjustment. Social adjustment can be considered at two levels—functioning within the microenvironment (e.g., family and friends) and the macroenvironment (e.g., work, community, and school). Abundant evidence indicates, for example, that family disruption may be the most salient problem contributing to alcohol or drug use for one person, whereas occu-pational maladjustment may be most problematic for another. Also, for some individuals, chronic substance abuse is associated with generalized psychosocial maladjustment or an antisocial disposition. For others, the psychosocial disturbance may be circumscribed and confined only to one or a few particular areas of functioning. The point to be emphasized is that psychosocial adjustment is not a unitary dimension but rather consists of numerous processes. Disturbances in one or more of these processes may either presage or emerge as a result of prolonged alcohol or drug abuse. Moreover, the particular areas of disturbance vary widely in the population. If the matter is considered in the context of heterogeneous presentation in the previously discussed areas of cognitive and psychological functioning, it is apparent that the overall clinical presentation for any given individual is unique. In other words, substance abuse dichotomies such as primary–secondary (Tarter, McBride, Buonpane, & Schneider, 1977), essential–reactive (Rudie & McGaughran, 1974), or type 1–type 2 (Cloninger, Bohman, & Sigvardsson, 1981) are, at best, general categorizations. Subtyping substance abusers into larger categories is similarly beset with the problem of obscuring the marked individuality of antecedent characteristics and potential range of consequences. Thus, from a clinical perspective, the evaluation must be idiographic to the extent that it identifies the unique characteristics and their interrelationships within the client to help the clinician arrive at an understanding of the current predicament. In this way, a comprehensive psychometric evaluation surpasses merely assigning the person to a diagnostic category.

Evaluating social adjustment is an integral component of the overall clinical examination. Commonly, social stress precipitates substance use, which can subsequently evolve into a substance use disorder. Under these circumstances, substance use may reflect an attempt by the individual to cope with a discrete stressor (e.g., death of parent, loss of employment, accidental injury, and chronic illness) or cumulative conflicts in meeting the challenges of everyday living. Furthermore, a change in lifestyle may trigger substance use. In this regard, it is noteworthy that the risk for substance abuse is augmented among newly retired individuals, who may for the first time in their lives have extensive free time and an accompanying lack of daily challenges revolving around their job or parenting responsibilities. The point is that disturbed psychosocial processes can be either etiologically related to a substance use disorder or consequential to such a condition. This disturbance can involve any of a number of social roles (e.g., parent, spouse, and employee) or center around interpersonal matters (e.g., conflicts and social skill deficits). In conducting the psychometric evaluation, it is essential, therefore, that information be obtained about the specific areas of maladjustment, as well as the time of their emergence in the context of the natural history of the substance use disorder.

In summation, the three broadly defined categories of functioning—cognitive processes, psychological processes, and social adjustment—form an interrelated unity. A disruption in one area may affect other areas of functioning. Hence, a severe emotional disorder, for example, can produce disturbances in cognitive efficiency and capacity as well as in psychosocial adjustment. Many different patterns of disturbance may be manifested. In substance abusers, a disturbance may be confined to one area of functioning, may pervade all psychological domains, or (theoretically, at least) may not be present in any of the three areas. The major objective of the psychometric assessment is to analyze the relationships among these three categories of functioning with respect to the etiology and consequences of alcoholism and other types of substance abuse. The next section describes the procedures for accomplishing this objective.

METHODS OF PSYCHOMETRIC ASSESSMENT

Evaluation in the three broad areas described previously, namely, cognitive, psychological, and social processes, is useful only to the extent that the information obtained contributes to a better understanding of the onset and course of substance abuse, so that affected individuals may be effectively treated. The evaluation must entail identifying the individual's specific problems that are amenable to intervention. The psychometric techniques employed need to focus on characterizing the client–environment interrelationship to elucidate how each reciprocally affects the other to culminate in substance abuse. Hence, interventions can be directed to changing either the individual's psychological makeup or the environment that may have triggered or helped maintain the substance abuse disorder.

In addition to promoting an intervention strategy, psychometric assessment offers the opportunity to quantitatively monitor changes occurring during the course of treatment. The use of brief standardized self-report checklists or rating scales, for example, facilitates the objective and systematic charting of therapeutic progress. This information not only provides feedback to the clinician but also serves the purpose of goal setting for the client. Furthermore, demonstrating to the client via objective and quantitative indices that he or she is benefiting from treatment serves the important purpose of sustaining motivation for continued involvement in rehabilitation.

Alcohol or drug abuse is almost invariably embedded in a variety of other psychological, social, or psychiatric disturbances. Within the three categories or processes, seven specific domains comprise the comprehensive psychometric evaluation:

- Alcohol and drug use history
- Health status/medical history
- Psychiatric status and history
- Personality
- Cognition: General cognitive functioning, neuropsychological deficits
- Family functioning: Cohesion, adaptability, communication
- Social adjustment: Social support, social roles, peer affiliation, social skills, vocational adjustment, school adjustment, recreation/leisure

Alcohol and Drug Use

The first requirement in the assessment is to characterize the substance use behavior. The onset of each type of substance used needs to be documented so that drug use progression may be explicitly described. As each type of substance emerges in the person's history, it is essential to ascertain whether it reached problematic severity to warrant a diagnosis of abuse or dependence. In addition, the occurrence of remission and number of lifetime episodes should be described. Also, the quantity and frequency of consumption within a typical 30-day period should be recorded for each episode so that a picture of the person's total involvement with alcohol and drugs can be obtained. In addition, polydrug use should be investigated because of the substantial lethal risk posed by the synergistic effects of the combined use of psychoactive drugs. For example, conjointly using alcohol and benzodiazepines is especially dangerous because of the risk of respiratory arrest.

To date, no single assessment measure evaluates all aspects and ramifications of substance abuse. Certain instruments measure quantity and frequency, others severity, and yet others measure patterns of current and lifetime abuse. With this in mind, the purpose of assessment dictates the instrument.

For adults, a number of unidimensional rating scales quantifying severity of alcohol problems are routinely used. The Michigan Alcoholism Screening Test (MAST; Selzer, 1971) is best known for this purpose. The MAST is easy to administer because it consists of 25 true–false statements. Like the MAST, the Drug Abuse Screening TEST (DAST; Skinner, 1982) is a self-report measure that is brief (5 minutes to administer) and easy to score (20 items). The DAST provides information on the consequences of drug abuse. Also, it can be used as part of an interview or as a self-report measure and can be used in a variety of settings.

Alcohol problems can also be evaluated from a multivariate perspective employing the Alcohol Use Inventory (AUI; Wanberg & Horn, 1985). The specific scales of the AUI are listed in Table 3.1. This instrument attempts to capture both the motivational and consequential aspects of alcohol use. The AUI consists of 228 items in a self-report format and can be given to individuals or to groups. A limiting characteristic of the AUI is that it is not well suited as a baseline measure of functioning because the questions are without reference to a specific time frame.

Drug problem severity can be quantified using the Addiction Severity Index (ASI; McClellan, Luborsky, Woody, & O'Brien, 1980). This semistructured interview yields an evaluation of the impact of drug use on various aspects of daily living. Information obtained from the ASI, a 147-item interview, can be helpful in treatment planning. The ASI is also useful in that it provides both self-report data on severity of abuse as well as clinical ratings regarding the severity of abuse.

A subscale of the Minnesota Multiphasic Personality Inventory (MMPI)—the MacAndrew Alcoholism Scale (MAC)—consists of 49 items that can be used to differentiate between persons with purely psychiatric disorders and those with substance abuse disorders. Another important feature of the MAC is that it assists in the assessment of particular characteristics associated with addiction such as impulsivity, poor judgment, and sensation-seeking behavior. Also, when analyzed within the context of a full MMPI profile that makes use of the validity scales, the MAC can identify those persons who might be minimizing their substance abuse by subscribing to socially desirable responses. It is important to note that individuals with substance abuse disorders who might be legally mandated to receive a drug and alcohol evaluation are often motivated to hide or minimize their substance abuse and thus often respond defensively (Shaffer, 1992).

TABLE 3.1. Scales of the Alcohol Use Inventory

Primary scales

Drinking to improve sociability
Drinking to improve mental functioning
Gregarious versus solo drinking
Sustained drinking
Obsessive–compulsive drinking
Guilty and worry associated with drinking
Drinking helps manage mood
Prior attempts to stop drinking
Lose control over behavior when drinking
Social role maladaption
Psychoperceptual withdrawal
Psychophysical withdrawal
Quantity of daily alcohol use
Drinking used to cope with marital stress
Marital problems associated with drinking

Secondary scales

Drinking to enhance functioning
Obsessive sustained drinking
Anxious concern about drinking
Uncontrolled, life-functioning disruption (1)
Uncontrolled, life-functioning disruption (2)

General factor

General alcohol involvement

Psychometric tests for known or suspected adolescent drug users have been recently validated. The Personal Experience Inventory (PEI; Henly & Winters, 1988) and the Chemical Dependency Assessment Survey (Oetting, Beauvais, Edwards, & Waters, 1984) are the two best-developed instruments, with the PEI being more suitable for a clinical population. The PEI assesses multiple domains of experience affected by substance abuse. The PEI evaluates the substance use itself (i.e., quantity, frequency, and severity) as well as the context of abuse (i.e., the family) and social and environmental influences. A teen version of the ASI is presently undergoing psychometric validation (Kaminer, Bukstein, & Tarter, 1991).

Finally, the Drug Use Screening Inventory (DUSI; Tarter, 1990) has also been developed. This self-report has homologous forms for adolescents and adults. It profiles substance use involvement in conjunction with severity of disturbance in nine spheres of everyday functioning. Absolute and relative severity scores ranging from 0 to 100% quantify the magnitude of problems in 10 domains: (1) substance use, (2) psychiatric disorder, (3) health, (4) behavior, (5) school, (6) work, (7) social competence, (8) peer relationships, (9) family, and (10) leisure and recreation. Psychometric statistics have documented the reliability and validity of the DUSI in conjunction with generation of norm and cutoff scores for diagnosis (Kirisci, Hsu, & Tarter, 1994; Tarter & Kirisci, 1997).

It is readily apparent that psychometric techniques have not been developed to encompass the measurement of alcohol and drug abuse in all of their multifaceted aspects. The previously described procedures only clarify present or current use patterns and problem severity. Other types of information are also important to obtain and these can most easily be gathered during the course of an interview or from self-report that can additionally contribute to the comprehensive description of substance use behavior. Questioning should, therefore, be directed to determine the following: (1) patterns of substance use (e.g., episodic vs. continuous), (2) context of substance use (solitary vs. social consumption), (3) availability of drugs and opportunity to access drugs in the social environment, (4) perceived importance of drugs, (5) expected and experienced effects of drugs on mood and behavior, and (6) family history of drug and alcohol abuse.

Health Status

At the present time, there is no standardized assessment measure of health status in individuals with substance abuse disorders. This lack of instrumentation in a critical area of health care is the result of current health policy which has shifted the emphasis from health status to emphasis on health care delivery and quality of life. Although these latter two areas of health care are important, a need still exists for research in health status itself not just its ramifications. Some general health surveys, not specific to substance abuse but which can be applied to this population, are the Nottingham Health Profile (Hunt, McEwen, & McKenna, 1985), the Duke–UNC Health Profile (Parkerson et al., 1981), and the General Health Survey (Stewart, Hays, & Ware, 1988).

Psychiatric History

Substance abuse can occur conjointly with virtually any Axis I or Axis II psychiatric disorder. This has important treatment implications of which the most obvious is that for some individuals, alcohol or drug consumption may constitute an attempt at self-medication. Hence, treatment of the primary disorder may in some circumstances be sufficient to ameliorate the substance use disorder. Alternatively, prolonged drug abuse may precipitate a psychiatric disturbance, either directly by inducing neurochemical changes or indirectly through the stress or maladjustment concomitant to a substance abusing lifestyle. A major task, therefore, is to delineate the type and severity of psychiatric morbidity that may be present and to determine whether it preceded or developed after the substance use disorder.

Structured diagnostic interviews have been increasingly utilized in the objective formulation of substance use disorder diagnoses as well as other psychiatric diagnosis. Several instruments, all with good reliability, are currently available. The Structured Clinical Interview for DSM-III-R (SCID; Spitzer, Williams, & Gibbon, 1987) is the most recent interview schedule to be introduced.

Other structured interviews are the Diagnostic Interview Schedule (DIS; Robins, Helzer, Croughan, & Ratcliff, 1981) and the Schedule for Affective Disorders and Schizophrenia (SADS; Spitzer, Endicott, & Robins, 1975); both of these latter instruments are based on the older criteria according to the third edition of the *Diagnostic and Statistical Manual of Mental Disorders* (DSM-III). By employing a structured interview, it is possible, at the diagnostic threshold level of psychiatric disorder, to relate substance use behavior to psychiatric status. The ramification for treatment is that the information gleaned may suggest a particular type of intervention. For example, if an affective disorder preceded the substance use disorder and is still present at the time of the assessment, it would suggest the need to treat this disorder as the primary condition.

There are some important characteristics and differences among the SCID, DIS, and SADS. In contrast to the SCID and SADS, which are semistructured interviews requiring a high level of clinical sophistication, the DIS is a fully structured interview that can be used by paraprofessionals, thus making it useful as a research diagnostic instrument. The DIS also captures the lifetime history of substance abuse by documenting episodes and duration of abuse. Both the DIS and SADS provide an abundance of comparative data. The DIS has been used extensively as a cross-cultural epidemiological research instrument (Helzer & Canino, 1991). As such, national and international norms are available. Similarly, the SADS was developed and implemented by a national study on depression that has provided extensive data that can be used as a comparative sample.

Three diagnostic interviews are available for adolescents. These include the Diagnostic Interview Schedule (Revised) for Children (Costello, Edelbrock, & Costello, 1984), the Kiddie Schedule for Affective Disorders and Schizophrenia (Orvaschel, Puig-Antich, Chambers, Tabrizi, & Johnson, 1982), and the Diagnostic Interview for Children and Adolescents (Wellner, Reich, Herianic, Jung, & Amado, 1987). Each of these interviews also has a version to be administered to a parent to obtain convergent validity of the findings accrued from the youngster.

Self-report questionnaires can also reveal important information by quantifying the presence and severity of psychiatric disorder that may not be severe enough to warrant a diagnosis (e.g., an affective disturbance that although not qualifying for a diagnosis, may nonetheless be a contributor to or a consequence of substance abuse). Thus, self-rating scales may provide a more valid picture of the severity of psychopathology than that afforded by only an interview. For example, the MMPI (Hathaway & McKinley, 1951) contains three validity scales that also measure some test-taking attitudes, Hence, truthfulness or a response bias toward either over- or underreporting symptoms is documented. A disadvantage is that the profile obtained from the

MMPI does not translate to diagnosis in any taxonomic system but rather quantifies severity across multiple dimensions. However, the configuration of scores among the scales, in conjunction with the many specialized scales that have been derived from the MMPI, makes it possible to comprehensively identify personality disorders, family problems, health disturbances, and social maladjustment.

Other self-report dimensional rating scales can be employed when either the time or expertise is not available to conduct a structured interview or to obtain an MMPI profile. The most commonly used test in this regard is the Symptom Checklist 90—Revised (SCL-90-R; Derogatis, 1983). This self-rating scale is brief and easily scored and yields indices of severity of psychopathology across nine specific dimensions of psychopathology in addition to three summary global scales.

Table 3.2 presents the primary scales for the MMPI and the SCL-90-R. However, with respect to the MMPI, it should be noted that the richness of clinical information lies in the configuration comprising the overall profile of the primary scales, combined with the numerous other specialized scales.

The importance of evaluating psychopathology in the substance abuse disorders cannot be overemphasized. Treatment of the underlying psychiatric disorder may itself be, in many cases, sufficient to ameliorate a substance abuse disorder. For this reason, it is essential to document the type, onset, and presentation of psychopathology as it relates to alcohol or drug use behavior. In addition, documentation of psychiatric illness in other family members, using such instruments as the Family History Chart (Mann, Sobell, Sobell, & Pavan, 1985) or the Family Informant Schedule and Criteria (Manuzza, Fryer, Endicott, & Klein, 1985), can assist in obtaining a clear picture of the primary psychiatric disorder when it is unclear whether the substance abuse or another psychiatric disturbance constitutes the fundamental problem.

Personality

Certain dispositional behaviors or personality traits of the individual are commonly associated with the etiology and maintenance of alcohol or drug

TABLE 3.2. Minnesota Multiple Personality Inventory and Symptom Checklist 90—Revised Scales

MMPI scales		
Hypochondriasis	Psychopathic Deviate	Psychasthenia
Depression	Masculinity–Femininity	Schizophrenia
Hysteria	Paranoia	Hypomania
		Social Introversion

SCL-90-R scales		
Somatization	Obsessive–Compulsive	Interpersonal Sensitivity
Depression	Anxiety	Hostility
Phobic Anxiety	Paranoid Ideation	Psychoticism

abuse. The extent to which certain personality traits presage the onset of substance use or are shaped by the long-term consequence of drug abuse needs to be ascertained on a case-by-case basis. Features such as low self-esteem, impulsivity, aggressiveness, and behavioral disinhibition are more prevalent in the drug-abusing than in the normal population.

No single instrument currently assesses all dimensions of personality that may be relevant to understanding drug use behavior. The MMPI, described previously, is very useful for profiling psychopathology and facilitating the formulation and testing of heuristic hypotheses about specific personality characteristics. However, more specialized personality assessment focusing on discrete traits is required to determine which dispositional behaviors are linked to drug use motivation. The Multidimensional Personality Questionnaire (MPQ) provides information about personality traits that have frequently been found to be deviant in alcoholics or drug abusers. Significantly, the scales comprising the MPQ are quite independent of one another and measure traits having a strong heritable basis (Tellegen, 1982, 1985; Tellegen et al., 1988). Table 3.3 summarizes the MPQ scales. Numerous other personality questionnaires have been developed; however, none measures traits that are so integrally linked to substance abuse as those assessed by the MPQ.

Self-esteem disturbances may be also related in some individuals to substance use. Low self-esteem can occur in a number of areas of daily living and may be secondary to psychopathology. The Self-Esteem Inventory (Epstein, 1976) is a multidimensional scale with good breadth of coverage and superior psychometric properties. Table 3.4 lists the scales comprising this inventory. As can be seen, the test taps aspects of psychological well-being that are not ordinarily covered by personality tests and that may contribute to a better understanding of the causes and consequences of a substance use disorder in the individual.

Cognition

A neuropsychological evaluation is important for a variety of reasons. It provides information regarding the amenability of the person to respond to treatment. For example, individuals who have mental retardation, have suffered severe neurological injury, or have dementia as a result of their alcoholism or drug use are unlikely to profit from insight-oriented forms of

TABLE 3.3. Multidimensional Personality Questionnaire Scales

Well-being	Control (vs. Impulsiveness)
Social Potency	Harm Avoidance
Achievement	Traditionalism
Social Closeness	Absorption
Stress Reaction	Positive Affectivity
Alienation	Negative Affectivity
Aggression	Constraint

TABLE 3.4. Multidimensional Self-Esteem Inventory

Global Self-Esteem	Competence
Lovability	Likability
Self-Control	Personal Power
Moral Self-Approval	Body Appearance
Body Functioning	Identity Integration
	Defensive Self-Enhancement

therapy. In the early stages of withdrawal, cognitive assessment can help determine whether mental confusion is present to a degree that it would militate against any benefits accrued from individual or group therapy. The high prevalence of acute neurological injury from trauma, fights, and falls as well as automobile accidents is also important to document insofar as they have an impact on cognitive capacity. Knowing this information can also help characterize the person's lifestyle and overall association with psychoactive drugs. In addition, the behavioral changes associated with these types of injuries, such as behavioral disinhibition, social inappropriateness, and emotional lability, may impede rehabilitation. Hence, clarifying cognitive impairment due to CNS injury and dysfunction enables the comprehensive characterization of neuropsychiatric disorder, which in turn has treatment and posttreatment ramifications. Moreover, by delineating the person's cognitive strengths and weaknesses, these specialized psychometric tests afford the important advantage of yielding information pertinent to vocational rehabilitation, educational planning, and treatment.

The National Institute on Drug Abuse (NIDA) has emphasized the importance of including an assessment of the cognitive consequences of substance abuse. In 1989, NIDA funded the development of a substance abuse assessment project to evaluate the multiple problem areas affected by addiction. In fact, it is the primary objective of the Drug Abuse Treatment Outcome Study (DATOS) conducted by the Research Triangle Institute to conceptualize and implement the use of a standardized comprehensive assessment protocol to be used in treatment settings to evaluate the multifactorial nature of substance abuse.

An important feature of DATOS assessment battery is the use of a neuropsychological screening tool to assess whether further evaluation of cognitive functioning is needed. For the sake of efficiency and clinical utility, the DATOS model of assessment proposes the use of the Trail Making Test, a well-known gross measure of general cognitive function (Armitage, 1946). If the client performs poorly on this test, the Mini-Mental Status Examination (MMSE; Folstein, Folstein, & McHugh, 1975) would be administered. As described by (Tarter & Edwards, 1987), the purpose of the initial neuropsychological screening is to determine whether there is evidence for the presence of a nonspecific CNS disturbance. That is, this stage of testing will ascertain whether there is any general gross disturbance using sensitive but nonspecific tests. The second stage of the evaluation involves the delineation of cognitive abilities and limitations. Using standardized batteries, complemented when necessary by specialized tests, the severity of cognitive impairment is quantified. The processes evaluated typically include speech and language, attention, psychomotor skill, learning and memory, and abstract reasoning ability. At this stage of the evaluation, hypotheses can be formulated about lesion localization and lateralization. Several standardized neuropsychological batteries are currently in wide use. The Halstead–Reitan Battery (Reitan, 1955), Luria–Nebraska Neuropsychological Test Battery (Golden, 1981), and the Pittsburgh Initial Neuropsychological Test System (Goldstein, Tarter, Shelly, & Hegedus, 1983) are perhaps the most comprehensive in that they pandemically survey the major cognitive domains. Then, if significant impairment is noted in a specific cognitive domain, specialized comprehensive testing should be conducted to elucidate its severity and breadth. This is the third stage of the assessment. It is not only important for purposes of lesion localization but perhaps even more critical for posttreatment planning. For example, it is important to fully describe psychomotor impairments if the client works with power machinery or when there are other safety risks. Visuoperceptual disturbances must be comprehensively documented if the person drives a car, especially when driving at night might pose a significant risk. Similarly, when the clinician identifies learning or memory deficit in stage two, it should be further evaluated if the posttreatment plan included educational or vocational rehabilitation. For example, memory testing at stage three can be most easily accomplished using the California Verbal Learning Test (Fridlund & Dellis, 1987). This test provides detailed information about learning and memory when the stage two assessment uncovers evidence of a memory disorder. From such comprehensive evaluation of memory capacities, targeted cognitive rehabilitation can then be implemented. In the same vein, specialized tests are also available for other aspects of cognitive and psychomotor abilities which could yield the data essential for making decisions about the client's treatment needs. It is also important to note that, generally speaking, individuals under the age of 40 with a shorter history of substance abuse are more likely to regain premorbid cognitive functioning than are older individuals with a more chronic course of abuse (Mearns & Lees-Haley, 1993).

In interpreting the results of a neuropsychological evaluation, it is important to be cognizant of the multifactorial etiology of any identified impairment. Not only do alcohol and other drugs act directly on the brain, but their use may also induce organ/system injury which in turn can disrupt CNS integrity. For example, cirrhosis, independent of alcoholism, is associated with an hepatic encephalopathy, Thus, neuropsychological defects seen in alcoholics may be, in large part, a result of liver disease (Tarter, Van Thiel, & Moss, 1988). This fact is not inconsequential because treatment of low-grade hepatic encephalopathy caused by alcoholic liver disease has been tentatively shown to improve cognitive capacities (McClain, Potter, Krombout, & Zieve, 1984). Thus medically significant problems should be recorded, particularly hypertension, malnutrition, and pulmonary insufficiency, insofar as these latter disturbances are correlated with impaired cognitive capacity. Other neurological problems frequently found in alcoholics and drug abusers are developmental disability and head trauma. The extent to which these factors contribute to neuropsychological test performance should be studied, particularly if they presaged the substance use disorder. It is not sufficient merely to describe the presence of a neuropsychological disorder. It is essential also to attempt to identify the causes underlying the manifest impairments. This latter objective can be accomplished when the neuropsychological assessment is conducted in tandem with documentation of the medical and psychiatric history.

Family Adjustment

Family organization and interactional patterns contribute to the etiology and maintenance of substance abuse. Indeed, the transmission of alcoholism across generations is to some degree influenced by familial attitudes and rituals surrounding consumption and the meanings attached to ingestion (Steinglass, Bennett, Wolin, & Reiss, 1987). Given that the family is the primary influence shaping the values and behavioral patterns of children, parenting style and family environment exercise a profound influence on the child's development until at least the time of adolescence, when psychoactive substance use may first become problematic. From the standpoint of clinical diagnosis, a number of issues must be addressed. First, it is essential to characterize the contribution of psychiatric disorder, including substance abuse, in the family. The greater the density and pervasiveness of psychiatric disorder in family members of the client undergoing evaluation, the more problematic the family and the client are likely to be. Among young substance-abusing clients, it may be especially important to record the presence or history of physical or sexual abuse toward the client as one critical index of family dysfunction. Second, the causal relationship between family dysfunction and drug use behavior needs to be ascertained. How substance abuse precipitated the family problems or conversely how family problems triggered substance abuse needs to be investigated in the course of the diagnostic evaluation. Third, the reinforcement contingencies, if any, exercised by the family on the member with the substance abuse problem needs to analyzed. That is, is substance abuse ignored, punished, or positively reinforced? Fourth, the roles and status of each family member must be understood to the extent that maladjustment, conflict, or instability is a contributor to family dysfunction that propels one member to seek alcohol or drugs as a means of coping with the ensuing stress.

Assessment of family functioning and its impact on each individual family member is predicated on making the distinction between whether the evaluative material is collected from the "insider's perspective" (i.e., self-report measures) or from the "outsider's perspective" (i.e., behavioral rating scales and observational techniques) (Olson, 1977). The issue is not whether one approach is more valid than another. Clearly, both methods of gathering information would provide a particular perspective that would contribute to a comprehensive evaluation of family functioning. Whereas both approaches to data collection might be more feasible in a research setting, data collection in a clinical environment is usually restricted to self-report measures.

Five self-report instruments quantifying family functioning are standards in the field of family studies. Each of these instruments adheres to a theoretical model from work espoused by Olson et al. (1989) that encompasses three dimensions in understanding the dynamics, functioning, and roles of any given family: *cohesion, adaptability,* and *communication.* Table 3.5 lists each of the five self-report measures according to these three theoretical dimensions as well as delineating the scales of each instrument according to each dimension.

The earliest developed self-report measure of family functioning is the Family Environment Scale (FES; Moos, 1974; Moos & Moos, 1981). The length of the FES (n = 90 items) in true–false format makes it a relatively easy instrument to administer. The FES is divided in to three major dimensions: Relationship Dimension, Personal Growth Dimension, and the Systems Maintenance Dimension. The Relationship Dimension is composed of scales that measure cohesion, expressiveness, and conflict. The Personal Growth Dimen-

TABLE 3.5. Family Adjustment Measures

Inventory	Cohesion	Adaptability	Communication	Other
Family Adaptability and Cohesion Evaluation Scales (FACES III)	• Cohesion	• Adaptability	• Marital Communication • Parent–Adolescent Communication	
Family Assessment Device (FAD)	• Affective Involvement	• Problem Solving • Behavior Control • Roles	• Communication • Affective Responsiveness	
Family Assessment Measure (FAM III)	• Affective Involvement	• Task Accomplishment • Control • Role Performance	• Communication • Affective Expression	• Values and Norms
Family Environment Scale (FES)	• Cohesion • Independence	• Organization Control	• Expressiveness Conflict	• Achievement • Active–Recreational • Moral–Religious • Intellectual Cultural
Self-Report Family Inventory (SFI)	• Positive Emotional Expression • Cohesion	• Leadership	• Communication • Conflict Resolution	• Family Health

Note. From Olson & Tiesel (1993).

sion includes scales on independence, achievement, intellectual–cultural orientation, active–recreational scale, and the moral–religious scale. The Systems Maintenance Dimension includes one scale on family organization and another on family rules/control.

The Self-Report Family Inventory (SFI) is based on the theoretical orientation of the Beavers Systems Model of Family Functioning (Beavers & Hampson, 1990). Although initially constructed to be used with observational rating scales, the SFI has been found to have clinical utility as a self-report measure of family functioning. The SFI contains six scales measuring each family member's perception of their family's health/competence, level and type of conflict, communication patterns, cohesiveness, leadership, and expression of positive emotional regard.

Epstein, Baldwin, and Bishop (1983) developed the Family Assessment Device (FAD) to assess the entire family and current level of functioning. The instrument is clinically useful especially as it is easy to score and can be used in children as young as age 12. In addition to providing a general functioning scale (GFS), the FAD also provides useful information across six conceptual dimensions: affective involvement, behavioral control, family roles, problem-solving abilities and styles, communication patterns, and affective responsiveness.

The Family Assessment Measure (FAM III) emphasizes individual perceptions and interactional patterns among family members (Skinner, Steinhauer, & Santa Barbara, 1983; Steinhauer, Santa Barbara, & Skinner, 1984). That is, although the FAM measures overall family functioning as measured by a General Scale, the FAM also provides information on specific couplings of family members as measured by the Dyadic Relationship Scale, and a Self-Rating Scale provides a measure of each individual's perception of how he or she is functioning within the family. An important feature of the FAM is that the General Scale assesses an individual's response style as measured by social desirability and defensiveness. Particular variables that are assessed by various scales of the FAM are affective involvement, control, role performance, task accomplishment, communication patterns, affective expression, and implicit/explicit family values and norms. The FAM has proven clinical utility in its relative ease of administration (30–45 minutes) and its use in younger family members (age 10 and older).

The Family Adaptability and Cohesion Evaluation Scales (FACES) is also a measure of family functioning. This has high clinical utility in that it can be administered in 10–15 minutes and can be used in younger children (ages 10–12). FACES was developed by Olson, Russell, and Sprenkle (1980, 1983) and Olson et al. (1989) as an instrument that could easily be used in both research settings and treatment facilities. FACES assesses three dimensions of family functioning: cohesion (degree of emotional bonding), adaptability (family power/roles/rules), and communication (dyadic patterns/styles). The FACES assessment instrument is especially helpful in discriminating between clinical and control families, or discriminating between "problem" and "non-problem" families (Thomas & Olson, 1991).

Besides identifying liabilities, the evaluation should also clarify the family's resources or strengths. This is particularly important for engaging the family in a therapeutic alliance. Although most evaluations of the family are typically limited to a description of its structure, it is more important to understand the family as an organizational system involving complex interactional patterns. It is these dynamic relationships occurring within the family as well as values and rituals transmitted across generations that most influence the onset and persistence of substance abuse.

Social Adjustment

For the purpose of this review, the concept of social adjustment encompasses far-reaching and diverse domains of a person's world. Included under this heading are social support, social roles, social skills, peer affiliation, school and vocational adjustment, and recreation and leisure activities. Each domain is addressed separately. The extent to which one has achieved adequate social functioning is especially important for the purposes of predicting treatment outcome. Conflicts in this sphere can delimit treatment progress.

Generally speaking, social adjustment can be defined in broad terms as the individual's capacity to fulfill designated social roles (Weissman, 1975) and, further, the individual's ability not only to fulfill these roles but that do so according to predetermined expectations of functioning (Barrabee, Barrabee, & Finesinger, 1955). With this in mind, the concept of social support can be understood as the network of relationships that are available to the individual to achieve adaptive role functioning. The extent to which a person's system of social support can provide a structure for the achievement of the multiple roles they inhabit is the extent to which social support can alleviate environmental stressors. This is especially significant if stress contributes to one's substance abuse.

Social Functioning/Social Support

Although there are many good measures of social functioning, three are included here due to the expanse of the content areas that are assessed. Table 3.6 presents a brief review of each measure.

As previously discussed, the ASI (McLellan et al., 1980) is a semistructured interview profiling an individual's problem areas as well as the severity of the problem. The ASI consists of the following scales: chemical abuse, medical status, psychological status, legal status, family/social status, vocational status, and social support. The ASI was normed on male substance abusers; thus it is not applicable to adolescents.

The Substance Abuse Problem Checklist (SAPC; Carroll, 1983) has good clinical utility as an easy-to-administer self-report checklist that assesses social functioning with application to treatment planning. An especially useful feature of the SAPC is its assessment of a client's readiness or motivation to engage in substance abuse treatment. Other categories that the SAPC evaluates

TABLE 3.6. Social Adjustment Measures

Factors	Addiction Severity Index	Substance Abuse Problem Checklist	Social Relationship Scale
Construct			
Social functioning	×	×	
Social support			×
Measurable domains			
Health		×	×
Behavior	×	×	
Family	×		×
School/work	×	×	×
Religion		×	
Legal		×	
Social	×	×	×
Recreation	×	×	×
Psychometric properties			
Reliability	×	×	×
Validity	×	×	×
Norms	×		×

are health status, personality, social relationships, vocational status, leisure time, religious status, and legal status.

The Social Relationship Scale (SRS; McFarlane, Neale, Norman, Roy, & Steiner, 1981) is one of the few assessment instruments that measures social support. The SRS assesses three aspects of social support: the total number of individuals who make up one's social support network, the type of relationship, and perhaps most important, the quality of the relationship. These factors are then evaluated as to their usefulness in moderating or buffering stress in a number of life events. Again, the concept of social support is especially useful in treatment planning. Indeed, as emphasized in the treatment outcome research of McLellan (1986) and Woody et al. (1983) a strong, intact, social support network is a positive prognostic indicator.

Peer Affiliation

A social network in which drug use is commonplace will increase the likelihood that the individual will also engage in this behavior. Drug and alcohol accessibility and availability are thus important to evaluate because ameliorating the substance use disorder may require abandoning long-standing peer affiliations. Hence, changing peer involvement may be necessary for preventing relapse. The extent to which peer relationships are embedded in a pattern of nonnormative or antisocial behavior also needs to be evaluated because such maladjustment interacts with other aspects of role performance maladjustment at work, at school, and in family life. Standardized psychometric instruments for evaluating peer affiliation patterns have not been developed. Consequently, this information must be accrued during the course of the diagnostic interview. One newly developed self-report measure, the Drug Use Screening Inventory (Tarter, 1990), enables assessment of peer problems in adolescents.

Because the social environment is a major source of reinforcement, it is essential to learn about the reward contingencies, role models, and social contextual characteristics associated with alcohol or drug use for the individual. It should be recognized that the individual not only responds to the particular social environment but also seeks out an environment that has reinforcing value. Hence, during the course of the psychometric assessment, attempts should be made to learn why the drug- or alcohol-abusing client seeks out social interactions that have maladaptive consequences. From such an evaluation, social needs and motivational patterns may be elucidated which bear directly on the etiology and persistence of substance abuse for the individual.

Social Skills

Social skill deficits are common among substance abusers (Van Hasselt, Hersen, & Milliones, 1978). Deficiencies in assertiveness skills, refusal skills, and compliment-giving skills have all been well documented. Poor ability to manage conflict in interpersonal situations may also be linked to alcohol or drug abuse. Moreover, the exacerbation of poor social skills by the stress or anxiety they induce may lead to substance use as a learned coping response. Consequently, coping style needs to be determined as one component of social skills assessment.

There are currently no psychometrically standardized instruments for evaluating social skills. Various self-rating scales, although lacking in normative scores, have been employed for identifying the presence and severity of social skill deficits and for targeting behaviorally focused interventions. The same limitations exist with respect to coping style; however, two measures that have been found to be informative are the Ways of Coping Scale (Folkman & Lazarus, 1980) and the Constructive Thinking Inventory (Epstein, 1987). Table 3.7 lists the scales comprising these two instruments.

TABLE 3.7. Assessment of Coping Skills

Ways of Coping Scale	
Conformative coping	Accepting responsibility
Distancing	Escape–avoidance
Self-controlling	Planful problem solving
Seeking social support	Positive reappraisal

Constructive Thinking Inventory	
Constructive thinking	Categorical thinking
Emotional coping	Superstitious thinking
Behavioral coping	Naive optimism
	Negative thinking

In addition to social skills, the comprehensive evaluation should document the individual's capacity to exercise the skills required for everyday living. As society becomes more and more technologically complex, it is desirable to learn whether the individual is capable of performing everyday tasks required for adaptive social adjustment. For example, can the individual manage a bank account, use bankcard machines, access directories, obtain appropriate service information, utilize public transportation, satisfy personal needs with respect to food and clothing, or apply for a job? Deficiencies in any of these areas may exacerbate the level of experienced stress and thus further alcohol or drug abuse.

School Adjustment

It is important to document the school adjustment and performance of young alcohol or drug abusers. The school is the primary social environment during adolescence. Drug accessibility and opportunity in school, and particularly the peer affiliation network of the adolescent, are especially influential as determinants of drug use initiation. Conduct problems and deviance from normative behavior are commonly associated with current substance abuse and future psychopathology. The teacher version of the Child Behavior Checklist (CBCL; Achenbach & Edelbrock, 1983) affords the opportunity to identify and quantify severity of behavioral problems in the school environment. Also, comparing the findings to the parallel parent version enables the clinician to ascertain whether adjustment problems are confined to school or are also present in the home. Table 3.8 presents the scales comprising the CBCL.

Assessing the teacher's perceptions of a child's behavior in the classroom is an essential component of a comprehensive evaluation. The Disruptive Behavior Rating Scale (Pelham & Murphy, 1987) is a measure based on DSM-III-R (American Psychiatric Association, 1987) criteria for diagnosing conduct disorder, attention-deficit/hyperactivity disorder, and oppositional defiant disorder. Another brief symptom rating scale that can be completed by the teacher is the Iowa Conners Teachers Rating Scale (Loney & Milich, 1982).

One important aspect of social adjustment is the extent to which the child participates in athletics and other extracurricular activities. These types of activities indicate how well a person is socially integrated and accepted by peers. In addition, it is essential to evaluate academic achievement and learning

TABLE 3.8. Child Behavior Checklist

Externalizing factors	Internalizing factors
Hyperactivity	Schizoid Withdrawal
Aggression	Depression
Delinquency	Uncommunicativeness
Sexual Activity	Obsessive–Compulsive Phenomena
Cruelty	Somatization
	Immaturity

aptitude in the basic skills areas. For example, learning disability compounded by low self-esteem may be a major factor propelling a youngster toward drug use as well as other nonnormative behaviors. Standardized learning and achievement tests may need to be administered to the substance-abusing adolescent to document the extent to which cognitive impairments and low achievement are involved in the motivation to use alcohol or drugs. A quick indication of whether such testing is necessary is whether the client has been held back at least two grades or cannot master specific subjects. The Peabody Individual Achievement Test (PIAT; Dunn & Markwardt, 1970) and the Wide Range Achievement Test (WRAT; Jastak & Wilkinson, 1984) are the tests most commonly used by psychologists to evaluate a learning disability, in conjunction with the Wechsler Intelligence Scale for Children—Revised (WISC-R). However, testing by a learning disabilities specialist may be required to reveal the array of cognitive processes that are developmentally delayed. In the context of such an evaluation, emphasis should be placed on the child's ability to use language. Communication skills are integral to social adjustment, because language mediates or regulates overt behavior. The Test of Language Competence (TLC; Wiig, 1985) is specifically developed to assess everyday or practical language capacity.

Vocational Adjustment

The rapid expansion of employee assistance programs illustrates the extent to which alcohol or drug abuse affects the workplace and the extent to which the workplace may influence alcohol or drug use. Stress in the workplace can have a multifactorial basis: It may occur as a consequence of inability to meet performance standards, conflicts with other employees or supervisors, disruptive work schedules, and low job satisfaction. In the most extreme cases, unemployment as well as underemployment needs to be evaluated as one factor underlying substance abuse. In addition, for some individuals, extensive travel and associated social obligations place the individual in social situations where alcohol consumption is expected. It is apparent that no single factor in the workplace predisposes a person to substance abuse. Hence, for the individual presenting for drug abuse or alcoholism treatment, it is necessary to analyze, in detail, performance and adjustment in the workplace as an etiological determinant.

Besides evaluating the job demands and workplace environment, it is necessary to evaluate the client's behavioral disposition. For example, premorbid personality disorders (particularly Antisocial Personality Disorder or social phobias) may contribute to job failure, which in turn may predispose the individual to a substance use disorder. Furthermore, it is important to evaluate the particular job in the context of normative behaviors with respect to alcohol and drug use. Access to addictive substances places the person at heightened risk simply by virtue of availability. Not surprisingly, physicians have a very high prevalence of opiate abuse. The vocational evaluation must therefore not only identify specific job-related characteristics that predispose a client to alcohol or drug abuse but also elucidate the personality and behavioral characteristics of the person. In particular, it should clarify how the vocational maladjustment results from an interaction between the person and the job environment.

Recreation/Leisure Activities

Alcohol and drug use is commonly associated with recreational and leisure-time activities. An individual who does not have socially satisfying recreational activities, hobbies, or other leisure-time opportunities may resort to the use of alcohol or drugs as a means of passing time or otherwise coping with the stress of boredom. This may be particularly problematic among members of the elderly population who are no longer gainfully employed and productive and have not developed adequate or satisfying substitute behaviors. A somewhat similar problem may confront members of the adolescent population who have substantial free or unstructured time.

Assessment and counseling related to recreational and leisure-time activities constitute a newly developing specialty. Presently, there are no standardized evaluation procedures. It therefore remains for the clinician to gather this information informally. Once it is determined that the absence of positively reinforcing pastimes may be associated with substance abuse, or that the recreational activities in which the client engages involve peers who use psychoactive substances, it is possible to help the person to restructure this important aspect of his or her life.

SUMMARY: FROM ASSESSMENT TO TREATMENT

Decision-Tree Procedure

Based on a three-stage evaluation, a decision-tree procedure described in Figure 3.1 provides a format for assessment that links evaluation to treatment. This approach enables an integration of diagnostic findings to be applied to specific treatment needs. This approach is based on an initial assessment using the DUSI (Tarter, 1990), which identifies explicit areas of possible disturbance that then points to the need for comprehensive evaluation.

There are several advantages to using a decision-tree multistage evaluation procedure:

1. The areas of disturbance can be quickly identified and at minimal cost.
2. Labor-intensive comprehensive diagnostic evaluation will only be targeted to specific areas suggested by initial screening.
3. Based on the aggregate findings from initial screening and the comprehensive diagnostic evaluation, the client's rehabilitation needs are clearly delineated.

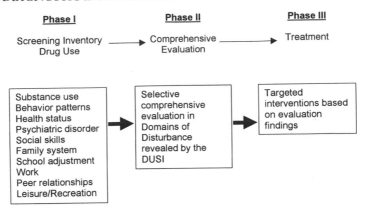

FIGURE 3.1. Decision tree.

4. Once the required treatment interventions are specified, a coordinated intervention program can be developed. In this fashion, evaluation and treatment are integrally linked in an ongoing reciprocal and interactive manner.

Linking Assessment with a Specific Treatment Modality

A recent avenue of investigation in research on addictive behaviors focuses on matching assessment instruments to specific treatment approaches. The cognitive-behavioral approach to treatment is the theoretical model that has proven efficacious in application to other psychological disorders. The work of Annis and colleagues at the Addiction Research Foundation in Canada exemplifies this approach (Annis & Graham, 1995). The focus of their work is on linking treatment planning, including relapse prevention counseling, to particular client profiles identified by the Inventory of Drinking Situations (IDS; Annis, 1982). The IDS is a 100-item self-report questionnaire that was developed to ascertain the antecedents to periods of alcohol abuse in the previous year. The IDS then categorizes heavy alcohol users by four profile types that are characterized by different precursors to periods of heavy alcohol use: (1) the negative profile—individuals whose alcohol abuse is a consequence of negative emotions (e.g., boredom, anxiety, and depression); (2) the positive profile—individuals who drink heavily due to social pressure, wanting to have a good time/celebrate, or wanting to relax; (3) the low-testing personal control individual whose abuse of alcohol is undifferentiated, possibly due to lack of motivation to change and lack of awareness of the antecedents of abuse; and (4) the low-physical-discomfort individual who also presents with an undifferentiated profile characterized by very little use of alcohol.

The cognitive-behavioral approach to substance abuse treatment can be individualized according to the four IDS client profiles. In the case of the negative and positive profilers, the focus of intervention can be on teaching alternate ways of coping with social pressure or interpersonal conflict, teaching alternate forms of relaxation, providing assertiveness training, or resolving specific areas of conflict. In the latter two profiles that are undifferentiated, the focus of treatment could be on enhancing awareness of environmental and psychological stressors that then lead to periods of heavy alcohol consumption. This could involve having clients chart their emotional responses by keeping a journal of daily events.

In summation, the current trend to match assessment profiles to specific treatment modalities has implications not only for individual treatment outcome but, on a much larger scale, for program planning and social policy in substance abuse. Much research needs to be done in this area, especially in the application of research results to diverse racial and ethnic populations.

REFERENCES

Achenbach, T., & Edelbrock, C. (1983). *Manual for the Child Behavior Checklist and Revised Child Behavior Profile.* Burlington: University of Vermont, Department of Psychiatry.

American Psychiatric Association. (1980). *Diagnostic and statistical manual of mental disorders* (3rd ed.). Washington, DC: Author.

American Psychiatric Association. (1987). *Diagnostic and statistical manual of mental disorders* (3rd ed., rev.). Washington, DC: Author.

Annis, H. M. (1982). *Inventory of Drinking Situations (IDS-100).* Toronto, Canada: Addiction Research Foundation of Ontario.

Annis, H. M., & Graham, J. M. (1995). Profile types on the Inventory of Drinking Situations: Implications for relapse prevention counseling. *Psychology of Addictive Behaviors, 9,* 176–182.

Armitage, S. (1946). An analysis of certain psychological tests used for the evaluation of brain surgery. *Psychological Monographs, 60* (Whole No. 277).

Barrabee, R., Barrabee, E. L., & Finesinger, J. E. (1955). A normative social adjustment scale. *American Journal of Psychiatry, 112,* 252–259.

Beavers, W. R., & Hampson, R. B. (1990). *Successful families: Assessment and Intervention.* New York: Norton.

Buchsbaum, M., & Ludwig, A. (1980). Effects of sensory input and alcohol administration on visual evoked potentials in normal subjects and alcoholics. In H. Begleiter (Ed.), *Biological effects of alcohol.* New York: Plenum.

Carroll, J. F. (1983). *Substance Abuse Problem Checklist manual.* Eagleville, PA: Eagleville Hospital.

Cloninger, C., Bohman, M., & Sigvardsson, S. (1981). Inheritance of alcohol abuse: Cross fostering analysis of adopted men. *Archives of General Psychiatry, 38,* 361–868.

Costello, J., Edelbrock, C., & Costello, A. (1984). *The reliability of the NIMH Diagnostic Interview Schedule for Children: A comparison between pediatric and psychiatric referrals.* Pittsburgh: Western Psychiatric Institute and Clinic.

Dackis, C. A., Gold, M. S., Pottash, A. L. C., & Sweeney, D. R. (1985). Evaluating depression in alcoholics. *Psychiatry Research, 17,* 105–109.

Daley, D., Moss, H. B., & Campbell, F. (1987). *Dual disorders: Counseling clients with chemical dependency and mental illness.* Center City, MN: Hazelden.

Derogatis, L. R. (1983). *SCL-90-R: Administration, scoring and procedures manual II* (rev.). Towson, MD: Clinical Psychometric Research.

Dodes, L. M. (1990). Addiction, helplessness, and narcissistic rage. *Psychoanalytic Quarterly, 59,* 398–419.

Dunn, L. M., & Markwardt, F. C. (1970). *Peabody Individual Achievement Test.* Circle Pines, MN: American Guidance Service.

Epstein, N. B., Baldwin, L., & Bishop, D. (1983). The McMaster Family Assessment Device. *Journal of Marital and Family Therapy, 9,* 213–228.

Epstein, S. (1976). Anxiety, arousal and the self-concept. In I. G. Sarason & C. D. Spielberger (Eds.), *Stress and anxiety.* Washington, DC: Hemisphere.

Epstein, S. (1987). *The constructive thinking inventory.* Amherst: University of Massachusetts, Department of Psychology.

Ewusi-Mensah, I., Saunders, J., & Williams, R. (1984). The clinical nature and detection of psychiatric disorders in patients with alcoholic liver disease. *Alcohol and Alcoholism, 39,* 297–302.

Folkman, S., & Lazarus, R. (1980). An analysis of coping in middle aged community sample. *Journal of Health and Social Behavior, 21,* 219–239.

Folstein, M. F., Folstein, S. E., & McHugh, P. R. (1975). Mini mental state. *Journal of Psychiatric Research, 12,* 189–198.

Fridlund, A. J., & Dellis, D. C. (1987). *California Verbal Learning Test* (research ed.). New York: Psychological Corporation.

Golden, C. J. (1981). A standardized version of Luria's neuropsychological tests. In S. Filskov & T. J. Boll (Eds.), *Handbook of clinical neuropsychology.* New York: Wiley-Interscience.

Goldstein, G., Tarter, R., Shelly, C., & Hegedus, A. (1983). The Pittsburgh Initial Neuropsychological Testing System (PINTS): A neuropsychological screening battery for psychiatric patients. *Journal of Behavioral Assessment, 5,* 227–238.

Goldstein, S., Deysach, R., & Kleinknecht, R. (1973). Effect of experience and amount of information on identification of cerebral impairment. *Journal of Consulting and Clinical Psychology, 41,* 30–34.

Grant, I., Adams, K., & Reed, R. (1979). Normal neuropsychological abilities of alcoholic men in their late thirties. *American Journal of Psychiatry, 136,* 1263–1269.

Grant, I., & Judd, L. (1976). Neuropsychological and EEG disturbances in polydrug users. *American Journal of Psychiatry, 133,* 1039–1042.

Grant, I., Mohns, L., Miller, M., & Reitan, R. (1976). A neuropsychological study of polydrug users. *Archives of General Psychiatry, 33,* 973–978.

Haertzen, C. A. (1974). *An overview of Addiction Research Center Inventory scales (ARCI): An appendix and manual of scales* (DHEW Publication No. ADM 74-92). Rockville, MD: National Institute on Drug Abuse.

Handelsman, L., Cochran, K. J., Aronson, M. J., Ness, R., Rubinstein, K. J., & Kanof, P. D. (1987). Two new rating scales for opiate withdrawal. *American Journal of Drug and Alcohol Abuse, 13,* 293–308.

Hathaway, S. R., & McKinley, J. C. (1951). *The Minnesota Multiphasic Personality Inventory manual* (rev.). New York: Psychological Corporation.

Helzer, J. E., & Canino, G. (1991). *Alcoholism in North America, Europe, and Asia.* New York: Oxford University Press.

Helzer, J. E., & Pryzbeck, T. R. (1988). The co-occurrence of alcoholism with other psychiatric disorders in the general population and its impact on treatment. *Journal of Studies on Alcohol, 49,* 219–224.

Henly, G., & Winters, K. (1988). Development of problem severity scales for the assessment of adolescent alcohol and drug abuse. *International Journal of the Addictions, 23,* 65–85.

Hunt, S. M., McEwen, J., & McKenna, S. P. (1985). Measuring health status: A tool for clinicians and epidemiologists. *Journal of the Royal College of General Practitioners, 35,* 185.

Jacobson, G., Pisani, V., & Berenbaum, H. (1970). Temporal stability of field dependence among hospitalized alcoholics. *Journal of Abnormal Psychology, 76,* 10–12.

Jastak, S. F., & Wilkinson, G. S. (1984). *Wide Range Achievement Test—Level I and II* (rev. ed.). Wilmington, DE: Jastak.

Kaminer, Y., Bukstein, O. G., & Tarter, R. E. (1991). The Teen Addiction Severity Index: Rationale and reliability. *International Journal of the Addictions, 26.*

Karp, S., Kissin, B., & Hustmeyer, F. (1970). Field-dependence as a predictor of alcoholic therapy dropouts. *Journal of Nervous and Mental Disease, 15,* 77–83.

Khantzian, E. J. (1985). The self-medication hypothesis of addictive disorders: Focus on heroin and cocaine dependence. *American Journal of Psychiatry, 142,* 1259–1264.

Kirisci, L., Hsu, T., & Tarter, R. (1994). Fitting a two-parameter logistic item response model to clarify the psychometric properties of the Drug Use Screening Inventory for adolescent alcohol and drug abusers. *Alcoholism: Clinical and Experimental Research, 18,* 1335–1341.

Kissin, B., Platz, A., & Su, W. (1970). Social and psychological factors in the treatment of chronic alcoholism. *Journal of Psychiatric Research, 8,* 13–27.

Loney, J., & Milich, R. (1982). Hyperactivity, inattention, and aggression in clinical practice. In M. Wolraich & D. Routh (Eds.), *Advances in developmental and behavioral pediatrics.* Greenwich, CT: JAI.

Mann, R. E., Sobell, L. C., Sobell, M. B., & Pavan, D. (1985). Reliability of family tree questionnaire for assessing family history of alcohol problems. *Drug and Alcohol Dependence, 15,* 61–67.

Manuzza, S., Fryer, A. J., Endicott, J., & Klein, D. F. (1985). *Family Informant Schedule and Criteria (FISC).* New York: New York State Psychiatric Institute.

McFarlane, A. H., Neale, K. A., Norman, G. R., Roy, R. G., & Steiner, D. L. (1981). Methodological issues in developing a scale to measure social support. *Schizophrenia Bulletin, 7,* 90–100.

McLellan, A. (1986). "Psychiatric severity" as a predictor of outcome from substance abuse treatments. In R. E. Meyer (Ed.), *Psychopathology and addictive disorders* (pp. 97–139). New York: Guilford Press.

McLellan, A., Luborsky, L., Woody, G., & O'Brien, C. (1980). An improved diagnostic evaluation instrument for substance abuse patients: The Addiction Severity Scale Index. *Journal of Nervous and Mental Disease, 168,* 26–33.

Mearns, J. & Lees-Haley, P. R. (1993). Discriminating neuropsychological sequelae of head injury from alcohol-abuse-induced deficits: A review and analysis. *Journal of Clinical Psychology, 49,* 714–720.

Moos, R. (1974). *Combined preliminary manual for the family, work, and group environment scales.* Palo Alto, CA: Consulting Psychologists Press.

Moos, R., & Moos, B. (1981). *Family Environment Scale manual.* Palo Alto, CA: Consulting Psychologists Press.

Oetting, E., Beauvais, F., Edwards, R., & Waters, M. (1984). *The drug and alcohol assessment system.* Fort Collins, CO: Rocky Mountain Behavioral Sciences Institute.

Olson, D. H. (1977). Insiders and outsiders views of relationships: Research studies. In

G. Levinger & H. L. Raush (Eds.), *Close relationships: Perspectives on the meaning of intimacy* (pp. 115–135). Amherst: University of Massachusetts Press.

Olson, D. H., McCubbin, H. I., Barnes, H. L., Larsen, A. S., Muxen, M. J., & Wilson, M. A. (1989). *Families: What makes them work* (updated ed.). Newbury Park, CA: Sage.

Olson, D. H., Portner, J., & Lavee, Y. (1985). *FACES III: Family Adaptability and Cohesion Evaluation Scales.* St. Paul: University of Minnesota Press.

Olson, D. H., Russell, C. S., & Sprenkle, D. H. (1980). Circumplex Model of marital and family systems. II. Empirical studies and clinical intervention. In J. Vincent (Ed.), *Advances in family intervention, assessment and theory* (Vol. I, pp. 129–179). Greenwich, CT: JAI.

Olson, D. H., Russell, C. S., & Sprenkle, D. H. (1983). Circumplex model of marital and family systems. VI. Theoretical update. *Family Process, 22,* 69–83.

Olson, D. H., & Tiesel, J. W. (1993). Assessment of family functioning. In B. J. Rounsaville, F. M. Tims, A. M. Horton, & B. Sowder (Eds.), *Diagnostic source book on drug abuse research and treatment* (NIH Publication No. 96-3508, pp. 60–61). Rockville, MD: NIDA.

Orvaschel, H., Puig-Antich, J., Chambers, W., Tabrizi, M. A., & Johnson, R. (1982). Retrospective assessment of prepubertal major depression with the Kiddie-SADS-E. *Journal of the American Academy of Child Psychiatry, 21,* 392–397.

Parkerson, G. R., Gehlbach, S. H., Wagner, E. H., James, S. A., Clapp, N. E., & Muhlbaier, L. H. (1981). The Duke–UNC health profile: An adult health status instrument for primary care. *Medical Care, 19,* 806.

Parsons, A., & Farr, S. (1981). The neuropsychology of alcohol and drug abuse. In S. Filskov & T. Boll (Eds.), *Handbook of clinical neuropsychology* (pp. 320–365). New York: Wiley.

Peace, K., & Mellsop, G. (1987). Alcoholism and psychiatric disorder. *Australian and New Zealand Journal of Psychiatry, 21,* 94–101.

Pelham, W. E., & Murphy, D. A. (1987). *The DBD rating scale: A parent and teacher rating scale for the disruptive behavior disorders of childhood in DSM-III-R.* Unpublished manuscript, University of Pittsburgh.

Reitan, R. (1955). An investigation of the validity of Halstead's measures of biological intelligence. *Archives of Neurology and Psychiatry, 73,* 28–35.

Robins, L., Helzer, J., Croughan, J., & Ratcliff, K. (1981). National Institute of Mental Health Diagnostic Schedule: Its history, characteristics and validity. *Archives of General Psychiatry, 38,* 381–389.

Rounsaville, B. J. (1993). Overview: Rationale and guidelines for using comparable measures to evaluate substance abusers. In B. J. Rounsaville, F. M. Tims, A. M. Horton, & B. J. Sowder (Eds.), *Diagnostic source book on drug abuse research and treatment* (pp. 1–10). Rockville, MD: National Institute on Drug Abuse.

Rudie, R., & McGaughran, L. (1974). Differences in developmental experience, defensiveness and personality organization between two classes of problem drinkers. *Journal of Abnormal and Social Psychology, 83,* 655–666.

Schooler, C., Zahn, T., Murphy, D., & Buchsbaum, M. (1978). Psychological correlates of monoamine oxidase activity in normals. *Journal of Nervous and Mental Disease, 166,* 177–186.

Selzer, M. (1971). The Michigan Alcoholism Screening Test: The quest for a new diagnostic instrument. *American Journal of Psychiatry, 127,* 1653–1658.

Shaffer, H. J. (1992). The psychology of stage change: The transition from addiction to recovery. In J. H. Lowinson, P. Ruiz, & R. B. Millman (Eds.), *Substance abuse: A comprehensive textbook* (pp. 1019–1033). Baltimore: Williams & Wilkins.

Skinner, H. A. (1982). The Drug Abuse Screening Test. *Addictive Behaviors, 7,* 363–371.

Skinner, H. A., Steinhauer, P. D., & Santa Barbara, J. (1983). The Family Assessment Measure. *Canadian Journal of Community Mental Health, 2,* 91–105.

Spitzer, R. L., Endicott, J., & Robins, E. (1975). Clinical criteria for psychiatric diagnosis and DSM-III. *American Journal of Psychiatry, 132,* 1187–1192.

Spitzer, R. L., Williams, J. B. W., & Gibbon, M. (1987, April 1). *Instruction manual for the Structured Clinical Interview for DSM-III-R* (rev.). New York: New York State Psychiatric Institute.

Steinglass, P., Bennett, L., Wolin, S., & Reiss, D. (1987). *The alcoholic family.* New York: Basic Books.

Steinhauer, P. D., Santa-Barbara, J., & Skinner, H. A. (1984). The process model of family functioning. *Canadian Journal of Psychiatry, 29,* 77–88.

Stewart, A. L., Hays, R. D., & Ware, J. E. (1988). The MOS short form general health survey: Reliability and validity in a patient population. *Medical Care, 27,* S12–S26.

Sugerman, A., & Schneider, D. (1976). Cognitive styles in alcoholism. In R. Tarter & A. Sugerman (Eds.), *Alcoholism: Interdisciplinary approaches to an enduring problem.* Reading, MA: Addison-Wesley.

Tarter, R. (1990). Evaluation and treatment of adolescent substance abuse: A decision tree method. *American Journal of Drug and Alcohol Abuse, 16,* 1–46.

Tarter, R., Alterman, A., & Edwards, K. (1985). Vulnerability to alcoholism in men: A behavior genetic perspective. *Journal of Studies on Alcohol, 46,* 329–356.

Tarter, R., & Edwards, K. (1985). Neuropsychology of alcoholism. In R. Tarter & D. Van Thiel (Eds.), *Alcohol and brain: Chronic effects.* New York: Plenum.

Tarter, R., & Edwards, K. (1987). Brief and comprehensive neuropsychological assessment of alcoholism and drug abuse. In L. Hartlage, M. Ashen, & L. Hornsby (Eds.), *Essentials of neuropsychological assessment* (pp. 138–162). New York: Springer.

Tarter, R., Edwards, K., & Van Thiel, D. (1986). Hepatic encephalopathy. In G. Goldstein & R. Tarter (Eds.), *Advances in clinical neuropsychology* (Vol. 3, pp. 243–263). New York: Plenum.

Tarter, R., & Kirisci, L. (1997). The Drug Use Screening Inventory for adults: Psychometric structure and discriminative sensitivity. *American Journal of Drug and Alcohol Abuse, 23,* 207–219.

Tarter, R., McBride, H., Buonpane, N., & Schneider, D. (1977). Differentiation of alcoholics: Childhood history of minimal brain dysfunction, family history and drinking pattern. *Archives of General Psychiatry, 34,* 761–768.

Tarter, R., & Ryan, C. (1983). Neuropsychology of alcoholism: Etiology, phenomenology, process and outcome. In M. Galanter (Ed.), *Recent developments in alcoholism* (pp. 449–469). New York: Plenum.

Tarter, R., Van Thiel, D., & Moss, H. (1988). Impact of cirrhosis on the neuropsychological test performance of alcoholics. *Alcoholism: Clinical and Experimental Research, 12,* 619–621.

Tellegen, A. (1982). *A manual for the Differential Personality Questionnaire.* Unpublished manuscript.

Tellegen, A. (1985). Structures of mood and personality and their relevance to assessing anxiety with an emphasis on self-report. In A. H. Tuma & J. D. Maser (Eds.), *Anxiety and the anxiety disorders.* Hillsdale, NJ: Erlbaum.

Tellegen, A., Lykken, D., Bourchard, T., Wilcox, K., Segal, N., & Rich, S. (1988).

Personality similarity in twins reared apart and together. *Journal of Personality and Social Psychology, 54,* 1031–1039.

Thomas, V., & Olson, D. H. (1991). Problem families and the Circumplex Model: Observational assessment using the Clinical Rating Scale (CRS). *Journal of Marital and Family Therapy, 19,* 159–175.

Van Hasselt, V. B., Hersen, M., & Milliones, J. (1978). Social skills for alcoholics and drug addicts: A review. *Addictive Behaviors, 3,* 221–233.

Von Knorring, A., Bohman, M., Von Knorring, L., & Oreland, L. (1985). Platelet MAO activity as a biological marker in subgroups of alcoholism. *Acta Psychiatrica Scandinavica, 72,* 51–58.

Wanberg, K., & Horn, J. (1985). *The Alcohol Use Inventory: A guide to the use of the paper and pencil version.* Fort Logan, CO: Multivariate Measurement Consultants.

Weissman, M. (1975). The assessment of social adjustment: A review of techniques. *Archives of General Psychiatry, 32,* 357–365.

Weissman, M. (1988). Anxiety and alcoholism. *Journal of Clinical Psychiatry, 49,* 17–19.

Wellner, Z., Reich, W., Herjanic, B., Jung, D., & Amado, K. (1987). Reliability, validity and parent–child agreement studies of the Diagnostic Interview for Children and Adolescents (DICA). *Journal of the American Academy of Child Psychiatry, 26,* 649–653.

Wiig, E. H. (1985). *Test of Language Competence.* San Antonio, TX: Psychological Corporation.

Wilkinson, D., & Carlen, P. (1980). Relationship of neuropsychological test performance to brain morphology in amnesic and non-amnesic chronic alcoholics. *Acta Psychiatrica Scandinavica, 62,* 89–102.

Woody, G. E., Luborsky, L., McLellan, A. T., O Brien, C. P., Beck, A. T., Blaine, J., Herman, I., & Hole, A. (1983). Psychotherapy for opiate addicts: Does it help? *Archives of General Psychiatry, 40,* 639–645.

Zuckerman, M., Bone, R., Neary, R., Mangelsdorff, D., & Brastman, B. (1972). What is the sensation seeker?: Personality and trait experience correlates of the Sensation Seeking Scales. *Journal of Consulting and Clinical Psychology, 39,* 308–321.

4

❑ ─────────────────────────────────────

Laboratory Testing

KARL VEREBEY

BETTY J. BUCHAN

CARLTON E. TURNER

INTRODUCTION

With the advent of drug-free workplace programs in private enterprise, federal workplace drug-testing programs, and laboratory certification programs, the reliability of laboratory testing for drug abuse is at an all-time high. Properly certified laboratories produce quality drug analysis that protects the rights and freedoms of the testee as well as providing valuable and reliable information to the clinician. Certified laboratories follow standardized guidelines which place the highest degree of expectation of accuracy on the drug-testing process.

The confusion surrounding drug abuse testing today may be a result of many variables. Each individual drug is unique. Detectability depends on the type of drug, size of the dose, frequency of use, the route of administration, differences in individual drug metabolism, the sample collection time, and the sensitivity of the analytical method used to test the sample. All these variables make each test request an individual case, and general rules for all drugs and all situations are extremely difficult to set.

Modern analytical toxicology deals with the detection and identification of minute amounts of drugs or alcohol in biological specimens. This branch of science has grown, become organized and efficient, and expanded tremendously in the last decade. The recognition of widespread drug abuse in the United States and its impact on our economy and work force has enhanced the development and need of improved drug abuse testing facilities.

Qualified drug-testing laboratories, providing objective qualitative and quantitative results, are now easily accessible to physicians. However, the physician must check laboratory accreditations before ordering tests because poor quality laboratories still exist. This chapter examines the availability and usefulness of various biological specimens for drug testing, the common analytical methodology used, and the clinical and forensic utility of drug abuse testing.

RATIONALE FOR TESTING

Drug abuse is characterized by impulsive drug-seeking behavior, with paroxysmal breaks in use and almost certain relapses. A common feature of all drug abusers is denial. The patients lie to themselves, as well as to the forbidding outside world, to protect the continuity of their obsessive addiction to drugs and/or alcohol. For this reason, physicians dealing with drug abusers are seldom given voluntarily the diagnostically important information about the patients' addictive habits.

The drug abuse pattern is an important part of the medical history, as the presentation of drug abuse is often quite nonspecific. It is not uncommon for substance abuse to be mistaken for other medical or psychiatric conditions. The attending physician cannot properly design treatment when kept in the dark about a patient's addiction. Depending on the drug or drugs used, symptoms of physical and/or psychiatric illness may be simulated by the presence or the absence of the particular drug(s). The dichotomy of symptoms associated with drug presence or absence is best illustrated with the opioid class of drugs (Jaffe & Martin, 1985). While under the influence of an opioid, the addict experiences euphoria, anxiolytic sedation, mental clouding, sweating, and constipation. In the absence of opioid, the common withdrawal signs and symptoms appear: pupillary mydriasis, agitation, anxiety, panic, muscle aches, gooseflesh, rhinorrhea, salivation, and diarrhea. Thus, the two different sets of diagnostic symptoms belong to the abuse of the same drug, observed at different times in the presence and absence of an opioid.

Behavior similar or identical to textbook descriptions of psychosis can be triggered in predisposed individuals by drugs. For example, phencyclidine (PCP), D-lysergic acid diethylamide (LSD), amphetamines, or cocaine can cause toxic psychosis that is indistinguishable from paranoid schizophrenia; drug-induced model psychosis can be produced in anyone given the adequate dose of one of these drugs. Drug-induced psychosis has a different prognosis and must be treated differently from psychosis related to endogenous organic, anatomical, or neurochemical disorders (Gold, Verebey, & Dackis, 1985).

Treatment of identified drug abusers would be extremely handicapped if drug abuse testing were not utilized. Therefore, comprehensive drug testing is important for psychiatrists in making precise follow-up evaluations and selecting appropriate treatments for their patients. The first good reason for laboratory drug testing is to provide objective identification of drug abusers and the substances they are abusing (Pottash, Gold, & Extein, 1982).

Testing is also of great value after drug abusers are identified. Current treatment strategies are intimately tied to frequently scheduled urinalyses to monitor recovering addicts. Negative results support the success of treatment, whereas positive test results alert the treating physician to relapses. This is the reason that objective testing is a necessary component of modern treatment of ex-drug abusers.

Drug abuse testing, in some cases, is forensic in nature. Ex-drug abusers, after release from incarceration, are monitored by parole officers. A positive drug test may invalidate the parole and signal to law enforcement the involvement of the parolee with criminal elements.

Professional athletes often abuse drugs. Teams and national or international sport associations may prohibit the use of performance-enhancing drugs, and staying drug-free is often the condition athletes must fulfill to be allowed to compete. Laboratory testing of body fluids for drugs of abuse is the objective technique used to enforce these rules (Wadler & Heinline, 1989).

Finally, the conduct of business and the public safety may be endangered by drug-impaired employees. Bankers and stockbrokers handle investors' money; such business professionals should not be influenced by psychoactive drugs, especially drugs that cause delusions and impulsive risk-taking behavior. During 1991–1993, the highest rates of current and past-year illicit drug use were reported by workers in the following occupations: construction, food preparation, and waiters and waitresses. Heavy alcohol use followed a similar pattern, although auto mechanics, vehicle repairers, light truck drivers, and laborers also had high rates of heavy alcohol use (Hoffman, Brittingham, & Larison, 1996). The National Institute on Drug Abuse (NIDA) has estimated that if every worker ages 18–40 were tested for drug use on any given day, 14–25% would test positive for marijuana, cocaine, barbiturates, or other controlled substances (NIDA, 1989). And economists now say that workplace drug abuse costs us somewhere between $60 billion and $100 billion a year in lost productivity (Schwab, 1997). As a result, the military services, regulated transportation and nuclear industries, many federal and state agencies, and private businesses and industries conduct routine employee drug testing. Those employees who have positive test results may be denied employment, be fired from a job, be court-martialed, or suffer a loss of reputation.

Drug abuse has also been identified among airline pilots, bus drivers, railroad engineers, and police officers. In all these examples, drug abuse testing is advantageous to both the drug abuser and his or her environment (family and the general public). The abuser gets early treatment and a chance for early rehabilitation, and the public is saved from potential wrongdoing under the influence of drugs.

Success of drug abuse testing by decreasing drug abuse has been clearly demonstrated in the military. Prior to the institution of testing in 1981, 48% of armed services personnel used illegal drugs. After 3 years of testing, fewer than 5% were found to be using drugs (Willette, 1986). Although critics often attack testing as ineffective, drug use clearly decreases when serious drug testing is in place.

TESTS AVAILABLE

A number of different laboratory methods are available for comprehensive drug screening. When the drug abuse habit of the patient is unknown, physicians request a "comprehensive drug screen" (Verebey, Martin, & Gold, 1986). Some laboratories usually perform the most inexpensive procedure, the relatively insensitive thin-layer chromatography (TLC) test. Many results are negative because of the low sensitivity of this screening procedure, not because a drug or its metabolite is not present in the sample. By "comprehensive drug testing," different laboratories mean different things. Unless the physician is familiar with the laboratory procedures and technical language, he or she will be less effective in diagnosing drug-induced psychiatric symptoms when the use of drugs is the true cause of a patient's problems.

Urine samples are most commonly sent for "routine drug screen" analysis. Psychiatrists and other physicians may assume that this test will detect all abused drugs. The problem is that the TLC drug screen will detect only high-level drug use of a select group of drugs. TLC is not sensitive enough to detect marijuana, PCP, LSD, 3,4-methylenedioxyamphetamine (MDA), 3,4-methylenedioxymethamphetamine (MDMA), mescaline, and fentanyl, among others. Thus, a negative TLC drug screen does not mean that the patient has not used drugs. What it means is that there is no evidence of high-dose abuse of morphine, quinine (a diluent of heroin), methadone, codeine, dextromethorphan, propoxyphene, barbiturates, diphenylhydantoin, phenothiazines, cocaine, amphetamine, or phenylpropanolamine. Again, low-dose abuse of these drugs is not likely to be detected. Thus, false negatives are very high for the routine drug screen performed by TLC (Manno, 1986); therefore, TLC is not as commonly used in a urine drug testing laboratory as it once was.

For example, if a physician suspects marijuana abuse, he or she must specifically request that a marijuana screen be performed, usually by enzyme immunoassay (EIA; Verebey et al., 1986). Currently, screening for prescription drugs and drugs of abuse is most often performed by EIA, such as the enzyme multiplied immunoassay test (EMIT); radioimmunoassay (RIA); fluorescent polarization immunoassay (FPIA); and a modern version of the TLC, called "ToxiLab," which has improved sensitivity over conventional TLC systems. In exceptional laboratories, drug screening is performed by capillary gas–liquid chromatography (GLC) equipped with nitrogen–phosphorous detector (NPD). In a single analysis, 25 compounds or more can be identified. This system is advantageous when there is no clue to the identity of the abused or toxic substance in the sample; however, GLC-NPD is time-consuming, labor-intensive, and usually expensive. High-performance liquid chromatography (HPLC) is similar to GLC in principle. It is usually less sensitive than GLC but sample preparation is easier. The EMIT and RIA tests are significantly cheaper and more practical than the more specific gas chromatography (GC) and gas chromatography/mass spectrometry (GC/MS) methods. The EIA and FPIA have technical advantages over other screening techniques for urine specimens in that no extraction of drugs or metabolites is required. Thus, these procedures are easily adaptable for high-volume automated screening analysis of drugs in urine. In fact, most good laboratories offer a 5- or 10-drug panel with or without alcohol (Hawks, 1986). These tests are usually performed by EIA. Table 4.1 presents an example of EIA selection of a 10-drug panel plus alcohol.

ANALYTICAL METHODOLOGY

The choice of methods for the identification of drugs or their metabolites in body fluids and tissues depends on the patient's history, physical examination, past history, and available biological samples. Sometimes there is some hint or knowledge about the type of substances used by the subject. This is the simplest and best situation because it allows the analyst and physician to determine the most appropriate biological specimen and analytical method to be used to confirm the suspected drug. Also, the method of choice is determined by knowledge of the drug's biotransformation pathway, and pharmacokinetic pattern (Chiang & Hawks, 1986).

Most often, however, there is no clue about the substance(s) used. Such samples are tested to rule out the drug-related symptoms. In this case, a broad drug screen is required.

Thin-Layer Chromatography

TLC is a technique utilized to separate different molecules in a mixture, based on their polarity and their chemical interaction with developing solvents and the thin-layer coating. It is a qualitative method and it is the least sensitive analytical technique for most drugs. Visualization of the spots on TLC is achieved by illumination with ultraviolet or fluorescent lights or by color reactions of the spots after spraying with chemical dyes. Identical molecules are expected to migrate to the same area and to give specific color reactions. Thus migration and color give TLC specificity not recognized in recent years with the advancement of more sophisticated techniques.

TABLE 4.1. Ten Drugs and Alcohol Screened by Enzyme Immunoassay

Alcohol (ethanol)
Amphetamine
Barbiturate
Benzodiazepines (including Librium, Valium, and Dalmane)
Cannabinoids (THC metabolites)
Cocaine and metabolite (benzoylecgonine)
Methadone
Methaqualone (Quaalude)
Opiates: morphine, codeine, monoacetyl morphine (heroin metabolite), and hydrocodone (Dilaudid)
PCP (phencyclidine)
Propoxyphene (Darvon)

Enzyme Immunoassay and Radioimmunoassay

The various immunoassays operate on the principle of antigen–antibody interactions. These techniques are commonly used to measure hormones, neurochemicals, and drugs. Antibodies are used to seek out specific drugs in biofluids. In the sample containing one or more unknown drugs, competition exists for available antibody-binding sites between the tagged drug in the test and drug(s) in the unknown sample. The binding ratio determines the presence or absence of specific drugs.

The specificity and sensitivity of the antibodies to a given drug compound differ, depending on the particular assay and the manufacturer. Immunoassay can be very specific; however, compounds structurally similar to the drug of interest (their metabolites) often do cross-react. Lack of specificity may be an advantage in some cases because interaction of the antibody with drugs plus metabolites in a sample increases sensitivity in "total" detection of a drug class.

EIA systems are very popular and commonly used for urine drug screening because no extraction or centrifugation is required, and the system lends itself to easy automation. EIA is more sensitive for most drugs and detects lower drug concentrations than TLC.

"On-Site" Screening Immunoassays

The increased prevalence of drug use has prompted the development of new drug screening technology that will produce results in as little as 10 minutes. Many situations require immediate testing and results for drugs of abuse. Hospital emergency departments have an immediate need for detecting drug overdoses. In addition, rapid results are useful for monitoring psychiatric patients, monitoring compliance within a drug rehabilitation program, and supervising parolees. Because these tests are designed to be performed "on-site," they may be performed directly in front of the person being tested or, certainly, at the site of collection. The "on-site" procedure has been successfully used for preemployment screening, random or probable-cause workplace testing, and for workplace accident-related injuries.

Visually interpreted competitive immunoassays have been developed in recent years that do not require instrumentation. These kits are particularly effective because there is no calibration, maintenance, or downtime required and no special skills are needed to perform these tests. Most kits have built-in quality control zones in each panel that ensures reagent integrity, and they may be kept at room temperature due to an extended shelf-life.

There are currently a half dozen or more "on-site" kits on the market. Two particular kits have novel approaches. The Triage® Panel for Drugs of Abuse plus Tricyclic Antidepressants (Biosite Diagnostics, Inc., San Diego, CA) is based on the use of Ascend® MultImmunoassay (AMIA™) technology for simultaneous detection of multiple analytes in a sample. Figure 4.1 shows the Triage® test device. A urine sample is placed in the reaction cup in contact

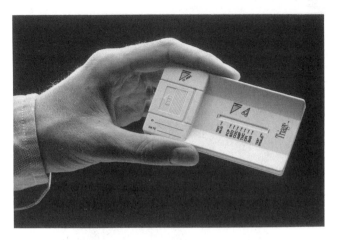

FIGURE 4.1. Triage® test device.

with lyophilized reagents and the reaction mixture is allowed to come to equilibrium for 10 minutes. The chemically labeled drugs (drug conjugate) compete with drugs that may be present in the urine for antibody binding sites. The reaction mixture is transferred to the solid phase membrane in the detection area that contains various immobilized antibodies in discrete drug-class-specific zones. After a washing step, the operator visually examines each zone for the presence of a red bar. The method incorporates preset threshold concentrations that are independent for each drug. The assay response is proportional to the concentration of the unbound drug conjugate so that no signal is observed at drug concentrations less than the threshold concentrations (Buechler et al., 1992). A positive specimen produces a distinct red-colored bar in the drug detection zone adjacent to the drug's abbreviated name. Testing time is about 10 to 12 minutes. A negative specimen does not produce a colored bar. The Triage® Panel for Drugs of Abuse plus Tricyclic Antidepressants is available for the following drugs with their respective threshold or cutoff concentrations: PCP (25 ng/ml), benzodiazepines (BZO) (300 ng/ml), cocaine (COC) (300 ng/ml), amphetamines/methamphetamines (AMP) (1,000 ng/ml), tetrahydrocannabinol (THC) (50 ng/ml), opiates (OPI) (300 ng/ml), barbiturates (BAR) (300 ng/ml), and tricyclic antidepressants (TCA) (1,000 ng/ml).

The OnTrak TesTcup™ Collection/Urinalysis Panel (Roche Diagnostic Systems, Inc., Somerville, NJ) is another new and unique screening device. The OnTrak TesTcup™, shown in Figure 4.2, simultaneously tests for the presence of four drugs (with respective threshold/cutoff concentrations): COC (300 ng/ml), tetrahydrocannabinol (THC) (50 ng/ml), morphine (MOR) (300 ng/ml), and amphetamine (AMP) (1,000 ng/ml) and will soon have the capability for a total of five different drugs. OnTrak TesTcup® assays are based on the principle of microparticle capture inhibition. The test relies on

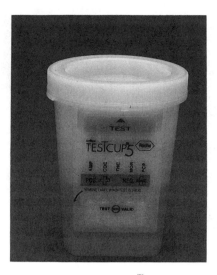

FIGURE 4.2. TesTcup® test device.

the competition between drug, which may be present in the urine being tested, and drug conjugate immobilized on a membrane in the test chamber. Urine is collected directly in the OnTrak TesTcup™ and therefore provides the advantage of eliminating transfer or direct contact with the sample. After closing the cap and moving it to the test position, the sample reservoir is filled by tilting the cup for 5 seconds. Urine proceeds down immunochromatographic strips by capillary action and reacts with antibody-coated microparticles and drug conjugate present on the membrane. In approximately 3 to 5 minutes, the test valid bars appear, a decal is removed from the detection window, and the results are interpreted as positive or negative. In the absence of drug, the antibody is free to interact with the drug conjugate, causing the formation of a blue band (negative sign). When a drug is present in the specimen, it binds to the antibody-coated microparticles and no blue band is formed. A positive sample causes the membrane to remain white (positive sign) (OnTrak TesTcup® package insert, September 1996).

These "on-site" screening kits demonstrate greater than 97% agreement with confirmatory tests such as GC/MS (Buechler et al., 1992). However, it must be stressed that these kits provide only preliminary analytical test results just like immunoassay tests run in a laboratory. A more specific alternate chemical method must be used to confirm positive screening results.

Gas–Liquid Chromatography and Gas Chromatography/Mass Spectrometry

GLC is an analytical technique that separates molecules by migration as described for TLC. The TLC plate is replaced by lengths of glass or metal tubing called columns, which are packed or coated with stationary materials of variable polarity. The extracted analyte is carried through the column to the detector by a steady flow of heated gas. The detector responds to the drugs and other molecules. This response is graphically recorded and quantified and is proportional to the amount of substance present in the sample. Identical compounds travel through the column at the same speed because they have identical interaction with the stationary column packing. The time between injection and an observed response at the recorder is the retention time. Identical retention times of substances on two different polarity columns constitute strong evidence that the substances are identical.

Stronger evidence can be obtained by the use of GC/MS, the most specific confirmation method, which identifies substances by GLC separation and MS fragmentation patterns. Not all bonds in molecules are of equal strength. The weak bonds are more likely to break under stress. In the MS detector, electron beam bombardment of molecules breaks weak bonds. The mass detector measures the exact mass and quantity of the molecular fragments or breakage products. The breakage of molecules results in fragments unique for a drug. They occur in specific ratios to one another, thus the GC/MS method is often called "molecular fingerprinting." GC/MS is the most reliable, most definitive procedure in analytical chemistry for drug identification (Hawks, 1986).

The fragmentation pattern of unknowns is checked against a computer library that lists the mass of drugs and related fragments. Matching a control's fragments and fragment ratios is considered absolute confirmation of a particular compound. The sensitivity of GLC for most drugs is in the nanogram range, but with special detectors some compounds can be measured at picogram levels. GLC and GC/MS can also be used quantitatively, which provides additional information helping to interpret a clinical syndrome or explain corroborating evidence in forensic cases.

When a routine toxicology screen is ordered, the physician is often not aware that options are available for more specific screening and confirmation. Table 4.2 shows the performance characteristics of different types of assays for drugs of abuse.

TABLE 4.2. Performance Characteristics of Different Types of Assays for Drugs of Abuse

Assay	Sensitivity	Specificity	Accuracy	Turnaround time	Cost
On-site	Moderate–high	Moderate	Qualitative[a]	Minutes	$4–25
EMIT; FPIA; RIA; KIMS	Moderate–high	Moderate	Moderate–high	1–4 hours	$1–5
TLC	Low–high	High	Qualitative[a]	1–4 hours	$1–4
GLC	High	High	High	Days	$5–20
GC/MS	High	High	High	Days	$10–100

Note. EMIT, enzyme multiplied immunoassay technique; FPIA, fluorescent polarization immunoassay; RIA, radioimmunoassay; KIMS, kinetic interaction of microparticles in solution; TLC, thin-layer chromatography; GLC, gas–liquid chromatography; GC/MS, gas chromatography/mass spectrometry.
[a]Results for on-site tests and TLC assays are generally expressed only in qualitative terms (i.e., positive/negative); consequently, accuracy may be difficult to assess.

THE CHOICE OF BODY FLUIDS AND TIME
OF SAMPLE COLLECTION

Some drugs are metabolized extensively and are very quickly excreted, whereas others stay in the body for an extended period of time. Thus, success of detection depends not only on the time of sample collection after the last drug use but also on the particular drug used and whether the analysis is performed for the drug itself or for its metabolites. Table 4.3 illustrates the typical screening and confirmation cutoff concentrations and the expected time scales of detectability for some commonly abused drugs.

When drug abuse detection is the goal, the following questions should be asked:

1. How long does the particular drug stay in the body, or what is its half-life?
2. How extensively is the drug biotransformed? Thus, should one look for the drug itself or its metabolite(s)?

TABLE 4.3. Typical Screening and Confirmation Cutoff Concentrations and Detection Times for Drugs of Abuse

Drug	Screening cutoff concentrations	Analyte tested in confirmation	Confirmation cutoff concentrations	Urine detection time
Amphetamine	1,000	Amphetamine	500	2–4 days
Barbiturates	200	Amobarbital; secobarbital; other barbiturates	200	2–4 days for short acting; up to 30 days for long acting
Benzodiazepines	200	Oxazepam; diazepam; other benzodiazepines	200	up to 30 days
Cocaine	300	Benzoylecgonine	150	1–3 days
Codeine	300	Codeine; morphine	300; 300	1–3
Heroin	300	Morphine; 6-acetylmorphine	300; 10	1–3 days
Marijuana	100; 50; 20	Tetra-hydrocannabinol	15	1–3 days for casual use; up to 30 days for chronic use
Methadone	300	Methadone	300	2–4 days
Methamphetamine	1,000	Methamphetamine; amphetamine	500; 200	2–4 days
Phencyclidine	25	Phencyclidine	25	2–7 days for casual use; up to 30 days for chronic use

Note. From Cone (1996).

3. Which body fluid should be analyzed, or what is the major route of excretion (Chiang & Hawks, 1986)?

The importance of asking these questions is illustrated by cocaine and methaqualone (Quaalude), which are biotransformed significantly differently.

Cocaine has a half-life of about 1 hour in humans. It is rapidly biotransformed into two inactive major metabolites of benzoylecgonine and ecgonine methylester. Less than 10% of unchanged cocaine and more than 45% of benzoylecgonine is excreted into the urine. Unchanged cocaine is detectable only from 0 to 12 hours after use. What does all this suggest to the clinician who wants to know whether or not a patient is taking cocaine? The short half-life indicates that unless use is suspected within hours, or the patient is suspected of being currently under the influence of cocaine, the parent compound is not likely to be found in detectable concentration in either the blood or the urine. However, a blood test that includes cocaine and the cocaine metabolite may be reliable for many hours after use to document or exclude recent exposure to cocaine. Plasma enzymes continue to metabolize cocaine even after the blood is taken from the subject. Therefore, blood samples should be collected into sodium fluoride, which inactivates these enzymes. Benzoylecgonine is the major metabolite of cocaine; its half-life is about 6 hours, and, as noted previously, it is excreted in urine at levels totaling approximately 45% of the dose. Clearly, detection is best accomplished by collecting urine and analyzing it for benzoylecgonine. In one study, it was observed that of those subjects who had enough benzoylecgonine in their urine to be detected, only 2% had enough cocaine present for detection. Thus, 98% of the subjects, if tested for cocaine specifically, would have been found negative (Verebey, 1987).

A contrasting example is methaqualone. This substance is, like cocaine, extremely lipid-soluble, but it has a half-life of 20 to 60 hours. Because it is not biotransformed rapidly, either blood or urine tests are effective for detection of the parent compound itself. In our studies, we were able to detect methaqualone for 21 days in the urine after a single 300-mg oral dose, and in blood for 7 days (Kogan, Jukofsky, Verebey, & Mule, 1978). Thus information about pharmacokinetics and excretion is important in deciding which chemical to look for and in which body fluid. Many physicians prefer blood to urine for drug screening because they believe that blood levels constitute stronger evidence of recent use and that they are more closely related to brain levels and drug-related behavioral changes than urine levels.

The collection of urine specimens must be supervised to ensure that the person in question is the source of the sample and to guarantee the integrity of the specimen. It is not unusual to receive someone else's or a highly diluted sample when collection of samples is not supervised or screened by the laboratory for pH, specific gravity, or creatinine. First morning urine samples are preferred because they are more concentrated and drugs are more readily detected (Verebey et al., 1986). The decision to use blood or urine should be based on the specific drug's pharmacokinetic and excretion data. As a rule, urine drug levels are higher and are most often the biofluid of choice for drug and metabolite detection.

RECENT DEVELOPMENTS IN DRUG TESTING: SALIVA, SWEAT, AND HAIR

Most drugs enter saliva by passive diffusion. The major advantages of saliva as a test specimen are that it is readily available, its collection is noninvasive, the presence of parent drug is in higher abundance than metabolites, and a high correlation of saliva drug concentration can be compared with the free fraction of drug in blood (Cone, 1996). The use of saliva to predict blood concentrations is limited because of the possibility of contamination of saliva from drug use by oral, smoked, and intranasal routes. Cone (1993) reported that marijuana smoking produced contamination of the oral cavity by THC. Even though saliva concentrations of THC were derived from contamination, they were highly correlated with plasma concentrations (Cone, 1996). However, even with this precaution in mind, and the short window of detectability of drugs in saliva, saliva measurements can be used to detect very recent drug use.

Sweat is approximately 99% water and is produced by the body as a heat regulation mechanism. Because the amount of sweat produced depends on environmental temperatures, routine sweat collection is difficult due to a large variation in the rate of sweat production and the lack of adequate sweat collection devices. However, cocaine, morphine, nicotine, amphetamine, ethanol, and other drugs have been identified in sweat (Cone, 1996). A recently developed "sweat patch" resembles a Band-Aid® and is applied to the skin for a period of several days to several weeks. Sweat is absorbed and concentrated on the cellulose pad which is then removed from the skin and tested for drug content. Cone, Hillgrove, Jenkins, Keenan, and Darwin (1994) recently evaluated sweat testing for cocaine. Generally, there appeared to be a dose–concentration relationship; however, there was wide intersubject variability which is a disadvantage of this technology. Research in this testing technology is still developing and is indicating apparent advantages of the sweat patch such as high subject acceptability of wearing the patch for drug monitoring and the ability to monitor drug intake for a period of several weeks with a single patch (Cone, 1996)

Testing for drugs in hair is also a recent addition to the drug abuse detection technology (Baumgarten, Hill, & Blahd, 1989). Because of the very low concentrations of drugs incorporated in hair, sensitive methodology must be used. Screening is performed by RIA with ultrasensitive antibodies and confirmation by GC/MS or MS/MS. Drug representatives from virtually all classes of abused drugs have now been detected in hair (Cone, 1996). It remains unclear how drugs enter the hair although the most likely entry routes involve (1) diffusion from blood into the hair follicle and hair cells with subsequent binding to hair cell components, (2) excretion in sweat which bathes hair follicles and hair strands, (3) excretion in oily secretions into the hair follicle and onto the skin surface, and (4) entry from the environment (Cone, 1996). Two controversial issues in hair drug testing are the environmental contamination of hair, which may result in a false-positive test result, and the interpretation of dose and time relationships. Although it has been generally assumed that the hair strand, when sectioned, provides a long-term time course of drug abuse history, studies with labeled cocaine have not supported this interpretation. Henderson, Harkey, and Jones (1993) concluded that "there is not, at present, the necessary scientific foundation for hair analysis to be used to determine either the time or amount of cocaine use." In spite of some controversial aspects of hair testing, this technique is being used on an increasingly broad scale in a variety of circumstances (Cone, 1996). This technology may be used to estimate the drug abuse habit of the patient who is in denial. Self-reported drug use over a period of several months can be compared to hair test results from a hair strand (approximately 3.9 cm length) representative of the same time period (Cone, 1996). It is expected that this type of comparison would be more effective than urine testing because urine provides a historical record of only 2–4 days under most circumstances (Cone, 1996). Because denial is a major problem with drug abusers, this technology may be an invaluable tool in drug abuse diagnosis and therapy. Table 4.4 illustrates the comparison of usefulness of urine, saliva, sweat and hair as a biological matrix for drug detection.

TABLE 4.4. Comparison of Usefulness of Urine, Saliva, Sweat, and Hair as a Biological Matrix for Drug Detection

Biological matrix	Drug detection time	Major advantages	Major disadvantages	Primary use
Urine	2–4 days	Mature technology; on-site methods available; established cutoffs	Only detects recent use	Detection of recent drug use
Saliva	12–24 hours	Easily obtainable; samples "free" drug fraction; parent drug presence	Short detection time; oral drug contamination; collection methods influence pH and submaxilary/parotid saliva ratios; only detects recent use	Linking positive drug test to behavior and performance impairment
Sweat	1–4 weeks	Cumulative measure of drug use	High potential for environmental contamination	Detection of recent drug use
Hair	Months	Long-term measure of drug use; similar sample can be recollected	High potential for environmental contamination; new technology	Detection of drug use in recent past (1–6 months)

THE MEANING OF POSITIVE AND NEGATIVE REPORTS

Psychoactivity of most drugs lasts only a few hours after drug ingestion, whereas urinalysis can detect many drugs and/or metabolites for days or even weeks. Thus, the qualitative presence of drugs (or metabolites) in urine is only an indication of prior exposure, not proof of intoxication or impairment at the time of sample collection. In some cases, quantitative data in blood or urine can corroborate observed behavior or action of a subject, especially when the levels are so high that it is impossible for the subject to be free of drug effects. Thus, drug-induced behavior and laboratory data should be interpreted by experts in pharmacology, toxicology, and pharmacokinetics (Verebey et al., 1986).

When one receives drug analysis reports, whether positive or negative, there are certain questions about the absolute truth of the results. The questions following should be asked to clarify issues about the testing procedure:

1. What method was used? (If the lab does not make this clear on the report, the clinician should call and ask.)
2. Did the assay analyze for the drug alone, metabolite only, or both? What is the "cutoff" value for the assay? (Again, the clinician should call and ask if anything seems unclear.)
3. Was the sample time close enough to the suspected drug exposure? (This information is usually unavailable, since denial is one of the most typical features of drug abusers. Their use pattern is usually hidden.)

First, let us examine positive results. Some scrutiny of the method is needed to determine whether or not a false-positive result is a possibility. Knowledge of the method of determination is helpful. TLC, although not very sensitive, is reasonably specific for drugs that have both the parent drug and its metabolite identified on the TLC plate. Also, specific color reactions help to eliminate false positives for certain drugs. However, if GLC or GC/MS is the analytical technique, positive results are usually acceptable. Either RIA or EMIT is considered rather sensitive, but chemically similar compounds may cross-react with the antibody, registering positive results. Cross-reactivity depends on the specificity of the antibody used for a particular drug and drug metabolite. Some antibodies are more specific than others; therefore, each test should be individually evaluated for specificity. Positive test results for amphetamines and opiates must be further defined for specific substances if the results are to be legally and medically acceptable. Usually, an immunoassay can be confirmed by a chromatographic procedure, and vice versa.

False-negative results can occur more easily than false positives. Generally once a test is screened negative it is not tested further. Also, negative reports based on TLC alone are not conclusive. In addition, if the screening method is RIA or EIA, the cutoff that separates positives and negatives may have been set too high. Another possibility for false negatives is that the sample was obtained too long after the last drug exposure. Whatever the case may be, if the suspicion of drug use is strong, the clinician should have the testing repeated and inquire at the laboratory for more sensitive drug-screening procedures.

In general, analytical toxicology methods have significantly improved in the past decades, and the trend is toward further improvement. As technology continues to improve, more drugs and chemicals will be analyzed in biofluids at the nanogram and picogram level. Advancement, however, does not mean that modern methodologies are infallible, nor do they replace the clinician. Theoretically and practically, technical or human error can influence testing results. A solid laboratory, locally and nationally certified, with a full spectrum of drug abuse tests, enables the well-trained clinician to make drug abuse diagnoses that were not possible in the past. With knowledge of the available analytical methods, one can scrutinize the laboratory test results and be more confident about their validity.

ETHICAL CONSIDERATIONS

The legitimate utilization of drug abuse testing in the clinical setting is indisputable. Denial makes identification of drug abuse difficult; therefore, testing is necessary both in identification and in monitoring treatment outcome. However, drug testing at the workplace and in sports is more controversial. For example, positive test results may be used (or abused) in termination of longtime employees or refusal to hire new ones.

Private companies feel that it is their right to establish alcohol- and drug-free workplaces and sports arenas. The opposition feels that it is ill advised to terminate individuals for a single positive test result even when it is confirmed by forensically acceptable procedures. A testing program is more reasonable when a chance for rehabilitation is offered. Probationary periods would provide individuals with an opportunity to stop using drugs through treatment or self-help programs (Verebey et al., 1986). Employee assistance programs, which refer employees to drug counseling, are available in larger companies and governmental organizations.

It is important that this new powerful tool, drug testing, be used not as a weapon but judiciously as a means of early detection and prevention of disability. Test results must be interpreted only by individuals who understand drugs of abuse medically and/or pharmacologically. The federal government requires that in its drug-testing program the results go directly to medical review officers, who are trained to interpret such reports. Improper testing in the laboratory or improper interpretation of drug-testing data, which may destroy innocent lives, must be prevented.

Federal employees may be tested for drugs of abuse only by locally and nationally certified laboratories. The two most respected regulatory agencies for forensic toxicology laboratories are the Department of Health and Human Services/Substance Abuse and Mental Health Services Administration (SAM-

HSA) National Laboratory Certification Program and the College of American Pathologists (CAP) Forensic Toxicology Proficiency Program. Only the most proficient and competent laboratories in the nation are certified by these organizations. The laboratories must pass a stringent 2-day "on-site" inspection and frequent proficiency testing throughout the year. Because of the serious consequences of positive test results, employee and preemployment testing by private companies should also be conducted in certified laboratories.

Is society placed in jeopardy by the drug-related actions of certain drug abusers? How should the test results be used? Who should know the results and under what circumstances? These are just some of the questions asked by private citizens. The verdict on random testing is not yet decided, but in a case of "for-cause testing," the U.S. Supreme Court was on the side of testing. The Court determined that public safety supersedes individual rights to privacy, especially when the job in question has a significant impact on society. It is predictable that the controversy regarding the civil rights issues and legality of drug abuse testing will continue for some time.

CONCLUSIONS

As long as illegal drug use is prevalent in our society, drug abuse testing will have an important clinical and forensic role. Testing in the clinical setting will aid the physician in treating subjects with psychiatric signs and symptoms secondary to drug abuse, in monitoring treatment outcome, and in handling serious overdose cases. Drug testing in the forensic setting will be used in the workplace and in monitoring parolees convicted of drug-related charges.

Several civil rights concerns must be enforced to protect the innocent. Names of subjects should be known only to the medical office where the sample is collected. Testing must follow strict chain-of-custody procedures to ensure anonymity and prevent sample mixup during testing. Most progressive laboratories have instituted bar-code labeling of samples and related documents to ensure confidentiality. Bar coding also improves the accuracy of reporting, tracking of samples, and locating records. This system ultimately prevents sample mixup due to human error during accessioning.

The reliability of testing procedures is also of foremost importance. Good laboratories institute internal (both open and blind samples) and external quality control systems to ensure high quality of testing (Blanke, 1986).

Before issuing licenses, governmental agencies require laboratories to adhere to strict standards in personnel qualifications, experience, quality control, quality assurance programs, chain-of-custody procedures, and multiple data review prior to the reporting of results.

Two nationally recognized agencies are protecting the rights of individual citizens who might be tested by assuring proper procedures in forensic drug testing: SAMHSA (through its National Laboratory Certification Program) and CAP (through its Forensic Toxicology Proficiency Program). In addition, numerous city and state regulatory agencies inspect and license drug-testing laboratories. Good laboratories are easily identified by having current certificates of qualification and licenses issued by national and local regulatory agencies.

Drug abuse testing has come a long way in accuracy and reliability (Frings, Battaglio, & White, 1989). Testing started in traditional "wet chemistry" laboratories, using huge sample volumes and crude methodologies of low sensitivity. Now autoanalyzers and on-site testing kits perform hundreds of tests on minute sample volumes, measuring accurately low-nanogram amounts of substances. Thus, the insecurity sometimes expressed in the popular press about drug abuse testing should not be a concern to anyone using properly certified, licensed laboratories.

REFERENCES

Baumgarten, W. A., Hill, V. A., & Blahd, W. H. (1989). Hair analysis for drugs of abuse. *Journal of Forensic Science, 34*(6), 1433–1453.

Blanke, R. V. (1986). Accuracy in urinalysis. In R. L. Hawks & N. C. Chiang (Eds.), *Urine testing for drugs of abuse* (NIDA Research Monograph No. 73, pp. 43–53). Washington, DC: U.S. Government Printing Office.

Buechler, K. F., Moi, S., Noar, B., McGrath, D., Villela, J., Clancy, M., Shenhav, A., Colleymore, A., Valkirs, G., Lee, T., Bruni, J. F., Walsh, M., Hoffman, R., Ahmuty, F., Nowakowski, M., Buechler, J., Mitchell, M., Boyd, D., Stiso, N., & Anderson, R. (1992). Simultaneous detection of seven drugs of abuse by the Triage panel for drugs of abuse. *Clinical Chemistry, 38,* 1678–1684.

Chiang, N. C., & Hawks, R. L. (1986). Implications of drug levels in body fluids: Basic concepts. In R. L. Hawks & N. C. Chiang (Eds.), *Urine testing for drugs of abuse* (NIDA Research Monograph No. 73, pp. 62-83). Washington, DC: U.S. Government Printing Office.

Cone, E. J. (1993). Saliva testing for drugs of abuse. In D. Malamud & L. Tabak (Eds.), *Saliva as a diagnostic fluid* (pp. 91–127). New York: New York Academy of Sciences.

Cone, E. J. (1996). New developments in biological measures of drug prevalence. In L. D. Harrison & A. Hughes (Eds.), *The validity of self-reported drug use: Improving the accuracy of survey estimates* (NIDA Research Monograph No. 167, pp. 104–126).Washington, DC: U.S. Government Printing Office.

Cone, E. J., Hillsgrove, M. J., Jenkins, A. J., Keenan, R. M., & Darwin, W. D. (1994). Sweat testing for heroin, cocaine, and metabolites. *Journal of Analytic Toxicology, 18*(6), 298–305.

Frings, C. S., Battaglio, D. J., & White, R. M. (1989). Status of drugs of abuse testing in urine under blind conditions: An AACC study. *Clinical Chemistry, 35*(5), 891–844.

Gold, M. S., Verebey, K., & Dackis, C. A. (1985). Diagnosis of drug abuse, drug intoxication and withdrawal states. *Fair Oaks Hospital Psychiatry Letter, 3*(5), 23–34.

Hawks, R. L. (1986). Analytical methodology. In R. L. Hawks & N. C. Chiang (Eds.), *Urine testing for drugs of abuse* (NIDA Research Monograph No. 73, pp. 30–42). Washington, DC: U.S. Government Printing Office.

Henderson, G. L., Harkey, M. R., & Jones, R. (1993, September). *Hair analysis for drugs of abuse* (Final Report, Grant No. NIJ 90-HIJ-CX-0012). Washington, DC: National Institute on Justice, National Institute on Drug Abuse.

Hoffman, J. P., Brittingham, A., & Larison, C. (1996). *Drug use among U.S. workers: Prevalence and trends by occupation and industry categories* (DHHS Publication No. SMA 96-3089, p. 1). Washington, DC: U.S. Government Printing Office.

Jaffe, J. H., & Martin, W. R. (1985). Opioid analgesics and antagonists. In A. G. Gilman, L. S. Goodman, T. W. Rall, & F. Murad (Eds.), *The pharmacological basis of therapeutics* (7th ed., pp. 491–531). New York: Macmillan.

Kogan, M. J., Jukofsky, D., Verebey, K., & Mule, S. J. (1978). Detection of methaqualone in human urine by radioimmunoassay and gas-liquid chromatography after a therapeutic dose. *Clinical Chemistry, 24,* 1425–1427.

Manno, J. E. (1986). Interpretation of urinalysis results. In R. L. Hawks & N. C. Chiang (Eds.), *Urine testing for drugs of abuse* (NIDA Research Monograph No. 73, pp. 54–61). Washington, DC: U.S. Government Printing Office.

National Institution on Drug Abuse. (1989). *Drug abuse curriculum for employee assistance program professionals* (DHHS Publication No. ADM 89-1587, pp. I–VI, 98). Washington, DC: U.S. Government Printing Office.

Pottash, A. L. C., Gold, M. S., & Extein, I. (1982). The use of the clinical laboratory. In L. Sederer (Ed.), *Inpatient psychiatry: Diagnosis and treatment* (pp. 205–221). Baltimore: Williams & Wilkins.

Schwab, P. (1997, April 28). *Scientific meeting on drug testing of alternative specimens and technologies: Proceedings of the DHHS/Public Health Service/Substance Abuse and Mental Health Services Administration/Drug Testing Advisory Board.* Rockville, MD: National Institute of Drug Abuse.

Verebey, K. (1987). Cocaine abuse detection by laboratory methods. In A. M. Washton & M. S. Gold (Eds.), *Cocaine: A clinician's handbook* (pp. 214–228). New York: Guilford Press.

Verebey, K., Martin, D., & Gold, M. S. (1986). Drug abuse: Interpretation of laboratory tests. *Psychiatric Medicine, 3*(3), 155–166.

Wadler, G. I., & Heinline, B. (1989). *Drugs and athletes: Contemporary exercise and sports medicine.* Philadelphia: F. A. Davis.

Willette, R. E. (1986). Drug testing programs. In R. L. Hawks & N. C. Chiang (Eds.), *Urine testing for drugs of abuse* (NIDA Research Monograph No. 73, pp. 5–12). Washington, DC: U.S. Government Printing Office.

Part III

Psychoactive Substance Disorders

5

Alcohol

PATRICIA I. ORDORICA
EDGAR P. NACE

INTRODUCTION

Alcoholism continues to be one of medicine's most devastating diseases both at the individual and the societal level. Estimates are that at least 9 million Americans are alcohol dependent and about 6 million abuse alcohol. Approximately 40 million family members are affected by a loved one's alcoholism. Alcoholism is a significant risk factor for violence, with nearly half of all deaths from accidents, suicide, and homicide related to alcohol use. In the United States, direct and indirect costs secondary to alcoholism are on the order of $85 billion annually.

Alcoholism has been acknowledged by the American Medical Association as a disease since 1956. Jellinek's seminal work (1960), *The Disease Concept of Alcoholism,* served as major factor in changing professional and public attitudes toward alcoholism. Despite these developments, many people continue to view this disorder as a result of moral weakness or willful misconduct. The stigma attached to alcoholism has resulted in the relatively low priority our society places on the funding of treatment and research when compared with other major health concerns. The term "alcoholism" has many definitions but generally is a condition in which an individual continues to use alcohol despite significant impairment in social and physical functioning. The fourth edition of the *Diagnostic and Statistical Manual of Mental Disorders* (DSM-IV; American Psychiatric Association, 1994) includes alcohol use disorders, alcohol dependence and alcohol abuse, and alcohol-induced disorders, which includes alcohol intoxication and alcohol withdrawal and those which cause a variety of symptoms characteristic of other mental disorders.

DIAGNOSIS

Alcohol use may lead to two alcohol-use disorders (abuse and dependence) and 12 alcohol-induced disorders (see section "Clinical Features"). DSM-IV (American Psychiatric Association, 1994) requires that three or more criteria for dependence occur at any time within a 12-month period (see Table 5.1). The necessity for occurrence of three or more criteria within a 12-month time frame is more diagnostically rigorous than was the case with the criteria of the third revised edition of the DSM (DSM-III-R; American Psychiatric Association, 1987). In contrast to DSM-III-R, DSM-IV lists only seven criteria under dependence; a former criteria—"substance often taken to relieve or avoid withdrawal symptoms"—has been subsumed under the withdrawal criteria; and the criteria on failure to fulfill major role obligations at work, school, or home have been shifted to the abuse criteria (Table 5.1).

Alcohol abuse criteria (Table 5.1) have been expanded from two criteria in DSM-III-R to four criteria in DSM-IV. Alcohol abuse requires at least one of the criteria to have occurred within a 12-month period.

Proper diagnosis requires adherence to these criteria. The distinctions between alcohol abuse and alcohol dependence (alcoholism) are clinically useful. For example, if only criteria for abuse are met it can be assumed that the patient is not alcohol dependent (and is, therefore, not an "alcoholic"). Such an individual is more likely to benefit from controlled drinking strategies and to be able to return to nonpathological use of alcohol than is the person who reaches criteria for dependence where abstinence would be the preferred treatment goal.

The symptoms associated with alcohol abuse and alcohol dependence are far-ranging and involve biological, psychological, and social domains. The presenting symptoms vary from patient to patient, and such heterogeneity should be appreciated by the clinician making a diagnosis.

In assessing a patient for alcoholism, the clinician should consider problems related to the drinker, the family, and the community (Moser, 1980). Problems for the drinker may include declining job performance, joblessness, divorce, arrests (especially for driving while intoxicated and public intoxication), accidents, withdrawal symptoms, broken relationships, and associated medical and psychiatric illnesses. Assessment of family functioning may reveal marital discord, spousal abuse, child abuse, financial problems, depression or anxiety syndromes, child neglect, child developmental problems, school dropout, and delinquency. At the community level, manifestations may include violence, accidents, property damage, economic costs of welfare or health services, and decreased work productivity.

Screening

Several instruments and interviewing techniques enable the clinician to screen for an alcohol use disorder. Interview techniques include the CAGE (Ewing, 1984) and the TWEAK (Russell et al., 1991). "CAGE" is a mnemonic device

TABLE 5.1. DSM-IV Diagnostic Criteria for Substance-Related Disorders

Criteria for substance abuse

A. A maladaptive pattern of substance use leading to clinically significant impairment or distress, as manifested by one (or more) or the following, occurring within a 12-month period:

    (1) recurrent substance use resulting in a failure to fulfill major role obligations at work, school, or home (e.g., repeated absences or poor work performance related to substance use; substance-related absences, suspensions, or expulsions from school; neglect of children or household)

    (2) recurrent substance use in situations in which it is physically hazardous (e.g., driving an automobile or operating a machine when impaired by substance use)

    (3) recurrent substance-related legal problems (e.g., arrests for substance-related disorderly conduct)

    (4) continued substance use despite having persistent or recurrent social or interpersonal problems caused or exacerbated by the effects of the substance (e.g., arguments with spouse about consequences of intoxication, physical fights)

B. The symptoms have never met the criteria for Substance Dependence for this class of substance.

Criteria for substance dependence

A maladaptive pattern of substance use, leading to clinically significant impairment or distress, as manifested by three (or more) of the following, occurring at any time in the same 12-month period:

    (1) tolerance, as defined by either of the following:

        (a) a need for markedly increased amounts of the substance to achieve intoxication or desired effect

        (b) markedly diminished effect with continued use of the same amount of the substance

    (2) withdrawal, as manifested by either of the following:

        (a) the characteristic withdrawal syndrome for the substance (refer to Criteria A and B of the criteria sets for Withdrawal from the specific substances)

        (b) the same (or a closely related) substance is taken to relieve or avoid withdrawal symptoms

    (3) the substance is often taken in larger amounts or over a longer period than was intended

    (4) there is a persistent desire or unsuccessful efforts to cut down or control substance use

    (5) a great deal of time is spent in activities necessary to obtain the substance (e.g., visiting multiple doctors or driving long distances), use the substance (e.g., chain-smoking), or recover from its effects

    (6) important social, occupational, or recreational activities are given up or reduced because of substance use

    (7) the substance use is continued despite knowledge of leaving a persistent or recurrent physical or psychological problem that is likely to have been caused or exacerbated by the substance (e.g., current cocaine use despite recognition of cocaine-induced depression, or continued drinking despite recognition that an ulcer was made worse by alcohol consumption)

Note. From the American Psychiatric Association (1994, pp. 181–183). Copyright 1994 by the American Psychiatric Association. Reprinted by permission.

(Cut down: "Has anyone ever recommended that you cut back or stop drinking?"; Annoyed: "Have you ever felt annoyed or angry if someone comments on your drinking?"; Guilt: "Have there been times when you've felt guilty about or regretted things that occurred because of drinking?"; Eye-opener: "Have you ever used alcohol to help you get started in the morning, to steady your nerves?" Positive answers to three of these four questions strongly suggest alcoholism. "TWEAK" is a similar mnemonic device but more useful than the CAGE in interviews with women. T assesses tolerance—"How many drinks can you hold or how many drinks does it take to get high?"; W: "Have close friends or relatives worried about your drinking?"; Eye-opener: "Do you sometimes take a drink in the morning to wake up?"; Amnesia: "Has a friend or family member ever told you things you said or did while you were drinking that you could not remember?"; K (cut): "Do you sometimes feel the need to cut down on your drinking?" Three points or more suggests alcoholism.

Laboratory tests are useful for detecting heavy drinking. Serum γ-glutamyltransferase (GGT) has been established as a sensitive test of early liver dysfunction. The GGT is elevated in 70% of alcoholics and heavy drinkers (Kristenson, Trell, Fex, & Hood, 1980). In a study of patients admitted for alcoholism treatment at the Mayo Clinic, 63% had an elevated GGT, and 48% an elevated serum glutamic–oxaloacetic transferase (SGOT) (Morse & Hurt, 1979).

Another useful screening test is increased erythrocyte mean corpuscular volume (MCV), which was elevated in 26% of the patients in the Mayo Clinic study. In both male and female alcoholics, the combinations of elevated GGT and MCV identified 90% of alcoholic patients (Skinner, 1981). Other tests that may be elevated are triglycerides, serum alkaline phosphatase, serum bilirubin, and uric acid.

A relatively new test which may gain increased clinical utility is carbohydrate-deficient transferrin (CDT). CDT levels correlate significantly with the amount of alcohol ingested in the past month (Schellenberg, Benard, LeGoff, Bourdin, & Weill, 1989). A review of 2,500 subjects (Stibler, 1991) found sensitivities averaging 82% and specificities averaging 97%.

COMORBIDITY

The compelling data of the early 1990s on the high rate of the comorbidity of alcoholism with other psychiatric disorders has significant implications for an integrative approach in treatment strategies. The Epidemiologic Catchment Area (ECA) study, involving 20,000 adults in the general public, found a lifetime prevalence of alcoholism to be 16% in the general population. Individuals with alcoholism were found to have a 36.6% lifetime prevalence of another nonaddictive mental disorder or twice the rate observed in those without alcoholism (Regier et al., 1990).

Each of the psychiatric disorders studied was more likely to occur in the alcoholic population than in the general population. In the National Comorbidity Survey (NCS), which was designed to evaluate the comorbidity of substance use disorders and other psychiatric disorders, similar increased rates are seen with one-sixth of the population having a history of three or more disorders (Kessler et al., 1994). Follow-up analysis found that 86% of alcohol dependent women and 78% of alcohol dependent men had a lifetime co-occurrence of an additional mental disorder (Kessler et al., 1997). Patient treatment matching based on assessment of comorbid psychiatric disorders may improve treatment outcomes. (McLellan, Luborsky, & Woody, 1983). With the exception of depression among alcoholic women, the occurrence of comorbid psychiatric disorders usually confers a poor treatment prognosis (Rounsaville, Dolinski, & Babor, 1987).

Drug Abuse/Dependence

The most frequent comorbidity associated with alcoholism is drug abuse/dependence. Within the general population, 3.5% of people who are not alcoholic meet criteria for a diagnosis of alcohol abuse/dependence. In contrast, 18% of the population with a diagnosis of alcohol abuse/dependence also meet criteria for drug abuse/dependence (Helzer & Pryzbeck, 1988). In a clinical sample of over 500 patients, the overlap of alcohol abuse/dependence and drug abuse/dependence was 38% (Ross, Glaser, & Germanson, 1988).

The more serious the drug abuse disorder, the more likely it is that alcohol abuse/dependence will be found. For example, the ECA data indicate that if no drug abuse problem exists, the rate of alcohol abuse/dependence is 11% (compared to 13% for the total population). When tetrahydrocannabinol abuse/dependence is present, the prevalence of alcohol abuse/dependence rises to 36%. The rates of alcohol abuse/dependence rise even further with amphetamines (62%), opioids (67%), barbiturates (71%), and cocaine (84%) (Helzer & Pryzbeck, 1988).

Anxiety Disorders

Anxiety disorders are the most common psychiatric disorders found in the general population. The 1-month prevalence rate is 7.3%, and the lifetime prevalence rate is 14.6%. Alcohol abuse/ dependence has a 1-month prevalence rate of 2.8%, and a lifetime rate of 13.3% (Regier et al., 1988).

Given these two commonly occurring disorders, it is not surprising to find considerable comorbidity. A diagnosis of generalized anxiety was made in 26% of patients presenting to a large substance abuse program, although nearly 52% met criteria for a lifetime diagnosis of generalized anxiety disorder (Ross et al., 1988).

The same treatment center has reported the rate of phobic disorders among alcoholics to be 30% (Ross et al., 1988). Among these disorders, the most common is agoraphobia, followed by simple phobia, social phobia, and agoraphobia with panic attacks (Ross et al., 1988).

Panic disorder is also found at considerably greater rates in the alcoholic population. In the general population, the lifetime prevalence of panic disorder is 2% for females and 1% for men. In treatment programs, the disorder is found in approximately 9% of patients (Ross et al., 1988). Female alcoholics are three times more likely to have panic disorder than male alcoholics (Helzer & Pryzbeck, 1988).

Obsessive–compulsive disorder is found in about 2.5% of the adult population according to ECA lifetime prevalence data (Regier et al., 1988). This disorder may have been overlooked in earlier studies of anxiety and alcoholism, but recent data indicate an increased comorbidity in alcoholic patients.

The available data indicate that generalized anxiety disorder is the only anxiety disorder for which alcoholism is more likely than not to precede the development of symptoms. At least 51% of patients with a lifetime history of alcoholism and generalized anxiety disorder were determined to have the alcoholism at least 1 year prior to the anxiety disorder. However, some studies have demonstrated that most anxiety disorders among patients in addiction treatment are substance induced (Anthenelli & Schuckit, 1993).

Posttraumatic stress disorder (PTSD) commonly occurs with other psychiatric disorders including substance use disorders (Brady, 1997). Data from a recent epidemiological survey indicate that approximately 80% of individuals with PTSD meet criteria for at least one other psychiatric diagnosis. Individuals with PTSD should be screened for alcoholism.

Mood Disorders

Depression has long been linked with alcoholism, but the nature of this linkage has only gradually been understood. ECA data (Helzer & Pryzbeck, 1988) indicate that major depression and dysthymia occur between 1.5 and 2 times more commonly in alcoholics. In male alcoholics, major depression has a 5% lifetime prevalence rate, compared to 3% for the total male population. Female alcoholics, however, have a prevalence rate of major depression of 19%, compared to 7% in the total female population.

Clinical samples report higher rates of depression in alcoholics. In a combined outpatient and inpatient sample using the National Institute of Mental Health Diagnostic Interview Schedule, major depression was found in nearly 23% of alcoholics and dysthymia in 13%. If both alcoholism and drug abuse were present, the respective rates increased to 36% and 23% (Ross et al., 1988).

There is a strong sex difference in order of onset. In males, alcoholism precedes depression in 78% of cases. For women the reverse is true: Depression is the antecedent diagnosis in 66% of cases (Helzer & Pryzbeck, 1988).

ECA data have revealed considerable comorbidity between alcoholism and bipolar affective disorder. Mania occurs in the population at a lifetime prevalence rate of 0.3% in men and 0.4% in females. However, the alcoholic woman has a tenfold increased risk of mania and the alcoholic male has a risk three times greater. Approximately 2–3% of hospitalized alcoholics are found to have bipolar disorder (Hesselbrock, Meyer, & Keener, 1985; Ross et al., 1988).

Schizophrenia

Among the general population, 1% have a schizophrenic disorder. Among schizophrenic patients, 47% have an alcohol and other drug use disorder. According to ECA data (Helzer & Pryzbeck, 1988), the alcoholic individual is four times more likely to have schizophrenia than the nonalcoholic. In a large clinical sample of alcoholics, 8% were also schizophrenic and at least 50% developed alcoholism after the onset of schizophrenia (Ross et al., 1988). The difficult clinical course of the patient with both schizophrenia and alcoholism has become increasingly apparent as we seek to develop effective treatment strategies for this population. Treatment models that include individual case management, persuasion groups, active treatment groups, and abstinence support groups have met some success. (Minkoff & Drake, 1991; Ries, 1993).

Personality Disorders

The assumption that alcoholism and personality disorders are linked in some fashion has a long history. Earlier editions of the DSM (DSM-I and DSM-II) classified alcoholism along with personality disorders. By 1980, with publication of DSM-III, substance use disorders (including alcoholism) were understood as entities independent of the personality disorders. However, the comorbidity of alcoholism and personality disorders is extensive, and our knowledge of comorbidity has been improved by the use of standardized diagnostic instruments.

Generally, antisocial personality disorder (APD) is the most prevalent personality disorder associated with alcoholism when samples from public treatment centers are studied, and borderline personality disorder (BPD) is the most common in studies from private treatment facilities. In a sample of alcoholics consecutively admitted to a private psychiatric hospital, 13% were found to have BPD according to conservative diagnostic criteria (Nace, Saxon, & Shore, 1983). In a more recent private psychiatric hospital sample, 57% of substance-abusing patients met DSM-III-R criteria for a personality disorder; in this latter sample, BPD was the most commonly occurring personality disorder (Nace, Davis, & Gaspari, 1991).

Personality disorder occurs more commonly in alcoholics than in the general population. A prospective long-term study of a nonclinical sample (Drake & Vaillant, 1985) determined that by age 47, 23% of males met criteria for a personality disorder. However, the alcoholic males in the sample met criteria for a personality disorder in 37% of cases. Personality disorders are more common in alcoholics than among general psychiatric patients. In a review of over 2,400 psychiatric patients (Koenigsberg, Kaplan, Gilmore, & Cooper,

1985), 36% were found to have a personality disorder. The alcoholics in this clinical sample, however, had a personality disorder in 48% of cases. In this sample, BPD was most common personality disorder (43%), followed by APD (21%) and mixed personality disorder (17%). In a review of alcoholism and APD, a positive association was found in 11 of 14 studies (Grande, Wolfe, Schubert, Patterson, & Brocco, 1984). Estimates of APD in clinical samples vary from 20% to 49% in males and from 5% to 20% in females (Schuckit, 1973). ECA study data document APD in 15% of alcoholic men and 4% of alcoholic women. These prevalences exceed the rate of APD in the total population by 4 times for men and 12 times for women (Helzer & Pryzbeck, 1988).

ETHNICITY AND ALCOHOLISM

The prevalence of alcohol abuse and alcohol dependence among individuals of different ethnic groups is likely mediated by unique genetic and environmental factors. Cultural attitudes exert a powerful influence on drinking behaviors and response to treatment. It has been shown that although cultural approval may increase the accessibility of alcohol, ritualistic use of the drug by the culture may help to inhibit abuse or dependence (Westermeyer, 1986). The lower rates of drinking problems among Italian Americans, Italians, and Jews have been explained by the traditional use of wine in these groups; integration of drinking into family life; and, in the Jewish drinkers, the religious significance attached to alcohol (Snyder, 1958). However, even ethnic groups with ritualistic use patterns do not consistently show low incidences of alcoholism or alcoholic complications. For example, the French and Italians have relatively high rates of alcoholism, with the French having the highest rate of cirrhosis in the world.

Native Americans

Many Native American tribal groups have high rates of alcohol-related problems (Westermeyer, 1986). However, attitudes toward drinking vary considerably from tribe to tribe. Westermeyer also noted increasing rates of alcoholism and medical complications secondary to alcohol as Native American tribes have moved from their rural tribal areas to cities. Among Native Americans residing in Los Angeles, 16% have been found to drink heavily, compared with 5.8% of California Indians in rural areas (Weibel-Orlando, Weisner, & Long, 1984). A recent study contradicted the "firewater myth," the theory that Native Americans are more sensitive to the effects of alcohol. (Garcia-Andrade, Wall, & Ehlers, 1997). Their data found that the Mission Indian men were generally less sensitive to alcohol effects, a physiological characteristic shown to be associated with a greater risk for alcoholism in Caucasian populations.

Many Native American tribal groups have high rates of alcohol-related problems (Westermeyer, 1986). Traditionally, Apaches had relatively few problems with alcoholism, but more recently they have developed higher rates of drinking problems. Westermeyer has noted increasing rates of alcoholism and medical complications secondary to alcohol as Native American tribes have moved from their native lands to "integrated" towns.

African Americans

Epidemiological data on alcohol use among African Americans reveal a high number of deaths related to alcoholic cirrhosis (Nace, 1984) and high rates of homicide in association with alcohol use. A 1996 report by the Group for the Advancement of Psychiatry (GAP), on alcohol abuse among African Americans says that little difference in the lifetime prevalence of alcoholism was found between African Americans and whites. Also, the prevalence of alcoholism among African Americans is greatest in middle age. The alcoholism prevalence for African Americans is low in the young adult group and then increases, in contrast to the alcoholism prevalence for whites, which starts at moderately high levels in the young group and then decreases. Deaths from alcohol-induced causes are about 2.5 times higher in the black population than in the white population. Overall heavy drinking among black and white appears to be similar (GAP, 1996).

Asian Americans

A finding that may be linked to the lower level of alcoholism among Orientals is that as many as 50% of Orientals do not possess ALDH-1, one of four clinically significant isoenzymes of aldehyde dehydrogenase (ALDH). The higher rate of facial flushing is probably a result of acetaldehyde accumulation due to the absence of this isoenzyme. Sue (1987) has cautioned that although many consider Asian Americans to be at low risk for developing alcoholism, subgroups with patterns of high rates of alcohol consumption suggest other factors and vulnerability. Japanese Americans and Korean Americans may have the highest proportion of heavy drinkers and Chinese Americans the lowest proportion (Chi, Lubben, & Kitano, 1989).

Hispanic Americans

The recent GAP report, in regard to alcohol in Hispanic Americans, concluded that Hispanic American men drink more during their young adult and early middle age years. Hispanic American women drink more during their young adult and middle age years. Hispanic American men drink more than Hispanic American women regardless of age. Mexican American men drink more and abstain less than either Puerto Rican or Cuban American men. Hispanic American men and women drink more as their income increases (GAP, 1996). Mexican Americans make up the largest subgroup among the Hispanic population of the United States and have been studied the most frequently in regard to manifestation and treatment of alcoholism. The findings of group differences in expectancies toward drinking of alcoholic beverages and toward excessive drinking between Mexican Americans and non-Hispanic whites support the need for culturally appropriate interventions that target group-specific beliefs. (Marin, 1996). In regard to alcohol in Hispanic Americans, the recent GAP report concluded that Hispanic American men drink more during their young adult and early middle age years. Hispanic American women drink more during their young adult and middle age years. Hispanic American men drink more than Hispanic American women regardless of age. Mexican American men drink more and abstain less than either Puerto Rican or Cuban American men. Hispanic American men and women drink more as their income increases.

PHARMACOLOGY OF ALCOHOL

Alcohol refers to compounds with a hydroxyl group, that is, an oxygen and hydrogen (-OH) bonded to a carbon atom. Beverage alcohol consists of ethanol, which occurs naturally as a fermentation product of sugars and grains. The ethyl alcohol molecule is hydrophilic and affects all cells of the body.

Alcohol is absorbed from the stomach and the proximal part of the small bowel. Ninety-five percent of alcohol is metabolized in the liver by alcohol dehydrogenase (ADH), which converts alcohol to the toxic substance acetaldehyde. The stomach contains at least three isoenzymes of alcohol dehydrogenase. Women have less gastric ADH (Frezza et al., 1990) and, therefore, may metabolize alcohol less efficiently. If gastric emptying is slowed, as with ingestion of food or with drugs having anticholinergic properties, more metabolism of alcohol by gastric ADH occurs, resulting in a lower blood alcohol concentration (Wedel, Pieters, Pikaar, & Ockhuizen, 1991). Alternatively, aspirin and cimetidine inhibit gastric ADH and may lead to an increased blood alcohol concentration (Roine, Gentry, Hernandez-Munoz, Baraona, & Lieber, 1990).

The principal route of metabolism of alcohol is through the ADH pathway, which eliminates approximately one drink (13 g of alcohol) per hour. The major product is the toxic substance acetaldehyde. Acetaldehyde is further broken down to acetic acid via the enzyme ALDH, and subsequently goes through the citric acid cycle to become carbon dioxide and water. Both ADH and ALDH possess several distinct isoenzymes that may reflect a genetic predisposition to alcoholism. Another pathway for oxidation, the microsomal ethanol-oxidizing system (MEOS), is induced by chronic ingestion of alcohol. The increase in the activity of the MEOS pathway can increase the rate of elimination by 50–70%. The MEOS may be responsible for the increased metabolic tolerance seen in chronic alcoholics for other hypnotic-sedative drugs as well as for alcohol.

The MEOS system contains the enzyme cytochrome P450 IIEI, which has the potential to generate free radicals from the metabolism of alcohol. Other excessive metabolic by-products of alcohol include increased fatty acid esters and increased acetaldehyde, both of which are implicated in the disruption of normal protein formation (Tuma, Newman, Donohue, & Sorrell, 1987).

The specific mechanisms of alcohol on the central nervous system (CNS) remain under investigation. The theory that alcohol may produce a morphine-like substance in the brains of certain individuals led to a greater focus on the neurochemical changes in the brain that result from alcohol ingestion. The effect of alcohol on neurotransmitters such as dopamine or serotonin may produce morphine-like compounds such as tetrahydropapaverolines and tetra-hydrocarbolines (Davis & Walsh, 1970).

One action of ethanol is the disruption of the phospholipid molecular chain in the nerve cell membrane. The result is an increased "fluidity" of the membrane. This disturbance in the structure of the membrane affects the functional protein system (enzymes, receptors, and ionophores), which is attached to the membrane (Tabakoff & Hoffman, 1988). For example, adenylate cyclase and monoamine oxidase activity are lower in alcoholics than in controls. Adenylate cyclase is important in the formation of cyclic adenosine monophosphate (CAMP), which, in turn, influences metabolism within the cytoplasm. Of particular interest is the finding that adenylate cyclase remains inhibited in alcoholics 12 to 48 months following abstinence (Tabakoff et al., 1988).

The glutamate system and the glutamate receptor, N-methyl-D-aspartate (NMDA), may mediate acute effects of alcohol. Alcohol inhibits the activity of glutamate, possibly by blocking NMDA-stimulated calcium uptake. The NMDA receptor is believed to be a factor in consolidation of long-term memory. When abnormally excited (e.g., when alcohol is withdrawn), hypoxic damage and seizure activity may result. Alcohol's action at the NMDA site may partially account for such alcohol-related problems as memory dysfunction, seizures, and brain damage (Chandler, Sumners, & Crews, 1991).

Low doses of ethanol activate norepinephrine systems via the reticular activating system in the brain stem. This effect activates behavior and arousal by increasing the flow of sensory input to the cortex. As the concentration of ethanol in the brain increases, the dopamine pathways in the mesolimbic system assume importance as a reward center. This system, which involves the ventral tegmental area and projections to the nucleus accumbens, is the same neuronal system activated by opiates and cocaine. Alcohol at this concentration, with its impact on dopamine, becomes a primary reinforcer (i.e., a reward unto itself rather than an enhancement of experience by increased arousal). Tolerance develops within the dopamine system, necessitating higher concentrations of alcohol to capture the "reward" (Tabakoff & Hoffman, 1988).

Low brain serotonin levels have been associated with increased spontaneous alcohol consumption in rodents, and serotonin uptake inhibitors have been associated with decreased alcohol consumption in humans (Gill & Amit, 1989).

The major inhibitory system of the brain has been demonstrated to be affected by alcohol. The γ-amino butyric acid (GABA) receptor/chloride channel complex is the site for GABA (the brain's major inhibiting neurotransmitter) and is also the recognition site for barbiturates and benzodiazepines. The binding of these latter compounds to their recognition sites on the receptor causes an ion channel to open temporarily to emit chloride ions into the cell (Suzdak, Glowa, Crawley, Skolnick, & Paul, 1988). The chloride ion influx is enhanced by the presence of alcohol and may represent one of the mechanisms for alcohol's anxiolytic effects (Linnoila, 1989).

CLINICAL FEATURES

DSM-IV (American Psychiatric Association, 1994) lists, in addition to the syndromes of alcohol abuse and alcohol dependence, 12 alcohol-induced disorders. This is an addition of six new disorders over DSM-III-R (American Psychiatric Association, 1987). Alcohol idiosyncratic intoxication ("pathological intoxication") is deleted in DSM-IV.

Alcohol Intoxication

Alcohol intoxication is the most common alcohol-induced disorder. It is a reversible syndrome characterized by slurred speech, impaired judgment, disinhibition, mood lability, motor incoordination, cognitive impairment and impaired social or occupational functioning. These effects vary according to setting, mental set, dose, and tolerance of the individual and are a result of a direct stimulant effect of alcohol on norepinephrine and dopamine systems combined with inhibition of the stimulating effect of the glutamate-mediated NMDA receptor and facilitation of the inhibiting function of the GABA system.

A blood alcohol level of 30 mg% will produce a euphoric effect in most individuals who are not tolerant. At 50 mg%, the CNS depressant effects of alcohol become prominent, with associated motor coordination problems and some cognitive deficits. In most states, the legal level of intoxication is 100 mg%. There is evidence that even at blood alcohol levels of 15 mg%, present after approximately one drink, there is impairment in the ability to operate a motor vehicle (Moskowitz, Burns, & Williams, 1985). At levels greater than 250 mg%, significant confusion and a decreased state of consciousness may occur. Alcoholic coma may occur at this level, and at greater than 400 mg%, death may result. Secondary to an established high tolerance, some heavy drinkers may not show these effects even at high blood levels.

Alcohol Withdrawal

Prolonged and heavy alcohol use results in alcohol withdrawal when drinking is stopped or reduced. The intensity of withdrawal symptoms vary according to the magnitude of drinking and the general physical condition of the patient.

The typical symptoms are increased autonomic nervous system activity (sweating, elevated blood pressure, increased respiratory rate, and increased pulse), hand tremors, insomnia, anxiety, agitation, nausea, and vomiting.

Grand mal seizures and illusions or hallucinations also occur but are less common. Grand mal seizures occur during withdrawal in approximately 10% of alcoholics (Espir & Rose, 1987), have a peak occurrence at 24 hours after cessation of alcohol, and usually occur within a range of 7 to 38 hours (Holloway, Hales, & Watanabe, 1984). Almost one-third of patients with withdrawal seizures progress to delirium tremens (DTs, or alcohol withdrawal delirium) and approximately 2% progress to status epilepticus (Adams and Victor, 1989).

Alcohol withdrawal may be accompanied by perceptual disturbances and is coded accordingly if the perception disturbance occurs with intact reality testing (i.e., the person knows that the perceptions are caused by alcohol). The perceptual disturbances may be auditory, visual, or tactile hallucinations or illusions. They are transitory and usually develop within 48 hours of cessation of drinking. "Alcohol hallucinosis" is a clinical term commonly applied to these perceptual disturbances.

Delirium

An alcohol-induced delirium may occur during intoxication (alcohol intoxication delirium) or during withdrawal (DTs).

Alcohol intoxication delirium (unlike delirium from stimulants or hallucinogens which may emerge in hours) requires days of heavy use of alcohol to occur. Evidence for a delirium would include a disturbance in consciousness manifested by inability to shift, sustain, or focus one's attention; reduced awareness of the environment; and cognitive impairment such as disorientation, memory deficits, and language disturbance (e.g., mumbling). The symptoms would fluctuate during the course of a day and would be linked by history and physical or laboratory data to the use of alcohol (American Psychiatric Association, 1994).

The onset is usually around 72 hours after cessation of drinking and rarely lasts longer than 7 days. Vivid, frightening visual hallucinations are usually present. Delusions may be elicited and the patient typically is in a state of extreme autonomic nervous system hyperactivity as evidenced by profuse sweating, tachycardia, tremors, and fever.

The syndrome is life-threatening, with a mortality rate of about 10 to 15% (Adinoff, Bone, & Linnoila, 1988). The DTs are more likely to occur in chronic alcoholics—5 or more years sustained heavy drinking—and in alcoholics with a concomitant fracture, infection, or other medical problem.

Alcohol-Induced Persisting Amnestic Disorder

Alcohol-induced persisting amnestic disorder constitutes a continuum involving Wernicke's acute encephalopathy, the amnestic disorder per se (commonly known as Korsakoff's psychosis), and cerebellar degeneration. Alcohol-induced persisting amnestic disorder typically follows an acute episode of Wernicke's encephalopathy. The latter consists of ataxia, sixth cranial nerve (abducens) paralysis, nystagmus, and confusion. Wernicke's often clears with vigorous thiamine treatment, but 50% to 65% of patients show persistent signs of amnesia.

The amnesia is characterized by anterograde amnesia (inability to form new memories due to failure of information acquisition), retrograde amnesia (loss of previously formed memories), and cognitive deficits such as loss of concentration and distractibility.

The etiology is based on nutritional factors, specifically on the thiamine deficiency present with chronic alcohol use. Other factors, such as familial transketolase deficiency may be important in the pathogenesis of this syndrome in a subgroup of individuals.

The disorder in memory that persists is best correlated with lesions in the diencephalon, specifically the dorsomedial nucleus of the thalamus.

In contrast to other dementias, intellectual function is typically preserved. In a review of Wernicke–Korsakoff syndrome, McEvoy (1982) points out that 20% of patients show complete recovery over a period of months to years, 60% show some improvement, and 20% show minimal improvement. Previously believed to be a distinct clinical entity, alcoholic cerebellar degeneration may be indistinguishable clinically and pathophysiologically from the cerebellar dysfunction seen with Wernicke–Korsakoff syndrome.

Alcoholic amnestic disorder should not be confused with "blackouts," which are periods of retrograde amnesia during periods of intoxication. Blackouts, caused by high blood alcohol levels, may occur in nonalcoholics as well as at any time in the course of alcoholism.

Alcohol-Induced Persisting Dementia

This disorder develops in approximately 9% of alcoholics (Eckardt & Martin, 1986) and consists of memory impairment combined with aphasia, apraxia, agnosia, and impairment in executive functions such as planning, organizing, sequencing and abstracting. These deficits are not part of a delirium and persist beyond intoxication and withdrawal.

Models of cognitive impairment in alcoholics include "premature aging," which means that alcohol accelerates the aging process and/or that vulnerability to alcohol brain damage is magnified in people over the age of 50; the "right hemisphere model," which is derived from the evidence that nonverbal skills (e.g., reading maps, block design tests, etc.) are more profoundly impaired in alcoholics than left hemisphere tasks (language functions); and the "diffuse brain dysfunction" model, which proposes that chronic alcoholism leads to widespread brain damage (Ellis & Oscar-Berman, 1989).

Personality changes, irritability, and mild memory deficits in an abstinent individual with a history of alcoholism are early clues suggestive of alcohol-induced persisting dementia.

Alcohol-Induced Anxiety, Affective, or Psychotic Disorder

If symptoms of an anxiety disorder, affective disorder (depressive, manic, or mixed), or psychotic disorder (hallucinations or delusions) develop during or within 1 month of intoxication or withdrawal, an alcohol-induced anxiety, affective or psychotic disorder may be diagnosed. If the patient has insight that hallucinations are alcohol-induced, an alcohol-induced psychotic disorder is not diagnosed. The anxiety and affective symptoms must exceed the usual presentation of such symptoms as they commonly occur during intoxication or withdrawal (DSM-IV).

These disorders must be distinguished from comorbid psychiatric disorders (see section on "Comorbidity"). A careful history eliciting the onset of symptoms and the course of the symptoms during abstinence or reexposure to alcohol will help distinguish alcohol-induced syndromes from psychiatric comorbidity.

Alcohol-Induced Sleep Disorder

Alcohol's effect on sedation is biphasic with stimulating effects prevailing at low doses and during the ascending limb of blood alcohol concentration. At higher doses and during the descending limb of blood alcohol concentration, sedation prevails. As dosage increases, sleep latency decreases and a sedative effect can be expected for at least 2 hours after the blood alcohol concentration reaches zero (Petrucelli, Roehrs, Wittig, & Roth, 1994).

Alcohol use decreases REM (rapid eye movement) sleep in the first few hours of sleep, with REM returning to normal or increasing in the terminal hours of sleep. Alcohol use also decreases the amount of Stage IV sleep, therefore interfering with the most restful stage of sleep.

Alcohol-induced sleep disorder refers to a sleep disorder arising from intoxication or withdrawal (DSM-IV). The most typical disorder is insomnia occurring during alcohol withdrawal. A rebound increase in REM sleep can be expected during withdrawal leading to vivid dreaming. Chronic alcoholics may complain of light or fragmented sleep for years secondary to decrements in slow-wave sleep.

Alcohol-Induced Sexual Dysfunction

Sexual dysfunction refers to impairment in sexual desire, arousal, or orgasm or presence of pain associated with intercourse as a result of alcohol use. Alcohol-induced sexual dysfunction differs from a primary sexual disorder in that improvement would be expected with abstinence from alcohol.

A national survey of drinking and reproductive dysfunction (Wilsnack, Klassen, & Wilsnack, 1984) found a strong association between dysmenorrhea, heavy menstrual flow, and premenstrual discomfort in women as drinking levels increased. Secondary sexual characteristics in women may be affected by alcohol such as decreased breast tissue and increased pelvic accumulation of fat. Ovarian atrophy has been found in women who died of cirrhosis, including those under 40 years of age (U.S. Department of Health and Human Services, 1983).

In males, erectile dysfunction may occur transiently with alcohol use, especially at blood alcohol levels above 50 mg/100 ml. Decreased libido, erectile dysfunction and gonadal atrophy are reported in chronic alcoholics (Adler, 1992).

Chronic male alcoholics, even without liver dysfunction, commonly demonstrate primary hypogonadism as evidenced by decreased sperm count and motility and altered sperm morphology. Increases in luteinizing hormone and a decrease in the free androgen index was reported in noncirrhotic males and was related to lifetime quantity of ethanol intake (Villalta et al., 1997).

However, a controlled study of abstinent alcohol males selected for absence of physical illness and use of medications found that sexual dysfunction, level of lutenizing hormone, and level of bioavailable testosterone did not differ between the controls and the alcoholics (Schiave, Stimmel, Mandeli, & White, 1995).

Normal sexual functioning in abstinent alcoholic men can be expected in the absence of sexually impairing medications (e.g., disulfiram), liver disease, or gonadal failure.

MEDICAL COMPLICATIONS OF ALCOHOLISM

Gastrointestinal Tract and Pancreas

Secondary to vitamin deficiencies, alcoholics suffer from inflammation of the tongue (glossitis), inflammation of the mouth (stomatitis), caries and periodontitis. A low protein diet, associated with alcoholism, can lead to a zinc deficiency which impairs the sense of taste and further curbs the appetite of the alcoholic. Parotid gland enlargement may be noted (Bode & Bode, 1992).

Alcohol causes decreased peristalsis and decreased esophageal sphincter tone, which leads to reflux esophagitis with pain and stricture formation (Mezey, 1982). The Mallory–Weiss syndrome refers to a tear at the esophageal–gastric junction caused by intense vomiting. Another source of bleeding from the esophagus is esophageal varices secondary to the porta/hypertension of cirrhosis.

Alcohol decreases gastric emptying and increases gastric secretion. As a result, the mucosal barrier of the gastrium is disrupted allowing hydrogen ions to seep into the mucosa, which releases histamine and may cause bleeding. Acute gastritis is characterized by vomiting (with or without hematemesis), anorexia, and epigastric pain. It remains uncertain whether chronic alcohol abuse increases the risk of ulcer disease (Thomson & Pratt, 1992).

The small intestine shows histological changes and contractual pattern changes even with adequate nutrition. Acute alcohol consumption impairs absorption of folate, vitamin B-12, thiamine, and vitamin A as well as some amino acids and lipids (Mezey, 1982).

Acute pancreatitis occurs in 5–10% of alcoholics usually after 10 years of heavy drinking, and chronic pancreatic insufficiency may develop in the absence of acute episodes (Korsten & Lieber, 1982).

The actual mechanism by which alcohol injures the pancreatic acinus is unclear. During acute pancreatitis, intense pancreatic inflammation results from intracellular activation and release of proteolytic enzymes. Autodigestion of the pancreas produces interstitial edema, necrosis, and hemorrhage. The end result of acute alcoholic pancreatitis may be chronic pancreatitis. Acute pancreatitis presents as a dull, steady epigastric pain that may radiate to the back. Bending or sitting may partially relieve the pain, confirming its retroperitoneal origin. Pain may be precipitated or aggravated by meals and relieved by meals or by vomiting. The serum amylase is the most sensitive test for acute pancreatitis. An amylase level 1.5 to 2 times the upper limit of normal has a sensitivity of 95% and specificity of 98% for the diagnosis of acute pancreatitis. The management of acute pancreatitis includes intravenous fluids, nasogastric suction, and parenteral analgesics. Uncomplicated pancreatitis will usually resolve in 2 to 4 days with these supportive measures. Severe pancreatitis may lead to shock, renal failure, coagulopathy, adult respiratory distress syndrome, pancreatic abscess, and pancreatic pseudocyst. The mortality of severe pancreatitis with complications may exceed 30% (Ranson, 1984). Cessation of alcohol intake may diminish the pancreatic pain but does not necessarily halt the progression of pancreatic exocrine and endocrine dysfunction.

Liver

Three histologically distinct lesions occur in the evaluation of alcohol-induced liver disease. The most common, occurring in 90% of heavy drinkers, is fatty liver (hepatic steatosis); 40% of heavy drinkers acquire evidence of alcoholic hepatitis and 15–20% alcohol cirrhosis (fibrosis, nodules, loss of normal structure).

Hepatic steatosis is a common, reversible condition that may progress to cirrhosis in about 7% of cases (Gish, 1996). Signs and symptoms of alcoholic steatosis include nausea, vomiting, hepatomegaly, right-upper-quadrant pain, and tenderness. Ascites and jaundice are uncommon. Laboratory data may reveal mild elevation of transaminases, alkaline phosphatase, or bilirubin. Clinically, fatty liver may mimic or coexist with alcoholic hepatitis. Symptoms of alcoholic fatty liver should resolve within 2 weeks of abstinence (Lieber & Leo, 1982).

Alcoholic hepatitis frequently coexists with fatty liver and cirrhosis. Symptoms include anorexia, nausea, vomiting, fever, chills, and abdominal pain. Hepatomegaly and right-upper-quadrant tenderness are common. Transaminase levels rarely exceed 500 International Units (IU), with a typical ratio of aspartate aminotransferase to alanine aminotransferase of 2:1 to 5:1. Liver biopsy can be helpful in distinguishing fatty liver from mild hepatitis. Ascites, encephalopathy, high bilirubin levels, and prolongation of the prothrombin time are poor prognostic indicators that portend an increased mortality. Treatment consists of abstinence and nutritional support. Treatment with steroids, propylthiouracil, and colchicine has yielded mixed results. Histological recovery from alcoholic hepatitis can require from 6 weeks to 6 months. Of patients with alcoholic hepatitis who continue to drink, 50% will develop cirrhosis (Galamos, 1985).

Nonwhite males carry the highest risk for cirrhosis followed by white males, nonwhite females, and white females (Grant, Debakey, & Zobeck, 1991). The risk for cirrhosis increases when the daily intake of alcohol exceeds 80 g (6.2 ounces of alcohol) in males and 20 g (1.5 ounces of alcohol) in females (Parrish, Higuchi, & Dufour, 1991).

Alcoholic cirrhosis develops as a result of prolonged hepatocyte damage, leading to centritobular inflammation and fibrosis. The latter pathology causes portal hypertension and the development of varices. Esophageal varices may bleed spontaneously or bleeding may be precipitated by respiratory tract infections, nonsteroidal anti-inflammatory drugs, and alcohol. Cirrhosis also leads to ascites, clotting deficiencies, secondary malnutrition, and hepatic encephalopathy (Sutton & Shields, 1995).

Nutrition

Several mechanisms cause alcohol to interfere with normal nutrition. Alcoholics are especially susceptible to deficiencies of thiamine, folate, B vitamins, and ascorbic acid. Ethanol can suppress appetite through its effect on the CNS. Gastric, hepatic, and pancreatic disease may further decrease enteral intake and contribute to maldigestion or malabsorption. Signs of malnutrition include thinning of the hair, ecchymosis, glossitis, abdominal distention, peripheral edema, hypocalcemic tetany, and neuropathy. Nutritional management consists of abstinence and institution of a well-balanced diet and multivitamins plus thiamine and vitamin B supplements when indicated.

Cardiovascular System

It is well established that alcoholic heart muscle disease is a complication of long-term alcoholism and not malnutrition or other possible causes of dilated cardiomyopathy. The contractility of heart muscle is decreased by alcohol through alcohol's effect of increased calcium flow into muscle cells, decreased protein synthesis (possibly secondary to increased acetaldehyde), and mitochondrial disruption (e.g., depressed adenosine triphosphate [ATP] level, leakage of enzymes, and accumulation of glycogen) (Davidson, 1989).

Alcoholic cardiomyopathy is related to the frequency and duration of drinking and involves decreased cardiac output compared to beriberi heart disease (thiamine deficiency), which results in increased cardiac output (Urbano-Marquez et al., 1989). Alcoholic cardiomyopathy should not be confused with heart disease occasionally resulting from congeners, as occurred in the 1960s, when cobalt was added to beer to stabilize the foam (Friedman, 1984).

The symptoms are similar to other forms of congestive heart failure and begin with shortness of breath and fatigue. Abstinence is necessary for recovery: a 54% morality rate from this disease is reported in those who continue to drink compared to 9% who abstain (Regan, 1990).

Transient hypertension is noted in nearly 50% of alcoholics undergoing detoxification and is related to quantity of drinking and severity of other withdrawal symptoms. Epidemiological studies have demonstrated that alcohol elevates blood pressure independently of age, body weight, or cigarette smoking (Coates, Corey, Ahsley, & Steele, 1985; Klatsky, Friedman, & Armstrong, 1986). The blood pressure–elevating effect of alcohol is relatively small compared to the effects of age and body fat, but heavy drinking increases the risk of developing hypertension, especially in men (MacMahon, Blacket, MacDonald, & Hall, 1984).

Alcohol is associated with strokes in the brain in a dose-dependent manner and involves cerebral infarction, intracerebral hemorrhage, and subarachnoid hemorrhage. The strongest association is seen in people younger than age 50 (Hillborn, 1987). Compared with nondrinkers, light drinkers (two to three drinks per day) double the risk of stroke and heavier drinkers almost triple the risk (Donahue, Abbott, Reed, & Yano, 1986). Alcohol has been shown directly to cause vasoconstriction of cerebral blood vessels, and this effect can be reversed or prevented by calcium-channel blocking drugs and by magnesium (Altura & Altura, 1989).

Thus far the effects of alcohol on the cardiovascular system are distinctly negative—cardiomyopathy, hypertension, and strokes. Yet, a beneficial effect has been observed in that people who drink low to moderate amounts of alcohol are at lower risk for coronary artery disease. Light drinkers (up to three drinks per day) have a 30% reduction in risk for coronary artery disease (Gruchow, Hoffman, Anderson, & Barbaoriak, 1982). The protective effect of alcohol seems to follow a U-shaped curve, with nondrinkers and heavy drinkers showing greater risk for coronary artery disease (Criqui, 1990). Hypertension in heavy drinkers is the most plausible explanation for the lack of protective effect as drinking increases (Criqui, 1990).

The mechanism by which alcohol provides some protective effect against coronary artery disease is in the elevation of high-density lipoproteins (HDL). The subspecies HDL2 and HDL3 are both raised by alcohol and both seem to offer protection against coronary artery disease (Salonen, Seppanen, & Rauramaa, 1988).

Nervous System

Ethanol damages the CNS and peripheral nervous system by altering neurotransmitter levels, cell membrane fluidity, and function. Alcoholic dementia and Wernicke–Korsakoff syndrome were discussed earlier. Hepatic encephalopathy occurs in the setting of severe liver failure as a result of either severe alcoholic hepatitis or cirrhosis. Early manifestations of encephalopathy include inappropriate behavior, agitation, depression, apathy, and sleep disturbance. Confusion, disorientation, and depressed mental status develop in the advanced stages of encephalopathy. Physical examination may demonstrate asterixis, tremor, rigidity, hyperreflexia, and fetor hepaticas. Treatment requires the elimination of the offending condition, dietary protein restriction, and removal of nitrogenous waste from the gut with osmotic laxatives and antibiotics (lactulose, neomycin).

Alcoholic peripheral neuropathy is the result of alcohol toxicity and B vitamin deficiency. Pain, paresthesias, and weakness of alcoholic peripheral neuropathy begin in the lower extremities. Advanced neuropathy can assume the classic stocking-glove distribution similar to that seen in diabetic neuropathy. Involvement of the motor nerves results in muscular atrophy and weakness. Physical findings include stocking-glove anesthesia, decreased deep tendon reflexes, dorsal column dysfunction, hyperhidrosis, and postural orthostasis. Treatment consists of abstinence and B vitamin supplements. Phenytoin, carbamazepine, tricyclic antidepressants, and nerve blocks all have been used with variable success (Adams & Victor, 1981).

Hematology

Alcohol interferes with the oral intake and intestinal uptake of vitamins and minerals essential for normal hematopoiesis and may be intrinsically toxic to the bone marrow (Hebert, 1980).

Anemia can result from hemorrhage, hemolysis, or bone marrow hypoplasia. Marrow hypoplasia can result from the toxic effect of alcohol on the bone marrow of folate deficiency. The bone marrow changes of megaloblastosis secondary to folate deficiency are reversible with one day of folate supplementation. Macrocytosis can also occur in the absence of folate deficiency, although the mechanism is unknown.

Leukopenia is less common, resulting from the same mechanisms of toxic and nutritional factors already enumerated. Hypersplenism, an irreversible complication, may also contribute to leukopenia, thrombocytopenia, and anemia. Bone marrow recovery with resolution of leukopenia usually occurs after 1 to 2 weeks of abstinence.

Abnormalities of hemostastis results from the diminished production of the vitamin K-dependent clotting factors (prothrombin, VII, IX, and X), fibrinolysis, and occasionally disseminated intravascular coagulation. Thrombocytopenia may result from decreased production (bone marrow suppression, folate deficiency) or hyperplenism.

Endocrine System

Alcohol interferes with gonadal function even in the absence of cirrhosis by inhibiting normal testicular, pituitary, and hypothalamic function. In males, hypogonadism may cause testicular atrophy, low testosterone levels, decreased beard growth, diminished sperm count, and a loss of libido. Similarly, alcoholism in women is associated with amenorrhea, ovulation, and late luteal phase dysfunction and may also increase the risk of spontaneous abortion as well as induced early menopause (Lex, 1991).

Musculoskeletal System

Acute alcoholic myopathy (rhabdomyolysis) may cause painful tender swelling of one or more large muscle groups. Diagnosis depends on a high index of clinical suspicion, elevation of serum creatine phosphokinase, and myoglobinuria. Chronic alcoholic myopathy may accompany alcoholic poly-neuropathy, presenting as painless progressive muscle weakness and wasting.

Immune System

The effect of alcohol on the immune system includes a direct cell-mediated action that is manifested by depression of the natural killer cell activity and lymphocyte transformation. The effects of heavy alcohol consumption, and the possible increased susceptibility of individuals to human immunodeficiency virus (HIV) and its possible progress to acquired immune deficiency syndrome (AIDS), have been studied. (Petrakis, 1985). The association between alcohol abuse and high-risk behaviors for contracting AIDS has recently been demonstrated by the finding of a substantial prevalence of HIV infection among clients in alcohol treatment programs (Avins et al., 1994).

Skin

Skin disorders can serve as early markers of alcohol misuse. Psoriasis in men has been associated with alcohol abuse and the treatment responsiveness of psoriasis is significantly reduced when daily alcohol use exceeds 80 g per day (Gupta, Schork, Gupta, & Ellis, 1993). Other early skin markers of excessive alcohol use include discoid eczema (coin-shaped, scaly lesions usually on the lower legs), rosacea, and skin infections such as tinea pedis, pityriasis, and onychomycosis (Higgins & du Vivier, 1992). Immunosuppression secondary to alcohol intake is the likely mechanism for the increased incidences of these skin infections (Delune, Mendenhall, & Rosella, 1989). Late states of alcoholism may reveal cigarette burns, bruises, acne, and cutaneous stigmata of liver disease such as spider nevi and palmer erythema.

Cancer

It is unclear whether alcoholics have an increased risk of dying from cancer. The American Cancer Society has estimated that 4% of all cancers in men and 1% of all cancers in women can be directly attributed to alcohol abuse. Studies have shown an increase in breast cancer in women who were light or moderate drinkers (Harvey, Scheiner, Brinton, Hoover, & Fraucueri, 1987; Willet et al., 1987). A recent meta-analysis suggested a modest but positive association between alcohol use and breast cancer. Alcohol abuse probably increases the risk of carcinoma of the pharynx, esophagus, liver, and rectum (Breeden, 1984). The combination of tobacco and alcohol is clearly synergistic, markedly increasing the incidence of cancer of the mouth and esophagus. In epidemiological and case-controlled studies, it is difficult to separate the effects of alcohol from those of tobacco.

Fetal Effects

The fetal effects of maternal alcohol abuse manifest as the congenital abnormalities in fetal alcohol syndrome (FAS), identified in 1973. The fetus is most vulnerable to the effects of alcohol during the first trimester. Neurological features of FAS range from mild CNS dysfunction (attention deficit disorders and hyperactivity) to severe mental retardation. Commonly recognized somatic abnormalities include short palpebral fissures, midfacial hypoplasia, absence of the philtrum, and a thin upper lip. FAS has been shown to occur in 33% of infants born to women who drink more than 150 g per day during pregnancy (Greenfield, Weiss, & Mirin, 1997). This estimate for the United States is a rate of 19.5 newborns with FAS per 10,000 births. (Stratton, Howe, Battaglia, & Institute of Medicine, 1995). The number of children with fetal alcohol effects who have a less severe variant is estimated to be triple the number with full-blown FAS.

TREATMENT PRIORITIES

Comorbidity with other psychiatric disorders is common in alcoholic patients. A recent epidemiological study (Kessler et al., 1997) found that 86% of alcohol-dependent women and 78% of alcohol-dependent men had a lifetime co-occurrence of an additional psychiatric disorder (including drug abuse or dependence). For alcohol abuse co-occurrence was found in 72% of women and 57% of men.

This potential multiplicity of clinical problems raises questions about what condition is treated first, which setting, and what modalities. Several guidelines can be offered.

1. The issues of acuity and safety must receive priority (Nace, 1995). A patient who presents as acutely suicidal would necessarily be placed in an inpatient setting capable of offering close or constant observation. An acutely delusional patient would require the intensity of an inpatient psychiatric unit as well.

2. Alcohol-related disorders and co-occurring disorders should be treated in parallel or synchronously. For example, a suicidal patient requiring the

protection of a locked psychiatric unit may also require detoxification simultaneously with efforts to diminish suicidal potential.

3. Sufficient time free of alcohol may clarify the issue of comorbidity. Alcohol-related anxiety amd affective or psychotic disorders are expected to resolve in about 4 weeks (DSM-IV), although clinical judgment is more appropriate than fixed time intervals in determining whether symptoms are alcohol-related or part of a comorbid condition. If symptoms abate as alcohol is withdrawn, the likelihood of a co-occurring disorder diminishes. If symptoms persist or new symptoms emerge in the absence of alcohol, a co-occurring disorder is likely.

4. Severe symptoms, even if alcohol-induced, require appropriate medication and management. Panic attacks occurring in association with alcohol may require relief with alprazolam or other suitable drugs. Addressing acute symptoms pharmacologically does not imply that an additional dependency will be established or alcohol dependence will be prolonged.

5. Each disorder requires treatment. The severely depressed patient cannot be expected to respond to Twelve-Step programs or rehabilitation efforts if they are not simultaneously receiving appropriate pharmacology and psychotherapy. Nor will a bipolar patient be likely to achieve stabilization if his or her alcoholism or alcohol abuse is not arrested.

The question of which disorder to treat first oversimplifies the process. The treatment of co-occurring "dual disorders" is more likely to be done in parallel or in synchrony than in a discrete temporal sequence. While acute symptoms (e.g., hallucinations) are being treated, a therapeutic alliance can be developed with the patient, from which the dependent state can be modified by elimination of denial and restoration of adult ego skills. Specific treatments for anxiety, affective, or other co-occurring disorders may be provided within the treatment setting of a psychiatrically based substance abuse program. For example, antidepressants may be prescribed for depression, biofeedback or buspirone may be useful in modifying anxiety disorders, and lithium and neuroleptics are essential for manic or psychotic patients.

Research on medications to treat alcoholism has flourished in the last five years. The most promising are the opiate antagonists and acamprosate, a synthetic compound with a chemical structure similar to that of GABA acid. These anticraving compounds have recently been approved for the maintenance of abstinence after detoxification from alcohol in the United States (naltrexone) and in various European countries (acamprosate). These medications and others are discussed in the chapter on pharmacological treatments.

The synchronous treatment of alcoholism and comorbid disorders is well illustrated in the personality-disordered alcoholic patient. The recovery process from alcohol dependence provides a paradigm for ego strengthening and personality growth. Successful treatment of alcoholism involves the patient's development of tolerance for frustration, the ability to delay gratification, the capacity to anticipate consequences of behavior, and a tolerance for affect.

These skills are integral to the modification of character pathology as well. Hence, key therapeutic issues in both the treatment of alcoholism and personality disorders are addressed during the recovery process (Nace, 1995).

Depending on the severity of the patient's alcoholism, the medical status, and the severity of additional psychiatric symptoms, the evaluation and treatment for comorbidity may occur in either an inpatient or an outpatient setting.

CONCLUSION

This chapter emphasizes that alcoholism is a disease that manifests itself through social or medical symptoms. Alcohol dependence and alcohol abuse are amenable to reliable diagnostic criteria. The expressions of alcohol dependence across family, occupational, and social settings often conceal from the naive observer the internal suffering of the alcoholic patient. Subjectively, the alcoholic struggles with prolonged craving for the substance, fear of functioning without alcohol, and doubts about his or her ability to abstain and hence to recover. Concomitant with the ambivalent struggle to change, the alcoholic endures remorse, regret, guilt, and shame.

The physician, if not cognizant of the protean manifestations of this disease, or blinded to the suffering of the patient by the alcoholic's often outrageous behavior, may miss or decline to take the opportunity for a life-changing clinical encounter. On the other hand, the physician prepared for the diagnosis and treatment of addictive disorders will find clinical experiences that contradict the pessimism often instilled during training years.

The psychiatrist's role in the treatment of alcoholism is especially pertinent given the significant issue of comorbidity and the biopsychosocial orientation of modern psychiatry. This chapter presented extensive data on the comorbidity of alcoholism with other psychiatric disorders. With an understanding of the overlapping relationships between substance use disorders and other psychiatric disorders, and an ability to establish treatment priorities, the psychiatrist is in a unique position to provide medical leadership to effectively treat this complex biopsychosocial disorder.

REFERENCES

Adams, R. D., & Victor, M. (1989). Alcohol and alcoholism. In *Principles of neurology* (pp. 870–888). New York: McGraw-Hill.

Adinoff, B., Bone G. H. A., & Linnoila, M. (1988). Acute ethanol poisoning and ethanol withdrawal syndrome. *Medical Toxicology, 3*(2), 172–196.

Adler, R. A. (1992). Clinically important effect of alcohol on endocrine function. *Journal of Clinical Endocrinology and Metabolism, 74*, 957–960.

Altura, B. A., & Altura, B. T. (1989). Cardiovascular functions in alcoholism and after acute administration of alcohol: Heart and blood vessels. In H. W. Goedde & D.

P. Agarwal (Eds.), *Alcoholism: Biochemical and genetic aspects* (pp. 167–215). New York: Pergamon Press.

American Psychiatric Association. (1987). *Diagnostic and statistical manual of mental disorders* (3rd ed., rev.). Washington, DC: Author.

American Psychiatric Association. (1994). *Diagnostic and statistical manual of mental disorders* (4th ed.). Washington, DC: Author.

Anthenelli, R. M., & Schuckit, M. A. (1993). Affective and anxiety disorders and alcohol and drug dependence: Diagnosis and treatment. *Journal of Addictive Diseases, 12*(3), 73–87.

Avins, A. L., Woods, W. J., Lindan, C. P., et al. (1994). HIV infection and risk behaviors among heterosexuals in alcohol treatment programs. *Journal of the American Medical Association, 271,* 515–518.

Bode, J. C., & Bode, C. (1992). Alcohol malnutrition and gastrointestinal tract. In R. R. Watson & B. Watzl (Eds.), *Nutrition and alcohol* (pp. 402–428). Boca Raton, FL: CRC Press.

Brady, K. T. (1997). Posttraumatic stress disorder and comorbidity: Recognizing the many faces of PTSD. *Journal of Clinical Psychiatry, 58*(Suppl. 9), 12–15.

Breeden, J. H. (1984). Alcohol, alcoholism, and cancer. *Medical Clinics of North America, 68,* 163–171.

Chandler, L. H., Sumners, C., & Crews, F. T. (1991). Ethanol inhibits NMDA-stimulated excitotoxicity. *Alcohol, 15,* 323.

Chi, I., Lubben, J. E., & Kitano, H. H. (1989). Differences in drinking behavior among three Asian American groups. *Journal of Studies on Alcohol, 50*(1), 15–23.

Coates, R. A., Corey, P. N., Ashley, M. J., & Steele, C. A. (1985). Alcohol consumption and blood pressure: Analysis of data from the Canada Health Survey. *Preventive Medicine, 14*(1), 1–14.

Criqui, M. H. (1990). The reduction of coronary heart disease with light to moderate alcohol consumption: Effect or artifact. *British Journal of Addiction, 85,* 854–857.

Davidson, D. M. (1989). Cardiovascular effects of alcohol. *Western Journal of Medicine, 151*(4), 430–439.

Davis, V. E., & Walsh, M. D. (1970). Alcohol, amines and alkaloids: A basis for alcohol addiction. *Science, 167,* 1005–1007.

Delune, N. E., Mendenhall, C. L., & Rosella, G. A. (1989). Cell mediated immune responses associated with short term alcohol intake: Time course and dose dependency. *Alcoholism: Clinical and Experimental Research, 13,* 201–205.

Donahue, R. P., Abbott, R. D., Reed, D. M., & Yano, K. (1986). Alcohol and hemorrhagic stroke: The Honolulu heart program. *Journal of the American Medical Association, 255*(17), 2311–2314.

Drake, R. E., & Vaillant, G. E. (1985). A validity study of Axis II of DSM-III. *American Journal of Psychiatry, 142,* 553–558.

Eckardt, M. J., & Martin, P. R. (1986). Clinical assessment of cognition in alcoholism. *Alcoholism: Clinical and Experimental Research, 10*(2), 128–137.

Ellis, R. J., & Oscar-Berman, M. (1989). Alcoholism, aging, and functional cerebral asymmetries. *Psychological Bulletin, 106*(1), 128–147.

Espir, M. L., & Rose, F. C. (1987). Alcohol, seizures, and epilepsy. *Journal of Social Medicine, 9,* 542–543.

Ewing, J. A. (1984). Detecting alcoholism: The CAGE questionnaire. *Journal of the American Medical Association, 252*(14), 1905–1907.

Frezza, M., DiPadova, C., Pozzato, G., Terpin, M., Baraona, E., & Lieber, C. S. (1990). High blood alcohol levels in women: The role of decreased gastric alcohol dehydrogenase activity and first-pass metabolism. *New England Journal of Medicine, 322*(2), 95–99.

Friedman, H. S. (1984). Cardiovascular effects of alcohol with particular reference to the heart. *Alcohol, 1*(4), 333–339.

Galamos, J. T. (1985). Alcoholic liver disease: Fatty liver, hepatitis, and cirrhosis. In J. E. Berk (Ed.), *Gastroenterology* (pp. 2985–3048). Philadelphia: Saunders.

Garcia-Andrade, C., Wall, T. L., & Ehlers, C. L. (1997, July). The firewater myth and response to alcohol in Mission Indians. *American Journal of Psychiatry, 154*(7), 983–988.

Gill, K., & Amit, Z. (1989). Serotonin uptake blockers and voluntary alcohol consumption: A review of recent studies. In M. Galanter (Ed.), *Recent developments in alcoholism* (Vol. 7, pp. 225–248). New York: Plenum.

Gish, R. (1996, November 30). *Rational evaluation of liver dysfunction of the chemically dependent patient and diagnosis and treatment of hepatitis C.* Audiotape of presentation at the 7th annual meeting and symposium of the American Academy of Addiction Psychiatry, San Francisco.

Grande, T. P., Wolfe, A. W., Schubert, D. S. P., Patterson, M. B., & Brocco, K. (1984). Associations among alcoholics, drug abuse, and anti-social personality: A review of the literature. *Psychological Reports, 55,* 455–474.

Grant, B. F., DeBakey, S., & Zobeck, T. S. (1991). Liver cirrhosis mortality in the United States, 1973–1988 (NIAAA Surveillance Report No. 18, DHHS Publication No. ADM 281-89-0001). Washington, DC: U.S. Government Printing Office.

Greenfield, S. F., Weiss, R. D., & Mirin, S. M. (1997). Psychiatric substance use disorders. In A. J. Gelenberg & E. L. Bassuk (Eds.), *The practitioner's guide to psychoactive substances.* New York: Plenum.

Group for the Advancement of Psychiatry. (1996). *Alcoholism in the United States: Racial and ethnic considerations* (Report No. 141, VII–X). 1–111. Washington, DC: American Psychiatric Press.

Gruchow, H. W., Hoffman, R. G., Anderson, A. J., & Barbaoriak, J. J. (1982). Effects of drinking patterns on the relationship between alcohol and coronary occlusion. *Atherosclerosis, 43*(2, 3), 393–404.

Gupta, M. A., Schork, N. J., Gupta, A. K., & Ellis, C. N. (1993, May 28). Alcohol intake and treatment responsiveness of psoriasis: A prospective study. *Journal of American Academy of Dermatology, 5*(pt. 1), 730–732.

Harvey, E. B., Scheiner, C., Brinton, L. A., Hoover, R. N., & Fraucueri, J. F. (1987). Alcohol consumption and breast cancer. *Journal of the National Cancer Institute, 78,* 657–661.

Hebert, V. (Ed.). (1980). Hematologic complications of alcoholism [Special issue]. *Seminars in Hematology, 17,* 83–176.

Helzer, J. E., & Pryzbeck, T. R. (1988). The co-occurrence of alcoholism with other psychiatric disorders in the general population and its impact on treatment. *Journal of Studies on Alcohol, 49*(3), 219–224.

Hesselbrock, M. N., Meyer, R. E., & Keener, J. J. (1985). Psychopathology in hospitalized alcoholics. *Archives of General Psychiatry, 42,* 1050–1055.

Higgins, E. M., & du Vivier, A. W. P. (1992). Alcohol and the skin. *Alcohol, 27,* 595–602.

Hillborn, M. E. (1987). What supports the role of alcohol as a risk factor for stroke? [Review]. *Acta Medica Scandinavica, 717*(Suppl.), 93–1169.

Holloway, H. C., Hales, R. E., & Watanabe, H. K. (1984). Recognition and treatment of acute alcohol withdrawal syndromes. *Psychiatric Clinics of North America, 7*(4), 729–743.

Jellinek, E. M. (1960). The disease concept of alcoholism. New Haven, CT: Hillhouse.

Kessler, R. C., Crum, R. M., Warner, L. A., Nelson, C. B., Schulenberg J., & Anthony, J. C. (1997). Lifetime cooccurrence of DSM-III-R alcohol abuse and dependence with other psychiatric disorders in the National Comorbidity Survey. *Archives of General Psychiatry, 54,* 313–321.

Kessler, R. C., McGonagle, K. A., Zhao, S., et al. (1994). Lifetime and 12 month prevalence of DSM-III-R psychiatric disorders in the United States. *Archives of General Psychiatry, 51,* 8–19.

Klatsky, A. L., Friedman, G. D., & Armstrong, M. A. (1986). Relationships between alcoholic beverage use and other traits to blood pressure: A new Kaiser Permanente study. *Circulation, 73*(4), 628–636.

Koenigsberg, H. W., Kaplan, R. D., Gilmore, M. M., & Cooper, A. M. (1985). The relationship between syndrome and personality disorder in DSM-III: Experience with 2,462 patients. *American Journal of Psychiatry, 142*(2), 207–212.

Korsten, M. A., & Lieber, C. S. (1982). Liver and pancreas. In E. M. Patterson & E. Kaufman (Eds.), *Encyclopedic handbook of alcoholism* (pp. 225–244). New York: Gardner Press.

Kristenson, J., Trell, E., Fex G., & Hood, B. (1980). Serum Y-flutamyltransferase: Statistical distribution in a middle-aged male population and evaluation of alcohol habits in individuals with elevated levels. *Preventive Medicine, 9,* 108–119.

Lex, B. W. (1991). Gender differences and substance abuse. In N. K. Mello (Ed.), *Advances in substance abuse: Behavioral and biological research* (Vol 4, pp. 225–296). London: Jessica Kingsley.

Lieber, C. S., & Leo, M. A. (1982). Alcohol and the liver. In C. S. Lieber (Ed.), *Medical disorders of alcoholism: Pathogenesis and treatment* (pp. 259–312). Philadelphia: Saunders.

Linnoila, M. I. (1989). Anxiety and alcoholism. *Journal of Clinical Psychiatry, 50*(Suppl. 11), 28–29.

MacMahon, S. W., Blacket, R. B., MacDonald, G. J., & Hall, W. (1984). Obesity, alcohol consumption and blood pressure in Australian men and women: The National Heart Foundation of Australia risk factor prevalence study. *Journal of Hypertension 2*(1), 85–91.

Marin, G. (1996, July–August). Expectancies for drinking and excessive drinking among Mexican-Americans and non-Hispanic whites. *Addictive Behaviors, 21*(4), 491–507.

McEvoy, J. P. (1982). The chronic neuropsychiatric disorders associated with alcoholism. In E. M. Pattison & E. Kaufman (Eds.), *Encyclopedic handbook of alcoholism* (pp. 167–179). New York: Gardner Press.

McLellan, A. T., Luborsky, L., & Woody, G. E. B. (1983). Predicting response to alcohol and drug abuse treatments. *Alcohol and Drug Abuse, 40,* 620–625.

Mezey, E. (1982). Alcoholic liver disease. In H. Popper & F. Schoffner (Eds.), *Progress in liver disease* (Vol. 7). New York: Grune & Stratton.

Minkoff, K., & Drake, R. E. (Eds.). (1991). *Dual diagnosis of major mental illness and substance disorder.* San Francisco: Jossey-Bass.

Morse, R. M., & Hurt, R. D. (1979). Screening for alcoholism. *Journal of the American Medical Association, 242*(24), 2688–2690.

Moser, J. (1980). *Prevention of alcohol-related problems.* Toronto: Alcoholism and Drug Addiction Research Foundation.

Moskowitz, H., Burns, M., & Williams, A. (1985). Skills performance at low blood alcohol levels. *Journal of Studies on Alcohol, 46,* 482–485.

Nace, E. P. (1984). Epidemiology of alcoholism and prospects for treatment. *Annual Review of Medicine, 35,* 293-309.

Nace, E. P. (1995). *Achievement and addiction: A guide to the treatment of professionals.* New York: Brunner/Mazel.

Nace, E. P., Davis, C., & Gaspari, J. D. (1991). Axis II comorbidity in the substance abuse sample. *American Journal of Psychiatry, 148.*

Nace, E. P., Saxon, J. J., & Shore, N. (1983). A comparison of borderline and non-borderline alcoholic patients. *Archives of General Psychiatry, 40,* 54–56.

Parrish, K. M., Higuchi, S., & Dufour, M. C. (1985). Alcohol consumptions and the risk for developing liver cirrhosis: Implications for future research. *Journal of Substance Abuse, 3*(3), 325–335.

Petrakis, P. L. (1985). *The effects of alcohol on the immune system: Summary of a workshop.* Rockville, MD: National Institute on Alcohol Abuse and Alcoholism.

Petrucelli, N., Roehrs, T. Z., Wittig, R. M., & Roth, T. (1994). The biphasic effects of ethanol on sleep latency. *Sleep Research, 23,* 75.

Ranson, J. H. C. (1984). Acute pancreatitis: Pathogenesis, outcome, and treatment. *Clinical Gastroenterology, 13*(3), 343–363.

Regan, R. J. (1990). Alcohol and the cardiovascular system. *Journal of the American Medical Association, 264*(3), 377–381.

Regier, D. A., Boyd, J. H., Burke, J. D. Jr., Rae, D. S., Myers, J. K., Kramer, M., Robins, L. N., George, L. K., Karns, M., & Locke, B. Z. (1988). One month prevalence of mental disorders in the United States. *Archives of General Psychiatry, 45,* 977–985.

Regier, D. A., Farmer, M. E., Rae, D. S., Locke, B. Z., Keith, S. J., Judd, L. L., & Goodwin, K. K. (1990). Comorbidity of mental disorders with alcohol and other drug abuse. *Journal of the American Medical Association, 264,* 2511–2518.

Ries, R. K. (1993). The dually diagnosed patient with psychotic symptoms. *Journal of Addictive Diseases, 12*(3), 103–122.

Roine, R., Gentry, R. T., Hernandez-Munoz, R., Baraona, E., & Lieber, C. S. (1990). Aspirin increases blood alcohol concentrations in humans after ingestion of ethanol. *Journal of the American Medical Association, 264*(18), 2406–2408.

Ross, H. E., Glaser, F. B., & Germanson, T. (1988). The prevalence of psychiatric disorders in patients with alcohol and other drug problems. *Archives of General Psychiatry, 45,* 1023–1031.

Rounsaville, B. J., Dolinski, I. S., & Babor, T. S. (1987). Psychopathology as predictors of treatment outcome in alcoholics. *Archives of General Psychiatry, 44,* 505–513.

Russell, M., Martier, S. S., Sokol, R. J., Jacobson, S., Jacobson, J., & Bottoms, S. (1991). Screening for pregnancy risk-drinking: TWEAKING the tests [Abstract]. *Alcoholism: Clinical amd Experimental Research, 15*(2), 368.

Salonen, J. T., Seppanen, K., & Rauramaa, R. (1988). Serum high-density lipoprotein cholesterol subfractions and the risk of acute myocardial infarction: A population study in Eastern Finland. *Circulation, 78*(Suppl. II), 281.

Schellenberg, F., Benard, J. Y., LeGoff, A. M., Bourdin, C., & Weill, J. (1989). Evaluation of carbonhydrate-deficient transferrin compared with TF index and other markers of alcohol abuse. *Alcoholism: Clinical and Experimental Research, 13*(5), 605–610.

Schiave, R. C., Stimmel, B. B., Mandeli, J., & White, D. (1995). Chronic alcoholism and male sexual function. *American Journal of Psychiatry, 152,* 1045–1051.

Schuckit, M. A. (1973). Alcoholism and sociopathy: Diagnostic confusion. *Journal of Studies on Alcohol, 34,* 157–164.

Skinner, H. (1981). Early identification of alcohol abuse. *Canadian Medical Journal, 124,* 1279–1295.

Snyder, C. R. (1958). *Alcohol and the Jews: A cultural study of drinking and sobriety.* New Brunswick NJ: Rutgers Center for Alcohol Studies.

Stibler, H. (1991). Carbonhydrate-deficient transferrin in serum: A new marker of potentially harmful alcohol consumption reviewed. *Clinical Chemistry, 37*(12), 2029–2037.

Stratton, K., Howe, C., Battaglia, F., & Institute of Medicine. (1995). *Fetal alcohol syndrome: Diagnosis, epidemiology, prevention, and treatment.* Washington, DC: National Academy Press.

Sue, D. (1987). Use and abuse of alcohol by Asian Americans. *Journal of Psychoactive Drugs, 19*(1), 23–26.

Sutton, R., & Shields, R. (1995). Alcohol and esophageal varices. *Alcohol, 30*(5), 581–589.

Suzdak, P. D., Glowa, J. R., Crawley, J. N., Skolnick, P., & Paul, S. M. (1988). Is ethanol antagonist selective for ethanol? *Science, 239,* 648–650.

Tabakoff, B., & Hoffman, P. L. (1988). A neurobehavioral theory of alcoholism. In C. D. Chaudron & D. A. Wilkinson (Eds.), *Theories of alcoholism* (pp. 29–72). Toronto, Canada: Addiction Research Foundation.

Tabakoff, B., Hoffman, P. L., Lee, J. M., Saio, T., Willard, B., & DeLeon-Jones, R. (1988). Differences in platelet enzyme activity. *New England Journal of Medicine, 313,* 134–139.

Thomson, A. D., & Pratt, O. E. (1992). Interaction of nutrients and alcohol: Absorption, transport, utilization, and metabolism. In R. R. Watson & B. Watzl (Eds.), *Nutrition and alcohol* (pp. 75–100). Boca Raton, FL: CRC Press.

Tuma, D. J., Newman, M. R., Donohue, T. M., & Sorrell, M. F. (1989). Covalent binding of acetaldehyde to proteins: Participation of lysine residues. *Alcoholism: Clinical and Experimental Research, 11*(6), 579–584.

Urbano-Marquez, A., Estruch, R., Navarro-Lopez, F., Grau, J. M., Mont, L., & Rubin, E. (1989). The effects of alcoholism on skeletal and cardiac muscle. *New England Journal of Medicine, 320*(7), 409–415.

U.S. Department of Health and Human Services. (1983). *Alcohol and health: Fifth special report to the U.S. Congress* (DHHS Publication No. ADM 84-1291). Washington, DC: U.S. Government Printing Office.

Villalta, F., Ballesca, J. L., Nicholas, J. M., Martinez di Osaba, M. J., Antunez, E., & Pimentel, C. J. (1977, February). Testicles function in asymptomatic chronic alcoholics: Relation to ethanol intake. *Alcoholism: Clinical and Experimental Research, 21*(1), 128–133.

Wedel, M., Pieters, J. E., Pikaar, N. A., & Ockhuizen. (1991). The application of a three-compartment model to a study of the effects of sex, alcohol dose and concentration, exercise, and food consumption on the pharmacokinetics of ethanol in healthy volunteers. *Alcohol, 26*(3), 329–336.

Weibel-Orlando, J., Weisner, T., & Long, J. (1984). Urban and rural Indian drinking patterns: Implications for intervention and policy development. *Substance and Alcohol Actions Misuse, 5,* 45–57.

Westermeyer, J. (1986). *A clinical guide to alcohol and drug problems.* New York: Praeger.

Willett, W. C., Stamfer, M. J., Colditz, G. A., Rosner, B. A., Hennekens, C. H., & Speizer, F. E. Moderate alcohol consumption and the risk of breast cancer. *New England Journal of Medicine, 316,* 1174–1180.

Wilsnack, S. C., Klassen, A. D., & Wilsnack, R. W. (1984). Drinking and reproductive dysfunction among women in a 1981 national survey. *Alcoholism: Clinical and Experimental Research, 8*(5), 451–458.

6

❑ _____

Sedatives/Hypnotics
and Benzodiazepines

ROBERT L. DuPONT
CAROLINE M. DuPONT

INTRODUCTION

The other drugs with which this book deals—whether legal, such as alcohol, or illegal, such as cocaine and marijuana—are not used routinely in medical practice. By contrast, the sedatives and the hypnotics, especially the benzodiazepines, are widely used in medical practice in the treatment of anxiety, insomnia, epilepsy, and for several other indications (Baldessarini, 1996). The combination of abuse by alcoholics and drug addicts and the withdrawal symptoms on discontinuation leads to the view that these are potentially "addictive" drugs (DuPont, 1997a). The pharmacology and the epidemiology of sedatives and hypnotics are reviewed in this chapter, which focuses on the needs of the clinical practitioner in dealing with the risks and benefits of the benzodiazepines in the treatment of anxiety and in addiction medicine (Salzman & Freeman, 1998).

The Epidemiologic Catchment Area (ECA) study of the National Institute of Mental Health (NIMH) found that over their lifetimes, 24% of American men and 4.5% of American women will be diagnosable as suffering from alcohol and/or drug abuse, and that 8% of the men and 19.5% of the women will be diagnosable as suffering from an anxiety disorder, while a more recent study in the National Comorbidity Survey (NCS) found that 17.2% of the population reported an anxiety disorder in the past 12 months and 24.9% reported a lifetime history of an anxiety disorder (DuPont et al., 1996; Kessler et al., 1994, 1996; Robins et al., 1984). These studies establish that the anxiety disorders are most prevalent mental disorders (DuPont, 1995, 1997c).

A recent study using the standard human capital approach to estimate the social costs of illnesses showed that in 1990, the anxiety disorders produced a total social cost of $47 billion (DuPont et al., 1996). A more recent update through 1994 showed that the costs of anxiety disorders had risen to $65 billion, of which only $15 billion was the cost of all treatment, and that $50 billion was due to lost productivity because of the seriously disabling nature of these illnesses (DuPont, 1997c). For comparison, the costs of all mental illnesses in 1994 was $204 billion, of which the affective disorders totaled $42 billion and schizophrenia totaled $45 billion.

The benzodiazepines were introduced as comparatively problem free compared to the barbiturates they replaced, and their popularity reached unprecedented levels in the early 1970s. However, a growing backlash labeled the "social issues" began to emerge (DuPont, 1986). This backlash caused a drop in the use of the benzodiazepines during the 1980s, even though there was a rise in the prevalence of the disorders for which they are used (DuPont, 1988).

As the benzodiazepines have become more controversial, and as various regulatory approaches have been employed to limit their use in medical practice, there is a danger that clinicians will revert to the older and generally more toxic sedatives and hypnotics, which, in the era of the benzodiazepines, have become unfamiliar (Juergens, 1997). Thus, there is more than historical interest in looking at these earlier sedatives because for some younger medical practitioners they are new drugs. However, the use of sedatives and hypnotics for the treatment of anxiety and insomnia in patients with addiction to alcohol and other drugs entails additional risks, especially when the benzodiazepines are used (Johnson & Longo, 1998).

DISTINGUISHING MEDICAL AND NONMEDICAL USE

To understand the place of the benzodiazepines in contemporary medical practice, it is important to clearly distinguish appropriate medical use from inappropriate nonmedical use. Five characteristics distinguish medical from nonmedical use of all controlled substances as medicines, including the benzodiazepines.

1. *Intent*. Is the substance used to treat a diagnosed medical problem, such as anxiety or insomnia, or is it to get high (or to treat the complications of the nonmedical use of other drugs)? Typical medical drug use occurs without use of multiple nonmedical drugs, whereas nonmedical drug use is usually polydrug abuse. Although alcoholics and drug addicts sometimes use the language of medicine to describe their reasons for using drugs nonmedically, "self-administration" or "self-medication" of an intoxicating substance

outside the legal and ordinary practice boundaries of medical care is a hallmark of drug abuse.

2. *Effect.* What is the effect of the drug use on the user's life? The only acceptable standard for medical use is that it helps the user live a better life. Typical nonmedical drug use is associated with deterioration in the user's life, even though continued use and denial of these negative consequences are universal.

3. *Control.* Is the substance use controlled only by the user, or does a fully knowledgeable physician share the control of the drug use? Medical drug use is controlled by the physician as well as the patient, whereas typical nonmedical drug use is solely controlled by the user.

4. *Legality.* Is the use legal or illegal? Medical drug use is legal; with the exception of alcohol use by adults, nonmedical drug use is illegal.

5. *Pattern.* What is the pattern of the substance use? Typical medical drug use of controlled substances is similar to the use of the penicillin or aspirin in that it occurs in a medically reasonable pattern to treat an easily recognized health problem other than addiction. Typical use of nonmedical drugs (e.g., alcohol or marijuana), in contrast, takes place at parties or in other social settings. Medical substance use is stable and at a moderate dose level. Nonmedical drug use is usually polydrug abuse at high and/or unstable doses.

Warning signs of possible addiction to alcohol and other drugs in the context of using prescribed benzodiazepines are as follows:

1. Frequent or everyday use of the benzodiazepines at levels far above the maximum dose levels established in the *Physicians' Desk Reference* (PDR; Medical Economics Data Production, 1997).
2. Simultaneous use of alcohol or other drugs nonmedically.
3. "Addict behavior," such as "losing" prescriptions or medicine, getting controlled or dependence-producing drugs from multiple physicians, often through dishonesty.
4. Poor therapeutic response.

DRUG DEPENDENCE VERSUS PHYSICAL DEPENDENCE

Drug dependence is a mental or a behavioral disorder defined in the fourth edition of the *Diagnostic and Statistical Manual of Mental Disorders* (DSM-IV; American Psychiatric Association, 1994). It includes out-of-control drug use, use outside social and medical sanctions, use despite clear evidence of drug-caused problems, and a drug-centered lifestyle. Physical dependence (including withdrawal on discontinuation) is, in contrast to addiction, a pharmacological phenomenon in which the user experiences a specific constellation of symptoms for a relatively short period when use of the substance is abruptly discontinued. Physical dependence may, but often does not, accompany substance use disorder (abuse or dependence).

A patient who seeks to continue using a medicine because it is helpful is no more demonstrating "drug-seeking behavior" than is a patient who finds eyeglasses helpful in the treatment of myopia demonstrating "glasses-seeking behavior" if deprived of a corrective lens. Drug abuse and drug dependence are characterized by use despite problems caused by that use (loss of control) and by denial (and dishonesty)—neither of which is seen in appropriate medical treatment (DuPont & Gold, 1995).

Precisely the same confusion of medically trivial physical dependence with serious substance use disorder (addiction) occurs in regard to the use of opiates in the treatment of severe pain. Many patients and many physicians undertreat severe pain because they are unable to distinguish physical dependence, the benign pharmacological fact of neuroadaptation in medical patients, from the abuse of opiates by drug addicts, a malignant biobehavioral disorder (Melzack, 1990).

MEDICAL USE AND ABUSE

Within medical practice, the benzodiazepines have largely displaced the barbiturates for all the common indications, including antianxiety, anti-insomnia, and anticonvulsant effects, as well as for their muscle-relaxing and preanesthetic properties. Before there were barbiturates, which became widely used in medical practice when phenobarbital became available in 1912, alcohol was the substance most commonly used for these purposes (Hobbs, Rall, & Verdoorn, 1996; O'Brien, 1996). Even today, some people who are neither drug addicts nor alcoholics occasionally use alcohol to reduce anxiety and insomnia. However negatively one might view the benzodiazepines, they are a substantial improvement over either alcohol or barbiturates in terms of both safety and efficacy.

The benzodiazepines are among the most widely prescribed psychotropic medicines in the world. The World Health Organization (1988) labeled them "essential drugs" that should be available in all countries for medical purposes. They are also the least likely to cause any adverse effects, including serious medical complications and death, of the widely used psychotropic drugs (DuPont, 1988).

Several other important health concerns unrelated to addiction have been expressed, especially about the long-term use of benzodiazepines, including the effects on the brain, the possibility of cerebral atrophy associated with prolonged benzodiazepine use, and other problems, such as memory loss and personality change (Golombok, Moodley, & Lader, 1988; Lader, Ron, & Petursson, 1984; American Psychiatric Association Task Force on Benzodiazepine Dependence, Toxicity and Abuse, 1990; Uhde & Kellner, 1987). The evidence for these problems is both preliminary and disputed, except for the well-studied acute effect of benzodiazepines on memory, which has no clinical significance for most patients.

PHARMACOLOGY

"Sedative" refers to daytime calming, whereas "hypnotic" refers to nighttime promotion of sleep. These are two closely related, if not identical, pharmacological target symptoms; thus it is not surprising that, in general, the same classes of substances are used to produce both daytime and nighttime calming, or what used to be called "tranquilization."

The barbiturates presented several serious problems, however, that limited their usefulness for these indications. They were a major cause of overdose death from accidental poisonings and suicide, and they produced lethargy and drowsiness even at therapeutic doses. In addition, although it was less noticed at the time than the first two effects, alcoholics and drug addicts frequently abused them (Hobbs et al., 1996). Compared to the benzodiazepines, the barbiturates are more dangerous because they induce hepatic enzymes causing more drug interactions, they produce more tolerance, they are more reinforcing for alcoholics and drug addicts, and they produce more severe withdrawal symptoms (Juergens, 1997).

Workplace drug testing is usually limited to identification of marijuana, cocaine, morphine/codeine, amphetamine/methamphetamine, and phencyclidine (PCP). However, benzodiazepines and barbiturates may be added to the test panel (Roy-Byrne & Cowley, 1990). Laboratory positive test results from patients with legitimate prescriptions for benzodiazepines and barbiturates are reported to employers by medical review officers (MROs) as negative, as are other laboratory results that reflect appropriate medical treatment with other controlled substances (DuPont, 1990a).

In this section, the sedatives and hypnotics are divided for convenience into three groups: the barbiturates, "other sedatives and hypnotics," and the benzodiazepines. We also discuss the newer agents, which are alternatives to the benzodiazepines.

Barbiturates

Barbital was introduced into medical practice in 1903, and phenobarbital in 1912. Their rapid success led to the development of over 2,000 derivatives of barbituric acid, with more than 50 being used in medical practice. The only sedatives to precede the barbiturates were bromides and chloral hydrate, both of which were in widespread use before the end of the 19th century.

The most commonly used barbiturates today are amobarbital (Amytal), butabarbital (Butisol), mephobarbital (Mebaral), pentobarbital (Nembutal), secobarbital (Seconal), and phenobarbital (Luminal). The first four are intermediate in their duration of action whereas the last, phenobarbital, has a long duration of action. Short-acting barbiturates are used as anesthetics but not in outpatient medicine.

Barbiturates reversibly suppress the activity of all excitable tissue, with the central nervous system (CNS) being particularly sensitive to these effects. Except for the antiepileptic effects of phenobarbital, there is a low therapeutic index for the sedative effects of the barbiturates, with general CNS depression being linked with the desired therapeutic effects. The amount of barbiturates that can cause a fatal overdose is only about 10 to 20 times the usual one-night hypnotic dose and well within the usual size of a single prescription. A common problem with the medical use of the barbiturates for both sedation and hypnosis is the rapid development of tolerance, with a common tendency to raise the dose on chronic administration. The barbiturates also affect the γ-aminobutyric acid (GABA) system, producing both a cross-tolerance to other sedating drugs, including alcohol and the benzodiazepines, and a heightened risk of fatal overdose reactions.

The use of barbiturates does continue in two areas of medical practice: to treat headaches (e.g., Fiorinal [butalbital, aspirin, and caffeine]) and to treat irritable bowel syndrome (IBS) and other functional gastrointestinal disorders (e.g., Donnatal [phenobarbital, hyoscyamine sulfate, atropine sulfate, and scopolamine hydrobromide]). Phenobarbital is used both as a sedative and in the management of epilepsy. Phenobarbital received unwelcome publicity as an easily available suicide agent in the mass suicide at Rancho Santa Fe, California, in 1997.

Other Sedatives and Hypnotics

Chloral hydrate (Notec), ethchlorvynol (Placidyl), ethinamate (Valmid), glutethimide (Doriden), meprobamate (Miltown, Equanil), methyprylon (Noludar), and paraldehyde (Paral) belong in this large and heterogeneous class of seldom-used drugs.

Chloral hydrate, the oldest of these medicines, produces a decrease in sleep latency and, in therapeutic doses, little effect on respiration or blood pressure. Toxic doses, however, produce severe respiratory depression and hypotension. Chloral hydrate has an unpleasant taste and is irritating to the skin and mucous membranes. Gastric irritation is common, especially if the drug is not well diluted or if it is taken on an empty stomach.

There is little to recommend the use of glutethimide and methyprylon because of their addictive potential and the severity of withdrawal, as well as because the treatment of overdoses from these drugs is particularly hazardous.

Meprobamate was introduced in 1955 and was the first of the postbarbiturate antianxiety medicines. It enjoyed a sudden, wide popularity because of the dissatisfaction with barbiturates at the time, but meprobamate was rapidly and virtually completely replaced by the benzodiazepines in the early 1960s. The largest group of patients using meprobamate today are those who started in the late 1950s and continue taking this medicine because they have been unable or unwilling to stop meprobamate use.

Methaqualone is a hypnotic that possesses anticonvulsant, antispasmodic, local anesthetic, and weak antihistaminic properties. It also has antitussive properties similar to codeine. Within a short time of its introduction, it achieved popularity with drug abusers because of its dissociative "high" and reputed aphrodisiac properties. It has been withdrawn from the medical market because of its abuse and because of its lack of unique therapeutic properties.

Paraldehyde is an old-fashioned hypnotic that has survived in medical practice for a century but deserved to be retired decades ago. It produces rapid onset of sleep but may cause excitement in the presence of pain. Although it produces few effects on respiration and blood pressure at therapeutic doses, it causes potentially lethal respiratory depression and hypotension in overdose situations.

This class of hypnotics is of general pharmacological and historical interest, but it does not contain medicines that have a useful place in contemporary medical practice. These drugs have a narrow therapeutic index (i.e., there is relatively little difference between the therapeutic dose and the toxic dose), and they have substantial potential for both abuse and overdose death.

Benzodiazepines

The benzodiazepines were recognized in animal experiments in the 1950s for their ability to produce calm without sedation. Cats, which are extremely sensitive to even small electrical shocks, were obviously sedated when given enough alcohol or barbiturates to prevent "anxious" avoidance behavior of impending shocks. But when given benzodiazepines, the cats appeared normal in all their behavior except that they did not show the exaggerated anticipatory sensitivity to mild electrical shocks that they showed prior to treatment with a benzodiazepine.

After the synthesis in the late 1950s of chlordiazepoxide (Librium), the first benzodiazepine, more than 3,000 additional benzodiazepines have been synthesized, of which about 50 have been used clinically (Baldessarini, 1996). In recent years, several benzodiazepines, including alprazolam (Xanax), diazepam (Valium), lorazepam (Ativan), and clonazepam (Klonopin) have been among the most frequently prescribed medicines worldwide.

The identification of the benzodiazepine receptors in 1977 began the modern era of benzodiazepine research, establishing this class as the best understood of all the psychiatric medicines. The benzodiazepine receptors are found in approximately 30% of all CNS synapses and in all species above the level of the shark, demonstrating their fundamental biological importance. The benzodiazepine receptors are part of the GABA complex, which is a major quieting, or inhibiting, system in the CNS.

Alcohol and barbiturates also work through the GABA complex. Unlike the benzodiazepines, however, alcohol and barbiturates have potent, direct effects reducing neuronal transmission. This may explain why alcohol and barbiturates cause respiratory depression and death in high doses. The benzodiazepines potentiate GABA, which opens the chloride channel, hyper-polarizing these inhibitory neurons. The fact that benzodiazepines potentiate GABA but (unlike alcohol and barbiturates) do not directly activate the inhibitory GABA system appears to explain the important clinical observation that benzodiazepines potentiate the sedating and the CNS depression effect (and overdose potential) of alcohol and barbiturates but do not produce unconsciousness or death when taken alone.

There are 12 benzodiazepines marketed in the United States today to treat anxiety and insomnia (Woods, Katz, & Winger, 1988). Although all ben-zodiazepines have anticonvulsant properties, three are used clinically to treat epilepsy (clonazepam, diazepam, and clorazepate [Tranxene]). Benzodiazepi-nes are also used as muscle relaxants and supplemental anesthetic agents. There are pharmacological differences among the individual benzodiazepines that have important clinical significance. The differences among the ben-zodiazepines resemble the differences within the two other major classes of psychotropic medicines: the antipsychotics and the antidepressants. Although there are many overlapping effects within each class, there are also important differences among the medicines in each class so that the medicines within a class cannot be used interchangeably. These pharmacological differences include the rapidity of onset (distributional half-life), persistence of active drug and/or metabolite in the body (elimination half-life), major metabolic break-down pathways (conjugation vs. oxidation), and specific molecular structure (e.g., alprazolam has a unique triazolo ring that may account for some differences in its clinical effects). Table 6.1 summarizes these differences for the most widely used benzodiazepines. Clinically important pharmacological characteristics are summarized as they relate to the use and abuse of the benzodiazepines (Scharf, Jennings, & Graham, 1988). Benzodiazepines may produce some clinically relevant effects by mechanisms that do not involve GABA-mediated chloride conductance (Burt & Kamatchi, 1991). The ben-zodiazepines have only a slight effect on rapid eye movement (REM) sleep but they do suppress deeper, stage 4 sleep. Although this effect is probably of no clinical significance, diazepam has been used to prevent "night terrors" that arise in stage 4 sleep.

Speed of Onset

The most important distinction among the benzodiazepines in the substance abuse context is the speed of onset, which reflects abuse potential. Those benzodiazepines that have a slow onset (either because they are slowly absorbed or because they must be metabolized to produce an active substance) have a relatively lower abuse potential; those that rapidly reach peak brain levels are relatively more likely to produce euphoria, and therefore abuse, among alcoholics and drug addicts (Arendt, Greenblatt, Liebisch, Luu, & Paul,

TABLE 6.1. Pharmacological Characteristics of Benzodiazepines

Drug	Trade name	Rate of oral absorption	Rate of metabolism	Metabolized primarily by liver oxidation	Active metabolites	Elimination half-life (hours)	Maximum usual dose (mg/day)
			Used primarily to treat anxiety				
Alprazolam	Xanax	Intermediate	Intermediate	Yes	Yes	12–15	4
Chlordiazepoxide hydrochloride	Librium	Intermediate	Long	Yes	Yes	5–30	100
Clonazepam	Klonopin	Fast	Long	Yes	No	18–50	2
Clorazepate dipotassium	Tranxene	Fast	Long	Yes	Yes	36–200	60
Diazepam	Valium	Fast	Long	Yes	Yes	20–50	40
Halazepam	Paxipam	Intermediate	Long	Yes	Yes	50–100	160
Lorazepam	Ativan	Intermediate	Short	No	No	10–14	6
Oxazepam	Serax	Slow	Short	No	No	5–10	60
Prazepam	Centrax	Slow	Long	Yes	Yes	36–200	60
			Used primarily to treat insomnia				
Flurazepam hydrochloride	Dalmane	Intermediate	Long	Yes	Yes	40–150	30
Quazepam	Doral	Fast	Long	Yes	Yes	20–120	30
Temazepam	Restoril	Intermediate	Short	No	Yes	8–12	30
Triazolam	Halcion	Intermediate	Short	Yes	No	2–5	0.25

Note. Adapted from DuPont (1990b). Copyright 1990 by *The Western Journal of Medicine.* Adapted by permission.

1987). Diazepam is the most rapidly absorbed and the most effective producer of euphoria. It may, therefore, be the most abusable of the benzodiazepines. In contrast, the most slowly absorbed and activated benzodiazepines, such as oxazepam (Serax) and prazepam (Centrax), appear to have a lower abuse potential. Clorazepate and prazepam, with inactive parent compounds, are also less likely to be abused for their euphoric effects because of slower onset of action. Oxazepam and the other slow-onset benzodiazepines may be like phenobarbital compared to other barbiturates, or codeine compared to other opiates, in that they all show relatively low abuse potentials despite being representative of a class of relatively highly abused medicines.

The relative rapidity of onset of diazepam does not mean that this benzodiazepine is reinforcing or likely to lead to abuse by medical patients who have no addiction history. None of the benzodiazepines, including diazepam, are reinforcing for patients who do not have a history of addiction. On the other hand, the pharmacology of the benzodiazepines suggests that, for patients with a history of addiction to alcohol and other drugs, diazepam is more likely to be abused than oxazepam or prazepam. In terms of the abuse potential of benzodiazepines for alcoholics and drug addicts, lorazepam and alprazolam appear to pose an intermediate risk: less than diazepam, more than oxazepam.

Differences in abuse liability among the benzodiazepines may have implications for scheduling of the benzodiazepines, all of which are now Schedule IV (Benet, 1996). The Food and Drug Administration (FDA) has held hearings on this subject (Nightingale, 1997). Some serious students of the pharmacology of benzodiazepines believe that abuse is no more likely for diazepam than for oxazepam (Woods et al., 1988). The greater liking found for diazepam, in this view, is the result of the dose: Raise the dose of oxazepam in the double-blind studies, and the liking scores of oxazepam are similar to those of diazepam. In contrast, other well-respected researchers are convinced that diazepam, lorazepam, and alprazolam have greater abuse potential—not solely because of dosage factors—because of their more rapid absorption and penetration of the blood–brain barrier due to greater lipid solubility (Griffiths & Sannerud, 1987).

Metabolic Pathway

The metabolic pathway of the various benzodiazepines is important clinically because those benzodiazepines that are metabolized by oxidation in the liver may alter the effects of other drugs. This is illustrated by the "boosting" effect of some benzodiazepines when used by methadone-maintained patients. Although the pharmacology of this effect is not well understood, it appears that simultaneous use of a drug (e.g., diazepam or alprazolam) that competes with methadone for oxidative pathways in the liver produces higher peak levels of methadone in the blood (and brain) shortly after methadone administration. Thus, prior use of some benzodiazepines may enhance brain reward for an hour or so after oral methadone dosages.

Benzodiazepines that have conjugation as the major metabolic pathway are not dependent on liver functioning, so they are less likely to raise methadone plasma levels or to build up plasma levels of the active benzodiazepine in patients who have compromised liver functioning, including alcoholics and the elderly. The benzodiazepines metabolized by conjugation include lorazepam, oxazepam, and temazepam (Restoril). Thus, these are less "liked" by methadone-maintained patients and may be better choices for these patients and for patients with compromised liver functioning if any benzodiazepine is to be used.

Oxazepam is both a slow-onset and a conjugated benzodiazepine, making it perhaps the best choice for methadone-maintained patients who are treated with a benzodiazepine. On the other hand, oxazepam has a short elimination half-life, meaning it must be taken three or four times a day for continuous therapeutic effects, and it is no less likely to produce physical dependence (including difficulties on discontinuation) than any other benzodiazepine. Oxazepam is a widely used benzodiazepine in Europe (but not in the United States) where it is commonly abused by drug addicts and alcoholics. Thus whatever benefit it may possess for alcoholics and drug addicts compared to other benzodiazepines is relative and not absolute.

Persistence

Persistence of the benzodiazepine (or an active metabolite) in the body is important clinically because it governs the rapidity of onset of withdrawal symptoms after the last dose for people who have used benzodiazepines for prolonged periods. The benzodiazepines with shorter elimination half-lives are more likely to produce early and pronounced withdrawal symptoms, whereas those with longer elimination half-lives generally produce more delayed and attenuated withdrawal symptoms. In general, alprazolam, lorazepam, and oxazepam are more rapidly eliminated than are clorazepate, diazepam, flurazepam (Dalmane), and prazepam. Thus, these first three benzodiazepines, with shorter elimination half-lives, are more likely to produce acute withdrawal on abrupt cessation after prolonged use. Clonazepam has a longer elimination half-life than alprazolam or lorazepam, so it is less likely to produce interdose withdrawal symptoms and it is more appealing as a withdrawal agent (for the same reason, methadone and phenobarbital are attractive as agents in opiate withdrawal and sedative/hypnotic withdrawal).

When discontinuing treatment with a benzodiazepine abruptly, the speed of onset and the severity of symptoms are greater for benzodiazepines with shorter elimination half-lives (e.g., alprazolam or lorazepam) than for benzodiazepines with a longer half-life (such as clonazepam). However, abrupt discontinuation is not appropriate medical treatment for benzodiazepine discontinuation after prolonged, everyday use. When short-acting benzodiazepines are withdrawn gradually over several weeks or longer, they do not produce more symptoms of withdrawal than do longer-acting benzodiazepines (Sellers et al., 1993).

Although a long half-life may be beneficial in reducing the speed of onset and severity of benzodiazepine withdrawal on abrupt discontinuation, it can be more problematic in other situations. A recent article found an increase in motor vehicle crash involvement in the elderly using long half-life benzodiazepines whereas shorter half-life benzodiazepines showed no increase in the probability of crashes in the elderly compared to people of the same age who did not use a benzodiazepine (Hemmelgarn, Suissa, Huang, Boivin, & Pinard, 1997).

Reinforcement

Three additional aspects of benzodiazepine pharmacology are relevant to the treatment of addicted patients: reinforcement, withdrawal, and tolerance. Reinforcement is the potential for these drugs to be abused or "liked" by alcoholics and drug addicts. Controlled research now shows that the benzodiazepines are not reinforcing or "liked" by either normal or anxious subjects. For example, normal and anxious subjects, given a choice between placebos and benzodiazepines, more often choose the placebo in double-blind acute dose experiments, regardless of the specific benzodiazepine given. In contrast, subjects with a history of addiction, also in double-blind studies, commonly prefer benzodiazepines to placebos. These same studies with alcoholics and drug addicts have demonstrated that people with a history of addiction show a greater preference for intermediate-acting barbiturates and stimulants, as well as narcotics, than for benzodiazepines. Thus, the benzodiazepines are reinforcing for alcoholics and drug addicts (though not for anxious people or for people who do not have a history of addiction). The benzodiazepines are relatively weak reinforcers compared to opiates, stimulants, and barbiturates among alcoholics and drug addicts.

This research confirms the common clinical observation that benzodiazepines are rarely drugs of choice among addicted people for their euphoric effects (DuPont, 1984). Although it remains unclear why alcoholics and drug addicts react differently to the benzodiazepines than do normal or anxious subjects, this phenomenon exists with abused drugs in general and is not limited to the benzodiazepines. Normal subjects do not generally "like" other abused drugs either, including stimulants, narcotics, and even alcohol, in double-blind studies. People who are not addicted to alcohol and other drugs do not like the feeling of being intoxicated. Whether addicted people learn to like the intoxicated feeling or whether they have some innate (perhaps genetically determined) difference that explains this characteristic response to alcohol and controlled substances remains an unanswered question of great importance to the prevention of addiction.

Alcoholics and drug addicts react differently from others not only to the drugs they prefer or have had trouble with in the past but to all "abused" or controlled drugs, whether those drugs are taken medically or nonmedically. In medical practice, this is called "cross-addiction." It means that the abuse or loss of control of the abused substance is potentially associated with the abuse or loss of control of all other intoxicating substances. This makes the point of the unity of addiction—addiction is not "substance specific."

A related clinically important point is that once a person is addicted to alcohol and other drugs, he or she remains permanently addicted, even after stopping use of all abused drugs (DuPont, 1997a). An addicted person is said to be "in recovery" or to be "recovering" when the person has a stable abstinence from all use of alcohol and other abused drugs and is actually participating in a Twelve-Step program such as Alcoholics Anonymous (AA) or Narcotics Anonymous (NA) (DuPont & McGovern, 1994). Although many recovering alcoholics and drug addicts have stable, lifelong patterns of abstinence, the vulnerability to relapse to addictive use and the special reactivity to abusable drugs persist for the lifetimes of recovering alcoholics and drug addicts. There are many circumstances in which medical use of controlled drugs in such patients can be appropriate and safe, but vigilance and honesty need to be maintained, especially if the controlled substance is used on an outpatient basis and if this use is prolonged.

When it comes to the outpatient treatment of anxiety in patients with active addiction (e.g., still or recently abusing alcohol or other drugs), the use of a controlled substance, including a benzodiazepine, is generally contraindicated. A number of alternative treatments for anxiety are available, including nonpharmacological treatments, some antidepressants, and buspirone (BuSpar), a nonsedating antianxiety drug with no abuse potential. (See Table 6.2.) As a general principle, the use of psychotropic medicines, whether controlled substances (e.g., benzodiazepines) or noncontrolled substances (e.g., antidepressants or antipsychotics), is unlikely to produce a therapeutic benefit for the actively using addicted patient. Stable abstinence is required for these brain-affecting medicines to produce positive results (DuPont, 1997b).

TABLE 6.2. Alternative Medicines to Benzodiazepines for the Treatment of Anxiety and Insomnia in Outpatients

Medicine	Comments
For anxiety	
BuSpar	Slower onset, less dramatic benefits Not effective against panic Seldom useful for patients who have previously used a benzodiazepine
Antidepressants (SSRIs, tricyclic antidepressants, and others)	Slower onset, everyday use for months or years Not effective for simple phobia
For insomnia	
Ambien	Similar profile to benzodiazepines
Sedating antidepressants (e.g., amitriptyline and trazodone) Sedating antihistamines, (Benadryl)	May have less efficacy than benzodiazepines and more side effects

For patients who have been stable in recovery (including recovering alcoholics) and who need treatment for anxiety, it is advisable not to use benzodiazepines unless the physician can be sure that the patient uses the benzodiazepine only as prescribed and in the absence of any nonmedical drug use, including alcohol use. Many recovering people who have used benzodiazepines successfully in the treatment of their anxiety disorders have not had their sobriety threatened by this use of the benzodiazepines. We have seen many more patients in recovery who do not want to use any controlled substance and who have done well with their anxiety problems without using a benzodiazepine.

If a benzodiazepine is to be used by a recovering person, it may be prudent to use one of the slow-onset medicines (e.g., oxazepam, clorazepate, or prazepam) and to include a family member as well as the sponsor from a Twelve-Step fellowship in the therapeutic alliance to help ensure that there is no abuse of the benzodiazepine or any other drug, including alcohol.

Some recovering people believe that they are more likely to have withdrawal symptoms when they discontinue a benzodiazepine, even if it has been taken within medical guidelines. Research on the topic suggests that this is not the case, but it is best dealt with as an unresolved question in clinical practice.

Withdrawal

All the drugs that influence the GABA system show cross-tolerance and similar withdrawal patterns. Because of cross-tolerance within this class of sedatives and hypnotics, an alcoholic or barbiturate addict can be withdrawn under medical supervision using a benzodiazepine. For the same reason, phenobarbital can be used to manage benzodiazepine withdrawal.

The sedatives/hypnotics withdrawal syndrome, including the potential for withdrawal seizures on abrupt discontinuation, is also a phenomenon of this class of drugs. This phenomenon argues powerfully against abrupt discontinuation of any of these drugs after daily use for more than a few weeks. Cessation of use of the benzodiazepines, along with the other sedatives and hypnotics, can cause withdrawal seizures because they all are potent antiepilepsy drugs that raise the seizure threshold. Any medicine that raises the seizure threshold when abruptly discontinued produces a rebound drop in the seizure threshold that may cause seizures, even in people who have not previously had an epileptic seizure (Hobbs et al., 1996).

Tolerance

Tolerance is rapid, and all but complete, to the sedative and to the euphoric effects of the benzodiazepines on repeated administration at a steady dose level for even a few days. This rapidly developing tolerance for both sedation and euphoria/reward is seen clinically when these medicines are used to treat anxiety. Patients often experience sedation or drowsiness when they take their first few benzodiazepine doses, but within a few days of steady dosing the symptoms of sedation lessen and, for most patients, disappear.

By contrast, tolerance to the antianxiety and antipanic effects of the benzodiazepines is clinically nonexistent. Medical patients who are not alcoholics or drug addicts and who use a benzodiazepine to treat chronic anxiety obtain substantial beneficial effects at standard doses. They do not escalate their doses beyond common therapeutic levels, even after they have taken benzodiazepines for many years.

This distinction between rapid tolerance to the sedating and the euphoric effects and the absence of tolerance to the antianxiety effects of benzodiazepines is important for the clinician, as patients who use benzodiazepines to get high typically add other substances and escalate their benzodiazepine dose over time. This commonly observed pattern reflects the existence of tolerance to the euphoric effects of benzodiazepines among addicted people. In contrast, typical medical patients using benzodiazepines for their antianxiety effects take them at low and stable doses, without the addition of other drugs, including alcohol.

Some patients who use benzodiazepines daily, even after a long time, escalate their dose beyond the usually prescribed level, add other drugs (especially alcohol), and/or have a poor clinical response to the benzodiazepine use (inadequate suppression of anxiety). Usually, but not always, these patients have a personal and a family history of addiction to alcohol and other drugs. These same patients sometimes have unusual difficulty in discontinuing. This syndrome of problems with long-term benzodiazepine use is commonly seen in treatment programs for alcoholics and drug addicts, tending to reinforce the view in the addiction field that benzodiazepines are ineffective, problem-generating medications, especially after long-term use. Although this pattern certainly exists, it is, in our experience, uncommon in the typical medical or psychiatric practice dealing with anxious patients who do not have a history of addiction. Nevertheless, when it occurs, the best response is discontinuation of benzodiazepine use, which may require inpatient treatment.

Epidemiology

The epidemiology of sedative and hypnotic use has evolved into the epidemiology of the benzodiazepines. However, a review of the most recent drug abuse data from the Drug Abuse Warning Network (DAWN), operated by the Substance Abuse and Mental Health Services Administration (SAMHSA), shows that some of the nonbenzodiazepine sedatives and hypnotics are continuing to cause problems. In 1994, the most recent year for which data are available, DAWN captured the data on 518,521 emergency room (ER) episodes from 488 hospitals in 21 metropolitan areas and 8,426 drug-related deaths in 138 medical examiner (ME) facilities in 42 metropolitan areas (U.S. Department of Health and Human Services, 1996a, 1996b). Of the top 40 drugs in the ER reports, 6 were sedatives and hypnotics. In order of their occurrence on the list, they were as follows: alprazolam (9), diazepam (10), lorazepam (11), clonazepam (12), unspecified benzodiazepine (16), and temazepam (31). In the first edition of this book, the 1988 data from DAWN showed that 12 of the top 40 drug mentions were sedatives and hypnotics (U.S. Department of Health and Human Services, 1988a, 1988b). To put the abuse of benzodiazepines in perspective, the top five spots in the DAWN ER reports in 1994 were taken, in order, by alcohol (in combination with other drugs) (1), cocaine (2), heroin/morphine (3), marijuana/hashish (4), and acetaminophen (5). The number five drug, acetaminophen, was responsible for 38,674 mentions (7.46% of the total), more than one-half (57%) of all the 6 sedatives and hypnotics in the top 40 DAWN ER mentions combined.

All six of the sedatives and hypnotics on the DAWN top 40 ER list were benzodiazepines. The other sedatives and hypnotics among the 132 drugs listed in DAWN's ER sample were: phenobarbital (46), butabarbital combination (56), methaqualone (85), chloral hydrate (100), and butalbital (114).

In the ME data the sedatives and hypnotics were equally prominent. Nine members of this class were in the top 40, as follows: diazepam (5), unspecified benzodiazepine (16), phenobarbital (20), alprazolam (23), butalbital (26), chlordiazepoxide (27), meprobamate (31), temazepam (38), and flurazepam (40). Three of these 9 sedatives and hypnotics on the top 40 ME list were not benzodiazepines.

Medical Use

A series of national surveys tracking the medical use of the benzodiazepines has shown that their use peaked in 1976 and by the late 1980s had fallen about 25% off that peak rate (DuPont, 1988). A survey of medical use of the benzodiazepines, taken in 1979 (near the peak of benzodiazepine use in the United States), showed that 89% of Americans ages 18 years and older had not used a benzodiazepine within the previous 12 months. Of those who had used a benzodiazepine, most (9.5% of total adults) had used the medicine either less than every day or for less than 12 months or both, whereas a minority (1.6% of the adult population) had used a benzodiazepine on a daily basis for 12 months or longer. This long-term user group was two-thirds female; 71% were ages 50 or older, and most had chronic medical problems as well as anxiety (DuPont, 1988).

Of those with anxiety disorders, three-fourths were receiving no treatment at all, including not using a benzodiazepine. The 1.6% of the population who are chronic benzodiazepine users can be compared to the 8% of the population who are suffering from anxiety disorders. This statistic led many observers to conclude that the benzodiazepines not only are not overprescribed but may actually be underprescribed because of the reluctance of both physician and patients to use these medicines (Mellinger & Balter, 1981).

Nonmedical Use

The Public Health Service collects data on the nonmedical use of benzodiazepines in the general population, surveying all Americans over the age of 12 in the National Household Survey on Drug Abuse, as well as separately surveying high school seniors (Johnston, 1997; U.S. Department of Health and Human Services, 1997). The Household Survey has been conducted every few years for the last two decades; high school seniors have been surveyed annually since 1975. Both surveys show a substantial decline of nonmedical use of benzodiazepines since the peak in the mid-1970s. The high school senior data from 1975 through 1996 are reported in Figure 6.1.

To put numbers of people who use benzodiazepines nonmedically into context, the number of people who had used drugs nonmedically in the last month before the 1996 Household Survey (U.S. Department of Health and Human Services, 1997) is shown in Figure 6.2. Only 1.0 million had used a tranquilizer. Recall that most of these people who had used a benzodiazepine nonmedically had done so only a few times in their lifetimes. Nonmedical benzodiazepine use is different from, and far rarer than, medical use of the benzodiazepines; it is a small part of the overall nonmedical drug problem in the nation.

There are a number of publications on the diagnosis and treatment of chronic anxiety (DuPont, Spencer, & DuPont, 1998); Physicians Postgraduate Press, 1997; Ross, 1994). The benzodiazepines can be used to treat either acute or chronic anxiety as well as the panic attacks that are commonly associated with anxiety disorders. The benzodiazepines can be used either as needed or every day, and they can be used either alone or with other medicines, most often in psychiatry with antidepressants (Davidson, 1997).

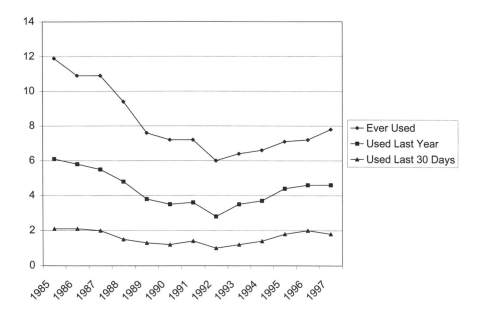

FIGURE 6.1. Nonmedical use of tranquilizers by high school seniors, 1985–1997. From Johnston (1997).

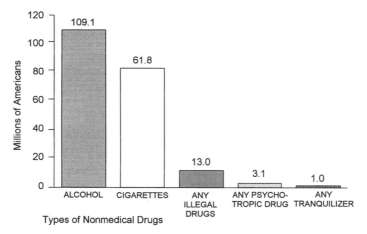

FIGURE 6.2. Nonmedical drug use (in millions) during previous month by Americans 12 years of age and older, 1996. From U.S. Department of Health and Human Services (1997).

Newer Antianxiety Agents

In recent years a variety of alternatives to the benzodiazepines have become available to treat both anxiety and insomnia. Buspirone (BuSpar) has been shown to reduce anxiety in generalized anxiety disorders, but it does not suppress panic attacks and is not used as a primary treatment of obsessive–compulsive disorder. It is not abused by alcoholics and drug addicts, and it does not produce withdrawal symptoms on abrupt discontinuation. Like the antidepressants, buspirone requires several weeks of daily dosing to produce antianxiety effects, which are less dramatic from the patients' point of view than are the effects produced by the benzodiazepines.

Zolpidem (Ambien) is a rapid onset, short-duration of action imidazopyridine that acts on the benzodiazepine receptor of the GABA system. It has been shown to reduce insomnia and has largely replaced the benzodiazepines as hypnotic medicines, although it lacks the anxiolytic, anticonvulsant, and muscle-relaxant properties of the benzodiazepines (Scharf, Mayleben, Kaffeman, Krall, & Ochs, 1991). Zolpidem is reinforcing to alcoholics and drug addicts and it does impair memory and performance of complex tasks similar to the acute use of benzodiazepines. It does not affect stage 4 sleep, as do the benzodiazepines.

The antidepressants as a class have been shown to possess antipanic and antianxiety effects opening up a new range of uses for these nonbenzodiazepine medicines in the treatment of anxiety disorders. The selective serotonin reuptake inhibitors (SSRIs) have emerged as first-line treatment for many anxiety disorders (DuPont, 1997d; Jefferson, 1997). Although the earlier antianxiety and anti-insomnia medicines focused exclusively on the benzodiazepine receptors in the GABA complex, the recognition of the importance of serotonin and norepinephrine neurotransmitters in the management of anxiety and insomnia and the success of buspirone, have stimulated a search for a new generation of antianxiety medicines that are not controlled substances (e.g., they are not abused by alcoholics and drug addicts). Recognition of the withdrawal symptoms associated with abrupt discontinuation of some antidepressants (especially those with shorter half-lives and more anticholinergic properties) has raised doubts about the effort to reduce or eliminate withdrawal symptoms after abrupt discontinuation for future anxiolytics (DuPont, 1997d).

IDENTIFICATION OF PROBLEMS AMONG LONG-TERM BENZODIAZEPINE USERS

Physicians frequently encounter patients, or family members of patients, who are concerned about the possible adverse effects of long-term use of a benzodiazepine in the treatment of anxiety or insomnia. In helping to structure the decision making for such a patient, we use the Benzodiazepine Checklist (DuPont, 1986; see Table 6.3). There are four questions to be answered:

1. *Diagnosis.* Is there a current diagnosis that warrants the prolonged use of a prescription medicine? The benzodiazepines are serious medicines that should only be used for serious illnesses.

2. *Medical and nonmedical substance use.* Is the dose of the benzodiazepine the patient is taking reasonable? Is the clinical response to the benzodiazepine favorable? Is there any use of nonmedical drugs, such as cocaine or marijuana? Is there any excessive use of alcohol (e.g., a total of more than four drinks a week, or more than two drinks a day)? Are there other medicines being used that can depress the functioning of the CNS?

3. *Toxic behavior.* Is there any evidence of slurred speech, staggering, accidents, memory loss, or other mental deficits or evidence of sedation?

4. *Family monitor.* Because people who abuse drugs deny drug-caused problems, or even lie to their doctors, and because many family members are

---

TABLE 6.3. Benzodiazepine Checklist for Long-Term Use

---

1. *Diagnosis.* Does the patient's diagnosis, with accompanying disability and distress, warrant long-term medical treatment?
2. *Drug and alcohol use.* Does the patient's use of the benzodiazepine and of other psychotropic substances demonstrate good therapeutic response to the benzodiazepine with no drug or alcohol abuse?
3. *Toxic behavior.* Is there no evidence of any benzodiazepine-caused problem?
4. *Family monitor.* Does a family member confirm the effectiveness of the benzodiazepine use and the lack of impairment and addiction?

Standard for continued benzodiazepine use: A "yes" to all four questions.

If problems are identified, benzodiazepine discontinuation is probably indicated.

concerned about long-term benzodiazepine use, we generally ask that a family member come to the office with the patient who is taking a benzodiazepine for a prolonged period. This gives us an opportunity to confirm, with the family member, that the benzodiazepine use produces a therapeutic benefit without problems. If there is a problem of toxic behavior or abuse of other drugs, we are more likely to identify it when we speak with the patient's family member; if not, we have an opportunity to educate and reassure both the patient and the family member when they are seen together.

After completion of the Benzodiazepine Checklist, if there is clear evidence that the long-term benzodiazepine use is producing significant benefit and no problems, and if the patient wants to continue using the benzodiazepine (which is, in our experience, a common set of circumstances for chronically anxious patients), then we have no hesitancy in continuing to prescribe a benzodiazepine, even for the patient's lifetime.

On the other hand, many anxious patients do want to stop using benzodiazepines. Other patients do not want to stop but show signs of poor clinical response or trouble with the use of a benzodiazepine. In either case, discontinuation is in order and is an achievable goal.

Some critics of benzodiazepines, including Stefan Borg and Curtis Carlson of St. Goran's Hospital in Stockholm, Sweden (Allgulander, Borg, & Vikander, 1984), have expressed concerns about the possibility that benzodiazepine abuse may lead to alcohol problems, especially in women. The simple advice to a long-term medical user of a benzodiazepine is not to use alcohol or to use alcohol only occasionally and never more than one or two drinks in 24 hours. Most anxious patients who do not have a prior history of addiction either do not use alcohol at all or use it only in small amounts. The Benzodiazepine Checklist helps the physician, the patient, and the patient's family identify any problems (including alcohol abuse) at early stages and thus facilitates constructive interventions.

LONG-TERM DOSE AND ABUSE

One clinical observation helps the physician identify people who have addiction programs among anxious benzodiazepine users. Most anxious medical users of benzodiazepines have used them at low and stable doses over time, often for many years, with good clinical responses. Dose is a critical and distinguishing variable in long-term benzodiazepine use. People who are addicted to alcohol and other drugs commonly abuse benzodiazepines in high and unstable doses; anxious patients who are not addicted do not. People with active addiction (e.g., currently using illegal drugs and/or abusing alcohol) seldom report a good clinical response to low and stable doses of benzodiazepines.

We use a simple assessment of dose level: If the patient's typical benzodiazepine dose level is stable at or below one-half the ordinary clinical maximum dose of the prescribed benzodiazepine as recommended in the PDR (Medical Economics Data Production, 1997) or in the package insert approved by the FDA for the prescribed benzodiazepine, we call this the "green light" benzodiazepine dose zone. Thus, patients whose daily benzodiazepine dose is stable at or less than 2 mg of alprazolam, 20 mg of diazepam, 5 mg of lorazepam, 4 mg of clonazepam, or 60 mg of oxazepam are in the relatively safe or green-light zone.

The "red light" or danger zone is above the FDA-approved maximum daily dose (e.g., above 4 mg of alprazolam or 40 mg of diazepam). Except in the treatment of panic, when doses up to two or three times the FDA maximum for chronic anxiety are occasionally needed, it is unusual to see an anxious non-alcohol- or non-drug-abusing patient taking benzodiazepine doses that are this high. Most panic disorder patients, after a few months of treatment, are able to do well (with good panic suppression) in the green-light zone without the physician or the patient making any special effort to restrain the benzodiazepine dose level. If vigilance and control are required by the physician to limit the benzodiazepine dose to levels below the maximum recommended doses, this is a poor prognostic sign and a signal that addiction to alcohol and other drugs may be a confounding, comorbid disorder.

One common clinical problem is to see a patient, a family member, or sometimes a physician or therapist who is concerned about "tolerance" and "addiction" because the patient feels compelled to raise the dose of the benzodiazepine over time. In our experience, such worries among patients who lack a personal history of addiction to alcohol or other nonmedical drugs are usually the result of underdosing with the benzodiazepine rather than evidence of addiction. Although some patients with such a presentation are more comfortable taking no medicine at all, most need education about the proper dose of the benzodiazepine. Once the benzodiazepine dose is raised to an ordinary therapeutic level (e.g., well within the green-light zone), the patient usually feels much better and has no inner pressure to raise the benzodiazepine dose further.

Within the addicted population, several patterns of benzodiazepine abuse can be identified. The most common pattern is the use of a benzodiazepine to "self-medicate" the adverse effects of the abuse of other, more preferred drugs. Typical is the "self-medication" of hangover and other withdrawal phenomena from alcohol use with a benzodiazepine. Patients waking up in the morning after an alcoholic binge may take 10 to 40 mg or more of diazepam, for example, "just to face the day."

Other common patterns of self-medication are to use the benzodiazepines (often alprazolam or lorazepam) concomitantly with stimulants (often cocaine) to reduce the unpleasant experience of the stimulant use, and/or to use benzodiazepines (often triazolam [Halcion]) to treat the insomnia that often accompanies stimulant abuse.

Benzodiazepines are occasionally used as primary drugs of abuse; in this case, they are typically taken orally at high doses. Addicted patients report using doses of 20 to 100 mg or more of diazepam or the equivalent doses of other benzodiazepines, for example, at one time. Such high-dose oral use is often repeated several times a day for long periods or on binges. Although, in our experience, such benzodiazepine abuse without simultaneous use of other drugs is unusual, it does occur. The common hallmarks of benzodiazepine abuse by addicted people are high and unstable dosing, simultaneous alcohol and polydrug abuse, and poor antianxiety and anti-insomnia results.

Preventing, Detecting, and Treating Benzodiazepine Abuse

With respect to the abuse of alcohol and other drugs, it is important for the prescribing physician to clearly identify patients who have a current or past addiction to alcohol and other drugs. Although benzodiazepines have been accepted in the inpatient withdrawal treatment of patients dependent on alcohol and other depressant substances, the use of benzodiazepines in outpatient settings by actively addicted people, even if they have stable sobriety, is generally discouraged (Castaneda & Cushman, 1989; Ditman, 1964; Kissin & Platz, 1968; Miller, 1994a, 1994b; Sellers, Naranjo, & Peachey, 1981). Although it is clear that using potentially abusable medicines is hazardous in the treatment of patients with a history of addiction, even for people who are not currently using, it is also unwise to completely prohibit the medical treatment of serious psychiatric disorders experienced by patients with a history of addiction, even with controlled substances.

Our treatment guidelines for addicted patients with anxiety disorders and/or insomnia who are still using alcohol and other nonmedical drugs are as follows:

1. Do not use benzodiazepines in outpatient treatment.
2. Refer the patient to addiction treatment and Alcoholics Anonymous or Narcotics Anonymous.
3. Refer family members to Al-Anon.
4. Work with the patient to find nonbenzodiazepine treatments for the anxiety and/or insomnia.

Other treatment alternatives to the benzodiazepines with or without comorbid addiction are as follows:

1. Education and support about the problem (help the patient put panic and anxiety into perspective).
2. Nonpharmacological treatments:
   a. Cognitive-behavioral treatments.
   b. Psychotherapy.
   c. Relaxation training.
   d. Assertiveness training.
   e. Aerobic exercise.

(See Barlow, 1988, 1997, for a discussion of nonpharmacological treatments of anxiety disorders).

As a general principle, drug abuse treatment programs should treat benzodiazepine abuse as they treat the abuse of any other drug, applying the routine sanctions for this behavior if it persists during treatment for addiction. We conducted a study in two methadone maintenance programs, looking for prevalence of abuse of two classes of drugs not often tested for: benzodiazepines and marijuana. We found that the rates of positive urine for marijuana were 27% and 51% in the two programs, whereas the rates for benzodiazepines were 4% and 7% (DuPont & Saylor, 1989).

Discontinuation of Benzodiazepine Use

Discontinuation of sedatives and hypnotics, including the benzodiazepines, can be divided into three categories: (1) long-term low-dose benzodiazepine use, (2) high-dose benzodiazepine abuse and multiple drug abuse, and (3) high-dose abuse of nonbenzodiazepine sedatives and hypnotics (especially intermediate-acting barbiturates). The first group of patients can usually be discontinued on an outpatient basis. Some of the second and even the third group can be treated as outpatients, but most will require inpatient care. Inpatient discontinuation today with managed care is generally reserved for patients who fail at outpatient discontinuation and for patients who demonstrate acutely life-threatening loss of control over their drug use.

With respect to withdrawal from benzodiazepines in the context of addiction treatment, the most common problem treatment professionals experience is that some of the patients who take benzodiazepines also suffer chronically from underlying anxiety disorders and panic attacks. Therefore, when the patients stop taking benzodiazepines, they experience a short-term rebound increase in these distressing symptoms. These rebound symptoms, including panic attacks, are difficult for the patients or the physicians to separate from withdrawal symptoms because they are similar and because the time course is also similar, with both types of symptoms occurring at low benzodiazepine doses and peaking during the first or second drug-free week.

There is abundant evidence that most patients who take benzodiazepines at prescribed dose levels can discontinue using them with quite moderate symptoms if the dose reduction is gradual (Busto, Simpkins, & Sellers, 1983; Rickels, Schweizer, Csanalosi, Case, & Chung, 1988). One study found that about half of long-term benzodiazepine users could stop with no withdrawal symptoms (Tyrer, Rutherford, & Huggett, 1981). However, some patients who stop benzodiazepine use, especially after use for many years, do have symptoms that are either prolonged or severe (Noyes, Garvey, Cook, & Perry, 1988). It has been found that about one-third of medical patients with long-term use of a benzodiazepine will have clinically significant withdrawal symptoms, even after gradual tapering, and that about one in eight patients stopping a benzodiazepine will have prolonged and/or severe symptoms (DuPont, 1988). In any case, discontinuation symptoms (except for abrupt cessation, which can produce seizures and is not indicated) from benzodiaze-pines are "distressing but not dangerous" (DuPont et al., 1992; Sellers et al., 1993).

Two common clinical errors occur in dealing with benzodiazepine dis-continuation symptoms: underestimating the symptoms and overestimating them. Unfortunately, patients taking benzodiazepines today have no trouble finding physicians who do both. Our recommendation is to state the following clearly to the patient: "Withdrawal, especially after many years of daily use of a benzodiazepine, can be hard, but it is not dangerous. It is a solvable problem that is of fairly short duration."

We have found that it is rarely necessary to hospitalize a long-term low-dose benzodiazepine user who is not a drug abuser for benzodiazepine discontinuation. The preferred treatment is gradual reduction of the dose of the usually taken benzodiazepine over a 6- to 12-week period on an outpatient basis.

Outpatient Discontinuation

The simplest discontinuation technique on an outpatient basis is to gradually reduce the patient's dose of the currently used benzodiazepine over a 6- to 12-week period or longer (DuPont, 1987, 1990b, 1990c; Sellers, 1988). Patients need education and support in this process because they are likely to feel uncomfortable and to worry about the painful and distressing rise of their anxiety and insomnia symptoms during benzodiazepine discontinuation. It is helpful to schedule weekly visits to the physician and to help the patient carefully structure a discontinuation program in which each dose is planned in advance. It often helps if the patient has the opportunity to take a small "extra dose" (e.g., 2 mg of diazepam or 0.25 mg of alprazolam) any day during discontinuation, so that the feeling of being trapped by the dose-reduc-tion schedule is lessened. Patients are reassured to know that their discomfort during dose reduction means that their bodies are getting used to no longer having the benzodiazepine. This discomfort of withdrawal is both healthy and temporary.

Benzodiazepine discontinuation symptoms are likely to be most intense at the lowest dose levels and during the first drug-free week. This information helps patients to know what to expect; otherwise they experience the building up of symptoms as they approach zero dose as if the worsening trend would increase endlessly. The acute benzodiazepine withdrawal symptoms subside by the second drug-free week. Chronic, generally low-level withdrawal distress may continue for several months, or even a year, after becoming drug free.

Along with total duration of benzodiazepine use and maximum dose used, personality factors play a major role in the severity and duration of withdrawal symptoms (DuPont, 1988; Rickels, Schweizer, Case, & Garcia-Espana, 1988). The longer the patient has used the benzodiazepine, the higher the dose used, and the more chronic character pathology the patient has, the more likely the benzodiazepine withdrawal is to be difficult. Nevertheless, in our experience, it is not possible to predict accurately with any particular patient how mild or how severe the benzodiazepine (or other) withdrawal symptoms will be.

It is of considerable academic interest that three distinct types of symptoms occur on benzodiazepine discontinuation: withdrawal (a response to physical dependence), relapse (of the underlying anxiety disorder), and rebound (a temporary exaggeration of the underlying anxiety disorder, mixed with withdrawal that occurs just at the time of stopping the medication) (DuPont & Pecknold, 1985). All these symptoms overlap both in quality of the experience and in time course, so it is difficult for either the patient or the physician to distinguish them. The clinically important point is that the upsurge of symptoms from all three sources during discontinuation is temporary. If the patient sticks with the benzodiazepine discontinuation program, these symptoms can all be overcome.

If gradual benzodiazepine dose reduction does not succeed (though for most anxious patients taking therapeutic doses of a benzodiazepine, it will succeed), there are two alternatives: using a longer-acting cross-tolerant medication and/or using a medicine to suppress the withdrawal symptoms.

The best choices for cross-tolerant long-acting agents are clonazepam and phenobarbital. For patients taking the usual therapeutic doses of a benzodiazepine, the standard approach with clonazepam is to give the patient 0.5 or 1.0 mg at bedtime for 1 week. During that week, the patient may continue to take his or her regular benzodiazepine on an as-needed (p.r.n.) basis, up to the total dose taken prior to the start of discontinuation. After 1 week taking clonazepam, the patient is to stop all use of the original benzodiazepine and to continue taking the clonazepam at the same dose (e.g., usually 0.5 or 1.0 mg at bedtime; however, the dose of clonazepam can be higher or lower and may be divided if the patient has problems with sedation, the most common side effect of clonazepam use). Then the patient reduces the clonazepam dose by 0.25 mg (half a tablet) each week, until reaching a zero dose. This approach, developed by Jerrold Rosenbaum, has been labeled the "Klonopin switch" (Herman, Rosenbaum, & Brotman, 1987).

Some patients who use benzodiazepines medically without any nonmedical drug use find it helpful to join in mutual-aid groups, such as Drugs Anonymous (formerly Pills Anonymous) or other Twelve-Step programs that focus particularly on the problems of prescription drug dependence as part of their efforts to stop benzodiazepine use. The Twelve-Step programs are the foundation of the treatment of all addicted patients who discontinue benzodiazepines.

Inpatient Discontinuation

Inpatient withdrawal is indicated for patients using sedatives and hypnotics other than the benzodiazepines (especially if that use is at doses higher than usually prescribed), for patients exhibiting polydrug abuse, for patients with severe medical or psychiatric complications, and for patients who have failed in outpatient benzodiazepine discontinuation programs. In general, inpatient care permits a more controlled and more rapid benzodiazepine discontinuation because patients can tolerate more distressing symptoms when in a hospital and because they can be observed and managed medically more carefully. Perhaps the most striking observation of the care of patients discontinuing benzodiazepines in hospitals, compared to patients stopping other abused drugs, is the severity of their insomnia and the prolonged nature of their distress during and after benzodiazepine discontinuation.

Inpatient benzodiazepine discontinuation allows more careful monitoring of sedation and possible side effects of adjunctive treatment (especially leukopenia for carbamazepine [Tegretol] and hypotension for propranolol [Inderal] and clonidine [Catapres]). If the patient has concomitantly abused other drugs, especially alcohol, that needs to be considered during the detoxification process.

For patients using sedatives and hypnotics other than the benzodiazepines, especially at high doses, it may be desirable to use the classic pentobarbital challenge test to set the original dose and then to withdraw the patient gradually from this intermediate-acting barbiturate (Schuckit, 1984).

The underlying principle is the same with all patients being withdrawn from any of the sedatives and hypnotics: Either gradually reduce the dose of the original substance or find a roughly equivalent dose of a cross-tolerant substance (of which there are several alternatives, most notably clonazepam and phenobarbital) and then gradually reduce the dose. First reduce the dose of the benzodiazepine and then reduce the dose of the cross-tolerance medicine to zero. For inpatient discontinuation, the period of withdrawal is usually 1 or 2 weeks (followed by a week or two of stabilization off all medicines), whereas on an outpatient basis the duration for dose reduction of a benzodiazepine is longer, usually 6 weeks or more.

REFERENCES

Allgulander, C., Borg, S., & Vikander, B. (1984). A 4-6 year follow-up of 50 patients with primary dependence on sedative and hypnotic drugs. *American Journal of Psychiatry, 141,* 1580–1582.

American Psychiatric Association. (1994). *Diagnostic and statistical manual of mental disorders* (4th ed.). Washington, DC: Author.

American Psychiatric Association Task Force on Benzodiazepine Dependence, Toxicity and Abuse. (1990). *Benzodiazepine dependence, toxicity and abuse: A task force report of the American Psychiatric Association.* Washington, DC: American Psychiatric Press.

Arendt, R. M., Greenblatt, D. J., Liebisch, D. C., Luu, M. D., & Paul, S. M. (1987). Determinants of benzodiazepine brain uptake: Lipophilicity versus binding affinity. *Psychopharmacology, 93,* 72–76.

Baldessarini, R. J. (1996). Drugs and the treatment of psychiatric disorders—psychosis and anxiety. In J. G. Hardman & L. E. Limbird, (Eds.), *Goodman and Gilman's the pharmacological basis of therapeutics* (9th ed., pp. 399–430). New York: McGraw-Hill.

Barlow, D. H. (1988). *Anxiety and its disorders: The nature and treatment of anxiety and panic.* New York: Guilford Press.

Barlow, D. H. (1997). Antidepressants in panic disorder. *Journal of Clinical Psychiatry,* 58(Suppl. 2), 32–37.

Benet, L. Z. (1996). Principles of prescription order writing and patient compliance instructions. In J. G. Hardman & L. E. Limbird, (Eds.), *Goodman and Gilman's the pharmacological basis of therapeutics* (9th ed., pp. 1697–1706). New York: McGraw-Hill.

Burt, D. R., & Kamatchi, G. L. (1991). GABA receptor subtypes: From pharmacology to molecular biology. *FASEB Journal, 5,* 2916–2923.

Busto, U., Simpkins, J., & Sellers, E. M. (1983). Objective determination of benzodiazepine use and abuse in alcoholics. *British Journal of Addiction, 48,* 429–435.

Castañeda, R., & Cushman, P. (1989). Alcohol withdrawal: A review of clinical management. *Journal of Clinical Psychiatry, 50,* 278–284.

Davidson, J. R. T. (1997). Use of benzodiazepines in panic disorder. *Journal of Clinical Psychiatry,* 58(Suppl. 2), 26–31.

Ditman, K. S. (1964). Review and evaluation of current drug therapies in alcoholism. *Psychosomatic Medicine, 28,* 667–677.

DuPont, R. L. (1984). *Getting tough on gateway drugs: A guide for the family.* Washington, DC: American Psychiatric Press.

DuPont, R. L. (1986). *Benzodiazepines: The social issues.* Rockville, MD: Institute for Behavior and Health.

DuPont, R. L. (1987). Discontinuation of benzodiazepine use: A clinician's guide. In F. Flach (Ed.), *Directions in psychiatry* (Vol. 7, Lesson 12:1–8). New York: Hatherleigh.

DuPont, R. L. (Ed.). (1988). Abuse of benzodiazepines: The problems and the solutions. *American Journal of Drug and Alcohol Abuse, 14*(Suppl. 1).

DuPont, R. L. (1990a). Medicines and drug testing in the workplace. *Journal of Psychoactive Drugs, 22,* 451–459.

DuPont, R. L. (1990b). A physician's guide to discontinuing benzodiazepine therapy. *The Western Journal of Medicine* [Special issue], *152,* 600–603.

DuPont, R. L. (1990c). A practical approach to benzodiazepine discontinuation. *Journal of Psychiatric Research, 24*(Suppl. 2), 81–90.

DuPont, R. L. (1995). Anxiety and addiction: A clinical perspective on comorbidity. *Bulletin of the Menninger Clinic, 59*(Suppl. A), A53–A72.

DuPont, R. L. (1997a). *The selfish brain: Learning from addiction.* Washington, DC: American Psychiatric Press.

DuPont, R. L. (1997b). Panic disorder and addiction: The clinical issues of comorbidity. *Bulletin of the Menninger Clinic, 61*(Suppl. A), A54–A65.

DuPont, R. L. (1997c, March). *Update of the costs of mental illness in the United States.* Presentation to the 17th annual conference, Anxiety Disorders Association of America, New Orleans.

DuPont, R. L. (1997d). The pharmacology and drug interactions of the newer antidepressants. *Essential Psychopharmacology, 2,* 7–31.

DuPont R. L., & Gold, M. S. (1995) Withdrawal and reward: implications for detoxification and relapse prevention. *Psychiatric Annals, 25,* 663–668.

DuPont, R. L., & McGovern, J. P. (1994). *A bridge to recovery—An introduction to 12-step programs.* Washington, DC: American Psychiatric Press.

DuPont, R. L., & Pecknold, J. C. (1985, May). *Symptoms after alprazolam discontinu-*

ation: Withdrawal or relapse? Paper presented at the annual meeting of the American Psychiatric Association, Dallas.

DuPont, R. L., Rice, D. P., Miller L. S., Shiraki, S. S., Rowland, C. R., & Harwood, H. J. (1996). Economic costs of anxiety disorders. *Anxiety, 2,* 167–172.

DuPont, R. L., & Saylor, K. E. (1989). Marijuana and benzodiazepines in patients receiving methadone treatment. *Journal of the American Medical Association, 261,* 3409.

DuPont, R. L., Spencer, E. D., & DuPont, C. M. (1998). *The anxiety cure: An eight step program for getting well.* New York: Wiley.

DuPont, R. L., Swinson, R. P., Ballenger, J. C., Burrows, G. D., Noyes, R., Rubin, R. T., Rifkin, A., & Pecknold, J. C. (1992). Discontinuation effects of alprazolam after long-term treatment of panic-related disorders. *Journal of Clinical Psychopharmacology, 12,* 352–354.

Golombok, S., Moodley, P., & Lader, M. (1988). Cognitive impairment in long-term benzodiazepine users. *Psychological Medicine, 18,* 365–374.

Griffiths, R. R., & Sannerud, C. A. (1987). Abuse of and dependence on benzodiazepines and other anxiolytic/sedative drugs. In H. Meltzer, B. S. Bunney, & J. T. Coyle (Eds.), *Psychopharmacology: The third generation of progress* (pp. 1535–1541). New York: Raven Press.

Hemmelgarn, B., Suissa, S., Huang, A., Boivin, J.-F., & Pinard, G. (1997). Benzodiazepine use and the risk of motor vehicle crash in the elderly. *Journal of the American Medical Association, 278,* 27–31.

Herman, J. B., Rosenbaum, J. F., & Brotman, A. W. (1987). The alprazolam to clonazepam switch for the treatment of panic disorder. *Journal of Clinical Psychopharmacology, 7,* 175–178.

Hobbs, W. R., Rall, T. W., & Verdoorn, T. A. (1996). Hypnotics and sedatives; ethanol. In J. G. Hardman & L. E. Limbird (Eds.), *Goodman and Gilman's the pharmacological basis of therapeutics* (9th ed., pp. 361–396). New York: McGraw-Hill.

Jefferson, J. W. (1997). Antidepressants in panic disorder. *Journal of Clinical Psychiatry, 58*(Suppl. 2), 20–25.

Johnson, B., & Longo, L. P. (Eds.). (1998). Treating the anxious person with an addiction. *Psychiatric Annals, 28* (entire issue).

Johnston, L. D. (Principal Investigator). (1997, December 18). Drug use among American teens shows some signs of leveling after a long rise [News release]. *Monitoring the future study.* Ann Arbor: University of Michigan, Institute for Social Research.

Juergens, S. M. (1997). Benzodiazepines, other sedative, hypnotic, and anxiolytic drugs, and addiction. In N. S. Miller (Ed.), *The principles and practice of addictions in psychiatry* (pp. 177–187). Philadelphia: Saunders.

Kessler, R. C., McGonagle, K. A., Zhao, S., Nelson, C. B., Hughes, M., Eshleman, S., Wittchen, H. U., & Kendler, K. S. (1994). Lifetime and 12-month prevalence of *DSM-III-R* psychiatric disorders in the United States: Results from the National Comorbidity Survey. *Archives of General Psychiatry, 51,* 8–19.

Kessler, R. C., Nelson, C. B., McGonagle, K. A., Edlund, M. J., Frank, R. G., & Leaf, P. J. (1996). The epidemiology of co-occurring mental disorders and substance abuse disorders in the National Comorbidity Survey: Implications for prevention and service utilization. *American Journal of Orthopsychiatry, 66,* 17–31.

Kissin, B., & Platz, A. (1968). The use of drugs in the long term rehabilitation of alcoholics. In D. H. Efron (Ed.), *Psychopharmacology: A review of progress, 1957–1967* (PHS Publication No. 1836). Washington, DC: U.S. Government Printing Office.

Lader, M. H., Ron, M., & Petursson, H. (1984). Computed axial brain tomography in long-term benzodiazepine users. *Psychological Medicine, 14,* 203–206.

Medical Economics Data Production. (1997). *Physicians' desk reference.* Montvale, NJ: Author.

Mellinger, G. D., & Balter, M. B. (1981). Prevalence and patterns of use of psychotherapeutic drugs: Results from a 1979 national survey of American adults. In G. Tognoni, C. Bellantuono, & M. Lader (Eds.), *Epidemiological impact of psychotropic drugs* (pp. 117–135). Amsterdam: Elsevier.

Melzack, R. (1990). The tragedy of needless pain. *Scientific American, 262,* 27–33.

Miller, N. S. (1994a) Medicines used with the dually diagnosed. In N. S. Miller (Ed.), *Treating coexisting psychiatric and addiction disorders* (pp. 143–160). Center City, MN: Hazelden.

Miller, N. S. (Ed.). (1994b). *Principles of addiction medicine.* Chevy Chase, MD: American Society of Addiction Medicine.

Nightingale, S. L. (1997). From the Food and Drug Administration. *Journal of the American Medical Association, 278,* 15.

Noyes, R., Garvey, M. J., Cook, B. L., & Perry, P. J. (1988). Benzodiazepine withdrawal: A review of the evidence. *Journal of Clinical Psychiatry, 49,* 382–389.

O'Brien, C. P. (1996). Drug addiction and drug abuse. In J. G. Hardman & L. E. Limbird (Eds.), *Goodman and Gilman's the pharmacological basis of therapeutics* (9th ed., pp. 557–577). New York: McGraw-Hill.

Physicians Postgraduate Press. (1997). Treatment of panic disorder: The state of the art. *Journal of Clinical Psychiatry, 58*(Suppl. 2).

Rickels, K., Schweizer, E., Case, G. W., & Garcia-Espana, F. (1988). Benzodiazepine dependence, withdrawal severity, and clinical outcome: Effects of personality. *Psychopharmacology Bulletin, 24,* 415–420.

Rickels, K., Schweizer, E., Csanalosi, I., Case, G. W., & Chung, H. (1988). Long-term treatment of anxiety and risk of withdrawal. *Archives of General Psychiatry, 45,* 444–450.

Robins, L. N., Helzer, J. E., Weissman, M. M., Orvaschel, H., Burke, J. D., & Regier, D. A. (1984). Lifetime prevalence of specific psychiatric disorders in three sites. *Archives of General Psychiatry, 41,* 949–958.

Ross, J. (1994). *Triumph over fear: A book of help and hope for people with anxiety, panic attacks, and phobias.* New York: Bantam Books.

Roy-Byrne, P. P., & Cowley, D. S. (1990). The use of benzodiazepines in the workplace. *Journal of Psychoactive Drugs, 22,* 461–465.

Salzman, C., & Freeman, S. A. (1998). Benefits versus risks of benzodiazepines. *Psychiatric Annals, 28,* 139–141.

Scharf, M. B., Jennings, S. W., & Graham, J. P. (1988, December). Therapeutic substitution: Clinical differences among benzodiazepine compounds. *U.S. Pharmacist,* pp. H1–H13.

Scharf, M. B., Mayleben, D. W., Kaffeman, M., Krall, R., & Ochs, R. (1991). Dose response effects of zolpidem in normal geriatric subjects. *Journal of Clinical Psychiatry, 52,* 77–83.

Schuckit, M. A. (1984). *Drug and alcohol abuse: A clinical guide to diagnosis and treatment.* New York: Plenum.

Sellers, E. M. (1988). Alcohol, barbiturate and benzodiazepine withdrawal syndromes: Clinical management. *Canadian Medical Association Journal, 139,* 113–120.

Sellers, E. M., Ciraulo, D. A., DuPont, R. L., Griffiths, R. R., Kosten, T. R., Romach,

M. K., & Woody, G. E. (1993). Alprazolam and benzodiazepine dependence. *Journal of Clinical Psychiatry, 54*(Suppl.), 64–74.

Sellers, E. M., Naranjo, C. A., & Peachey, J. E. (1981). Drugs to decrease alcohol consumption. *New England Journal of Medicine, 305,* 1255–1262.

Tyrer, P., Rutherford, D., & Huggett, D. (1981). Benzodiazepine withdrawal symptoms and propranolol. *Lancet, i,* 520–522.

Uhde, T. W., & Kellner, C. H. (1987). Cerebral ventricular size in panic disorder. *Journal of Affective Disorders, 12,* 175–178.

U.S. Department of Health and Human Services. (1988a). *A decade of DAWN: Benzodiazepine-related cases, 1976–1985* (DHHS Publication No. ADM 88-1575). Washington, DC: U.S. Government Printing Office.

U.S. Department of Health and Human Services. (1988b). *Annual data 1987: Data from the Drug Abuse Warning Network (DAWN)* (DHHS Publication No. ADM 88-1584). Washington, DC: U.S. Government Printing Office.

U.S. Department of Health and Human Services. (1996a). *Annual emergency department data 1994: Data from the Drug Abuse Warning Network (DAWN)* (Series I, Number 14-A). Rockville, MD: Substance Abuse and Mental Health Services Administration, Office of Applied Studies.

U.S. Department of Health and Human Services. (1996b). *Annual Medical Examiner data 1994: Data from the Drug Abuse Warning Network (DAWN)* (Series I, Number 14-B). Rockville, MD: Substance Abuse and Mental Health Services Administration, Office of Applied Studies.

U.S. Department of Health and Human Services. (1997, July). *Preliminary results from the 1996 National Household Survey on Drug Abuse* (DHHS Publication No. SMA 97-3149). Rockville, MD: Substance Abuse and Mental Health Services Administration, Office of Applied Studies.

Woods, J. H., Katz, J. L., & Winger, G. (1988). Use and abuse of benzodiazepines: Issues relevant to prescribing. *Journal of the American Medical Association, 260,* 3476–3480.

World Health Organization. (1988). *The use of essential drugs: Third report of the World Health Organization expert committee* (WHO Technical Report Series No. 770). Geneva: Author.

7

Opioids

LISA A. DARTON
STEPHEN L. DILTS

INTRODUCTION

Opioids constitute a group of compounds whose pharmacological effects resemble those of morphine. Opioids are commonly used medically for the relief of pain, as an adjunct to anesthesia, for the prevention of an abstinence syndrome, for cough suppression, and occasionally for sedation in the agitated patient. Frequently opioids are also abused for their intoxicating effects.

The history of opioid use goes back thousands of years in human history. The Ebers Papyri from approximately 7000 B.C. refer to the use of opium in children suffering from colic (Deneau & Mule, 1981). In the Victorian era, the use of laudanum was socially acceptable. In the present day, opioids are severely regulated, especially in the United States; however, demand by addicts results in the existence of a "black market" characterized by crime, disease, poverty, and loss of personal and social productivity. The sexually promiscuous intravenous heroin user is a most effective spreader of the deadly acquired immune deficiency syndrome (AIDS) virus, as well as other venereal and infectious diseases. High overall death rates are associated with opioid abuse, approximately 10–15 per 1,000 in the United States (Jaffe, 1989). The Drug Abuse Warning Network (Substance Abuse and Mental Health Services Administration,1995) indicates an alarming increase in the use of opioids, especially in young people. Opioids have the capacity to commandeer all of an individual's attention, resources, and energy, and to focus these exclusively on obtaining the next dose at any cost. This vicious cycle repeats itself every few hours, 24 hours a day, 365 days a year, for years on end. Comprehending the implications of opioid abuse shocks and staggers the inquiring mind.

150

DEFINITIONS

As a group, the opioids are addicting; that is, they produce a well-defined syndrome characterized by repeated self-administration over time, tolerance to the effects of the drug, and an abstinence syndrome when the drug is no longer available. "Cross-tolerance" is the ability of any drug in the opioid class to produce similar effects and block the abstinence syndrome associated with opioids in general as long as equivalent doses are used.

Morphine, codeine, and thebaine are phenanthrane alkaloids naturally occurring in opium, the milky exudate from the unripe capsule of the poppy plant, *Papaver somniferum.* Raw opium contains 4–21% morphine and 0.7–2.5% codeine and is refined to produce these medically useful products. In practice, most codeine is actually converted directly from morphine, which also can be used to produce hydromorphone (Dilaudid). Thebaine, found in very small concentrations in raw opium, is similar to morphine. It is converted into medically useful compounds such as codeine, hydrocodone (Vicodin), oxycodone (Percodan, Percocet, Tylox), oxymorphone (Numorphan), nalbuphine (Nubain), and diacetylmorphine (heroin). Naloxone (Narcan) is also produced from morphine but lacks euphoric and analgesic properties; its use in humans is discussed later in this chapter. Etorphine (M99), which is produced from thebaine, is a potent opioid useful mainly in the immobilization of large animals. Raw opium, morphine, codeine, and thebaine are referred to as naturally occurring opioids, whereas those compounds mentioned previously, which are produced directly from these naturally occurring compounds, are called semisynthetic opioids.

Attempts to synthesize opioid-like compounds have produced a variety of agents that are chemically distinct from morphine yet seem to act via similar mechanisms and also exhibit cross-tolerance. These include meperidine (Demerol), propoxyphene (Darvon), and methadone (Dolophine). Fentanyl (Sublimaze) is a very potent short-acting opioid used mainly as an anesthetic. Buprenorphine is a partial μ agonist which may prove useful in the treatment of heroin addiction. These compounds are collectively referred to as the synthetic opioids.

Most opioids are legitimately used medically for pain relief and therefore are referred to commonly as analgesics; yet not all analgesics are opioid-like in their mechanisms of action, nor do they exhibit complete cross-tolerance with the naturally occurring, semisynthetic, and synthetic opioids. Initial hopes were that a nonaddicting analgesic with the same potent pain-relieving properties as the opioids could be produced; unfortunately, this has not come to pass, and the following examples are known to produce dependence along with analgesia. Pentazocine (Talwin) and butorphanol (Stadol) produce analgesia in the opioid-free individual, but when given to someone who is opioid dependent, they produce an abstinence syndrome. The semisynthetic compound nalbuphine, mentioned earlier, has similar properties. Tramadol (Ultram), a synthetic aminoncyclohexanol, binds to μ opioid receptors and inhibits reuptake of norepinephrine and serotonin; there have been increasing reports of tramadol abuse. This mixed agonist–antagonist phenomenon highlights an important aspect of opioid pharmacology, the "opioid receptor."

Discovery of the opioid receptor in relation to both endogenous and exogenous compounds that may bind to it has broadened the definition of "opioid" to include any substance that binds specifically to the opioid receptor site and produces an agonistic action. Further investigations have described opioid receptor subtypes. For example, the μ receptor is occupied preferentially by the classic morphine-like opioids, but butorphanol (Stadol) and nalbuphaine prefer the κ receptor. Both receptors are highly specific, and an abstinence syndrome mediated by the κ receptor will not be relieved if a μ receptor compound is administered. There are also compounds that bind selectively to the receptor site yet produce no agonistic action. These compounds are antagonistic in nature because they occupy the receptor site and exclude agonist opioids; examples include naloxone and naltrexone (Revia). These opioid antagonists are useful as treatment agents and are discussed later in the chapter in connection with pharmacotherapy. Also of interest is the discovery and description of endogenous opioid substances in humans, operating at the κ receptor site along the spectrum from agonistic to antagonistic function. To date, no endogenous μ receptor opioid has been discovered (Jaffe, 1989).

DIAGNOSIS

In the framework provided by the fourth edition of the *Diagnostic and Statistical Manual of Mental Disorders* (DSM-IV; American Psychiatric Association, 1994), the problem of opioid abuse is divided into four categories, among which there may be some overlap. Opioid-induced organic mental disorders of two types are defined: intoxication and withdrawal. Opioid intoxication is defined in Table 7.1, and opioid withdrawal is defined in Table 7.2. Facility in making these diagnoses requires a clear understanding of the clinical features associated with opioids, as discussed later in this chapter. In addition to intoxication or withdrawal, it is important to characterize the individual's relationship to the use of opioids over time. Tables 3.1 and 3.2 (Chapter 3, this volume) give the DSM-IV criteria for psychoactive substance dependence and abuse, respectively.

Initial assessment always includes a thorough history of the individual's substance use over time, with corroboration from outside sources if possible. This corroboration of the individual's history is essential because of the universal presence of denial in the nonrecovered substance abuser. Minimization of the frequency and amounts of opioid use is common, as is the illusion of control characterized by the often-heard phrase, "I can stop any time I want to." Progression in the pattern of usage is the rule, as the reinforcing qualities of the opioid and tolerance exert their powerful influence. Critical to the initial assessment is an accurate answer to this question: "When did you last use and how much did you use?" With this information, one can

TABLE 7.1. DSM-IV Diagnostic Criteria for Opioid Intoxication

A. Recent use of an opioid.

B. Clinically significant maladaptive behavioral or psychological changes (e.g., initial euphoria followed by apathy, dysphoria, psychomotor agitation or retardation, impaired judgment, or impaired social or occupational functioning) that developed during, or shortly after, opioid use.

C. Pupillary constriction (or pupillary dilation due to anoxia from severe overdose) and one (or more) of the following signs, developing during, or shortly after, opioid use:
(1) drowsiness or coma
(2) slurred speech
(3) impairment in attention or memory

D. The symptoms are not due to a general medical condition and are not better accounted for by another mental disorder.

Note. From American Psychiatric Association (1994, p. 250). Copyright 1994 by the American Psychiatric Association. Reprinted by permission.

begin to assess the impact of intoxication or withdrawal upon the immediate clinical presentation. It is also necessary to understand the crises or events precipitating contact with the health care system to assess whether the patient has truly "hit bottom" or merely experienced a temporary loss of ability to obtain opoids. This information may be useful in predicting readiness to accept treatment interventions.

A family history of substance abuse provides data reflective of the genetic influences in opioid dependence, as well as the contribution of learned behavior and sanction of substance abuse within the family structure. This

TABLE 7.2. DSM-IV Diagnostic Criteria for Opioid Withdrawal

A. Either of the following:
(1) cessation of (or reduction in) opioid use that has been heavy and prolonged (several weeks or longer)
(2) administration of an opioid antagonist after a period of opioid use

B. Three (or more) of the following, developing within minutes to several days after Criterion A:
(1) dysphoric mood
(2) nausea or vomiting
(3) muscle aches
(4) lacrimation or rhinorrhea
(5) pupillary dilation, piloerection, or sweating
(6) diarrhea
(7) yawning
(8) fever
(9) insomnia

C. The symptoms in Criterion B cause clinically significant distress or impairment in social, occupational, or other important areas of functioning.

D. The symptoms are not due to a general medical condition and are not better accounted for by another mental disorder.

Note. From American Psychiatric Association (1994, p. 251). Copyright 1994 by the American Psychiatric Association. Reprinted by permission.

information is particularly useful in planning a strategy for recovery and relapse prevention. Returning an individual to contact with family members and/or friends who are still using opioids and other drugs will virtually guarantee a quick relapse.

Also important are inquiries into the individual's functioning in the workplace, at home, and in the social arena. Trouble may occur in each area because of the competition between dependence-driven, drug-seeking behavior and the demands of everyday living. It is important to ask specifically about legal difficulties, arrests, convictions, or restrictions of freedom (e.g., loss of professional licensure).

A medical review of systems in tandem with a thorough physical examination, including a neurological examination and a mental status examination, will almost always reveal actual signs of intoxication or withdrawal as outlined later. Stigmata of opioid use, such as fresh or old needle marks (tracks) around superficial veins in the extremities and neck, are readily observed. These often appear as increased lines of pigmentation. There may be evidence of old and new skin abscesses, clotted or thrombosed veins, an enlarged and tender liver, swollen lymph nodes, a heart murmur caused by endocarditis; hypo- or hyperactive bowel sounds, and pupillary abnormalities, which depend on the stage of intoxication or withdrawal. Significant weight loss is common, though weight gain is occasionally reported.

Useful laboratory studies include serum liver function studies, which may show inflammation in the form of elevated serum glutamic-oxaloacetic transferase, serum glutamic-pyruvic transferase, bilirubin, or alkaline phosphatase, and reduction in total protein and immunoglobulins. Blood urea nitrogen may also be elevated, though the meaning of this finding is unclear. Further testing should include hepatitis A, B, and C screening; human immunodeficiency virus (HIV) testing; complete blood count; and urine and/or serum analyses for the presence of opioids, cocaine metabolites, marijuana, alcohol, benzodiazepines, barbiturates, other stimulants, and hallucinogens. If possible, the collection of urine samples should be actively observed to ensure that the samples are not falsified in some manner by the individual. "Scams" for avoiding detection of illicit drugs in urine are diverse and imaginative: Some men have provided "clean" urine from a small tube alongside the penis, and some women have concealed a balloon of "clean" urine in the vagina to be lacerated with a fingernail, while apparently positioning the specimen cup near the urethral meatus as the sample is collected.

As evidence of opioid abuse or dependence grows, the clinician can mount a firm but respectful confrontation of the individual, who will frequently admit the problem because he or she now recognizes that there may exist an opportunity for treatment. The "addiction as an illness" concept can be useful at this critical juncture in the physician's interactions with an opioid-dependent person. If the patient's denial prevents engagement in treatment, leverage on his or her behavior may be gained by involving significant others, employers, or the legal system.

CLINICAL FEATURES AND PHARMACOLOGY

Clinical features of opioid abuse are logically divided into three categories: intoxication, withdrawal, and overdose. These features are outlined in Tables 7.3, 7.4, and 7.5, respectively. The features listed in these tables are directly related to the pharmacological actions of the opiates and are uniform in humans, with the occasional exception of the individual who experiences an idiosyncratic reaction.

Analgesia is the principal useful effect of the opioids. It seems not to matter whether the pain is physical or emotional; relief is significant. The addiction potential of a given opioid appears to be at least partly related to the analgesic affect. Analgesia is increased in a dose-related manner, to a point beyond which larger doses cause greater side effects but no greater analgesia (Deneau & Mule, 1981). Contravening side effects include respiratory depression, sedation, seizures, and loss of motor control. Heroin, morphine, and hydromorphone are among the best analgesics because of rapid absorption into the central nervous system and a relatively higher threshold for side effects. Meperidine and codeine are less effective in this regard. Route of administration significantly affects analgesic effectiveness. Parenteral use is the most efficient because oral administration subjects the opioid to erratic absorption in the gastrointestinal tract as well as passage through the portal system before reaching the central nervous system. Codeine and methadone are reliably absorbed orally; morphine and meperidine are not.

Opioids are potent suppressors of the cough reflex, and this antitussive action is most often accomplished with codeine or hydrocodone. A related phenomenon is that of respiratory depression. Opioids cause the central respiratory center to become less sensitive to carbon dioxide, which in rising concentrations ordinarily stimulates breathing. The mechanism of death in acute opioid overdose is respiratory arrest.

Opioids have pronounced gastrointestinal effects. Initially the user may experience nausea and emesis due to central stimulation; however, this is followed by depression of the central structures controlling emesis, and even

TABLE 7.3. Signs of Opioid Intoxication

1. Euphoria immediately following ingestion; profound relief from anxiety and tension.
2. Apathy following euphoria.
3. An initial mild to moderate burst of energy in the minutes following ingestion, ultimately replaced with psychomotor retardation.
4. "Nodding," a "twilight state" in between alertness and sleep during which the individual is quiescent but arousable.
5. Pupillary constriction (myosis).
6. Hypoactive bowel sounds.
7. Slow regular respiration.
8. Slurred speech.
9. Impaired judgment, attention, concentration, and memory.
10. Physical evidence of recent use, including needle marks, hyperemic nasal mucosa if insufflation was the route of administration, and positive opioid blood or urine screen.

TABLE 7.4. Opioid Withdrawal

Stage I—begins within hours of last dose and peaks at 36–72 hours:
1. Craving for the drug.
2. Tearing (lacrimation).
3. "Runny nose" (rhinorrhea).
4. Yawning.
5. Sweating (diaphoresis).

Stage II—begins at 12 hours and peaks at 72 hours:
1. Mild to moderate sleep disturbance.
2. Dilated pupils (mydriasis).
3. Loss of appetite (anorexia).
4. "Goose flesh" or "cold turkey" (piloerection).
5. Irritability.
6. Tremor.

Stage III—begins at 24–36 hours and peaks at 72 hours:
1. Severe insomnia.
2. Violent yawning.
3. Weakness.
4. Nausea, vomiting, diarrhea.
5. Chills, fever.
6. Muscle spasms or "kicking the habit" (especially in the lower extremities).
7. Flushing.
8. Spontaneous ejaculation.
9. Abdominal pain.

emetic agents frequently fail to produce vomiting. The intestinal smooth muscle is stimulated to contract by opioids, thus reducing peristalsis. Although this action may be desirable in preventing loss of water through diarrhea, the related undesirable effect of constipation routinely appears.

Smooth muscle in the urinary bladder is also stimulated by opioids, sometimes resulting in an unpleasant sensation of nearly constant urinary urgency. Although uterine muscle is not seriously affected by opioids, labor is frequently prolonged. Because opioids do cross the placental barrier, newborn infants can show all the adult signs of intoxication, withdrawal, and overdose.

TABLE 7.5. Opioid Overdose

1. Signs of recent ingestion.
2. Profoundly decreased respirations or apnea.
3. Pale skin and blue mucous membranes.
4. Pinpoint pupils unless prolonged cerebral apnea has caused some brain damage, in which case pupillary dilatation may occur.
5. Pulmonary edema resulting in characteristic gasping and audible rhonchi; occasional froth in the upper airway.
6. Cardiovascular collapse.
7. Cardiac dysrhythmias.
8. Convulsions, especially with meperidine, propoxyphene, or codeine.
9. Semicoma or coma.

Blood vessels in the periphery are generally dilated as a result of opioid-induced histamine release; this sometimes causes a blush of the skin with itching, especially in the face. By a separate mechanism, reflex vasoconstriction is inhibited, resulting in significant orthostasis. This opioid effect usually disappears as tolerance develops.

Some endocrine effects have also been noted. Thyroid activity, output of gonadotropins, and adrenal steroid output are all reduced. These effects are caused by opioid actions on the pituitary gland.

The concept of tolerance has been previously mentioned. Repeated administration of opioids results in decreasing levels of euphoria and analgesia over time. The user also becomes less affected by respiratory depression, nausea and emesis, and impairment of consciousness. Less tolerance develops to orthostasis and very little to myosis, constipation, and urinary urgency; however, these side effects may be counteracted by the euphoric and analgesic properties of opioids, in which individuals remain aware of unpleasant physical sensations but insist that they are no longer bothered by these. Tolerance is reversed during periods of abstinence.

Tolerance is the direct result of neuroadaptive change at the opioid receptor site during a period of continuous occupation by an exogenous opioid. A state of physical dependence is reached when removal of the opioid from its receptor site produces an abstinence syndrome. A more sudden removal of the opioid from its receptor site produces a more intense abstinence syndrome. The most rapid removal of opioid from its receptor site is accomplished by the opioid antagonists, which selectively compete for the site but have no agonist properties. Shorter-acting opioids exit the receptor site system more quickly than opioids with longer half-lives. Thus heroin and morphine produce intense abstinence syndromes with relatively rapid onset and progression, whereas methadone produces an abstinence syndrome of less overall intensity but with slower progression through the stages of acute abstinence to resolution, which, for a short-acting drug such as heroin, arrives at 5–10 days. Abrupt methadone withdrawal produces an abstinence syndrome that is largely resolved at 14–21 days. Following resolution of the acute abstinence syndrome, a more subtle abstinence syndrome may occur and last for many months. Symptoms include hyposensitivity to the respiratory stimulant effect of carbon dioxide, disturbed sleep, preoccupation with physical discomfort, poor self-esteem, and diminished ability to tolerate stress. Risk of relapse is higher during this period (Martin & Jasinski, 1969).

COURSE

Many complex factors influence the natural history of opioid addiction. Overall, the course is one of relapse and remission. Attempts to define the opioid abusers as a group have been limited because long-term contact with these frequently itinerant persons is difficult and because only a minority of opioid abusers can be studied effectively (namely, those who elect to enter treatment). Given these obstacles to accurate understanding, some generalizations can still be made. The vast majority of active opioid abusers are between the ages of 20 and 50 years. Age at first use is usually in the teens or 20s. Race, ethnicity, and socioeconomic status variables are important. Though opioid addiction affects persons from all groups in the United States, black or Hispanic persons who are poor are overrepresented. True iatrogenic opioid dependence rarely persists to become chronic, although the risk exists for those with chronic, painful medical or surgical problems. Although men and women seek treatment in roughly equal numbers, women who are mothers of dependent children may benefit from a more favorable prognosis.

, Opioid addiction follows a relapsing and remitting course until middle age, when its relentless grip on the individual seems to abate slowly and spontaneously. Some experts have estimated 9 years as the average duration of active opioid addiction (Jaffe, 1989). Criminal activity, usually in support of addiction, is very common during periods of active use. In periods of remission, criminal activity drops off significantly. The overall death rate in opioid abusers is estimated to be as much as 20 times that of the general population. The proximate cause of death is usually overdose, use-related infections, suicide, homicide, or accidental death.

, Significant psychiatric comorbidity has been observed; depression and personality disorder are the most frequent diagnoses. Polysubstance abuse is common in opioid addicts. Many are nicotine addicted, and many have serious alcohol-related problems as well. Benzodiazepine use is common and probably underestimated because it may not be specifically assayed in urine specimens. Sporadic use of cocaine and other stimulants is common, as is the use of marijuana. A few opioid addicts also use hallucinogens or toxic vapors.

The medical complications of opioid abuse are many and diverse. They stem most commonly from (1) the failure to use aseptic techniques during injection, (2) the presence of particulate contaminants in the injected solution, and (3) the direct pharmacological actions of the drug. The consequences of infection are the most frequently encountered medical complications of opioid abuse. Skin abscesses, lymphadenopathy, osteomyelitis, septic emboli in the lungs, endocarditis, septicemia, glomerulonephritis, meningitis, and brain abscesses are encountered with regularity when "dirty needles" are used. A low-level immunodeficiency exists in chronic opioid addicts, causing them to be more susceptible to infectious processes such as tuberculosis, syphilis, malaria, tetanus, and hepatitis (Senay, 1983). HIV infection may result from sharing needles with an infected individual. Risk of this complication is highest in the northeastern United States, where a survey of opioid addicts in methadone treatment programs showed seropositivity in 60% of those who reported sharing needles (Jaffe, 1989). Fortunately, the percentage drops dramatically in most other parts of the country, and aggressive efforts at education of both addicts and those who treat them in clinics and elsewhere have helped slow the spread of this deadly virus.

Addicts frequently inject opioid solutions contaminated with adulterants such as talc and starch; these substances are used to increase the bulk of the illicit powder and thus to increase profits for the drug dealer. Addicts mix the powder with water, heat it, and use cotton or a cigarette filter to block the entry of undissolved particles as the solution is drawn into the syringe. As a result, fibers enter the venous blood stream and lodge in the lungs, where conditions become favorable for the development over time of pulmonary emboli, pulmonary hypertension, and right-side heart failure. Opioid abusers are at further risk of compromised pulmonary function if they use cigarettes and marijuana, as they usually do. The antitussive effect of opioids also compromises pulmonary function, contributing to frequent pneumonia and other respiratory tract infections.

A number of lesions may occur in the central nervous system of those persons who have survived overdoses that featured anoxia and coma. The residual effects of such trauma include partial paralysis, Parkinsonism, intellectual impairment, personality changes, peripheral neuropathy, acute transverse myelitis, and blindness.

Psychiatric complications caused by opioid dependence occur most frequently in the form of depression. When depression is observed during the recovery period, treatment with antidepressants and psychotherapy is indicated and frequently helpful if the individual is abstinent from illicit drug use.

⋆ Psychiatric comorbidity is also common. Though not necessarily caused by drug abuse, the following disorders are seen in association with opioid dependence:

1. Depression.
2. Antisocial personality disorder.
3. Anxiety disorders.
4. Other personality disorders, including paranoid, schizoid, schizotypal, histrionic, narcissistic, borderline, dependent, compulsive, passive–aggressive, and mixed.
5. Organic brain syndrome (rare).
6. Schizophrenia (very rare). ⋆

Mood disorders may be diagnosable in many opioid addicts (Mirin, Weiss, Michael, & Griffin, 1989). Major depression is the most common mood disorder, diagnosed at almost 16% (Brooner, King, Kidorf, Schmidt, & Bigelow, 1997); it may have preceded the onset of drug abuse as chronic, episodic low-grade depression or dysthymia, and a full-blown major depressive episode may develop in the stressful and traumatic context of opioid addiction. Depression occurs more frequently in women than in men. Depression coexisting with opioid dependence is more strongly associated with a history of concomitant polydrug abuse.

Of the personality disorders, antisocial personality disorder is the most commonly diagnosed and can be seen in as many as 25% of opioid abusers seeking treatment; this is noted in men the vast majority of the time (Brooner et al., 1997). It is inaccurate to assume that drug-seeking behavior learned during years of addiction is responsible for the high percentage of antisocial personalities among opioid addicts. Antisocial personality disorder can be reliably diagnosed historically in most individuals at a young age prior to the onset of opioid dependence. The relationship between opioid abuse and antisocial personality is complicated and appears to be influenced by a non-sex-linked genetic factor. When antisocial personality and opioid dependence are found together, the treatment course is frequently challenging, and the overall outcome is poor with regard to adequate length of time in treatment, relapse, criminal behavior during treatment, and ability to establish rapport with a therapist or counselor. The one exception appears to be the antisocial addict who also has a diagnosable depression. This group responds much better to treatment, on a par with the average opioid addict without significant psychiatric comorbidity (Woody, McLellan, Luborsky, & O'Brien, 1985).

Anxiety disorders, such as panic disorder, obsessive–compulsive disorder, generalized anxiety disorder, and phobia, are seen in approximately 10% of opioid addicts. This group is typically somewhat younger in age and higher in socioeconomic status, and their drug use histories are not as extensive.

Personality disorders from DSM-IV Axis II are regularly found coexisting with opioid abuse, with antisocial personality disorder being the most significant factor in treatment. Organic brain syndrome and psychotic disorders such as schizophrenia, mania, and psychotic depression are not usually seen in opioid clinic populations. The presence of both a DSM-IV Axis I diagnosis (depression or an anxiety disorder) and an Axis II diagnosis (a personality disorder) in the same opioid-dependent individual is frequently observed; the proportion of such patients may approach 50% in clinic populations (Khantzian & Treece, 1985).

TREATMENT

The various nonpharmacological treatment modalities used to treat other types of substance abusers are also useful in treating opioid addicts and are discussed in Chapter 19 (this volume). The focus of this chapter is on pharmacotherapy of situations commonly found in the context of opioid abuse, including overdose, withdrawal, detoxification, and maintenance. In addition, we discuss the usefulness of blocking agents and some experimental agents currently on the horizon.

The management of opioid overdose is best accomplished in a medical facility with the availability of sophisticated expertise and technology. These can be brought to bear on the potential "worst-case scenario," for example, opioid overdose in a pregnant female with septicemia, pulmonary edema, and coma. In addition to intensive physiological support needed in opioid overdose, the use of an opioid antagonist can be life saving. Naloxone is the drug of choice because it does not further depress respiratory drive (Berger & Dunn, 1986). A regimen of 0.4 to 0.8 mg, administered intravenously several times over the course of 20 to 30 minutes, is conservative but avoids the pitfall of precipitating full-blown opioid withdrawal, which can be a greater threat than respiratory depression because of the possible occurrence of emesis, seizure, or combative delirium. If after 10 mg of naloxone there is no improvement in the patient's condition, one must question the diagnosis of opioid overdose. Other drugs may be involved, or other central nervous system processes may exist. One also must remember that the action of naloxone almost always will be shorter than the action of the opioid, necessitating close attention to the reemergence of the opioid's physiological effects (Wilford, 1981).

The opioid withdrawal syndrome can easily be suppressed by administering any opioid with significant same-receptor activity as the drug that originally produced the addiction. However, it is more useful to prevent opioid withdrawal symptoms pharmacologically with a nonaddicting drug. This approach furthers the goals of detoxification and abstinence. When circumstances force addicts to treat their withdrawal symptoms without opioids, they most commonly use alcohol and/or benzodiazepines. The main disadvantage to this approach is that because of the lack of cross-tolerance between opioids and alcohol/benzodiazepines, blockade of withdrawal symptoms requires the ingestion of large amounts of these sedatives to achieve suppression, thus rendering the individual almost totally nonfunctional during the course of acute withdrawal.

Clonidine, an α_2 agonist originally marketed as an antihypertensive, represents an effective and safer alternative for the treatment of opiate withdrawal symptoms (Koob & Bloom, 1988; O'Connor et al., 1995). It can partially suppress many (but not all) elements of opioid withdrawal, so that the risk of immediate relapse is reduced (Jasinski, Johnson, & Kocher, 1985). Clonidine is most effective for those motivated persons who are involved in their overall treatment program and are using small amounts of opioid (Kleber et al., 1985). Outpatients who are on less than 20 mg of methadone per day and detoxifying at rates approaching 1 mg per day make ideal candidates for the adjunctive use of clonidine. These individuals can be given 0.1 to 0.3 mg up to three or four times a day throughout the withdrawal period with good effect. Sometimes only small amounts of clonidine (on the order of 0.1 mg per day) may be useful, to be administered at the time of day that is most difficult for the patient. Clonidine is not generally useful beyond 2 weeks after the last dose of methadone (Gold, Pottash, Sweeney, & Kleber, 1980). A transdermal delivery system (Catapres-TTS), which is active over a 7-day period, is useful in the outpatient setting because the indiscriminate use of large amounts of clonidine by the individual can be avoided, thus limiting the risk of adverse reactions (Spencer & Gregory, 1989). A major side effect of clonidine is hypotension, which can be profound. Lethargy is also a common side effect.

In a hospital setting, clonidine has been used in concert with abstinence and an opioid antagonist to produce tolerable withdrawal and detoxification in a short period (5–6 days) for persons on methadone doses of 50 mg or less; various protocols exist (Charney, Heninger, & Kleber, 1986). This treatment can be complicated by delirium and/or psychosis (Brewer, Rezae, & Bailey,

1988). The treatment involves sudden cessation of opioid ingestion, precipitation of an acute abstinence syndrome with an opioid blocker, and aggressive treatment of the withdrawal symptoms with large doses of clonidine throughout the day and benzodiazepines at night. Over the 5- to 6-day course, the clonidine and opioid blocker are tapered. Naltrexone and buprenorphine have been used successfully (Gerra et al., 1995; Cheskin, Fudala, & Johnson, 1994). Benzodiazepines are not routinely used after the second or third night. A more time-consuming approach would involve abstinence not precipitated suddenly by an opioid blocker and more aggressive use of clonidine than would be practical in an outpatient setting. These approaches are appropriate for those individuals who are highly motivated to become drug-free quickly in a controlled manner, for reasons related to employment or to impending incarceration.

It is generally recognized that abrupt withdrawal from opioids is almost always followed by relapse. The risk of relapse can be lessened by following a rational plan for detoxification, using decreasing amounts of an opioid over time. In this way the withdrawal syndrome is minimized, rendering the individual more responsive to other, nonpharmacological therapies during this high-risk phase of treatment. In the United States, the usual first step toward detoxification is to switch the addicted individual to a longer-acting opioid. Methadone is the obvious choice, with a half-life of 15–25 hours in comparison to 2–3 hours for morphine, heroin, and many other commonly available opioids. In addition to methadone, levo-α-acetyl methadol (LAAM) was approved in 1993 as a maintenance treatment agent for opioid dependence. Both methadone and LAAM are strictly controlled, and clinicians should refer to federal, state and local regulations regarding their use. LAAM is similar to methadone but is longer acting and may be given three times per week instead of daily. LAAM is a μ agonist with a slow onset of action. Its half life is 2.6 days, and cessation produces no withdrawal for 72–96 hours. No take-out doses are allowed with LAAM. LAAM doses in the range of 60 to 100 mg three times a week have been shown to reduce opioid use comparable to therapy with 50 to 100 mg of methadone daily (Ling, Rawson, & Compton, 1994). Generally speaking, for every 2 mg of heroin, 1 mg of methadone may be substituted. The same is true for 4 mg of morphine, 20 mg of meperidine, 50 mg of codeine, and 12 mg of oxycodone. Other equivalencies are available in standard pharmacology texts.

Usually, it is not possible to know how much heroin a user is actually administering in a 24-hour period because of the impure nature of the product available on the street. Experience shows that an initial dose of 20–30 mg of methadone will block most withdrawal symptoms in moderate to heavy users who may inject from 4 to 12 or more times in 24 hours. For those who inject two to three times per day, a starting dose of 10–20 mg of methadone is usually sufficient. Methadone may be given every 24 hours, and the dose may be adjusted daily up or down by 5- to 10-mg increments, based on observable symptoms of withdrawal or intoxication. The peak plasma levels from methadone occur between 2 and 6 hours after ingestion. Over time, methadone becomes tissue bound throughout the body, creating a buffer against significant withdrawal in those persons who occasionally miss a daily dose. This phenomenon also facilitates a smooth detoxification over time as daily dosage is reduced. Stabilization on methadone can usually be accomplished with 20–50 mg daily. Detoxification may then begin.

Regulations at the various levels of government historically mandated that detoxification be accomplished within 21 days. Unfortunately, this period was too short for all but the most minimally addicted individuals and frequently resulted in relapse. Fortunately, the regulations have been liberalized, largely because of recognition that HIV/AIDS is spread very rapidly among intravenous drug abusers who share needles. Changes in the regulations are intended to allow more addicts to enter and stay in treatment. As a practical matter, 30 days is the minimum amount of time required for successful detoxification, and often 45 days or more may be needed; relapse still is a definite risk. For those individuals with long abuse histories and high doses of opioids, 6 months or more may be required. Veteran opioid users are extremely sensitive to even small reductions in their daily dose of methadone. The critical stage of detoxification occurs below 20 mg of methadone daily, and the use of clonidine is helpful in blocking withdrawal symptoms. In some individuals detoxification is successful, but symptoms of insomnia, malaise, irritability, fatigue, gastrointestinal hypermotility, and even premature ejaculation may persist for months. Clonidine is less effective in this situation.

After detoxification, relapse prevention must be actively addressed with whatever treatment interventions are available. A pharmacological agent in the form of an opioid antagonist can be a useful adjunct in relapse prevention. A long-acting agent such as naltrexone is effective in blocking the euphoric effects of opioids and ultimately leads to the extinction of operantly conditioned drug-seeking behaviors. Naltrexone is given orally in the opioid-free individual three times a week in doses of 50–150 mg, and it blocks the effects of relatively large doses of opioids. This adjunctive therapy works best in the context of ongoing treatment and support. Its administration should be monitored over time because compliance with voluntary, unsupervised self-administration of naltrexone is notoriously poor. Length of treatment with this agent is a therapeutic issue, having mainly to do with the individual's ability to embrace a drug-free lifestyle consistently over time.

Some addicts seem unable to tolerate acute withdrawal, to succeed at controlled detoxification, or to remain drug free. Methadone maintenance may then become the treatment of choice. Administered on a once-a-day schedule, methadone in appropriate doses blocks opioid withdrawal, thus reducing compulsive drug-seeking behavior and use. The individual may then focus energy and attention on more productive behaviors. Indications for the use of methadone maintenance include (1) a history of chronic high-dose opioid abuse; (2) repeated failures at abstinence; (3) history of prior successful methadone maintenance; (4) history of drug-related criminal convictions or incarcerations; (5) pregnancy, especially first and third trimesters; and (6) HIV seropositivity.

Relative contraindications to methadone maintenance include (1) being less than 16 years of age, (2) the expectation of incarceration within 30–45 days, and (3) history of abuse of methadone maintenance, including diversion of methadone to "the street" and failure to cease illicit use despite adequate doses.

The administration of methadone, as noted earlier, is heavily regulated by federal and state governments. Specific requirements must be met by individuals and clinics offering this service. Generally, after the individual's history and physical condition are assessed, methadone dosing begins according to the protocol previously described. A period of 4–10 days may be required to stabilize the patient at an appropriate dose. When stabilization has occurred, the individual's illicit drug use should cease, as evidenced by regular monitored urinalysis showing only methadone. Methadone maintenance programs that maintain an overall average dose of 60–100 mg a day yield consistently better results in decreasing illicit opioid use. Doses in excess of 120 mg a day are seldom needed (Gerstein, 1990). A pitfall here is that individuals may supplement their maintenance dose with "black market" methadone. Urinalyses will not be helpful in detecting this behavior as quantification techniques are not generally employed. Dosage requirements should not change after stabilization unless something has occurred to change the body's absorption, metabolism, distribution, or excretion of methadone. Emesis within 20–30 minutes after the oral ingestion of methadone is an obvious example of disruption to absorption. Metabolism of methadone may be affected by the use of phenytoin, rifampin, barbiturates, carbamazepine, and some tricyclic antidepressants, all of which can precipitate withdrawal symptoms by reducing methadone plasma levels. Concealed regular use of other opiates in addition to methadone will result in the user's asking for more methadone because the development of tolerance has outpaced current stable dosing. Abusive use of alcohol and/or benzodiazepines with methadone maintenance will also cause individuals to request more methadone, possibly because of enhanced hepatic metabolization and/or significant withdrawal symptoms from these agents that do not share cross-tolerance with methadone. Administering disulfiram with methadone is a common and highly useful therapeutic approach.

Certain individuals report that heavy labor with much perspiration reduces the effectiveness of methadone in a 24-hour period. This phenomenon is usually easily addressed with a small increase in dose unless the individual is not being truthful. After months or years of methadone maintenance, most individuals are able to tolerate a slow taper of a few milligrams per week or month. For those persons who become suspicious or psychologically unstable as their dose is lowered, a "blind" detoxification schedule may be used in which the individual never knows the exact amount of methadone he or she is receiving.

Pregnancy is a special situation for which continued methadone maintenance is recommended as any withdrawal symptoms place the fetus at risk (Finnegan, 1979). In addition, relapse to street drugs after detoxification also places the fetus at risk. Therefore, maintenance at a level of 20 mg is the safest plan. Slow detoxification down to this level can be achieved safely during the second trimester.

Other agents may be useful in maintenance of opioid users. LAAM has more side effects than methadone, including some that are stimulant-like; in addition, its pharmacology is complicated, requiring the attention of a sophisticated clinician. For these and possibly other reasons, dropout rates for LAAM exceed those for methadone in maintenance settings (Blaine, Thomas, Barnett, Whysner, & Renoult, 1981). Another agent, buprenorphine, is a mixed agonist–antagonist agent that has been shown to be acceptable to addicts, is long acting (daily administration is sufficient), and blocks the effects of other opiates. An additional benefit is that it can be discontinued more easily than methadone because it produces less physical dependence. Unfortunately, it appears that buprenorphine cannot be substituted completely for methadone without some withdrawal symptoms appearing during the transition period (Bickel et al., 1988). Neither of these agents has compelling advantages over methadone as an agent for maintenance in opioid addiction but may be preferred by some patients (Ling et al., 1994).

Although this section presented only pharmacotherapies for opioid addiction, it is crucial that psychosocial interventions be used to help these patients change their lifestyles. It is generally accepted that escape from drug seeking and the accompanying antisocial impulses requires a change in deeply rooted behavioral patterns. Individual and group psychotherapy may be useful in approaching this goal. The various Twelve-Step programs such as Narcotics Anonymous are also useful adjuncts to treatment and facilitate significant degrees of change. For those persons who continue to relapse in less restrictive treatment settings, a "therapeutic community" may be the appropriate next step (O'Brien & Biase, 1981). These nonhospital, community-based, 24-hour live-in programs are geared to subject the addict to continuous treatment pressure for as long as 1 or 2 years. Personal freedom is severely curtailed and community rules are rigorously enforced. The goal is to use nonviolent but highly confrontational tactics in the context of peer pressure, for the purpose of breaking down denial and exposing destructive attitudes and behaviors that formerly led to drug use (Rosenthal, 1989). A growth process may then occur, allowing the individual to achieve a degree of personal integrity that is unrelated to the former identity of drug abuser. When successful, this type of personal transformation can lead to permanent recovery. However, this form of treatment requires a total commitment, which many opioid abusers are unable to make; thus the dropout rate is high. As with any treatment modality, selection of appropriate candidates leads to greater success.

REFERENCES

American Psychiatric Association. (1994). *Diagnostic and statistical manual of mental disorders* (4th ed.). Washington, DC: Author.

Berger, P. A., & Dunn, M. J. (1986). The biology and treatment of drug abuse. In S.

Arieti (Ed.), *American handbook of psychiatry* (Vol. 8, pp. 811–822). New York: Basic Books.

Bickel, W. K., Stitzer, M. L., Bigelow, G. E., Liebson, I. A., Jasinski, D. R., & Johnson, R. E. (1988). A clinical trial of buprenorphine: Comparison with methadone in the detoxification of heroin addicts. *Clinical Pharmacology and Therapeutics, 43,* 72–78.

Blaine, G. D., Thomas, D. B., Barnett, G., Whysner, J. A., & Renoult, P. F. (1981). Levo-α-acetylmethadol (LAAM): Clinical utility and pharmaceutical development. In J. H. Lowinson & P. Ruiz (Eds.), *Substance abuse: Clinical problems and perspectives* (pp. 356–370). Baltimore: Williams & Wilkins.

Brewer, C., Rezae, H., & Bailey, C. (1988). Opioid withdrawal and naltrexone induction in 48–72 hours with minimal drop-out, using a modification of the naltrexone–clonidine technique. *British Journal of Psychiatry, 153,* 340–343.

Brooner, R. K., King, V. L., Kidorf, M., Schmidt, C. W. Jr., & Bigelow, G. E. (1997). Psychiatric and substance use comorbidity among treatment-seeking opioid abusers. *Archives of General Psychiatry, 54,* 71–80.

Charney, D. S., Heninger, G. R., & Kleber, H. D. (1986). The combined use of clonidine and naltrexone as a rapid, safe, and effective treatment of abrupt withdrawal from methadone. *American Journal of Psychiatry, 143,* 831–837.

Cheskin, L. J., Fudala, P. J., & Johnson, R. E. (1994). A controlled comparison of buprenorphine and clonidine for acute detoxification from opioids. *Drug and Alcohol Dependence, 36,* 115–121.

Deneau, G. A., & Mule, S. J. (1981). Pharmacology of the opiates. In J. H. Lowinson & P. Ruiz *(Eds.), Substance abuse: Clinical problems and perspectives* (pp. 129–139). Baltimore: Williams & Wilkins.

Finnegan, L. P. (Ed.). (1979). *Drug dependency in pregnancy: Clinical management of mother and child.* Rockville, MD: National Institute on Drug Abuse.

Gerra, G., Marcato, A., Caccavari, R., Fontanesi, B., Deisignore, R., Fertonani, G., Avanzini, P., Rustichelli, P., & Passeri, M. (1995). *Journal of Substance Abuse Treatment, 12,* 35–41.

Gerstein, D. R. (1990). The effectiveness of treatment. In D. R. Gerstein & H. J. Harwood (Eds.), *Treating drug problems* (Vol. 1, pp. 132–199). Washington, DC: National Academy Press.

Gold, M. S., Pottash, A. C., Sweeney, D. R., & Kleber, H. D. (1980). Opiate withdrawal using clonidine. *Journal of the American Medical Association, 243*(4), 343–346.

Jaffe, J. H. (1989). Psychoactive substance use disorders. In H. I. Kaplan & B. J. Sadock (Eds.), *Comprehensive textbook of psychiatry* (5th ed., pp. 642–698). Baltimore: Williams Wilkins.

Jasinski, D. R., Johnson, R. E., & Kocher, T. R. (1985). Clonidine in morphine withdrawal: Differential effects on signs and symptoms. *Archives of General Psychiatry, 42,* 1063–1066.

Khantzian, E. J., & Treece, C. (1985). DSM-III psychiatric diagnosis of narcotic addicts: Recent findings. *Archives of General Psychiatry, 42,* 1067–1071.

Kleber, H. D., Riordan, C. E., Rounsaville, B., Kosten, T., Charney, D., Gaspari, J., Hogan, I., & O'Connor, C. (1985). Clonidine in outpatient detoxification from methadone maintenance. *Archives of General Psychiatry, 42,* 391–394.

Koob, G. F., & Bloom, F. E. (1988). Cellular and molecular mechanisms of drug dependence. *Science, 242,* 715–723.

Ling, W., Rawson, R. A., & Compton, M. A. (1994). Substitution pharmacotherapies for opioid addiction: from methadone to LAAM and buprenorphine. *Journal of Psychoactive Drugs, 26,* 119–128.

Martin, W. R., & Jasinski, D. R. (1969). Physiological parameters of morphine dependence in men: Tolerance, early abstinence, protracted abstinence. *Journal of Psychiatric Research, 7,* 9–17.

Mirin, S. M., Weiss, R. D., Michael, J., & Griffin, M. L. (1989). Psychopathology in substance abusers: Diagnosis and treatment. *American Journal of Drug and Alcohol Abuse, 14,* 139–157.

O'Brein, W. B., & Biase, D. V. (1981). The therapeutic community: The family-milieu approach to recovery. In J. H. Lowinson & P. Ruiz (Eds.), *Substance abuse: Clinical problems and perspectives* (pp. 303–316). Baltimore: Williams & Wilkins.

O'Connor, P. G., Waugh, M. E., Carroll, K. M., Rounsaville, B. J., Diagkogiannis, I. A., & Schottenfeld, R. S. (1995). Primary care-based ambulatory opioid detoxification: The results of a clinical trial. *Journal of General Internal Medicine, 10,* 255–260.

Rosenthal, M. S. (1989). The therapeutic community: Exploring the boundaries. *British Journal of Addiction, 84*(2), 141–150.

Senay, E. C. (1983). *Substance abuse disorders in clinical practice.* Littleton, MA: John Wright/PSG.

Spencer, L., & Gregory, M. (1989). Clonidine transdermal patches for use in outpatient opiate withdrawal. *Journal of Substance Abuse, 6,* 113–117.

Substance Abuse and Mental Health Services Administration. (1995, November). *Preliminary estimates from the Drug Abuse Warning Network* (Advance Report 11). Washington, DC: Author.

Wilford, B. B. (1981). *Drug abuse for the primary care physician.* Chicago: American Medical Association.

Woody, G. E., McLellan, A. T., Luborsky, L., & O'Brien, C. P. (1985). Sociopathy and psychotherapy outcome. *Archives of General Psychiatry, 42,* 1081–1086.

8

Cocaine and Stimulants

LORI D. KARAN
DEBORAH L. HALLER
SIDNEY H. SCHNOLL

ETHNOGRAPHY

Data from the 1995 National Household Survey on Drug Abuse (National Institute on Drug Abuse, 1997b) estimates that 1.5 million Americans or 0.7% of the population ages 12 and older are current cocaine users. This number has been essentially level since 1992, after declining from 5.7 million or 3% of the population in 1985. In 1995, the past year prevalence of cocaine use among youth 12–17 years of age was higher for blacks (1.1%), than Hispanics (0.7%) or whites (0.6%). Users were more likely to be young adults ages 18–25 (1.3%) and ages 26–34 (1.2%) than youth ages 12–17 (0.8%) or adults 35 years and older (0.4%). Men (1%) had higher use rates than women (0.4%). In addition, current cocaine use was inversely correlated with educational status and was higher among the unemployed (2.1%) than the employed (0.7%). Thus, it is the general population but not the socioeconomically disadvantaged who have diminished their use of cocaine over the last decade. However, because socioeconomically disadvantaged persons are still a minority population, cocaine users are more often white, employed, and high school graduates (Johanson & Schuster, 1995).

Despite diminishing numbers of cocaine users, information collected from the Drug Abuse Warning Network (DAWN; National Institute on Drug Abuse, 1997a) shows that the number of hospital emergencies associated with the use of cocaine increased from 5,000 in 1981 to 29,000 in

1985 and 142,000 in 1995. Crack (freebase cocaine that can be smoked) may be responsible for this trend as its strength and nearly immediate onset of action cause increased toxicity. In 1987, more than one out of every five homicide victims in the United States had evidence of recent cocaine use in the blood or body tissues. Budd (1989) analyzed cause of death in the first 114 Los Angeles County Coroner's cases with positive drug toxicology for cocaine in the period from January 1, 1988, to February 24, 1988. He found that 61.4% died a violent death, with more than 68% of deaths resulting from shootings and stabbings; nonviolent deaths included overdose (73%), illness (20.5%), and stillbirth (6.8%). Although blacks compose only 15% of the Los Angeles County population, they were overrepresented in both violent (36%) and nonviolent (18%) deaths. In another study (Lindenbaum, Carroll, Daskal, & Kapusnick, 1989) more than half of the patients at Albert Einstein Medical Trauma Center in New York City tested positive for cocaine, and approximately 50% of these had been involved in a violent crime.

PREPARATION AND ROUTES OF ADMINISTRATION

Cocaine is a benzoylmethylecgonine. It is an ester of benzoic acid and a nitrogen-containing base. Cocaine occurs naturally in the leaves of erythroxylon coca and other species of erythroxylon indigenous to Peru, Bolivia, Java, and Columbia. Andean natives who chew coca leaves experience diminished hunger and fatigue and an improved sense of well-being without evidence of chronic toxicity and dependence. However, other preparations and routes of administration of cocaine have a more rapid onset of action and are more problematic.

Cocaine hydrochloride is frequently snorted (insufflation) or "tooted" in "lines" or "rails" about one-half to 2 inches long and one-eighth of an inch thick. Users pour the powdered cocaine onto a hard surface such as a mirror, glass, or slab of marble and arrange it into lines with a razor blade, knife, or credit card. One line is snorted into each nostril via a rolled bill, straw, or miniature coke spoon or a specially grown fingernail. A street purchase of a single gram of cocaine, about 30 lines can be made from each, averaging 10–35 mg of powder. The actual amount of cocaine hydrochloride present in each line depends on the purity of the drug. The bioavailability of intranasal cocaine is about 60%. Peak plasma levels occur over a range of 30–120 minutes (Barnett, Hawkes, & Resnick, 1981). Intranasal cocaine limits its own absorption by causing vasoconstriction of the nasal mucous membranes. Cocaine is a topical anesthetic and causes numbness of the nose during snorting. Nasal congestion with stuffiness and sneezing may occur after snorting cocaine due to its vasoconstrictive properties as well as the contaminants in the preparation. Users may flush out the inside of the nose with a salt water mixture after a round of snorting and decongestants, and they commonly employ antihistamines to relieve symptoms.

Cocaine can also be injected intravenously: "shooting" or "mainlining." The cocaine is mixed in a spoon or bottle cap with water to form a solution. Unlike heroin, cocaine hydrochloride may not need to be heated over a candle to enter solution. "Kicking" or "booting" refers to drawing blood from the vein back into the syringe and reinjecting it with each cocaine mixture. Injection drug users feel that this produces a heightened drug sensation or "rush," despite the lack of a pharmokinetic basis. Following intravenous administration, users achieve peak plasma levels almost instantaneously.

The smoking of coca paste, popularly "pasta" or "bazooka," is prevalent in South America and also occurs in the United States. The paste is an intermediate product in the processing of cocaine hydrochloride. This results in a gray–white or dull brown powder with a slightly sweet smell which is 40–85% cocaine sulfate.

Freebase cocaine is obtained by extracting cocaine hydrochloride with an alkali such as buffered ammonia and then mixing it with a solvent, which is usually ether. The solvent fraction is separated and volatilized, leaving very small amounts of residual freebase material. Cocaine freebase is most often smoked in a water pipe with a fine stainless steel screen on which the cocaine is vaporized. Cigarettes are rarely used because only a small amount of cigarette smoke actually enters the lungs, wasting valuable cocaine. Cocaine hydrochloride is soluble in water and has a melting point of 195° C. In contrast, cocaine freebase is lipid soluble and has a melting point of 98° C. Thus, cocaine freebase vaporizes and readily crosses the blood–lung barrier (DePetrillo, 1985), resulting in nearly immediate peak plasma levels which are achieved at a rate similar to that of injecting cocaine hydrochloride.

"Crack" or "rock" is a preprepared, ready-to-use form of base cocaine that is inexpensive and has been widely available on the streets in many U.S. cities since 1985. It is processed from cocaine hydrochloride to a base by adding ammonia or baking soda and water and heating it rather than the more volatile method of preparation which uses ether. The processing does not necessarily remove the impurities and adulterants in the cocaine or the baking soda which is now present as table salt. "Crack" is named for the crackling sound heard when the mixture is heated and "rock" describes its crystalline appearance. The drug is sold in vials or foil packets and is smoked in a pipe. Its rapid onset of action and rapid dissipation are problematic because the user wants to repeat the effects of the intense but short-lived high. The cost of a 300-mg dose on the street has been reported to be as low as $5 to $10. Crack cocaine can be injected as well as smoked. This practice originated in the United Kingdom and it is now a trend in the United States (Johnson & Ouellet, 1996). To prepare crack cocaine for injection, the crack is dissolved in water or alcohol either by heating the solution or by acidifying it. The resultant viscous solution, which is too thick for use in standard insulin syringes, requires a larger bore needle. Because these are considerably harder to obtain, the incidence of needle sharing along with the risk of HIV infection is greater.

In the United States, popular street names for cocaine include blow, flake, girl, white lady, nose candy, paradise, and snow. Adulterants commonly found in illicitly purchased cocaine include inert substances such as talc, flour, cornstarch, and various sugars (lactose, inositol, sucrose, maltose, and mannitol). Local anesthetics such as procaine, lidocaine, tetracaine, and benzocaine may be added to replace or enhance the local anesthetic effect of cocaine. Cheaper stimulants including amphetamines, caffeine, methylphenidate, ergotamine, aminophylline, and strychnine ("death hit") may also be added to the preparation. Quinine may be added for taste and other compounds such as thiamin, tyramine, sodium carbonate, magnesium silicate, magnesium sulfate, salicylamide, and arsenic (Lombard, Levin, & Weiner, 1989) may be found. Contaminants may include bacteria, fungi, and viruses. Users frequently take cocaine in combination with other drugs, citing the need to take the edge off the abrupt effects and "crash" from cocaine. Intravenous injection of heroin and cocaine mixed together is called speedballing, and ingesting alcohol in conjunction with taking cocaine may be referred to as liquid lady. Any drug combination is possible and other opioids and depressants, as well as hallucinogens, phencyclidine (PCP), and marijuana are all frequently used in conjunction with cocaine.

COCAETHYLENE

When alcohol use precedes cocaine use, the normal hydrolysis of cocaine to benzoylecgonine by hepatic carboxyesterase enzymes is inhibited, higher levels of cocaine remain, and from this the body produces cocaethylene, an ethyl ester (Andrews, 1997). Cocaethylene substitutes for cocaine in animal drug discrimination experiments (Schechter, 1994). Cocaethylene is the only known example in which the human body forms a new psychoactive compound from two other psychoactive substrates. Cocaethylene has been found to bring an 18- to 25-fold increase over cocaine alone in the risk for immediate death (Xu, Crumb, & Clarkson, 1994). This is frightening because it is estimated that between 62–90% of cocaine abusers are concurrent ethanol abusers (McCance, Price, Kosten, & Jatlow, 1995). Cocaethylene is bound to two human serum proteins and has a plasma half-life three to five times that of cocaine. Cocaethylene also has greater cardiac toxicity than cocaine. It causes substantial and sustained increases in heart rate and blood pressure, and decreases in ventricular contractility. In addition to myocardial infarctions, cerebrovascular accidents, and arrhythmias, cocaethylene is associated with seizures, liver damage, and immune compromise in adults (Andrews, 1997). Animal fetal models demonstrate hypoxia with diminished cerebral blood flow and a decreased cerebral metabolic rate of oxygen (Albuquerque, Kurth, Monitto, Sha, & Anday, 1995).

NEUROTRANSMITTERS AND
BEHAVIORAL PHARMACOLOGY

Cocaine is both a stimulant of the central nervous system and a local anesthetic. Cocaine facilitates the effects of dopamine, norepinephrine, and serotonin by binding to their respective transporters and inhibiting their reuptake back into the presynaptic neuronal terminal. Animal studies have demonstrated significant correlations between cocaine self-administration and blockade of dopamine uptake. However, similar reinforcement has not been shown with the blockade of norepinephrine or 5-hydroxytryptamine (5-HT) uptake (Johanson & Schuster, 1995; Kuhar, Ritz, & Sharkey, 1988). Both the nucleus accumbens and the medial prefrontal cortex receive dopamine projections from the ventral segmental area and may be important areas in drug reinforcement and reward. Microdialysis studies have demonstrated increases in extracellular dopamine in the nucleus accumbens when cocaine is self-administered (Pettit & Justice, 1989). Injections of the dopaminergic neurotoxin 6-hydroxydopamine into the mesolimbic/mesocortical dopaminergic neuronal pathway (including the ventral tegmentum, nucleus accumbens, and ventral pallidum) attenuate cocaine self-administration. Animals, when allowed to freely self-administer cocaine, rapidly escalate their doses and prefer taking cocaine to meeting their biological and psychological needs. Dose escalation with cocaine occurs more rapidly, resulting in death of the animal, than does dose escalation with amphetamines or heroin (Johanson, Balster, & Bonese, 1976).

It is now recognized that there are subtypes of dopamine receptors. Antagonists to the D1 and D2 receptors reduce the acute reinforcing effects of cocaine, whereas agonists of the D3 receptors sensitize or facilitate cocaine self-administration (Koob, 1997). Self, Barnhart, Lehman, and Nestler (1996) have discerned that D1- and D2-like dopamine receptor agonists produce opposite modulation of cocaine-seeking behavior.

Identification and characterization of cocaine's site of action at the dopamine transporter and the cloning of this transporter have provided further evidence for dopamine's role in mediating the behavioral actions of cocaine. Transfection of COS cells, which do not take up dopamine or bind cocaine, with a single DNA for the dopamine transporter confers both dopamine uptake and cocaine-binding activity simultaneously on the cells (Shimada et al., 1991). It has been found that the important structural features of cocaine in its binding activity at the dopamine transporter include a levorotatory configuration, a beta-oriented substituent at C-2 and C-3, and a benzene ring at the C-3 carbon (Ritz, Cone, & Kuhar, 1990). Cloning and expression experiments have shown that the binding sites for dopamine and cocaine on the dopamine transporter are overlapping but not identical. Medication development initiatives are under way to utilize such differences to develop a cocaine antagonist that does not interfere with normal dopamine transport.

Although there are many experimental data to indicate a prominent role for dopamine, it remains likely that significant interactions between other neurochemical mediator systems will be discovered that modulate the rein-forcing actions of cocaine and related compounds. Research is taking place to understand the roles of 5-HT, glutamate, opiates, and corticotropin releasing factor in cocaine addiction. 5-HT may have an important role in cocaine's activity. Buydens-Branchey, Branchey, Fergeson, Hudson, and McKernin (1997) found that meta-chlorophenylpiperazine, a 5-HT partial agonist, di-minished the patients' craving for cocaine significantly over placebo in 31 cocaine-dependent male inpatients undergoing withdrawal from cocaine.

Glutamate may also have a modulatory role on the reinforcing effects of cocaine. It has been shown that injections of 2-amino-5-phosphonovaleric acid, a selective N-methyl-D-aspartate (NMDA) receptor antagonist, into the nucleus accumbens decreases the effective reinforcing dose of cocaine, and MK-801, a noncompetitive NMDA antagonist, also has been shown to interfere with the acquisition and maintenance of cocaine self-administration (Pulvirenti, Maldonado-Lopez, & Koob, 1992).

In the setting of chronic "binge" pattern cocaine administration, Unter-wald, Rubenfeld, and Kreek (1994) found enhanced μ and κ opioid receptor binding in regions of the mesolimbic–mesocortical and nigrostriatal dopamin-ergic systems which have abundant dopaminergic terminals. There is also significant and persistent upregulation of dynorphin gene expression mRNA levels in the caudate putamen (Spangler, Unterwald, & Kreek 1993). Prelimi-nary studies in humans have demonstrated a lowering of dopaminergic tone as evidenced by a dose-dependent rise in prolactin release after the intravenous administration of dynorphin A1-13 (Kreek, Ho, & Borg, 1994). Under the direction of Mary Jeanne Kreek, MD, this laboratory has a novel approach to medications development for cocaine addiction. They are investigating whether dynorphin or a synthetic congener could be used to modulate dopaminergic tone in basal states, and whether such modulation and/or normalization of some of the disruptions seen in the setting of cocaine dependency would occur with use of κ receptor selective ligands.

Corticotropin-releasing factor (CRF) controls the pituitary adrenal re-sponse to stressors. According to Koob (1997), preliminary evidence indicates that before the end of a cocaine binge and during withdrawal, CRF levels in the amygdala increase. Evidence shows that CRF levels are sensitized during ethanol withdrawal and opiate withdrawal. CRF is a neurotransmitter that may have a common function in adaptation to drugs of abuse.

CLINICAL FEATURES

Intoxication/Overdose

With intoxication, cocaine blocks monoamine neuronal reuptake, initially leading to increased dopamine and norepinephrine availability at receptor sites. Acute dopaminergic stimulation of the endogenous pleasure center results in euphoria, increased energy and libido, decreased appetite, hyperalertness, and increased self-confidence when small initial doses of cocaine are taken. Exaggerated responses such as grandiosity, impulsivity, hyperawareness of the environment, and hypersexuality may also occur. The acute noradrenergic effects of small doses of cocaine include a mild elevation of pulse and blood pressure. Insomnia results from both increased dopamine and norepinephrine concentrations and decreased serotonin synthesis and turnover. Higher doses of cocaine are accompanied by increasing toxicity. Not only is there intensification of the "high," but anxiety, agitation, irritability, confusion, paranoia, and hallucinations may occur. Sympathomimetic effects include dizziness, tremor, hyperreflexia, hyperpyrexia, mydriasis, diaphoresis, tachypnea, tachycardia, and hypertension. These symptoms can be accompanied by a sense of impending doom and they may have important ramifications in overdose situations. Overdose complications may become manifest as muscle twitching, rhabdomyolysis, convulsions, cerebral infarction and hemorrhage, cardiac ischemia and arrhythmias, and respiratory failure. Acute intoxication with cocaine is more frequently characterized by convulsions and cardiac arrhythmias than intoxication with other amphetamines, possibly due to cocaine's lack of tolerance to these effects and its local anesthetic qualities. Death may be caused by peripheral autonomic toxicity and/or paralysis of the medullary cardiorespiratory centers (Gay, 1982).

Chronic Use

In contrast to acute cocaine intoxication, chronic cocaine administration is believed to result in neurotransmitter depletion. This is evidenced by a compensatory increase in postsynaptic receptor sensitivity for dopamine and noradrenaline, increased tyrosine hydroxylase activity (a major enzyme in norepinephrine and dopamine synthesis), and hyperprolactinemia. These are expected results for a negative feedback system. Clinical features of chronic cocaine use include depression, fatigue, poor concentration, loss of self-esteem, decreased libido, mild Parkinsonian features (myoclonus, tremor, bradykinesis), paranoia, and insomnia. Tolerance to the stimulant effects of cocaine, particularly the anorexic effects, develops rapidly. However, repeated phasic use of low-dose cocaine can lead to enhanced sensitivity and potentiation of motor activity, including exaggerated "startle" reactions, dyskinesias, and postural abnormalities. Increased stereotypical behavior and a toxic psychosis can occur after repeated cocaine use. The elimination half-life of cocaine is under 1 hour by the intravenous route and just over 1 hour by the intranasal route. The physiological and subjective effects due to cocaine correlate well with plasma levels (Javaid, Fischman, Schuster, Dekirmenjian, & Davis, 1978) although, with repeated use, pharmacodynamic tachyphylaxis does occur. Cocaine euphoria is of short duration, with a 10- to 20-second "rush" followed by 15–20 minutes of a lower level of euphoria and the subsequent onset of irritability and craving. Cocaine users who try to maintain the euphoric state readminister the drug frequently until their supply disappears. Cocaine binges average 12 hours but can last as long as 7 consecutive days.

Withdrawal

A withdrawal syndrome, often referred to as the crash, has been demonstrated consisting of strong craving, electroencephalograph abnormalities, depression, alterations in sleep patterns, hypersomnolence, and hyperphagia (Jones, 1984). However, because abrupt discontinuation of cocaine does not cause any major physiological sequelae, cocaine is stopped and not tapered or substituted by a cross-tolerant drug during medically supervised withdrawal. Following the resolution of intoxication and acute withdrawal symptoms, there is a 1- to 10-week period of chronic dysphoria, anergia, and anhedonia. Relapses frequently occur because the memory of cocaine euphoria is quite compelling in contrast to a bleak background of intense boredom. If patients can remain abstinent from illicit mood altering drugs during this period, the dysphoria gradually improves. Thereafter, intense cocaine craving is replaced by episodic craving which is frequently triggered by environmentally conditioned cues during an indefinite extinction phase.

Abuse and Addiction

The National Institute on Drug Abuse (NIDA) estimates that, of 30 million Americans who have tried cocaine intranasally, 20% become regular users and 5% develop compulsive use or addiction (Gawin & Ellinwood, 1988). Whether or not a given recreational cocaine user will become chemically dependent is difficult to predict. Abusers report that controlled use commonly shifts to compulsive use either when they attain increased access to cocaine and therefore escalate their dosage or when they switch to a more rapid route of administration (e.g., from intranasal administration to intravenous injection or smoking freebase or crack).

With recreational use, the cocaine user's initial experience of elation and heightened energy, with increased sexuality and self-esteem, appears to be free of negative consequences. Abusers may experience occasional problems associated with their drug use. Because cocaine use in the United States is illegal, recreational users can be considered abusers. Persons addicted to cocaine, however, have a compulsion to use this drug despite disastrous consequences. In search of the illusive "high," increased doses are taken with more rapid routes of administration and increased frequency. In comparison to daily use, which is common with alcohol and opiate dependence, binge use is more frequent with cocaine dependence. With chronic and increased use there is increased drug toxicity, dysphoria, and depression. The addict has irresistible cravings for cocaine. He or she focuses on pharmacologically based cocaine euphoria despite progressive inability to attain this state and adverse physical, psychological, and social sequelae. Loved ones are neglected, responsibility becomes immaterial, financial hardships occur, and nourishment, sleep, and health care are ignored. It is lucky that most addicts, unlike most animal models, deplete their cocaine supplies or are confronted by the harsh reality of their losses before death occurs.

GENETIC FACTORS

Studies in rodents suggest that genetic variation influences several aspects of the response to cocaine, including preference, stimulant effects, and sensitization (Schuster, Yu, & Bates, 1977; Miner & Marley, 1995). Twin and adoption studies in man suggest that genetic factors play an important role in the use and abuse of the licit psychoactive substances of ethanol (Begleiter & Kissin, 1995) and nicotine (Kendler et al., 1993). Studies of illicit drug abuse in general and cocaine specifically are, however, much more limited. Prior family studies suggest that drug abuse "runs" in families (Mirin, Weiss, Griffin, & Michael, 1991). However, familial aggregation could be the result either of genetic factors or a range of cultural/psychological factors that could both run in families and influence the risk for substance abuse. In humans, this "nature/nature" problem can be addressed by two quasi-experimental methods: adoption studies and twin studies. In a series of adoption studies, Cadoret and colleagues suggest that alcohol abuse and/or antisocial traits in biological parents predisposes to substance abuse in adoptees (Cadoret, Yates, Troughton, Woodworth, & Stewart, 1995, 1996). One large-scale twin study of substance use and abuse in male U.S. veterans found that genetic factors played a substantial etiological role in the abuse of stimulants—defined as including both amphetamine-like compounds and cocaine (Tsuang et al., 1996). The only genetically informative study of which we are aware that focuses specifically on cocaine use, abuse, and dependence was conducted in over 800 pairs of female–female twins ascertained from the population-based Virginia Twin Registry (Kendler & Prescott, in press). Cocaine use, abuse, and dependence were all found to be strongly influenced by genetic factors with heritabilities ranging from 69% to 81%. Although much further work remains to be done, the current evidence supports the hypothesis that the liability to cocaine use, abuse, and dependence in humans is substantially influenced by genetic risk factors, the exact nature of which remain to be identified.

PSYCHIATRIC COMORBIDITY AND SEQUELAE

Among clinical populations, psychiatric comorbidity varies by treatment setting and sample. More than half of cocaine abusers meet criteria for a current psychiatric diagnosis and nearly three-fourths meet criteria for a lifetime diagnosis (Ziedonis, Rayford, Bryant, Kendall, & Rounsaville, 1994). The most frequent co-occurring substance use disorder is alcoholism; 29% of cocaine abusers have a current psychoactive alcohol diagnosis whereas 62% have a lifetime diagnosis (Rounsaville et al., 1991). Individuals with both cocaine and alcohol dependencies manifest a more severe form of cocaine dependence, with onset of cocaine abuse typically preceding onset of alcohol abuse (Carroll, Rounsaville, & Bryant, 1993). Cocaine use disorders are common among opioid abusers as well. In fact, two-thirds of patients in methadone maintenance abuse cocaine (Kosten, Rounsaville, & Kleber, 1987) and three-fourths of the heroin addicts admitted to methadone programs identify cocaine as their secondary drug of abuse (New York State Division of Substance Abuse Services, 1990). Although some patients reduce their cocaine use during methadone treatment (Magura, Siddiqi, Freeman, & Lipton, 1991), most do not. A national survey of 15 clinics (General Accounting Office, 1990) revealed continued cocaine use in as many as 40% after 6 months of treatment. Ongoing cocaine use suggests the need for modifications to traditional methadone treatment programs to successfully address this concurrent problem.

Nonsubstance Axis I disorders are also common among cocaine addicts. The rates for current depressive disorders vary between 11% and 50% (Carroll et al., 1994; Haller, Knisely, Dawson, & Schnoll, 1993; Griffin, Weiss, Mirin, & Lange 1989; Kleinman et al., 1990; Rounsaville et al., 1991, whereas those for lifetime disorder range from 40% to 60% (Kleinman et al., 1990). Because of the specific actions and effects of cocaine, it is sometimes difficult to determine whether depression is independent of cocaine use or the result of chronic self-administration. However, depression that predates drug use or persists beyond the 1–2 weeks characteristic of cocaine withdrawal may indicate a coexisting disorder. In addition, if a cocaine abuser becomes acutely depressed or suicidal after ingesting only very small amounts of the drug, a primary depressive disorder may be indicated (Kosten et al., 1987).

Panic disorder is also prevalent among cocaine abusers and the literature contains a number of case reports of individuals who developed panic disorder following cocaine use (Aronson & Craig, 1986; Bystritsky, Ackerman, & Pasnau, 1991). Even more telling, Rosen and Kosten (1992) reported an increase (over a 10-year period) in the incidence of panic attacks observed among methadone patients; this increase (from 1% to 6–13%) was attributed to multiple factors, one'of which was increased use of cocaine.

Another Axis I disorder that is overrepresented among cocaine abusers is attention-deficit/hyperactivity disorder (ADHD). Approximately 35% of cocaine addicts meet childhood criteria (Rounsaville et al., 1991; Carroll & Rounsaville, 1993). Compared to cocaine abusers without comorbid ADHD, those with ADHD are more likely to be male and to also meet criteria for conduct disorder and antisocial personality (ASP). Cocaine abusers with ADHD evidence earlier age of onset of use, more frequent and severe use, more alcoholism, and more prior treatment episodes. Men who score high on an ADHD measure also report more use of cocaine for purpose of self-medication (Horner, Scheibe, & Stine, 1996). Although somewhat controversial, several case reports suggest that stimulants (e.g., magnesium pemoline, and methylphenidate) can be successfully used to treat patients with comorbid cocaine abuse and ADHD (Khantzian, Gawin, Kleber, & Riordan, 1984; Weiss, Pope, & Mirin, 1985). This treatment effect appears to be selective as non-ADHD cocaine abusers derive no apparent benefit from stimulants but do manifest cross-tolerance (Gawin, Riordan, & Kleber, 1985).

Most comorbidity studies are conducted in drug treatment programs;

consequently, study samples generally do not include the seriously mentally ill. However, this subgroup of cocaine abusers should not be overlooked because coexisting major mental illness can be an important determinant to both the course and the outcome of treatment. In terms of prevalence, Brady, Casto, Lydiard, and Malcolm (1991) found that 64% of admissions to an inpatient psychiatry unit were current substance abusers with 29% meeting diagnostic criteria according to the revised third edition of the *Diagnostic and Statistical Manual of Mental Disorders* (DSM-III-R; American Psychiatric Association, 1987). Cocaine was the second most abused substance (17%), following alcohol (68%). No differences in comorbitity rates were detected for patients with schizophrenia, major depression, and bipolar disorder. Rosenthal, Hellerstein, Miner, and Christian (1994) reported that 93% of schizophrenics regularly abuse cocaine, alcohol, and 100% marijuana. Cocaine-abusing schizophrenics have fewer negative signs (Lysaker, Bell, Beam-Goulet, & Milstein, 1994) but more depression and anxiety at time of hospital admission compared to nonabusing schizophrenics (Serper, Alpert, Richardson, & Dickson, 1995); posttreatment, no differences in negative signs or mood are observed, suggesting that differences were a result of the effects of cocaine. Schizophrenics who abuse cocaine have increased morbidity, which is evidenced by higher rates of hospitalization, greater suicidality, and the need for higher doses of neuroleptics than either users of other drugs or nonusers (Seibyl, Satel, Anthoy, & Southwick, 1993).

Cocaine use may itself induce noxious psychiatric effects, some of them psychotic in nature. Bruxism, picking at the face and body, and other stereotypical or repetitious behaviors may occur. Cocaine hallucinosis may include visual, tactile, auditory, and olfactory hallucinations along with delusions. Cocaine users may also perceive "cocaine bugs" on their skin as well as visual "snow lights." In less severe cases, the user is aware that the hallucinations and delusions are not real. However, in more severe cases, individuals may show a full-blown toxic psychosis with extreme paranoia, hypervigilance, and ideas of persecution. This toxic psychosis can potentially lead to unusual aggressiveness, damaged property, and homicidal or suicidal behavior. Fortunately, these effects are generally limited to the time of cocaine intoxication.

Comorbid Axis II disorders are even more prevalent than Axis I disorders. Cocaine addicts with personality disorders tend to have greater psychiatric severity than those without personality disorders. Among cocaine-abusing outpatients, 48% have at least one personality disorder whereas 18% have two or more (Barber, Frank, Weiss, & Blane, 1996). Even more compelling, 65% of those with a comorbid Axis II diagnosis have a Cluster B disorder, ASP and borderline personality (BPD) being the most frequent. For intensive outpatients, the rates of co-occurring personality disorders are higher; three-fourths meet criteria for at least one Axis II diagnosis and more than one-third have two or more (Haller et al., 1993; Marlowe, Husband, Lamb, & Kirby, 1995). Males are more likely to have comorbid alcohol dependence, stimulant dependence, ASP, and narcissistic personality (NPD), whereas females are more likely to be diagnosed with mood disorders and BPD. The Haller et al. (1993) study also found significant rates of paranoid, self-defeating, and dependent personality disorder (approximately 20% each) for females. Three-fourths of inpatients also meet diagnostic criteria for an Axis II disorder (Kranzler, Satel, & Apetr, 1994; Weiss, Mirin, Griffin, & Gunderson, 1993); the most common are BPD (34%), ASP and NPD (28% each), avoidant and paranoid (22% each), obsessive–compulsive (16%), and dependent (10%). Collectively, these studies show that personality disorders are common among cocaine addicts in all treatment settings. Unfortunately, personality disorders (particularly Cluster B disorders) have the potential to disrupt treatment and negatively impact outcome. Therefore, it is important to routinely evaluate patients for Axis II disorders at point of treatment entry and to design drug treatment programs that provide adequate attention to these comorbid conditions.

In summary, cocaine use disorders commonly co-occur with other substance use disorders as well as nonsubstance Axis I and Axis II disorders. More than a decade ago, Weiss and Mirin (1986) identified five subtypes of cocaine abusers. These included (1) depressed patients who obtain euphoric effects from the drug, (2) bipolar or cyclothymic patients who use cocaine to regulate their mood, (3) patients with ADHD who benefit from the paradoxical effects of cocaine (e.g., increased attention), (4) patients with BPD/NPD who use cocaine to bolster self-esteem, and (5) patients with ASP. The recent literature on comorbidity appears to support this typology. Unfortunately, psychiatric comorbidity has negative implications for symptom expression, prognosis, medical compliance, and services utilization (Bartels et al., 1993; Moos & Moos, 1995; Moos, Mertens, & Brennan, 1994; Pristach & Smith, 1990). It is therefore important for substance abuse and mental health clinicians to become aware of patterns of comorbidity among their patients and to develop treatment plans that address dual disorders simultaneously. Awareness of subtypes of cocaine abusers should guide treatment, both pharmacological and psychological.

To determine the proper interventions for cocaine abusers with co-occurring psychiatric disorders, it may be useful to distinguish primary from secondary disorders. Most of the work in this area has focused on alcoholics; however, the concepts apply to cocaine abusers as well. For instance, Schuckit (1985) argues that antisocial behavior that predates the onset of heavy drinking differs from antisocial behavior occurring within the context of addiction. The temporal relationships between onset of drug use, period(s) of drug abstinence, and psychiatric symptoms are key in determining whether or not a comorbid psychiatric disorder is "independent" of drug use. For example, because cocaine intoxication and withdrawal can cause various psychiatric disturbances, a careful history and psychiatric assessment needs to be completed after the period of acute withdrawal and before diagnosis is finalized.

MEDICAL COMPLICATIONS

Direct Results of Cocaine Use

Medical consequences of acute and chronic cocaine abuse may be categorized as those caused directly by cocaine, those due to adulterants, and those related to route of administration. An increasing number of cases relating cardiovascular toxicity to cocaine use and withdrawal are being reported. Cocaine may decrease coronary flow during a period of increased oxygen demand. Cocaine increases heart rate and blood pressure, produces focal coronary vasospasm, and induces platelet aggregation (Schrank, 1993). Cocaine's peripheral actions involve the release of adrenaline and noradrenaline from the adrenals (Chiueh & Kopin, 1978), inhibition of noradrenaline reuptake sites in myocardial tissue (Iversen, 1965), and local anesthetic effects in myocardial cells (Seifen, Plunkett, & Kennedy, 1989). Cocaine is directly toxic to the myocardium, and positive emission tomography (PET) studies by Volkow (Volkow, Fowler, & Ding, 1996) demonstrate significant uptake of [^{11}C]cocaine by the human heart.

There have been reports of cocaine-induced coronary artery vasoconstriction both during cocaine intoxication and withdrawal. In one study (Lange et al., 1989), persons undergoing cardiac catheterization for the evaluation of chest pain were given intranasal cocaine (2 mg/kg body weight). Although no patient had chest pain or electrocardiographic evidence of myocardial ischemia, the heart rate and arterial pressure rose, the coronary–sinus blood flow fell, and the diameter of the left coronary artery decreased by 8–12% following the application of cocaine. These values returned to baseline after administration of phentolamine, an alpha adrenergic blocking agent. Another study (Nademanee et al., 1989) related ST elevation upon Holter monitoring to cocaine withdrawal. Eight of 21 consecutive male patients admitted to a 28-day inpatient treatment program for cocaine addiction had a total of 45 episodes of ST elevation during the first several weeks of their withdrawal. Eighty-seven percent of these episodes of ST elevation were not accompanied by chest pain and the mean duration of each episode was 57 ± 77 minutes. It is possible that a deficiency of dopamine could cause coronary vasoconstriction and release norepinephrine at the presynaptic junction. Alternatively, cocaine may affect vascular smooth muscle tone by affecting calcium channels. In addition, procoagulant effects of combined protein C and antithrombin III depletion have been found in a person with cocaine-related arterial thromboses (Chokshi, Miller, Rongione, & Isner, 1989). Singly or in combination, these factors may lead to vasospasm and myocardial ischemia. Cocaine is also arrhythmogenic. Sinus tachycardia, ventricular premature contractions, ventricular tachycardia, and fibrillation and asystole may occur as results of the direct effect of cocaine, its effects on catecholamines, or myocardial ischemia. Cocaine blocks sodium channels and does interfere with the action potential in cardiac cells (Andrews, 1997).

Central nervous system manifestations of cocaine abuse include seizures, status epilepticus, cerebral hemorrhage, cerebral vascular accidents, and transient ischemic attacks. Cocaine may produce hyperpyrexia through its direct effect on thermoregulatory centers. Depression of the medullary centers may result in respiratory paralysis and sudden death may be caused by respiratory arrest, myocardial infarction or arrhythmia, or status epilepticus (Cregler & Mark, 1986). Migraine-like headaches have been associated with cocaine withdrawal and may be linked to serotonin disregulation (Satel & Gawin, 1989). Rhabdomyoloysis is a complication of cocaine use. When it is accompanied by acute renal failure, severe liver dysfunction, and disseminated intravascular coagulation, the fatality rate is high (Roth, Alarcon, Fernandez, Preston & Bourgoignie, 1988).

Given cocaine's widespread use, the relatively low frequency of cocaine-induced morbidity is surprising. Predictors of these medical sequelae have not yet been ascertained. It is possible that low cholinesterase activity and/or liver disease can impede the metabolism of cocaine and result in increased toxicity at lower cocaine doses. Preexisting conditions such as coronary artery disease, seizures, and hypertension also place a person at higher risk of medical complications.

Difficulties associated with chronic cocaine use include weight loss, dehydration, nutritional deficiencies (particularly of vitamins B_6, C, and thiamine), and endocrine abnormalities. Neglect of self-care may be evident, including multiple dental caries and periodontitis exacerbated by bruxism. Addicts may medicate their pain with cocaine or other mood-altering drugs and seek medical attention only after prolonged existence of their problem(s).

Results of Adulterants and Routes of Administration

Adulterants also play a role in the development of medical complications. Local anesthetics and stimulants may increase cocaine's inherent toxicity by increasing the risk of hypertension and cardiovascular complications. Sugars, though relatively benign, may encourage development of bacteria that becomes problematic when injected intravenously.

Other complications of cocaine may be due to the route of administration. Intestinal ischemia caused by vasoconstriction and reduced blood flow in the mesenteric vasculature from catecholamine stimulation of alpha receptors has been reported after oral cocaine ingestion (Texter, Choe, Merrill, Laureton, & Frohlich, 1964). A 58% mortality rate has occurred in smugglers or "body packers" of cocaine whose packets have ruptured (McCarron & Wood, 1983). This problem is also seen in persons who swallow their cocaine stores to escape police, either because an actual "bust" is occurring or because they are paranoid about the potential of this event. Depending on the packaging material, partially radiopaque material or gas halos can be seen on abdominal roentgenography. In recent years, professional smugglers have been using more durable packages with multiple layers instead of condoms and plastic food wrap. Treatment consists of activated charcoal and sorbitol to absorb released cocaine and to facilitate expulsion. Nonstimulant laxatives are used to avoid compromising the integrity of the packets. Endoscopic removal can sometimes be performed in those whose packets have been recently swallowed. Surgical removal of packets lower in the intestine should be reserved for cases of gastrointestinal obstruction or serious intoxication. The patient needs to be monitored until all packets are expelled.

Complications of intranasal administration include loss of sense of smell, atrophy and inflammation, and necrosis and perforation of the nasal septum. Snorting cocaine may anesthetize and paralyze the pharynx and larynx, causing hoarseness and predisposing the person to aspiration pneumonia (Estroff & Gold, 1986). There is a report of osteolytic sinusitis with optic disc swelling, optic atrophy, and visual field defects (Newman, Diloreto, Ho, Klein, & Birnbaum, 1988).

Pneumomediastinum and cervical emphysema have been reported after smoking freebase cocaine due to alveolar rupture with prolonged deep inspiration and Valsalva's maneuver (Aroesty, Stanley, & Crockett, 1986). Other respiratory complications of inhaling or smoking freebase cocaine include abnormal reductions in carbon monoxide diffusing capacity (Itkonen, Schnoll, & Glassroth, 1984), granulomatous pneumonitis (Cooper, Bai, Heyderman, & Lorrin, 1983), and pulmonary edema (Allred & Ewer, 1981). Inhalation of hot cocaine vapors may also result in bilateral loss of eyebrows and eyelashes (Tames & Golderning, 1986), and preparation of freebase cocaine with solvents such as ether may result in accidental burns and explosions.

Complications of intravenous cocaine use are multiple and include skin abscesses, phlebitis and cellulitis, and septic emboli resulting in pneumonia, pulmonary abscesses, subacute bacterial endocarditis, ophthalmological infections, and fungal cerebritis (Wetti, Weiss, Cleary, & Gyori, 1984). Injected talc and silicate may cause granulomatous pneumonitis with pulmonary hypertension as well as granulomata of the liver, brain, or eyes (Estroff & Gold, 1986). Hepatitis B, hepatitis C, and delta agent are all too frequently by-products of intravenous drug abuse. In the past several years, concomitantly with the increase in HIV infection, there has been an increase in pneumonia, endocarditis, tuberculosis, hepatitis delta, and other sexually transmitted diseases in drug users.

HIV/AIDS

Although the role of injection drug use in transmission of the HIV virus is well-known, the specific role of cocaine has been less emphasized. Specifically, cocaine use has been associated with increased numbers of injections, needle sharing, and sexual intercourse without condoms (Bux, Lamb, & Iguchi, 1995; Longshore & Anglin, 1995). An increase in the rate of "blood booting" (blood drawn up in syringe and reinjected) is likewise associated with cocaine use, and injecting "speedball" (cocaine and heroin mixed together) is more frequent than heroin use alone (Greenfield, Bigelow, & Brooner, 1992).

The HIV risk profile may be even worse for users of crack than other forms of cocaine. Crack users engage in more high-risk sexual behavior, have more sex partners, higher rates of sexually transmitted diseases and are more likely to exchange sex for money or drugs (Booth, Waters, & Chitwood, 1993; McCoy & Inciardi, 1993). Cocaine injectors and crack users are more likely to exchange sex for money or drugs than other drug use subgroups (Hudgins, McCusker, & Stoddard, 1995), and ethnographic studies suggest that female crack addicts involved in sex work transmit the virus more effectively than women addicted to other forms of cocaine or heroin (Bowser, 1989). The important link between cocaine use and risky sexual behaviors (Ickovics & Rodin, 1992) cannot be overemphasized. Among cocaine abusers who exchange sex for cocaine, approximately one-third of men and nine-tenths of women have had more than 100 sexual partners in the past 30 days (Inciardi, 1995).

OBSTETRIC COMPLICATIONS

In the United States, more than 100,000 babies are prenatally exposed to cocaine each year (Office of the Inspector General, 1990). Dubbed "crack babies," these infants and their mothers began attracting national attention during the late 1980s. Early reports of pregnancy complications and adverse birth outcomes were highly publicized by the media and led to public outcry. NIDA responded by allocating millions of dollars to treatment demonstration projects focusing on perinatal addiction (the "Perinatal 20"). Today, funding for pregnant/postpartum programs comes largely from the Substance Abuse Mental Health Services Administration (both Center for Substance Abuse Treatment [CSAT] and Center for Substance Abuse Prevention [CSAP]).

Like other drugs of abuse, cocaine readily crosses the placental barrier (Moore, Sorg, Miller, Key, & Resnik, 1986). Due to the fetus's immature metabolic, hepatic, and renal systems, the drug is poorly metabolized and, consequently, the half-life is longer (Chasnoff & Schnoll, 1987). Cocaine inhibits reuptake of norepinephrine and dopamine, resulting in increased extracellular levels of these catecholamines at synapses leading to subsequent activation of the adrenergic system (Farrar & Kearns, 1989). These altered circulating levels of neurotransmitters (e.g., dopamine depletion) may be responsible for observed adverse developmental outcomes (Volpe, 1992). Research has also shown that maternal intake of cocaine results in increased fetal systolic blood pressure, decreased uterine blood flow, and decreased fetal oxygenation (Moore et al., 1986); the implications for fetal development, given this scenario, are obvious.

Maternal cocaine use may result in complications of labor and delivery as well as influence the outcome of pregnancy. Increases in spontaneous abortion, preterm labor, and abruptio placentae have all been reported; even when women discontinue use during the first trimester, they remain at risk for preterm labor (Chasnoff, Griffith, MacGregor, Dirkes, & Burns, 1989). There are also reports of cocaine-exposed infants with genitourinary abnormalities, including ambiguous genitalia, hypospadias, "prune belly," and hydronephrosis. Finally, ileal atresia, seizures, and cerebral infarction have been observed in neonates whose mother's use of cocaine has been observed

(Chasnoff, 1988; Chasnoff & Schnoll, 1987). Although these outcomes are quite serious, they are rare and the majority of concerns for prenatal children continue to fall in the neurobehavioral realm.

Although initial research suggested significant developmental and/or neurobehavioral abnormalities for infants prenatally exposed to cocaine, findings from recent studies have been less negative. For instance, although there have been numerous reports of prematurity and intrauterine growth retardation (IUGR) among prenatally exposed infants (Chasnoff, 1988; Coles, Platzman, Smith, James, & Falk, 1992; Hurt et al., 1995; Woods, Eyler, Behnke, & Conlon, 1993), no differences in growth or morphology were found when demographic factors differentiating cocaine using and nonusing mothers were controlled (e.g., age, race, marital status, and other drug use) (Richardson & Day, 1994). Findings pertaining to long-term outcomes are perhaps of even greater importance. Here, the data are complex and somewhat difficult to interpret. For instance, at birth cocaine-exposed neonates evidence less optimal neurobehavioral development on the Brazelton Scale than controls. However, by 6 weeks of age the only remaining differences are related to autonomic stability (Black, Schuler, & Nair, 1992). Hurt et al. (1995) failed to detect differences between low socioeconomic cocaine exposed and control children on the Bayley Scales of Infant Development (BSID) over a 30-month follow-up period although both groups had lower scores than a comparison group of children of higher socioeconomic status. Although cognitive and language development were similar for cocaine exposed and nonexposed preschoolers, the exposed group evidenced greater emotional and behavioral difficulties (Hawley, Halle, Drasin, & Thomas, 1995). Azuma and Chasnoff (1993) reported lower IQ scores (though still normal range) on the Stanford–Binet for children prenatally exposed to cocaine in combination with other drugs; this study also identified mediating variables such as home environment, head circumference, and child behavior, however. Finally, 2-year-olds who had been prenatally exposed to both PCP and cocaine were found to utilize less mature play strategies and to evidence less sustained attention, more deviant behaviors, and poorer quality interactions with caregivers (Beckwith et al., 1994).

In summary, findings on the consequences of prenatal cocaine exposure relative to child development are inconsistent, although early concerns about severe, permanent neurobehavioral deficits appear to have been exaggerations. In studying this population, it will be essential for researchers to control for confounding factors such as age, race, socioeconomic status, and other drug use; this is especially true as some studies have found environmental factors to be as or even more important determinants of functioning.

ASSESSMENT

Initial evaluation of the cocaine abuser begins with a medical, psychiatric, and psychosocial history as well as physical examination. Confirming and augmenting the patient's history through collateral reports of family members and significant others is often helpful. On an emergency basis, the following laboratory tests need to be considered based on the patient's clinical presentation: complete blood count, chemical profile (SMA 12), urinalysis, urine and/or blood toxicology, electrocardiogram, and chest X-ray. Indications for acute hospitalization include (1) serious medical or psychiatric problems either caused by the stimulant drugs or independently coexisting and (2) concurrent dependency on other drugs such as alcohol or sedative hypnotics, necessitating a more closely supervised withdrawal. A validated widely accepted tool to assess addiction severity specifically to cocaine has not yet been developed. However, DSM-IV (American Psychiatric Association, 1994) diagnostic criteria for cocaine intoxication, withdrawal, delirium, delusional disorder, dependence, and abuse are based on the symptoms described in this chapter. Evaluation to guide addiction treatment needs to address a variety of issues, including the dosage, patterns, chronicity, and method of cocaine use; other drug use; antedating and drug-related medical, social, and psychological problems; the patient's cognitive ability and social skills; and the patient's knowledge, motivation, attitude, and expectations of treatment (Washton, Stone, & Hendrickson, 1988). Additional factors indicating increased severity of addiction which may necessitate inpatient treatment include chronic smoking of freebase or intravenous cocaine use, the demonstrated inability to abstain from use while in outpatient treatment, and the lack of family and social supports.

Once the patient is stabilized and assigned to an appropriate level of care, a more detailed medical, psychiatric, and psychosocial history and physical examination should be performed. The search for evidence of medical and psychiatric sequelae should be stressed as well as consequences of self-neglect. The following laboratory tests should be considered supplements to those obtained previously on an acute care basis: pulmonary function testing with diffusing capacity of carbon monoxide (DLCO, DCO) in smokers of freebase and crack cocaine and purified protein derivative (PPD) tubercular skin testing with controls, rapid plasma reagin agglutination test (RPR; syphilis serology), hepatitis B surface antigen, hepatitis C antigen, and HIV serology in intravenous users. Because these patients generally have poor follow-up rates, immunizations should be given and general preventive health maintenance should be performed at this time as well.

TREATMENT

Overdose

In the case of a massive cocaine overdose, patients are likely to present with advanced cardiorespiratory distress and seizures. Treatment is life support. The principles of resuscitation along with the administration of thiamine, glucose, and naloxone (Narcan) are necessary. Naloxone is important because narcotics and cocaine are often taken concomitantly. Oxygen is helpful in light of increased anaerobic metabolism with muscle hyperactivity, seizures, and hyperthermia. Treatment of metabolic and lactic acidosis, often accompanied by respiratory alkalosis due to hyperventilation, is critical.

Suggestions for symptom-specific therapies to counteract the effects of cocaine overdose follow. Oxygen and sedation with a benzodiazepine are helpful in treating myocardial ischemia, infarction, tachyarrhythmias, and hypertension (Goldfrank & Hoffman, 1991). Nitrates and calcium channel blockers can be used for coronary artery spasm. Although there is substantial evidence that nitroglycerine alleviates cocaine-induced coronary vasoconstriction in both diseased and nondiseased arteries (Brogan, Lange, Kim, Moliterno, & Hills, 1991), there is less clinical experience with the calcium channel blockers. Aspirin can help alleviate cocaine-mediated platelet aggregation. Thrombolytic agents should be used cautiously in the face of hypertension and potential cerebrovascular complications. Tachyarrhythmias can be treated with oxygen and a benzodiazepine for sedation. Atrial arrhythmias can be treated with a calcium channel blocker or mixed alpha and beta adrenergic blockade, as well as cooling if the patient is febrile. Ventricular arrhythmias can be treated with lidocaine or sodium bicarbonate (Goldfrank & Hoffman, 1993).

Sodium nitroprusside, phentolamine and calcium channel blockers are effective therapies for hypertension. Propranolol is controversial due to resultant unopposed alpha receptor stimulation. Dantrolene is advocated for severe hyperthermia in addition to physical cooling techniques and possibly muscle paralysis. Paralysis with pancuronium (Pavulon) may be helpful to allow intubation of the patient or control persistent seizure activity. Succinylcholine has rapid paralytic effects, but it can worsen muscle fasiculations and aggravate hyperthermia. Benzodiazepines, such as diazepam, lorazepam, or barbiturates, are helpful to control severe agitation or seizure activity. Whenever seizures occur, their etiology should be carefully assessed, as these may not be stimulant related. Hypotension may necessitate norepinephrine tartrate (Levophed) and/or dopamine (Intropin). A pneumomediastinum or pneumothorax may require a chest tube but can often be treated supportively.

Intoxication

Intoxicated persons who seek assistance with less severe cocaine complications are more likely to present panic, irritability, hyperreflexia, paranoia, hallucinations, and stereotyped repetitive movements. Assurance in a calm, nonthreatening environment is a prerequisite for successful patient management. Psychosis can be treated with haloperidol although caution is necessary as this medication can lower the seizure threshold. Monoamine oxidase inhibitors are contraindicated because they block cocaine degradation. Infectious diseases and other complications need to be treated appropriately.

Withdrawal

Benzodiazepines may be considered to ameliorate the "crash" or early phase withdrawal from cocaine. However, the high abuse potential of benzodiazepines limits their therapeutic value (Kosten, 1988). The most serious complication of early withdrawal is depression with the potential for suicide. Patients must be watched closely when manifesting depression and agitation. If symptoms of depression do not remit within 10 days to 2 weeks and with relative normalization of sleep patterns, underlying major depression requiring psychiatric intervention is suggested.

Pharmacological Treatment of Chronic Cocaine Addiction

Clinical researchers have tried to identify drugs to reduce cocaine craving and prevent relapse. Numerous drugs looked promising in initial open label trials but did not prove efficacious in subsequent placebo-controlled studies. These pharmacological treatments have included dopaminergic agonists (e.g., monamine oxidase inhibitors, amantadine, mazindol, methylphenidate, pemoline, bromocriptine, L-dopa and pergolide), neurotransmitter precursors (L-tyrosine, L-tryptophan, multivitamins with B complex), carbamazepine, and antidepressants including desipramine and fluoxetine. Clinical trials with bupropion, olanzapine, naltrexone, buprenorphine, and other drugs are ongoing. As our understanding of the neurobiological basis of cocaine addiction becomes further refined, new pharmacological strategies are emerging. Potential targets include specific dopamine, 5-HT, and other receptor subtypes, neuroendocrine peptides (i.e., CRF), and biogenic amine transporters including the dopamine reuptake transporter. These pharmacotherapies and the potential development of a vaccine to prevent cocaine from reaching its central nervous system site of action are covered in Chapter 25 (this volume).

Cognitive, Behavioral, and Nonpharmacological Treatments

Cocaine disorders have proven to be refractory to psychological as well as pharmacological treatment. Consequently, considerable energy has been directed toward developing and testing the efficacy of new psychotherapeutic approaches in the treatment of cocaine use disorders. Many of these therapies have been adapted from ones originally developed to treat alcoholism. One approach that has received attention is cognitive-behavioral relapse prevention (RP). RP strives to teach the addict how to recognize high-risk situations and deal with these using cognitive strategies that have been well rehearsed. RP recognizes that with a chronic disorder such as addiction, relapses and remissions are expected. When a relapse occurs, more intense treatment and cognitive restructuring are necessary to help prevent a "slip" from escalating. Reminding patients of their prior progress, focusing on making the "slip" an isolated event, and maximizing the learning value of this experience are constructive ways of handling the situation. The literature on efficacy of RP in the treatment of cocaine dependence is mixed. In a review of 24 randomized clinical trials of RP for drug abuse (including cocaine), Carroll (1996) concluded that RP is superior to no treatment, although superiority to other active therapies is less evident.

A somewhat different approach has been taken by researchers studying the role of conditioned cues or "reminders" of cocaine use (O'Brien, Childress, Arndt, & McLellan, 1988); this approach deigns to extinguish conditioned responses to these cocaine cues, thereby reducing the chances for relapse. Desensitization training requires patients to be repeatedly exposed to drug stimuli and then given the opportunity to deal with them in real-life situations. Behavioral rehearsal is key to being prepared to deal with the drug-laden situations that exist outside the protection of the treatment center. In one study (O'Brien, Childress, McLellan, & Ehrman, 1990), 30 drug-free cocaine addicts were repeatedly exposed to cocaine cues within a controlled setting. Subjects reported experiencing strong physiological arousal including cocaine craving, highs, and withdrawal in response to exposure. However, by the sixth hour of extinction (repeated nonreinforced exposure to cocaine cues), highs and withdrawal were no longer reported and, by the fifteenth hour, craving was no longer experienced. Despite the strong extinction of arousal, these effects diminished over time unless they were reinforced with repeated cue exposure sessions.

Voucher-based reinforcement strategies have also shown considerable promise (Higgins, Budney, Bickel, & Hughes, 1993; Higgins, Budney, Bickel, & Foerg, 1994; Higgins et al., 1995). Silverman et al. (1996) studied the impact of contingent vouchers on cocaine abstinence among 37 methadone-maintained patients. Compared to controls (who received vouchers of equal value independent of urinalysis results), those in the reinforcement group achieved significantly longer periods of cocaine abstinence. Also, urine benzoylecgnonine concentrations were reduced by half for the reinforcement group but not for the control group. Higgins et al. (1993) compared the efficacy of multicomponent behavioral treatment (based on community reinforcement approach) to drug abuse counseling (based on disease model). Subjects in the behavioral group also received incentives for cocaine-free urine samples. Although 58% of the behavioral group completed the 24-week treatment program, only 11% of the drug counseling group completed this program. Also, 68% of the behavioral group achieved 8 weeks of continuous cocaine abstinence and 42% achieved 16 weeks; in comparison, documented continuous abstinence was achieved by only 11% and 5% of the drug counseling group for the 8 and 16 weeks, respectively. Finally, Higgins, Budney, Bickel, and Foerg (1994) demonstrated that voucher incentives (in combination with comprehensive behavioral intervention) enhanced retention in the 24-week-long treatment program for those receiving both interventions (75%) over those receiving behavioral therapy only (40%). In addition, those in the voucher group had greater continuous abstinence and evidenced greater improvements on the ASI Drug and Psychiatric scales than those not receiving vouchers.

Unfortunately, not all substance abusers are motivated to change their drug use behavior; this is particularly true of patients with comorbid psychiatric disorders who may be overwhelmed by their multiple problems and prior treatment failures (Martino, McCance-Katz, Workman, & Boozang, 1995; Ziedonis & Fischer, 1996). Motivational enhancement therapy (MET), a nonconfrontational approach, developed by Miller and Rollnick (1991), was originally designed for working with problem drinkers. In numerous trials, the principles of motivational interviewing have been shown to be effective, sometimes after only one or two sessions (Bien, Miker, & Tonigan, 1993; Brown & Miller, 1993). Because of promising results with alcoholics, MET is currently being adapted for use with drug abusers, including those with cocaine dependence and psychiatric comorbidity. MET works in tandem with the stages-of-change model of Prochaska, DiClemente, and Norcross (1992). The model postulates five distinct stages: precontemplation, contemplation, action, maintenance, and relapse; these stages can be assessed via paper and pencil instruments such as the University of Rhode Island Change Assessment (URICA). Different therapeutic strategies are employed based on the patient's designated stage of change. MET represents a clear departure from traditional drug abuse counseling strategies. Because acceptance of the addict identity is considered unimportant, patients are less likely to manifest overt resistance. Rather than emphasize powerlessness this approach assumes that people have within themselves the capacity to change. Although the efficacy of MET for cocaine abusers has yet to be proven, it would appear that its unique focus on readiness should, at minimum, help patients to engage in other forms of therapy.

The approaches described (i.e., relapse prevention, cue exposure/desensitization, contingency management, and motivational interviewing) are somewhat technical and require specific training and supervision. Research-based interventions such as these appear to be the wave of the future, and most can be adapted for use in community-based programs. Frequently, treatment of cocaine dependence takes place within the context of a comprehensive drug treatment program. Although therapeutic modalities may be the same as for other drug abusers (e.g., education and individual and group therapy), the intensity of treatment must be greater. An emphasis must be placed on the acquisition of skills that will enable the cocaine abuser to have more internal control, greater self-efficacy, and reduced likelihood of relapse. This means that treatment must have multiple "practical" components.

The first goal of treatment is to interrupt recurrent binges or daily use of cocaine and overcome drug craving. For patients who do not have serious psychiatric comorbidity, a structured outpatient program can be attempted prior to physically removing the person from the drug-using environment for treatment in a residential setting. While attempting to initiate abstinence, treatment should include daily or multiple weekly contacts and urine monitoring with as many external controls as possible. Explicit practical measures to limit exposure to stimulants and high-risk situations should be individualized but might include monitoring and support by drug-free "significant others," the discarding of drug supplies and paraphernalia, breaking off relationships with dealers and drug-using comrades, limiting finances, changing one's telephone number and/or geographic location, and structuring one's time during all waking hours. Instead of simply replacing cocaine's central role in one's existence, emphasizing lifestyle changes including stress reduction, wellness, exercise and leisure activities is important. This may be more difficult for persons of lower socioeconomic classes and/or those with an earlier onset of addiction. These persons lack the knowledge, experience, and resources with which to make these changes. Such patients may need linkage to other social services and habilitation in addition to the rehabilitation just discussed. The involvement of significant others in the treatment of cocaine use disorders can have a positive impact. For instance, Higgins, Budney, Bickel, and Badger (1994) recently showed that patients who had family involvement were 20 times more likely to complete treatment. Finally, supportive therapies including self-help groups may provide positive role models, a group spirituality, and the backing needed to assist in change. Special Cocaine Anonymous (CA) groups may be beneficial in addressing issues pertinent to cocaine's strong reinforcing properties and associated lifestyle. On the other hand, CA meetings may have detrimental effects by continuing to foster a sense of cocaine separatism.

METHAMPHETAMINE

D-Methamphetamine hydrochloride is a stimulant that produces many subjective effects similar to those of cocaine, although its 10–12-hour half-life is 6 to 30 times as long as the 20- to 120-minute duration of cocaine (Gold, Miller, & Jonas, 1992). Its' street names include "crank," "go," "crystal," and "crystal meth." Methamphetamine can be snorted, taken orally, injected intravenously, or inhaled, but it must be purified before it can be smoked. "Ice" is the purified form of the d-isomer that is frequently sold as large crystals which are smoked. The freebase form of methamphetamine is a liquid at room temperature. Rocks are made by melting, cooling, and cutting the methamphetamine crystals, which are often done in an aluminum turkey roasting pan. Methamphetamine can be smoked by inhaling it from a straw placed on aluminum foil or inhaling it through a glass pipe. Methamphetamine pipes differ from those for crack cocaine because the drug vaporizes at a much lower temperature (Cook, 1991). Methamphetamine is heated by a lighter held under a large glass ball at the end of the pipe. Air flow is regulated by a finger placed over a hole on the top of the pipe.

Clandestine laboratories synthesize methamphetamine from pseudoephedrine, ephedrine, phenylpropanolamine, and phenyl-2-propanone. The recipes for manufacturing methamphetamine are continuously shifting due to changes in precursor availability and legal controls by the Drug Enforcement Administration. President Clinton signed into law "The Comprehensive Methamphetamine Control Act of 1996" to abate this problem, diminishing precursor supply and enacting stiffer penalties on the illicit manufacturing of methamphetamine. Regional "pockets" of misuse have been found in San Diego, San Francisco, Los Angeles, Denver, Seattle, Minneapolis, Dallas, Iowa, Oklahoma, Hawaii, the Pacific Northwest, and Guam (Heischober & Miller, 1991; Miller, 1991; Suwaki, 1991; Cho, 1991; Hall & Broderick, 1991).

Methamphetamine elevates blood pressure, speeds heart rate, raises body temperature, dilates pupils, reduces food intake, and diminishes sleep. Low doses initially are associated with increased alertness and vigilance, and higher doses result in anxiety, irritability, tremors, paranoia, and stereotypical behavior. Tolerance (needing more drug to achieve a given effect) or sensitization (needing less drug to achieve a given effect) may occur upon continued methamphetamine exposure. Different drug effects may have varying rates of either tolerance or sensitization (Lukas, 1997). Tolerance to methamphetamine euphoria occurs more quickly than tolerance to its tachycardic or anorexic effects. Being more prone to seizures and psychosis after repeated dosing with methamphetamine is an example of sensitization (Koob, 1997).

Methamphetamine toxicity can affect many organ systems. Methamphetamine cardiotoxicity is related to catechol excess and may result in myocardial infarction and/or arrhythmias. Pulmonary hypertension, rhabdomyolysis, and idiosyncratic liver necrosis are a few of the morbidities associated with methamphetamine use. Paranoid delusions occur in more than 80% of the cases of toxic psychosis.

Methamphetamine enters the nerve terminal via the synaptic or membrane transporter and then enters the storage vesicles through vesicular transporters, forcing out neurotransmitters such as dopamine and norepinephrine. Methamphetamine is basic and disrupts the acidic interior of the synaptic vesicles, inactivating the proton pump necessary to transport dopamine back inside the vesicle. The dopamine in the cytoplasm undergoes autooxidation, which produces toxic peroxides, oxygen radicals, and hydroxylquinones, which can cause damage in such dopamine-rich areas of the brain as the ventral tegmentum and substantia nigra (Seiden, 1991; Seiden & Sabol, 1996). Dopamine and serotonin and their precursor enzymes tyrosine hydroxylase and tryptophan hydroxylase are depleted, which, in turn, affects levels of the major metabolites of these transmitters, their receptors, and their reuptake transporters. Nitric oxide may have a role in methamphetamine-induced behavioral sensitization and neurotoxicity. When mice were given methamphetamine after pretreatment with the neuronal nitric oxide synthase inhibitor 7-nitroindazole, the animals were protected against depletion of dopamine, its metabolites, and dopamine transporter binding sites (Itzhak, Huang, & Ali, 1997). Susceptible neuronal axons and axon terminals rather than cell bodies seem to be damaged. This toxicity depends on dosage, dosing interval, route of administration, chronicity of use, and the animal species studied. The permanency of methamphetamine damage dependent on these factors is not yet fully characterized.

Given an unlimited supply, animals will self-administer methamphetamine, like cocaine, until its toxic effects cause death. The animals that most readily learn methamphetamine self-administration are those that are more reactive to novel environments. The animals respond less in progressive reinforcement schedules to obtain methamphetamine than cocaine, but this may be due to methamphetamine's longer duration of action.

Other than symptomatic treatment of drug-induced sequelae, there are no specific pharmacological treatments for methamphetamine addiction (Lukas, 1997). Continued progress in understanding the neurobiological basis for methamphetamine addiction as well as medication development initiatives aimed at cocaine and other drugs may benefit methamphetamine pharmacotherapy in the future. Nonpharmacological therapies for methamphetamine addiction are similar to those for other chemical dependencies but need take into account methamphetamine's longer duration of action, withdrawal period, and potentially longer recovery phase.

CONCLUSION

Since the initial draft of this chapter 7 years ago, much knowledge has been gained about cocaine use, abuse, and dependency. Over time, the epidemiology of the cocaine epidemic has shifted. Most notably, cocaine dependence now appears to be differentially affecting poor, minority individuals who live in the intercity. This same population is overrepresented in the AIDS population. This confluence is not surprising as both sex risk (including sex work) and needle risk are associated with chronic use of cocaine. It therefore appears that these two epidemics are interconnected in a way that deserves close attention.

At the same time, there may be reason for cautious optimism with regard to the long-term effects of prenatal exposure to cocaine. Some of the early claims of devastating physical consequences to "crack babies" have proven to be exaggerated; experts in the perinatal addiction field now consider the many factors (e.g., poverty, poor maternal nutrition/health, smoking, and exposure to violence) that combine to influence development. Molecular mechanisms of developmental neuroadaptation are at the same time beginning to be studied. In the future we hope to better understand the physiological basis for the observed clinical events.

In the basic sciences arena, we have come to understand more about the interactions of various neurotransmitters, drug reinforcement, and the reward pathway. Receptors are being subtyped and cloned. Signal transduction pathways with their longer range on protein synthesis and genetic regulation are being explored. Inroads are beginning in our understanding of sensitization and tolerance. Although pharmacological treatments for cocaine addiction have not yet proven successful in clinical trials, there are many exciting new avenues of pursuit. These prospects for pharmacological intervention are based on the remarkable advances in neuroscience being made this decade.

Researchers also have been hard at work testing psychotherapeutic solutions to this complex problem. Cocaine dependence should not be viewed in isolation from other psychiatric conditions and life problems. Rather, we must consider how to best address the problem in the presence of other psychoactive substance use and nonsubstance use Axis I and Axis II disorders. Depending on the larger clinical picture, successful treatment may require multiple or highly select therapies that are matched to the patient's pathology and adaptive strengths and resources. It is clear that a "one size fits all" approach to treatment of cocaine dependence is inappropriate; instead, an array of assessment tools is necessary to determine patient needs, along with a menu of cost-effective and readily available therapeutic strategies. Although American Society of Addiction Medicine (Hoffman, Halikas, Mee-Lee, & Weedman, 1991) criteria facilitate placement in an appropriate treatment setting based on addiction severity, they provide little guidance in terms of specific interventions to be delivered within those settings. Clinical research aimed at developing therapies for specific subtypes of cocaine addicts in a variety of settings is the most promising approach we now have.

ACKNOWLEDGMENTS

Special thanks to Kenneth S. Kendler, MD, Rachel Brown Banks Distinguished Professor of Psychiatry and Professor of Human Genetics, Medical College of Virginia of Virginia Commonwealth University, Richmond, Virginia, for contributing to the genetic factors section of this chapter.

REFERENCES

Albuquerque, M., Kurth, C. D., Monnitto, C., Shaw, L., & Anday, E. (1995). Ethanol, morphine and barbiturate alter the hemodynamic and cerebral response to cocaine in newborn pigs. *Biology of the Neonate, 67,* 432–440.

Allred, R. J., & Ewer, S. (1981). Fatal pulmonary edema following intravenous "free base" cocaine use. *Annals of Emergency Medicine, 10,* 441–442.

American Psychiatric Association. (1987). *Diagnostic and statistical manual of mental disorders* (3rd ed., rev.). Washington, DC: Author.

American Psychiatric Association. (1994). *Diagnostic and statistical manual of mental disorders* (4th ed.). Washington, DC: Author.

Andrews, P. (1997). Cocaethylene toxicity. *Journal of Addictive Diseases, 16*(3), 75–84.

Aroesty, D. J., Stanley, R. B., Jr., & Crockett D. M. (1986). Pneumomediastinum and cervical emphysema from inhalation of "free based" cocaine: Report of three cases. *Otolaryngology: Head and Neck Surgery, 94,* 372–374.

Aronson, T., & Craig, T. (1986). Cocaine precipitation of panic disorder. *American Journal of Psychiatry, 143*(5), 643–645.

Azuma, S. D., & Chasnoff, I. J. (1993). Outcome of children prenatally exposed to cocaine and other drugs: A path analysis of three-year data. *Pediatrics, 92*(3), 396–402.

Barber, J., Frank, A., Weiss, R., & Blane, J. (1996). Prevalence and correlates of personality disorder diagnoses among cocaine dependent outpatients. *Journal of Personality Disorders, 10*(4), 297–311.

Barnett, G., Hawks, R., & Resnick, R. (1981). Cocaine pharmacokinetics in humans. *Journal of Ethnopharmacology, 3,* 353–366.

Bartels, S., Teague, G., Drake, R., Clark R., Bush, P., & Noordsy, D. (1993). Service utilization and costs associated with substance abuse among rural schizophrenic patients. *Journal of Nervous and Mental Disease, 181,* 227–276.

Beckwith, L., Rodning, C., Norris, D., Phillipsen, L., Khandabi, P., & Howard, J. (1994).

Spontaneous play in two-year-olds born to substance-abusing mothers. *Infant Mental Health Journal, 15*(2), 189–201.

Begleiter, H., & Kissin, B. (Eds.). (1995). *The genetics of alcoholism.* New York: Oxford University Press.

Bien, T., Miker, W., & Tonigan, S. (1993). Brief interventions for alcohol problems: A review. *Addictions, 8,* 305–325.

Black, M., Schuler, M., & Nair, P. (1992). Prenatal drug exposure: Neurodevelopmental outcome and parenting environment. *Journal of Pediatric Psychology, 18*(5), 605–620.

Booth, R., Watters, J., & Chitwood, D. (1993). HIV risk-related sex behaviors among injection drug users, crack smokers, and injection drug users who smoke crack. *American Journal of Public Health, 83*(8), 1144–1148.

Bowser, B. (1989). Crack and AIDS: An ethnographic impression. *Journal of the National Medical Association, 5,* 538–540.

Brady, K., Casto, S., Lydiard, R., & Malcolm, R. (1991). Substance abuse in an inpatient psychiatric sample. *American Journal of Drug and Alcohol Abuse, 17*(4), 389–397.

Brogan, W. C., Lange, R. A., Kim, A. S., Moliterno, D. J., & Hills, L. D. (1991). Alleviation of cocaine-induced coronary vasoconstriction by nitroglycerine. *Journal of the American College of Cardiology, 18,* 581–586.

Brown, J., & Miller, W. (1993). Impact of motivational interviewing on participation and outcome in residential alcoholism treatment. *Psychology of Addictive Behaviors, 7,* 211–218.

Budd, R. D. (1989). Cocaine abuse and violent death. *American Journal of Drug and Alcohol Abuse, 15*(4), 375–382.

Bux, D., Lamb, R., & Iguchi, M. (1995). Cocaine use and HIV risk behavior in methadone maintenance patients. *Drug and Alcohol Dependence, 37*(1), 29–35.

Buydens-Branchey, L., Branchey, M., Fergeson, P., Hudson, J., & McKernin, C. (1997). Craving for cocaine in addicted users: Role of serotonergic mechanisms. *American Journal on Addictions, 6,* 65–93.

Bystritsky, A., Ackerman, D., & Pasnau, R. (1991). Low dose desipramine treatment of cocaine-related panic attacks. *Journal of Nervous and Mental Disease, 179*(12), 755–758.

Cadoret, R. J., Yates, W. R., Troughten, E., Woodworth, G., & Stewart, M. A. (1995). Genetic–environmental interaction in the genesis of aggressivity and conduct disorders. *Archives of General Psychiatry, 52*(11), 916–924.

Cadoret, R. J., Yates, W. R., Troughten, E., Woodworth, G., & Stewart, M. A. (1996). An adoption study of drug abuse/dependency in females. *Comprehensive Psychiatry, 37*(2), 88–94.

Carroll, K. (1996). Relapse prevention as a psychosocial treatment: A review of controlled clinical trials. *Experimental and Clinical Psychopharmacology, 4*(1), 46–54.

Carroll, K., & Rounsaville, B. (1993). History and significance of childhood attention deficit disorder in treatment-seeking cocaine abusers. *Comprehensive Psychiatry, 34*(2), 75–82.

Carroll, K., Rounsaville, B., & Bryant, K. (1993). Alcoholism in treatment seeking cocaine abusers: Clinical and prognostic significance. *Journal of Studies on Alcohol, 54*(2), 199–208.

Carroll, K., Rounsaville, B., Gordon, L., Nich, C., Jatlow, P., Bisighini, R., & Gawin, F. (1994). Psychotherapy and pharmacotherapy for ambulatory cocaine abusers. *Archives of General Psychiatry, 51,* 177–187.

Chasnoff, I. J. (1988). *Cocaine use in pregnancy: Pre- and postnatal effects.* Paper presented at a technical review meeting, Clinical Applications of Cocaine Research: From Bench to Bedside, National Institute on Drug Abuse, Rockville, MD.

Chasnoff, I. J., Griffith, D. R., MacGregor, S., Dirkes, K., & Burns, K. A. (1989). Temporal patterns of cocaine use in pregnancy. *Journal of the American Medical Association, 261,* 1688–1689.

Chasnoff, I. J., & Schnoll, S. H. (1987). Consequences of cocaine and other drug use in pregnancy. In A. Washton & M. S. Gold (Eds.), *Cocaine: A clinician's handbook* (pp. 241–251). New York: Guilford Press.

Chiueh, C. C., & Kopin, I. J. (1978). Endogenous epinephrine and norepinephrine from the sympathoadrenal medullary system of unanesthetized rats. *Journal of Pharmacology and Experimental Therapeutics, 205,* 148–154.

Cho, B. I. (1991). Trends and patterns of methamphetamine abuse in the Republic of Korea. In M. A. Miller & N. J. Kozel (Eds.), *Methamphetamine abuse: Epidemiologic issues and implications* (NIDA Research Monograph No. 115, DHHS Publication No. ADM 91-1836, pp. 99–108). Washington, DC: U.S. Government Printing Office.

Chokshi, S. K., Miller, G., Rongione, A., & Isner, J. M. (1989). Cocaine and cardiovascular diseases: The leading edge. *Cardiology, 111,* 1–6.

Coles, C., Platzman, K., Smith, I., James, F., & Falk, A. (1992). Effects of cocaine and alcohol use in pregnancy on neonatal growth and neurobehavioral status. *Neurotoxicology Teratology, 14,* 23–33.

Cook, C. E. (1991). Pyrolytic characteristics, pharmacokinetics, and bioavailability of smoked heroin, cocaine, phencyclidine, and methamphetyamine. In M. A. Miller & N. J. Kozel (Eds.), *Methamphetamine abuse: Epidemiologic issues and implications* (NIDA Research Monograph No. 115, DHHS Publication No. ADM 91-1836, pp. 6–23). Washington, DC: U.S. Government Printing Office.

Cooper, C. B., Bai, T. R., Heyderman, C., & Lorrin, B. (1983). Cellulose granulomas in the lungs of a cocaine sniffer. *British Medical Journal, 286,* 2121–2022.

Cregler, L. L., & Mark, H. (1986). Special report: Medical complications of cocaine abuse. *New England Journal of Medicine, 315,* 1495–1500.

DePetrillo, P. (1985). Getting to the base of cocaine. *Emergency Medicine, 8,* 8.

Estroff, T. W., Gold, M. S. (1986). Medical and psychiatric complications of cocaine abuse with possible points of pharmacological treatment. In B. Stimmel (Ed.), *Controversies in alcoholism and substance abuse* (pp. 61–75). New York: Haworth Press.

Farrar, H., & Kearns, G. (1989). Cocaine: Clinical pharmacology and toxicology. *Journal of Pediatrics, 115,* 665–675.

Gawin, F. H., & Ellinwood, E. H., Jr. (1988). Cocaine and other stimulants: Actions, abuse, and treatment. *New England Journal of Medicine, 318,* 1173–1182.

Gawin, F. H., Riordan, C., & Kleber, H. (1985). Methylphenidate treatment of cocaine abusers without attention-deficit disorder: A negative report. *American Journal of Drug and Alcohol Abuse, 11,* 193–197.

Gay, G. R. (1982) Clinical management of acute and chronic cocaine poisoning. *Annals of Emergency Medicine, 11,* 562–572.

General Accounting Office. (1990). *Methadone maintenance: Some treatment programs are not effective, greater federal oversight needed.* Washington, DC: Author.

Gold, M. S., Miller, N. S., & Jonas, J. M. (1992). Cocaine (and crack) neurobiology. In J. H. Lowinson, P. Ruiz, & R. B. Millman (Eds.), *Substance abuse: A comprehensive textbook* (2nd ed., pp. 222–235). Baltimore: Williams & Wilkins.

Goldfrank, L. R., & Hoffman, R. S. (1991). The cardiovascular effects of cocaine. *Annals of Emergency Medicine, 20,* 165–175.

Goldfrank, L. R., & Hoffman, R. S. (1993). The cardiovascular effects of cocaine—update 1992. In H. Sorer (Ed.), *Acute cocaine intoxication: Current methods of treatment* (NIDA Research Monograph No. 123, NIH Publication No. 93-3498, pp. 70–109). Washington, DC: U.S. Government Printing Office.

Greenfield, L., Biglow, G., & Brooner, R. (1992). HIV risk behavior in drug users: Increased blood "booting" during cocaine injection. *AIDS Education and Prevention, 4*(2), 95–107.

Griffin, M. L., Weiss, R. D., Mirin, S. M., & Lange, U. (1989). A comparison of male and female cocaine abusers. *Archives of General Psychiatry, 46,* 122–126.

Hall, J. N., & Broderick, P. M. (1991). *Community networks for response to abuse outbreaks of methamphetamine and its analogs.* In M. A. Miller & N. J. Kozel (Eds.), *Methamphetamine abuse: Epidemiologic issues and implications* (NIDA Research Monograph No. 115, DHHS Publication No. ADM 91-1836, pp. 109–120). Washington, DC: U.S. Government Printing Office.

Haller, D., Knisely, J., Dawson, K., & Schnoll, S. (1993). Perinatal substance abusers: Psychological and social characteristics. *Journal of Nervous and Mental Disease, 181*(8), 509–513.

Hawley, T. L., Halle, T. G., Drasin, R. E., & Thomas, N. G. (1995). *American Journal of Orthopsychiatry, 65*(3), 364–379.

Heischober, B., & Miller, M. A. (1991). Methamphetamine abuse in California. In M. A. Miller & N. J. Kozel (Eds.), *Methamphetamine abuse: Epidemiologic issues and implications* (NIDA Research Monograph No. 115, DHHS Publication No. ADM 91-1836, pp. 60–71). Washington, DC: U.S. Government Printing Office.

Higgins, S., Budney, A., Bickel, W., & Badger, G. (1994). Participation of significant others in outpatient behavioral treatment predicts greater cocaine abstinence. *American Journal of Drug and Alcohol Abuse, 20*(1), 47–56.

Higgins, S., Budney, A., Bickel, W., Badger, G., Foerg, F., & Ogden, D. (1995). Outpatient behavioral treatment for cocaine dependence: One-year outcome. *Experimental and Clinical Psychopharmacology, 3*(2), 205–212.

Higgins, S., Budney, A., Bickel, W., & Foerg, F. (1994). Incentives improve outcome in outpatient behavioral treatment for cocaine dependence. *Archives of General Psychiatry, 51*(7), 568–576.

Higgins, S., Budney, A., Bickel, W., & Hughes, J. (1993). Achieving cocaine abstinence with a behavioral approach. *American Journal of Psychiatry, 150*(5), 763–769.

Hoffman, N. G., Halikas, J. A., Mee-Lee, D., & Weedman, R. D. (1991). *Patient placement criteria for the treatment of psychoactive substance use disorders.* Washington, DC: American Society of Addiction Medicine.

Horner, B., Scheibe, K., & Stine, S. (1996). Cocaine abuse and attention-deficit hyperactivity disorder: Implications of adult symptomatology. *Psychology of Addictive Behaviors, 10*(1), 55–60.

Hudgins, R., McCusker, J., & Stoddard, A. (1995). Cocaine use and risky injection and sexual behaviors. *Drug and Alcohol Dependence, 37*(1), 7–14.

Hurt, H., Brodsky, N., Betancourt, L., Braitman, L., Malmud, E., & Giannetta, J. (1995). Cocaine exposed children: Follow-up through 30 months. *Developmental and Behavioral Pediatrics, 16*(1), 29–35.

Ickovics, J., & Rodin, J. (1992). Women and AIDS in the United States: Epidemiology, natural history, and mediating mechanisms. *Health Psychology, 11,* 1–16.

Inciardi, J. (1995). Crack, crack house sex, and HIV risk. *Archives of Sexual Behavior,* 24(3), 249–269.

Itkonen, J., Schnoll, S., & Glassroth, J. (1984). Pulmonary dysfunction in free base cocaine users. *Archives of Internal Medicine, 144,* 2195–2197.

Itzhak, Y., Huang, P., & Ali, S. F. (1997). *Methamphetamine-induced behavioral sensitization and neurotoxicity: Role for nitric oxide synthase* [Abstract]. Fifty-ninth annual scientific meeting of the College on Problems of Drug Dependence, p. 70.

Iversen, L. L. (1965). Inhibition of noradrenaline uptake by drugs. *Journal of Pharmaceutics and Pharmacology, 17,* 62–64.

Javaid, J. I., Fischman, M. W., Schuster, C. R., Dekirmenjian, H., & Davis, J. M. (1978). Cocaine plasma concentration: Relation to physiological and subjective effects in humans. *Science, 202,* 227–228.

Johanson, C. E., Balster, R. L., & Bonese, K. (1976). Self-administration of psychomotor stimulant drugs: The effects of unlimited access. *Pharmacology Biochemistry and Behavior, 4,* 45–51.

Johanson, C. E., & Schuster, C. R. (1995). Cocaine. In F. L. Bloom & D. J. Kupfer (Eds.), *Psychopharmacology: The fourth generation of progress* (pp. 1685–1697). New York: Raven Press.

Johnson, W., & Ouellet, L. (1996). [Letter]. *American Journal of Public Health, 86,* 266.

Jones, R. T. (1984). The pharmacology of cocaine. In J. G. Grabowski (Ed.), *Cocaine: Pharmacology, effects and treatment of abuse* (DHHS Publication No. ADM AD4-1325, pp. 34–53). Washington, DC: U.S. Government Printing Office.

Kendler, K. D., Neale, M. C., MacLean, C. J., Heath, A. C., Eaves, L. J., & Kessler, R. C. (1993). Smoking and major depression: a causal analysis. *Archives of General Psychiatry, 50,* 36–43.

Kendler, K. D., & Prescott, S. C. (in press). Cocaine use, abuse and dependence in a population-based sample of female twins. *British Journal of Psychiatry.*

Khantzian, E. J., Gawin, F., Kleber, H. D., & Riordan, C. E. (1984). Methylphenidate treatment of cocaine dependence: A preliminary report. *Journal of Substance Abuse Treatment, 1,* 107–112.

Kleinman, P., Miller, A., Millman, R., Woody, G., Todd, T., Kemp, J., & Lipton, D. (1990). Psychopathology among cocaine abusers entering treatment. *Journal of Nervous and Mental Disease, 178,* 442–447.

Koob, G. F. (1997). Neurochemical explanations for addiction. *Hospital Practice: A Special Report,* pp. 12–15.

Kosten, T. R. (1988) *Cocaine treatment: Pharmacotherapies.* Paper presented at a technical review meeting, Clinical Applications of Cocaine Research: From Bench to Bedside, National Institute on Drug Abuse, Rockville, MD.

Kosten, T. R., Rounsaville, B. J., & Kleber, H. D. (1987). A 2.5 year follow-up of cocaine use among treated opioid addicts: Have our treatments helped? *Archives of General Psychiatry, 44,* 281–284.

Kranzler, H., Satel, S., & Apetr, A. (1994). Personality disorders and associated features in cocaine-dependent inpatients. *Comprehensive Psychiatry, 35*(5), 335–340.

Kreek, M. J., Ho, A., & Borg, L. (1994). Dynorphin A1-13 administration causes elevation of serum levels of prolactin in human subjects. In L. S. Harris (Ed.), *Problems of drug dependence, 1993. Proceedings of the 55th annual scientific meeting of the College on Problems of Drug Dependence* (NIDA Research Monograph No. 141, NIH Publication No. 94-3749, pp. 108). Washington, DC: U.S. Government Printing Office.

Kuhar, M. J., Ritz, M. D., & Sharkey, J. (1988). Cocaine receptors on dopamine transporters medicate cocaine-reinforced behavior. In D. Clouet, A. Khurshee, & R. Brown (Eds.), *Mechanisms of cocaine abuse and toxicity* (NIDA Research Monograph No. 88, DHHS Publication No. ADM 88-1585, pp. 14–22). Washington, DC: U.S. Government Printing Office.

Lange, R. A., Cigarroa, R. G., Yancy, C. W., Jr., Willard, J. E., Popma, J. J., Sills, M. N., McBride, W., Kim, A. S., & Hillis, L. D. (1989). Cocaine-induced coronary-artery vasoconstriction. *New England Journal of Medicine, 321,* 1557–1562.

Lindenbaum, G. A., Carroll, S. F., Daskal, I., & Kapusnick, R. (1989). Patterns of alcohol and drug abuse in an urban trauma center: the increasing role of cocaine abuse. *Journal of Trauma, 29,* 1654–1658.

Lombard, J., Levin, J. H., & Weiner, W. J. (1989). Arsenic intoxication in a cocaine abuser. *New England Journal of Medicine, 320*(13), 869.

Longshore, D., & Anglin, D. (1995). Number of sex partners and crack cocaine use: Is crack an independent marker for HIV risk behavior? *Journal of Drug Issues, 25*(1), 1–10.

Lukas, S. E. (1997). *Proceedings of the national consensus meeting on the use, abuse, and sequelae of abuse of methamphetamine with implications for prevention, treatment and research* (DHHS Publication No. SMA 96-8013, pp. 1–37). Washington, DC: U.S. Government Printing Office.

Lysaker, P., Bell, M., Beam-Goulet, J., & Milstein, R. (1994). Relationship of positive and negative symptoms to cocaine abuse in schizophrenia. *Journal of Nervous and Mental Disease, 182*(2), 109–122.

Magura, S., Siddiqi, Q., Freeman, R., & Lipton, L. (1991). Changes in cocaine use after entry to methadone treatment. *Journal of Addictive Disorders, 4,* 31–35.

Marlowe, D., Husband, S., Lamb, R., & Kirby, K. (1995). Psychiatric co-morbidity in cocaine dependence: Diverging trends, Axis II spectrum, and gender differentials. *American Journal on Addictions, 4*(1), 70–81.

Martino, S., McCance-Katz, E., Workman, J., & Boozang, J. (1995). The development of a dual diagnosis partial hospital program. *Continuum, 2,* 145–165.

McCance, E., Price, L., Kosten, T., & Jatlow, P. (1995) Cocaethylene: pharmacology, physiology and behavioral effects in humans. *Journal of Pharmacology and Experimental Therapeutics, 266,* 1364–1373.

McCarron, M. M., & Wood, J. D. (1983). The cocaine "body packer" syndrome: diagnosis and treatment. *Journal of the American Medical Association, 250,* 1417–1420.

McCoy, V., & Inciardi, J. (1993). Women and AIDS: Social determinants of sex-related activities. *Women and Health, 20*(1), 69–86.

Miller, M. A. (1991) Trends and patterns of methamphetamine smoking in Hawaii. In M. A. Miller & N. J. Kozel (Eds.), *Methamphetamine abuse: Epidemiologic issues and implications* (NIDA Research Monograph No. 115, DHHS Publication No. ADM 91-1836, pp. 72–83). Washington, DC: U.S. Government Printing Office.

Miller, W., & Rollnick, S. (1991). *Motivational interviewing: Preparing people to change addictive behavior.* New York: Guilford Press.

Miner, L. L., & Marley, R. J. (1995). Chromosomal mapping of the psychomotor stimulant effects of cocaine in BXD recombinant inbred mice. *Psychopharmacology, 122,* 209–214.

Mirin, S. M., Weiss, R. D., Griffin, M. L., & Michael, J. L. (1991). Psychopathology in drug abusers and their families. *Comprehensive Psychiatry, 32,* 36–51.

Moore, T., Sorg, J., Miller, L., Key, T., & Resnik, R. (1986). Hemodynamic effects of intravenous cocaine on the pregnant ewe and fetus. *American Journal of Obstetrics and Gynecology, 155,* 838–888.

Moos, R. H., Mertens, J. R., & Brennan, P. L. (1994). Rates and predictors of four-year readmission among late, middle-aged, and old substance abuse patients. *Journal of Studies on Alcohol, 55,* 561–570.

Moos, R. H., & Moos, B. S. (1995). Stay in residential facilities and mental health care as predictors of readmission for with patients with substance use disorders. *Psychiatric Services, 46,* 66–72.

Nademanee, K., Gorelick, D., Josephson, M., Ryan, M., Wildins, J., Robertson, H., Mody, F. V., & Intarachot, V. (1989) Myocardial ischemia during cocaine withdrawal. *Annals of Internal Medicine, 111,* 876–880.

National Institute on Drug Abuse. (1997a). Drug Abuse Warning Network (DAWN) [Data file]. Rockville, MD: Author.

National Institute on Drug Abuse. (NIDA). (1997b). National Household Survey [Data file]. Rockville, MD: Author.

Newman, N. M., Diloreto, P. A., Ho, J. T., Klein J. C., & Birnbaum, N. S. (1988). Bilateral optic neuropathy and osteolytic sinusitis. *Journal of the American Medical Association, 259,* 72–74.

New York State Division of Substance Abuse Services. (1990). [Data file]. Albany, NY: Author.

O'Brien, C., Childress, A., Arndt, I., & McLellan, T. (1988). Pharmacologic and behavioral treatments of cocaine dependence: Controlled studies. *Journal of Clinical Psychiatry, 49*(Suppl.), 17–22.

O'Brien, C., Childress, A., McLellan, T., & Ehrman, R. (1990). Integrating systematic cue exposure with standard treatment in recovering drug dependent patients. *Addictive Behavior, 15*(4), 355–365.

Office of the Inspector General, Office of Evaluation and Inspections, & Department of Health and Human Services. (1990). *Crack babies.* Washington, DC: U.S. Government Printing Office.

Pettit, H., & Justice, J. Jr. (1989). Dopamine in the mucleus accumbens during cocaine self-administration as studied by in vivo microdialysis. *Pharmacology, Biochemistry and Behavior, 34,* 899–904.

Pristach, C. A., & Smith, C. M. (1990). Medication compliance and substance abuse among schizophrenic patients. *Hospital and Community Psychiatry, 41*(12), 1345–1348.

Prochaska, J., DiClemente, C., & Norcross, J. (1992). In search of how people change: Applications to addictive behavior. *American Psychologist, 47*(9), 1102–1114.

Pulvirenti, L., Maldonado-Lopez, R., & Koob, G. F. (1992). MNDA receptors in the nucleus accumbens modulate intravenous cocaine but not heroin self-administration in the rat. *Brain Research, 594,* 327–330.

Richardson, G., & Day, N. (1994). Detrimental effects of prenatal cocaine exposure: Illusion or Reality. *Journal of the American Academy of Child and Adolescent Psychiatry, 33*(1), 28–34.

Ritz, M. C., Cone, E. J., & Kuhar, M. J. (1990). Cocaine inhibition of ligand binding at dopamine, norepinephrine and serotonin transporters: A structure-activity study. *Life Sciences, 28,* 755–760.

Rosen, M., & Kosten, T. (1992). Cocaine-associated panic attacks in methadone maintained patients. *American Journal of Drug and Alcohol Abuse, 18*(1), 57–62.

Rosenthal, R., Hellerstein, D., Miner, C., & Christian R. (1994). Positive and negative syndrome typology in schizophrenic patients with psychoactive substance use disorders. *Comprehensive Psychiatry, 35*(2), 91–98.

Roth, D., Alarcon, F. J., Fernandez, J. A., Preston, R. A., & Bourgoignie, J. J. (1988). Acute rhabdomyolysis associated with cocaine intoxication. *New England Journal of Medicine, 319,* 673–677.

Rounsaville, B., Anton, S., Carroll, K., Budde, D., Prusoff, B., & Gawin, F. (1991). Psychiatric diagnoses of treatment-seeking cocaine abusers. *Archives of General Psychiatry, 48*(1), 43–51.

Satel, S. L., & Gawin, F. H. (1989). Migraine-like headache and cocaine use. *Journal of the American Medical Association, 261,* 2995–2996.

Schechter, M. (1994). Cocaethylene produces discriminative stimulus properties in the rat: Effect of cocaine and ethanol coadministration. *Pharmacology, Biochemistry and Behavior, 51,* 285–289.

Schrank, K. S. (1993). Cocaine-related emergency department presentations. In H. Sorer (Ed.), *Acute cocaine intoxication: Current methods of treatment* (NIDA Research Monograph No. 123, NIH Publication No. 93-3498, pp. 110–128). Washington, DC: U.S. Government Printing Office.

Schuckit, M. A. (1985). The clinical implications of primary diagnostic groups among alcoholics. *Archives of General Psychiatry, 42,* 1043–1049.

Schuster, C. L., Yu, G., & Bates, A. (1977). Sensitization to cocaine stimulation in mice. *Psychopharmacology, 52,* 185–190.

Seibyl, J., Satel, S., Anthoy, D., & Southwick, S. (1993). Effects of cocaine on hospital course in schizophrenia. *Journal of Nervous and Mental Disease, 181*(1), 31–37.

Seiden, L. S. (1991). Neurotoxicity of methamphetamine: Mechanisms of action and issues related to aging. In M. A. Miller & N. J. Kozel (Eds.), *Methamphetamine abuse: Epidemiologic issues and implications* (NIDA Research Monograph No. 115, DHHS Publication No. ADM 91-1836, pp. 24–32). Washington, DC: U.S. Government Printing Office.

Seiden, L. S., & Sabol, K. E. (1996). Methamphetamine and methylenedioxymethamphetamine neurotoxicity: Possible mechanisms of cell destruction. In M. D. Majewska (Ed.), *Neurotoxicity and neuropathology associated with cocaine abuse* (NIDA Research Monograph No. 163, NIH Publication No. 96-4019, pp. 251–276). Washington, DC: U.S. Government Printing Office.

Seifen, E., Plunkett, L. M., & Kennedy, R. H. (1989). Cardiovascular and lethal effects of cocaine in anesthetized dogs and guinea pigs. *Archives of Internal Pharmacodynamics, 300,* 241–253.

Self, D. W., Barnhart, W. J., Lehman, D. A., & Nestler, E. J. (1996) Opposite modulation of cocaine-seeking behavior by D1 and D2-like dopamine receptor agonists. *Science, 271,* 1586–1589.

Serper, M., Alpert, M., Richardson, N., & Dickson, S. (1995). Clinical effects of recent cocaine use on patients with acute schizophrenia. *American Journal of Psychiatry, 152*(10), 1464–1469.

Silverman, K., Higgins, S., Brooner, R., Montoya, I., Cone, E., Schuster, C., & Preston, K. (1996). Sustained cocaine abstinence in methadone maintenance patients through voucher-based reinforcement therapy. *Archives of General Psychiatry, 53,* 409–415.

Silverman, S. (1989). Scope, specifics of maternal drug use, effects on fetus are beginning to emerge from studies. *Journal of the American Medical Association, 261,* 1688–1689.

Spangler, R., Unterwald, E. M., & Kreek, M. J. (1993). "Binge" cocaine administration induces a sustained increase of prodynorphin mRNA in rat caudate-putamen. *Molecular Brain Research, 19*(4), 323–327.

Suwaki, H. (1991). Methamphetamine abuse in Japan. In M. A. Miller & N. J. Kozel (Eds.), *Methamphetamine abuse: Epidemiologic issues and implications* (NIDA Research Monograph No. 115, DHHS Publication No. ADM 91-1836, pp. 84–98). Washington, DC: U.S. Government Printing Office.

Tames, S. M., & Goldenring, J. M. (1986). Madarosis from cocaine use. *New England Journal of Medicine, 314,* 1324.

Texter, E. C., Chou, C. C., Merrill, S. L., Laureton, H. C., & Frohlich, E. D. (1964). Direct effects of vasoactive agents on segmental resistance of the mesenteric and portal circulation: Studies with l-epinephrine, levarterenol, angiotensin, vasopressin, acetylcholine, methacholine, histamine, and serotonin. *Journal of Laboratory and Clinical Medicine, 64,* 624–633.

Tsuang, M. T., Lyons, M. J., Eisen, S. A., Goldberg, J., True, W., Meyer, J. M., & Eaves, L. J. (1996). Genetic influences on abuse of illicit drugs: a study of 3,297 twin pairs. *American Journal of Medical Genetics, 67,* 473–477.

Unterwald, E. M., Rubenfeld, J. M., & Kreek, M. J. (1994) Repeated cocaine administration upregulates kappa and mu, but not sigma opioid receptors. *Neuroreport, 5*(13), 1613–1616.

Volkow, N. D., Fowler, J. S., & Ding, Y-S. (1996). Cardiotoxic properties of cocaine: studies with positron emission tomography. In M. D. Majewska (Ed.), *Neurotoxicity and neuropathology associated with cocaine abuse* (NIDA Research Monograph 163, NIH Publication No. 96-4019, pp. 159–174.). Washington, DC: U.S. Government Printing Office.

Volpe, J. (1992). Effect of cocaine use on the fetus. *New England Journal of Medicine, 327,* 399–407.

Washton, A. M., Stone, N. S., & Hendrickson, E. C. (1988). Cocaine abuse. In D. M. Donovan & G. A. Marlatt (Eds.), *Assessment of addictive behaviors* (pp. 364–389). New York: Guilford Press.

Weiss, R., Mirin, S., Griffin, M., & Gunderson, J. (1993). Personality disorders in cocaine dependence. *Comprehensive Psychiatry, 34*(3), 145–149.

Weiss, R. D., Pope, H., & Mirin, S. (1985). Treatment of chronic cocaine abuse and attention-deficit disorder, residual type, with magnesium pemoline. *Drug and Alcohol Dependence, 15*(1–2), 69–72.

Wetti, C. V., Weiss, S. D., Cleary, T. J., & Gyori, E. (1984). Fungal cerebritis from intravenous drug use. *Journal of Forensic Science, 29,* 260–268.

Woods, N., Eyler, F., Behnke, M., & Conlon, M. (1993). Cocaine use during pregnancy: Maternal depressive symptoms and infant neurobehavior over the first month. *Infant Behavior and Development, 16,* 83–98.

Xu, Y. Q., Crumb, W. J., Jr., & Clarkson, C. W. (1994). Cocaethylene, a metabolite of cocaine and ethanol, is a potent blocker of cardiac sodium channels. *Journal of Pharmacology and Experimental Therapeutics, 271*(1), 319–325.

Ziedonis, D., & Fischer, W. (1996). Motivation-based assessment and treatment of substance abuse in patients with schizophrenia. *Directions in Psychiatry, 16,* 1–7.

Ziedonis, D., Rayford, B., Bryant, B., Kendall, J., & Rounsaville, B. (1994). Psychiatric comorbidity in white and African-American cocaine addicts seeking substance abuse treatment. *Hospital and Community Psychiatry, 45*(1), 43–49.

9

Hallucinogens, Phencyclidine, Marijuana, Inhalants

CAROL J. WEISS
ROBERT B. MILLMAN

HALLUCINOGENS

The term "hallucinogens" describes a group of naturally occurring and synthetic drugs that alter consciousness or produce changes in thought, mood, and perception. "Hallucinogen" is not an accurate term, however, as the drugs in this group rarely produce true hallucinations. Rather, pseudohallucinations or perceptual distortions are more common.

The major effects of hallucinogens—their mind-altering and perceived mystical/transcendent effects—inspired the term "psychedelic" (mind manifesting, mind revealing) for this class of drugs, as well as other less popular names including "psychodysleptic" (mind disrupting), "psycholytic" (mind loosening), and "mysticomimetic" (Grinspoon & Bakalar, 1986; Hollister, 1984). Current terms for this class of drugs are "entheogen" (the divine within) (Gehr, 1996; Lucas, 1995) and "enactogen" (touch within) (Nichols, 1986). "Psychotomimetic" is also a term sometimes applied to this drug class, though it too is not adequate: It describes an inconsistent effect that may also occur with use of many licit and illicit drugs other than hallucinogens, such as stimulants and steroids.

Classification

The hallucinogens are primarily derivatives of indoles or phenylalkylamines, though other drugs may also be classified as part of this group, such as phencyclidine (PCP) and ketamine (see the section on "Phencyclidine").

There are about a dozen natural hallucinogens and over 100 synthetic ones (Grinspoon & Bakalar, 1986). The drugs in this class that are most abused in Western society are as follows (this summary draws on the reviews of Climko, Roehrich, Sweeney, & Al-Razi, 1986–1987; Cohen, 1989; Ungerleider & Pechnick, 1992):

Indolealkylamine derivatives

1. D-Lysergic acid diethylamide (LSD; "acid"). Synthesized from ergot (*Claviceps purpurea*), a fungus, and chemically related to certain alkaloids found in morning glory seeds. First synthesized in 1938.
2. Psilocybin (dimethyl-4-phosphoryltryptamine; "magic mushrooms"). Found in *Psilocybe mexicana* and over 100 related species of mushrooms.
3. DMT (dimethyltryptamine). Found in cohaba snuff from the seeds of *Piptadenia peregrina,* but made synthetically for street sales.
4. Harmine, harmaline, and ibogaine. Naturally occurring, rarely used in Western societies.

Phenylalkylamine derivatives

1. Mescaline (3,4,5-trimethoxyphenylethylamine). Found in the buttons of the peyote cactus (*Lophophora Williamsii*). Available legally in the United States as part of Native American religious ceremonies.
2. Ring-substituted amphetamines
   a. 3,4-Methylenedioxyamphetamine (MDA). Known as Ecstasy before MDMA became popular; differs from it by one methyl group. First synthesized in 1910. Widely used in the United States between 1960 and 1973. Classified as a Schedule I drug in 1973.
   b. 3,4-Methylenedioxymethamphetamine (MDMA), also known as Ecstasy, X, XTC, MDM, and Adam. First synthesized in 1914. Classified as a Schedule I drug in 1985.
   c. 3,4-Methylenedioxyethamphetamine (MDE or MDEA), also called Eve. A weaker version of MDMA, classified as a Schedule 1 drug, and not widely used.
   d. 2,5-Dimethoxy-4-methylamphetamine (DOM, STP).

Other

1. Salvinorin A (also known as divinorin A). A neoclerodane diterpene isolated from the plant *Salvia divinorum,* a vision-inducing mint used by the Mazatec people of Oaxaca, Mexico. It is a legal hallucinogen grown in California and other parts of the United States (Valdes, 1994).

MDA, MDMA, and MDEA are considered "designer drugs" (i.e., new chemical analogues or variations of existing controlled substances that have high potential for abuse). These drugs are outlawed by the Controlled

Substances Analog Act ("designer drug" bill). Other designer drugs include fentanyl and meperidine analogues.

History

Ritual and recreational use of naturally occurring hallucinogens goes back to antiquity (Siegel, 1984). Mescaline is still used in certain Native American rituals. The modern age of synthetic hallucinogens began with the first "trip" taken in 1943 by Albert Hoffman when he accidentally ingested the LSD he had created 5 years earlier (Ungerleider & Pechnick, 1992).

Fascination with hallucinogens was a prominent feature of the social, cultural, and sexual revolution of the 1960s. "Psychedelic" art, language, music, and clothing suffused the culture; all were referential to the hallucinogen experience. Though this experience could be hedonic and sensory, it was also perceived by many to be meaningful and enlightening.

Hallucinogens, particularly LSD, psilocybin, and mescaline, were investigated as a possible adjunct to psychotherapy. By the time LSD became illegal in the mid-1960s, more than 1,000 articles on its use had appeared in the medical literature (Ungerleider & Pechnick, 1992). By virtue of the drug's unpredictability and the poorly controlled studies done, it was not shown to be helpful for the many conditions for which it was tried. In the early 1970s, MDMA began to replace LSD as the psychotherapy adjunct that might promote insight and therapeutic communication (Greer & Strassman, 1985). Though many psychotherapists were dismayed by the Drug Enforcement Agency's emergency classification of MDMA into Schedule I in 1985, little exists in the medical literature supporting its actual therapeutic value. At the same time, some workers believe that if better research could be done, appropriate indications for the use of these substances might be found (Strassman, 1995; Szara, 1994; Riedlinger & Riedlinger, 1994).

A significant resurgence of hallucinogens occurred in the late 1980s, especially in the context of clubs and "raves"—all-night dance parties that originated in England (Millman & Beeder, 1994; Beck & Rosenbaum, 1994).

Epidemiology

Use of hallucinogens peaked during the era of a media-popularized counterculture in the late 1960s and early 1970s, in association with remarkable increases in the use of marijuana and other drugs. It has been estimated that at least one-third of college students experimented with it in the 1969–1972 period. In the 1980s, the numbers dropped and then rose again in the 1990s.

It should be noted, however, that most epidemiological studies of drug abuse are limited. Many surveys are conducted in treatment or academic facilities; the significant number of drug users in disenfranchised, illiterate, and homeless populations are not represented. Many people may use them rarely on special occasions and do not develop adverse sequelae. Also, responses to self-report surveys are often colored by what the respondent believes is an acceptable response. Moreover, given the prevalence of polysubstance abuse, the variable quality of drugs, the uncertain composition of street drugs, and confusion resulting from intoxication, many drug users themselves do not truly know what they use, how much, and how often. Interestingly, many hallucinogen users of the 1960s were "purists" and did not use other classes of drugs, whereas contemporary users tend to use a variety of drugs.

According to the National Annual High School Senior and Young Adult Survey, in 1996, the annual prevalence of hallucinogens among 50,000 students in the 8th, 10th, and 12th grades continued to rise as it had been doing since 1991 (Johnston, O'Malley, & Bachman, 1997). Lifetime prevalence of LSD use among 12th-graders was 12.6% in 1996, up from 7.2% in 1986 and 11.3% in 1975. Lifetime prevalence of all hallucinogens among 12th-graders was 14% in 1996, up from 9.7% in 1986, but not as high as the 16.3% of 1975. Lifetime prevalence of hallucinogen use among 10th- and 8th-graders was 10.5% and 5.9%, respectively. Lifetime prevalence of MDMA use among 12th-, 10th-, and 8th-graders was 6.1%, 5.6%, and 3.4%, respectively.

Pharmacology

LSD is the most potent of the hallucinogens, with effects recorded after 20 to 30 micrograms; most of the agonist effects of the other hallucinogens are similar to that of LSD. The usual street dose of LSD ranges from 10 to 300 micrograms. It is 4,000 to 6,000 times more potent than mescaline and 100 to 200 times more potent than psilocybin (Halikas, Weller, & Morse, 1982). LSD is usually ingested in the form of impregnated paper or sugar cubes, capsules, and tablets. Intravenous use is rare (Millman, 1982).

The physiological effects of LSD and mescaline are seen within 20 minutes after ingestion; the psychoactive effects within 2 to 4 hours. LSD effects may last 6 to 24 hours; mescaline effects may last 6 to 10 hours, and psilocybin effects 2 to 6 hours. DOM effects last more than 24 hours. DMT—the "businessman's LSD" for its rapid onset (15 to 30 minutes) and short duration of action (60 to 120 minutes)—has a mothball aroma. DMT must be injected, sniffed, or smoked.

The usual dose of MDMA is 75 to 150 mg. It is commonly available on the street in 100-mg gelatin capsules or loose powder. It is occasionally insufflated (sniffed) and rarely injected by intramuscular or subcutaneous route. It has a rapid onset, usually within 30 minutes, and its duration of action is 4 to 8 hours. The leaves of *Salvia divinorum* can be chewed or dried and smoked. The latter form is extremely potent, effective in doses of 200 to 500 micrograms. It is the most potent naturally occurring hallucinogen (Valdes, 1994).

Most hallucinogens produce central sympathomimetic stimulation: mydriasis, hyperthermia, tachycardia, palpitations, and slightly elevated blood pressure. Piloerection, blurring of vision, flushed face, diaphoresis, quickened reflexes, tremors, incoordination, and increased alertness may also be present.

Delirium and sedation are rare. Peyote characteristically causes dramatic nausea and emesis.

Tolerance to the euphoric and psychedelic effects develops and is lost rapidly. LSD, mescaline, and psilocybin are cross-tolerant. Little tolerance develops to the autonomic effects. True craving and physiological dependence do not occur. There is no hallucinogen withdrawal syndrome or need for detoxification. There is no known pharmacologically lethal dose of LSD. Cases have been reported of people surviving 10,000 mg of LSD (Cohen, 1982).

Pattern of Use and Abuse

Hallucinogens are generally used intermittently by youthful people to punctuate an occasion such as a concert or party. Some adolescents take the drug more regularly, sometimes every day, though this pattern usually lasts only for short periods. When used in this way, the hallucinogen's effects are decreased because of the advent of tolerance. In the language of the fourth edition of the *Diagnostic and Statistical Manual of Mental Disorders* (DSM-IV; American Psychiatric Association, 1994), the diagnostic classification system developed by the American Psychiatric Association, the main distinction between Hallucinogen Dependence and Abuse is frequency of use.

Effects*

Varied and often quite poetic descriptions have been used to convey the psychological aspects of the hallucinogen experience. The experience varies remarkably from person to person and in the same person under different conditions (Zinberg, 1984). Usually perceptions are heightened and may become overwhelming. Afterimages are prolonged and overlap with ongoing perceptions. Objects may seem to move in a wavelike fashion or to melt. Overflow of one sense modality to another are common. There may be a sense of unusual clarity, and one's thoughts may assume unusual importance. Time may seem to pass slowly. Illusions and body distortions are commonly perceived. True hallucinations with loss of insight may occur in susceptible individuals. Mood is highly variable and labile and may range from euphoria and self-confidence to depression and panic (Millman, 1982).

The ring-substituted amphetamines have different and varying properties. MDA is mildly hallucinogenic and has been described as producing "a warm glow," increased esthetic sense, increased spirituality and sense of "oneness," and heightened tactile sensation. It has also been described as producing increased desire for interpersonal contact, increased sense of well-being, increased insight, heightened self-awareness, and diminished anxiety and defensiveness (Climko et al., 1986–1987). MDMA has minimal hallucinogenic properties. It appears to produce fewer perceptual phenomena, less emotional lability, less

---

*For a presentation of effects and treatment, see Table 9.1 on pages 208–209.

depersonalization, and fewer disturbances of thought than do other hallucinogens. Its popularity is attributed mostly to such effects as positive mood changes, enhanced communication and intimacy, improved interpersonal relationships, and increased self-esteem. Though MDMA has been called a sex drug, a survey of 76 users in San Francisco did not confirm any actual aphrodisiacal properties; in fact, decreased ability to reach orgasm or ejaculation was reported by 70% of males surveyed (Buffum, & Moser, 1986).

Adverse Psychological Effects

Adverse psychological effects are classified as acute or chronic. The main acute adverse reaction is the "bad trip." This a general term used to describe an acute anxiety/panic reaction, dysphoric reaction, or paranoid state. These are a result of a combination of factors, including the user's psychological state before using, the environment in which the drug is being used, the quality of the drug, and the nature of the user's drug-induced distorted perceptions. The reactions vary in intensity and on rare occasions lead to suicide attempts and accidents.

Chronic adverse effects include a prolonged psychotic state resembling schizophrenia or mania (Bowers, 1977; Lake, Stirba, Kinneman, Carlson, & Holloway, 1981), depression, chronic anxiety state, and chronic personality changes, sometimes with persistent evidence of magical thinking. Some users continue to experience, for months to years, mild perceptual changes such as intensified colors and sounds or trails of images from moving objects. These symptoms are often experienced within a context of otherwise normal functioning.

Sequelae that last more than 4 to 6 weeks often suggest the likelihood of a premorbid vulnerability to psychiatric illness uncovered or exposed by the drug experience. One wonders whether the person would have developed the chronic state if he or she had never used the drug. Did the drug open the gate, or kindle certain neurotransmitters, that led to psychosis or schizoid personality? And once the gate was opened, could it not be closed? In one 2- to 6-year follow-up study of hallucinogen-induced prolonged psychotic reactions, half of the 15 patients had poor outcome, including 2 who committed suicide (Bowers, 1977).

"Flashbacks" are recurrences of the drug-induced state that may appear days to years after the drug exposure. They can be pleasurable or distressing, depending on their content and the context in which they occur. They are usually brief and spontaneous, though stress, fatigue, and certain drugs such as marijuana may precipitate them (Cohen, 1989). Flashbacks have been divided into three categories: perceptual, somatic, and emotional. Perceptual flashbacks are the most common; they are most often visual, although any sensory modality may be affected. Somatic flashbacks can consist of feelings of depersonalization, and emotional flashbacks often consist of distressing emotions originally associated with the acute LSD reaction (Shick & Smith, 1970).

TABLE 9.1. Hallucinogens, Arylcyclohexylamine, Cannabinoids, and Inhalants: Effects and Treatment

	Hallucinogens	Arylcyclohexylamine	Cannabinoids	Inhalants
Included in drug class	LSD, mushrooms (psilocybin), peyote (mescaline), MDMA (Ecstasy)	Phencyclidine (PCP), ketamine ("Special K")	Marijuana, hashish	Amyl nitrite (poppers), butyl nitrite, toluene (glue, paint thinner), nitrous oxide (whippets)
Intoxication: physiological	Dilated pupils; increased pulse, blood pressure, temperature, and reflexes; piloerection, tremor, nausea (peyote)	Increased reflexes, temperature, pulse, and blood pressure; constricted pupils, diaphoresis, ataxia, incoordination, nystagmus, numbness	Increased pulse, injected conjunctivae, dry mouth, increased appetite	Lightheadedness, dizziness, headache, blurred vision, dysarthria, nystagmus, tremor, paresthesia, ataxia, incoordination, muscle weakness, decreased reflexes
Intoxication: behavioral	Dream-like feelings, perceptual distortions, altered time sense, depersonalization, intensified and labile moods, delusions	Euphoric, floating feeling, perceptual disturbance, disinhibition, confusion, disorientation, schizophrenia-like psychotic state, severe anxiety, panic, rage, aggression, violence, agitation and/or catatonia	Euphoria, hilarity, enhanced sensory awareness, distorted sense of time and perception, slowed reaction time, anxiety, paranoia, panic	Disinhibition, euphoric rush, giddiness, disorientation, hallucinations, confusion, agitation, irritability
Acute toxic effects/overdose	Acute anxiety/panic reaction ("bad trip"); delirium and overdose rare except with MDMA; hyperthermia, cerebral infarct, and death seen with MDMA	Dramatic hypertension, muscular rigidity, seizure, increased secretions, profuse sweating, delirium, coma; cardiac, respiratory, and renal failure	Anxiety, paranoia, panic; delirium rare; no reported overdose	Delirium, seizure, arrhythmia, coma, anoxia

Withdrawal: physiological	No physiological withdrawal	Physiological withdrawal not demonstrated	No physiological withdrawal; may see tremor and chills	No physiological withdrawal; may see tremor, diaphoresis, nausea
Withdrawal: behavioral			May see anxiety, irritability, insomnia, and decreased appetite	May see sleep disturbance, irritability, fleeting illusions
Detoxification: physiological	No specific medical detoxification; sedatives useful for management of agitation or anxiety; use of neuroleptics controversial; dantrolene or cooling blanket for hyperthermia	No specific medical detoxification; benzodiazepines and/or neuroleptics with low anticholinergic properties may be used for agitation; for overdose: gastric lavage, acidify urine, support vital functions, body cooling, dantrolene	No specific medical detoxification; sedatives and clonidine may be helpful; neuroleptics usually not necessary	No specific medical detoxification
Detoxification: behavioral	"Talking down" helpful	Low-stimulation environment	"Talking down"	
Nonpharmacological treatments	Self-help groups, inpatient or outpatient rehabilitation, multimodal therapies including individual, behavioral, group, and family therapy; acupuncture	Same as hallucinogens	Same as hallucinogens	Same as hallucinogens

Shared paranoid disorder—as seen with Charles Manson and his "family"—has been described in connection with the use of hallucinogens (Cohen, 1989). However, this phenomenon is usually complicated by factors other than drugs, including the presence of psychiatric illness in the group, isolation, or the power of a charismatic leader and group forces.

Medical Consequences

Despite numerous articles and great concern in the late 1960s that LSD might cause chromosomal damage, there are no convincing data showing that LSD is a mutagen. Any mutagenic effects shown were more likely to be due to the lifestyle of the user or to impurities (Cohen, 1989).

Most hallucinogens act as 5-HT^2 agonists. Neurotoxic effects of MDMA have been demonstrated in rats and monkeys but not yet in humans. To date, studies are suggestive of neurotoxic effects in humans (Fischer, Hatzidimitrou, Wlos, Katz, & Ricaurte, 1995; Ungerleider & Pechnick, 1992).

The ring-substituted amphetamines (MDMA, MDA, DOM, etc.) may produce amphetamine-like stimulant effects such as hyperthermia, rhabdomyolysis, severe hyponatremia, and cerebral infarction ("Acute Reaction to Drugs of Abuse," 1996).

Deaths have been reported among users of MDMA, especially at "raves." It is felt that the combination of direct toxicity, strenuous physical exertion, and dehydration contribute to the risk of death (Green, Cross, & Goodwin, 1995). Often, other drugs are also involved.

Treatment

Treatment of the acute medical reactions include decreasing body temperature and possible use of dantrolene and sedatives (Green et al., 1995). Treatment of the acute psychological reaction should be directed toward relieving patients' overwhelming anxiety and protecting them from harm. The person should be placed in a calm environment with someone present to provide reassurance by "talking down." He or she should be told that the present state is due to the drug and will soon pass. Patient should be frequently oriented and discouraged from closing their eyes, as this may worsen the symptoms. Restraints should be avoided, though they may be necessary if agitation becomes too severe. The preferred medication is a benzodiazepine, such as lorazepam or diazepam. Chlorpromazine or haloperidol may be necessary if there is no response to the benzodiazepine, though, in this context, adverse reactions have been seen in response to the neuroleptics, such as seizures and neuroleptic malignant syndrome.

Treatment is often complicated by use of other psychoactive drugs or a toxic reaction to an adulterant. In these instances, too, benzodiazepines are preferred over neuroleptics as the first treatment choice. The presence of a clear sensorium can help differentiate an acute hallucinogen reaction from a toxic reaction; a clouded sensorium or delirium is more common in the latter condition.

Chronic states should be treated with the modality appropriate for that disorder. Neuroleptics, antidepressants, benzodiazepines, psychotherapy, and/or behavioral interventions should be used when indicated. Serotonergic agents have been suggested for persistent perceptual disorders, though these data are based on anecdotal reports.

Few patients use hallucinogens compulsively or require traditional chemical dependency rehabilitation for their hallucinogen use. This may be indicated, however, if other drugs are also being abused. Some young people use these drugs as self-medication of severe premorbid psychopathology; they are attempting to distance themselves from their functional psychopathology with the hallucinogen.

Cultural biases in diagnosing mental illness may arise when one is evaluating a hallucinogen user. Today, one might diagnose a hallucinogen user who extols the magical and mystical states induced by frequent hallucinogen use as a schizotypal personality or worse. Twenty years ago, the same patient might have been perceived as a normal college student or professor seeking deeper meaning.

PHENCYCLIDINE

PCP is an inexpensive, easily available, widely abused drug that alters perception and affect. It has been associated with violence, psychosis, and delirium, although it shares some properties with LSD and other hallucinogens, it is sufficiently different to be considered as a separate entity.

Classification

PCP (1-[1-phenylcyclohexyl] piperidine monohydrochloride) and related aryl-cyclohexylamines are classified as dissociative or cataleptoid anesthetics. PCP is classified as a Schedule II drug along with morphine and amphetamines. It has approximately 30 chemical analogues, several of which have appeared on the illicit market (Grinspoon & Bakalar, 1986). These include PCE (N-ethyl-1-phencyclohexalamine), TCP (1-[1-2-thienyl-cyclohexyl] piperidine), PHP (1-[1-phencyclohexyl] pyrrolidine), PCC (1-piperidinocyclohexane carbonitrile), and ketamine (2-2-[chlorophenyl]-2-[methylamino]-cyclohexanone).

On the street, PCP has many names, including "angel dust," "mist," "THC," "PeaCePill," "Shermans," "tranq," "HOG," and "whack" (Schuckit, 1985). A general rule of thumb is that a new drug with a strange name that profoundly alters perception in a bizarre way is likely to be PCP unless proven otherwise (Luisada, 1981). Because it is so inexpensive, PCP has been used to adulterate or enhance other drugs, such as LSD, cannabis, and cocaine.

Ketamine is often called "Special K," "K," and "Vitamin K," and is often confused with MDMA ("Ecstasy") by users.

History

PCP was developed in the late 1950s as an anesthetic agent. It was found to have a calming and sedating effect on nonhuman primates. When used in humans, it had the advantage of inducing anesthesia through a dissociative state without significant depression of vital signs. However, as patients emerged from anesthesia, some became agitated, bizarre, psychotic, or delirious. These were called emergent reactions. PCP was quickly removed from the market as a human anesthetic but became valuable as a research drug that could induce psychosis. Numerous studies of the drug's psychotomimetic effects in humans were published prior to 1965, when PCP was withdrawn from human experimentation. PCP is now used legally only as a veterinary tranquilizer under the trade name Sernylan. Most of the drug that is available for street use has been produced in illicit laboratories.

Ketamine was synthesized in 1962 and has been easily available by prescription since 1969 as a veterinary, surgical, and pediatric anesthetic. Most abused ketamine is purchased from wholesale veterinary drug suppliers. It has anesthetic effects similar to PCP and has become increasingly popular in the 1990s among the homosexual population and young club-goers. It is often used in the same context as MDMA (Ecstasy).

PCP first appeared as a drug of abuse in the mid-1960s in San Francisco and New York City. It was ingested in the form of a pill called the PeaCePill, but it did not become a widely abused drug because of a high incidence of adverse reactions (Smith, Wesson, Buxton, Seymour, & Kramer, 1978).

A few years later, PCP emerged as a white powder or solution that could be insufflated or ingested or combined with parsley, tobacco, or marijuana leaves that would be suitable for smoking. The smokable form became particularly popular because it offered a rapid onset and short duration of psychoactive effects. It was also easily synthesized in illicit laboratories, so that it was inexpensive and widely available. The current popularity of "crack" use owes much to similar factors.

Epidemiology

PCP is used primarily by young adults, adolescents, and even young children, most of whom also abuse other substances, particularly marijuana and alcohol. The prevalence of PCP-related problems appears to be higher among males (about twofold), among those between ages 20 and 40 years, and among ethnic minorities (about twofold). Males comprise about three-quarters of those with PCP-related emergency-room visits (American Psychiatric Association, 1994). PCP abuse has tended to be a regional phenomenon; it has been a much greater problem in Los Angeles and Washington, DC, than in New York City, and in inner-city minority groups rather than the middle class.

According to the Annual National High School Senior and Young Adult Survey, PCP use has increased since 1988 (Johnston et al., 1997). In 1996,

4% of high school seniors had ever used PCP, up from 2.9% in 1988, but down from 12.8 in 1979; 2.6% had used in the past year, up from 1.2% in 1988, but down from 7% in 1979; 1.3% had used in the past month, up from 0.3% in 1988, and down from 2.4% in 1979.

Unfortunately, there are no reported studies of ketamine use, though its increasing incidence is clinically evident and supported by information available from the Internet (ketamine.info@www.lycaeum.org).

Pharmacology

PCP is usually smoked, though it can also be insufflated in powder form or ingested in pill or liquid form. Intravenous or intramuscular use is rare. There is great variation in the amount of PCP per cigarette or capsule, ranging from 2 to 25 mg (Grinspoon & Bakalar, 1986; Schuckit, 1985). Incoordination, a euphoric floating feeling, and heightened emotionality can be experienced with 1 to 5 mg of PCP and usually lasts hours; 5 to 10 mg can produce an intoxicated state marked by numbness of extremities and perceptual illusions (Schuckit, 1985). Experienced users report that the effects of 2 to 3 mg of smoked PCP begin within 5 minutes and plateau within 30 minutes. The effects usually last 4 to 6 hours, though it may take 1 to 2 days to recover completely. Toxic effects may persist for significantly longer periods.

PCP is metabolized by the liver, is stored in adipose tissue, and has a long half-life (up to 3 days). Craving has been reported by chronic users. Both tolerance and withdrawal symptoms have been demonstrated in animals but not clearly demonstrated in humans. Anecdotally, many chronic users report tolerance.

It is now known that the PCP receptor is a binding site of the NMDA (N-methyl-D-aspartic acid) channel and PCP is an NMDA channel blocker or antagonist (Zukin & Zukin, 1992).

Ketamine HCl is available as Ketaset (injectable form for veterinary use) in 10-ml bottles of 100 mg/ml. The liquid is ineffective when ingested (usual dose 200 to 400 mg) and is usually injected subcutaneously, intramuscularly (25 to 100 mg), or intravenously (5 to 50 mg). Alternatively, the liquid can be heated leaving a white crystal powder which can be insufflated (100 to 300 mg) or smoked. Onset of effects usually occurs after 4 to 5 minutes and is called a K wave. Effects may last 5 to 75 minutes. A lethal dose is 2 to 3 grams (www.lycaeum.org).

Patterns of Use and Abuse

Individuals with phencyclidine dependence, as defined by DSM-IV, often smoke PCP at least two to three times per day. Individuals who abuse PCP use the substance much less often than those with dependence, though they may repeatedly fail to fulfill major role obligations at school, work, or home because of PCP intoxication.

Effects*

Intoxication

The PCP user is seeking an altered state of consciousness marked by bizarre perceptions. If perceptual disturbances occur with intact reality testing and the absence of a delirium, the state meets criterion for PCP intoxication. If delirium is present, a diagnosis of PCP intoxication delirium or PCP-induced psychotic disorder should be considered. Perceptual distortions may or may not accompany PCP intoxication.

Behavioral changes include confusion, disorientation, and impaired judgment. The user may appear agitated and hyperactive or catatonic and withdrawn or may unpredictably vacillate between these two states. The agitated state is notable for its high incidence of belligerence, assaultiveness, and impulsiveness. The catatonic state is marked by a blank stare, facial grimacing, stereotyped movements, little spontaneous speech, and, at times, waxy flexibility. Speech, when present, is often slurred or perseverative.

Characteristic physiological hallmarks of PCP intoxication include both sympathomimetic and cholinergic effects. Sympathomimetic properties account for increased muscle tone; increased deep tendon reflexes; and moderately increased temperature, pulse, blood pressure, and respiration. Cholinergic effects are increased lacrimation, salivation, diaphoresis, and pupillary constriction. Cerebellar disturbances such as dizziness, ataxia, incoordination, and nystagmus are common. Horizontal nystagmus should be present; vertical nystagmus may be absent at lower doses. Nystagmus may persist for 48 hours after cessation of drug use (Luisada, 1981). Anesthetic effects include numbness or diminished responsiveness to pain.

Overdose, Poisoning, Toxic Reaction

The primary distinction between intoxication and overdose is level of consciousness and autonomic hyperactivity. Doses greater than 10 mg can produce delirium, catalepsy, mutism, severe sedation, and stupor; greater than 20 mg may produce convulsions and/or coma.

The overdose state is marked by dramatic and persistent hypertension. Hypertensive crisis has been reported to persist for up to 3 days after PCP ingestion. Muscular rigidity and horizontal and vertical nystagmus are invariably present. Increased oral and bronchial secretions and profuse sweating are common. Repetitive purposeless movements may be present. Cardiac, respiratory, and renal failure are life-threatening complications.

The PCP coma can last up to 10 days leaving a residual organic brain syndrome that can last over a month.

In most PCP-related deaths, other drugs are involved. Many PCP-related deaths are due to homicides and accidents.

---

*For a presentation of effects and treatment, see Table 9.1 on pages 208–209.

Organic Brain Syndrome, Delirium

A waxing and waning confusional state, disorientation, and clouded sensorium are characteristic of PCP-induced intoxication, overdose, and psychosis. The organic brain syndrome may occur as an element of the acute effects, though it may last for more than a month after the acute effects have resolved. The presence of an organic brain syndrome often helps to differentiate PCP-related disturbances from hallucinogen effects or functional psychoses.

Psychosis

The most common PCP-induced disorder is a psychotic disorder, though PCP-induced mood disorder and anxiety disorder may also occur. PCP can precipitate a psychotic reaction in normals, though this disorder is more likely in predisposed individuals. The drug may markedly exacerbate a psychotic disorder in schizophrenic patients. PCP psychosis is defined as a schizophreniform psychosis that occurs after PCP use and persists for days or weeks with no additional PCP use. The features that differentiate this disorder from functional schizophrenia, other than a history of recent PCP use, are a higher incidence of violent behavior and clouded sensorium, though these distinctions may not be present. Patients with functional psychosis tend to have poorer premorbid functioning than those admitted with PCP psychosis. Schizophrenic patients admitted with exacerbations due to PCP tend to exhibit more violent and unpredictable behavior during their PCP-related admissions than during admissions not related to PCP. It should be understood that a PCP-precipitated psychotic disorder, if it persists, may be indistinguishable from a functional psychotic reaction (Zukin & Zukin, 1992).

The psychosis has been characterized as having three phases, each lasting from 1 day to more than 1 week, though these have not been well documented (Luisada, 1981). The initial (agitated) phase is characterized by violent, psychotic behavior. During the second (mixed) phase, behavior is more controlled, but patients remain restless and unpredictable. Resolution of psychotic processes occurs in the final (resolution) phase. A clouded sensorium may be present or may remit during any of these phases.

According to one study, one-fourth of the patients treated for PCP psychosis returned to the hospital within a year with a schizophrenic psychosis in the absence of drug use (Luisada, 1981). These patients tended to be the ones with the longest initial PCP-related psychosis.

Treatment

Treatment is aimed at four functions: protecting the patient and others from harm, maintaining necessary life support, enhancing excretion of the toxic agent, and ameliorating symptoms with medication.

Violent or medically ill patients require hospitalization, often against their will. Restraints may exacerbate muscle damage and agitation and should be avoided, but at times they may be necessary.

A toxic reaction to PCP should be considered a medical emergency. Vital functions may need to be supported. Body cooling and antihypertensive agents may be required, as well as intravenous benzodiazepines to treat convulsions. Use of the muscle relaxant dantrolene might be considered if severe hyperthermia and rhabdomyolysis are present ("Acute Reaction to Drugs of Abuse," 1996).

When PCP has been taken orally, gastric lavage with activated charcoal may prevent further absorption of the drug (Schukit, 1985). To enhance excretion of the drug, the urine should be acidified to a pH of less than 5.0 with 500 mg of intravenous ammonium chloride every 4 hours or 500 mg of oral ascorbic acid every 4 hours, though this should only be attempted in an appropriately equipped and staffed medical setting. Repeated monitoring of blood pH, blood gases, blood urea nitrogen, blood ammonia, and electrolytes are necessary.

Mild psychiatric symptomatology including anxiety and paranoia, should be treated with reassurance in a warm, supportive, low-stimulation atmosphere ("talking down"), as with hallucinogens and marijuana. Sensory deprivation should be avoided. More severe acute psychiatric complications usually do not respond to this intervention and may necessitate minimization of sensory inputs and pharmacotherapy early on. Benzodiazepines are preferable to neuroleptics, as the latter may exacerbate cholinergic imbalance, muscle damage, or vulnerability to seizures. There is no evidence to support earlier concerns that benzodiazepines might delay excretion of PCP. Low-potency neuroleptics, such as chlorpromazine and thioridazine, have undesirable anticholinergic effects that may worsen the delirium and psychosis (Miller, Gold, & Millman, 1988). High-potency neuroleptic medication is recommended for patients who do not respond to benzodiazepines or who develop protracted psychoses. PCP-induced psychotic disorders that persist for weeks after the drug ingestion should be treated as a functional psychosis.

One recent study suggests that ascorbic acid may enhance the therapeutic effects of haloperidol in the treatment of PCP psychosis (Giannini, Loiselle, DiMarzio, & Giannini, 1987). Electroconvulsive therapy has also been recommended as an effective treatment for patients with PCP psychosis who are refractory to antipsychotic medication (Rosen, Mukherjee, & Shinbach, 1984).

Chronic PCP users often abuse other substances and/or have concomitant psychiatric illnesses. After the resolution of acute symptoms, conventional chemical dependency treatment should be provided to promote abstinence and prevent relapse. Severe psychopathology must be treated with the drug dependence. Psychiatric evaluation should continue throughout the early treatment stages because symptomatology may change with continued abstinence (Daghestani & Schnoll, 1989).

MARIJUANA

Marijuana is the most widely used illicit substance in Western society. The term "marijuana" refers to various preparations obtained from the upper leaves and flowering tops of the Indian hemp plant, *Cannabis sativa*. The resin obtained from the plant contains over 60 cannabinoids and 400 different chemicals, of which delta-9-tetrahydrocannabinol (THC) is the major chemical with psychoactive properties. The THC content can vary from 0.1% in the type of plant grown for fiber to 60% in hashish oil, a concentrated resin distillate (Cohen, 1986; Grinspoon & Bakalar, 1992). Marijuana as used in the United States may contain from 1% to 10% THC. In recent years, the cultivated plant has yielded preparations with increasingly high THC content. The least potent grade of cannabis, "bhang," is derived from uncultivated flowers and tops with a low resin content comprising 1 to 2% THC. Most of the marijuana used in the United States is of this grade. "Ganja" is the product of the carefully cultivated flowers with a high resin content. "Hashish" is an extremely potent form of cannabis derived mostly from the resin itself. "Sinsemilla" is a potent cannabis preparation that can contain THC concentrations of greater than 10%.

Although marijuana alters perceptions and heightens sensory awareness as do the hallucinogens, the drug differs from this class of substances in a number of ways and should therefore be classified separately. In distinction to the hallucinogens, it is generally smoked; its consciousness-altering properties at the doses generally used are less profound; and it is sedating, whereas LSD and most of the other hallucinogens are activating.

History and Epidemiology

Like the other naturally occurring drugs of abuse, cannabis has been used since ancient times, having first been described in an ancient Chinese medical text. It has been used all over the world in a variety of ways by diverse people including religious mystics, Persian and Jamaican laborers, and European literati.

In the mid-19th century, marijuana was introduced to England and the United States as both a medicinal agent and euphoriant. Prior to World War II in the United States, the use of marijuana was confined to the very wealthy, the underworld classes, and the entertainment profession (Millman & Sbriglio, 1986). Following the war, use increased significantly in urban ghetto populations in association with other drugs of abuse such as heroin and cocaine. During the 1960s and 1970s, marijuana use assumed epidemic proportions, spreading to the middle class as well as to youthful, female, and rural populations. Cannabis use disorders appear more often in males, and prevalence is most common in persons between ages 18 and 30 years.

According to the Annual National High School Senior and Young Adult Survey, marijuana use has experienced a strong resurgence since its low point in 1992 but is still not at the peak it reached in 1979 (Johnston et al., 1997). Among 8th-graders, annual prevalence rose from 6% in 1991 to 18% in 1998. Among 10th-graders, annual prevalence rose from 15% in 1992 to 34% in 1996. Among 12th-graders, it increased from 22% in 1992 to 36% in 1996 (vs. 50% in 1978). Daily use was reported in 4.9% of 12th-graders (vs. 11% in 1978), 3.5% of 10th-graders, and 1.5% of 8th-graders.

The authors of the study speculate that this increase is possibly related to four factors: (1) "generational forgetting"—this cohort grew up in a period in which drug use rates were down, offering them less opportunity to learn from others' mistakes; (2) a decline in drug education among parents, schools, and the media; (3) pro-drug music; and (4) substantial increase in cigarette smoking.

One study of 757 African American and Hispanic 7th-graders showed marijuana use to be predicted by inadequate social and refusal skills as well as the most admired person's marijuana use (Epstein, Botvin, Diaz, Toth, & Schinke, 1995)

Marijuana has been called a gateway drug, leading to the abuse of other classes of drugs (Golub & Johnson, 1994; Clayton & Voss, 1981; O'Donnell et al., 1976). Alcohol and tobacco have a similar correlation with other drug use. It is likely that positive experiences with one illicit psychoactive drug may encourage use of other drugs; the extent of marijuana use correlates positively with the use of other drugs (Halikas et al., 1982). Also, the acquisition and use of marijuana usually encourages association with people who use or have access to other drugs (Cohen, 1986; Millman, 1989).

Marijuana has long been advocated by some as a useful medical treatment for glaucoma and an antiemetic agent for chemotherapy patients. Though the utility of marijuana for these medical purposes has been much debated, in 1996, marijuana was legalized in California and Arizona for medical use (Grinspoon & Bakalar, 1995; Lowenthal, Bennetts, Nahas, & Manger, 1995; Doblin & Kleinman, 1995).

Patterns of Use and Abuse

The patterns of marijuana use are quite varied and depend on social and cultural factors as well as individual personality factors. Many young people experiment with the drug for a time and then relegate it to a peripheral status in their lives or they stop completely; others continue to use it intermittently to punctuate particular occasions. Regular smokers include those who use the drug three to five times a week; chronic use refers to those who smoke every day, often throughout the day so that they remain intoxicated.

Dependence on marijuana and compulsive use is often associated with psychopathology, though the relationship is often complex. In some cases, the drug may be a cause of the psychopathology noted, though in others it may be seen as self-medication of a preexisting psychological disorder. For example, some people use the drug for its sedative properties, to decrease symptoms of anxiety or depression. It is striking that a subset of chronic psychiatric patients, including those with psychotic disorders, will use a drug that may increase their feelings of paranoia or unreality and that often results in their readmission to hospitals. It is as if they are seeking distance from their symptoms, or some control over their thoughts and feelings. Perhaps they are able to derive some comfort from the idea that their symptoms are drug induced, under their control, and not due to their own psychopathology. It is also somewhat more socially acceptable to be a "drug abuser" or a "pothead" than it is to be a "mental patient."

The complex relationship between use, abuse, and psychopathology was demonstrated in a long-term study following 101 children of both sexes from ages 5 to 18 (Shedler & Block, 1990). Personality tests were given at ages 7, 11, and 18. Parent–child interactions were studied at age 5. By the end of the study, 68% had used marijuana, and 39% had used it once a week or more. Three main groups were distinguished: 29 abstainers, 36 experimenters (used marijuana no more than once a month and had tried at most one other drug), and 20 frequent users (used marijuana at least once a week and had used at least one other drug). The three groups had consistent personality traits at ages 7, 11, and 18.

Frequent users were described as having few friends; being uncooperative, insecure, and impulsive; and having lower high school grades than the other two groups. Abstainers were described as inhibited, shy, neat, tense, and lacking in personal charm. Their high school grades were average. Experimenters, the largest group, were more likely to be described as warm, curious, and cheerful. They had good relations with others and were able to employ rational self-control.

A study of college-age marijuana smokers showed no significant demographic or psychiatric features that differentiated occasional from heavy smokers (Kouri, Pope, Yurgelon-Todd, & Gruber, 1995).

Pharmacology

Marijuana is generally smoked, though it can be ingested. When it is smoked, much of the THC content is lost by pyrolysis. After smoking, effects begin within minutes and last 2 to 4 hours; after ingestion, effects begin within 30 to 60 minutes and last 5 to 12 hours (Jaffe, 1990). The delay in effects after ingestion is not satisfying to most drug users who are seeking rapid change in affect or perceptual state. Moreover, this delay makes it difficult to titrate dosage against effects; often, larger quantities of the drug are consumed because no immediate effects are experienced. This in part contributes to the greater incidence of adverse sequelae experienced with oral ingestion.

THC is highly lipid soluble and quickly passes from the blood to the brain and other lipid-rich tissues (Cohen, 1986). It is extensively metabolized in the liver. The metabolites are excreted in the bile, urine, and feces. After high-dose or chronic use, traces of THC and its metabolites persist in blood for several days or weeks and even longer in urine.

Significant tolerance develops to the physiological effects of the drug;

tolerance to its psychoactive subjective effects is markedly variable. According to DSM-IV, the diagnosis of cannabis dependence may occur with or without physiological dependence. After cessation of high-dose chronic use, a mild withdrawal syndrome occurs, though the diagnosis of cannabis withdrawal is not included in DSM-IV. This is characterized by 4 to 5 days of irritability, restlessness, nervousness, decreased appetite, weight loss, and insomnia (with rebound increase in rapid eye movement [REM] sleep) (Jaffe, 1990). This syndrome is quite variable and much influenced by set and setting. Fatal overdoses due to marijuana alone have not been reported.

Effects*

The physiological effects of marijuana include a rise in systolic blood pressure while supine and a decrease while standing (though these changes are inconsistent), tachycardia, conjunctival vascular injection, and dry mouth. There is no significant change in pupil size (Jaffe, 1990). REM sleep decreases. Appetite is increased, though it seems to be quite dependent upon expectation and setting.

The psychoactive effects of cannabis are remarkably varied and are profoundly dependent on the personality of the user, his or her expectation, and the setting, though relaxation, a sense of well-being, and enhanced somatosensory perceptions are quite common.

Marijuana intoxication is often associated with labile affect, impaired short-term memory, and altered time perception (such that time seems to pass more slowly). Enhanced sociability and giddy laughter occur, but so may social withdrawal and extreme self-consciousness. Information processing is altered such that boring and repetitive tasks may be performed with enhanced interest and concentration whereas the ability to carry out complex goal-oriented tasks is impaired. Ideas may seem to change in importance and relevance. Impaired judgment and impaired motor coordination may be present.

Adverse Psychological Effects

The most common acute adverse psychological reactions to marijuana are anxiety reactions and frank panic attacks. These reactions are usually brief and do not persist beyond the period of intoxication. The anxiety can range from mild to severe, depending on the amount used, the degree of experience of the user, the setting in which the drug is used, and the psychological predisposition of the user.

Cannabis-induced panic attacks may occur in patients with no psychiatric history, though they occur more often in those with a history of a panic

---

*For a presentation of effects and treatment, see Table 9.1 on pages 208–209.

disorder, a generalized anxiety disorder, or other related psychopathology. Most users who develop panic attacks while intoxicated do not continue to experience these reactions; others find that these reactions occur frequently with the drug and thus discontinue its use. Some patients develop panic attacks and/or agoraphobia that continue to recur despite the cessation of marijuana use. It may be postulated that in these instances, the drug and its psychoactive sequelae represented a sensitization or kindling phenomena that led to the persistence of psychiatric symptomatology.

Frank hallucinations and/or delusions occur infrequently with acute marijuana reactions. They are usually associated with high doses, oral ingestion, or psychiatric vulnerability. Rarely, these symptoms may be manifestations of a hallucinogen flashback precipitated by marijuana, the most common precipitant. Delirium is rare but can occur in the setting of high-dose use, particularly after oral ingestion. Adulterants such as PCP may be associated with delirium or other adverse effects.

Psychotic disorders precipitated by cannabis use are usually short-lived but may last days to weeks or longer. Prolonged and severe psychotic disorders indistinguishable from schizophrenia have been attributed to high dose and chronic cannabis use, though it is likely these reactions occurred in predisposed individuals whose drug use triggered expression of premorbid psychopathology.

An "amotivational" or "chronic" cannabis syndrome, marked by apathy, dullness, diminished goal-directed activities, impaired concentration, and deterioration in personal appearance, has been described in some chronic marijuana users (Stefanis, Boulougouris, & Liakos, 1976). It is likely that the psychoactive effects of the drug in the setting of premorbid psychopathology may present as this syndrome. In the absence of severe psychopathology, cessation of drug use leads to improvement in symptoms and performance; for others, abstinence may reveal the complex and disturbing symptoms that were previously being medicated with the drug.

A subgroup of chronic users who have been described as having an amotivational syndrome actually manifest remarkable energy and enthusiasm in the pursuit of their goals, such as involvement with particular kinds of music or identification with drug using cults. The term "aberrant motivational syndrome" has been suggested as a more precise description of the phenomenon (Millman & Sbriglio, 1986).

The evidence for long-term cognitive impairments associated with chronic use of cannabis has been inconclusive. One study of regular and infrequent marijuana users on a college campus showed residual neuropsychological effects even after a day of abstinence. Heavy users displayed significantly greater impairment than light users on attention and learning measures (Pope & Yurgelon-Todd, 1996).

Medical Consequences

The most notable adverse physiologic effects of marijuana smoking are its effects on the lung and pulmonary function. These effects are proportionally greater than the effects of smoking tobacco and may be additive with tobacco. Habitual smoking of three to four marijuana cigarettes is associated with the same frequency of bronchitis and the same epithelial damage in the central airways as regular smoking of more than 20 tobacco cigarettes a day (Wu, Tajhkin, Djghed, & Rose, 1988). These differences are due to the irritants in marijuana as well as the smoking behavior of marijuana users, who take larger and longer inhalations than cigarette smokers.

Aphrodisiac properties have been attributed to marijuana, as well as to many of the other drugs of abuse. Self-report surveys support claims of both enhanced and impaired sexual function secondary to marijuana use (Cohen, 1982; Halikas et al., 1982). Cannabis may lower testosterone levels after chronic and acute use and may affect all phases of reproductive physiology in both sexes (Kolodny, Masters, Kolodner, & Toro, 1974; Kolodny, Lessin, Toro, Masters, & Cohen, 1976; Powell & Fuller, 1983). Gynecomastia may occur in male chronic users. Chromosomal damage, teratological effects, and increased fetal loss have been suggested but not documented.

Treatment

Treatment of the acute adverse effects of cannabis, including anxiety reactions, panic attacks, and flashbacks, consists of calm and gentle reassurance in a warm and supportive atmosphere ("talking down"). When these people are brought to an emergency room, an attempt should be made to find a quiet place for them out of the mainstream of traffic (Millman, 1989). It is useful to remind the patient that the symptoms are drug induced and will pass quickly. When necessary, a benzodiazepine anxiolytic should be administered. As with adverse reactions from hallucinogens, neuroleptics are usually not necessary and should be avoided except when severe agitation has not been adequately managed with benzodiazepines. Protracted psychotic symptoms, when severe, usually require neuroleptics. The presence of delirium necessitates the consideration of etiologies other than cannabis. Management is similar to that of any delirium: close monitoring of vital functions and metabolic status and supportive care. Benzodiazepines are indicated if withdrawal from depressants is also suspected. Low-dose high-potency neuroleptics may also be used.

It is necessary to define the meaning of the drug for individual patients to develop the most appropriate treatment for chronic users. The therapist or counselor needs to be mindful of the interrelationship of character, psychopathology, and addictive behavior when evaluating any substance abuse patient. Moreover, this evaluation should be an ongoing process, with new information being uncovered as the patient faces the challenges of the treatment process.

Chronic marijuana users and chemically dependent patients who also abuse marijuana should be afforded treatment based on the disease model of chemical dependence, including Twelve-Step programs as well as relapse prevention techniques. Although most marijuana-dependent people can be managed as outpatients, institutionalization in a therapeutic community, rehabilitation program, or psychiatric hospital with a coordinated drug treatment program may be indicated. Surprisingly, given the widespread use and abuse of this substance, few Twelve-Step groups are specifically aimed at marijuana users.

Treatment programs for marijuana-dependent people, many of whom are adolescents, are often indistinguishable from those aimed at adults who are dependent on alcohol and other drugs. These programs may not be sensitive to the particular needs and cultural mores of this youthful population. Many young people are unable or unwilling to accept the tenets of adult programs, such as the admission that they have the disease of chemical dependence and that they may never again use another psychoactive drug, including alcohol. Programs aimed specifically at this younger population, which emphasize identification with a non-drug-using group and the development of alternatives to drug use, have shown promise.

Treatment of patients with premorbid psychopathology depends on the characterization of symptomatology and behavioral patterns after cessation of marijuana use. This may take days or weeks. It may be necessary to institute treatment presumptively before abstinence is obtained or drug effects have disappeared. Patients should be carefully educated with respect to relapse prevention techniques and their attempts at self- medication or rationalization of their psychopathology (Millman, 1989).

INHALANTS

The term "inhalants" refers to a category of diverse substances that produce psychoactive but generally short-lived effects after inhalation. They are relatively inexpensive, easily available, and subject to a wide variety of abuse patterns.

Classification

Many substances that are classified as inhalants are quite disparate; they may contain multiple ingredients, with differing desired and toxic effects. The inhalants that are commonly subject to abuse are listed next, with their general composition (Fornazzari, 1988; Sharp & Rosenberg 1992; Dinwiddie, 1994). Disorders resulting from the use of anesthetic gases (e.g., nitrous oxide and ether) and short-acting vasodilators (e.g., alkyl nitrites) are excluded from the DSM-IV category of "inhalant-related disorders" and should be classified under "other substance-related disorders."

Commonly abused inhalants

Alkyl nitrites—amyl nitrite ("amies," "poppers," "snappers"), butyl nitrite ("Rush," "Locker room"). Amyl nitrite is available by prescription; butyl nitrites are available over the counter.

Glues, adhesives, cements.
Paints and paint thinners.
Gasoline, lighter fluid.
Aerosols—includes nitrous oxide ("whippets").
Nail polish remover.
Dry-cleaning fluid, cleaning solutions.
Typewriter correction fluid.
Antifreeze.

Common contents of inhalants

Amyl nitrite, butyl nitrite.
Toluene and toluene mixtures—glues, adhesives, cements, paint and cement cleaners and thinners.
Benzene and substances containing benzene—gasoline, glues, paints.
Hexane—gasoline, some glues, spray adhesives, rubber cement.
Ketones—rubber cement, printing ink, paint, nail polish remover (acetone).
Halogentated hydrocarbons (halocarbons): methylene chloride—spray paints, paint thinner; trichloroethylene—typewriter correction fluid, dry cleaning solvent; Halothane—surgical anesthetic; chloroform, methylchloroform—typewriter correction fluid, household cleaning fluids.
Fluorocarbons—aerosols, Freon.
Nitrous oxide—aerosols.
Ethylene glycol—antifreeze.

Epidemiology and Patterns of Use and Abuse

The fact that certain smells and vapors alter consciousness has been known since antiquity, though the first characterization of glue and gasoline sniffing as substance abuse and dependence did not occur in the United States until the 1950s (Brecher, 1972). Abuse of these substances increased significantly in the late 1960s and early 1970s in association with the increased use of other psychoactive substances.

According to the National High School Senior and Young Adult Survey, inhalant use stabilized in 1996 after a 4-year steady increase (Johnston et al., 1997). In 1996, annual prevalence among 8th-, 10th-, and 12th-graders was 12.2%, 9.5%, and 7.6%, respectively. Lifetime prevalence was 21.2%, 19.3%, and 16.6%. This stabilization is paralleled by an increase in the proportion of students indicating that they view inhalants as dangerous.

Inhalants come in a variety of forms, from tanks of nitrous oxide to ampules of butyl nitrite or bottles of occupational fluids. Nitrous oxide is also available as cartridges that are used in whipped cream dispensers (hence the name "whippets"). These cartridges can be purchased in large quantities in hardware, gourmet, restaurant supply, and drug paraphernalia stores. The cartridge is placed in an empty whipped cream canister or a special "charger" that can be purchased at a drug paraphernalia store. The user places his or her mouth over the dispensing spout and pushes down on the dispensing lever, which punctures the opening to the ampule, releasing its contents. Some adolescents have learned to extract the gas from whipped cream dispensers on supermarket shelves, leaving behind a contaminated can of flat whipped cream to be sold to unwitting customers.

Amyl nitrite ampules are available by prescription, whereas the butyl nitrites may be purchased in drug paraphernalia stores as "aromas." The ampule is broken and inhaled, or placed in a metal container to prolong its effects. During the peak of nitrite popularity in the mid-1970s, the wearing of the metal container around one's neck conferred a status akin to wearing a cocaine spoon.

Organic solvents can be inhaled from a hand, rag ("huffing"), or jar. Gasoline is commonly inhaled from portable plastic gas cans. An opening is created as a vent, and the user places his or her mouth over the spout. Solvents such as glue or cement are often deposited in a plastic bag, which is secured around the face or head so as to create a closed system ("bagging").

Most surveys report a marked male preponderance of users. Initial and experimental use is generally by young people in a group setting; chronic or compulsive use is generally a solitary practice. Solitary use is also more common with older users. Most users state that inhalants are not their drug of choice; abuse of other substances is common. One analysis of the 1990 National Household Survey on Drug Abuse found that inhalant users were more than five times more likely than nonusers to have injected drugs (Schutz, Chilcoat, & Anthony, 1994).

Though solvent abuse is frequently perceived as a problem of adolescence, abuse among adults, including the educated and middle class, is not uncommon. During the 1970s and 1980s, alkyl nitrites became popular with young adults (most visibly, homosexual men) to enhance social and sexual encounters. Nitrite inhalants were investigated as a possible co-factor in the development of Kaposi's sarcoma among HIV-infected homosexual men (Beral et al., 1992). It was ultimately determined that the stronger correlation was between nitrite use and unprotected receptive anal intercourse (Seage et al., 1992).

Reports of nitrous oxide abuse by dentists, who have access to large quantities of it, are not uncommon. Intermittent and compulsive use of nitrous oxide cartridges continues to be common. High-functioning individuals, the affluent, and the educated middle class are attracted to nitrous oxide or the nitrites because of their legality and easy availability.

Pharmacology

Inhalants are quickly absorbed over the large surface of the lungs, accounting for its almost instantaneous psychoactive effects. It has been estimated that solvent abusers inhale a concentration of about 1,000 to 5,000 parts per million, as compared to factory workers, who may be exposed to solvent concentrations not greater than 100 to 500 parts per million (Fornazzari, 1988; Ron, 1986). The solvents are deposited in organs and tissues with high lipid contents, including the central nervous system. Inhalant effects generally persist for minutes, though some of the preparations may exert effects for up to 1 hour. Inhalation can be repeated an indefinite number of times; some users do it more than 100 times a day. It is likely that the rapid onset and waning of effects account for the liability to develop compulsive use. Abusers seek rapid, predictable change, often in any direction, and continue to seek this change. The drugs are reinforcing rather than classically addicting.

Tolerance has been reported with toluene and nitrous oxide; some degree of subjective tolerance probably occurs with all of the inhalants. Whereas profound dependence marked by craving and compulsive use is common, a physiological withdrawal syndrome does not occur with these drugs, though one case of a phenomenon similar to delirium tremens has been reported (Ron, 1986).

A possible withdrawal syndrome beginning 24 to 48 hours after cessation of use and lasting from 2 to 5 days has been described, with symptoms including sleep disturbance, tremor, irritability, diaphoresis, nausea, and fleeting illusions. This syndrome has not been well documented; thus inhalant withdrawal is not necessary to qualify for the DSM-IV diagnosis of inhalant dependence.

Contrary to popular belief, many of the inhalants or their metabolites can be detected in blood and urine, albeit very transiently. For toluene, the blood concentration reaches its peak 15 to 30 minutes after use and cannot be detected after 4 to 6 hours. Urine levels are at their peak after 1 hour and rapidly wane after 4 hours (Ron, 1986). According to one report, toluene is detectable by portable mass spectrometry 4 days after the last inhalation (Fornazzari, 1988).

It is believed that the mechanism of action of most inhalants is to reduce excitatory impulses on neuronal membranes, possibly after an initial enhanced excitation. The nitrites differ from the other inhalants in that they are smooth muscle relaxants and dilate blood vessels; this may relate to their use as a sexual aid.

Psychoactive Effects and Toxicity*

Initial psychoactive effects of the various inhalants have some features similar to alcohol intoxication. Users seek the "rush," the rapid onset of a euphoric feeling that may be associated with a sensation of floating and decreased inhibitions. The initial excitation is generally followed by sedation. Irritability may occur with continued use. Nitrous oxide use is characteristically accompanied by giddy laughter. Though use of all inhalants is associated with the

---

*For a presentation of effects and treatment, see Table 9.1 on pages 208–209.

rapid onset of effects, the nitrite "rush" is most often associated with the attempt to enhance sexuality, particularly the experience of orgasm.

To qualify for the DSM-IV diagnosis of inhalant intoxication, significant maladaptive behavioral changes such as belligerence, assaultiveness, apathy, impaired judgment, or impaired social or occupational functioning must be present as well as two or more of the following physiological signs: dizziness, nystagmus, incoordination, slurred speech, unsteady gait, lethargy, depressed reflexes, psychomotor retardation, tremor, generalized muscle weakness, blurred vision or diplopia, stupor or coma, and euphoria.

Tinnitus, eye irritation, light sensitivity, and a characteristic taste in the mouth are common concomitants of nitrite use. Sneezing, rhinorrhea, and coryza often occur after chronic use. Illusions, hallucinations, other perceptual distortions, delusions, and clouding of consciousness may occur, especially after chronic use. Chronic users often appear to be intoxicated, though the characteristic inhalant breath smell or perioral rash are useful diagnostic clues.

Aftereffects of the inhalants almost invariably include headache; gastrointestinal symptoms such as abdominal cramps, nausea, vomiting, and diarrhea may be present. Transient central nervous system toxicity is manifested by cerebellar dysfunction, parasthesias, and (rarely) seizures.

Arrhythmias secondary to cardiac toxicity have been reported with use of the solvents. Other associated medical complications include restrictive ventilatory defects, bronchitis, and pneumonias. Acidosis and hyperchloremia may be present in plasma or cerebrospinal fluid (Fornazzari, 1988). Asphyxiation and death have occurred when the plastic bag that was used to increase the concentration of organic solvents collapsed around the user's head. Anoxia and death have also occurred when users inhaled nitrous oxide with a fixed face mask that did not allow sufficient oxygen to enter the closed system.

Multiple organ systems are adversely affected by the various inhalants. Benzene can produces hematotoxic changes such as anemia, leukopenia, pancytopenia, and leukemia. The halogenated hydrocarbons are associated with significant hepatorenal toxicity including renal tubular acidosis. The hydrocarbons are also associated with carcinogenesis, abortions, and developmental defects. Halothane has been associated with delayed-onset behavioral changes after perinatal exposure. Toluene can cause hypokalemia, hypophosphatemia, renal tubular acidosis, and complications of pregnancy including fetal growth retardation and perinatal death. The fluorocarbons are significantly cardiotoxic and are the primary etiological agent in deaths due to cardiac sensitization (Sharp & Rosenberg, 1992). Methemoglobin is formed after nitrite inhalation. Though hemoglobin is reformed from the methemoglobin, patients with an enzyme deficiency or cardiac sensitivies are at risk for serious complications.

Many of the inhalants are associated with the development of both transient and persistent neuropathies. The production of ketones has been implicated as the cause of the most rapidly developing neuropathies. Hexane is especially associated with sensorimotor neuropathies due to myelin degeneration, characterized by symmetrical numbness, weakness, and ataxia. Benzene's motor and sensory neurotoxic effects are characterized by dysmetria and dysarthria. Toluene actually presents a low risk for the development of neuropathies, though rare optic neuropathy and sensorineural hearing loss has been reported with its use. The distal paresis and numbness reported with nitrous oxide use is also likely to be due to a neuropathic process.

A persistent cerebellar syndrome characterized by nystagmus, titubating gait, ataxia, and limb tremor has been convincingly attributed to toluene. ("Titubating gait" is a characteristic staggering gait seen in cerebellar diseases.) These findings were correlated with cerebellar atrophy on computed tomography (Fornazzari, 1988). The same author has also demonstrated cerebral atrophy associated with toluene use, though complicating factors (such as other drug use) and lack of controls were not adequately addressed (Ron, 1986).

Many studies have attempted to demonstrate a causal relationship between persistent neuropsychological deficits and inhalant use. To date, studies addressing cognitive, reading, and memory impairment and defective visual scanning have all been inconclusive (Ron, 1986).

Severe psychiatric morbidity (including a dementia, delirium, psychotic reactions, and anxiety, mood, and personality disorders) is frequent in chronic inhalant abusers, though it has been difficult to determine whether the inhalant use is causal, what the contribution of other drug use is, or whether the psychopathology preceded the inhalant use and may have determined the drug abuse pattern. As with all substance abusers who present with psychiatric illness, a careful and ongoing evaluation is critical to determine the relationship of the drug and the psychiatric symptomatology.

Treatment

Intermittent or experimental inhalant users do not generally come to medical attention. Inhalant abuse is often considered unimportant and frivolous both by the users themselves and by health professionals, possibly because the substances are legal and are an integral part of every day life. However, because of their short duration of action, easy availability, cheapness, and licitness, inhalants lend themselves to compulsive use patterns which may be associated with severe behavioral and psychiatric impairment. Other drug use is generally present as well.

Inhalant abusers should be treated in well-coordinated chemical dependency treatment programs; adolescents should optimally be treated in programs focused particularly on this age group. Although outpatient treatment should be attempted initially, institutionalization is indicated when the use cannot be controlled or severe psychiatric sequelae are present. A number of studies indicate that adolescent inhalant abusers tend to respond poorly to traditional treatment programs (Mason, 1979). This result is attributed to a number of factors, including a high incidence of antisocial personality disorders and other severe psychopathology.

Hospitalization is required for such severe medical sequelae as arrythmia, seizure, coma, or unmanageable agitation. Most neurological symptoms, such as cerebellar disturbance or paresthesias, are quickly reversible. Psychiatric disturbances are also usually transient and will remit with no medication or, on occasion, benzodiazepines. In more severe or protracted disturbances, neuroleptics may be necessary.

Methylene blue has been suggested as a treatment for high methemoglobin levels due to nitrous oxide abuse. Renal tubular acidosis, associated with fluorocarbon use, responds to intravenous bicarbonate and potassium chloride (Sharp & Rosenberg 1992).

Prevention programs aimed at making inhalants and related paraphernalia less accessible or adding noxious additives to the substances of abuse have been suggested but not instituted.

REFERENCES

Acute Reaction to Drugs of Abuse. (1996, May 10). *Medical Letter on Drug Therapy, 38*(974), 43–46.

American Psychiatric Association. (1994). *Diagnostic and statistical manual of mental disorders* (4th ed.). Washington, DC: Author.

Beck, J., & Rosenbaum, M. (1994). *Pursuit of ecstasy: The MDMAA experience.* Albany: State University of New York Press.

Beral, V., Bull, D., Darby, S., Weller, I., Carne, C., Beecham, M., & Jaffe, H. (1992). Risk of Kaposi's sarcoma and sexual practices associated with faecal contact in homosexual or bisexual men with AIDS. *Lancet, 339*(8794), 632–635.

Bowers, M. (1977). Psychoses precipitated by psychomimetic drugs. *Archives of General Psychiatry, 34,* 832–835.

Brecher, E. M. (1972). *Licit and illicit drugs.* Boston: Little, Brown.

Buffum, J., & Moser, C. (1986). MDMA and human sexual function. *Journal of Psychoactive Drugs, 18*(4), 355–359.

Clayton. R. R., & Voss, H. L. (1981). *Young men and drugs in Manhattan: A causal analysis* (NIDA Research Monograph No. 39). Washington, DC: U.S. Government Printing Office.

Climko, R. P., Roehrich, H., Sweeney, D. R. & Al-Razi, J. (1986–1987). Ecstasy: A review of MDMA and MDA. *International Journal of Psychiatry in Medicine, 16*(4), 359–371.

Cohen, S. (1982). Cannabis and sex. *Journal of Psychoactive Drugs, 14*(1–2), 55–58.

Cohen, S. (1986). Marijuana. In A. J. Frances & R. Hales (Eds.), *American Psychiatric Association annual review* (Vol. 5). Washington, DC: American Psychiatric Press.

Cohen, S. (1989). The hallucinogens. In T. B. Karasu (Ed.), *Treatment of psychiatric disorders.* Washington, DC: American Psychiatric Press.

Daghestani, A. N., & Schnoll, S. H. (1989). Phencyclidine abuse and dependence. In T. B. Karasu (Ed.), *Treatments of psychiatric disorders* Washington, DC: American Psychiatric Press.

Dinwiddie, S. H. (1994). Abuse of inhalants: A review. *Addiction, 89*(8), 925–939.

Doblin, R., & Kleiman M. A. R. (1995). The medical use of marijuana: The case for clinical trials. *Journal of Addictive Diseases, 14*(1), 5–15.

Epstein, J. A., Botvin, G. J., Diaz, T., Toth, V., & Schinke, S. P. (1995). Social and personal factors in marijuana use and intentions to use drugs among inner city minority youth. *Journal of Development Behavior in Pediatrics, 16*(1), 14–20.

Fischer, C., Hatzidimitrou, G., Wlos, J., Katz, J., & Ricaurte, G. (1995). Reorganization of ascending 5HT axon projections in animals previously exposed to MDMA. *Journal of Neuroscience, 15,* 5476–5485.

Fornazzari, L. (1988, June). Clinical recognition and management of solvent abusers. *Internal Medicine, 9*(6), 99–109.

Gehr, R. (1996, November 5). The state of the stone. *Village Voice,* pp. 33–36.

Giannini, A. J., Loiselle, R. H., DiMarzio, L. R., & Giannini, M. C. (1987). Augmentation of haloperidol by ascorbic acid in phencyclidine intoxication. *American Journal of Psychiatry, 144*(9), 1207–1209.

Golub, A., & Johnson, B. D. (1994). The shifting importance of alcohol and marijuana as gateway substances among serious drug abusers. *Journal of Studies on Alcohol, 55*(5), 607–614.

Green, A. R., Cross, A. J., & Goodwin, G. M. (1995). Review of the pharmacology and clinical pharmacology of MDMA. *Psychopharmacology (Berlin), 119*(3), 247–260.

Greer, G., & Strassman, R. J. (1985). Information on "Ecstasy." *American Journal of Psychiatry, 142*(11), 1391.

Grinspoon, L., & Bakalar, J. B. (1986). Psychedelics and Arylcyclohexylamines. In A. J. Frances & R. Hales (Eds.), *American Psychiatric Association annual review* (Vol. 5). Washington, DC: American Psychiatric Press.

Grinspoon, L., & Bakalar, J. B. (1992). Marihuana. In J. H. Lowinson, P. Ruiz, & R. B. Millman (Eds.), *Substance abuse: A comprehensive textbook.* Baltimore: Williams & Wilkins.

Grinspoon, L., & Bakalar, J. B. (1995). Marihuana as medicine: A plea for reconsideration. *Journal of the American Medical Association, 273,* 1875–1876.

Halikas, J., Weller, R., & Morse, C. (1982). Effects of regular marijuana use on sexual performance. *Journal of Psychoactive Drugs, 14*(1–2), 59–70.

Hollister, L. E. (1984). Effects of hallucinogens in humans. In B. L. Jacobs (Ed.), *Hallucinogens: Neurochemical, behavioral, and clinical perspectives.* New York: Raven Press.

Jaffe, J. (1990). Drug addiction and drug abuse. In A. G. Gilman, T. W. Rall, A. S. Niesi, & P. Taylor (Eds.), *Goodman and Gilman's the pharmacological basis of therapeutics* (8th ed.). New York: Macmillan.

Johnston, L. D., O'Malley, P. M., & Bachman, J. G. (1997). *National Annual High School Senior and Young Adult Survey.* Washington, DC: U.S. Government Printing Office.

Kolodny, R. C., Lessin, P., Toro, G., Masters, W. H., & Cohen, S. (1976). Depression of plasma testosterone with acute marijuana administration. In M. C. Braude & S. Szara (Eds.), *The pharmacology of marijuana.* New York: Raven Press

Kolodny, R. C., Masters, W. H., Kolodner, R. M., & Toro, G. (1974). Depression of plasma testosterone levels after chronic intensive marijuana use. *New England Journal of Medicine, 290*(16), 872–874.

Kouri, E., Pope, H. G., Yurgelun-Todd, D., & Gruber, S. (1995). Attributes of heavy vs. occasional marijuana smokers in a college population. *Biological Psychiatry, 38*(7), 475–481.

Lake, C. R., Stirba, A. L., Kinneman, R. E., Carlson, B., & Holloway, H. C. (1981). Mania associated with LSD ingestion. *American Journal of Psychiatry, 138*(11), 1508–1509.

Lowenthal, E. A., Bennetts, R. W., Nahas, G. G., & Manger, W. M. (1995). Marijuana as medicine [Letters]. *Journal of the American Medical Association, 274*(23), 1837–1838.

Lucas, A. M. (1995). Entheology. *Journal of Psychoactive Drugs, 27*(3), 293–295.

Luisada, P. V. (1981). Phencyclidine. In J. H. Lowinson & P. Ruiz (Eds.), *Substance abuse: Clinical problems and perspectives.* Baltimore: Williams & Wilkins.

Mason, T. (1979). *Inhalant use and treatment* (NIDA Research Monograph). Washington, DC: U.S. Government Printing Office.

Miller, N. S., Gold, M. S., & Millman, R. B. (1988). PCP: A dangerous drug. *American Family Physician, 38*(3), 215–218.

Millman, R. B. (1982). Psychedelics. In J. B. Wyngaarden & L. H. Smith (Eds.), *Cecil textbook of medicine* (16th ed.) Philadelphia: Saunders.

Millman, R. B. (1989). Cannabis use and dependence. In T. B. Karasu (Ed.), *Treatments of psychiatric disorders.* Washington, DC: American Psychiatric Press.

Millman, R. B., & Beeder, A. B. (1994). The new psychedelic culture: LSD, ecstasy, "rave" parties and the Grateful Dead. *Psychiatric Annals, 24*(3), 148–150.

Millman, R. B., & Sbriglio, R. (1986). Patterns of use and psychopathology in chronic marijuana users. *Psychiatric Clinics of North America, 9*(3), 533–545.

Nichols, D. E. (1986). Difference between the mechanisms of actions of MDMA, MBDB, and the classic hallucinogens. *Journal of Psychoactive Drugs, 18*, 305–313.

O'Donnell, J. A., Voss, H. L., Clayton, R. R., et al. (1976). *Young men and drugs: A nationwide survey* (NIDA Research Monograph No. 42, DHEW Publication No. ADM 76-311). Washington, DC: U.S. Government Printing Office.

Pope, H. G., & Yurgelun-Todd, D. (1996). The residual cognitive effects of heavy marijuana use in college students [Comments 560–561]. *Journal of the American Medical Association, 275*(7), 521–527.

Powell, D. J., & Fuller, R. W. (1983). Marijuana and sex. *Journal of Psychoactive Drugs, 15*(4), 269–280.

Riedlinger, T. J., & Riedlinger, J. E. (1994). Psychedelic and entactogenic drugs in the treatment of depression. *Journal of Psychoactive Drugs, 26*(1), 41–55.

Ron, M. A. (1986). Volatile substance abuse: A review of possible long-term neurological, intellectual, and psychiatric sequelae. *British Journal of Psychiatry, 148*, 235–246.

Rosen, A. M., Mukherjee, S., & Shinbach, K. (1984). The efficacy of ECT in phencyclidine-induced psychosis. *Journal of Clinical Psychiatry, 45*(5), 220–222.

Schick, J. F., & Smith, D. E. (1970). Analysis of the LSD flashback. *Journal of Psychedelic Drugs, 3*, 13–19.

Schuckit, M. A. (1985). *Drug and alcohol abuse.* New York: Plenum.

Schutz, C. G., Chilcoat, H. D., & Anthony, J. C. (1994). The association between sniffing inhalants and injecting drugs. *Comprehensive Psychiatry, 35*(2), 99–105.

Seage, G. R. III, Mayer, K. H., Horsburgh, C. R. Jr., Holmberg, S. D., Moon, M. W., & Lamb, G. A. (1992). The relation between nitrite inhalants, unprotected receptive anal intercourse, and the risk of human immunodeficiency virus infection. *American Journal of Epidemiology, 135*(1), 1–11.

Sharp, C. W., & Rosenberg, N. L. (1992). Volatile substances. In J. H. Lowinson, P. Ruiz, & R. B. Millman (Eds.), *Substance abuse: A comprehensive textbook.* Baltimore: Williams & Wilkins.

Shedler, J., & Block, J. (1990). Adolescent drug use and psychological health: a longitudinal inquiry. *American Psychologist, 45*, 612–630.

Shick, J. F., & Smith, D. E. (1970). Analysis of the LSD flashback. *Journal of Psychedelic Drugs, 3*, 13–19.

Siegel, R. K. (1984). The natural history of hallucinogens. In B. L. Jacobs (Ed.),

Hallucinogens: Neurochemical, behavioral, and clinical perspectives. New York: Raven Press.

Smith, D. E., Wesson, D. R., Buxton, M. E., Seymour, & Ratkramer, H. M. (1978). The diagnosis and treatment of the PCP abuse syndrome. In *PCP abuse: An appraisal* (NIDA Research Monograph No. 21). Washington, DC: U.S. Government Printing Office.

Stefanis, C., Boulougouris, I., & Liakos, A. (1976). Clinical and psychophysiological effects of cannabis in long term users, In M. C. Braude & S. Szara (Eds.), *Pharmacology of marijuana.* New York: Raven Press.

Strassman, R. J. (1995). Hallucinogenic drugs in psychiatric research and treatment. *Journal of Nervous and Mental Disease, 183*(3), 127–138.

Szara, S. (1994). *Are hallucinogens psychoheuristic?* (NIDA Research Monograph No. 146). Washington, DC: U.S. Government Printing Office.

Ungerleider, J. T., & Pechnick, R. (1992). Hallucinogens. In J. H. Lowinson, P. Ruiz, & R. B. Millman (Eds.), *Substance abuse: A comprehensive textbook.* Baltimore: Williams & Wilkins.

Valdes, L. J. (1994). Salvia divinorum and the unique diterpene hallucinogen, Salvinorin (divinorin) A. *Journal of Psychoactive Drugs, 26*(3), 277–283.

Wu, T. C., Tashkin, D. P., Djahed, B., & Rose, J. E. (1988). Pulmonary hazards of smoking marijuana as compared with tobacco. *New England Journal of Medicine, 318,* 347–351.

Zinberg, N. (1984). *Drug, set, and setting.* New Haven, CT: Yale University Press.

Zukin, S. R., & Zukin, R. S. (1992). Phencyclidine. In J. H. Lowinson, P. Ruiz, & R. B. Millman (Eds.), *Substance abuse: A comprehensive textbook.* Baltimore: Williams & Wilkins.

10

☐

Tobacco

NORMAN HYMOWITZ

INTRODUCTION

The use of tobacco (*Nicotine tobaccum*) has been traced to early American civilizations, where it played a prominent role in religious rites and ceremonies. Among the ancient Maya, tobacco smoke was used as "solar incense" to bring rain during the dry season. Shooting stars were believed to be burning butts cast off by the rain god (Schultes, 1978). The Aztecs employed tobacco (*Nicotine rustica*) as a power, which was used in ceremonial rites as well as chewed as a euphoric agent with lime (Schultes, 1978).

In 1492, Columbus and his crew observed natives lighting rolls of dried leaves, which they called *tobacos* (cigars), and "swallowing" the smoke (Schultes, 1978). Twenty years later, Juan Ponce de Leon brought tobacco back to Portugal, where it soon was grown on Portuguese soil. Sir Walter Raleigh introduced smoking to England in 1565, and the English, too, successfully grew their own tobacco (Vogt, 1982). The growth of world trade led to the spread of tobacco to every corner of the globe.

The popular "weed" was not without its detractors. James I of England published a "counterblaste to tobacco" in 1604, and he arranged a public debate on the effects of tobacco in 1605. Pope Urban III condemned tobacco use in 1642, threatening excommunication of offenders. In Russia, a decree in 1634 punished tobacco users by nose slitting, castration, flogging, and banishment. These harsh measures were abolished by Peter the Great, who took to smoking a pipe in an effort to open a window to the West (Van Lancker, 1977).

It is believed that the smoking of cigarettes first occurred in Mexico, where chopped tobacco was wrapped in corn husks (Van Lancker, 1977). The most popular forms of tobacco use in the United States in the past were chewing and dipping snuff, as evidenced by spittoons in homes and public places. In the late 1800s, cigarette smoking grew in popularity. James Buchanan Duke brought Polish and Russian Jews to the United States to manufacture cigarettes in 1867, and he used advertising to enlighten Americans about the pleasures of smoking. Cigarettes were first mass produced in Durham, North Carolina, in 1884, when Washington Duke used a newly invented cigarette machine to produce some 120,000 cigarettes per day, thus ushering in the era of cheap, abundant tobacco products for smoking and setting the stage for 20th-century epidemics of lung cancer, emphysema, and coronary heart disease (Vogt, 1982).

In 1990, the total consumption of cigarettes in the United States was 2.5 billion (U.S. Department of Health and Human Services [DHHS], 1989a), and cigarette smoking was largely restricted to males. Major advances in agriculture, manufacturing, and marketing; two world wars; and changing cultural norms led to a marked increase in smoking rates. In the United States, total consumption of cigarettes increased from 2.5 billion in 1900 to 631.5 billion in 1980 (DHHS, 1989a). Cigarette consumption peaked in 1981 (640 billion) but has since declined to an estimated 574 billion in 1987 (DHHS, 1989a), the equivalent of more than 6 trillion doses of nicotine (Jones, 1987). By 1935, 52.5% of adult American males smoked cigarettes, and at the age of peak smoking prevalence (roughly from the age of 20 through the early 30s), more than 70% of all American males were smokers in 1947 (Warner, 1986).

While tobacco consumption is declining in the United States, global tobacco consumption is rising (Pierce, 1991). World consumption of tobacco probably will double before the turn of the century. Of this projected growth in demand, 60% is expected to come from Asia (particularly China), and another 25% will come from the Far East countries. About 10% will come from Africa and Latin America (Pierce, 1991).

Cigarettes are the nation's most heavily advertised consumer product (Warner, 1986). Advertising expenditures were estimated at more than $2 billion for 1985—twice the annual expenditures of the National Cancer Institute (American Cancer Society, 1986). By 1990, cigarette advertising and promotional expenditures grew to almost $4 billion (DHHS, 1994a), and expenditures continue to increase. Tobacco advertisers have expanded existing markets and opened new ones, contributing to significant changes in the demography of smoking. Tobacco advertisements in magazines targeted to women (Albright, Altman, Slater, & Maccoby, 1988) and minorities (Cummings, Giovino, & Mendicino, 1987) have increased markedly, as have smoking rates in both population groups. American women are now almost as likely to smoke as men, and teenage girls are more likely to begin smoking than teenage boys (DHHS, 1989a). The prevalence of smoking among blacks is higher than among whites (DHHS, 1989a), as are rates of lung cancer (Devesa & Diamond, 1983; DHHS, 1995) and coronary heart disease (Sempos, Cooper, Kovar, & McMillan, 1988; DHHS, 1995).

Considerable amounts of tobacco company dollars have been specifically directed toward capturing the attention of young people (DHHS, 1994a;

Evans, Farkas, Gilpin, Berry, & Pierce, 1995). Some conclusions from the 1994 Surgeon General's report, "Preventing Tobacco Use among Young People," are as follows:

- Young people continue to be a strategically important market for the tobacco industry.
- Young people are currently exposed to cigarette messages through print media and through promotional activities, such as sponsorship of sporting events and public entertainment, point-of-sale displays, and distribution of specialty items.
- Cigarette advertising uses images rather than information to portray the attractiveness and function of smoking.
- Cigarette advertisements capitalize on the disparity between an ideal and actual self-image and imply that smoking may close the gap.
- Cigarette advertising appears to affect young people's perceptions of the pervasiveness, image, and function of smoking. Because misperceptions in these areas constitute psychosocial risk factors for the initiation of smoking, cigarette advertising appears to increase young people's risk of smoking.

The occurrence of cigarette smoking as a mass phenomenon in the 20th century gave rise to new information about the adverse health consequences of smoking. Dr. Luther Terry, who served as Surgeon General of the U.S. Public Health Service from 1961 to 1965, noted that the landmark 1964 Surgeon General's Advisory Committee Report, "Smoking and Health," was the culmination of growing scientific concern over a period of more than 25 years (Terry, 1983). This report also recognized the "habitual" nature of tobacco use but stopped short of recognizing tobacco use as an addiction.

Data on the health effects of cigarette smoking and other forms of tobacco continue to accumulate, documenting adverse effects of maternal smoking on the developing fetus (Asmussen, 1980) and of "secondhand" smoke on non-smokers (Kauffmann, Tessier, & Oriol, 1983; Samet, Lewit, & Warner, 1994). The 1979 Report of the Surgeon General presented the most comprehensive review of health effects of smoking ever published (U.S. Department of Health, Education and Welfare [DHEW], 1979). Subsequent reports focused on women, the "changing cigarette," cancer, cardiovascular disease, chronic obstructive lung disease, the workplace, and involuntary smoking (DHHS, 1989a), reducing the health consequences of smoking (25 years of progress) (DHHS, 1989a), health benefits of cessation (DHHS, 1990), smoking and health in the Americas (DHHS, 1992), and prevention (DHHS, 1994a).

Major conclusions from the 1988 Surgeon General's report (DHHS, 1988) were as follows: (1) cigarettes and other forms of tobacco are addicting, (2) nicotine is the drug in tobacco that causes addiction, and (3) the pharmacological and behavioral processes that determine tobacco addiction are similar to those that determine addiction to drugs such as heroin and cocaine.

These conclusions were based on years of observation and study. Nicotine was isolated from tobacco leaves in 1828 by Posselt and Reimen, pharmacological studies of the physiological actions of nicotine were well under way by the end of the 19th century, and the central nervous system effects of nicotine were clearly documented in the 1950s (Henningfield & Jasinski, 1988). Attempts to market nicotine-free cigarettes have been commercial failures. Relapse rates among ex-smokers are remarkably similar to relapse rates among ex-heroin and alcohol users (cf. Hunt & Bespalec, 1974), and persons trying to quit smoking or other forms of tobacco use often experience intense withdrawal symptoms that can be relieved by ingestion of nicotine (Russell, 1986).

Studies of the conditioned, discriminative, and reinforcing functions of nicotine, in animals as well as humans (Henningfield & Goldberg, 1988), have underscored nicotine's dependence potential. Experiments in behavioral pharmacology showed that pretreatment of smokers with nicotine led to a reduction in smoking (Lucchesi, Schuster, & Emley, 1967), that smokers compensated for lower-nicotine cigarettes by smoking more (Ashton, Watson, Marsh, & Sadler, 1970), and that central nicotine antagonists, such as mecamylamine, led to an increase in cigarette smoking (Stolerman, Goldfarb, Fink, & Jarvik, 1973). These findings suggest that nicotine regulation plays an important role in smoking behavior, and that the effects of nicotine on the brain may be an important factor in understanding tobacco use. Studies of nicotine receptors in the brain (e.g., Sloan, Todd, & Martin, 1984), and a greater understanding of the role of cigarettes and other forms of tobacco as "nicotine delivery systems" (see Henningfield & Goldberg, 1988), served as additional bases for the 1988 report.

DEFINITIONS

Henningfield (1986) compared tobacco dependence to other forms of drug dependence and concluded that there are more similarities than differences. He noted that (1) tobacco dependence, like other forms of drug dependence, is a complex process, involving interactions between drug and nondrug factors; (2) tobacco dependence is an orderly and lawful process governed by the same factors that control other forms of drug self-administration; (3) tobacco use, like other forms of drug use, is sensitive to dose manipulation; (4) development of tolerance (diminished response to repeated doses of a drug or the requirement for increasing the dose to have the same effect) and physiological dependence (termination of nicotine followed by a syndrome of withdrawal phenomena) when nicotine is repeatedly administered is similar to the development of tolerance and dependence of other drugs of abuse; and (5) tobacco, like many other substances of abuse, produces effects often considered a utility or benefit to the user (e.g., relief of anxiety or stress, avoidance of weight gain, alteration in mood) (see also Henningfield, Cohen, & Pickworth, 1993).

Although the similarities between tobacco or nicotine dependence and other forms of drug dependence are noteworthy, there are features of tobacco use that make it unique. In contrast to many other drugs of abuse, tobacco products are legal and readily available. When used as intended, tobacco products lead to disease and death. Unlike alcohol, a legal drug that can be consumed socially and in moderation without ill effects, all levels of tobacco use are harmful (DHHS, 1988).

Large sums of money are spent each year to advertise and market tobacco products, particularly cigarettes. This adds an important dimension to tobacco dependence that is not present to the same degree with other substances, with the possible exception of alcohol. Few children in our society grow up free of the tobacco advertisers' reach; this provides unique opportunities for the tobacco companies to teach them about the virtues of tobacco, the manner in which it should be used, and the role it should play in their daily lives. So pervasive is the positive imagery associated with cigarette smoking that it is almost impossible to distinguish the reinforcing qualities of cigarettes that derive from past conditioning and learning from those that derive from nicotine per se.

Subtle behavioral factors may also assume a relatively greater role in controlling smoking than other forms of substance dependence. Daily, repetitive smoking patterns make cigarette smoking an overpracticed, unconscious behavior that is associated via conditioning mechanisms with almost every other behavior in the smoker's repertoire. So insidious is the moment-to-moment role of smoking in daily life that smokers often do not even know what to do with their hands when they stop smoking.

DIAGNOSIS

According to the fourth edition of the *Diagnostic and Statistical Manual of Mental Disorders* (DSM-IV; American Psychiatric Association, 1994), nicotine dependence is considered to be a substance-related disorder. The key features of substance dependence are a cluster of cognitive, behavioral, and physiological symptoms indicating that the individual continues use of the substance despite significant substance-related problems. There is a pattern of repeated self-administration that usually results in tolerance, withdrawal, and compulsive drug-taking behavior (American Psychiatric Association, 1994). Specific criteria for substance dependence are shown in Table 10.1.

The diagnosis of nicotine dependence in DSM-IV is fairly straightforward. Information needed to make the diagnosis can be obtained through interview and questionnaire and can readily be collected along with other medical history data. Two National Institutes of Health publications (DHHS, 1986, 1989b) and a recent report prepared by the American Psychiatric Association (1996) provide guidelines to help physicians inquire about smoking, assess their patient's needs, and encourage patients to quit smoking. The American Heart Association and the American Academy of Family Physicians also have

TABLE 10.1. DSM-IV Criteria for Substance Dependence

A maladaptive pattern of substance use, leading to clinically significant impairment or distress, as manifested by three (or more) of the following, occurring at any time in the same 12-month period:

(1) tolerance, as defined by either of the following:
   (a) a need for markedly increased amounts of the substance to achieve intoxication or desired effect
   (b) markedly diminished effect with continued use of the same amount of the substance
(2) withdrawal, as manifested by either of the following:
   (a) the characteristic withdrawal syndrome for the substance
   (b) the same (or a closely related) substance is taken to relieve or avoid withdrawal symptoms
(3) the substance often taken in larger amounts or over a longer period than was intended
(4) there is a persistent desire or unsuccessful efforts to cut down or control substance use
(5) a great deal of time is spent in activities necessary to obtain the substance (e.g., visiting multiple doctors or driving long distances), use the substance (e.g., chain smoking), or recover from its effects
(6) important social, occupational, or recreational activities are given up or reduced because of substance use
(7) the substance use is continued despite knowledge of having a persistent or recurrent physical or psychological problem that is likely to have been caused or exacerbated by the substance (e.g., current cigarette smoking despite recognition that a heart ailment was made worse by smoking)

Note. From American Psychiatric Association (1994, p. 181). Copyright 1994 by the American Psychiatric Association. Reprinted by permission.

prepared "quit-smoking kits" to enable physicians to intervene on smoking in their offices.

It is important to be aware that verbal report data can be misleading. Patients may underreport the number of cigarettes smoked per day and, depending on the "demand" characteristics of the situation, may report that they have stopped smoking when they have not. Objective measures of smoking, such as expired air carbon monoxide, serum or saliva thiocyanate, and cotinine (DHEW, 1979), are available and readily applicable to clinical and research settings. Self-monitoring of smoking behavior and verification of smoking status by checking with an informant are additional ways of improving or monitoring the accuracy of verbal reports.

Most of the criteria for psychoactive substance dependence are characteristic of cigarette smoking and other forms of tobacco use. Cigarette smokers often smoke more than they intend to, have difficulty quitting or simply cutting down, spend a great deal of time procuring cigarettes and smoking them, persist in smoking despite known risk and/or current illness, and readily develop tolerance, enabling them to smoke a larger number of cigarettes per day than they did when they first started smoking. The fact that most smokers who quit smoking in the past did so on their own, without formal treatment, seems to be somewhat at odds with the popular notion of addiction. However, it is important to note that most former heroin users also gave up heroin without formal treatment (Johnson, 1977).

When smokers stop smoking, they may experience nicotine withdrawal as defined by DSM-IV (American Psychiatric Association, 1994). About 50% of adults who attempt to stop smoking will meet DSM-IV criteria for nicotine dependence (American Psychiatric Association, 1996). Diagnostic criteria for nicotine withdrawal are presented in Table 10.2. Associated features include craving, a desire for sweets, and impaired performance on tasks requiring vigilance (American Psychiatric Association, 1994). Depression and difficulty sleeping are not uncommon. Associated laboratory findings include a slowing on electroencephalograph, decreases in catecholamine and cortisol levels, rapid eye movement (REM) changes, impairment on neuropsychological testing, and decreased metabolic rate (American Psychiatric Association, 1994). Nicotine withdrawal also may be associated with a dry or productive cough, decreased heart rate, increased appetite or weight gain, and a dampened orthostatic response (American Psychiatric Association, 1994).

When smokers quit smoking, there is a fairly high probability that they will return to smoking (relapse). Smokers often quit many times before they succeed in remaining abstinent. Relapse is most likely to occur soon after quitting, and studies of quit-smoking programs show that most smokers relapse within about 3 months. Although ex-smokers are less likely to relapse after they have been abstinent for 3 months, the potential for relapse remains present for many years (Ockene, Hymowitz, Lagus, & Shaten, 1991).

In general, the more highly addicted the smoker, the more difficult it is for the smoker to quit smoking and remain cigarette free (Hymowitz et al., 1997). Severity of addiction can be readily assessed by questioning the smoker. Smokers who report smoking 25 or more cigarettes per day, report smoking

---

TABLE 10.2. DSM-IV Diagnostic Criteria for Nicotine Withdrawal

A. Daily use of nicotine for at least several weeks.

B. Abrupt cessation of nicotine use, or reduction in the amount of nicotine used followed within 24 hours by four (or more) of the following signs:
   (1) dysphoric or depressed mood
   (2) insomnia
   (3) irritability, frustration, or anger
   (4) anxiety
   (5) difficulty concentrating
   (6) restlessness
   (7) decreased heart rate
   (8) increased appetite or weight gain

C. The symptoms in Criterion B cause clinically significant distress or impairment in social, occupational, or other important areas of functioning.

D. The symptoms are not due to a general medical condition and are not better accounted for by another mental disorder.

Note. From American Psychiatric Association (1994, pp. 244–245). Copyright 1994 by the American Psychiatric Association. Reprinted by permission.

the first cigarette of the day soon after waking, and smokers who either never quit smoking in the past or who had a difficult time in the past (gained excessive amounts of weight, were burdened by cravings, experienced difficulty sleeping, etc.) are likely to have a very difficult time stopping smoking. It is important to inquire about past quit attempts, learn from them, and develop a new quitting plan for the future. As noted later, nicotine replacement therapy may be particularly helpful to highly addicted smokers.

CLINICAL FEATURES

Under normal circumstances, cigarette smoking and other forms of tobacco use do not cause obvious states of intoxication, nor does their chronic use lead to organic brain damage, although acute effects of nicotine may affect vigilance and memory (DHHS, 1988). Overdose typically is not a problem, and acute effects of nicotine on health have received less attention in the medical literature than have chronic effects.

A number of poisonings and deaths from ingestion of nicotine, primarily involving nicotine-containing pesticides, have been reported, and acute intoxication has been observed in children after swallowing tobacco materials (DHHS, 1988). The lethal oral dose of nicotine in adults has been estimated at 40–60 mg (DHHS, 1988). Nicotine intoxication produces nausea, vomiting, abdominal pain, diarrhea, headaches, sweating, and pallor. More severe intoxication results in dizziness, weakness, and confusion, progressing to convulsions, hypotension, and coma. Death is usually due to paralysis of respiratory muscles and/or central respiratory control (DHHS, 1988).

The chronic effects of cigarette smoking take a massive toll. The role of cigarette smoking in the pathogenesis of coronary heart disease, lung and other cancers, and chronic obstructive lung disease, as well as many other forms of illness, has been dramatically documented in a series of reports by United States surgeon generals dating back to 1964 (U.S. Public Health Service, 1964). Cigarette smoking has been cited as the chief avoidable cause of death and morbidity in our society and the number one public health problem of our time (DHHS, 1989a). Tobacco is responsible for more than 400,000 deaths each year in the United States alone (Bartecchi, Mackenzie, & Schrier, 1994). These include 179,820 deaths due to cardiovascular diseases, 119,920 due to lung cancer, 31,402 due to other cancers, and 84,475 deaths due to respiratory diseases (Bartecchi et al., 1994).

The problems of cigarette smoking and tobacco-related diseases are not limited to the United States. According to the World Health Organization (American Cancer Society, 1997), approximately 3 million people die worldwide each year as a result of smoking. Approximately half of all continuing smokers will die prematurely from smoking. Of these, approximately half die in middle age (35–69), losing an average of 20–25 years of life expectancy.

The acute effects of nicotine also are important, having been implicated in sudden heart attack death and stroke (Black, 1990). Cigarette smoking and other forms of tobacco use are contraindicated in patients with heart disease, hypertension, diabetes, chronic obstructive lung disease, and diseases of the gastrointestinal tract for fear that nicotine and other components of tobacco will exacerbate existing illness as well as contribute to progressive pathogenesis (DHEW, 1979). Direct effects of nicotine on heart rate, cerebral blood flow, blood pressure, platelet aggregation, and fibrinogen are just a few of the mechanisms by which nicotine and cigarette smoking exert acute influences on health and well-being (Black, 1990).

Evidence of the harmful effects of cigarette smoking also may be observed in smokers in whom frank disease has not yet developed. Shortness of breath, cough, excessive phlegm, and nasal catarrh are common symptoms, which readily subside when smokers stop smoking (Hymowitz, Lasser, & Safirstein, 1982). Smokers often report a dulling of the senses of taste and smell, and smokers, as well as their family members, generally experience more colds and illness than nonsmokers (DHEW, 1979). Tobacco smoke and products may interact with other drugs that patients are taking ("Pharmacists' 'helping smokers quit' program," 1986). Drugs that show the most significant interactions with tobacco smoke include oral contraceptives, theophylline, propranolol, and other antianginal drugs. Drugs with moderately significant clinical interactions with smoking include propxyphene, pentazocine, phenylbutazone, phenothiazine, tricyclic antidepressants, benzodiazepines, amobarbital, heparin, furosemide, and vitamins ("Pharmacists' 'helping smokers quit' program," 1986).

A recent study (Bansil, Hymowitz, & Keller, 1989) showed that schizophrenic outpatients who smoked cigarettes required significantly more neuroleptic medication to control psychiatric symptoms than comparable nonsmokers, despite the fact that the patients were identical with respect to initial severity of illness. Multivariate analyses showed that the difference between the groups was not due to age, weight, sex, alcohol consumption, or tea/coffee intake. In view of the side effects profile of many drugs used in psychiatry, and the fact that the prevalence of tardive dyskinesia may be higher in mentally ill patients who smoke than in patients who do not smoke (Yassa, Lal, Korpassy, & Ally, 1987), it is important to achieve clinical effectiveness with as low a dose as possible. Cigarette smoking compromises this important goal.

The evidence clearly indicates that smokers benefit in many ways when they stop smoking (DHHS, 1990). Carbon monoxide is eliminated from their systems within 24 hours, and within a few months ex-smokers report a lessening of pulmonary symptoms, such as shortness of breath, cough, phlegm, and nasal catarrh (Hymowitz et al., 1982). Their senses of taste and smell return, peripheral vascular circulation improves, and ex-smokers may experience an improvement in small-airway disease and a slowing in the rate of decline of pulmonary function (DHEW, 1979). Most important, risk of serious disease and premature death declines markedly over the course of several years following smoking cessation, and in people already disabled by frank disease, prospects for recovery improve greatly (DHEW, 1979).

COURSE

Cigarette smoking starts at an early age, usually in response to peer pressure and/or curiosity (Lynch & Bonnie, 1994). Personal characteristics, family, social norms, and cigarette marketing (DHHS, 1989a) exert important influences. A sizable proportion (one-third or more) of children as young as 9 years old have engaged in experimental "puffing," and there is a steady rise with age in the proportion of children who report becoming involved with smoking (Oei & Fea, 1987). Among American children 13 years old and older, only about one-third of those surveyed had not at least puffed a cigarette (Chassin et al., 1981). By age 14 or 15, smoking or nonsmoking behavior is an established pattern, and little experimentation takes place thereafter (Aitken, 1980).

The issue of smoking by youth is of great interest and importance to the public health community as well as to the tobacco industry. If people do not start smoking by their late teens, they are unlikely to smoke as adults. Cross-sectional surveys of adults who smoke daily show that 89% began using cigarettes and 71% began smoking daily by or at age 18 (Lynch & Bonnie, 1994). For the public health community, the prevention of smoking onset by youth is the key to stemming the tide of tobacco addiction and tobacco-related disease. For the tobacco industry, young people *must* take up smoking or else they could very well go out of business. Collectively, the tobacco industry spent more than 4.6 billion dollars in 1991 to advertise and promote tobacco products, and much to the chagrin of the public health community, approximately 3,000 young people become regular smokers every day (Lynch & Bonnie, 1994).

Despite a marked decline in adult smoking rates (from 40.4% of the adult population in 1965 to 25.7% in 1991), the estimated prevalence of smoking among adults appears to have leveled off (Lynch & Bonnie, 1994). In 1994, smoking prevalence for white men 18 years or older was 28%; for black men, 34%. For white women, the smoking prevalence was 23%; for black women, 22% (American Cancer Society, 1997). Among youth, there has been little, if any, decline in smoking rates since 1980. Among eighth-grade students in 1993, 16.7% were current smokers and 8.3% smoked daily. Among high school seniors, 29.9% were current smokers (smoked within the past 30 days) and 19% smoked daily. In 1980, the prevalence of regular smokers among high school seniors was 30.5% and the prevalence of daily smokers was 21.3% (Lynch & Bonnie, 1994). With the exception of African American female students, the prevalence of high school students who smoke frequently increased from 1991 to 1995 for all racial, ethnic, and gender groups (American Cancer Society, 1997).

Researchers have suggested that substance use, in general, increases between adolescence and young adulthood and then declines in the mid-20s. Individuals may discontinue substance use in adulthood because the responsibilities and demands of marital, occupational, and parental roles are incompatible with substance use (Yamaguchi & Kandel, 1985). In work by Chassin,

Presson, Rose, and Sherman (1996), age-related trends for cigarette smoking paralleled those for other drugs in showing a significant increase between adolescence and young adulthood. However, unlike other forms of drug use, they found no significant decline in cigarette smoking in the late 20s. The authors suggested that the persistence of cigarette smoking into the late 20s (and beyond) may be due to three factors: (1) nicotine dependence may contribute to low cessation rates, (2) the negative health impacts of cigarette smoking may not be encountered until later ages, and (3) because smoking is a legal behavior whose pharmacological effects are not incompatible with the day-to-day demands of adult roles, role socialization pressure for cessation may be less intense (Chassin et al., 1996).

Although psychosocial factors play a major role in the initiation of smoking in adolescence, pharmacological and conditioning factors are also important. Like adults, young people often have difficulty stopping smoking (Green, 1980). The reasons they give for this difficulty—social pressure, urges, and withdrawal symptoms—implicate behavioral and physiological dependence on tobacco (Biglan & Lichtenstein, 1984). Hansen (1983) studied abstinence and relapse in high-school-age smokers (16–18 years old) who smoked an average of 15–20 cigarettes per day. As with adults, most relapse occurred within 3 months of stopping smoking. Variables that predicted relapse were the number of cigarettes smoked per day and the regularity of a teenager's smoking pattern—findings that are also indicative of tobacco dependence.

As noted earlier, the early initiation of smoking is of considerable concern to the public health community. The pathogenesis of diseases such as chronic obstructive lung disease and atherosclerotic heart disease begins early in life, and duration of exposure to tobacco contributes to the likelihood of suffering adverse consequences as an adult (DHEW, 1979). However, it is not necessary to wait until adulthood to see signs of impaired health. Seely, Zuskin, and Bouhuys (1971) reported that cough, phlegm, and shortness of breath were more common among high school students who smoked than among non-smokers, with no significant differences between sexes. Pulmonary function testing showed that maximum ventilation (V max) at both 50% and 25% vital capacity (midmaximal flow rates) were significantly below expected levels in boys who smoked more than 15 cigarettes per day and in girls who smoked more than 10 cigarettes per day (Seely et al., 1971). The authors concluded that regular smoking for 1–5 years is sufficient to cause demonstrable decreases in lung function (see also DHHS, 1994a).

After high school, there is a gradual transition to regular adult smoking levels, and the relative influence of dependence on nicotine increases (Sachs, 1986). For most, smoking rates will hover around one pack per day and remain quite stable for most of their adult lives. Others will progress to higher smoking rates, again revealing marked day-to-day stability in nicotine ingestion. Recent surveys have shown that the percentage of adult smokers who smoke 25 or more cigarettes per day (heavy smokers) has increased since the 1960s, primarily because heavy smokers are least likely to stop smoking on their own or in formal smoking cessation programs (DHHS, 1988).

Inevitably, adverse consequences of cigarette smoking and other forms of tobacco use take their toll. Smokers experience excess illness and absence from work, diseases of the small and large airways of the lungs, and adverse complications of diseases that are exacerbated but not caused by smoking, such as diabetes and hypertension (DHEW, 1979). Most important, risk of life-threatening illness, such as chronic obstructive lung disease, lung cancer, and coronary heart disease, is significantly higher in smokers than in non-smokers (DHEW, 1979). Most smokers are aware of these facts, and a majority admit that they would like to stop smoking (DHHS, 1989a). Approximately 2% per year succeed (DHHS, 1989a), most making a number of attempts before succeeding. Nearly half of all living adults who ever smoked have quit (DHHS, 1989a), and most did so "on their own" (Schachter, 1982).

Despite the fact that most ex-smokers reported quitting on their own, quit-smoking groups still have an important place in the antismoking arena (Fiore et al., 1990). Analysis of data from the 1986 Adult Use of Tobacco Survey showed that about 90% of successful quitters and 80% of unsuccessful quitters used individual methods of smoking cessation rather than organized programs (Fiore et al., 1990). Most used a "cold turkey" approach. Multivariate analysis showed that women, middle-age persons, more educated persons, persons who had made more quit-smoking attempts, and, particularly, heavier smokers were most likely to use a cessation program. Among smokers who had attempted to quit on their own within the previous 10 years, 47.5% were successful. Only 23.6% of persons who used cessation programs were successful. The authors concluded that formal cessation programs serve a small but important population of smokers that includes heavier smokers, those most at risk for tobacco-related morbidity and mortality (Fiore et al., 1990).

DIFFERENTIAL DIAGNOSIS

The diagnosis of nicotine dependence is relatively straightforward, particularly in adults. Most adults admit that they smoke cigarettes, and they typically smoke on a daily basis. For adolescents and teens, smoking may not occur on a daily basis. The physician should ask if they ever smoked, how frequently they smoke, and if they consider themselves to be smokers. Older teens, of course, are more likely to report that they smoke on a daily basis, although the number of cigarettes smoked per day may be fewer than adults.

The clinician often wishes to determine the severity of tobacco dependence, as such information provides insight into how difficult it will be for the smoker to quit and what kind of quitting strategy will be most effective. Fagerstrom (1978) developed a brief nicotine dependence questionnaire. Among the most discriminating questions are the following: "How soon after you wake up do you smoke your first cigarette?", "How many cigarettes a day do you smoke?", and "Have you stopped smoking or tried to stop smoking in the past?" (Kozlowski et al., 1989).

Smokers who smoke the most cigarettes, smoke soon after waking, and never quit smoking in the past are least likely to quit smoking on their own or with assistance (cf. Hymowitz et al., 1997). They also are the smokers who are most likely to benefit from nicotine replacement therapy (Fagerstrom, 1988). Despite the fact that many addicted smokers have a difficult time quitting, it is important to be optimistic and to join with them in planning new cessation strategies. It is possible to learn from past failures to motivate smokers anew and to consider new methods for cessation. Helping people stop smoking requires as much art as science, and factors such as warmth, concern, and support play a significant role. Stop-smoking aids and self-help books may help, and follow-up postcards and telephone contact may tip the balance toward success (cf. Lando, 1993).

Smokers with psychiatric illness, such as schizophrenia, alcoholism, and depression, have an extremely difficult time quitting smoking (Glassman, 1993; American Psychiatric Association, 1996) and for smokers who succeed in quitting, negative affect and stress play a major role in smoking relapse (Schiffman, 1986). Empathy and support often are essential to success. A large proportion of adult smokers have quit smoking in the past, and it is instructive to question them about past quitting methods and reasons for relapse. Each new quit attempt increases the likelihood of ultimate success.

ETHNICITY

According to the "State Tobacco Control Highlights, 1996" (Centers for Disease Control, 1996), there were 46,824,800 adult smokers (18 years and older) in the United States in 1993. The overall smoking rate in 1993 was 25%—27.7% for men and 22.5% for women. The smoking rate for adults with less than 12 years of education was 29.7%, compared to 19% for adults with more than 12 years of education. Of the major ethnic/racial groups, the highest rates of smoking were for American Indian/Alaska Native (38.7%) followed by black (26%), white (25.4%), Hispanic (20.4%), and Asian/Pacific Islanders (18.2%) (Centers for Disease Control, 1996).

Compared to whites, black smokers smoke fewer cigarettes per day (DHHS, 1988). This might suggest that blacks, as a group, may be less dependent on tobacco than whites. However, blacks are more likely than whites to smoke high-tar, high-nicotine cigarettes and mentholated brands, less likely to smoke "light" and "ultra light" brands, more likely to smoke soon after waking, and more likely to increase their rate of smoking on weekends (Hymowitz et al., 1995).

Although past surveys have shown that blacks have not quit smoking over the past decades at the same rate as the general population (Fiore et al., 1990), more recent data from large smoking intervention studies (e.g., Multiple Risk Factor Intervention Trial [MRFIT]; Hymowitz, Sexton, Ockene, & Grandits, 1991) and community studies (e.g., Community Intervention Trial for Smoking Cessation [COMMIT]; Hymowitz et al., 1997), revealed comparable quit rates for blacks and whites. Variables that did emerge as significant predictors of smoking cessation in these studies were older age, higher income, less frequent alcohol intake, lower levels of daily cigarette consumption, longer time to first cigarette in the morning, initiation of smoking after age 20, more than one previous quit attempt, a strong desire to stop smoking, absence of other smokers in the household, and male gender (Hymowitz et al., 1991, 1997).

Although it is generally true that smoking rates for males are higher than for females, for some racial/ethnic groups, the discrepancy is quit large. In China, for example, more than 60% of the males smoke, whereas less than 10% of the females smoke (Pierce, 1991). Similarly, in Catalonia, Spain, 58% of the males smoke cigarettes, whereas rates for women are less than 20%. Similar large discrepancies between male and female smoking are found in many countries of Eastern Europe (Peto, Lopez, Boreham, Thun, & Heath, 1994), the Caribbean, South America, and Central America (DHHS, 1992). When people from these countries immigrate to the United States, the sex differential in smoking rates diminish, as the smoking rates in women become more like women in their new country. This, in part, is a natural aspect of the acculturation process. However, it also reflects the marketing strategies of tobacco companies who specifically target females from countries with traditionally low female smoking rates (Pierce, 1991).

There is little evidence to suggest that smokers from different racial/ethnic groups respond differently to different smoking prevention and cessation strategies and methods. However, there is a growing appreciation for the need to take into account the smokers' racial/ethnic heritage when counseling them. New educational materials and self-help stop-smoking pamphlets available from the National Institutes of Health and voluntary agencies, such as the American Cancer Society, are sensitive to racial, ethnic, and cultural issues.

PHARMACOLOGY

Nicotine is a tertiary amine composed of a pyridine and a pyrolidine ring (DHHS, 1988). Absorption of nicotine across biological membranes depends on pH. Modern cigarettes produce smoke that is suitably flavored and sufficiently nonirritating to be inhaled deeply into lung alveoli (see Jones, 1987). When tobacco smoke reaches the small airways and alveoli of the lung, the nicotine is readily absorbed. The rapid absorption of nicotine from cigarette smoke thorough the lung occurs because of the huge surface area of the alveoli and small airways and because of the dissolution of nicotine at physiological pH, which facilitates transfer across cell membranes. Concentrations of nicotine in blood rise quickly during cigarette smoking and peak at its completion (DHHS, 1988).

Chewing tobacco, snuff, and nicotine polacrilex gum are of alkaline pH as a result of tobacco selection and/or buffering with additives by the manufacturer. The alkaline pH facilitates absorption of nicotine through mucous membranes. The rate of nicotine absorption from smokeless tobacco depends on the product and the route of administration. With fine-ground nasal snuff, blood levels of nicotine rise almost as fast as after cigarette smoking. The rate of nicotine absorption with the use of oral snuff, chewing tobacco, and nicotine polacrilex gum is more gradual (DHHS, 1988). Transdermal nicotine provides a stable source of nicotine while new products, such as nicotine nasal spray and inhaler, deliver a quicker bolus of nicotine to the brain which more closely matches what happens when a cigarette is inhaled. Swallowed nicotine is poorly absorbed because of the high acidity of the gut.

Nicotine inhaled in tobacco smoke enters the blood very rapidly, with uptake into the brain occurring within 1–2 minutes. After smoking, the action of nicotine on the brain occurs very quickly. Rapid onset of effects after a puff is believed to provide optimal reinforcement for the development of drug dependence (DHHS, 1988). The effects of nicotine decline after it is distributed to other tissues. The distribution half-life, which describes the movement of nicotine from the blood and other rapidly perfused tissues (such e.g., the brain) to other body tissues, is approximately 9 minutes (DHHS, 1988).

After absorption into the blood, which is at pH 7.4, about 69% of the nicotine is ionized and 31% nonionized. Binding to plasma protein is less than 5%. The drug is distributed to body tissues with a steady-state volume of distribution averaging 180 liters. Spleen, liver, lungs, and brain have a high affinity for nicotine, whereas the affinity of adipose tissue is very low (DHHS, 1988). Nicotine-binding sites or receptors in the brain have been identified and differentiated as very-high-affinity, high-affinity, and low-affinity types (DHHS, 1988). The most intense localization of labeled nicotine has been found in the interpeduncular nucleus and medial habenula.

Nicotine is extensively metabolized, primarily in the liver, but also to a small extent in the lung. Renal excretion of unchanged nicotine depends on urinary pH and urine flow and may range from 2% to 35% but typically accounts for 5–10% of elimination (DHHS, 1988).

The relationship between the dose of nicotine and the resulting response (dose–response relationship) is complex and varies with the specific response that is measured. Nicotine is commonly thought of as an example of a drug that in low doses causes ganglionic stimulation and in high doses causes ganglionic blockade following brief stimulation (DHHS, 1988). At very low doses, similar to those seen during cigarette smoking, cardiovascular effects appear to be mediated by the central nervous system, either through activation of chemoreceptor afferent pathways or by direct effects on the brain stem. The net result is sympathetic neural discharge with an increase in blood pressure and heart rate. At higher doses, nicotine may act directly on the peripheral nervous system, producing ganglionic stimulation and the release of adrenal catecholamine. With high doses or rapid administration, nicotine produces hypotension and slowing of heart rate, mediated either by peripheral vagal activation or by direct central depressor effects (DHHS, 1988).

Humans and other species readily develop tolerance of the effects of nicotine. Studies of tolerance to nicotine on *in vitro* tissue preparations may be summarized as follows: (1) with repeated dosing, responses diminished to nearly negligible levels; (2) after tolerance occurred, responsiveness could be restored by increasing the size of the dose; and (3) after a few hours without nicotine, responsiveness was partially or fully restored (DHHS, 1988). It is apparent that cigarette smokers reveal evidence for both acute tolerance (tachyphylaxis) and chronic tolerance to nicotine. This is consistent with the fact that smokers increase their tobacco consumption and intake of nicotine with experience (chronic tolerance). When they abstain for a while, the first few cigarettes they smoke produce a variety of bodily symptoms. Thereafter, they quickly become less sensitive (acute tolerance). Tolerance may be related to an increase in central nicotine-binding sites or to a decrease in their sensitivity (DHHS, 1988).

CLINICAL PRACTICE GUIDELINES

Physicians, in general, have a unique role to play in the antismoking arena (Sullivan, 1991), and recent reviews (Orleans, 1993), monographs (DHHS, 1994b), and guidelines (American Psychiatric Association, 1996) underscore the importance of physician intervention on smoking in a variety of medical settings. The Agency for Health Care Policy and Research (AHCPR) recently convened the Smoking Cessation Guidelines Panel to identify effective, experimentally validated smoking cessation treatments and practices (DHHS, 1996). The major findings and recommendations may be summarized as follow:

1. Effective smoking cessation treatments are available, and every patient who smokes should be offered one or more of these treatments.
2. It is essential that clinicians determine and document the tobacco-use status of every patient treated in a health care setting.
3. Brief cessation treatments are effective, and at least a minimal intervention should be provided to every patient who uses tobacco.
4. A dose–response relation exists between the intensity and duration of treatment and its effectiveness. In general, the more intense the treatment, the more effective the treatment, and the more effective it is in providing long-term abstinence from tobacco.
5. Three treatment elements, in particular, are effective, and one or more of these elements should be included in smoking cessation treatment:
   a. Nicotine replacement therapy (nicotine patches or gum and more recently, nasal spray).
   b. Social support (clinician-provided encouragement and assistance).
   c. Skills training/problem solving (techniques on achieving and maintaining abstinence).
6. Effective reduction of tobacco use requires that health care systems make institutional changes that result in systematic identification of, and intervention with, all tobacco users at every visit.

The AHCPR guidelines emphasize the importance of systematically identifying all smokers, strongly advising all smokers to quit, and determining the patients' willingness to make a quit attempt (DHHS, 1996). The patient not willing to commit to quitting should receive a motivational intervention to promote subsequent quit attempts (e.g., personalize the health message, provide brochures on smoking and health and how-to-quit, and discuss with the patient the "costs" and "benefits" of smoking and quitting). When the patient is willing to make a quit attempt, primary care clinicians may assist by encouraging the patient to set a quit date, preparing the patient for the quit date, encouraging nicotine replacement therapy, providing self-help materials, and providing key advice (DHHS, 1996). All patients attempting quitting should have follow-up contact.

Recommendations concerning pharmacotherapy are of particular interest. According to the expert panel, (1) transdermal nicotine approximately doubles 6- to 12-month abstinence rates over those produced by placebo interventions; (2) transdermal nicotine is consistently more efficacious than placebo treatment regardless of the intensity of any psychosocial interventions (however, intensive psychosocial interventions increase absolute abstinence rates); and (3) patients are more likely to comply with transdermal nicotine instructions than with nicotine gum instructions (DHHS, 1996).

The expert panel also concluded that nicotine gum improves smoking-cessation rates approximately 40–60% compared with control interventions through 12 months of follow-up (DHHS, 1996). Two other nicotine replacement interventions—a nicotine nasal spray and a nicotine inhaler—have recently been developed and tested. Published data on these products are limited but demonstrate a significant benefit compared with placebo interventions (Hjalmarson, Franzon, Westin, & Wiklund, 1994; Tonnesen, Norregaard, Mikkelsen, Jorgensen, & Nilsson, 1993). At the time of the AHCPR report, the products were not licensed for prescription use in the United States, and there were limited data regarding their use. Therefore, the panel drew no conclusions about their efficacy and made no recommendations regarding their use (nicotine nasal spray is now available as a prescription medication, "Nicotrol NS") (DHHS, 1996).

The panel also examined the efficacy of other pharmacological agents for smoking cessation. They found little support for the use of clonidine, either as a primary or as an adjunctive pharmacological treatment for smoking cessation, and they were silent about the efficacy of antidepressants and anxiolytics/benzodiazipines because of a paucity of published data (DHHS, 1996).

Since the publication of the AHCPR report, new data on the efficacy of antidepressants for smoking cessation have been published. Hurt et al. (1997) evaluated the efficacy and safety of a sustained-release form of bupropion (Zyban, Glaxo Wellcome) as an aid to smoking cessation in a double-blind, placebo-controlled trial involving 615 subjects. At the end of seven weeks of treatment, which also included behavioral counseling, the rates of smoking cessation, as confirmed by carbon monoxide measurements, were 19% in the placebo group, 28.8% in the 100-mg group, 38.6% in the 150-mg group, and 44.2% in the 300-mg group ($p < 0.001$). After 1 year, the respective quit rates were 12.4%, 19.6%, 22.9%, and 23.1%. The rates for the 150-mg and 300-mg groups, but not the 100-mg group, were significantly better than those for the placebo group. Zyban was recently approved by the Food and Drug Administration as a prescription drug for the indication of smoking cessation.

PSYCHOPHARMACOTHERAPY

Successful intervention on smoking and other forms of tobacco use must address many contributing factors. These include acquired associations between smoking and environmental events, the use of tobacco to regulate mood and cope with stress, subtle relationships between smoking and other features of the smoker's behavioral repertoire, many idiosyncratic ways in which tobacco dependence interweaves itself within the psychosocial fabric of each smoker's life, and pharmacological properties of tobacco. Withdrawal symptoms, the tendency for environmental stimuli to elicit the urge to smoke, and the need to cope actively with potential obstacles to abstinence represent important issues once smokers stop smoking.

There are numerous approaches to smoking cessation in adults, and many comprehensive reviews and critiques of the literature have been published (e.g., Leventhal & Cleary, 1980; Schwartz, 1987; Lando, 1993). Although many approaches to smoking cessation have been successful in the short run, few, if any, have proved satisfactory in terms of long-term abstinence. This is true for group and individual counseling, multicomponent behavioral interventions, and newer pharmacological interventions. Relapse seems to be the rule rather than the exception (Hunt & Bespelac, 1974), with most smokers relapsing within 3 months after the end of treatment. Of the many nonpharmacological approaches to smoking cessation, behavioral approaches are most germane to the present chapter: They have undergone the most extensive experimental study, they are suitable for office and clinic-based physician interventions, and they may be used in combination with pharmacological approaches to smoking cessation (Fagerstrom, 1988).

Behavioral programs, whether in group, individual, or "self-help" formats, typically include a number of strategies (self-monitoring, stimulus control procedures, behavioral contracting, relaxation training, advice on diet and exercise, "quit dates," self-management skill training for relapse prevention, etc.) to motivate smokers, to help them gain control over smoking, and to systematically eliminate smoking from their behavioral repertoire. Once smokers stop smoking, many of the very same behavioral skills that helped them quit smoking are used to help them cope with stress and problematic situations to prevent relapse. Aversive conditioning procedures also may be used, either alone or in combination with other behavioral techniques, and they are among the most successful approaches to initial smoking cessation

(Leventhal & Cleary, 1980). However, their initial success also is usually compromised by high relapse rates (Raw & Russell, 1980).

"Multicomponent" behavioral programs include diverse behavioral strategies to help smokers modify their behavior. Success rates vary, depending on selection factors, cost, and whether aversive conditioning procedures are used. Schwartz (1987) reported that 1-year quit rates for multicomponent programs average 40%. This figure seems somewhat inflated. When objective measures of smoking and completeness of follow-up are taken into account, 1-year quit rates of 20–30% are more common. End-of-treatment quit rates may be higher, but relapse again compromises the long-term success of the intervention.

The MRFIT employed diversified behavioral strategies for initial smoking cessation and long-term smoking abstinence (Hughes, Hymowitz, Ockene, Simon, & Vogt, 1981). The reported quit rates for special intervention (SI) men were 43.1% at year 1 and 50% at year 6 (Hymowitz, 1987). These quit rates were significantly superior to those for usual care (UC) participants (13% and 29% at years 1 and 6, respectively). When serum thiocyanate, a breakdown product of hydrogen cyanide, was used as an objective measure of smoking, the year 6 quit rate for SI participants was reduced to 46% (Hymowitz, 1987).

Most of the SI men quit smoking during the first year of the program, whereas quitting for UC men was more evenly distributed over the 6 years of the program (Ockene, Hymowitz, Sexton, & Broste, 1982). This is consistent with the overall trend toward quitting smoking in the United States during the same period (DHHS, 1989a). Of the SI smokers who reported not smoking at year 1, 65% continued to report abstinence at each follow-up visit through year 6 (DHHS, 1987). These findings compare quite favorably with those of most studies in the literature, and they show that large numbers of adult smokers can benefit from sustained behavioral intervention and follow-up (Hymowitz, 1987).

Heavy smokers in the MRFIT were less likely to stop smoking than light smokers. Ockene (1988) reported that the year 6 quit rate for SI light smokers (fewer than 25 cigarettes per day) was 61.6%. The quit rate for SI heavy smokers (more than 25 cigarettes per day) was 37.6%. A similar differential was observed for UC smokers. These findings, which are consistent with other reports in the literature (DHHS, 1988), suggest that the medical, educational, and behavioral strategies used in the MRFIT were more effective for the lighter smokers. Those at greatest risk of heart disease—the heavy smokers—were least likely to achieve abstinence.

In view of the fact that the proportion of smokers in our society who smoke heavily has increased over the past decade (DHHS, 1988), there is a need to develop interventions that are more helpful to heavy smokers. Pharmacological therapies may help fill this void. Lighter smokers generally report fewer or less intense withdrawal symptoms than heavier smokers (Stitzer & Gross, 1988), and it is likely that heavy smokers are relatively more dependent on nicotine than light smokers. Pharmacological agents that counteract withdrawal symptoms may be of particular value to heavy smokers, either when used alone or as a component of a multicomponent behavioral program.

The Lung Health Study, like the MRFIT, was a large-scale multicenter multiyear study in which smokers were exposed to comprehensive behavioral interventions (Anthonisen et al., 1994). In addition, SI participants in the Lung Health Study received nicotine replacement therapy (nicotine gum, 2 mg), as well as bronchodilator therapy for lung disease. Five-year cross-sectional quit rates, confirmed by expired air carbon monoxide and cotinine, were close to 40% for SI and 20% for UC, a highly significant difference. Like the MRFIT, the Lung Health Study demonstrates the importance of comprehensive sustained intervention on smoking. Unfortunately, such sustained and comprehensive intervention often is not possible or feasible in other studies or settings (cf. Hymowitz, 1987).

When smokers enroll in a quit-smoking program, one may be reasonably certain that they are at least motivated to try to quit smoking. This is not always true of patients seen in physician offices and other clinical settings. They generally come to the doctor for other reasons, such as a cold, and they may not even think about stopping smoking. Indeed, only about 10% of smokers are ready to try to quit (Prochaska & Goldstein, 1991). Yet, as we have seen, it is the physician's responsibility to ask about smoking and to encourage patients to quit.

According to the transtheoretical model of behavior change (Prochaska & DiClementi, 1983), smoking cessation is considered a process in which patients go through several distinct stages (precontemplation, contemplation, preparation, action, maintenance, and, all too often, relapse). Patients in the precontemplation stage, for example, are not even thinking about stopping smoking, and it probably would prove futile to try to convince such a patient to quit smoking. Rather, the physicians' task is to move the patient along the continuum of change until he or she is ready to try to quit.

Hence, physicians and other counselors ought to assess the patient's readiness for stopping smoking and to adjust their intervention accordingly (cf. Orleans, 1993). The physician might talk to patients in the precontemplation and contemplation stages about the health effects of smoking, allow them to weigh the costs and benefits of continuing to smoke (or to quit), perhaps give them some reading material, and follow up with them at a subsequent clinic/office visit. At a later date, the patient may be more ready to try to stop smoking, (preparation or action stages), at which time the physician may provide assistance.

Typically, physicians only have enough time to offer a brief intervention, often making strategic use of "clinical opportunities" for a personalized health message, to distribute self-help quit-smoking aids and material, and to arrange follow-up opportunities. It is often helpful to negotiate a quit date and then map out a strategy, with the patient as a partner in planning, so that the patient may prepare for quitting and remaining abstinent. The physician may encourage patients to monitor their smoking behavior and learn about factors that control it. They may encourage patients to begin cutting down on smoking, one step at a time, at the same time acquiring coping skills to deal, for example, with stress. Two to 3 weeks of modifying smoking, utilizing different techniques for cutting down, and preparing for the quit date often leads to a "stick point," a point beyond which it is difficult for the smoker to taper any more. At that time, smokers must consider going "cold turkey" on their quit date.

Staying cigarette free (maintenance stage) requires as much effort as stopping. Many ex-smokers use relaxation and stress management procedures, social support, and exercise to remain abstinent. Nicotine replacement therapy (gum, patch, nasal spray, or inhaler) also may be effective. A good time to start nicotine replacement is on the quit date. While on nicotine replacement, smokers may practice not smoking while avoiding withdrawal. At some point in time, smokers will stop using nicotine replacement, learn that they can get through life without a cigarette, and finally join the millions of ex-smokers who "kicked the habit."

The use of nicotine replacement therapy has grown in popularity and importance. The gum and patch now are available as over-the-counter products. In 20 cities which made up COMMIT, 12.8% of smokers (one out of eight) used the patch, making it the most popular method for stopping smoking (Cummings, Hyland, Ockene, Hymowitz, & Manley, 1997). By comparison, 1 out of 10 smokers used nicotine gum, 1 out of 13 attended a stop-smoking program, 1 out of 16 went to a hypnotist or acupuncturist, and 1 out of 20 used some other commercially available stop-smoking device (Cummings et al., 1997). Most important, among smokers who made an attempt to quit smoking, the likelihood of successful quitting was more than twice as high among patch users than among nonusers. Among patch users, the highest quit rates were observed among those who used the patch between 1 and 3 months (Cummings et al., 1997).

Compared to nonusers, patch users in COMMIT were more likely to be female and white, have higher annual incomes, be more motivated to stop smoking, and to smoke more heavily. Among low-income smokers, nicotine patch use was significantly higher among those who lived in a state where the public insurance program (i.e., Medicaid or MediCal) included the patch as a benefit (Cummings et al., 1997).

With nicotine replacement strongly endorsed as an effective therapy for smoking cessation, attention now is shifting toward ways of enhancing its effectiveness. Among areas of interest are studies of the effectiveness of higher doses of nicotine gum (Herrara et al., 1995) and patch (Dale et al., 1995; Jorenby et al., 1995) and combined use of gum and patch (Fagerstrom, Schneider & Lunell, 1993; Kornitzer, Boutsen, Dramaix, Thijs, & Gustavsson, 1995). In each case, the higher dose or combination therapy enhanced initial and long-term quit rates, particularly for the heavier, more dependent smoker. The American Psychiatric Association guidelines endorse the strategy of supplementing patch use with gum on an "as needed" basis (American Psychiatric Association, 1996).

Westman, Behm, and Rose (1995) studied the effects on smoking cessation of airway sensory replacement combined with the nicotine patch. In previous work in their laboratory, the investigators showed that airway sensory replacement reduced craving for cigarettes and improved 3-week smoking abstinence rates (Rose & Hickman, 1987; Levin, Rose, & Behm, 1990; Behm, Schur, Levin, Tashkin, & Rose, 1993; Levin et al., 1993). They noted that the satisfaction derived from smoking depends not only on the pharmacological effects of nicotine but also on the sensory stimulation from smoke inhalation (i.e., the tracheal "scratch"). A citric acid aerosol produces a similar tracheal "scratch" and provides some of the same satisfaction as cigarette smoke.

In Westman et al.'s (1995) study, subjects received either citric acid ($n = 41$) or lactose placebo ($n = 59$) inhalers to cope with smoking urges. Subjects also received self-help materials and nicotine patches for 6 weeks. Return visits were at weeks 1, 4, 6, and 10. The primary outcome of continuous abstinence at the end of the 10-week treatment period was 19.5% for the citric acid group compared to 6.8% for the lactose group, a statistically significant difference. In view of the low side effects profile of citric acid inhaler treatment and preliminary results which suggest that the citric acid inhaler may boost quit rates obtained with nicotine replacement therapy, the use of citric acid inhalers, alone or in combination with nicotine replacement therapy, appears to hold considerable promise (cf. American Psychiatric Association, 1996).

Mecamylamine has been marketed for many years as an antihypertensive agent—Inversine—but has been replaced by newer antihypertensive agents (Rose et al., 1994). The doses used to control blood pressure were typically 10–90 mg/day. In studies of nicotine dependence, doses of 2.5–20 mg have been administered acutely to human subjects. Mecamylamine has been shown to block many of the physiological, behavioral, and reinforcing effects of nicotine (cf. Rose et al., 1994).

As noted by Rose et al. (1994), the pharmacological actions of an agonist (nicotine) and an antagonist (mecamylamine) might be expected to oppose each other, nullifying any therapeutic effect. However, both nicotine and mecamylamine occupy receptors that would otherwise be acted on by nicotine from cigarettes. Thus, nicotine and mecamylamine may work in concert to attenuate the rewarding effects of cigarette smoking, thereby facilitating smoking abstinence. Also, the agonist and antagonist may be expected to offset each others' potential side effects.

To evaluate the effects of concurrent administration of mecamylamine and the nicotine skin patch on smoking cessation, 48 smokers who smoked at least one pack per day were assigned randomly to one of two conditions: nicotine skin patch (6–8 weeks) plus oral mecamylamine (2.5–5 mg twice per day for 5 weeks) or nicotine patch plus placebo (Rose et al., 1994). The continuous abstinence rate at 7 weeks was three times higher in the mecamylamine condition (50% vs. 16.7%), a highly significant difference. At follow-up, continuous abstinence remained higher for the mecamylamine condition (37.5% vs. 12.5% at 6 months; 37.5% vs. 4.2% at 12 months). Mecamylamine also significantly reduced craving for cigarettes, negative affect, and appetite (Rose et al., 1994). The American Psychiatric Association Practice Guidelines Panel (American Psychiatric Association, 1996) concluded that mecamylamine lacks sufficient evidence of efficacy to be classified as a recommended treatment, but it is considered promising. Clearly, more research on the use of mecamylamine for smoking cessation is warranted.

The effectiveness of other medications for stopping smoking has been examined (Schwartz, 1987; Hughes, 1994; American Psychiatric Association, 1996). Research findings on the efficacy of clonidine, naltraxone, benzodiazepine and nonbenzodiazepine anxiolytics, and beta blockers for smoking cessation have been either negative or inconsistent (Hughes, 1994). These medications may prove effective when used by skilled clinicians with selected patients. The American Psychiatric Association Guidelines Panel (American Psychiatric Association, 1996) classified clonidine, buspirone, antidepressants, and anorectics as promising regimens, worthy of further study and clinical testing. More recent studies of bupropion and nortryptiline (Benowitz, 1997; Hurt et al., 1997) suggest that antidepressant medications may have a particularly important role to play in the pharmacological management of smoking.

REFERENCES

Aitken, P. P. (1980). Peer group pressures, parental controls and cigarette smoking among ten-to-fourteen year olds. *British Journal of Social and Clinical Psychology, 19,* 141–146.

Albright, C. L., Altman, D. G., Slater, M. D., & Maccoby, N. (1988). Cigarette advertisements in magazines: Evidence for a differential focus on women's and youth magazines. *Health Education Quarterly, 15,* 225–233.

American Cancer Society. (1986). *Facts and figures on smoking, 1976–1986* (Publication No. 5650-LE). New York: Author.

American Cancer Society. (1997). *Cancer facts and figures—1997.* Atlanta: Author.

American Psychiatric Association. (1994). *Diagnostic and statistical manual of mental disorders* (4th ed.). Washington, DC: Author.

American Psychiatric Association. (1996, October). Practice guidelines for the treatment of patients with nicotine dependence. *American Journal of Psychiatry, 153*(Suppl.), 1–31.

Anthonisen, N. R., Connett, J. E., Kiley, J. P., Altose, M. D., Baily, W. C., Buist, A. S., Conway, Jr., W. A., Enright, P. L., Kanner, R. E., O'Hara, P., Owens, G. R., Scanlon, P. D., Tashkin, D. P., & Wise, R. A. (1994). Effects of smoking intervention and use of an inhaled anticholinergic bronchodilator on the rate of decline of FEV. The Lung Health Study. *Journal of the American Medical Association, 272,* 1497–1505.

Ashton, H., Watson, D. W., Marsh, R., & Sadler, J. (1970). Puffing frequency and nicotine intake in cigarette smokers. *British Medical Journal, iii,* 679–681.

Asmussen, I. (1980). Effects of maternal smoking on the fetal cardiovascular system. In R. M. Lauer & R. B. Shekelle (Eds.), *Childhood prevention of atherosclerosis and hypertension* (pp. 235–250). New York: Raven Press.

Bansil, R. K., Hymowitz, N., & Keller, S. (1989, May). *Cigarette smoking and neuroleptics.* Paper presented at the annual meeting of the American Psychiatric Association, San Francisco.

Bartecchi, C. E., Mackenzie, T. D., & Schrier, R. W. (1994). The human costs of tobacco use. *New England Journal of Medicine, 330,* 907–912.

Behm, F. M., Schur, C., Levin, E. D., Tashkin, D. P., & Rose, J. E. (1993). Clinical evaluation of a citric acid inhaler for smoking cessation. *Drug and Alcohol Dependence, 31,* 131–138.

Benowitz, N. L. (1997). Treating tobacco addiction—nicotine or no nicotine? *New England Journal of Medicine, 337,* 1230–1231.

Biglan, O., & Lichtenstein, E. (1984). A behavior-analytic approach to smoking acquisition: Some recent findings. *Journal of Applied Social Psychology, 14,* 207–223.

Black, H. R. (1990). Smoking and cardiovascular disease. In J. H. Laragh & B. M. Brenner (Eds.), *Hypertension: Pathophysiology, diagnosis, and management* (pp. 1917–1936). New York: Raven Press.

Centers for Disease Control and Prevention. (1996). State tobacco control highlights—1996 (CDC Publication No. 099-4895). Atlanta: Author.

Chassin, L., Corty, E., Presson, C. C., Olshovsky, R. W., Bensenberg, M., & Sherman, S. J. (1981). Predicting adolescents' intentions to smoke cigarettes. *Journal of Health and Social Behavior, 22,* 445–455.

Chassin, L., Presson, C. C., Rose, J. S., & Sherman, S. J. (1996). The natural history of cigarette smoking from adolescence to adulthood: Demographic predictors of continuity and change. *Health Psychology, 15,* 478–484.

Cummings, K. M., Giovino, G., & Mendicino, A. J. (1987). Cigarette advertising and black–white differences in brand preference. *Public Health Reports, 102,* 698–701.

Cummings, K. M., Hyland, A., Ockene, J. K., Hymowitz, N., & Manley, M. (1997). Use of the nicotine skin patch by smokers in 20 U.S. communities, 1992–1993. *Tobacco Control, 6*(Suppl. 2), S63–S70.

Dale, L. C., Hurt, R. D., Offord, K. P., Lawsen, G. M., Croghan, I. T., & Schroeder, D. R. (1995). High dose nicotine patch therapy. *Journal of the American Medical Association, 274,* 1353–1358.

Devesa, S. S., & Diamond, E. L. (1983). Socioeconomic and racial differences in lung cancer incidence. *American Journal of Epidemiology, 118,* 818–831.

Evans, N., Farkas, A., Gilpin, E., Berry, C., & Pierce, J. P. (1995). Influence of tobacco marketing and exposure to smokers on adolescent susceptibility to smoking. *Journal of the National Cancer Institute, 87,* 1538–1545.

Fagerstrom, K. O. (1978). Measuring degree of physical dependence to tobacco smoking with reference to individualization of treatment. *Addictive Behaviors, 3,* 235–241.

Fagerstrom, K. O. (1988). Efficacy of nicotine chewing gum: A review. In O. F. Pomerleau & C. S. Pomerleau (Eds.), *Nicotine replacement* (pp. 109–128). New York: Alan R. Liss.

Fagerstrom, K. O., Schneider, N. G., & Lunell, E. (1993). Effectiveness of nicotine patch and nicotine gum as individual versus combined treatments for tobacco withdrawal symptoms. *Psychopharmacology, 111,* 271–277.

Fiore, M. C., Novotny, T. E., Pierce, J. P., Giovino, G. A., Hatziendreu, E. J., Newcomb, P. A., Surawicz, T. S., & Davis, R. M. (1990). Methods used to quit smoking in the United States. Do cessation programs help? *Journal of the American Medical Association, 263,* 2760–2765.

Glassman, A. H. (1993). Cigarette smoking: Implications for psychiatric illness. *American Journal of Psychiatry, 150,* 546–553.

Gold, D. R., Wang, X., Wypij, D., Speizer, F. E., Ware, J. H., & Dockery, D. W. (1996). Effects of cigarette smoking on lung function in adolescent boys and girls. *New England Journal of Medicine, 335,* 931–937.

Green, D. E. (1980). Beliefs of teenagers about smoking and health. In R. M. Leauer & R. B. Shekelle (Eds.), *Childhood prevention of atherosclerosis and hypertension* (pp. 223–228). New York: Raven Press.

Hansen, W. B. (1983). Behavioral predictors of abstinence: Early indicators of a dependence on tobacco in adolescents. *International Journal of the Addictions, 18,* 913–920.

Henningfield, J. E. (1986). How tobacco produces drug dependence. In J. K. Ockene (Ed.), *The pharmacologic treatment of tobacco dependence: Proceedings of the World Congress* (pp. 19–31). Cambridge, MA: Institute for the Study of Smoking Behavior and Policy.

Henningfield, J. E., Cohen, C., & Pickworth, W. B. (1993). Psychopharmacology of nicotine. In C. T. Orleans & J. Slade (Eds.), *Nicotine addiction: Principles and management* (pp. 24–45). New York: Oxford University Press.

Henningfield, J. E., & Goldberg, S. R. (1988). Pharmacologic determinants of tobacco self-administration by humans. *Pharmacology, Biochemistry and Behavior, 30,* 221–226.

Henningfield, J. E., & Jasinski, D. R. (1988). *Pharmacologic basis for nicotine replacement.* New York: Alan R. Liss.

Herrara, N., Franco, R., Herrara, L., Partidas, A., Rolando, R., & Fagerstrom, K. O. (1995). Nicotine gum, 2 and 4 mg, for nicotine dependence. *Chest, 108,* 447–451.

Hjalmarson, A., Franzon, M., Westin, A., & Wiklund, O. (1994). Effects of nicotine nasal spray on smoking cessation. *Archives of Internal Medicine, 154,* 2567–2572.

Hughes, G. H., Hymowitz, N., Ockene, J. K., Simon, N., & Vogt, T. M. (1981). The Multiple Risk Factor Intervention Trial (MRFIT): V. Intervention on smoking. *Preventive Medicine, 10,* 476–500.

Hughes, J. R. (1994). Non-nicotine pharmacotherapies for smoking cessation. *Journal of Drug Development, 6,* 196–203.

Hunt, W. A., & Bespalec, D. A. (1974). An evaluation of current methods of modifying smoking behavior. *Journal of Clinical Psychology, 30,* 431–438.

Hurt, R. D., Sachs, D. P. L., Glover, E. D., Offord, K. P., Johnston, J. A., Dale, L. C., Khayrallah, M. A., Schroeder, D. R., Glover, P. N., Sullivan, C. R., Croghan, I. T., & Sullivan, P. M. (1997). A comparison of sustained-release bupropion and placebo for smoking cessation. *New England Journal of Medicine, 337,* 1195–1202.

Hymowitz, N. (1987). Community and clinical trials of disease prevention: Effects on cigarette smoking. *Public Health Reviews, 15,* 45–81.

Hymowitz, N., Corle, D., Royce, J., Hartwell, T., Corbett, K., Orlandi, M., & Piland, N. (1995). Smokers' baseline characteristics in the COMMIT Trial. *Preventive Medicine, 24,* 503–508.

Hymowitz, N., Cummings, K. M., Hyland, A., Lynn, W. R., Pechacek, T. F., & Hartwell, T. D. (1997). Pedictors of smoking cessation in a cohort of adult smokers followed for five years. *Tobacco Control, 6*(Suppl. 2), S57–S62.

Hymowitz, N., Lasser, N. L., & Safirstein, B. H. (1982). Effects of graduated external filters on smoking cessation. *Preventive Medicine, 11,* 85–95.

Hymowitz, N., Sexton, M., Ockene, J., & Grandits, G. (1991). Baseline factors associated with smoking cessation and relapse. *Preventive Medicine, 20,* 590–601.

Johnson, B. D. (1977). The race, class, and irreversibility hypotheses: Myths and research about heroin. In J. D. Rittenhouse (Ed.), *The epidemiology of heroin and other addicts* (NIDA Research Monograph No. 16, pp. 51–60). Washington, DC: U.S. Government Printing Office.

Jones, R. T. (1987). Tobacco dependence. In H. Y. Meltzer (Ed.), *Psychopharmacology: The third generation of progress* (pp. 1589–1595). New York: Raven Press.

Jorenby, D. E., Smith, S. S., Fiore, M. C., Hurt, R. D., Offord, K. P., Croghan, I. T., Hays, J. T., Lewis, S. F., & Baker, T. B. (1995). Varying nicotine patch dose and type of smoking cessation counseling. *Journal of the American Medical Association, 274,* 1347–1352.

Kauffmann, F., Tessier, J. F., & Oriol, P. (1983). Adult passive smoking in the home environment: A risk factor for chronic airflow limitation. *American Journal of Epidemiology, 117, 269.*

Kornitzer, M., Boutsen, M., Dramaix, M., Thijs, J., & Gustavsson, G. (1995). Combined use of nicotine patch and gum in smoking cessation: A placebo-controlled clinical trial. *Preventive Medicine, 24,* 41–47.

Kozlowski, L. T., Wilkinson, A., Skinner, W., Kent, C., Franklin, T., & Pope, M. (1989). Comparing tobacco cigarette dependence with other drug dependencies. *Journal of the American Medical Association, 261,* 898–901.

Lando, H. A. (1993). Formal quit smoking treatments. In C. T. Orleans & J. Slade (Eds.), *Nicotine addiction: Principles and management* (pp. 221–244). New York: Oxford University Press.

Leventhal, H., & Cleary, P. P. (1980). The smoking problem: A review of the research and theory in behavioral risk modification. *Psychological Bulletin, 88,* 370–405.

Levin, E. D., Behm, F., Carnahan, E., Le Clair, R., Shipley, R., & Rose, J. E. (1993). Clinical trials using ascorbic acid aerosol to aid smoking cessation. *Drug and Alcohol Dependence, 33,* 211–223.

Levin, E. D., Rose, J. E., & Behm, F. (1990). Development of a citric acid aerosol as a smoking cessation aid. *Drug and Alcohol Dependence, 25,* 273–279.

Lucchesi, B. R., Schuster, C. R., & Emley, A. B. (1967). The role of nicotine as a determinant of cigarette smoking frequency in man with observations of certain cardiovascular effects associated with the tobacco alkaloid. *Clinical Pharmacology and Therapeutics, 8,* 789–796.

Lynch, B. S., & Bonnie, R. J. (1994). *Growing up tobacco free.* Washington, DC: National Academy Press.

Ockene, J. K. (1988, March). *Why are there differences in reduction of lung cancer versus heart disease risk after quitting smoking?* Paper presented at the American Heart Association 28th annual conference on Cardiovascular Disease Epidemiology, Santa Fe, NM.

Ockene, J. K., Hymowitz, N., Lagus, J., & Shaten, B. J. (1991). Comparison of smoking behavior change for SI and UC study groups. *Preventive Medicine, 20,* 564–573.

Ockene, J. K., Hymowitz, N., Sexton, M., & Broste, S. K. (1982). Initial and long-term cessation of smoking after four years of the Multiple Risk Factor Intervention Trial (MRFIT). *Preventive Medicine, 11,* 621–638.

Oei, T. S., & Fea, A. (1987). Smoking prevention program for children: A review. *Journal of Drug Education, 17,* 11–42.

rleans, C. T. (1993). Treating nicotine dependence in medical settings: A stepped care model. In C. T. Orleans & J. Slade (Eds.), *Nicotine addiction: Principles and management* (pp. 145–161). New York: Oxford University Press.

Peto, R., Lopez, A. D., Boreham, J., Thun, M., & Heath, Jr., C. (1994). *Mortality from smoking in developed contries, 1950–2000.* New York: Oxford University Press.

Pharmacists' "helping smokers quit" program. (1986). *American Pharmacy, NS26*(7), 25–33.

Pierce, J. P. (1991). Progress and problems in international public health efforts to reduce tobacco usage. *Annual Reviews of Public Health, 12,* 383–400.

Prochaska, J. O., & DiClemente, C. C. (1983). Stages and processes of self-change of smoking: Toward an integrative model of change. *Journal of Consulting and Clinical Psychology, 51,* 390–395.

Prochaska, J. O., & Goldstein, M. G. (1991). Process of smoking cessation. *Clinics in Chest Medicine, 12,* 727–735.

Raw, M., & Russell, M. A. H. (1980). Rapid smoking, cue exposure, and support in the modification of smoking. *Behavior Research and Therapy, 18,* 363–372.

Rose, J. E., Behm, F. M., Westman, E. C., Levin, E. D., Stein, R. M., & Repha, G. V. (1994). Mecomylamine combined with nicotine skin patch facilitates smoking cessation beyond nicotine patch treatment alone. *Clinical Pharmacology and Therapeutics, 56,* 86–99.

Rose, J. E., & Hickman, C. S. (1987). Citric acid aerosol as a potential smoking cessation aid. *Chest, 92,* 1005–1008.

Russell, M. A. H. (1986). Conceptual framework for nicotine substitution. In J. K. Ockene (Ed.), *The pharmacologic treatment of tobacco dependence: Proceedings of the World Congress* (pp. 90–107). Cambridge, MA: Institute for the Study of Smoking Behavior and Policy.

Sachs, D. P. L. (1986). Nicotine polacrilex: Clinical promises delivered and yet to come. In J. K. Ockene (Ed.), *The pharmacologic treatment of tobacco dependence: Proceedings of the World Congress* (pp. 120–140). Cambridge, MA: Institute for the Study of Smoking Behavior and Policy.

Samet, J. M., Lewit, E. M., & Warner, K. E. (1994). Involuntary smoking and children's health. *The Future of Children, 4,* 94–114.

Schachter, S. (1982). Recidivism and self-cure of smoking and obesity. *American Psychologist, 37,* 436–444.

Schultes, R. E. (1978). Ethnopharmacological significance of psychotropic drugs of vegetal origin. In W. G. Clark & J. del Giudice (Eds.), *Principles of psychopharmacology* (pp. 41–70). New York: Academic Press.

Schwartz, J. L. (1987). *Smoking cessation methods: The United States and Canada, 1978–1985* (DHHS Publication No. NIH 87-2940). Washington, DC: U.S. Government Printing Office.

Seely, J. E., Zuskin, E., & Bouhuys, A. (1971). Cigarette smoking: Objective evidence for lung damage in teen-agers. *Science, 172,* 741–743.

Sempos, C., Cooper, R., Kovar, M. G., & McMillan, M. (1988). Divergence of the recent trends in coronary mortality for the four major race–sex groups in the United States. *American Journal of Public Health, 78,* 1422–1427.

Shiffman, S. (1986). A cluster-analytic typology of smoking relapse episodes. *Addictive Behaviors, 11,* 295–307.

Sloan, J. W., Todd, G. D., & Martin, W. R. (1984). Nature of nicotine binding to rat brain P 2 fraction. *Pharmacology, Biochemistry and Behavior, 20,* 899–909.

Stitzer, M. L., & Gross, J. (1988). Smoking relapse: The role of pharmacological and behavioral factors. In O. F. Pomerleau & C. S. Pomerleau (Eds.), *Nicotine replacement* (pp. 163–184). New York: Alan R. Liss.

Stolerman, I. P., Goldfarb, T., Fink, R., & Jarvik, M. E. (1973). Influencing cigarette smoking with nicotine antagonists. *Psychopharmacologia, 28,* 237–259.

Sullivan, L. W. (1991). To thwart the tobacco companies. *Journal of the American Medical Association, 266,* 2131.

Terry, L. L. (1983). The Surgeon General's first report on smoking and health. *New York State Journal of Medicine, 83,* 1254–1255.

Tonnesen, P., Norregaard, J., Mikkelsen, K., Jorgensen, S., & Nilsson, F. (1993). A double-blind trial of a nicotine inhaler for smoking cessation. *Journal of the American Medical Association, 269,* 1268–1271.

U.S. Department of Health and Human Services. (1986). *Clinical opportunities for smoking intervention: A guide for the busy physician* (NIH Publication No. 86-2178). Washington, DC: U.S. Government Printing Office.

U.S. Department of Health and Human Services. (1987). *Smoking and health: A national status report. A report to Congress* (DHHS Publication No. CDC 87-8396). Washington, DC: U.S. Government Printing Office.

U.S. Department of Health and Human Services. (1988). *The health consequences of smoking: Nicotine addiction. A report of the Surgeon General* (DHHS Publication No. CDC 88-8406). Washington, DC: U.S. Government Printing Office.

U.S. Department of Health and Human Services. (1989a). *Reducing the health consequences of smoking: 25 years of progress* (DHHS Publication No. CDC 89-8411). Washington, DC: U.S. Government Printing Office.

U.S. Department of Health and Human Services. (1989b). *How to help your patients stop smoking: A National Cancer Institute manual for physicians* (NIH Publication No. 89-3064). Washington, DC: U.S. Government Printing Office.

U.S. Department of Health and Human Services. (1990). *The health benefits of smoking cessation. A report of the Surgeon General* (DHHS Publication No. CDC 90-8416). Washington, DC: U.S. Government Printing Office.

U.S. Department of Health and Human Services. (1992). *Smoking and health in the Americas. A 1992 report of the Surgeon General, in collaboration with the Pan American Health Organization* (DHHS Publication No. CDC 92-8419). Washington, DC: U.S. Government Printing Office.

U.S. Department of Health and Human Services. (1994a). *Preventing tobacco use among young people. A report of the Surgeon General* (U.S. Department of Health and Human Services, Centers for Disease Control and Prevention, National Center for Chronic Disease Prevention and Health Promotion, Office on Smoking and Health). Washington, DC: U.S. Government Printing Office.

U.S. Department of Health and Human Services. (1994b). *Tobacco and the clinician* (NIH Publication No. 94-3693). Bethesda, MD: National Institutes of Health.

U.S. Department of Health and Human Services. (1995). *Healthy people 2000, midcourse review and 1995 revisions.* Washington, DC: U.S. Government Printing Office.

U.S. Department of Health and Human Services. (1996). *Clinical Practice Guideline No. 18: Smoking cessation* (AHCPR Publication No. 96-0692). Washington, DC: U.S. Government Printing Office.

U.S. Department of Health, Education and Welfare. (1979). *Smoking and health: A report of the Surgeon General* (DHEW Publication No. PHS 79-500066). Washington, DC: U. S. Government Printing Office.

U.S. Public Health Service. (1964). *Smoking and health* (Report of the Advisory Committee to the Surgeon General of the Public Health Service, U.S. Department of Health, Education, and Welfare, Public Health Service, Centers for Disease Control, PHS Publication No. 1103). Washington, DC: U.S. Government Printing Office.

Van Lancker, J. (1977). Smoking and disease. In M. E. Jarvik, J. W. Cullen, E. R. Gritz,

T. M. Vogt, & L. J. West (Eds.), *Research on smoking behavior* (NIDA Research Monograph No. 17, DHEW Publication No. ADM 78-581, pp. 230–283). Washington, DC: U.S. Government Printing Office.

Vogt, T. M. (1982). Cigarette smoking: History, risks, and behavior change. *International Journal of Mental Health, 11,* 6–43.

Warner, K. E. (1986). *Selling smoke: Cigarette advertising and public health.* Washington, DC: American Public Health Association.

Westman, E. C., Behm, F. M., & Rose, J. E. (1995). A randomized, placebo-controlled trial using a citric acid inhaler. *Chest, 107,* 1358–1364.

Yamaguchi, K., & Kandel, D. B. (1985). On the resolution of role incompatibility: A life event history analysis of family roles and marijuana use. *American Journal of Sociology, 90,* 1284–1325.

Yassa, R., Lal, S., Korpassy, A., & Ally, J. (1987). Nicotine exposure and tardive dyskinesia. *Biological Psychiatry, 22,* 67–72.

11

❑ _____

Special Problems of the Alcohol and Multiple-Drug Dependent
Clinical Interactions and Detoxification

NORMAN S. MILLER

INTRODUCTION

Multiple dependence on drugs other than alcohol by alcoholics and dependence on alcohol by drug dependents continue to be markedly observed in clinical practice and documented in research studies. The use of multiple drugs and alcohol is extraordinarily common (e.g., alcohol and cocaine, heroin and cocaine, and marijuana with alcohol or cocaine). The large overlap between the use of drugs and alcohol has had significant ramifications for diagnosis and treatment as they are traditionally practiced (Grant, 1996a; Kandel, Chen, Warner, Kessler, & Grant, 1997; Martin et al., 1996; Miller, 1997; Wiseman & McMillan, 1996).

Research models for dependence on alcohol and drugs are also affected by multiple use and dependence. In actual practice, one drug is frequently substituted for another, and the majority of the individuals develop combined alcohol and multiple-drug dependence. The concurrent and simultaneous occurrences of multiple-drug and alcohol dependence suggest an overlapping susceptibility to the various types of dependence (Denison, Paredes, & Booth, 1997; Kasselbaum & Chandler, 1994; Miller, Gold, Belkin, & Klahr, 1990; Miller, 1997).

This chapter defines multiple dependence as dependence on more than one psychoactive substance (drugs, alcohol) simultaneously or concurrently, including the common practice of hierarchial use of multiple substances. Simultaneous use of drugs and alcohol means within the same week, and concurrent use means within the last year. "Multiple dependence" as used here is more broadly defined than the diagnosis of "polysubstance dependence" according to criteria in the fourth edition of *Diagnostic and Statistical Manual of Mental Disorders* (DSM-IV; American Psychiatric Association, 1994). DSM-IV requires a period of at least 6 months in which the person has repeatedly used at least three categories of psychoactive substances (not including nicotine and caffeine) but no single psychoactive substance has predominated. During this period, the criteria should have been met for dependence on psychoactive substances as a group but not for any specific substance. Because most multiply dependent individuals use one particular drug or other predominantly, the term "polysubstance dependence" has limited application in actual clinical practice (American Psychiatric Association, 1994).

NATURAL HISTORY AND EPIDEMIOLOGY

Natural History of Multiple-Drug Dependence

Clinically, the course of alcoholism is often drastically telescoped with the need for earlier treatment because of the dependence on multiple drugs. Correspondingly, the course of a drug addiction is altered by repeated alcohol use, which may precipitate a relapse to other drugs (Babor et al., 1992; Blanken, 1993; Cornelius, Salloum, Day, Thase, & Mann, 1996; Grant, 1996a; Miller et al., 1990). The interaction of alcohol and multiple-drug dependence has altered treatment practices and recovery programs.

The widespread practice of multiple-drug and alcohol use began in adolescent cohorts as a cultural phenomenon in the 1960s with the "hippie" generation. Epidemiological evidence confirms that large numbers of individuals with extensive drug experiences entered the age of risk for alcoholism during their adolescence. The risk for alcoholics to develop a drug dependence is also high in early adolescence. On the other hand, on a cross-sectional analysis, a gradual transition from common to less common dependence on other drugs by alcoholics is evident as age increases, perhaps in a linear progression (Caeteno & Schafer, 1996; Hasin, Li, McCloud, & Endicott, 1996).

As far back as 1930 and throughout each decade into the 1980s, alcoholics have used other drugs in alarming frequency. Freed (1973) reviewed 15,447 cases in 46 studies carried out between the 1930s and 1970s and found 3,046 alcoholics who were also dependent on another drug—in other words, a 20% rate of drug dependence among alcoholics. Some of the drugs prevalent today were used then (i.e., barbiturates, opiates, benzodiazepines, and marijuana) (Freed, 1973).

Many current studies of both alcoholics and drug dependents of any age in general and patient populations indicate that alcohol is the first drug used and often addictively. The natural history of alcohol dependence in conjunction with drug dependence is highly variable and age dependent. Older alcoholics (over the age of 30) typically began drinking in adolescence and progressed to diagnosable alcohol dependence in their 20s. A certain proportion (perhaps 10–20%) began using cannabis in their 20s. Another 10% began using stimulants (including cocaine and amphetamines), whereas 20% began using sedative/hypnotics (predominantly benzodiazepines, barbiturates, and meprobamate). About 50% continue their alcohol dependence without significant use of any additional drugs (Hammer & Vaglum, 1992; Irwin et al., 1996).

Prevalence of Multiple-Drug Dependence in General Populations

The prevalence of drug dependence among alcoholics was reasonably high in the Epidemiologic Catchment Area (ECA) study, with as many as 30% of the alcoholics qualifying for a drug dependence (with marijuana dependence highest on the list). The reverse, the prevalence of alcohol dependence among drug dependents, was higher: Alcoholism among marijuana dependents was 36%; barbiturate dependents, 71%; amphetamine dependents, 62%; hallucinogen dependents, 64%; opiate dependents, 67%; and cocaine dependents, 84%. Clearly, in this survey of the general population, alcohol dependence was a common complicating dependence in the majority of those dependent on drugs. Furthermore, these estimates were conservative because they were based on self-report; drug dependents do not admit readily to type, amount, and duration of drug use (Robins, Helzer, Pryzbeck, & Regier, 1988).

Prevalence of Multiple-Drug Dependence in Treatment Populations

The prevalence of multiple use or dependence that includes alcohol is high for contemporary drug dependents being admitted in both inpatient and outpatient treatment programs. Over 80% of alcoholics in treatment populations are dependent on at least one other drug, and usually more than one. In large-scale studies of inpatient populations of adult and adolescent alcoholics and drug dependents in various treatment facilities, the number of cocaine dependents with the additional diagnosis of alcohol dependence was in the 70–90% range. Similar studies of methadone and heroin dependents show rates of alcohol dependence between 50% and 75%. Approximately 80–90% of admitted cannabis dependents also depend on alcohol (Craddock, Rounds-Bryant, Flynn, & Hubbard, 1997; Hoffman et al., 1996; Stein, Wilkinson, Berglas, & O'Sullivan, 1996).

A triad of alcohol, marijuana, and cocaine dependence is a regular occurrence among the alcoholics currently being admitted to inpatient and outpatient programs. According to these studies, the younger alcoholic begins using alcohol in early teenage years (i.e., at about 13 to 15 years of age) and progresses to dependent use of alcohol by 15 to 16 years of age. A year or two after the onset of alcohol and tobacco use, other drugs are tried and some used dependently, including marijuana, tobacco, and then cocaine, followed by hallucinogens (phencyclidine), benzodiazepines, and barbiturates in frequency. Cigarette smoking is particularly troublesome; unlike some other drug use, which may wax and wane, the use of tobacco often remains persistent well into adulthood, with its particularly well-known medical complications. The pattern of cocaine use has changed dramatically and continues to do so to the present day, most remarkably in the progressively earlier age of onset of use. The skillful marketing techniques for the initially cheaper form of cocaine, "crack," continue to lure younger individuals to addictive use (Grella, Anglin, & Wugalter, 1997; Kandel et al., 1997; National Institute on Drug Abuse, 1988).

The predictors of cessation of marijuana and cocaine use were examined in a longitudinal cohort of young adult men and women ($N = 1,222$). Six domains of predictors were examined: socioeconomic background variables, participation in the social roles of adulthood, degree of drug involvement, social context of drug use, health status, and deviant activities and conventionality of life experiences. Factors that predicted cessation of use in adulthood paralleled those that predicted lack of initiation in adolescence: conventionality in social role performance, social context unfavorable to the use of drugs, and good health. A most important predictor was prior degree of involvement in licit and illicit drugs (Kandel & Raveis, 1989).

Use of Alcohol with Other Drugs

A recent study of the population's use of alcohol and other drugs in combination or on the same day, termed "simultaneous polydrug use" (SPU), was conducted to assess patterns of SPU in 212 problem drinkers who participated in an alcohol treatment outcome study. Subjects were given a time-line follow-back interview, which assessed the use of alcohol and nine other drug classes for each day of the 120 days before treatment entry. A majority of subjects (61%) reported SPU during this assessment interval. Subjects who reported SPU were disproportionately younger, male, and unmarried, compared with those who did not report SPU. The most common alcohol/drug combinations were alcohol with cocaine (60% of subjects who reported SPU), alcohol with marijuana (51% of SPU subjects), and alcohol with sedatives (31% of SPU subjects). The most common three-drug combination was alcohol, cocaine, and marijuana (23% of SPU subjects) (Martin et al., 1996).

The use of alcohol and drugs on the same day was more frequent than expected by the daily base rates of the individual behaviors (Martin et al., 1996). The study suggested that for many problem drinkers who entered treatment, symptomatology and negative biomedical and psychosocial consequences could not be understood solely in terms of alcohol consumption. Research studies using alcohol-dependent and -abusing samples need to incorporate measures of polydrug use. The distinction between clinical research in alcohol versus drug addiction will continue to diminish in prevalence and importance (Martin et al., 1996).

Multiple-Drug Use by Adolescents

In a representative sample of 1,312 students 13 to 19 years of age from Mallorca, Spain, 19 variables from an anonymous questionnaire were used to define three groups of problems frequently found in adolescents: depression, deviant behaviors, and the use of alcohol, tobacco, and illicit drugs. A close relationship was evident between drug use and deviant behaviors but not with depressive symptoms. A small group used drugs without a relationship to deviant behaviors. There were also relationships between these problem behaviors and sleeping difficulties, enuresis, weight problems, family difficulties, and so on. A special relationship was found between the use of drugs and acting out. Nevertheless, there was a certain use of drugs unrelated to acting out, whereas the depressive manifestations did not appear to be related to the use of drugs (Calafat, Amengual, Palmer, & Saliba, 1997).

Use of Heroin with Other Drugs

A sample of 329 primary heroin users and a sample of 301 regular amphetamine users were analyzed to determine the extent and correlates of polydrug use among illicit drug users. Both samples exhibited high levels of polydrug use, with means of 5.2 (heroin) and 6.3 (amphetamines) drug classes used in the preceding 6 months. Multivariate analyses indicated that being younger, being male, not being in treatment, being an intravenous (IV) user, having recently borrowed injecting equipment, and being from the regular amphetamine-using sample were independently associated with higher levels of polydrug use. Illicit drug users appeared to reduce their range of drugs as they increased in age. The "pure" heroin or amphetamine user was extremely rare (Darke & Hall, 1995). After excluding the respective primary drug classes, the four most prevalent drugs were for heroin users: tobacco (94%), cannabis (84%), alcohol (78%), and benzodiazepines (64%). For the amphetamine sample, the corresponding classes were alcohol (94%), cannabis (93%), tobacco (92%), and hallucinogens (64%) (Darke & Hall, 1995).

Multiple-Drug Use with Disabilities

Among younger adults (18–24 years), persons with disabilities were more likely than those without disabilities to report that they had used heroin (adjusted odds ratios [OR] = 6.89; 95% confidence interval [CI] = 1.35, 35.1) or crack cocaine (OR = 6.38; 95% CI = 1.05, 38.6). Among older adults (35 years and older), persons with disabilities were more likely to report the use of sedatives (OR = 2.46; 95% CI = 1.21, 4.94) or tranquilizers (OR = 2.18; 95% CI = 1.08, 4.42) not medically prescribed (Gilson, Chilcoat, & Stapleton, 1996). For the youngest age group (ages 18 to 24), respondents with disabilities had higher odds of ever using heroin and cocaine than did the nondisabled. Higher odds for those with disabilities were found for the nonprescribed use of sedatives and tranquilizers among those in the oldest age range (Gilson et al., 1996). These results are consistent with the findings of Adlaf, Smart, and Walsh (1992) that subjects who were severely physically disabled reported higher use of sedatives and tranquilizers than nondisabled or partially disabled subjects (Gilson et al., 1996).

Multiple-Drug Use in Pregnancy

Of the 3,800 pregnant women seen in a clinic, 119 (3.1%) reported binge drinking during pregnancy; of the 19,991 women counseled by telephone, 153 (0.8%) reported binge drinking during pregnancy. The mean number of drinks per binge was 7.2 (standard deviation 2.5). None of the women was an alcoholic; 83.1% had binged fewer than 10 times during their pregnancy. A large majority (84%) of the women had a binge early in the first trimester (before 6 weeks' gestation). In comparison with control women, the women who had engaged in binge drinking were significantly younger (mean 30 vs. 27.9 years, $p < .0001$) and more likely to be single (12.2% vs. 54.6%, $p < .0001$), to be white (69.2% vs. 92.9%, $p < .004$), to smoke (19.3% vs. 57.1%, $p < .0001$), and to use cocaine (1.1% vs. 11.0%, $p < .0001$), marijuana (3.0% vs. 19.3%, $p < .0001$), and other illicit drugs (0.7% vs. 9.2%, $p < .0001$) (Gladstone, Levy, Nulman, & Koren, 1997; Jacob, Harrison, & Tigert, 1995).

Multiple-Drug Use in the Homeless

A countrywide probability sample of 564 homeless adults received structured interviews that included a standardized assessment of substance use disorders. Two-thirds of the sample (69.1%) had a lifetime history of a substance use disorder (including abuse of or dependence on alcohol [52.6%] or drugs [52.2%]); half had a current (52.4%) substance use disorder (including alcohol [38.8%] or drugs [31.3%]). Current drug disorders were higher among respondents who were younger, homeless longer, or sampled from the city of Oakland, California. Alcohol use disorders were higher among men than among women; surprisingly, drug use disorders were not. Rates of current drug use disorders for homeless adults were more than eight times higher than general population estimates (Robertson, Zlotnick, & Westerfelt, 1997).

Multiple-Drug Use in Homosexuals

Changes in substance use were evaluated in 321 gay men who used in the 90 days before entering treatment and who completed at least one follow-up interview, whether or not they continued in treatment. At baseline, 95% of the sample reported alcohol use in the prior 90 days; 64%, marijuana/hashish use; 46%, amphetamine use; 33%, inhalant nitrates use; and 31%, cocaine use. Most men were polydrug users: 10% reported using only one drug (including alcohol);

39% used four or more drugs. A marked reduction occurred in prevalence of use over time: declines on the order of 50% occurred in the first 90 days; prevalence then stabilized in remaining assessments. Frequency of usage by those reporting use of any given class of drugs also declined. No consistent predictors of reduction or cessation of use across different drug categories were found at 1 year (Paul, Barrett, Crosby, & Stall, 1996).

Multiple-Drug Use in Methadone Populations

A study of methadone-maintenance clients interviewed approximately 1 year after discharge from treatment revealed that outcomes differed between heavy-drinking clients who are alcohol dependent and those who are not. Alcohol-dependent clients seem to benefit more from treatment but continued to have severe cocaine use problems. The results emphasized the value in differentiating between these types of drinking clients. The role of alcohol consumption in treatment outcomes for methadone-maintenance clients was stressed (Chatham, Rowan-Szal, Joe, & Simpson, 1997).

Urinalysis data revealed a significant interaction for opiate urines, such that the treated alcohol-dependent clients showed significantly larger reductions in opiate use at follow-up ($F(1,81) = 5.8$, $p < .01$) than did nonalcohol-dependent clients. Urinalysis results obtained with cocaine revealed a marginally significant group effect ($F(1,81) = 3.7$, $p < .06$), with alcohol-dependent clients having more cocaine-positive urines than did the non-alcohol-dependent clients (Chatham et al., 1997).

The percentage of drug abuse patients who used cocaine while enrolled in methadone-maintenance programs has dramatically increased over the past 10 years. Currently, cocaine use is typically observed in approximately 50% of methadone treatment applicants. However, little is known about how much cocaine is used by these patients. Data regarding the quantity of cocaine used by methadone patients provide critical information for developing hypotheses about monetary and criminal involvement, disruption of social and other productive activity, and treatment prognosis (Kidorf & Stitzer, 1993).

A study examined the cocaine use of methadone-maintenance patients to determine amounts and patterns of use as well as use in combination with other drugs. Forty-five cocaine-using methadone-maintenance patients (78% used IV) reported their drug use for each day over the past 7 days after receiving information about their most recent urinalysis test results. Average reported use was 0.23 g cocaine/day on 3.4 days/week. Heroin and cocaine were typically used simultaneously, whereas only a subset of patients (47%) who used alcohol drank within close proximity to cocaine. Patients who used cocaine with alcohol and/or heroin on the same day ($N = 28$) reported more cocaine use ($M = 1$ g/week) than patients who used cocaine alone ($N = 17$; $M = 0.49$ g/week; Kidorf & Stitzer, 1993).

A number of studies have also documented that contemporary methadone patients abuse a number of drugs in addition to heroin and cocaine (e.g., alcohol, benzodiazepines, and marijuana), yet the relationship between cocaine and these other drugs has not been systematically explored. Methadone patients often used benzodiazepines and/or alcohol to counteract uncomfortable feelings following a period of cocaine use but did not report the frequency in which these combinations occurred. Heroin, alcohol, and/or benzodiazepines are likely used in close proximity to and in combination with cocaine. Thus, an assessment of when these drugs are used is crucial for understanding the role that they play in reinforcing and maintaining cocaine use (Kidorf & Stitzer, 1993).

HEREDITARY FACTORS IN GENERALIZED VULNERABILITY TO DRUG AND ALCOHOL ADDICTION

Family Studies

More than 50% of alcoholics have a family history positive for alcoholism. A child of an alcoholic is more likely to have certain neurophysiological and behavioral manifestations in common with other offspring of alcoholics than with matched controls without an alcoholic parent.

Corresponding studies for the prevalence of the family history of alcohol dependence in cocaine and opiate addicts and other drug dependents have been performed. In one study, the rate of the diagnosis of alcohol dependence in first- or second-degree relatives in the families of 263 cocaine dependents was greater than 50%; in other words, 132 cocaine dependents had at least one relative with alcohol dependence according to DSM-III-R (American Psychiatric Association, 1987) criteria (Miller et al., 1990).

Opiate dependents with a parental history of alcoholism were more frequently diagnosed with concurrent alcoholism. In one study, 21.3% of opiate dependents with a diagnosis of alcohol dependence ($N = 638$) had at least one parent with alcohol dependence. Opiate dependents without the diagnosis of alcohol dependence ($N = 422$) had a 12.5% rate of parental alcohol dependence. Among the opiate dependents with alcohol dependence, those with parental alcoholism had more severe problems with alcohol.

A study of young alcohol users in their 20s revealed a higher rate of alcohol-related problems and drug use if a family history of alcoholism was present in the first- and second-degree relatives. Young alcohol users without alcoholic relatives, or with fewer relatives with alcoholism, had a lower rate of alcohol-related problems and drug use (Schuckit, 1986). These genetic and familial studies of alcoholics and familial studies of drug dependents, in addition to the concept of the multiple-drug and alcohol dependent, support a possible common genetic transmission of alcohol and drug dependence.

Common versus Specific Transmission of Drug and Alcohol Use and Dependence in Families

The questions of familial transmission of nonalcohol drug use/dependence in combination and for specific drug types, with and without alcohol use/dependence, have not been completely studied. There is a high correlation between tranquilizer use in parents and both tranquilizer and cannabis use in offspring. Fawzy, Coombs, and Gerber (1983) (262 subjects) found a 78% prevalence of drug use in adolescent children of parents who admitted to using marijuana and hashish. In the studies on family drug use, predominant use by daughters and sons of multiple types of drugs including alcohol was found to parallel that of their parents.

In interviews with 32 alcoholics, 72 opiate addicts, and 42 alcoholic–opiate addicts, to a significant extent alcoholism tended to cluster in families, whereas alcoholism and opiate abuse did not occur in the same families significantly more or less often than expected by chance alone using the contingency chi-square analysis (Hill, Cloninger, & Ayre, 1977). It is important to note that overlap of alcoholism and opiate addiction did exist between relatives and probands, however, and that the lower rate of opiate addiction among alcoholic parents may have been due to a low rate of exposure to opiates in this generation. In addition, a more recent study examining this hypothesis failed to find specific intergenerational transmission of opiate use from parents to offspring independent of alcohol dependence (Rounsaville et al., 1991).

A study of younger drug addicts showed familial aggregation of drug abuse in 350 inpatients admitted for drug abuse in which 50% were opiate addicts, 33% were cocaine addicts, and the remainder (17%) were seda-tive/hypnotic addicts. The rate of familial drug abuse corresponded to the proband's drug of choice, from 16% of male relatives of cocaine addicts to 2% of male relatives of sedative/hypnotic addicts. Indicating a high association of familial alcoholism and drug abuse in the proband is the fact that the rate of alcoholism was the same across all proband groups regardless of drug type (Mirin, Weiss, Griffin, & Michael, 1991). Further support for a common transmission is a study of 41 male veterans that found an association between family history status of alcohol and drug dependence. Family history status did not discriminate onset of type of drug or alcohol abuse (i.e., "pure" alcohol abuse vs. mixed alcohol and drug abuse). Two-thirds of the subjects had combined drug and alcohol abuse, and only one-third met criteria for pure alcohol abuse or dependence. Thus, the distribution of alcohol or drug abuse in the proband was not related to the family history status (Moss, 1989).

Genetic Studies

Several adoption studies showed that sons of alcoholics raised by adoptive parents became alcoholics significantly more often than sons of nonalcoholics raised by adoptive parents. Similar results of three separate adoption studies conducted in Denmark, Sweden, and Iowa (United States) and a half-sibling study revealed the following: Sons of alcoholics were three to four times more likely to become alcoholics than were sons of nonalcoholics, whether the sons of alcoholics were raised by their alcoholic biological parent or by their nonalcoholic adoptive parents. The studies can be criticized on the basis of small numbers of subjects, criteria for diagnosis of alcoholism, and overlap between numbers of alcoholic parents of alcoholic and nonalcoholic adoptees. Nonetheless, the composite results and reliction in additional studies strongly support an inheritance factor in the development of alcoholism (Cloninger, 1988; Svikis & Pickens, 1988). Sons of alcoholics raised by nonalcoholic adoptive parents were no more susceptible to nonalcoholic adult psychiatric diagnoses than were sons of nonalcoholics raised by nonalcoholic adoptive parents. The Iowa study did find a higher rate of childhood conduct disorder in male offspring of alcoholics (Cloninger, 1988; Svikis & Pickens, 1988). No differences were found for female adoptees (Cloninger, 1988; Svikis & Pickens, 1988). Alcoholism and antisocial personality were genetically independent disorders for both males and females. The results of the Iowa study showed specificity of inheritance of antisocial and alcoholic condition, with two types of independent predispositions—one toward alcohol use and the other toward antisocial personality (Cloninger, 1988; Svikis & Pickens, 1988).

Adoption: Drug Addiction

An adoption study of genetic and environmental factors in drug abuse revealed that a biological background of alcohol problems predicted increased drug abuse in adoptees. Also, environmental factors, divorce, and psychiatric disturbance in the adoptive family were associated with increased drug abuse (Cadoret, Troughton, O'Gorman, & Heywood, 1986).

Twin Studies: Alcoholism

A Finnish (11,500 twin pairs) and a Swedish (7,500 male pairs) study showed drinking problems were greater in monozygotic twins than in dizygotic twins. Swedish (174 male pairs) and U.S. (15,924 male twins) studies showed that a diagnosis of alcoholism was more concordant in monozygotic twins than in dizygotic twins. Only one study conducted in England, enrolling the smallest number of twin pairs (56 twin pairs) of all the studies, did not show a difference in alcohol behavior between monozygotic twins and dizygotic twins.

A study of a U.S. treatment sample of 50 monozygotic and 64 dizygotic male twins and 31 monozygotic and 24 dizygotic female twins showed a significantly greater concordance rate for alcohol dependence in male and female twins and for alcohol abuse in males only (Pickens, Svikis, & McGue, 1991).

Twin Studies: Drug Addiction

In a U.S. study, only male monozygotic twins were significantly more concordant than dizygotic twins for other drug abuse/dependence and any substance abuse/dependence including alcohol dependence. However, the ratios of monozygotic to dizygotic concordance were comparable in the two sexes, suggesting that lack of significance in the female sample may be due to low statistical power (Kendler, Neale, Heath, Kessler, & Eaves, 1994).

BIOLOGICAL MECHANISMS IN MULTIPLE DEPENDENCE

Neurotransmitters

Several neurotransmitters may be involved in the various appetitive systems that underlie addictive behaviors. In studies, the major neurotransmitters identified in drug and alcohol addiction were the opioid peptides, dopamine, serotonin, and norepinephrine. These neurotransmitters had individual and interactive relationships in the reinforcement center and with the instinctual drive states. Together, this center and the drive states are thought to generate and underlie addictive use of drugs and alcohol. Findings have suggested that the common denominator for a wide range of classes of addictive drugs is their ability to activate the dopaminergic fibers in the mesolimbic system (Gardner, 1997; Wise, 1989).

Reinforcement Center

The reinforcement center has been shown to contain dopamine neurons that project from their location in the ventral tegmentum to the mesolimbic system in the forebrain. Opiate receptors were found on these dopamine neurons, and stimulation with opiates activated this dopamine system. Self-administration studies have shown that stimulation of the mesolimbic area supports addictive use of heroin, cocaine, and ethanol. Blockade of dopamine receptors prevented self-administration of opiates and cocaine, and blockade of norepinephrine sites reduced alcohol intake. Also, antagonism with narcotic-blocking agents attenuated reinforcement behavior from cocaine, heroin, and ethanol administration.

Other neurotransmitters may be involved in drug and alcohol use and addiction by serving a modulatory function. In humans, administration of serotonin reuptake inhibitors (zimelidine, fluoxetine, citalopram) to nondepressed heavy alcohol consumers and alcoholics has been associated with a reduction in the number of drinks consumed and an increase in abstinent days. A possible rationale is the influence of serotonin on other neurotransmitter systems. Serotonin neurons in the hypothalamus project to the metencephalon neurons, which inhibit mesencephalic endogenous opiate peptides and projections of γ-aminobutyric acid (GABA) neurons. GABA neurons interacted to inhibit dopamine neurons in the ventral tegmentum and other neurotransmitters and in doing so also performed widespread modulation functions (Gardner, 1997).

TIQs

Other more direct theories are based on the findings that alcohol, through the formation of condensation products termed "tetrahydroisoquinolines" (TIQs), may interact with opioid receptors to stimulate the mesolimbic catecholaminergic systems. TIQs that form following ethanol ingestion and metabolism can function as opiates and provide a link between the two-carbon ethanol molecule and the more complex phenanthrene alkaloids. The metabolic product from ethanol—acetaldehyde—condenses noncovalently with dopamine to form TIQs. The TIQs act as agonists at enkephalin- and endorphin-binding sites to further substantiate the link between alcohol and opiates through a common mechanism. A TIQ—salsolinol—has been found in the urine and in postmortem brains of alcoholics (Gardner, 1997).

Endogenous Opioids

Cerebrospinal fluid endorphin levels and plasma enkephalin levels are reduced in human alcoholics. Inbred mice (C57BL/6J) that show a preference for ethanol over water exhibit lower than normal levels of the opiate peptides, endorphins, and enkephalins than do mice (DBA2/J) that avoid alcohol. Long-term ethanol ingestion significantly reduces brain endorphins and enkephalins in animals. Acute and chronic treatment with the carboxypeptidase A (enkephalinase) inhibitors D-phenylalanine and hydrocinnamic acid, which raise brain enkephalin levels, significantly attenuate both forced and volitional ethanol intake in mice with a genetic preference for alcohol.

Generalized Biological Vulnerability

The theoretical implications extend to concepts of generalized biological vulnerability for drug and alcohol addiction. The co-occurrence of multiple drug and alcohol addiction and their common transmission in the adoption, twin, and familial studies suggest a genetic predisposition inclusive of a wide range of drugs and alcohol (Grant & Harford, 1990b). Although studies are inconclusive at this point, they do indicate that the genetic transmission for drugs may be similar to that for alcohol. Moreover, the genetic influence appears to be operative for both alcohol and drug addiction in the same individual and groups of ostensibly dissimilar individuals. These findings are consistent with the clinical observations that alcohol and drugs can be used interchangeably in the addictive mode and that distinct hierarchical combinations are apparent although alcohol is pervasive throughout subtypes (Freed, 1973; Kandel & Raveis, 1989; Needle, Lavee, Su, Brown, & Doherty, 1988). It is important to examine current and future generations of alcoholics and drug addicts for transmission of specific or common drug types (alcohol) in adoption, twin, and family cases. It is important to continue to assess for combined alcohol and drug use/dependence in multiply addicted individuals for epidemiological, diagnosis, and treatment implications. It is also important to continue to elucidate common brain mechanisms that underlie generalized biological vulnerabilities and identify specific brain targets for subtypes of alcohol and drug addiction for future treatments.

Environmental Factors

More research studies distinguishing between genetic and environmental determinants are necessary. Investigations of genetic and familial patterns of generational transmission of drugs and alcohol in relation to environmental influences regarding exposure to alcohol and drugs are needed. In a simplified formula, the addiction rate can be equated to vulnerability plus exposure: Genetic factors pertain to vulnerability, whereas environmental factors relate to exposure. Prevention and treatment may be more easily accomplished by manipulation of the environment than genetic alteration for the immediate future, whereas knowledge of genetic factors will provide direction for therapeutic agents for addictive disorders and genetic counseling (Kendler et al., 1994).

DIAGNOSIS

Clinical Criteria

The criteria for substance-related disorders in DSM-IV represent the manifestations of addictive use of alcohol/drugs (behavioral criteria 3–7) in addition to tolerance and dependence (pharmacological criteria 1 and 2) (American Psychiatric Association, 1994). The definition of addiction is (1) preoccupation with acquiring alcohol and drugs, (2) compulsive use (continued use despite adverse consequences from alcohol and drugs), and (3) a pattern of relapse to alcohol and drugs over time despite the reinstitution of adverse consequences. The definition of pharmacological tolerance is adaptation or loss of an effect with repeated use or the need to increase the dose to achieve the same effects. The definition of pharmacological dependence is deadaptation or the onset of predictable signs and symptoms of withdrawal on cessation of use or decreasing dose. The withdrawal syndrome is aborted or suppressed with resumption of adequate doses of the drug.

Addiction is drug seeking and can occur independently of tolerance and dependence (e.g., return to use of alcohol/drugs after a period of abstinence beyond the withdrawal period). Tolerance and dependence can occur without clinically observable signs of addiction (e.g., medications to which tolerance of pharmacological effects develops), and the onset of withdrawal without a return or relapse to the use of the medication ensues following discontinuation.

It is important to differentiate drug seeking in addictive use (biological drive) from the distress of withdrawal (physiological deadaptation): the former is the active pursuit of specific drug effects; the latter is the desire for relief of withdrawal symptoms. Drug/alcohol withdrawal is often short-lived (hours to days) and successfully treated with short-term substitution drug therapy or none at all. Treatment of addiction requires specific interventions to suppress the continual desire for drug effects (beyond the withdrawal period) that results in loss of control and endures indefinitely over the life of the alcohol/drug-addicted individual.

Diagnostic Features

The diagnostic features of alcohol and drug addiction have many parallels to the diagnosis of syphilis in the prepenicillin era. Before penicillin prevented the secondary and tertiary stages, syphilis was considered the great masquerader because it mimicked many other diseases. Manifestations of the spectrum of the disease of syphilis were confused with a variety of other medical and psychiatric disorders. The diagnosis often was overlooked if the suspicion of syphilis was not adequately high or avoided because of its moral implications. The long course, the wide systemic and neurological involvement, inadequate serological testing, and social stigmata associated with syphilis obscured and distracted making its diagnosis. Fortunately, because of early detection and adequate treatment, the many masks of syphilis are no longer seen as often.

Drug and alcohol addiction provides many and varied expressions of medical and psychiatric consequences, and moral implications. If the presence of drug and alcohol use and their significance are not recognized, the diagnosis and treatment of addiction will be obscured and the addictive disease will continue unabated.

Denial (minimization and rationalization) is important to the propagation of the drug and alcohol addiction. The denial is present not only in the addict (toward self and others) but also in those associated with the addict. Inherent in addictive illness is resistance by the addict and those affected by the addict to consider that drugs and alcohol can be problematic for the individual. Treatment of the alcohol and drug addiction often provides a solution to the related medical and personal adverse consequences produced by their addictive use.

Multiple-Drug Use

Studies indicate that 80% of alcoholics under the age of 30 years old use at least one other drug regularly and addictively. The propensity to freely exchange one drug for another or to use them simultaneously in an addictive way is common. The use of alcohol by the drug addict is also common, as 50 to 75% of heroin addicts, 80% of cocaine addicts, and 40% of cannabis addicts are addicted to alcohol (Grant, 1996a; Grant, 1996b).

In obtaining a history of alcohol intake and related consequences, a careful screen for other drugs is mandatory or vice versa, alcohol use in a history of drug intake. The vulnerability for abuse and addiction to alcohol and drugs appears to extend to a significant number of other drugs, suggesting a generalized susceptibility to addiction of chemicals possessed by alcoholics and drug addicts.

Because drug-seeking behavior appears to be common in alcoholics and drug addicts, careful, judicious, and sparing use of any medications should be exercised. Drug-seeking behavior for any drug or medication should be met with scrutiny and may require confrontation of the motivations behind medication requests and demands. Common illicit drugs and prescription medications used regularly by alcoholics include marijuana, cocaine, opiates, phencyclidine, hallucinogens, benzodiazepines, barbiturates, and anticholinergics (Miller, Gold, & Smith, 1997).

PHARMACOLOGY OF INTOXICATION AND WITHDRAWAL

Table 11.1 presents the intoxication syndromes for the various drugs and alcohol; Table 11.2 presents the withdrawal syndromes for the various drugs and alcohol.

Multiple-Drug Use

Multiple-substance use determines the clinical presentation of the acute and chronic intoxication syndromes in the multiply dependent individual. The clinical features are understandably a result of the combined effects of multiple substances during intoxication, withdrawal, and prolonged abstinence syndromes, as well as toxic and psychosocial consequences. The challenge to the physician to diagnose multiple dependence and to determine detoxification schedules has been increasing dramatically in recent years. The resultant mixture of signs and symptoms may complicate the clinical picture sufficiently to make the diagnosis of any one drug intoxication impossible. Furthermore, other psychiatric syndromes that may be induced by alcohol and particularly by drugs make diagnosis and treatment more complex.

Considerable overlap occurs among drug effects. The intoxicated state of one drug may mimic the withdrawal state of another. A stimulant picture is produced during intoxication and a depressant state during withdrawal by stimulants, whereas a depressant picture is produced during intoxication and a stimulant state during withdrawal by depressants. Psychotic symptoms are produced during intoxication by some drugs and during withdrawal by others (e.g., cocaine produces hallucinations and delusions during intoxication, and alcohol produces them during withdrawal). Moreover, because all the drugs involved in a multiple dependence produce psychiatric symptoms and syndromes, the clinical state of the multiply dependent individual frequently includes more severe psychopathological consequences.

Addicts use combinations of drugs for a variety of reasons. The high (euphoria) from a stimulant is better maintained with a depressant (e.g., alcohol is often used with cocaine for this reason). A drug may be used to "treat" unwanted side effects of another drug (e.g., the undesirable effects of a cocaine high can be counteracted by opioids, alcohol, or sedative/hypnotics). Moreover, depressants such as alcohol, opiates, or benzodiazepines are used to "come down" or to "sedate" a cocaine-induced anxiety. One drug may be used as a substitute for another drug (e.g., over-the-counter stimulants,

TABLE 11.1. Intoxication: Signs and Symptoms

Drug	Duration	Signs and symptoms
Alcohol	Hours	Alcohol intoxication is manifested in a broad range of clinical conditions. Commonly, alcohol is used in combination with other drugs. The signs and symptoms of intoxication include clouded sensorium, dysinhibition, impairment in motor and mental functions, poor insight and judgment, lethargy, stupor, and coma.
Benzodiazepines and other sedative/ hypnotics	Short-acting: hours Long-acting: days	Tranquilizers (benzodiazepines) and sedative/hypnotics (barbiturates, ethchlorvynol, glutethimide, and meprobamate) are depressants that suppress brain function. Manifestations of intoxication from sedatives and tranquilizers include sedation, slowed mentation and coordination, confusion, loss of consciousness, and coma. Depressants can cause hypotension, bradycardia, and slowed respiratory rate; as heart conduction slows, cardiac arrhythmias can occur. Prolonged slowing of the respiratory rate can lead to respiratory acidosis, arrest, and death.
Stimulants (cocaine, amphetamines, and derivatives)	Hours	Common examples of central nervous system stimulants are cocaine and amphetamines. Their short-term effect is to increase the release of dopamine and other catecholamines to act on postsynaptic receptors, but after prolonged use, they deplete the presynaptic supplies of these neurotransmitters. Signs and symptoms of cocaine and amphetamine intoxication are sympathomimetic: dilated and reactive pupils, tachycardia, elevated temperature, elevated blood pressure, dry mouth, perspiration or chills, nausea and vomiting, tremulousness, hyperactive reflexes, repetitious compulsive behavior, stereotypic biting or self-mutilation, cardiac arrhythmias, flushed skin, poor self-care, suicidal behaviors, violence and homicide, and seizures. Particularly common and serious psychiatric symptoms during intoxication are depression and suicidal and homicidal ideation.
Opiates (heroin)	Hours	During intoxication, centrally, opiate drugs cause a suppression of noradrenergic release. Mood and affect are depressed and inhibited. Important clinically, pupils are constricted and poorly reactive. Peripherally, hypotension and constipation from activation of noradrenergic alpha and beta receptors are common findings. If sufficient amounts of opiates are acutely used, medullary suppression in the brainstem can lead to respiratory suppression and cardiovascular arrest.
PCP/psychedelics	Hours to days	Cognitive or memory impairment, disorientation, and confusion often occur in intoxication from psychedelic use. Psychedelic agents also produce electroencephalographic changes similar to those seen during REM sleep, which may account for the dreamlike quality of the "high" reported by those using this class of drugs.
Nicotine	Hours to days	Exhilaration, sedation, anxiety, depression, elevated blood pressure, tachycardia.

anticholinergics, and antihistamines may be used in lieu of cocaine or opiates when the latter are not available). A withdrawal effect of one drug may be alleviated by the intoxicating effect of another drug (e.g., a cocaine-induced depression may be temporarily relieved by alcohol, opiates, benzodiazepines, or marijuana).

Cocaine and Alcohol (Cocaethylene)

Researchers have clearly demonstrated that in the presence of two drugs of abuse, cocaine and alcohol, the body creates a third. Additive myocardial depressant effects, not related to ischemia but, rather, a direct toxic effect of cocaine plus ethanol, have similarly been reported (Uszenski, Gills, Schaer, Analouei, & Kuhn, 1992). Small, "recreational" doses of cocaine produce coronary vasoconstriction and impair myocardial function. Ethanol has coronary vasoconstrictive and myocardial depressant effects as well. Additive effects on the nucleus locus coerleus may also contribute to the panic and anxiety produced by cocaine and alcohol. Because cocaine is most often taken with other drugs like alcohol, many of the findings that clinicians attribute to cocaine may in fact be due to the combination of drugs. Ethanol plus cocaine appears to increase the period associated with cocaine-related increases in blood pressure. Such an interaction between cocaine and alcohol might increase the likelihood of small vessel, intracerebral ischemic infarcts. Ethanol use increases cocaine use and liking for cocaine possibly by the association of combined use with cocaethylene production. In a recent study, nondependent cocaine users were chosen on the basis of ability to choose cocaine versus placebo. Thereafter they were pretreated with small social doses of alcohol and given choices of cocaine and money. Alcohol pretreatment significantly increased choice of cocaine over the alternative reinforcer, money (Higgins, Roll, & Bickel, 1996). Alcohol can make it particularly difficult to reduce or abstain from cocaine use.

Chronic cocaine addicts often experience persistent panic attacks or bouts of anxiety, which are reported to persist months after discontinuation of cocaine. These consequences may be linked to cocaine and alcohol use. Heuristically consistent with reports of cocaine kindling and cocaine modification of benzodiazepine receptor binding and withdrawal "anxiety" in animals combined use of cocaine and alcohol is quite common among cocaine users (Grant & Harford, 1990a) with approximately 12 million combination users (Randall, 1992). Although initially used by the addict to modify the anxiogenic effects of cocaine and reduce the likelihood of insomnia (Sands & Ciraulo, 1992) upon withdrawal, anxiety is increased and possibly prolonged well into abstinence (Prather & Lal, 1992).

The longer half-life of cocaethylene (2 hours compared with 38 minutes for cocaine) and addictive effect of cocaethylene on the dopamine transporter (Hearn et al., 1991) and the fortyfold greater affinity for the serotonin transporter may explain the occurrence of lethal heart attacks and stroke (eighteen fold increase in the risk of sudden death compared to cocaine alone) and the greater irritability, prolonged toxicity (Fowler et al., 1992), and withdrawal complaints.

Detoxification Treatment

Pharmacological therapies are indicated to prevent life-threatening withdrawal complications from addictive disorders such as seizures and delirium tremens and to increase compliance and retention with psychosocial forms of addiction treatment. Laboratory testing is indicated to assess the type and recency of drug use and to guide management of withdrawal and recovery from alcohol and drugs (see McCance & Kosten, Chapter 25, this volume; Miller et al., 1997).

From Alcohol

Management of alcohol withdrawal is based on history and current clinical status. The single best predictor of future withdrawal from alcohol is the previous history of withdrawal (e.g., presence or absence of seizures or delirium tremens). Treatment of alcohol withdrawal is accomplished by substitution of a pharmacological agent with cross-tolerance and dependence with alcohol. Diazepam, lorazepam, or phenobarbital is usually recommended (chlordiazepoxide or clorazepate are also commonly used because of their lower addiction potential). The usual initial dosage of diazepam 5 to 10 mg or lorazepam 1 to 2 mg is titrated according to elevations of blood pressure, pulse rate, agitation, and presence of delirium. In general, longer-acting preparations such as diazepam provide a smoother and safer withdrawal. Shorter-acting preparations such as lorazepam are indicated when elimination time for benzodiazepines is prolonged (e.g., significant liver disease).

A loading dose of a long-acting benzodiazepine such as diazepam or chlordiazepoxide can be given initially and allow the patient to self-taper. This method is often used in conjunction with a scale for detoxification (i.e., Clinical Inventory Withdrawal Assessment [CIWA]), and in an inpatient setting. Precautions are urged to screen the patient for other sedating drugs to avoid untoward drug–drug interactions, particularly oversedation. Typical loading doses for diazepam are 30 to 50 mg.

From Benzodiazepines and Other Sedative/Hypnotics

The signs and symptoms of withdrawal from benzodiazepines are similar to those for other sedative/hypnotics (barbiturates, ethchylorvynol, glutethimide, and meprobamate) (Table 11.2). The management of withdrawal for sedative/hypnotics (barbiturates) is similar to that for benzodiazepines (Table 11.3).

Withdrawal from benzodiazepines is not usually marked by significant elevations in blood pressure and pulse as with alcohol. Supplemental as-needed (prn) doses are usually not required for changes in vital signs as with alcohol

TABLE 11.2. Withdrawal: Signs and Symptoms

Drug	Peak period	Duration	Signs	Symptoms
Alcohol	1 to 3 days	5 to 7 days	Elevated blood pressure, pulse, temperature; hyperarousal, agitation, restlessness, cutaneous flushing, tremors, disphoresis, dilated pupils, ataxia, clouding of consciousness, disorientation	Anxiety, panic, paranoid delusions, illusions, visual and auditory hallucinations (often derogatory and intimidating)
Benzodiazepines and other sedative/hypnotics	Short-acting: 2 to 4 days Long-acting: 4 to 7 days	Short-acting: 4 to 7 days Long-acting: 7 to 14 days	Increased psychomotor activity, agitation, muscular weakness, tremulousness, hyperpyrexia, diaphoresis, delirium, convulsions, elevated blood pressure, pulse, temperature; tremor of eyelids, tongue, hands	Anxiety, depression, euphoria, incoherent thoughts, hostility, grandiosity, disorientation, tactile, auditory, visual hallucinations, suicidal thoughts
Stimulants (cocaine, amphetamines, and derivatives)	1 to 3 days	5 to 7 days	Withdrawn, psychomotor retardation, hypersomnia, hyperphagia	Depression, anhedonia, suicidal thoughts and behavior, paranoid delusions
Opiates (heroin)	1 to 3 days	5 to 7 days	Drug seeking, mydriasis, piloerection, diaphoresis, rhinorrhea, lacrimation, diarrhea, insomnia, elevated blood pressure and pulse (mild)	Intense desire for drugs, muscle cramps, arthralgia, anxiety, nausea, vomiting, malaise
PCP/psychedelics	days to weeks	days to weeks	Hyperactivity, increased pain threshold, nystagmus, hyperreflexia, hypertension and tachycardia, eyelid retraction (stare), agitation and hyperarousal, drug and erythematous skin, violent and self-destructive behaviors	Anxiety, depression, delusions, auditory and visual hallucinations, memory loss, irritable and angry mood and affect, suicidal thoughts
Nicotine	1 to 3 days	1 to 2 weeks	Elevated blood pressure and pulse (mild), agitation, ritual behaviors around smoking	Anxiety, dysphoria, malaise, desire for nicotine

withdrawal (Table 11.3) (Miller, 1994; Rickels, Schweizer, Case, & Greenblatt, 1990; Schweizer, Rickels, Case, & Greenblatt, 1990). Because benzodiazepines have cross-tolerance and dependence with each other, and other sedative/hypnotic drugs, benzodiazepines can be substituted for other sedative/hypnotics and vice versa. The conversion for equivalent doses can be calculated if doses are actually known prior to taper (Table 11.3). A long-acting benzodiazepine is more effective than short-acting preparations in suppressing withdrawal symptoms and in producing a gradual and smooth transition to the abstinent state. In general, greater patient compliance and less morbidity can be expected from the use of the longer-acting benzodiazepines, because of less intensely acute withdrawal.

A taper over 8 to 12 weeks or longer may be indicated for patients who have been on benzodiazepines chronically for years (e.g., low dose, have medical/surgical/psychiatric comorbidities, have been on higher doses of benzodiazepines, and have older age or protracted withdrawal symptoms). The rate of taper can be adjusted accordingly. The rate of taper is approximately 25% reduction in dose per quarter period (e.g., 25% per week for 1 month). Because of higher rates of withdrawal seizures from alprazolam, the use of phenobarbitol substitution is recommended for the taper.

From Stimulants (Cocaine, Amphetamines, and Derivatives)

Supportive treatment for withdrawal from stimulants is indicated. Observation and monitoring for depression and suicidal ideation during withdrawal are advised (Table 11.2). Because of irritability from stimulant withdrawal, diazepam 5 to 10 mg orally (po) every 6 hours either on a fixed schedule or prn for 2 to 3 days is recommended for mild to moderate withdrawal. For severe withdrawal with persistent depression (beyond a week), therapy can be initiated with desipramine at a dosage of 50 mg/day and titrated upward every other day in 50-mg increments until a dosage of 150 to 250 mg/day is attained. The dosage is maintained for 3 to 6 months and discontinued by gradually tapering off the drug over 2 weeks (Gorelick, 1993; Miller et al., 1997). Desipramine is not recommended routinely for management of withdrawal.

From Opiates

Withdrawal from heroin is predictable and identifiable (Table 11.2). Management of withdrawal can be accomplished with clonidine or methadone. Clonidine 0.1 mg to 0.2 mg four times a day (qid) is given for 1 to 2 weeks for symptoms and signs of acute withdrawal. Methadone 10 mg po test dose is given and repeated 6 hours later if tolerated (no significant sedation or hypotension). Methadone 20 to 30 mg po is given for 3 to 5 days and then tapered 5 mg po each day. Those patients for whom clonidine is indicated are those who are intranasal users, outpatients, and are motivated for the abstinent state. Those patients for whom methadone is more indicated are those who are IV users

TABLE 11.3. Detoxification/Withdrawal and Conversions

Part 1. Benzodiazepine (barbiturate) detoxification/withdrawal

Short-acting	Long-acting

7- to 10-day taper
  Day 1, diazepam 10 to 20 mg po qid with a gradual decremental reduction in dose to 5 to 10 mg po daily on last day; avoid prn. Adjustments in dose according to clinical state may be indicated.
	10- to 14-day taper
	  Day 1, diazepam 10 to 20 mg po qid with a gradual taper to 5 to 10 mg po daily on last day. Avoid prn. Adjustments in dose according to clinical state may be indicated.

Or	*Or*

7- to 10-day taper
  Calculate barbiturate or benzodiazepine equivalence and give 50% of the original dose, and taper (if actual dose is known before detoxification). Avoid prn.
	10- to 14-day taper
	  Calculate barbiturate or benzodiazepine equivalence and give 50% of the original dose and taper (if actual dose is known before detoxification). Avoid prn.

Part 2. Drug dose conversion (equivalent to 60 mg of diazepam and 180 mg of phenobarbital)[a] (conversion factor × dose = diazepam or phenobarbital dose equivalent ÷ 2)

Drug	Dose (mg)	Diazepam (60 mg)	Phenobarbital (180 mg)
Benzodiazepines			
Alprazolam	6	10×	30×
Chlordiazepoxide	150	0.4×	1.2×
Clonazepam	24	2.5×	7.5×
Flurazepam	90	0.6×	2.0×
Halazepam	240	0.25×	0.75×
Lorazepam	12	5.0×	15.0×
Oxazepam	60	1.0×	3.0×
Temazepam	60	1.0×	3.0×
Barbiturates			
Butabarbital	600	0.1×	0.3×
Pentobarbital	600	0.1×	0.3×
Secobarbital	600	0.1×	0.3×
Phenobarbital	180	0.33×	1.0×

[a]The diazepam or phenobarbital dose equivalent should be reduced by 50% for starting dose for taper.

and inpatients and have medical and psychiatric complications and poor compliance with withdrawal from opiates (Gold, 1995; Gorelick, 1993; Miller, 1994). Federal regulations do not allow the use of methadone for detoxification if opiate withdrawal is the primary diagnosis. However, methadone can be used if the primary diagnosis is a medical condition and the secondary condition is withdrawal from opiates.

From PCP and Other Psychedelic Agents

Acute symptoms of withdrawal are diminished or reversed by haloperidol 5 to 10 mg intramuscularly or po every 3 to 6 hours as needed for behavioral control. Lorazepam 1 to 2 mg IV or diazepam 5 to 10 mg po every

3 to 6 hours can be given as needed. Additional behavioral control may be indicated (e.g., isolation and restraints) (Giannini, 1991; Gorelick, 1993; Miller, 1994).

PSYCHOSOCIAL ADDICTIONS TREATMENT TO PREVENT RELAPSE

Relapse Prevention

Management of alcohol and drug withdrawal is often not sufficient to produce sustained abstinence from the use of alcohol and drugs. Further use of addictions treatment to prevent relapse to alcohol and drugs is indicated concurrently and following treatment of withdrawal (Miller, 1995).

Treatment Cost Benefits

Historically, addictions treatment has been marginalized and not integrated within the mainstream of the health care system. The available data actually show that addictions treatment is effective and reduces health care, as well as other costs. Accurate data on treatment outcomes and costs must become widely available so that informed and rational decisions about addiction treatment can be formulated by consumers, providers, primary care physicians, and policymakers. The results of several recent health services research studies unequivocally demonstrate the cost-effectiveness of addiction treatment (Ershoff, Radcliffe, & Gregory, 1996; Gerstein et al., 1994; Holder & Blose, 1992; Iglehart, 1992; Turnure, 1993).

Treatment Approaches and Effectiveness

The abstinence-based method is commonly used (95% of programs surveyed) to treat the disease of alcohol/drug addiction and utilizes cognitive behavioral techniques, and referral to Twelve-Step recovery programs, such as Alcoholics Anonymous (AA) and Narcotics Anonymous (Chappel, 1993; see Table 11.4).

One-year abstinence rates of 80% to 90% were achieved when weekly participation in continuing care and/or attendance at AA meetings followed the treatment program postdischarge. Also, medical and psychiatric utilization were reduced in association with 1-year abstinence rates (Miller, 1995; see Table 11.4).

Recovery in Alcoholics Anonymous

According to results of a survey conducted by AA in 1992, recovery rates achieved in the AA fellowship were as follows: (1) Of those sober in AA less than 1 year, 41% will remain in the AA fellowship another year; (2) of those sober more than 1 year and less than 5 years, 83% will remain in the AA

TABLE 11.4. Treatment Outcome

Part 1. 1-year abstinence by continuum of care and self-help support

	Inpatients (N = 6,508)		Outpatients (N = 1,572)	
	% Attending	% Abstinent	% Attending	% Abstinent
Months of continuing care attended in year				
0	42	53	34	48
1–5	32	55	33	61
6–11	19	71	18	68
12	8	88	14	89
AA attendance				
Nonattender	54	47	43	49
Regular attender	46	74	57	80

Part 2. Medical care utilization 1 year before and after treatment

	% Before	% After	% Before	% After
Hospitalizations				
Medical	23	10	16	7
Psychiatric	5	2	4	1
Detoxification	16	4	9	2
Any admission	28	14	21	9
Emergency room use				
Medical	31	22	29	22
Psychiatric	3	1	3	1
Any emergency room use	30	24	29	23

fellowship another year; (3) of those sober 5 years or more, 91% will remain in the AA fellowship another year (Chappel, 1993).

Of importance, attendance in an abstinence-based treatment program can increase the recovery rates in AA (e.g., 80% from 41%) with referral to AA following the treatment program (Chappel, 1993; Miller, 1995).

REFERENCES

Adlaf, E. M., Smart, R. G., & Walsh, G. W. (1992). Substance use and work disabilities among a general population. *American Journal of Drug and Alcohol Abuse, 18*(4), 371–387.

American Psychiatric Association. (1987). *Diagnostic and statistical manual of mental disorders* (3rd ed., rev.). Washington, DC: Author.

American Psychiatric Association. (1994). *Diagnostic and statistical manual of mental disorders* (4th ed.). Washington, DC: Author.

Babor, T. F., Hofmann, M., DelBoca, F. K., Hesselbrock, V., Meyer, R. E., Dolinsky, Z. S., & Rounsaville, B. (1992). Types of alcoholics, I. Evidence for an empirically derived typology based on indicators of vulnerability and severity. *Archives of General Psychiatry, 49*(8), 599–608.

Blanken, A. J. (1993). Measuring use of alcohol and other drugs among adolescents. *Public Health Reports, 108*(Suppl. 1), 25–30.

Cadoret, R. J., Troughton, E., O'Gorman, T. W., & Heywood, E. (1986). An adoption study of genetic and environmental factors in drug abuse. *Archives of General Psychiatry, 43*(12), 1131–1136.

Caetano, R., & Schafer, J. (1996). DSM-IV alcohol dependence and drug abuse/dependence in a treatment sample of whites, blacks and Mexican Americans. *Drug and Alcohol Dependence, 43*(1–2), 93–101.

Calafat, A., Amengual, M., Palmer, A., & Saliba, C. (1997). Drug use and its relationship to other behavior disorders and maladjustment signs among adolescents. *Substance Use and Misuse, 32*(1), 1–24.

Chappel, J. N. (1993). Long-term recovery from alcoholism. *Psychiatric Clinics of North America, 16*(1), 177–187.

Chatham, L. R., Rowan-Szal, G. A., Joe, G. W., & Simpson, D. D. (1997). Heavy drinking, alcohol-dependent vs. nondependent methadone-maintenance clients: A follow-up study. *Addictive Behaviors, 22*(1), 69–80.

Cloninger, C. R. (1988). Etiologic factors in substance abuse: An adoption study perspective. *National Institutes of the Sciences Drug Abuse Research Monograph Series, 89*, 52–72.

Cornelius, J. R., Salloum, I. M., Day, N. L., Thase, M. E., & Mann, J. J. (1996). Patterns of suicidality and alcohol use in alcoholics with major depression. *Alcoholism: Clinical and Experimental Research, 20*(8), 1451–1455.

Craddock, S. G., Rounds-Bryant, J. L., Flynn, P. M., & Hubbard, R. L. (1997). Characteristics and pretreatment behaviors of clients entering drug abuse treatment: 1969 to 1993. *American Journal of Drug and Alcohol Abuse, 23*(1), 43–59.

Darke, S., & Hall, W. (1995). Levels and correlates of polydrug use among heroin users and regular amphetamine users. *Drug and Alcohol Dependence, 39*, 231–235.

Denison, M. E., Paredes, A., & Booth, J. B. (1997). Alcohol and cocaine interactions and aggressive behaviors. *Recent Developments in Alcoholism, 13*, 283–303.

Ershoff, D., Radcliffe, A., & Gregory, M. (1996). The Southern California Kaiser-Permanente Chemical Dependency Recovery Program evaluation: Results of a treatment outcome study in an HMO setting. *Journal of Addictive Diseases, 15*(3), 1–25.

Fawzy, F. I., Coombs, R. H., & Gerber, B. (1983). Generational continuity in the use of substances: The impact of parental substance use on adolescent substance abuse. *Addictive Behaviors, 8*, 109–114.

Fowler, J. S., Volkow, N. D., MacGregor, R. R., Logan, J., Dewey, S. L., Gatley, S. J., & Wolf, A. P. (1992). Comparative PET studies of the kinetics and distribution of cocaine and cocaethylene in baboon brain. *Synapse, 12*, 220–227.

Freed, E. X. (1973). Drug abuse by alcoholics: A review. *International Journal of the Addictions, 8*, 451–473.

Gardner, E. L. (1997). Brain reward mechanisms. In J. H. Lowinson, P. Ruiz, R. B. Millman, & J. G. Langrod (Eds.), *Substance abuse: A comprehensive textbook* (3rd ed.). Baltimore: Williams & Wilkins.

Gerstein, D. R., Johnson, R. A., Harwood, H., Fountain, D., Suter, N., & Malloy, K. (1994). Evaluating recovery services. *The California Drug and Alcohol Treatment Assessment (CALDATA)*. Sacramento: California Department of Drug and Alcohol Programs.

Giannini, A. T. (1991). Phencyclidine. In N. S. Miller (Ed.), *Comprehensive handbook of drug and alcohol addiction* (pp. 383–394). New York: Marcel Dekker.

Gilson, S. F., Chilcoat, H. D., & Stapleton, J. M. (1996). Illicit drug use by persons with disabilities: insights from the National Household Survey on Drug Abuse. *American Journal of Public Health, 86*(11), 1613–1615.

Gladstone, J., Levy, M., Nulman, I., & Koren, G. (1997). Characteristics of pregnant women who engage in binge alcohol consumption. *Canadian Medical Association Journal, 156*(6), 789–794.

Gold, M. S. (1995). Pharmacological therapies of opiate addiction. In N. S. Miller & M. S. Gold (Eds.), *Pharmacologic therapies for drug and alcohol addictions.* New York: Marcel Dekker.

Gorelick, D. A. (1993). Overview of pharmacological treatment approaches for alcohol and other drug addiction. Intoxication, withdrawal, and relapse prevention. *Psychiatric Clinics of North America, 16*(1), 141–156.

Grant, B. F. (1996a). DSM-IV, DSM-III-R, and ICD-10 alcohol and drug abuse/harmful use and dependence, United States, 1992: A nosological comparison. *Alcoholism: Clinical and Experimental Research, 20*(8), 1481–1488.

Grant, B. F. (1996b). Prevalence and correlates of drug use and DSM-IV drug dependence in the United States: results of the National Longitudinal Alcohol Epidemiologic Survey. *Journal of Substance Abuse, 8*(2), 195–210.

Grant, B. F., & Harford, T. C. (1990a). Concurrent and simultaneous use of alcohol with cocaine: Results of a national survey. *Drug and Alcohol Dependence, 25,* 97–104.

Grant, B. F., & Harford, T. C. (1990b). Concurrent and simultaneous use of alcohol with sedatives and with tranquilizers: Results of a national survey. *Journal of Substance Abuse Treatment, 2,* 1–14.

Grella, C. E., Anglin, M. D., & Wugalter, S. E. (1997). Patterns and predictors of cocaine and crack use by clients in standard and enhanced methadone maintenance treatment. *American Journal of Drug and Alcohol Abuse, 23*(1), 15–42.

Hammer, T., & Vaglum, P. (1992). Further course of mental health and use of alcohol and tranquilizers after cessation or persistence of cannabis use in young adulthood: a longitudinal study. *Scandinavian Journal of Social Medicine, 20*(3), 143–150.

Hasin, D., Li, Q., McCloud, S., & Endicott, J. (1996). Agreement between DSM-III, DSM-III-R, DSM-IV and ICD-10 alcohol diagnoses in U.S. community-sample heavy drinkers. *Addiction, 91*(10), 1517–1527.

Hearn, W. L., Flynn, D. D., Hime, G. W., Rose, S., Cofino, J. C., Mantero-Atienza, E., Wetli, C. V., & Mash, D. C. (1991). Cocaethylene: A unique cocaine metabolite displays high affinity for the dopamine transporter. *Journal of Neurochemistry, 56*(2), 698–701.

Higgins, S. T., Roll, J. M., & Bickel, W. K. (1996). Alcohol pretreatment increases preference for cocaine over monetary reinforcement. *Psychopharmacology, 123,* 1–8.

Hill, S. Y., Cloninger, C. R., & Ayre, F. R. (1977). Independent familial transmission of alcoholism and opiate abuse. *Alcoholism: Clinical and Experimental Research, 1,* 335–342.

Hoffman, J. A., Caudill, B. D., Koman, J. J. III, Luckey, J. W., Flynn, P. M., & Mayo, D. W. (1996). Psychosocial treatments for cocaine abuse. 12-month treatment outcomes. *Journal of Substance Abuse Treatment, 13*(1), 3–11.

Holder, H. D., & Blose, J. O. (1992). The reduction of health care costs associated with alcoholism treatment: A 14 year longitudinal study. *Journal of Studies on Alcohol, 53*(4), 293–302.

Iglehart, J. K. (1992). The American health care system: Managed care. *New England Journal of Medicine, 337,* 742–747.

Irwin, K. L., Edlin, B. R., Faruque, S., McCoy, H. V., Word, C., Serrano, Y., Inciardi, J., Bowser, B., & Holmberg, S. D. (1996). Crack cocaine smokers who turn to drug injection: Characteristics, factors associated with injection, and implications for HIV transmission. The Multicenter Crack Cocaine and HIV Infection Study Team. *Drug and Alcohol Dependence, 42*(2), 85–92.

Jacob, J., Harrison, H. Jr., & Tigert, A. T. (1995). Prevalence of alcohol and illicit drug use by expectant mothers. *Alaska Medicine, 37*(3), 83–87.

Kandel, D., Chen, K., Warner, L. A., Kessler, R. C., & Grant, B. (1997). Prevalence and demographic correlates of symptoms of last year dependence on alcohol, nicotine, marijuana and cocaine in the U.S. population. *Drug and Alcohol Dependence, 44*(1), 11–29.

Kandel, D. B., & Raveis, V. H. (1989). Cessation of illicit drug use in young adulthood. *Archives of General Psychiatry, 46*, 109–116.

Kasselbaum, G., & Chandler, S. M. (1994). Polydrug use and self control among men and women in prisons. *Journal of Drug Education, 24*(4), 333–350.

Kendler, K. S., Neale, M. C., Heath, A. C., Kessler, R. C., & Eaves, L. J. (1994). A twin-family study of alcoholism in women. *American Journal of Psychiatry, 151*(5), 707–715.

Kidorf, M., & Stitzer, M. L. (1993). Descriptive analysis of cocaine use of methadone patients. *Drug and Alcohol Dependence, 32*, 267–275.

Martin, C. S., Clifford, P. R., Maisto, S. A., Earleywine, M., Kirisci, L., & Longabaugh, R. (1996). Polydrug use in an inpatient treatment sample of problem drinkers. *Alcoholism: Clinical and Experimental Research, 20*(3), 413–417.

Miller, N. S. (Ed.). (1994). *Principles of Addiction Medicine.* Washington, DC: American Society of Addiction Medicine.

Miller, N. S. (1995). *Treatment of the addictions: Applications of outcome research for clinical management.* New York: Haworth Press.

Miller, N. S. (1997). Generalized vulnerability to drug and alcohol addiction. In N. S. Miller (Ed.), *The principles and practice of addictions in psychiatry* (pp. 18–25). Philadelphia: Saunders.

Miller, N. S., Gold, M. S., Belkin, B., & Klahr, A. L. (1990). The diagnosis of alcohol and cannabis dependence in cocaine dependents and alcohol dependence in their families. *British Journal of Addiction, 84*, 1491–1498.

Miller, N. S., Gold, M. S., & Smith, D. E. (Eds.). (1997). *Manual of therapeutics for addictions.* New York: Wiley-Liss.

Mirin, S. M., Weiss, R. D., Griffin, M. L., & Michael, J. L. (1991). Psychopathology in drug abusers and their families. *Comprehensive Psychiatry, 32*(1), 36–51.

Moss, H. B. (1989). Psychopathy, aggression, and family history in male veteran substance abuse patients: A factor analytic study. *Addictive Behaviors, 14*, 565–570.

National Institute on Drug Abuse. (1988). *National household survey on drug abuse* (DHHS Publication No. ADM 89-1636). Washington, DC: U.S. Government Printing Office.

Needle, R., Lavee, Y., Su, S., Brown, P., & Doherty, W. (1988). Familial, interpersonal, and intrapersonal correlates of drug use: A longitudinal comparison of adolescents in treatment, drug-using adolescents not in treatment, and non-drug-using adolescents. *International Journal of the Addictions, 23*(12), 1211–1240.

Paul, J. P., Barrett, D. C., Crosby, G. M., & Stall, R. D. (1996). Longitudinal changes in alcohol and drug use among men seen at a gay-specific substance abuse treatment agency. *Journal of Studies on Alcohol, 57*, 475–485.

Pickens, R. W., Svikis, D. S., & McGue, M. (1991). Heterogeneity in the inheritance of alcoholism: A study of male and female twins. *Archives of General Psychiatry, 48,* 19–28.

Prather, P. L., & Lal, H. (1992). Protracted withdrawal: Sensitization of the anxiogenic response to cocaine in rats concurrently treated with ethanol. *Neuropsychopharmacology, 6,* 23–29.

Randall, T. (1992). Cocaine, alcohol mix in body to form even longer lasting, more lethal drugs. *Journal of the American Medical Association, 267,* 1043–1044.

Rickels, K., Schweizer, E., Case, G., & Greenblatt, D. J. (1990). Long-term therapeutic use of benzodiazepines. I: Effects of abrupt discontinuation. *Archives of General Psychiatry, 47,* 899–907.

Robertson, M. J., Zlotnick, C., & Westerfelt, A. (1997). Drug use disorders and treatment contact among homeless adults in Alameda County, California. *American Journal of Public Health, 87*(2), 221–228.

Robins, L. N., Helzer, J. E., Pryzbeck, T. R., & Regier, D. A. (1988). Alcohol disorders in the community: A report from the Epidemiologic Catchment Area. In R. M. Rose & J. Barrett (Eds.), *Alcoholism: Origins and outcome* (pp. 15–29). New York: Raven Press.

Rounsaville, B. J., Kosten, T. R., Weissman, M. M., Prusoff, B., Pauls, D., Anton, S. F., & Merikangas, K. (1991). Psychiatric disorders in relatives of probands with opiate addiction. *Archives of General Psychiatry, 48*(1), 33–42.

Sands, B. F., & Ciraulo, D. A. (1992). Cocaine drug-interactions. *Journal of Clinical Psychopharmacology, 12,* 49–55.

Schuckit, M. A. (1986). Genetic and clinical implications of alcoholism and affective disorders. *American Journal of Psychiatry, 143*(2), 140–147.

Schweizer, E., Rickels, K., Case, G., & Greenblatt, D. J. (1990). Long-term therapeutic use of benzodiazepines. II: Effects of gradual taper. *Archives of General Psychiatry, 47,* 908–915.

Stein, M. D., Wilkinson, J., Berglas, N., & O'Sullivan, P. (1996). Prevalence and detection of illicit drug disorders among hospitalized patients. *American Journal of Drug and Alcohol Abuse, 22*(3), 463–471.

Svikis, D. S., & Pickens, R. W. (1988). *Methodological issues in family, adoption, and twin research* (NIDA Research Monograph Series No. 89, pp. 120–133). Washington, DC: U.S. Government Printing Office.

Turnure, C. (1993). *Minnesota Consolidated Fund, annual cost offsets.* St. Paul: Minnesota Department of Human Services.

Uszenski, R. T., Gills, R. A., Schaer, G. L., Analouei, A. R., & Kuhn, F. E. (1992). Additive myocardial depressant effects of cocaine and ethanol. *American Heart Journal, 124,* 1276–1283.

Wise, R. A. (1989). The brain and reward. In J. M. Liebman & S. J. Cooper (Eds.), *The neuropharmacological basis of reward.* Oxford: Oxford University Press.

Wiseman, E. J., & McMillan, D. E. (1996). Combined use of cocaine with alcohol or cigarettes. *American Journal of Drug and Alcohol Abuse, 22*(4), 577–587.

Part IV

Treatment Issues for Special Populations

12

Substance Abuse and Psychiatric Disorders

ROGER D. WEISS
LISA M. NAJAVITS
STEVEN M. MIRIN

INTRODUCTION

The past decade has witnessed a burgeoning interest in individuals who are "dually diagnosed" with substance use disorders and psychiatric disorders. This increased interest has arisen as a result of two major factors: (1) the recognition of the high prevalence rate of this form of comorbidity and (2) the growing understanding by those in both the substance abuse field and in the mental health field that traditional approaches to the treatment of dually diagnosed patients were frequently unsuccessful. Indeed, a landmark series of studies performed by McLellan et al. in the early 1980s (McLellan, 1986; McLellan, Luborsky, Woody, O'Brien, & Druley, 1983) showed that the overall level of severity of psychiatric symptomatology was the most robust predictor of treatment outcome in patients with substance use disorders. The fact that patients with high levels of psychiatric severity responded poorly to traditional substance abuse treatment, combined with the growing recognition among those who treated psychiatrically ill patients that many of them suffered from coexisting substance use disorders, led clinical researchers to develop new, specific treatment approaches for dually disordered patients. As detailed later in this chapter, treatments that have been adapted for this patient population are now producing better outcomes than previously were achieved.

EPIDEMIOLOGY

A number of studies of clinical populations in the early and mid-1980s found that patients seeking treatment for substance use disorders had a relatively high prevalence rate of coexisting psychiatric disorders. Studies of patients in psychiatric treatment facilities also showed a higher prevalence rate of coexisting substance use disorders than would be expected in the general population. Treatment-seeking samples, unfortunately, may not be representative of community populations of individuals with a particular disorder, since they have higher rates of other disorders and may have more severe manifestations of the disorder. Therefore, studies of community samples are important in assessing the true comorbidity rate of disorders.

The Epidemiologic Catchment Area (ECA) study (Regier et al., 1990) and the more recent National Comorbidity Survey (NCS; Kessler et al., 1997) provided convincing evidence of the frequent co-occurrence of substance use disorders and psychiatric disorders. Although the results of these surveys differ somewhat, they are consistent in their finding that this form of comorbidity is quite common. The ECA study reported on the odds ratios (i.e., relative risk) associated with the coexistence of substance use disorders among individuals with various Axis I psychiatric disorders. This study found that individuals with a diagnosis of major depression had approximately twice the risk of having a coexisting substance use disorder when compared with people who do not have major depression. Panic disorder increased the odds of having a coexisting substance use disorder approximately by a factor of 3, and schizophrenia by a factor of 5. Interestingly, bipolar disorder was the Axis I disorder that placed individuals at greatest risk for coexisting substance use disorder, with an odds ratio of approximately 7. The NCS expanded on the ECA by studying a nationally representative household sample, as opposed to the ECA, which concentrated on five sites around the country. The NCS found large odds ratios for alcohol use disorders associated with conduct disorder, antisocial personality disorder, anxiety disorders, and mood disorders. Moreover, the NCS found that dually diagnosed individuals with alcohol use disorder usually had a later age of onset for that disorder than for at least one of their co-occurring disorders; this pattern was particularly true for women.

Studies have also documented high rates of Axis II disorders among individuals with substance use disorder. Of patients with substance use disorder, 50–91% have a co-occurring Axis II disorder, most commonly antisocial, borderline, and histrionic (Barber et al., 1996; Oldham et al., 1995). In the ECA study, antisocial personality disorder was more highly associated (84%) with having a substance use disorder than was any Axis I disorder. It should also be noted that the most common co-occurring diagnosis for any substance use disorder is actually another substance use disorder (Regier et al., 1990), with nicotine the most frequent.

No substance of abuse is more closely linked with psychiatric illness (particularly schizophrenia) than is nicotine. Indeed, one study has reported that 83% of patients hospitalized on a psychiatric unit at a Veterans Administration hospital smoked cigarettes (O'Farrell, Connors, & Upper, 1983). A wide variety of theories have been espoused to explain this link, including boredom, relief of extrapyramidal symptoms induced by neuroleptic medication, and a calming effect of nicotine. More recently, intriguing research regarding potential dysregulation of nicotinic neurotransmission among patients with schizophrenia has been discussed as a possible explanation for the use of nicotine by such a large proportion of patients with schizophrenia (Freedman, Hall, Adler, & Leonard, 1995).

THE MYTH OF THE TYPICAL DUAL-DIAGNOSIS PATIENT

When evaluating a patient with substance abuse and coexisting psychiatric problems, it is important to recognize the multiple possible relationships between substance abuse and psychopathology, as well as the heterogeneity of the population of patients labeled "dually diagnosed." We have previously written about the "myth of the typical dual-diagnosis patient" (Weiss, Mirin, & Frances, 1992b) (i.e., the notion that "dually diagnosed" patients represent a homogeneous population of patients who should receive "dual diagnosis treatment." This oversimplification is not characteristic of other fields of medicine; one would not find a specific ward in a general medical–surgical hospital devoted to the treatment of patients who all have two diseases. It is thus critical that patients with substance abuse and psychiatric illness be viewed as comprising many different subpopulations as well.

One way of conceptualizing dually disordered patients to balance a "lumping" and "splitting" approach is to divide dually disordered patients into four major subgroups, based on the severity of each respective disorder. Thus, we can classify a patient as having either a "major" or "minor" substance abuse problem and a major or minor psychiatric problem (Ries, Sloan, & Miller, 1997). Although this classification is somewhat crude, grouping dually diagnosed patients in this manner can be helpful in certain situations (e.g., when developing a group therapy program in a substance abuse outpatient clinic). Unfortunately, while grouping patients with some degree of homogeneity together is preferable (e.g., a group for patients with bipolar disorder and substance abuse), one needs a relatively large clinical population to recruit a sufficient number of patients for these groups. Moreover, even within diagnostically homogeneous groups, the level of functioning among patients may be quite varied.

THE RELATIONSHIP BETWEEN SUBSTANCE
ABUSE AND PSYCHOPATHOLOGY

When evaluating or treating a dually disordered patient, many clinicians initially focus on which is the "primary" disorder, frequently defined as the disorder that occurred first. Although this primary–secondary distinction can be useful in some instances (e.g., when conducting clinical research), it generally has less utility in clinical practice. With few exceptions (e.g., temporary psychiatric symptoms caused by substance use or withdrawal), an individual who has two discrete disorders needs treatment for both, even if the second disorder was directly related to the first (e.g., a patient with cocaine use disorder who develops panic attacks).

Meyer (1986) developed a comprehensive schema describing the relationship between substance abuse and psychopathology. Moving beyond the primary–secondary distinction, he described six ways in which substance abuse and psychopathology may be related.

1. *Psychopathology may serve as a risk factor for substance abuse.* As described earlier, the risk for having a coexisting substance use disorder is clearly elevated in individuals with Axis I or Axis II psychiatric disorders. For example, people with posttraumatic stress disorder (PTSD) sometimes use substances to blunt their painful PTSD symptoms, and people with bipolar disorder may drink much more heavily when manic than when euthymic.

2. *Psychiatric disorders and coexisting substance use disorders may affect the course of each other, including symptom picture, rapidity of onset, and response to treatment.* The impact of substance use on the course of psychiatric disorders (and vice versa) has been the subject of recent interesting research, indicating the adverse effect of substance use on the course of various psychiatric illnesses. For example, Gupta, Hendricks, Kenkel, Bhatia, and Haffke (1996) showed that among 22 patients with schizophrenia, those with substance abuse had significantly higher hospital readmission rates than did individuals who did not abuse substances. Interestingly, this increased readmission rate occurred independent of medication noncompliance because all the individuals in their study cohorts were treated with long-acting injectable neuroleptics.

Two studies show the public health impact of substance use among patients with major mental illness. In a study of 105 male patients with schizophrenia and cocaine dependence, Shaner et al. (1995) reported that a cyclical pattern of cocaine use, likely influenced by receipt of a disability check, led to an increased incidence of hospital admissions during the first week of each month, soon after the receipt of the disability payment. Dickey and Azeni (1996) found that among individuals with serious mental illness, psychiatric treatment costs among those with coexisting substance abuse problems were nearly 60% higher than costs of individuals with the same psychiatric diagnoses but no substance use disorder; most of the increased cost was associated with acute inpatient admissions.

Recent research has indicated that for certain people with psychiatric disorders, substance use that would be nonproblematic under other circumstances can adversely affect either the course of illness or treatment response. For example, Worthington et al. (1996) recently reported that among patients with major depressive disorder being treated with antidepressants, even social drinking was associated with a poorer antidepressant response.

As mentioned earlier, McLellan et al. (1983, 1986) showed that coexisting psychopathology has an adverse effect on the treatment outcome of patients with substance use disorders. This has been demonstrated to be true for a variety of disorders and drugs of abuse (Brooner, King, Kidorf, Schmidt, & Bigelow, 1997; Nace, Davis, & Gaspari, 1991; Rounsaville, Kosten, Weissman, & Kleber, 1986; Woody, McLellan, Luborsky, & O'Brien, 1985). However, the degree to which the poorer outcomes of this population are a reflection of misdiagnoses and unsuitable treatments is unclear, as opposed to severity of illness and coexisting problems. As innovative treatments for specific subpopulations of dually diagnosed patients are tested more thoroughly, the answer to this question should become clearer.

3. *Psychiatric symptoms may develop in the course of chronic intoxication.* The abuse of drugs or alcohol can lead to a wide variety of psychiatric symptoms, including depression, anxiety, psychosis, euphoria, and dissociative states. Most of these symptoms are time limited and disappear within hours of cessation of substance use. One example of this phenomenon is cocaine-induced paranoia (Satel, Southwick, & Gawin, 1991), which has some features in common with paranoia caused by other conditions. However, the time course of the two is quite different, with cocaine-induced paranoia typically lasting only minutes to hours, whereas paranoia due to other conditions ordinarily lasts longer. Moreover, the content of cocaine-induced paranoid thinking is also typically cocaine related, with fears about police and drug dealers most common; perceptual hallucinations and bizarre delusions are not typical features of this syndrome.

4. *Long-term use can precipitate psychiatric disorders that do not remit quickly.* The capacity for substances of abuse to precipitate enduring psychiatric disorders has generated a good deal of clinical interest and some controversy. Certain disorders, such as alcohol-induced organic disorders, are well-known sequelae of heavy, long-term use. One of the disorders that has recently received attention is cocaine-induced panic disorder (Louie et al., 1996), which has been found to differ from primary panic disorder by virtue of its decreased frequency of agoraphobia, increased frequency of psychosensory disturbances during panic attacks, and an atypical response to medication (exacerbation of the problem with antidepressant treatment, and a potentially better response to benzodiazepines and anticonvulsants).

5. *Substance abuse and psychopathological symptoms may he meaningfully linked.* Some individuals with psychiatric disorders use various drugs of abuse in a way that exacerbates their psychiatric symptoms. Thus, for example, certain individuals with eating disorders may use cocaine because it helps them to lose weight, some patients with antisocial personality disorder drink alcohol or use cocaine to facilitate disinhibition and aggression, and certain individuals with hypomania use cocaine or other stimulants to enhance their euphoric mood (Weiss, Mirin, Griffin, & Michael, 1988; Weiss, Mirin, Michael, & Sollogub, 1986). Thus, while some patients with psychiatric disorders may use drugs to "self-medicate" their symptoms (Khantzian, 1985, 1997), others may intentionally use drugs that highlight or enhance those symptoms.

6. *Some people may have a psychiatric disorder and an addictive disorder that are not related.* The coexistence of two disorders within the same individual does not imply a causal link. For example, a number of people have major depressive disorder and alcohol dependence but do not drink because they are depressed and are not depressed because they drink too much. Rather, they have two relatively common disorders, which are not necessarily linked. Brunette, Mueser, Xie, and Drake (1997) recently studied the relationship of severity of substance abuse and severity of schizophrenic symptoms in 172 patients with both disorders. They found very weak relationships between the two sets of symptoms, with no consistent pattern. Although substance use led to higher rates of hospitalization in this population, it did so through other means (i.e., through disinhibition, aggression, and other direct substance-induced symptoms). Thus, this research group concluded that patients with schizophrenia experience similar types of substance-related difficulties as do other people with substance abuse problems.

Vulnerability to Substance Abuse among Patients with Psychiatric Disorders

The "Self-Medication" Hypothesis

As described previously, numerous studies of clinical and community populations show that individuals with psychiatric illness have an increased likelihood of having a coexisting substance use disorder. However, this increased comorbidity rate does not explain why psychiatric illness should predispose an experimental drug user to subsequent abuse or dependence. Weiss (1992) hypothesized several different mechanisms by which having a psychiatric disorder may predispose an individual to developing a substance use disorder. First, certain drugs may be particularly reinforcing to patients with psychiatric disorders. In other words, some people with specific psychiatric symptoms may find that their symptoms are relieved or attenuated by particular substances of abuse. This theory, sometimes known as the "self-medication hypothesis" (Khantzian, 1985, 1997), has been the subject of a great deal of attention and controversy.

The self-medication hypothesis is based on several fundamental underlying assumptions, the first of which is that substances of abuse are used to relieve psychological pain, not just to induce euphoria. Second, the self-medication hypothesis ascribes a great deal of importance to a "drug of choice," which pharmacologically relieves specific intolerable emotions or symptoms. Thus, for example, the calming effect of opioids may have a specific effect in reducing the discomfort of those who experience intense anger, while cocaine may be eschewed by those same individuals because of its capacity to exacerbate angry feelings.

The self-medication hypothesis has been criticized because of its heavy reliance on anecdotal data from patients engaged in psychotherapy and the relative paucity of empirical studies testing the hypothesis. Moreover, it is important to note that the acute effects of various drugs of abuse on behavior and mood may be quite different from the effects one observes when the same drugs are taken chronically. Observations of heroin users in varying stages of intoxication and withdrawal illustrate this point. In the mid-1970s, members of our group (Meyer & Mirin, 1979) carried out a study in which previously detoxified heroin addicts were allowed to self-administer increasing doses of heroin over a 10-day period in a controlled research environment. Acute administration of heroin was quickly followed by euphoria and tension relief. With continued use, however, subjects developed increasing dysphoria, motor retardation, and social withdrawal. Although acute administration of heroin briefly reversed these chronic effects, tolerance eventually developed to the acute euphoric effects of the drug. A similar dichotomy between acute and chronic effects may be observed in cocaine users; whereas initial low-dose use often produces euphoria, chronic high-dose use is often accompanied by an agitated dysphoric state (Post, Kotin, & Goodwin, 1974). Seminal laboratory studies of alcoholics by Mendelson and Mello (1966) also illustrated the dysphoric effects of heavy drinking. The self-medication hypothesis may thus be better at explaining substance *use* than at explaining *dependence,* because all substance use can be seen as an attempt to change one's mood from its natural state to one of intoxication. Trying to explain continued use when the drug is exacerbating the symptoms that it is designed to escape is far more difficult, however.

Because of the discrepancy between some of the theoretical conceptualizations of self-medication espoused by Khantzian (1985) and empirical studies such as those described previously, our group (Weiss, Griffin, & Mirin, 1992a) conducted an empirical study of the self-medication hypothesis of drug abuse by examining motivation for drug use and drug effects in 494 patients consecutively admitted to McLean Hospital for drug-dependence treatment. We asked patients a series of questions regarding (1) their reasons for initiating the use of their drug of choice (e.g., because of problems sleeping, to relieve depression, when things are going well) and (2) effects that they typically experienced after taking this drug (e.g., improvement, worsening, or no effect on sleep, mood, appetite). We found that 63% of patients reported using their drug of choice in response to symptoms of depression, with no difference according to drug of choice (i.e., opioids, cocaine, or sedative/hypnotic drugs). However, women were significantly more likely to use drugs for depression than were men (76% vs. 58%). Moreover, patients with major depressive disorder were significantly more likely to use drugs in response to depressive symptoms than were patients without major depression (89% vs. 60%). Interestingly, this finding was true for men but not for women. All 21 of the men who had major depression reported using drugs when depressed, whereas only 55% of men without major depression did so. In contrast, women with or without major depression were nearly equally likely (81% vs. 75%) to use drugs in response to depressive symptoms. When we asked patients about their response to their drug of choice, 68% reported that their drug use improved their mood, with no difference based on gender, drug of choice, or presence or absence of major depression. However, it was notable that 26% of patients who initiated drug use when depressed reported that their drug use made their mood worse.

Finally, we were interested in the diagnostic significance of knowing whether or not a drug-dependent patient claimed to use drugs when depressed. We found that among women, this knowledge was not helpful in diagnosing major depression, although it was useful in men. Twenty percent of women who used drugs when depressed had a diagnosis of major depression, as compared with 15% of women who denied using drugs for depression. In contrast, 10% of men who used drugs for depression were diagnosed with major depressive disorder, whereas none of the 150 male patients who denied using drugs for depression received this diagnosis.

Khantzian (1997) recently answered some of the criticisms of the self-medication hypothesis, and some of his responses reflect the findings from our study. Specifically, he emphasized that the self-medication hypothesis does not apply primarily to discrete Axis I disorders but to psychological suffering in general. Indeed, some patients with subclinical symptoms of depression or anxiety may use drugs or alcohol to relieve these symptoms. Moreover, he stressed that many individuals use drugs or alcohol to escape uncomfortable feelings, whether that involves improving them or exchanging them for another set of uncomfortable feelings (Khantzian, 1989). Indeed, for many people with chaotic mood states, or for those whose lives have been influenced externally by forces or people out of their control (e.g., people who have been traumatized), the ability to change their mood, whether for better or worse, may feel as though it compensates for the negative consequences that often occur as a result of substance use.

Other Theories

A second potential explanation for the increased vulnerability among patients with psychiatric illness to developing substance abuse problems is their inability to appreciate the negative consequences that their substance use has caused or their failure to adapt their behavior to reflect that knowledge (Weiss, 1992). Thus, for example, although alcoholic patients with severe depression frequently understand the destructive effects of their drinking, many of them continue to abuse alcohol, fueled by the hopelessness of depressive thinking; they think that their lives cannot be made any worse than they already are, and they believe that intoxication will at least afford them an evening's reprieve from their psychological suffering (Beck, Wright, Newman, & Liese, 1993). Other psychiatric illnesses may also impair judgment. For example, patients with bipolar disorder may abuse substances during a manic episode, even though they might not do so when euthymic; their irritability, reckless-ness, and poor judgment lead them to make ill-advised decisions regarding spending money, sexual activity, substance use, and a wide variety of other behaviors.

DIAGNOSING PSYCHIATRIC DISORDERS
IN PATIENTS WITH SUBSTANCE USE DISORDERS

Because most substances of abuse can cause a wide variety of psychiatric disturbances, diagnosing independent psychiatric disorders in patients who have a known substance use disorder can be quite complex. In evaluating such patients, clinicians are often faced with the task of distinguishing whether the patients' presenting signs and symptoms are manifestations of a coexisting psychiatric disorder or consequences of drug intoxication or withdrawal. For example, when assessing someone with a long history of alcohol dependence and depressive symptoms, it is often difficult to discern whether the depression is the result of the direct pharmacological effects of alcohol, a response to the numerous losses that frequently occur in the lives of substance dependent persons, a manifestation of feelings of discouragement or desperation about being unable to stop drinking, or an independent mood disorder. Indeed, Jaffe and Ciraulo (1986) have pointed out that depression in alcohol-dependent individuals can occur as a result of these or a variety of other reasons, including metabolic disturbances, head trauma, or a coexisting personality disorder. Assessing the cause of depressive symptoms in patients with substance use disorder is even further complicated by the fact that depressive symptoms often serve as the precipitant for substance-dependent patients to seek treatment. Rounsaville and Kleber (1985), for example, found that a major feature distinguishing treatment-seeking opiate addicts from opiate addicts who continue to use drugs without seeking treatment is the presence of depressive symptoms.

How, then, should one proceed when trying to distinguish substance-related psychiatric symptoms from those that result from an independent psychiatric disorder? Some clinicians have developed rules that define the duration of a period of abstinence that is necessary to make a psychiatric diagnosis. For example, a typical rule may be, "a person has to be completely drug- and alcohol-free for 4 weeks before one can make a psychiatric diagnosis in a person with a substance use disorder." Although *guidelines* of this nature can be helpful, strict *rules* are not. Thus, the criteria for a substance-induced mood disorder according to the fourth edition of the *Diagnostic and Statistical Manual of Mental Disorders* (DSM-IV; American Psychiatric Association, 1994) offer a general guideline that an individual should achieve approximately 1 month of abstinence before a clinician can diagnose an independent mood disorder. However, these criteria include the caveat that clinicians should diagnose a mood disorder if the symptoms present are neither qualitatively nor quantitatively what they would expect from the amount and duration of substance(s) used.

When distinguishing substance-related psychiatric symptoms from those due to an independent disorder, clinicians should relate the symptoms the patient is having to the symptoms they would expect on cessation of the drug(s) the person has been taking. If there is substantial overlap between these two symptom pictures, the clinician should wait until (1) either the patient's symptoms resolve, or (2) the symptoms expected from drug cessation change and no longer match the observed clinical picture (e.g., the syndrome we would expect to see after 1 week vs. 1 month of cocaine abstinence). If there is little overlap between a patient's symptoms and the expected abstinence syndrome (e.g., symptoms of bulimia nervosa in an opioid-dependent individual), the diagnosis can be made without waiting.

DIAGNOSING SUBSTANCE ABUSE AMONG PATIENTS WITH PSYCHIATRIC DISORDERS

Detecting substance use among patients with psychiatric disorders presents a somewhat different problem from that frequently faced by clinicians trying to diagnose psychiatric illnesses among patients with substance use disorders. While many clinicians overdiagnose psychiatric disorders in substance abusers, substance use is frequently underdetected among patients with psychiatric disorders. Two studies, for example (Shaner et al., 1993; Stone, Greenstein, Gamble, & McLellan, 1993), demonstrated gross underreporting of drug use by patients with schizophrenia who had positive urine toxicology screens. Woodward, Fortgang, Sullivan-Trainor, Stojanov, and Mirin (1991) also found that substance use was likely to be underdetected among patients being admitted to a psychiatric hospital, particularly those with psychotic disorders. In contrast, Albanese, Bartel, and Bruno (1994) found that systematic administration of the Structured Clinical Interview for DSM-III-R—Patient Version (SCID-P; Spitzer, Williams, & Gibbon, 1992) was more likely to detect substance abuse in an inpatient psychiatric population than were an admission diagnostic assessment, a discharge diagnosis, or a urine toxicology screen. Moreover, our group (Weiss et al., 1998), found that in an outpatient population of patients dually diagnosed with substance use disorder and either bipolar disorder or PTSD, self-reports of substance use can be highly valid when urine screens are collected with patients' prior knowledge, when patients are well-known to staff, and when honest self-reporting is repeatedly encouraged.

Detecting substance abuse in patients with psychiatric illness, then, requires several factors (Drake, Alterman, & Rosenberg, 1993a). First, clinicians need to systematically ask about the presence of substance use. Woodward et al. (1991) hypothesized that substance use was underdetected in patients with psychotic illness partly because the acuity of the presenting illness led clinicians to eschew a systematic assessment of substance use. Accurate detection of substance use is also most likely to occur if the clinician uses multiple data sources. Therefore, the combination of a structured clinical assessment, a urine screen, and obtaining data from a collateral source (e.g., a family member) increases the likelihood of identifying a substance abuse problem. Urine toxicology screens alone are insufficient because they only detect recent use of drugs. However, if a patient knows that he or she will have a urine toxicology screen performed, the patient is more likely to be forthcoming in reporting substance use. Finally, it is important to understand the critical role that contingencies play in affecting an individual's substance use self-report. If patients know that a self-report of substance use will lead to a negative consequence (e.g., discharge from treatment or report to a probation officer or employer), they will most likely deny substance use, whether or not they have used drugs. However, if they are repeatedly encouraged to be honest in their self-reports, and if they are told and they believe that there are no negative contingencies attached to reporting substance use, the validity of their self-reports will increase substantially. Thus, self-reports in an emergency room setting or during an acute psychotic episode are likely to be suspect because the patient is unlikely to know the clinician and will probably not believe (whether or not it is true) that discussing recent illicit substance use will have no negative repercussions. In an outpatient treatment program, however, in which patients have seen other patients report substance use without experiencing negative consequences (indeed, they may have seen those patients benefit by discussing their recent episodes of substance use), self-reports are much more likely to be valid.

TREATMENT OF DUALLY DIAGNOSED PATIENTS

By the time they first present for treatment, many dually diagnosed patients have experienced some of the psychosocial sequelae of chronic drug use, including loss of relationships, occupational difficulties, legal problems, and repetitive relapses to substance use. In addition, they have experienced the impact of their co-occurring psychiatric disorder. The clinician may be overwhelmed by the myriad problems of the patient and may be uncertain about how to provide effective treatment. As noted by Lehman and Dixon (1995), the clinician's initial wish may be to refer the patient elsewhere. The all-too-frequent lack of coordination between the substance abuse and mental health treatment systems and declining resources in an era of managed care may add to the frustration.

In this section, our goal is to provide a basic foundation regarding what is known about treatment for dually diagnosed patients, However, it is worth noting that current empirically based understanding of treatment for this patient population is only in its infancy. Only recently have specific treatments been developed for subgroups of patients, and few treatment outcome studies have been performed. Where possible, we refer to research studies, drawing in addition from general treatment recommendations made by experts in the field.

Sequential, Parallel, and Integrated Treatment Models

Patients dually diagnosed with substance use disorder and psychiatric illness may receive treatment for these two disorders according to three major models of care: sequential, parallel, or integrated treatment. *Sequential treatment* consists of treating the most acute disorder first and then treating the other disorder; this may be done by the same staff or by transferring the patient from one facility or program to another. Sequential treatment is generally appropriate for the most severe manifestations of illness. For example, a patient who is acutely manic cannot be expected to identify relapse triggers for alcoholism. Conversely, a patient who is suffering from alcohol withdrawal delirium is in no position to discuss adherence to his or her antidepressant medication regimen. Rather, these issues should be addressed when the patient is more stable. The advantage of sequential treatment is the increased level of attention paid to the more acute disorder. However, the primary disadvantage of sequential treatment is the fact that patients are often transferred from one facility or program to another, so that the interrelationship of the two disorders may never be addressed adequately.

Parallel treatment consists of simultaneous treatment of patients in two different settings, e.g., an alcohol clinic and a mental health center. These programs are ordinarily staffed by different groups of clinicians, both of whom are knowledgeable in their own area but often not terribly well versed in the other. This leads to one of the difficulties inherent in parallel treatment (Mueser, Bellack, & Blanchard, 1992; Ridgely, Goldman, & Willenberg, 1990), the fact that substance abuse and mental health programs frequently have different philosophies of treatment, which may be confusing to the patients. For example, staff in substance abuse treatment programs may attribute psychiatric symptoms (e.g., depression and anxiety) to substance use and may see legitimate attempts by patients to seek symptom relief as "drug seeking." Conversely, staff in mental health programs frequently downplay the importance of substance use and do not stress its potential adverse effects on the patient's psychiatric symptoms and other life areas.

One advantage of parallel treatment is the fact that patients typically receive treatment from people who are knowledgeable in their own field. However, dually diagnosed patients who receive parallel or sequential treatment unfortunately are likely to have markedly different treatment experiences based on the treatment setting that they enter. Because patients in parallel treatment may receive contradictory feedback from staff members in different programs about the nature of their substance use or psychological symptoms, they may be left in the unfortunate position of trying to integrate these messages themselves. In a worst-case (but-all-too-common) scenario, patients who argue with treatment staff and present contradictory information from another program may be accused of "manipulating" and "splitting staff" and may thus be labeled "sociopathic" or "borderline."

In the past decade, a number of clinicians and researchers have argued the merits of *integrated treatment* for patients with dual disorders. Several studies in the late 1980s (Hellerstein & Meehan, 1987; Kofoed, Kania, Walsh, & Atkinson, 1986; Ries & Ellingson, 1989) found that integrating psychiatric and substance abuse treatment improved outcomes. In an integrated treatment model, dually diagnosed patients receive treatment for both illnesses from the same treatment staff in a single setting. Ideally, the staff in an integrated treatment program is knowledgeable about substance abuse, psychiatric illness, and its potential interrelationships. Although more attention may be paid to one disorder than another at any particular time, integrated treatment stresses the importance of a balanced approach. Drake, McHugo, and Noordsy (1993b) reported positive long-term results from an integrated approach; over 60% of patients with chronic mental illness achieved stable abstinence at 4-year follow-up after entering their program. Lehman, Herron, and Schwartz (1993), on the other hand, found no reduction in substance abuse among dually diagnosed patients who were treated for 1 year in an integrated program.

Although clinicians and researchers have cited the value of integrated treatment for the past decade, research support for this approach is relatively sparse. Most studies of integrated programs have consisted of isolated pilot projects, with very small sample sizes and no control groups. A recent controlled trial, however, which compared an integrated versus a parallel treatment model for patients with schizophrenia and substance use disorder, reported that engagement and retention in treatment were significantly better in the group receiving integrated treatment (Hellerstein, Rosenthal, & Miner, 1995). Moreover, a number of integrated treatment approaches are currently being studied for specific subpopulations of dually diagnosed patients, including those with a substance use disorder and schizophrenia (Ziedonis & Fisher, 1996), PTSD (Najavits, Weiss, Shaw, & Muenz, in press; Najavits, Weiss, & Liese, 1996), borderline personality disorder (Linehan, 1993), and bipolar disorder (Weiss, Najavits, & Greenfield, in press). Pilot results of these empirical trials have thus far been positive (Najavits et al., in press; Weiss et al., in press-a), and others should be forthcoming soon.

PSYCHOTHERAPY FOR DUALLY DIAGNOSED PATIENTS

As shown in Table 12.1, two types of psychotherapy studies have been performed with dually diagnosed patients: general studies of comorbid psychiatric illness and substance abuse and studies of particular diagnoses. In studies of the former type, psychiatric severity is typically assessed via a global rating scale of psychiatric severity (e.g., the Addiction Severity Index), without regard to the specific psychiatric diagnoses the patient has. In the second type of study, patients are assessed for particular DSM-IV disorders (e.g., bipolar disorder or antisocial personality disorder).

Several conclusions can be drawn from the existing work. First, as shown in Table 12.1, level of psychiatric severity, independent of specific diagnosis, appears to predict differential response to psychotherapeutic treatments. However, although this finding has been found across several studies, the exact nature of the relationship has been found to vary (which in part may be the result of differing methodologies and patient samples). For example, although high psychiatric severity among methadone-maintained opioid ad-

TABLE 12.1. Psychosocial Treatment Studies of Dually Diagnosed Patients

Citation	Psychiatric classification	Treatment(s)	Results
		General Studies[a]	
Woody et al. (1984, 1985)	Level of psychiatric severity	Cognitive psychotherapy (CT), supportive–expressive (SE) psychotherapy, Twelve-Step drug counseling (DC)	1. Patients with high psychiatric severity had better outcomes in CT + DC and SE + DC compared to drug counseling alone. 2. Patients with antisocial personality disorder had poor outcomes (but not when depression was also present)
Project MATCH (1997)	Level of psychiatric severity	Twelve-Step, CBT, motivational enhancement	Patients with low psychiatric severity had better outcomes in Twelve-Step than in CBT
Carroll et al. (1991)	Level of psychiatric severity	Relapse prevention therapy (RPT) versus interpersonal therapy (IPT)	Patients with high psychiatric severity had higher abstinence rates in RPT than in IPT
Carroll et al. (1994)	Level of psychiatric severity	RPT, clinical management, desipramine	Depressed patients in RPT stayed in treatment longer and had longer abstinence than those in clinical management
Kofoed et al. (1986)	"Severely mentally ill" patients with substance abuse	Integrated dual diagnosis treatment	Reduction in use of hospitalization
Ries & Ellingson (1989)	Psychiatric inpatients	Substance abuse discussion groups	Greater abstinence posttreatment
Lehman (1993)	Dually diagnosed patients	Integrated treatment	Null findings (no difference) after 1 year
Drake et al. (1993b)	Chronically mentally ill patients with substance abuse	Integrated treatment	60% abstinent at 4-year follow-up
		Specific diagnoses	
Weiss et al. (in press)	Bipolar disorder	Relapse prevention, integrated model	Patients receiving integrated treatment significantly improved compared to "treatment-as-usual" patients
Najavits et al. (1996)	PTSD	CBT group therapy, integrated model	Significant improvements pre- to posttreatment in a variety of domains
Hellerstein & Meehan (1987)	Schizophrenia	Outpatient dual-diagnosis group	Decrease in hospital days
Hellerstein et al. (1995)	Schizophrenia	Integrated treatment	Patients receiving integrated treatment had significantly better engagement and retention compared to patients receiving parallel treatment

[a]In these studies, psychiatric severity was measured in general terms, or the population consisted of patients with a variety of psychiatric disorders.

dicts predicted better outcome in psychotherapy compared to Twelve-Step counseling (Woody et al., 1985; Woody et al., 1984), a recent large-scale comparative treatment study (Project MATCH Research Group, 1997) found no such difference for alcoholics.

In terms of type of psychotherapy, the two main branches of treatment are based on cognitive-behavioral and psychodynamic principles (note that Twelve-Step treatment is considered counseling rather than psychotherapy because it was not designed to treat psychiatric disorders other than substance abuse). For patients with high levels of psychiatric severity, Woody et al. (1984, 1985) found equivalent results for cognitive-behavioral and psychodynamic treatments (CT and SE in the table), while Carroll, Rounsaville, and Gawin (1991) found improved outcomes for the cognitive-behavioral over the psychodynamic treatment (RPT and IPT, respectively) in a study of ambulatory cocaine abusers.

More consistent results have been found in studies that simply assessed outcomes within a particular treatment for dual-diagnosis patients (rather than comparing the effectiveness of different treatments). In all the studies in Table 12.1, except for Lehman et al. (1993), positive outcomes were found for treatments that attended to dually diagnosed populations. This was true for both general studies and for studies of specific disorders. However, it must be observed that the methodology of these studies is typically far inferior to the larger treatment outcome studies that assessed differential treatments; often they lacked control groups, standardized diagnostic assessments, or manuals that guided and structured the treatment approach. Thus, although a number of early outcome studies have shown that treatments specifically designed for dually diagnosed patients can be helpful, this area of research is still very new, with few controlled, rigorous trials.

Types of Psychosocial Treatment for Dually Diagnosed Patients

As described earlier, several prominent psychosocial treatments have been applied to dually diagnosed patients. Each was originally created for either substance abuse (e.g., motivational enhancement) or for psychiatric conditions (e.g., cognitive-behavioral) but has shown at least some positive outcomes in empirical studies with dually diagnosed patients (see Table 12.1). A brief description follows.

Relapse prevention therapy (RPT), developed by Marlatt and Gordon, (1985), and later studied by Carroll et al. (1991, 1994) emphasizes understanding the process of relapse to prevent it. RPT incorporates elements from cognitive therapy, social learning theory, behavioral skills training, and lifestyle change; it can be an adjunctive therapy or a treatment in and of itself. Specific strategies of RP include exploring ambivalence (e.g., listing pros and cons of drug use), avoiding high-risk triggers (e.g., seeing one's dealer), coping strategies (e.g., distraction), identifying the decisions that lead to drug use (e.g., rationalizations), making lifestyle modifications (e.g., taking up new hobbies), and learning from small episodes of substance use to prevent full relapse.

When applied to specific populations of dually diagnosed patients (e.g., patients with substance use disorder and bipolar disorder) (Weiss et al., in press), the treatment adapts these principles to also address the psychiatric disorder. For example, preventing relapse to both the substance abuse and the bipolar disorder is emphasized; patients are encouraged to adhere to their regimen of psychiatric medications to forestall relapse, and they are taught about triggers of both substance use and bipolar disorder (e.g., erratic sleep patterns).

Motivational interviewing (MI) was developed by Miller and Rollnick (1991; Project MATCH Research Group, 1997) as a hybrid approach derived from several theoretical models, including systems, client-centered, cognitive-behavioral, and social psychology. MI techniques are guided by five principles: expressing empathy, rolling with resistance (rather than direct confrontation), developing discrepancy (i.e., contrasting the patient's goals with current problem behavior), avoiding argumentation, and supporting self-efficacy by emphasizing personal responsibility. Treatment techniques include reflective listening, affirmation, open-ended questions, summarizing, and eliciting self-motivational statements (e.g., exploring pros and cons of behavior). MI is sometimes called motivational enhancement because it is typically a brief treatment conducted in as few as two sessions, sometimes aimed at helping the patient accept other psychotherapy. Empirical results for MI have been very positive (Holder, Longabaugh, Miller, & Rubonis, 1991), and in Project MATCH (1997) were notable in achieving equivalent results to treatments that were much longer in duration (4 sessions vs. 12).

The *stages-of-change* model (Prochaska, DiClemente, & Norcross, 1992; Prochaska, Norcross, & DiClemente, 1994) identifies five sequential phases of patients' readiness to recover from substance abuse: precontemplation (a patient continues to use substances, denying that it is a problem), contemplation (the patient continues to use but admits that substance use is a problem), preparation (the patient is using but is motivated to develop a plan in the near future to stop), action (the patient is willing to participate now in treatment and follow through to stop using), and maintenance (the patient has abstained from substance use for 6 months or more and is able to continue abstaining without great difficulty). In addition to being a popular model that intuitively matches many clinicians' experience with substance abuse patients, research on this model indicates a relationship between stage of change and treatment outcome (Prochaska et al., 1992). We know of no studies that have yet confirmed this with regard to dually diagnosed patients in particular, but efforts are under way to adapt and test the model for schizophrenic substance abusers (Ziedonis & Fisher, 1996). In addition, Osher and Kofoed (1989) articulated a conceptual model, similar to stages of change, for dually disordered patients.

Cognitive therapy (CT), developed by Beck (1979), was originated for the treatment of depression and anxiety (Beck, Emery, & Greenberg, 1985; Hollon & Najavits, 1988); it has subsequently been adapted for the treatment of substance abuse (Beck et al., 1993). Cognitive therapists seek to modify maladaptive thoughts as a means of decreasing negative feelings and behavior. For example, a depressed cocaine addict who believes, "I need to get high to feel better" will be more likely to use cocaine than will an individual who thinks, "Getting high will make me more depressed tomorrow." Specific CT interventions include guided questioning (e.g., "What are the implications of that belief?"), daily thought records to restructure cognitions, identifying a developmental history of beliefs related to substance use, and behavioral strategies such as relaxation training and goal setting. When adapted to specific dually diagnosed populations (e.g., PTSD), additional techniques include the identification of cognitive distortions associated with PTSD and substance use disorder (e.g., getting high now as a "reward" for having been deprived in the past), identifying meanings of substance use in the context of PTSD (e.g., as revenge against an abuser), and teaching new coping skills (e.g., boundary setting) (Najavits et al., 1996).

Supportive–expressive therapy (SE) is a treatment derived from psychoanalysis by Mark and Luborsky (Luborsky, 1984; Mark & Luborsky, 1992). "Supportive" refers to creating a strong alliance with the patient that allows the "expressive" component (interpretive work) to be conducted. The guideline for treatment is the "Core Conflictual Relationship Theme," a case conceptualization focused on three questions: (1) What is the patient's central wish in life? (2) What has the patient come to expect from others? (3) How has the patient responded to frustration in attaining his or her basic wishes? Interpretation and support are then used in treatment to guide the patient to resolve relationship dilemmas. In the treatment of substance abusers, SE also emphasizes several additional psychodynamic principles: resistance, attention to the patient's anxiety during the session, transference–countertransference, and focusing on the patient's responsibility. As noted in Table 12.1, this treatment was found equivalent to CT in the treatment of methadone-maintained opioid-dependent patients with high levels of psychiatric severity; both psychotherapies were found superior to Twelve-Step drug counseling alone for this group of patients (Woody et al., 1984, 1985).

Interpersonal therapy (IPT) was conceived by Klerman, Weissman, Rounsaville, and Chevron (1984) as a modification of psychodynamic therapy; it was adapted for substance abuse patients by Rounsaville, Glazer, Wilber, Weissman, and Kleber (1983). IPT is a short-term treatment that addresses several key problem areas in the patient's current interpersonal functioning. IPT emphasizes the patient's relationships with others, including interpersonal disputes, role transitions (coping with a changed social role such as divorce or a new job), and interpersonal deficits (such as social anxiety and isolation). Behavioral change strategies are also used, such as limit setting, advice and suggestions, education, and modeling. Carroll et al. (1991) found that this treatment was less effective than RPT for cocaine-dependent patients with high levels of psychiatric severity.

Twelve-Step drug counseling, which derives directly from principles of Alcoholics Anonymous (AA), has been adapted for use by professional alcohol and drug counselors (a necessary adaptation as AA was designed as a self-help group not led by professionals). Various versions of Twelve-Step drug counseling manuals exist (Mercer & Woody, 1992; Nowinski, Baker, & Carroll, 1995). Topics include learning the 12 steps of recovery, incorporating the use of spirituality as a recovery aid, making a commitment to abstinence, and utilizing the support of other alcoholics and addicts to maintain sobriety. As noted previously, some studies (Woody et al., 1984, 1985) have suggested that such a 12-step approach works best for patients with low levels of psychiatric severity (i.e., they primarily need to attend to substance abuse rather than to dual-diagnosis issues).

General Treatment Themes

Given the small number of empirical studies on the treatment of dually diagnosed patients, it may also be helpful to draw on general recommendations provided by various writers on this subject (Carey, 1995; Drake, Noordsy, & Ackerson, 1995, Najavits et al., 1996; Osher & Kofoed, 1989; Weiss & Najavits, 1998). Although treatment modalities differ, some common themes can help guide clinicians who must decide how to intervene with their patients. These suggestions are as follows:

- Provide support for the difficulty of living with two disorders.
- Teach patients to understand the symptoms of the two disorders, and the causal and etiologic connection between them.
- Monitor symptoms of both disorders (including use of urine screens for substance use).
- Monitor patients' medication compliance (e.g., lithium for bipolar disorder and naltrexone for opioid dependence) and boost efforts for patients to adhere to their medication regimens.
- To improve functioning, teach the patient skills that apply to both disorders (e.g., social skills).
- Attend to patient safety above all, including attention to human immunodeficiency virus (HIV) risk behaviors and suicidal ideation (both of which have been found increased in dually diagnosed patients) (Mahler, 1995; Weiss & Stephens, 1992).
- Have available resources to refer patients to self-help groups for each disorder.
- Discuss with the patient what to do and whom to call in case of emergency.
- Provide positive reinforcement for improvements, however small, in each disorder.
- Keep firm boundaries while maintaining a compassionate stance to minimize potential negative countertransference feelings.
- Expect occasional breaks in treatment attendance, and engage in active outreach.

PHARMACOTHERAPY FOR DUALLY
DIAGNOSED PATIENTS

The question of when to administer pharmacotherapy to dually diagnosed patients has long been a subject of controversy. For many years, physicians were reluctant to prescribe psychotropic medications for patients with substance use disorders. This consensus practice was based on a number of studies with significant methodological flaws, however. For example, Ciraulo and Jaffe (1981) found that studies examining the use of antidepressants in alcoholics (1) generally did not measure plasma antidepressant levels to ensure adequate dose and medication compliance, and (2) sometimes failed to measures changes in both depression and drinking in response to treatment.

Recent research on the effects of pharmacotherapy in dually diagnosed patients has been more encouraging. In general, these studies have shown that pharmacotherapy for patients dually diagnosed with substance use disorder and mood or anxiety disorder has had a beneficial effect on the psychiatric disorder and a less robust but not countertherapeutic effect on substance use (Weiss, Greenfield, & Najavits, 1995). Some studies, moreover, have shown some benefit for the substance use disorder as well.

The pharmacological treatment of patients with coexisting depression and substance use disorder has received the most research attention. Three recent studies in particular have shown that antidepressant treatment of alcoholics with depression may improve both depressive symptoms and drinking outcomes. McGrath et al. (1996) conducted a study of imipramine versus placebo in 69 actively drinking alcoholic outpatients with current depressive disorder, in which the first episode of depression preceded the alcohol abuse or occurred during long periods of sobriety. Depressive symptoms improved among the imipramine-treated sample, and patients whose mood improved showed a reduction in drinking that was more marked among those treated with imipramine. A preliminary report by Cornelius et al. (1995) also suggests that fluoxetine may reduce drinking in patients with coexisting major depressive disorder and alcohol dependence. Mason, Kocsis, Ritvo, and Cutler (1996) conducted a double-blind, placebo-controlled trial with desipramine in 71 alcohol-dependent patients with secondary major depression; depression was diagnosed after at least 1 week of abstinence. They found that these depressed patients had significantly greater improvement in depressed mood and were abstinent for significantly longer when receiving desipramine as opposed to placebo. This is a striking finding because clinicians have traditionally been least likely to consider antidepressant treatment for alcoholics whose depression was considered secondary to their drinking. Thus, recent data support the potential benefit of antidepressant treatment in patients with coexisting depression and alcoholism.

Many clinicians, however, are reluctant to use antidepressants to treat depressive symptoms in substance abusers. There are a number of reasons for this (Weiss & Najavits, 1998). First, they believe that the symptoms may remit as a result of abstinence alone. Second, clinicians fear a toxic interaction between their prescribed medication and the patient's substance(s) of abuse. Third, many clinicians fear that they may be "enabling" their patients by not allowing them to experience the naturalistic negative consequence of their substance use (i.e., depressed mood). The studies described previously should allay some of these fears because there were no serious adverse reactions reported and the fear of enabling (i.e., that the person's drinking will worsen as a result of antidepressant treatment) was not realized. Moreover, treatment of depression, an illness that is accompanied by substantial morbidity and mortality of its own, is an important goal in its own right. Therefore, successfully treating an alcohol-dependent patient's depression, even if not accompanied by improvement in drinking, can be seen as a successful outcome, analogous to the successful treatment of pneumonia in a patient with alcoholism. The difference between the treatment of depression and the treatment of pneumonia in an alcoholic is that the clinician may be disappointed in the former situation when the improvement in the target symptom (i.e., depression) is not accompanied by a reduction in drinking.

Pharmacological treatment of coexisting substance use disorders and anxiety disorders has generally received relatively little careful research attention. However, a double-blind, placebo-controlled study of 61 alcoholics who scored ≥ 15 on the Hamilton Anxiety Rating Scale after being abstinent from alcohol for a week showed that patients who received buspirone had better outcomes on measures of both anxiety and drinking than did patients who received placebo (Kranzler et al., 1994).

Very little research has been conducted on the pharmacotherapy of patients with coexisting substance use disorder and bipolar disorder. Only three small open trials have been conducted: two with lithium (one positive, one negative) and one positive study with valproate (Brady, Sonne, Anton, & Ballenger, 1995; Gawin & Kleber, 1984; Nunes, McGrath, Wager, & Quitkin, 1990). However, the extremely small sample sizes (total $N = 25$) and the open nature of these trials severely limit our ability to draw conclusions from these studies.

Most of the research that has been conducted on schizophrenia and substance use disorders has focused on psychosocial treatment methods, with patients receiving standard pharmacotherapy that is held constant (Weiss et al., 1995). Although case reports have described reduction in craving among patients receiving clozapine (Yovell & Opler, 1994) or mazindol (Siebel, Brenner, Krystal, Johnson, & Charney, 1992), we are aware of only one randomized pharmacotherapy study in this population. Ziedonis, Richardson, Lee, Petrakis, and Kosten (1992) found that among patients with schizophrenia and cocaine abuse, those who received desipramine in addition to antipsychotic medications had significantly fewer cocaine-positive urines during the third and final month of the trial when compared to patients who received antipsychotic medications alone.

The area of greatest difficulty and controversy in the pharmacological treatment of dually disordered patients involves the question of prescribing potentially abusable medications for this population. This comes up in two major areas: the use of benzodiazepines in patients with anxiety disorders, and the use of stimulants for patients with attention-deficit/hyperactivity disorder (ADHD). Some authors (Annitto & Dackis, 1990) have argued that the use of benzodiazepines is contraindicated in patients with substance use disorders outside of a detoxification setting; other authors (Adinoff, 1992; Ciraulo, Sands, & Shader, 1988; Lydiard, 1990) have supported their use in carefully selected situations (e.g., when patients either fail to respond to other pharmacotherapies or cannot take them). Similar issues arise in the treatment of patients with ADHD and substance use disorder. Although some case reports (Schubiner et al., 1995; Weiss, Pope, & Mirin, 1985) have shown the potential utility of these medications, other research has warned of the potential abuse of these medications by drug-dependent patients, particularly those who do not have true ADHD (Gawin, Riordan, & Kleber, 1985). A recent study of 27 cocaine-dependent patients found no differences in cocaine use between patients receiving methylphenidate and those receiving placebo (Roache, Thompson, Schmitz, & Grabowski, 1995). Several studies are currently under way to examine whether there are subgroups of this population who can use stimulants both safely and effectively.

In sum, then, pharmacotherapy of dually diagnosed patients is generally useful for the targeted psychiatric disorder, with typically less robust effects for the substance use disorder. Thus, it is generally more effective than its harshest critics would charge and less helpful than its most enthusiastic advocates would suggest. As more carefully designed trials are completed, the guidelines regarding which medications to use for which subgroups of dually diagnosed patients will be strengthened.

INTEGRATION OF PSYCHOTHERAPY AND PHARMACOTHERAPY FOR DUALLY DIAGNOSED PATIENTS

The predominance of sequential and parallel treatment over integrated treatment for dually diagnosed patients has been accompanied by a marked paucity of integration between pharmacological and psychotherapeutic approaches in the treatment of dually diagnosed patients (Weiss et al., 1995). Instead, most treatment studies for dually diagnosed patients have focused on either a pharmacological or a psychological treatment method, but rarely a combination of the two. This has varied to some extent by disorder, so that studies of patients with substance use disorders and depression or anxiety disorders have focused primarily on pharmacological treatments, while studies of innovative treatments for patients with substance use disorder and schizophrenia have generally emphasized psychosocial approaches. We are aware of only one study in which both an innovative psychotherapeutic and pharmacotherapeutic approach were studied at the same time (Ziedonis et al., 1992). More recent research efforts, however, have emphasized the importance of integrating pharmacological and psychotherapeutic treatments.

FUTURE DIRECTIONS

In recent years, the substance abuse and mental health fields have moved forward in the evaluation and treatment of dually diagnosed patients, from an appreciation of the high prevalence rate of comorbidity to an understanding of the need to adapt traditional treatments to suit this population, We have now entered an era in which these new treatments are being developed and rigorously tested through a series of empirical studies, which are evaluating psychosocial treatments, pharmacotherapies, and combinations of these modalities to develop optimal treatment methods for this widespread and traditionally difficult to treat patient population. In the next decade we anticipate that this research effort will translate into improved treatment methods and outcomes for this population.

ACKNOWLEDGMENTS

This work was supported by Grants DA09400, DA08631, DA07693, and KO2-DA00326 from the National Institute on Drug Abuse; and a grant from the Dr. Ralph and Marian C. Falk Medical Research Trust.

REFERENCES

Adinoff, B. (1992). Long-term therapy with benzodiazepines despite alcohol dependence disorder. *American Journal on Addictions, 1,* 288–293.

Albanese, M., Bartel, R., & Bruno, R. (1994). Comparison of measures used to determine substance abuse in an inpatient psychiatric population. *American Journal of Psychiatry, 151*(7), 1077–1078.

American Psychiatric Association. (1994). *Diagnostic and statistical manual of mental disorders* (4th ed.). Washington, DC: Author.

Annitto, W. J., & Dackis, C. A. (1990). Use of benzodiazepines by alcoholics. Reply. *American Journal of Psychiatry, 147,* 129.

Barber, J., Frank, A., Weiss, R., Blaine, J., Siqueland, L., Moras, K., Calvo, N., Chittams, J., Mercer, D., & Salloum, I. (1996). Prevalence and correlates of personality disorder diagnoses among cocaine dependent outpatients. *Journal of Personality Disorders, 10*(4), 297–311.

Beck, A. T. (1979). *Cognitive therapy of depression.* New York: Guilford Press.

Beck, A. T., Emery, G. E., & Greenberg, R. L. (1985). *Anxiety disorders and phobias: A cognitive perspective.* New York: Basic Books.

Beck, A. T., Wright, F. D., Newman, C. F., & Liese, B. S. (1993). *Cognitive therapy of substance abuse.* New York: Guilford Press.

Brady, K. T., Sonne, S. C., Anton, R., & Ballenger, J. C. (1995). Valproate in the treatment of acute bipolar affective episodes complicated by substance abuse: A pilot study. *Journal of Clinical Psychiatry, 56*(3), 118–121.

Brooner, R. K., King, V. L., Kidorf, M., Schmidt, C. W., & Bigelow, G. E. (1997). Psychiatric and substance use comorbidity among treatment-seeking opioid abusers. *Archives of General Psychiatry, 54,* 71–80.

Brunette, M. F., Mueser, K. T., Xie, H., & Drake, R. E. (1997). Relationships between symptoms of schizophrenia and substance abuse. *Journal of Nervous and Mental Disease, 185*(1), 13–20.

Carey, K. (1995). Treatment of substance use disorders and schizophrenia. In A. Lehman & L. Dixon (Eds.), *Double jeopardy: Chronic mental illness and substance use disorders* (pp. 85–108). Chur, Switzerland: Harwood.

Carroll, K., Rounsaville, B., & Gawin, F. (199 1). A comparative trial of psychotherapies for ambulatory cocaine abusers: Relapse prevention and interpersonal psychotherapy. *American Journal of Drug and Alcohol Abuse, 17,* 229–247.

Carroll, K. M., Rounsaville, B. J., Gordon, L. T., Nich, C., Jatlow, P., Bisighini, R. M., & Gawin, F. H. (1994). Psychotherapy and pharmacotherapy for ambulatory cocaine abusers. *Archives of General Psychiatry, 51*(3), 177–187.

Ciraulo, D. A., & Jaffe, J. H. (1981). Tricyclic antidepressants in the treatment of depression associated with alcoholism. *Journal of Clinical Pharmacology, 1,* 146–150.

Ciraulo, D. A., Sands, B. F., & Shader, R. 1. (1988). Critical review of liability for benzodiazepine abuse among alcoholics. *American Journal of Psychiatry, 145,* 1501–1506.

Cornelius, J. R., Salloum, I. M., Cornelius, M. D., Perel, J. M., Ehler, J. G., Jarrett, P. J., Levin, R. L., Black, A., & Mann, J. J. (1995). Preliminary report: Double-blind, placebo-controlled study of fluoxetine in depressed alcoholics. *Psychopharmacology Bulletin, 31,* 297–303.

Dickey, B., & Azeni, H. (1996). Persons with dual diagnoses of substance abuse and major mental illness: Their cost of psychiatric care. *American Journal of Public Health, 86*(7), 973–977.

Drake, R. E., Alterman, A. I., & Rosenberg, S. R. (1993a). Detection of substance use disorders in severely mentally ill patients. *Community Mental Health Journal, 29,* 175–192.

Drake, R. E., McHugo, G. J., & Noordsy, D. L. (1993b), Treatment of alcoholism among schizophrenic outpatients: 4-year outcomes. *American Journal of Psychiatry, 150,* 328–329.

Drake, R. E., Noordsy, D. L., & Ackerson, T. H. (1995). Integrating mental health and substance abuse treatments for persons with chronic mental disorders: A model. In A. F. Lehman & L. B. Dixon (Eds.), *Double jeopardy: Chronic mental illness and substance use disorders* (pp. 251–264). Chur, Switzerland: Harwood.

Freedman, R., Hall, M., Adler, L. E., & Leonard, S. (1995). Evidence in postmortem brain tissue for decreased numbers of hippocampal nicotinic receptors in schizophrenia. *Biological Psychiatry, 38,* 22–33.

Gawin, F. H., & Kleber, H. D. (1984). Cocaine abuse treatment: Open pilot trial with desipramine and lithium carbonate. *Archives of General Psychiatry, 41,* 903–909.

Gawin, F. H., Riordan, C., & Kleber, H. (1985). Methylphenidate treatment of cocaine abusers without attention-deficit disorder: A negative report. *American Journal of Drug and Alcohol Abuse, 11,* 193–197.

Gupta, S., Hendricks, S., Kenkel, A. M., Bhatia, S. C., & Haffke, E. A. (1996). Relapse in schizophrenia: Is there a relationship to substance abuse? *Schizophrenia Research, 20,* 153–166.

Hellerstein, D. J., & Meehan, B. (1987). Outpatient group therapy for schizophrenic substance abusers. *American Journal of Psychiatry, 144,* 1337–1339.

Hellerstein, D. J., Rosenthal, R., & Miner, C. (1995). A prospective study of integrated outpatient treatment for substance-abusing schizophrenic patients. *American Journal on Addictions, 4,* 33–42.

Holder, H., Longabaugh, R., Miller, W., & Rubonis, A. (1991). The cost effectiveness of treatment for alcoholism: A first approximation. *Journal of Studies on Alcohol, 52,* 517–540.

Holton, S. D., & Najavits, L. M. (1988). Review of empirical studies on cognitive therapy. In A. J. Frances & R. E. Hales (Eds.), *American Psychiatric Press review of psychiatry* (pp. 643–666). Washington, DC: American Psychiatric Press.

Jaffe, J. H., & Ciraulo, D. A. (1986). Alcoholism and depression. In R. E. Meyer (Ed.), *Psychopathology and addictive disorders* (pp. 293–320). New York: Guilford Press.

Kessler, R. C., Crum, R. C., Warner, L. A., Nelson, C. B., Schutenberg, J., & Anthony, J. C. (1997). Lifetime co-occurrence of DSM-III-R alcohol abuse and dependence with other psychiatric disorders in the National Comorbidity Survey. *Archives of General Psychiatry, 54,* 313–321.

Khantzian, E. J. (1985). The self-medication hypothesis of addictive disorders: Focus on heroin and cocaine dependence. *American Journal of Psychiatry, 142,* 1259–1264.

Khantzian, E. (1989). Addiction: Self-destruction or self-repair? *Journal of Substance Abuse Treatment, 6,* 75.

Khantzian, E. (1997). The self-medication hypothesis of substance use disorders: A reconsideration and recent applications. *Harvard Review of Psychiatry, 4,* 231–244.

Klerman, G., Weissman, M., Rounsaville, B., & Chevron, E. (1984). *Interpersonal psychotherapy of depression.* New York: Basic Books.

Kofoed, L., Kania, J., Walsh, T., & Atkinson, R. M. (1986). Outpatient treatment for patients with substance abuse and coexisting psychiatric disorders. *American Journal of Psychiatry, 143,* 867–872.

Kranzler, H. R., Burleson, J. A., Del Boca, F. K., Babor, T. F., Korner, P., Brown, J., & Bohn, M. J. (1994). Buspirone treatment of anxious alcoholics. *Archives of General Psychiatry, 51,* 720–731.

Lehman, A., & Dixon, L. (1995). Introduction. In A. Lehman & L. Dixon (Eds.), *Double jeopardy: Chronic mental illness and substance use disorders* (pp. 1–5). Chur, Switzerland: Harwood.

Lehman, A., Herron, J., & Schwartz, R. (1993). Rehabilitation for young adults with severe mental illness and substance use disorders: A clinical trial. *Journal of Nervous and Mental Disease, 181,* 86–90.

Linehan, M. (1993). Dialectical behavior therapy for treatment of borderline personality disorder: Implications for the treatment of substance abuse. In L. S. Onken, J. D. Blaine, & J. J. Boren (Eds.), *Behavioral treatments for drug abuse and dependence* (NIDA Research Monograph No. 137, DHHS Publication No. 93-3684, pp. 201–216). Washington, DC: U.S. Government Printing Office.

Louie, A. K., Lannon, R. A., Rutzick, E. A., Browne, D., Lewis, T. B., & Jones, R. (1996). Clinical features of cocaine-induced panic. *Biological Psychiatry, 40,* 938–940.

Luborsky, L. (1984). *Principles of psychoanalytic psychotherapy: A manual for supportive–expressive therapy.* New York: Basic Books.

Lydiard, R. B. (1990). Use of benzodiazepines by alcoholics [Letter to the editor]. *American Journal of Psychiatry, 147,* 128–129.

Mahler, J. (1995). HIV, substance abuse, and chronic mental illness. In A. Lehman & L. Dixon (Eds.), *Double jeopardy: Chronic mental illness and substance use disorders* (pp. 159–175). Chur, Switzerland: Harwood.

Mark, D., & Luborsky, L. (1992). A manual for the use of supportive–expressive psychotherapy in the treatment of cocaine abuse. Philadelphia: University of Pennsylvania, Department of Psychiatry.

Marlatt, G. A., & Gordon, J. R. (Eds.). (1985). *Relapse prevention: Maintenance strategies in the treatment of addictive behaviors.* New York: Guilford Press.

Mason, B. J., Kocsis, J. H., Ritvo, E., & Cutler, R. (1996). A double-blind, placebo-controlled trial of desipramine for primary alcohol dependence stratified on the presence or absence of major depression. *Journal of the American Medical Association, 275,* 761–767.

McGrath, P. J., Nunes, E. V., Stewart, J. W., Goldman, D., Agosti, V., Ocepek-Welikson, K., & Quitkin, F. M. (1996). Imipramine treatment of alcoholics with primary depression: A placebo-controlled clinical trial. *Archives of General Psychiatry, 53,* 232–240.

McLellan, A. T. (1986). "Psychiatric severity" as a predictor of outcome from substance abuse treatments. In R. E. Meyer (Ed.), *Psychopathology and addictive disorders.* (pp. 97–139). New York: Guilford Press.

McLellan, A. T., Luborsky, L., Woody, G. E., O'Brien, C. P., & Druley, K. A. (1983). Predicting response to alcohol and drug abuse treatments: Role of psychiatric severity. *Archives of General Psychiatry, 40,* 620–625.

Mendelson, J. H., & Mello, N. K. (1966). Experimental analysis of drinking behavior of chronic alcoholics. *Annals of the New York Academy of Sciences, 133,* 828–845.

Mercer, D., & Woody, G. (1992). *Addiction counseling.* Philadelphia: University of Pennsylvania/Philadelphia VAMC, Center for Studies of Addiction.

Meyer, R. (1986). How to understand the relationship between psychopathology and addictive disorders: Another example of the chicken and the egg. In R. Meyer (Ed.), *Psychopathology and addictive disorders* (pp. 3–16). New York: Guilford Press.

Meyer, R. E., & Mirin, S. M. (1979). The heroin stimulus: Implications for a theory of addiction. New York: Plenum.

Miller, W., & Rollnick, S. (1991). Motivational interviewing: Preparing people to change addictive behavior. New York: Guilford Press.

Mueser, K. T., Bellack, A. S., & Blanchard, J. J. (1992). Comorbidity of schizophrenia and substance abuse: Implications for treatment. *Journal of Consulting and Clinical Psychology, 60,* 845–856.

Nace, E. P., Davis, C. W., & Gaspari, J. P. (1991). Axis II comorbidity in substance abusers. *American Journal of Psychiatry, 148,* 118–120.

Najavits, L. M., Weiss, R. D., & Liese, B. S. (1996). Group cognitive-behavioral therapy for women with PTSD and substance use disorder. *Journal of Substance Abuse Treatment, 13,* 13–22.

Najavits, L. M., Weiss, R., Shaw, S., & Muenz, L. (in press). "Seeking safety": Outcome of a new cognitive-behavioral psychotherapy for women with posttraumatic stress disorder and substance dependence. *Journal of Traumatic Stress.*

Nowinski, J., Baker, S., & Carroll, K. (1995). *Twelve Step facilitation therapy manual: A clinical research guide for therapists treating individuals with alcohol abuse and dependence* (Vol. 1). Rockville, MD: National Institute on Alcohol Abuse and Alcoholism.

Nunes, E. V., McGrath, P. J., Wager, S., & Quitkin, J. M. (1990). Lithium treatment for cocaine abusers with bipolar spectrum disorders. *American Journal of Psychiatry, 147,* 655–657.

O'Farrell, T., Connors, G., & Upper, D. (1983). Addictive behaviors among hospitalized psychiatric patients. *Addictive Behaviors, 8,* 329–333.

Oldham, J. M., Skodol, A. E., Kellman, H. D., Hyler, S. E., Doidge, N., Rosnick, L., &

Gallaher, P. E. (1995). Comorbidity of axis I and Axis II disorders. *American Journal of Psychiatry, 152,* 571–578.

Osher, F. C., & Kofoed, L. L. (1989). Treatment of patients with psychiatric and psychoactive substance abuse disorders. *Hospital and Community Psychiatry, 40,* 1025–1030.

Post, R. M., Kotin, J., & Goodwin, F. R. (1974). The effects of cocaine on depressed patients. *American Journal of Psychiatry, 131,* 511–517.

Prochaska, J., DiClemente, C., & Norcross, J. (1992). In search of how people change: Applications to addictive behaviors. *American Psychologist, 47,* 1102–1114.

Prochaska, J., Norcross, J., & DiClemente, C. (1994). *Changing for good.* New York: William Morrow.

Project MATCH Research Group. (1997). Matching alcoholism treatments to client heterogeneity: Project MATCH posttreatment drinking outcomes. *Journal of Studies on Alcohol, 58,* 7–29.

Regier, D. A., Farmer, M. E., Rae, D. S., Locke, B. Z., Keith, S. J., Judd, L. L., & Goodwin, F. K. (1990). Co-morbidity of mental disorders with alcohol and other drug abuse: Results from the Epidemiologic Catchment Area (ECA) study. *Journal of the American Medical Association, 264,* 2511–2518.

Ridgely, M. S., Goldman, H. H., & Willenberg, M. (1990). Barriers to the care of persons with dual diagnosis: Organizational and financing issues. *Schizophrenia Bulletin,* pp. 123–132.

Ries, R. K., & Ellingson, T. (1989). A pilot assessment at one month of 17 dual diagnosis patients. *Hospital and Community Psychiatry, 41,* 1230–1233.

Ries, R. K., Sloan, K., & Miller, N. (1997). Dual diagnosis: concept, diagnosis, and treatment. In D. Dunner (Ed.), *Current psychiatric therapy* (pp. 173–180). Philadelphia: Saunders.

Roache, J. D., Thompson, W., Schmitz, J., & Grabowski, J. (1995). Methylphenidate effects in cocaine-dependent patients: Laboratory assessment and treatment outcome. In *Problems of drug dependence, 1995. Proceedings of the 57th annual scientific meeting of the College on Problems of Drug Dependence* (NIDA Research Monograph No. 153, p. 218). Washington, DC: U.S. Government Printing Office.

Rounsaville, B., Glazer, W., Wilber, C., Weissman, M., & Kleber, H. (1983). Short-term interpersonal psychotherapy in methadone-maintained opiate addicts. *Archives of General Psychiatry, 40,* 629–636.

Rounsaville, B. J., & Kleber, H. D. (1985). Untreated opiate addicts: How do they differ from those seeking treatment? *Archives of General Psychiatry, 42,* 1072–1077.

Rounsaville, B. J., Kosten, T. R., Weissman, M. M., & Kleber, H. D. (1986). Prognostic significance of psychopathology in treated opiate addicts. *Archives of General Psychiatry, 43,* 739–745.

Satel, S., Southwick, S., & Gawin, F. (1991). Clinical features of cocaine-induced paranoia. *American Journal of Psychiatry, 148,* 495–499.

Schubiner, H., Tzelepis, A., Isaacson, J. H., Warbasse, L. H., Zacharek, M., & Musial, J. (1995). The dual diagnosis of attention-deficit/hyperactivity disorder and substance abuse: Case reports and literature review. *Journal of Clinical Psychiatry, 56,* 146–150.

Shaner, A. M., Eckman, T. A., Roberts, L. J., & Wilkins, J. N., Tucker, D. E., Tsuang, J. W., & Mintz, J. (1995). Disability income, cocaine use, and repeated hospitalization among schizophrenic cocaine abusers: A government-sponsored revolving door. *New England Journal of Medicine, 333,* 777–783.

Shaner, A. M., Khalsa, M. E., Roberts, L., Wilkins, J., Anglin, D., & Hsieh, S. C. (1993). Unrecognized cocaine use among schizophrenic patients. *American Journal of Psychiatry, 150,* 758–762.

Siebel, J. P., Brenner, L., Krystal, J. H., Johnson, R., & Charney, D. S. (1992). Mazindol and cocaine addiction in schizophrenia. *Biological Psychiatry, 31,* 1172–1183.

Spitzer, R. L., Williams, J. B., & Gibbon, M. (1992). *The Structured Clinical Interview for DSM-III-R—patient version.* New York: Biometrics Research Institute.

Stone, A. M., Greenstein, R. A., Gamble, G., & McLellan, A. T. (1993). Cocaine use by schizophrenic outpatients who receive depot neuroleptic medication. *Hospital and Community Psychiatry, 44,* 176–177.

Weiss, R. D. (1992). The role of psychopathology in the transition from drug use to abuse and dependence. In M. Glantz & R. Picken (Eds.), *Vulnerability to drug abuse* (pp. 137–148). Washington, DC: American Psychological Association.

Weiss, R. D., Greenfield, S. F., & Najavits, L. M. (1995). Integrating psychological and pharmacological treatment of dually diagnosed patients. In L. S. Onken, J. D. Blaine, & J. J. Boren (Eds.), *Integrating behavior therapies with medication in the treatment of drug dependence* (NIDA Research Monograph No. 150, pp. 110–128). Washington, DC: U.S. Government Printing Office.

Weiss, R. D., Griffin, M. L., & Mirin, S. M. (1992a). Drug abuse as self-medication for depression: An empirical study. *American Journal of Drug and Alcohol Abuse, 18,* 121–129.

Weiss, R. D., Mirin, S. M., & Frances, R. J. (1992b). The myth of the typical dual diagnosis patient. *Hospital and Community Psychiatry, 43,* 107–108.

Weiss, R. D., Mirin, S. M., Griffin, M. L., & Michael, J. L. (1998). Psychopathology in cocaine abusers: Changing trends. *Journal of Nervous and Mental Disease, 176,* 719–725.

Weiss, R. D., Mirin, S. M., Michael, J. L., & Sollogub, A. (1986). Psychopathology in chronic cocaine abusers. *American Journal of Drug and Alcohol Abuse, 12,* 17–29.

Weiss, R. D., & Najavits, L. M. (1998). Overview of treatment modalities for dual diagnosis patients: Pharmacotherapy, psychotherapy, twelve-step programs. In H. Kranzler & B. Rounsaville (Eds.), *Dual diagnosis: Substance abuse and comorbid medical and psychiatric disorders* (pp. 87–105). New York: Marcel Dekker.

Weiss, R. D., Najavits, L. M., & Greenfield, S. F. (in press). A relapse prevention group for patients with bipolar and substance use disorders. *Journal of Substance Abuse Treatment.*

Weiss, R. D., Najavits, L. M., Greenfield, S. F., Soto, I. A., Shaw, S. R., & Wyner, D. (1998). Validity of substance use self-reports in dually diagnosed outpatients. *American Journal of Psychiatry, 155,* 127–128.

Weiss, R. D., Pope, H. G. J., & Mirin, S. M. (1985). Treatment of chronic cocaine abuse and attention deficit disorder, residual type, with magnesium pemoline. *Drug and Alcohol Dependence, 15,* 69–72.

Weiss, R. D., & Stephens, P. (1992). Substance abuse and suicide. In D. Jacobs (Ed.), *Suicide and clinical practice* (pp. 101–114). Washington, DC: American Psychiatric Press.

Woodward, B., Fortgang, J., Sullivan-Trainor, M., Stojanov, H., & Mirin, S. M. (1991). Underdiagnosis of alcohol dependence in psychiatric inpatients. *American Journal of Drug and Alcohol Abuse, 17,* 373–388.

Woody, G. E., McLellan, A., Luborsky, L., & O'Brien, C. (1985). Sociopathy and psychotherapy outcome. *Archives of General Psychiatry, 42,* 1081–1086.

Woody, G. E., McLellan, A. T., Luborsky, L., O'Brien, C., Blaine, J., Fox, S., Herman,

I., & Beck, A. T. (1984). Severity of psychiatric symptoms as a predictor of benefits from psychotherapy: The Veterans Administration–Penn Study. *American Journal of Psychiatry, 141,* 1172–1177.

Worthington, J., Fava, M., Agustin, C., Alpert, J., Nierenberg, A., Pava, J., & Rosenbaum, I. (1996). Consumption of alcohol, nicotine, and caffeine among depressed outpatients: Relationship with response to treatment. *Psychosomatics, 37,* 518–522.

Yovell, Y., & Opler, L. A. (1994). Clozapine reverses cocaine craving in a treatment-resistant mentally ill chemical abuser: A case report and a hypothesis. *Journal of Nervous and Mental Disease, 182,* 591–592.

Ziedonis, D., & Fisher, W. (1996). *Motivation-based assessment and treatment of substance abuse in patients with schizophrenia: Directions in psychiatry* (Vol. 16, Lesson 11). New York: Hatherleigh.

Ziedonis, D., Richardson, T., Lee, E., Petrakis, I., & Kosten, T. (1992). Adjunctive desipramine in the treatment of cocaine abusing schizophrenics. *Psychopharmacology Bulletin, 28,* 309–314.

13

AIDS and Addictions

CHERYL ANN KENNEDY
JAMES M. HILL
STEVEN J. SCHLEIFER

INTRODUCTION

Since its appearance in 1981, the HIV/AIDS pandemic has been the focus of global attention and remains a serious public health threat throughout the world. In 1996, health departments in the United States and U.S. territories reported more than 20,000 cases of acquired immunodeficiency syndrome (AIDS) in injecting drug users (IDUs), their sex partners, and children born to mothers who were IDUs or sex partners of IDUs. These IDU-associated AIDS cases accounted for more than one-third of AIDS cases in the U.S. reported in 1996 (Centers for Disease Control and Prevention [CDC], 1996a) when AIDS was the leading cause of death in U.S. adults ages 25–44 years (CDC, 1997). Within Europe, injecting drug use is the main transmission mode of newly diagnosed AIDS cases (Mann & Tarantola, 1996). HIV (human immunodeficiency virus) infection among IDUs has been reported in more than 80 countries worldwide and presents the risk of spreading to 40 more.

Seroprevalence rates among IDUs in U.S. cities range from 2% in southern New Jersey and New Orleans to 50-60% in New York City and northern New Jersey (Des Jarlais, Friedman, Choopanya, Varichseni, & Ward, 1992). Once the virus has been introduced into a local community of IDUs, spread is ordinarily rapid.

But, there is now evidence that IDUs can alter their behavioral risk patterns. In some regions where more than 50% of the IDU population reported changing risk behaviors, subsequent drops in HIV seroconversion rates and stabilization of seroprevalence were noted (Des Jarlais & Freidman, 1996). Given the continued incidence of HIV infection among IDUs and

319

injecting drug use–related transmission to the epidemiology of AIDS, it is essential that health and mental health professionals working with those with addictive disorders know the clinical parameters of this problem.

Whereas drug users who inject represent the major heterosexual at-risk population for HIV, other substance use, such as alcohol, other sedatives, and stimulants, plays an increasing, albeit less direct, role in HIV risk and disease progression. Impaired states caused by intoxicating doses of alcohol, other sedatives, or stimulants can influence sexual behavior through disinhibition and risk taking, leading to unsafe sexual practices that increase risk of exposure to HIV (Kennedy et al., 1993). Evidence also suggests that psychoactive substances such as alcohol and opioids may have suppressive effects on immune function, possibly increasing the risk for infection or further compromising the immune system of those already infected.

Multifaceted prevention and education strategies that emphasize safer sex through behavioral change, effective chemical dependency treatment, and innovative public health initiatives, which can curtail the epidemic, are required. This chapter reviews basic aspects of HIV and AIDS in substance users and the clinical relevance to health care providers.

ETIOLOGY AND PATHOGENESIS

AIDS is caused by infection with HIV (Fauci, 1985), a retrovirus only identified in the current epidemic. HIV is the primary cause of a progressive and life-threatening syndrome which results from impairment of the immune system. HIV is more complex than other known animal retroviruses and contains at least eight functional genes (Carpenter & Mayer, 1988; Fauci, 1988). Investigators have cloned and sequenced a large number of distinct HIV isolates (Pantaleo, Graziosi & Fauci, 1993), but, despite huge research efforts directed at developing a vaccine, none to date has been successful enough for widespread trials.

Immunity is mediated primarily by T- and B-lymphocytes, which regulate cell and humoral (antibody) mediated responses to antigenic challenge. T-suppressor cells dampen and terminate immune responses; T-helper cells are required for effective augmentation of responses to antigenic challenge. T-helper cells are detected by the expression of the phenotypical surface marker CD4. HIV has a particular affinity for CD4+ cells, which includes some cells in the central nervous system. It is the infection and destruction of these important immune system cells that are the primary source of morbidity in AIDS (Pantaleo, et al., 1993).

Specific cell surface genes mediate cell entry for the virus (Deng et al., 1996). Once in the cell, viral RNA is transcribed to DNA and integrated into the host cell chromosomal DNA. Subsequent cell activation, which may be triggered by host factors, results in transcription of viral RNA, protein synthesis, virus assembly, budding of the mature virus from the cell surface, cell death, and dissemination of viral particles (Fauci, 1988). Destruction or impaired function of T-helper lymphocytes results in diminished immune capacity for antigenic challenge and subsequent increased vulnerability to opportunistic infections and neoplasia.

DIAGNOSIS AND STAGING

Serum tests to detect antibody to HIV-1 are widely available and frequently used for screening and diagnosis. The enzyme-linked immunosorbent assay (EIA) detects viral antibodies in the blood. Positive EIA results must be confirmed by western blot, a more complicated serologic assay with higher predictive value. A negative western blot following a positive EIA should be repeated within 3 to 6 months.

Despite the accuracy of this two-step testing method (specificity = 99.9% and sensitivity in low prevalence populations = 99.9%), its drawbacks include a 1- to 2-week wait for definitive results. This wait may influence whether an individual returns for test results. In one study, up to 40% did not return (Kassler, Dillon, Haley, Jones, & Goldman, 1997). Concern about anonymity may prevent some individuals from being tested. Those who abuse substances may be more reluctant than others to be tested.

Home test kits for HIV received Food and Drug Administration approval in 1996. A blood sample collected at home is sent to a central laboratory and results are available by phone with a code within 3 to 7 days. Immediate and ongoing live counseling and referrals are made available to those who test positive. The full appraisal and evaluation of telecounseling and user-controlled testing of a sexually transmissible and blood-borne infection, such as HIV, are unknown. Despite some clinical advantages, it is not clear how widespread "personal testing" would affect the data gathered in the public health sector.

Rapid HIV testing is available in serological screening assays, which give results in 30 minutes or less. These tests are generally EIA testing meant solely for initial screening; any positive results must be confirmed by western blot.

Non-serum-based HIV testing using saliva or urine is also available for use in public health and clinic screening. These confer several advantages beyond conventional serum testing by eliminating needles and blood for specimen collection, easier waste disposal, and the need for only minimal training for sample collection. Both the oral fluid and urine screening tests for HIV use serum testing for confirmation. Conventional serum tests are used whenever higher sensitivity and specificity are required, as in blood banking.

Viral load can be measured in serum and other body tissue. The presence of clinical symptoms along with high viral load and intense immune activity comprises the acute retroviral syndrome and represents primary HIV infection. Antibodies to HIV are generally detectable within 4 to 12 weeks following exposure (Curran et al., 1985), but the newly infected may manifest symptoms of a flu-like illness. Although some may be clinically asymptomatic, many have a variety of clinical complaints, which range from mild to severe illness, including sore throat, weight loss, fatigue, and myalgias. Common physical findings include fever, lymphadenopathy, a macular erythematous rash, and orthostatic hypotension. Oral inflammations and ulcerations have been reported. The syndrome must be differentiated from Epstein–Barr virus, cytomegalovirus, influenza, acute toxoplasmosis, rubella, and syphilis.

Many clinicians recommend using antiretroviral therapy as soon as possible once a person is known to have acute retroviral syndrome, and they make the case for high-level clinical suspicion with widespread, frequent testing, especially for those at high risk or in high-prevalence areas (Rosenberg & Cotton, 1997). Researchers maintain that if early viral production can be acutely curtailed, the immune system can clear more of the virus. By using clinical data, researchers have developed mathematical models of viral kinetics which estimate that if the immune system does not become overwhelmed, HIV infection would be more manageable in the long term or even eradicated, in some, in the short term (Perelson, Neuman, Markowitz, Leonard, & Ho, 1996).

When AIDS has developed (the presence of an opportunistic infection or CD4+ lymphocytes less than 200/uL or less than 14% of total lymphocytes) (CDC, 1992), an individual's course may depend on type and experience of physician or facility where care is received (Kitahata et al., 1996; Paauw, Wenrich, Curtis, Carline, & Ramsey, 1995). CD4+ lymphocyte counts may remain important markers throughout the course of the disease (Poole et al., 1996), while viral load measurements, in serum and even in lymphoid tissue, can be used to evaluate benefits of drug therapies and to monitor HIV disease progression (Hammer et al., 1996; Katzenstein et al., 1996).

Those who inject drugs and have AIDS have an even more severe and rapidly progressive clinical course than other AIDS patients. Studies show a broad spectrum of severe HIV-associated diseases in IDUs. HIV infection often results in an exacerbation of illnesses common in IDUs, often by reactivation of latent disorders. Studies by Selwyn et al. and others (1988; Selwyn, Hartel, et al., 1989; Stoneburner, et al., 1988) found that deaths due to infections, endocarditis, and pulmonary tuberculosis occur more frequently among IDUs with HIV infection than among IDUs without HIV. IDUs have been shown to have substantially more pre-AIDS morbidity and mortality than non-IDUs (Selwyn et al., 1992). Other studies have confirmed that those infected with HIV who use either opioids or cocaine (by injection or other routes) require more resources and still have worse outcomes than those with HIV who do not use drugs (Scheidegger & Zimmerli, 1996).

NEUROPSYCHIATRIC COMPLICATIONS OF AIDS

Early in the HIV epidemic, the extent to which neuropsychiatric complications occur was not appreciated. Through a growing understanding of the neurological effects of HIV, it has become apparent that cognitive, affective, and behavioral symptoms are often manifestations of direct HIV infection in the central nervous system (CNS). These can be coupled with the psychological reactions to life-threatening illness or the deliria or meningitides associated with opportunistic infections or neoplasia. When working with substance users, clinical expertise is essential for accurate diagnosis and optimal management of the neurological and neuropsychiatric complications. The symptom overlap between the neurological effects of drug use and HIV-associated illnesses presents an important clinical challenge.

Laboratory and clinical findings implicate several mechanisms for HIV effects in the CNS: (1) direct effects of the virus on CNS macrophages, microglia, astrocytes, oligodendrocytes, and neurons (Michaels, Price, & Rosenblum, 1988; Peudenier, Hery, Montagnier, & Tardieu, 1991; Vazeux et al., 1987; Watkins et al., 1990); (2) opportunistic infections (Price & Worley, 1992), HIV-related CNS neoplasms (De Angelis, 1991; Remick et al., 1990; Shapshak et al., 1991), and CNS effects of systemic illness (Holtzman, Kaku, & So, 1989); and (3) CNS effects of antivirals and other medications often used simultaneously to treat related infections (antibacterial, antimycobacterial, antiparasitical, antifungal, among others). Although the impact of HIV on the CNS clearly adds substantial morbidity, the timing of these effects is poorly understood.

The clinical significance of CNS effects during seroconversion and asymptomatic phases is debatable, but physicians caring for high-risk persons must be sensitive to these effects so the likelihood of early detection is increased. Headaches and photophobia may be part of the acute retroviral syndrome associated with seroconversion (Tindall & Cooper, 1991; see "Diagnosis and Staging"). Although this acute syndrome is apparently common, it is frequently indistinguishable from other viral infections and often goes unreported or is not associated with HIV infection. Substance users have many potential barriers to early identification and intervention for HIV, and clinicians need a low threshold for considering neurological and cognitive symptoms as possible complications of undiagnosed HIV.

Mass lesions and infectious processes in the CNS, including cryptococcal infection, toxoplasmosis, cytomegalovirus, and lymphoma, are not uncommon and usually treatable. However, these account for only 30% of CNS complications of AIDS (Navia, Jordan, & Price, 1986). Progressive multifocal leukoencephalopathy (PML), a once rare demyelinating disease of the CNS associated with malignant proliferative disorders and impaired cell-mediated immunity, is now found more often in AIDS patients (Dix & Bredesen, 1988). Most frequently, end-stage AIDS patients develop a progressive dementia with diffuse cerebral atrophy demonstrable on computerized tomography (CT) or magnetic resonance imaging (MRI) scans. The terms "AIDS dementia complex" (ADC), "subacute encephalitis," or "subacute encephalopathy" have been used to describe this syndrome (Navia et al., 1986; Price, Sidtis, & Brew, 1991). Although ADC has been thought to affect the majority of AIDS patients prior to death (Price et al., 1991), some evidence suggests that antiviral therapies have lowered the incidence rate (Portegies et al., 1989).

Early detection of ADC is based on a careful tracking of mental status and cognitive changes. Formal neuropsychological testing has been effective in assessment. Differentiating the CNS effects of HIV from those related to drug and alcohol use may pose additional diagnostic concerns as many of the same neurological deficits are involved.

Abnormal findings on measures of dexterity, sensory processing, attention, concentration, language, verbal and nonverbal memory, abstraction, and problem solving have been demonstrated with chronic alcohol, cocaine, opiate, and polysubstance abuse (Ling, Compton, Rawson, & Wesson, 1996). In addition to the drug used, chronicity of use, age at use (Klisz & Parsons, 1977), history of impairment preceding use, gender (Fabian, Parsons, & Sheldon, 1985; Glenn & Parsons, 1992), and educational level (Grant & Reed, 1985) may further mediate neuropsychological findings in substance users.

Few studies have addressed the potential confounding effects of HIV and substance use on neuropsychological functioning. Wellman (1992) examined neuropsychological performance in symptomatic and asymptomatic HIV seropositive and seronegative substance users in recovery. She found deficits in attention, short-term memory and abstraction in asymptomatic seropositive persons. These deficits, usually associated with later HIV disease, were attributed to the effects of chronic drug use. Pakesh et al. (1992) found that both seropositive and seronegative opiate and polysubstance users performed worse than healthy controls on measures of short-term memory and concentration and they found no specific effect of HIV seropositivity. They concluded that the effects of substance use may mask the effects of HIV on cognitive functioning.

Silberstein et al. (1993) prospectively demonstrated a subtle decline in neuropsychological functioning for a seropositive methadone-maintenance group when compared to a similar seronegative cohort. Other researchers found that age and education are better predictors of neuropsychological functioning than HIV status or substance use history (Concha et al., 1992).

Neuropsychological impairments associated with substance use are often mild and often can be stabilized or reversed by abstinence. In the AIDS patient with ADC, the impairment is progressive and by the terminal phase of the disease severe. The differential diagnosis of HIV neuropsychiatric complications is complex but crucial for the best management of these patients, particularly to determine whether treatable conditions are present.

Serial mental status exams and assessment of neuropsychological functioning, coupled with neuroimaging procedures, cerebrospinal fluid exams, serological titers, toxic screens, and stereotaxic biopsy, can be used in evaluating substance-using AIDS patients with CNS dysfunction. ADC shows cerebral atrophy on either CT or MRI (Navia et al., 1986). In some ADC patients, MRI shows hemispheric white matter abnormalities and, less frequently, abnormalities in the basal ganglia or thalamus (Jarvik et al., 1988). Patients with PML have focal areas of low density, often with multiple areas of involvement confined to the white matter (Dix & Bredesen, 1988).

If ADC is established, antiretroviral drugs have reportedly lessened, slowed, or temporarily stabilized some cognitive losses. In early lab experiments, Nevirapine (Viramune), a nonnucleoside analog reverse transcriptase inhibitor, was shown to have good penetration through the blood–brain barrier (Yazdanian et al., 1997). A recent report has found indinivir (protease inhibitor) levels in cerebral spinal fluid comparable to trough plasma concentrations (Stahle, Martin, Svensson, & Sonnerborg, 1997). It is hoped that by reducing viral load or slowing viral replication some HIV damage in the CNS can be ameliorated. As in most CNS disturbances, psychotropics (antipsychotics, antidepressants, anxiolytics, etc.) may be used for specific symptom management, keeping in mind that patients with complicated CNS symptoms are apt to be very sensitive to all effects from psychotropic medications. Dosing and drug–drug interactions must be carefully monitored. Finally, supportive and insight-oriented psychotherapy with neuropsychoeducation may assist the patient and significant others with coping and adaptation.

SUBSTANCE USE AND RISK OF HIV INFECTION

A variety of exposure and host factors influence seroconversion and disease progression. Although not well understood, these may include altered baseline host immune capacity and viral load in the positive person. The presence of host-concurrent infections, most notably viral (herpes simplex, cytomegalovirus, the hepatitides), and bacterial infections in the bloodstream (endocarditis, others), may contribute to altered immunity, or, in the case of ulcerations or inflammation from sexually transmitted diseases, mucosal breaches can afford easy entry of microorganisms. In general, infections have increased prevalence in substance-using populations and because substance users often do not restrict their use to a single drug, some risk effects may be synergistic.

Opioids

In addition to the exceptionally high risk of HIV transmission in opiate abusers who inject, compromised immune function as a result of exposure to opiates may add to risk of infection and disease progression. Brown et al. (1974) found reduced lymphocyte stimulation in response to various mitogens in heroin addicts, suggesting a possible impairment in cell-mediated immunity. Other studies found that in addition to decreased lymphocyte functional responses, addicts had a significant reduction in numbers of T-cells when compared with nonaddicts (McDonough et al., 1980). Incubation of addicts' cells with naloxone (an opiate antagonist) reversed some of the immune effects. It has been postulated that opiates bind reversibly to lymphocytes, blocking T-cell receptors and diminishing the ability to proliferate when stimulated (MacGregor, 1988).

Other reported immune abnormalities in opiate addicts include hyperactive B-cell activity, hyperglobulinemia, and increased opsonic capacity (MacGregor, 1988). Studies by Bayer, Hernandez, Dunn, Melton, & Pellegrino (1996) suggest that many of the immunosuppressive effects of opiates are related to CNS effects of the drugs rather than to direct pharmacological suppression of the immune system. Others have demonstrated a range of opioid effects, enhancing as well as suppressive, related to different opioid receptors (Caroleo, Arbitrio, Melchiorri, & Nistico, 1994; Weber, Ikejiri, Rice, Pert, & Hagan, 1987). Experimental evidence suggests that morphine and other opioids may accelerate the course of bacterial as well as viral infections, including HIV, in the brain and other systems. The use of opioids may therefore, in addition to the well-described behavioral risk, have direct effects on HIV susceptibility and disease progression. Opiate addicts who enter methadone treatment are significantly less likely to become HIV infected in the first place (Metzger et al., 1993).

Alcohol

Alcoholics, many of whom use multiple drugs, may be at increased risk of exposure to HIV by high-risk behaviors while under the disinhibiting influence of the drug. Stall et al. (1986) examined sexual behaviors of homosexual men under the influence of alcohol and other drugs such as marijuana and amyl nitrate. Men with high-risk sexual behaviors were two to three-and-a-half times more likely to use drugs during their sexual encounters than men who were considered at no risk for HIV exposure. In follow-up, the men who remained at high risk were more than twice as likely to use alcohol during sexual activity, and eight times more likely to use other drugs (Stall et al., 1986). Homosexual and bisexual men who drank high volumes of alcohol had increased HIV seroconversion rates (Penkower et al., 1991). In a study at alcohol treatment centers, non-IDUs had higher than expected seroprevalence for HIV which was associated with a high prevalence of risky sexual behaviors (Avins et al., 1994). In a large study of sexually transmitted disease clinic attendees, alcohol was frequently used and was associated with other risk variables for HIV infection (Zenilman et al., 1994).

There is widespread use of alcohol among adolescents and the high prevalence presents significant threat to adolescent health. The use of alcohol and other drugs is associated with motor vehicle accidents, homicides, and suicides among adolescents as well as being associated with major medical, psychological, and social morbidity in U.S. teens (Singh, Kochaneck, & MacDorman, 1996). The use of alcohol and other drugs has been demonstrated to significantly increase adolescent risk behaviors for HIV transmission (Boyer & Ellen, 1994; Rotheram-Borus, Rosario, Reid, & Koopman, 1995). Cases of AIDS and rates of HIV infection are rapidly rising among adolescents particularly in those from risk groups not easily accessed (Kennedy & Eckholdt, 1997).

It has long been thought that alterations in immune function play a role in the increased susceptibility to infection found in alcoholics (Adams & Jordan, 1984; Smith & Palmer, 1976). Patients with a history of excessive prolonged consumption of alcohol (U.S. Department of Health and Human Services, 1987; Jerrels, Marietta, Bone, Weight, & Eckhardt, 1988) and alcoholic liver disease (Kanagasundaram & Leevy, 1979; MacGregor, 1988) have alterations in host defense mechanisms. A large study of Vietnam-era veterans found correlations between levels of alcohol use and both immuno-globulin and circulating lymphocyte levels (Mili, Flanders, Boring, Annest, & DeStefano, 1992). However, the extent to which clinically relevant immuno-suppression occurs in alcohol abusers without substantially compromised liver function is unclear. Natural killer cell activity (NKCA) has been reported to be suppressed *in vitro* (Ristow, Starkey, & Hass, 1982). *In vivo* when several hours of exposure of volunteers to alcohol was studied, NKCA was suppressed (Ochshorn-Andelson et al., 1994). Irwin et al. (1990) reported that NKCA is decreased in patients with major depression and in those with alcoholism, with an even greater decrease in patients with both alcoholism and depression. Liver function abnormalities did not appear to account for the effects. Cook et al. (1991, 1994) found selected shifts in CD4+ and CD8+ lymphocyte subsets that suggested abnormal activation of immune effector cells in alco-holics without liver disease. Improvement of CD4+ cell count has been demonstrated after alcohol withdrawal in some HIV-positive alcoholics (Pol, Artru, Thepot, Berthelot, & Nalpas, 1996). The preliminary analyses in a study of more than 300 inner-city alcoholics found that those without evidence of medical disorders or liver dysfunction showed modest changes in specific leukocyte and lymphocyte subsets and decreased phagocytosis, but substan-tially greater functional immune changes were found in alcoholics who had even modest medical or liver function abnormalities (Schleifer, Keller, Shiflett, & Eckholdt, 1995). It should also be noted that exposure to alcohol and other drugs may influence the symptomatic and pathological course of HIV in the CNS by additive effects on CNS function (Fein, Biggins, & MacKay, 1995) or by drug interactions with the neurotoxic effects of HIV (Tabakoff, 1994). Other researchers report no conclusive evidence for alcohol's effect on immu-nity (Bagasra, Pomerantz, & Kajidacsa-Balla, 1995).

Marijuana

Some animal studies have shown that the tetra-hydra-cannabinol (THC) in marijuana affects cell-mediated immunity (Holsapple & Munson, 1985). *In vivo* studies in rodents show decreased delayed hypersensitivity reactions, depressed lymphocyte transformation, and decreased natural killer cell activity (MacGregor, 1988). Human studies have been inconsistent and a range of effects have been described in a variety of experimental models for both THC and its metabolites. It has been suggested that THC use may exacerbate the course of viral and chronic diseases, but the clinical significance of such observations remains uncertain (Friedman, Kline, & Specter, 1991). Its active ingredient—congeners and marijuana, itself—have been used to battle the AIDS-wasting syndrome, nausea, vomiting, anorexia, and glaucoma.

Stimulants

Stimulant users, particularly, crack cocaine smokers or injecting stimulant users (cocaine, amphetamine) incur considerable risk for HIV. Those who inject, especially cocaine users, inject more frequently to maintain a quickly decaying "high." As with other disinhibiting drugs, users are apt to engage in risky sexual behavior fueled by these drugs' stimulant properties. Young people who are part of marginalized subcultures are at especially high risk of contracting HIV (Rotheram-Borus, Lune, Marotta, & Kelly, 1994).

Several studies have examined the effects of cocaine on the immune system. Studies done in rodents show suppressed antibody response (Faith & Valentine, 1983; Holsapple & Munson, 1985), whereas reports of cocaine's effects on cell-mediated immunity have been conflicting (MacGregor, 1988). Considering the continued role of injecting and noninjecting use in persons at risk for HIV transmission, potential direct and interacting immune effects of these agents are of serious concern. The increasing use of drugs in combination is especially worrisome, with generally unknown effects on the immune system. Shapshak et al. (1991) have reported accelerated progression of HIV in those who combine alcohol and cocaine.

Behavior–Immune Interactions

Other factors that are present in alcoholics and drug users may further compromise the immune system and increase the risk for poor outcomes. Malnutrition is an important immunosuppressive factor influencing various components of the immune system (Chedid, 1995; MacGregor, 1988). Immune effects associated with life stress, poor coping mechanisms, and depression, which are highly prevalent in alcoholics and other substance abusers (Jaffe & Ciraulo, 1986; Schuckit & Bogard, 1986), may further exacerbate AIDS risk and disease progression in these populations. The possible additive immunosuppressive effects of alcoholism and depression have already been noted (Irwin et al., 1990). Depressive symptoms have been linked with increased risk for mortality in HIV (Mayne, Vittinghoff, Chesney, Barrett, & Coates, 1996). Evans et al. (1995) have shown that the stress of HIV, even asymptomatic, may adversely affect the immune system.

Interventions to treat affective disorders in substance users may have medical as well as psychosocial benefits. Recent studies have begun to investigate more systematically the links among immunologically relevant psychosocial predictors, psychosocial interventions, and the course of disease, including HIV. Psychosocial effects have been reported for breast cancer (Spiegel, Bloom, Kraemer, & Gottheil, 1989), malignant melanoma (Fawzy et al., 1993), genital herpes (Kemeny, Cohen, Zegan, & Conant, 1989), Epstein–Barr virus (Glaser et al., 1991), and the common cold (Cohen, Tyrell, & Smith, 1991). Attention to a wider range of immune measures other than CD4+ cells alone and more extensive psychosocial assessments have found associations between specific stressors and depression and the course of HIV (Burack et al., 1993; Cole, Kemeny, Taylor, Visscher, Fahey, 1996; Evans et al., 1995; Goodkin et al., 1994).

AIDS IN DRUG ADDICTION TREATMENT

Introduction

Treatment of alcohol and drug abuse in persons infected with or at risk for HIV infection requires introduction of vigorous behavioral change strategies into treatment. AIDS education, prevention, and behavioral training are indicated as a regular and ongoing component of drug treatment and should be well integrated into the treatment protocol. Evaluators should use recognized general treatment principles such as those in the *Practice Guideline for Substance Use Disorders* (American Psychiatric Association, 1995) and widely accepted placement criteria (American Society of Addiction Medicine, 1996). Assessment of HIV risk behavior should be undertaken in the initial phases of treatment with frequent reassessments. Everyone should have safe sex training. This includes explicit discussion of proper techniques of latex condom usage and the importance of using condoms every time intercourse and other sex practices in which body fluids are transmitted or exchanged are initiated (CDC, 1993).

Those in treatment should receive a comprehensive physical examination. Psychiatric management and indicated pharmacotherapy are important components. In short, effective management of these persons requires a multidisciplinary team that can implement an individualized treatment plan structured to succeed within the constraints of available resources.

HIV testing for those in substance abuse programs entails special clinical considerations and should be addressed at intake. Testing could undermine participation in the program for some patients and, unless it is clinically indicated for medical reasons, might best be deferred until the patient has been engaged in substance use treatment. In any case, testing should be strongly encouraged, with emphasis placed on effective treatment and prophylactic measures that can be used if infection status is known (see "HIV Testing: Clinical Considerations").

Comprehensive counseling must accompany testing. For some individuals, either a positive or negative HIV test can be a powerful motivating factor for continued treatment for the addictive disorder (Perry, Fishman, Jacobsberg, Young, & Frances, 1991). Therapists and counselors can help facilitate positive motivation by stressing the beneficial effects that drug abstinence and other healthy lifestyle changes can have on the course of HIV infection.

Active alcohol and drug users encountered in other health care settings should be offered referrals and encouraged to enter treatment. It is apparent that altering risk behaviors in this population has many impediments. For the users who cannot or will not enter treatment, specific counseling methods should be employed to communicate effective harm reduction techniques. IDUs must be instructed on the hazards of needle sharing and, for those who do not stop injecting, emphasis must be placed on use of a new, sterile needle for each injection if blood-borne infections are to be prevented. Methods of needle decontamination, such as flushing with bleach, can reduce some exposure risk, but it is not as safe as using a fresh, unused needle for each injection (Gostin, Lazzarini, Jones, & Flaherty, 1997).

Counseling for noninjecting substance abusers is no less important—especially when sex partners may be IDUs (see "Prevention and Public Health"). Alcoholics, especially females and stimulant users, should be specifically targeted for counseling on sexual practices during intoxicated states. Commercial sex work, often found linked with drug use to support habits (Edlin et al., 1994) or bartering sex to obtain drugs, further adds to risk by introducing multiple partners (Catania et al., 1992; Catania et al., 1995) and circumstances where safe sex practices are unlikely to be easily maintained. All aspects of drug use must be critically addressed, even with those who only admit to very occasional or "recreational" use.

HIV Testing: Clinical Considerations

The CDC has suggested since 1988 that all patients admitted to substance abuse programs be screened for the presence of HIV antibody, and screening and treatment for HIV infection are often linked to substance abuse programs. Proponents of routine screening reason that knowledge of positive HIV status encourages safe sex practices and may discourage needle sharing. Literature on the behavioral impact of HIV testing is mixed. For some seropositive subjects, HIV testing and notification are catalysts for needle-use risk reduction among IDUs in treatment (Casadonte, Des Jarlais, Friedman, & Rotrose, 1990). In a study of 324 gay men, with a 3-month follow-up after testing, Farthing and Jesson (1987) concluded that the majority of men wanted to know their antibody status and having the test did encourage safer sex practices. Watkins, Metzger, Woody, and McLellan (1993) found that knowledge of HIV status was an important determinate of condom use among IDUs.

Knowledge of positive antibody status may have important implications for an individual's health care. Information on HIV status can aid physicians in evaluating patients with nonspecific medical, neurological, and psychiatric symptoms and assist in the prompt recognition and treatment of infection (Stimmel, 1988). Viral load testing can be used to stage treatment protocols for antiretroviral medications. In the immune compromised, some opportunistic infections can be prevented with pharmacotherapy; others can be prevented through environmental manipulations (avoidance of undercooked or contaminated food or water, for example). Furthermore, many clinicians now advocate early and potent treatment to reduce viral load (see "Diagnosis and Staging"). As the knowledge about more recent advances and advantages of treatment for HIV-related illnesses spreads, more and more people will be willingly tested.

Women with positive HIV status may wish to avoid pregnancy because there is a substantial risk (10–30%) of transmission to the fetus in utero (Abrams, 1987; Scott et al., 1985). The impact of HIV testing on pregnancy decisions is unclear. A Parisian study reported that 38% of women studied terminated their pregnancies after learning they were seropositive (Ciraru-Vigneron et al., 1988). In New York, it was reported that 67% of a group of women found to be seropositive opted to terminate their pregnancies, but this percentage was not significantly different from that of seronegative pregnant women (Selwyn, Carter, et al., 1989). The CDC now recommends that HIV-positive pregnant women receive zidovudine, which has been shown to reduce by about two-thirds the risk of HIV transmission in the newborn (CDC, 1994). Management of the HIV-positive pregnant woman who is undergoing treatment for a substance use disorder is best done with a specialty team or in a specially designed program (Lindberg, 1996).

Some individuals with substance use disorders may have underlying personality, behavioral, or affective problems that can provoke self-destructive behavior, including relapse. When confronted with HIV test results, whether positive or negative, substance users may also be less likely to respond appropriately in an emotional or behavioral way because HIV infection may be perceived as just one more in a long line of health risks identified by health care providers.

HIV Testing: Guidelines for Counseling

Before testing, written informed consent is obtained with the information imparted as pretest counseling. The counselor should first assess the person's current knowledge, attitude, and past experience with HIV/AIDS and HIV testing. The antibody test is explained in clear, easy-to-understand language. It is important to assess the individual's risk factors: What substances are used, in what quantity, over what time frame and in what social context? Does this person share needles and engage in risky sexual behaviors (especially when intoxicated)? Some persons who have engaged in illegal activities or behaviors stigmatized by the general public may be reluctant to disclose the nature and extent of their past risk. Once the degree of risk is identified, the person should be informed of the risk status and counseled on specific, effective means of reducing future risk behavior.

Significance of test results, positive and negative, are presented at posttest counseling and, again, must address issues of modifying such behaviors as needle sharing and risky sexual encounters. Individuals who are HIV positive should be alerted to the symptoms associated with altered immunity and the effects of alcohol and drugs on the immune system (Stimmel, 1988). Residential treatment programs should make information about HIV available and provide a variety of support mechanisms for those affected. Opponents argue that routine HIV screening may stigmatize those in high-risk groups leading to discrimination and denial of health insurance benefits. There are also reports of knowledge of positive HIV status having adverse psychological effects, including suicidal behavior (Glass, 1988). Ethical issues raised by HIV testing are not readily resolved. For example, if an individual is found to be HIV antibody positive, is there a duty to warn the sexual partner(s)? How will this affect the therapeutic relationship? Because public health regulations regarding these matters vary from state to state, practitioners need to be aware of local requirements.

The counselor or therapist should anticipate emotional and behavioral responses to a positive test result. Social support systems and coping strategies must be evaluated. Those newly tested positive for HIV must be advised of treatment options and available services. Counselors must be prepared to make adequate referrals, as indicated, especially for those who require medical evaluation or have psychiatric signs and symptoms that need further evaluation, particularly, if there is risk for suicide. Special attention should be given to those individuals with past or current depression and other mental disorders. Patients should be given an opportunity to ask questions about the test and respond to the results. Delayed emotional reactions are common. Hospitalized patients may be especially vulnerable to suicidal ideation and intent (Alfonso et al., 1994).

For persons testing negative, counseling should emphasize the testing limitations, including the possibility that they have, in fact, been infected, and the need for continued HIV precautions. Erroneous conclusions about negative tests in high-risk individuals should be preemptively addressed. Testing counselors should have a low tolerance of the need for specialized referral to mental health services, especially for individuals from groups who have endured multiple and ongoing losses to the AIDS epidemic.

Clinical Assessment and Management

AIDS has many physical and emotional effects that complicate the treatment of AIDS patients with chemical dependency. The presence of AIDS patients in drug treatment units elicits complex feelings in the staff and in other patients. Issues of death and dying are prevalent and patients may express feelings of hopelessness and question the value or practicality of abstinence from drug and alcohol use. Issues of compliance versus control become critical features in the care of these persons. Arrangements for aftercare and placement of patients with AIDS following inpatient detoxification or residential drug treatment may be difficult. Issues of confidentiality and required HIV testing are of special concern (see "Legal Issues").

Entrance into the treatment system can evolve through several routes. Those in drug treatment programs may be tested for HIV, and AIDS care is offered secondarily; others come to medical attention because of HIV/AIDS and then are additionally evaluated and referred to drug treatment programs. Combined diagnoses complicate treatment. Retention may be a problem: In one study, those with HIV who were receiving ambulatory psychiatric treatment were more likely to drop out of treatment if they drank or used drugs (Kennedy, Skurnick, & Lintott, 1994). The patient's family and significant others who can be instrumental in motivating drug-addicted individuals for treatment may, in the face of HIV, overlook or be reluctant to confront the substance abuse problem. Physicians and other health workers may minimize an individual's addiction in light of overwhelming physical illness.

Those with long-term addictions and multiple disabilities may be marginalized and have long been estranged from families. These patients have often alienated health care providers by inconsistent compliance with medical recommendations and subsequent emergency use of the system when life-threatening infections or overdoses occur. Such patients sometimes have a history of leaving the hospital against medical advice.

The medical, psychosocial, and social morbidity of substance use is no less catastrophic in the AIDS patient and may be exacerbated. For example, continued drug use in HIV-infected individuals may accelerate the course of AIDS (Rothenberg & Woefel, 1987). Dismissal of the patient's addiction problem may also convey the dehumanizing message to the patient that his problems of life are no longer relevant because he is "terminal" and "hopeless."

It is important not to focus on substance abuse issues alone to the point of excluding AIDS-related psychological needs. Anxiety and depression, complicated at times by cognitive impairment, may accompany disease progression, and, as noted, suicidal ideation is common. These symptoms should be evaluated frequently throughout the course of treatment. Addiction counselors and therapists should also know that patients may become overwhelmed by illness, grief, and a sense of loss that require a supportive, insight-oriented, and psychodynamically sound approach. Depressive symptoms have been associated with increased mortality from HIV infection (Mayne et al., 1996) and underscore the need for psychiatric services for this population.

Consultation–liaison psychiatrists face specific issues in the care of patients with HIV and addiction regardless of setting. A good working knowledge of current therapies and scientific advances for HIV infection is important. In addition, many patients will not have their wishes met regarding end-of-life care. Psychiatrists are in a unique position to assist those with HIV and those dying of AIDS to receive the type and level of care desired (Kennedy & Hill, 1997).

The family of HIV-infected substance abusers require special consideration. The HIV-positive individual may have difficulty confiding in family about his or her lifestyle, risk behaviors, or seropositivity or complicated needs for care. He or she may fear rejection or reprisal from others. Feelings of helplessness and hopelessness in the family may result in passive or active undermining of substance abuse treatment. A family may go through a bereavement process when their loved one is diagnosed with AIDS The therapist must be flexible, willing, and open.

Significant others may benefit from referral to AIDS support groups in their community during this time. Women may have special issues and suffer more psychological distress than men (Kennedy, Skurnick, Foley, & Louria, 1995). Nonjudgmental attitudes that convey a true sense of willingness to help have a better chance of building successful rapport with patients and may achieve a higher level of adherence to medical recommendations and lifestyle changes.

Patients do best with coordinated care at centers where there are specialized services, integrated care management, and a track record with HIV. A psychiatrist or therapist may be in a pivotal position to help coordinate and promote cooperation among the various caregivers.

Pitfalls for mental health professionals, addictions counselors, and other staff include countertransference issues linked to fear of contagion, addicto-phobia, racism, fear of homosexuality, denial of helplessness, and need for professional omnipotence. Mechanisms such as displacement and reaction formation can result in failure to maintain appropriate empathic distance from the patients. The therapist must avoid becoming overwhelmed by what he or she feels the patient is experiencing. Taking a moralistic attitude toward the patient's drug use and sexual behaviors will undermine treatment. Therapists must confront their own feelings and attitudes toward drug addiction, homo-sexuality, and AIDS.

Legal Issues

Issues of confidentiality arise when treating individuals with drug addiction and HIV infection. Pascal (1987) points out that federal law protects the confidentiality of patient records for those persons under treatment for drug abuse. This includes drug-abusing patients who have AIDS. (There is, how-ever, no general federal confidentiality protection for medical records of AIDS patients not being treated for drug abuse.) These federal regulations protect oral as well as written communications. In health care settings, the institution of universal precautions obviates the need to specifically identify any individ-ual as being HIV positive. Disclosure to those outside the clinical setting is permitted only with the patient's written consent. Reporting of HIV status to public health authorities may be required in some states and may be disclosed without patient consent to the extent required by law. In all other situations, disclosure without the patient's consent must be obtained through a court order based on a finding of good cause (Pascal, 1987). All employers should be aware of the provisions of the Americans with Disabilities Act.

Once a caregiver has knowledge of a positive HIV status, he or she is obligated to inform that individual. Failure to do so may make the caregiver liable for any harm that results to the individual or to the sexual partners (Pascal, 1987). Because AIDS is an often fatal, communicable disease, situ-ations may arise in which the physician or therapist is aware of a danger posed to a third party such as a sexual partner. HIV-positive patients must be counseled on their responsibilities and encouraged to voluntarily self-report to third parties who may be at risk for infection (Pascal, 1987). Some states have partner notification programs or requirements. If a substance abuse program considers it indicated to warn a third party concerning a patient's HIV status, the patient's consent must be obtained or a court order obtained to comply with federal confidentiality regulations. A policy of universal education for all patients, their spouses, significant others, and caregivers is often used and is consistent with the consensus public health viewpoint that education, prevention, and voluntary measures are the best approaches to stemming the AIDS epidemic and that punitive approaches are counterproductive (Pascal, 1987).

Single parents of minor children and, especially, women who are pregnant have special issues regarding custody and care should the mother or other primary caregiver become disabled, become incapacitated, or die. At the end stages of illness, many patients experience cognitive deficits; thus, issues of competency and future planning should be addressed in a timely and appropriate manner. Again, consultation psychiatrists are in a unique position to assist patients who are grappling with such difficult and serious matters. Many avenues and alternatives can be explored. Patients themselves prefer that physicians broach these subjects, and earlier rather than later (Kennedy & Hill, 1997).

PREVENTION AND PUBLIC HEALTH

As already noted, no effective cure for HIV infection has yet been identified; therefore, prevention is the strongest defense against spread of this blood-borne and sexually transmitted infection. Studies examining behavioral changes in response to the AIDS epidemic indicate that some IDUs are attempting risk reduction, especially in needle sharing (Des Jarlais et al., 1992; Des Jarlais & Friedman, 1987; Selwyn & Cox, 1985).

There is evidence that IDUs can reduce their risk by altering needle-sharing behaviors. In an early study of 59 patients attending a methadone-maintenance program, 59% reported some form of risk reduction, 31% increased their use of clean needles and/or the cleaning of needles, 29% reduced needle sharing, and 14% reported reduced drug injection (Des Jarlais & Friedman, 1987). More recently, injection users with appropriate AIDS knowledge have reported that their consistent use of sterile new needles depended on availability (Des Jarlais et al., 1992; Gostin, 1997). When sterile needles are unavailable, however, they use whatever is available.

Although needle sharing is quite common, it is not a universal pattern among IDUs. Sharing practices are influenced by many factors including economics, regional drug norms, needle availability, length of habit, drug of choice (i.e., heroin, cocaine, or drug combinations), and others. A large national survey of the regulations of syringes and needles concluded that deregulation of syringe sale and possession would reduce the morbidity and mortality associated with blood-borne infections, including HIV, among IDUs, their sexual partners, and their children (Gostin et al., 1997). Regulations vary throughout the United States, but despite a Government Accounting Office (1993) report and numerous other government task force recommendations that point out that new infections in IDUs have plateaued where needle exchanges have been tried, widespread support or federal backing for such strategies has been lacking. International studies show that needle exchange coupled with other risk-reduction education and available treatment slots has been successful (Des Jarlais et al., 1992). One evaluation of an experimental

U.S. needle exchange program showed that it was quickly adopted by IDUs and that an increase in injection and use did not occur (Watters, Estilo, Clark, & Lorvick, 1994). Lurie and Drucker (1997) estimated that from 4,000 to 10,000 HIV infections in the United States costing between $250,000 and $500,000 and untold amounts of human misery might have been prevented by needle exchange programs.

Prevention strategies to reduce the risk of exposure to contaminated needles include (1) cessation of injection drug use, (2) cessation of needle sharing and implementation of harm reduction methods, (3) methadone maintenance and drug-free treatment programs, and (4) needle exchange programs.

At present, IDU and sexual contact with IDUs is the most common mode of transmission for heterosexual cases of AIDS (CDC, 1996b). Male IDUs are an especially important vector for the spread of HIV into the general population. Murphy (1988) found that male IDUs reported a greater percentage of non-IDU heterosexual contacts than did female IDUs. Similar findings were reported by Des Jarlais et al. (1987). In contrast, female IDUs may be at particular risk for being exposed to HIV as a result of heterosexual behaviors and needle sharing. Des Jarlais (1987) reported that female IDUs were more likely than male IDUs to have sexual contacts who were also IDUs and who also tended to be needle sharers. Women who shared needles had twice as many IDU sexual partners as those who did not, whereas the majority of sexual partners of male needle sharers were not themselves needle sharers. Kennedy et al. (1993) found that high-risk women (those with HIV-positive male partners) were more likely to insist on condom use for sex if they were employed. Skurnick, Abrams, Kennedy, Valentin, and Cordell (in press) also found that heterosexual couples who practiced safe sex at a study entry were less likely to relapse into unsafe behaviors in 6 months if the female was employed. Unsafe sexual practices, most notably anal sex, are implicated in sexual transmission of HIV within heterosexual couples (Skurnick et al., 1998).

CONCLUSION

IDUs and other drug users are primary sources of HIV transmission to other adults and to children in the general population. Health care providers have a major responsibility to provide education and promote prevention in this group. HIV testing and counseling and drug treatment services must be readily available to those who desire it. Those drug users who are unable to abstain from injecting may benefit from therapeutic educational strategies concerned with reducing needle sharing and using sterile needles. Public health measures may have to be addressed through policy change. Counselors involved in the treatment of drug-addicted individuals should be prepared to explicitly discuss issues of safe sex and condom usage as well as to openly discuss the effects of intoxication on sexual behavior and HIV risk. Those involved in the care of addicted individuals should be aware of the wide range of presenting signs and symptoms of HIV infection as well as treatment choice options and difficult end-of-life decisions regarding care, treatments and legal issues, including estate planning and care of minor children.

The extraordinary rates of HIV infection among substance users suggest that these individuals will occupy an increasing proportion of health care resources, particularly as the disease is stretched into a chronic, ongoing state and those infected live longer. Treatment slots for those with HIV infection or AIDS will be increasingly required in alcohol and drug treatment programs. Education on HIV/AIDS and substance use disorders for medical staff and drug treatment staff is required to minimize difficulties and optimize treatment in managing these patients. As the incidence of HIV infection increases among the drug-addicted population, the potential for spread into other populations increases. For a successful battle against one part of the AIDS epidemic, additional resources for drug education, prevention, treatment, rehabilitation, and research are urgently needed.

REFERENCES

Abrams, E. (1987). *New York City Collaborative Study Group of maternal transmission of human immunodeficiency virus. Longitudinal study on infants born to women at risk for AIDS: One year report.* Paper presented at the 27th Interscience Conference on Antimicrobial Agents and Chemotherapy, New York.

Adams, H., & Jordan, C. (1984). Infections in the alcoholic. *Medical Clinics of North America, 68,* 179–200.

Alfonso, C. A., Cohen, M. A. A., Aladjem, A. D., Morrison, F., Powell, D. R., Winter, R. A., & Orlowski, B. K. (1994). HIV seropositivity as a major risk factor for suicide in the general hospital. *Psychosomatics, 35,* 368–373.

American Psychiatric Association. (1995). Practice guideline for the treatment of patients with substance use disorders: Alcohol, cocaine, opioids. *American Journal of Psychiatry, 152,* 5–59.

American Society of Addiction Medicine. (1996). Patient placement criteria for the treatment of substance related disorders (2nd ed.) (ASAM PPC-2). Chevy Chase, MD: Author.

Avins, A. L., Woods, W. J., Lindan, C. P., Hudes, E. S., Clark, W., & Hulley, S. B. (1994). Infection and risk behaviors among heterosexuals in alcohol treatment programs. *Journal of the American Medical Association, 271,* 515–519.

Bagasra, O., Pomerantz, R. J., & Kajidacsa-Balla, A. (1995). Do alcohol and other substances of abuse alter the natural evolution of and susceptibility to human immunodeficiency virus-1 infections? In R. R. Watson (Ed.), *Alcoholics, drugs of abuse, and immune function* (pp. 165–183). Boca Raton, FL: CRC Press.

Bayer, B. M., Hernandez, M. C., Dunn, K. L., Melton, R. D., & Pellegrino, T. C. (1996). Central pathways are involved in morphine and cocaine modulation of the immune system. *Journal of Neuroimmunology, 69,* 25–39.

Boyer, C. B., & Ellen, J. M. (1994). HIV risk in adolescents: The role of sexual activity and substance use behaviors. In R. J. Battjes, Z. Sloboda, & W. C. Grace (Eds.), *The context of HIV risk among drug users and their sexual partners* (NIDA

Research Monograph No. 143, pp. 135–154). Washington, DC: U.S. Government Printing Office.

Brown, S., Stimmel, B., Taub, R. N., Kochwa, S., & Rosenfield, R. E. (1974). Immunologic dysfunction in heroin addicts. *Archives of Internal Medicine, 134,* 1001–1006.

Burack, J. H., Barret, D. C., Stall, R. D., Chesney, M. A., Ekstrand, M. L., & Coates, T. J. (1993). Depressive symptoms and CD4 lymphocyte decline among HIV-infected men. *Journal of the American Medical Association, 270,* 2568–2575.

Caroleo, M. C., Arbitrio, M., Melchiorri, D., & Nistico, G. (1994). A reappraisal of the role of the role of the various opioid receptor subtypes in cell-mediate immunity. *Neuroimmunomodulation, 1,* 141–147.

Carpenter, C. J., & Mayer, K. (1988). Advances in AIDS and HIV Infection. *Advances in Internal Medicine, 33,* 45–80.

Casadonte, P., Des Jarlais, D., Friedman, S. R., & Rotrose, J. P. (1990). Psychological and behavioral impact of learning HIV test results. *International Journal of Addictions, 25,* 409–426.

Catania, J. A., Binson, D., Dolcini, M. M., Stall, R., Choi, K., Pollack, L. M., Hudes, E. S., Canchola, J., Phillips, K., Moskowitz, J. T., & Coates, T. J. (1995). Risk factors for HIV and other sexually transmitted diseases and prevention practices among U.S. heterosexual adults: Changes from 1990 to 1992. *American Journal of Public Health, 85,* 1492–1499.

Catania, J. A., Coates, T. J., Stall, R., Turner, H., Peterson, J., Hearst, N., Dolcini, M. M., Hudes, E., Gagnon, J., & Woley, J. (1992). AIDS-related risk factors and condom use in the United States. *Science, 258,* 1101–1106.

Centers for Disease Control and Prevention. (1992). 1993 revised classification system for HIV infection and expanded surveillance case definition for AIDS among adolescents and adults. *Morbidity and Mortality Weekly Report, 41*(RR-17), 1–19.

Centers for Disease Control and Prevention. (1993). Update: Barrier protection against HIV infection and other sexually transmitted diseases. *Morbidity and Mortality Weekly Report, 42,* 589–599.

Centers for Disease Control and Prevention. (1994). Zidovudine for the prevention of HIV transmission from mother to infant. *Morbidity and Mortality Weekly Report, 43,* 285–287.

Centers for Disease Control and Prevention. (1996a). *HIV/AIDS Surveillance Report, 8*(1), 8.

Centers for Disease Control and Prevention. (1996b) *HIV/AIDS Surveillance Report, 8,* 1–15.

Centers for Disease Control and Prevention. (1997). Update: Trends in AIDS incidence, deaths, prevalence—U.S. 1996. *Morbidity and Mortality Weekly Report, 46,* 1–6.

Chedid, A. (1995). Alcoholic liver disease, malnutrition, and the immune response. In R. R. Watson (Ed.), *Alcohol, drugs of abuse and immune function* (pp. 87–103). Boca Raton, FL: CRC Press.

Ciraru-Vigneron, N., Nguyen, T. L., Berau, G., Sauvanet, E., Bitton, C., Brunner, C., Boizard, B., Wautier, J. L., & Ravina, J. H. (1988). *Prospective study for HIV infection among high-risk pregnant women: Follow-up of 60 women, 37 children and 30 families.* Paper presented at the fourth international conference on AIDS, Stockholm, Sweden.

Cohen, S., Tyrell, A. J., & Smith, A. P. (1991). Psychological stress and susceptibility to the common cold. *New England Journal of Medicine, 325,* 606–612.

Cole, S. W., Kemeny, M. E., Taylor, S. E., Visscher, B. R., & Fahey, J. L. (1996). Accelerated course of human immunodeficiency virus infection in gay men who conceal their homosexual identity. *Psychosomatic Medicine 58,* 219–231.

Concha, M., Graham, N. M. H., Munoz, A., Vlahov, D., Royal, W. III, & Updike, M. (1992). Effect of chronic substance abuse on the neuropsychological performance of intravenous drug users with a high prevalence of HIV-1 seropositivity. *American Journal of Epidemiology, 36,* 1338–1348.

Cook, R. T., Garvey, M. J., Booth, B. M., Goeken, J. A., Stewart, B., & Noel, M. (1991). Activated CD-8 cells and HLA DR expression in alcoholic without overt liver disease. *Journal of Clinical Immunology, 11,* 246–253.

Cook, R. T., Waldschmidt, T. J., Bassas, Z. K., Cook, B. L., Booth, B. M., Stewart, B. C., & Garvey, M. J. (1994). Fine T-cell subsets in alcoholic as determined by the expression of L-selectin, leukocyte common antigen, and β-integrin. *Alcohol: Clinical and Experimental Research, 18,* 71–80.

Curran, J. W., Morgan, W., Hardy, A. W., Jaffe, H. W., Darrow, W. W., & Dowdle, W. R. (1985). The epidemiology of AIDS: Current status and future prospects. *Science, 229,* 1352–1357.

De Angelis, L. M. (1991). Primary CNS lymphoma: A new clinical challenge. *Neurology 41,* 619.

Deng, H. K., Liu, R., Ellmeier, W., Choe, S., Unutmas, D., Mukhart, M., Di Marzo, P., Marmon, S., Sutton, R. E., Hill, C. M., Davis, C. B., Peiper, S. C., Schall, T. J., Littman, D. R., & Landau, N. R. (1996). Identification of a major co-receptor for primary isolates of HIV-1. *Nature, 381,* 661–666.

Des Jarlais, D. C., & Friedman, S. (1987). HIV infection among intravenous drug users: Epidemiology and risk reduction. *AIDS, 1,* 67–76.

Des Jarlais, D. C., & Friedman, S. R. (1996). Risk reduction among injecting drug users. In J. Mann & D. Tarantola (Eds.), *AIDS in the world II* (pp. 264–267). New York: Oxford University Press.

Des Jarlais, D. C., Friedman, S. R., Choopanya, K., Varichseni, S., & Ward, T. (1992). International epidemiology of HIV and AIDS among injecting Drug Users. *AIDS, 6,* 1053–1068.

Des Jarlais, D. C., Wish, E., Friedman, S. R., Stoneburner, R., Yancovitz, S. R., Mildvan, D., el Sadr, W., Brady, E., & Cuadrado, M. (1987). Intravenous drug use and the heterosexual transmission of the human immunodeficiency virus: Current trends in New York City. *New York State Journal of Medicine, 3,* 283–286.

Dix, R. D., & Bredesen, D. E. (1988). Opportunistic viral infections in Acquired Immunodeficiency Syndrome. In M. L. Rosenblum, R. M. Levy, & D. E. Bredesen (Eds.), *AIDS and the nervous system* (pp. 221–261). New York: Raven Press.

Edlin, B. R., Irwin, K. L., Faruque, S., McCoy, C. B., Word, C., Serrano, Y., Inciardi, J. A., Bowser, B. P., Schilling, R. F., & Holmberg, S. D. (1994). Intersecting epidemics—crack cocaine use and HIV infection among inner city young adults. Multicenter crack cocaine and HIV infection study team. *New England Journal of Medicine, 331,* 1422–1427.

Evans, D. L., Leserman, J., Perkins, D. O., Stern, R. A., Murphy, C., Tamul, K., Liao, D., van der Horst, C. M., Hall, C. D., Folds, J. D., Golden, R. N., & Petitto, J. M. (1995). Stress-associated reductions of cytotoxic T-lymphocytes and natural killer cells in asymptomatic HIV infection. *American Journal of Psychiatry, 152,* 543–550.

Fabian, M. S., Parsons, O. A., & Sheldon, M. D. (1985). Effects of gender and alcoholism on verbal and visual–spatial learning. *Journal of Nervous and Mental Diseases, 172,* 16–20.

Faith, R. E., & Valentine, J. L. (1983). Effects of cocaine exposure on immune function. *Toxicology, 3,* 56.

Farthing, C. F., & Jesson, W. (1987). *The HIV antibody test: Influence on sexual behavior of homosexual men.* National Institutes of Health AIDS Conference (M6.4, p. 5), Bethesda, MD.

Fauci, A. S. (1985). The acquired immunodeficiency syndrome: An update. *Annals of Internal Medicine, 102,* 800–813.

Fauci, A. S. (1988). The human immunodeficiency virus: Infectivity and mechanisms of pathogenesis. *Science, 239,* 617–622.

Fawzy, F. I., Fawzy, N. W., Hyun, C. S., Elashoff, R., Guthrie, D., Fahery, J. L., & Morton, D. L. (1993). Malignant melanoma: Effects of an early structured psychiatric intervention, coping and affective state on recurrence and survival 6 years later. *Archives of General Psychiatry, 50,* 681–689.

Fein, G., Biggins, C. A., & MacKay, S. (1995). Alcohol abuse and HIV infection have additive effects on frontal cortex function as measured by auditory evoked potential P3A latency. *Biological Psychiatry, 37,* 183–195.

Friedman, H., Kline, T., & Specter, S. (Eds.). (1991). Immunosuppression by marijuana and its components. In R. Adler, D. L. Felten, & N. Cohen (Eds.), *Psychoneuroimmunology* (2nd ed., pp. 931–953). New York: Academic Press.

General Accounting Office. (1993). *Report to the Chairman, House Select Committee on Narcotics Abuse and Control.* Washington, DC: Author.

Glaser, R., Pearson, G. R., Jones, J. F., Hillihouse, J., Kennedy, S., Mao, H., & Kieclot-Glaser, J. (1991). Stress-related activation of Epstein–Barr virus. *Brain, Behavior and Immunity, 5,* 219–232.

Glass, R. M. (1988). AIDS and suicide [Editorial]. *Journal of the American Medical Association, 259,* 1369–1370.

Glenn, S. W., & Parsons, O. A. (1992). Neuropsychological efficiency measures in male and female alcoholics. *Journal of the Studies of Alcohol, 53,* 546–552.

Goodkin, K., Mulder, C. L., Blaney, N. T., Ironson, G., Kumar, M., & Fletcher, M. A. (1994). Psychoneuroimmunology and human immunodeficiency virus type 1 infection revisited. *Archives of General Psychiatry, 51,* 246–247.

Gostin, L. O., Lazzarini, S., Jones, S., & Flaherty, K. (1997). Prevention of HIV/AIDS and other blood-borne diseases among injection drug users. *Journal of the American Medical Association, 277,* 53–62.

Grant, I., & Reed, R. (1985). Neuropsychology of alcohol and drug abuse. In A. I. Alterman (Ed.), *Substance abuse and psychopathology* (pp. 289–341). New York: Plenum.

Hammer, S., Katzenstein, D. A., Hughes, M. D., Gundacker, H., Schooley, R. T., Haubrich, R. H., Henry, W. K., Lederman, M., Phair, J. P., Niu, M., Hirsch, M. J., & Merigan, T. C. (1996). A trial comparing nucleoside therapy monotherapy with combination therapy in HIV-infected adults with CD4 cell counts from 200–500 per cubic millimeter. *New England Journal of Medicine, 335,* 1081–1090.

Holsapple, M. P., & Munson, A. E. (1985). Immunotoxicology of abused drugs. In J. Dean et al. (Eds.), *Immunotoxicology and immunopharmacology* (pp. 381–392). New York: Raven Press.

Holtzman, D. M., Kaku, D. A., & So, Y. T. (1989). New onset seizures associated with human immunodeficiency virus infection: Causation and clinical features in 100 cases. *American Journal of Medicine, 87,* 173–180.

Irwin, M., Caldwell, C., Smith, T. L., Brown, S., Schuckit, M. A., & Gillin, J. C. (1990). Major depressive disorder, alcoholism, and reduced natural killer cell cytotoxicity. *Archives of General Psychiatry, 47,* 713–719.

Jaffe, J. H., & Ciraulo, D. A. (1986). Alcoholism and depression. In R. Meyer (Ed.), *Psychopathology and addictive disorders.* New York: Guilford Press.

Jarvik, J. G., Hesselink, J. R., Kennedy, C., Teschke, R., Wiley, C., Spector, S., Richman, D., & McCutchan, J. A. (1988). Acquired immunodeficiency syndrome: Magnetic resonance patterns of brain involvement with pathologic correlation. *Archives of Neurology, 45,* 731–739.

Jerrels, T. R., Marietta, C. A., Bone, G., Weight, F. F., & Echardt, M. J. (1988). Ethanol-associated immunosuppression. *Advances in Biochemical Psychopharmacology, 44,* 173–186.

Kanagasundaram, N., & Leevy, C. (1979). Immunologic aspects of liver disease. *Medical Clinics of North America, 63,* 631–642.

Kassler, W. J., Dillon, B. A., Haley, C., Jones, W. K., & Goldman, A. (1997). On-site, rapid HIV testing with same-day results and counseling. *AIDS, 11,* 1045–1051.

Katzenstein, D. A., Hammer, S. M., Hughes, M. D., Gundacker, H., Jackson, J. B., Fiscus, S., Rasheed, S., Elbeik, T., Reichman, R., Japour, A., Merigan, T. C., & Hirsch, M. C. (1996). The relation of virologic and immunologic markers to clinical outcomes after nucleoside therapy in HIV-infected adults with 200–500 CD4 cells per cubic millimeter. AIDS Clinical Trials Group Study 175 Virology Study Team. *New England Journal of Medicine, 10,* 1142–1149.

Kemeny, M. E., Cohen, F., Zegan, L. S., & Conant, M. A. (1989). Psychological and immunological predictors of genital herpes recurrence. *Psychosomatic Medicine, 51,* 195–208.

Kennedy, C. A., & Eckholdt, H. M. (1997). Diagnosis of AIDS in U.S. adolescents: 1983–1993. In L. Sherr (Ed.), *Adolescents and AIDS* (pp. 51–61). London: Hawthorn Academic Press.

Kennedy, C. A., & Hill, J. M. (1997). *Barriers to advance directives in hospitalized AIDS patients.* Paper presented at the annual meeting of the American Psychosomatic Association, Santa Fe, NM.

Kennedy, C. A., Skurnick, J. H., Foley, M., & Louria, D. (1995). Gender differences in HIV-related psychological distress in heterosexual couples. *AIDS Care, 7,* S33–S38.

Kennedy, C. A., Skurnick, J. H., & Lintott, M. (1994). *Evaluation of factors related to retention of HIV positive patients in ambulatory psychiatric treatment.* Paper presented at the annual meeting of the American Psychiatric Association, Philadelphia.

Kennedy, C. A., Skurnick, J., Wan, J. Y., Quattrone, G., Sheffet, A., Quinones, M., Wang, W., & Louria, D. B. (1993). Psychological distress, drug and alcohol use as correlates of condom use in HIV-serodiscordant heterosexual couples. *AIDS, 7,* 1493–1499.

Kitahata, M. M., Koepsell, T. D., Deyo, R. A., Maxwell, C. L., Dodge, W. T., & Wagner, E. H. (1996). Physician's experience with the acquired immunodeficiency syndrome as a factor in patients survival. *New England Journal of Medicine, 334,* 701–706.

Klisz, D. K., & Parsons, O. A. (1977). Hypothesis testing in younger and older alcoholic. *Journal of the Studies of Alcohol, 38,* 1718–1729.

Lindberg, C. (1996). *HIV and pregnancy: Information for service providers.* New Brunswick, NJ: New Jersey Women and AIDS Network.

Ling, W., Compton, P., Rawson, R., & Wesson, D. (1996). Neuropsychiatry of alcohol and drug abuse. In B. Fogel, R. Schiffer, & S. Rao (Eds.), *Neuropsychiatry* (pp. 679–722). Baltimore: Williams & Wilkins.

Lurie, P., & Drucker, E. (1997). An opportunity lost: HIV infections associated with lack of a national needle-exchange programme in the USA. *Lancet, 349,* 604–608.

MacGregor, R. (1988). Alcohol and drugs as co-factors for AIDS. *Advances in Alcohol and Substance Abuse, 7,* 47–51.

Mann, J. M. & Tarantola, D. J. M. (Eds.). (1996). *AIDS in the world II.* New York: Oxford University Press.

Mayne, T. J., Vittinghoff, E., Chesney, M. A., Barrett, D. C., & Coates, T. J. (1996). Depressive affect and survival among gay and bisexual men infected with HIV. *Archives of Internal Medicine, 156,* 2233–2238.

McDonough, R. J., Madden, J. J., Falek, A., Shafer, D. A., Pline, M., Gordon, D., Bokos, P., Kuehale, J. C., & Mendelson, J. (1980). Alteration of T- and null lymphocyte frequencies in the peripheral blood of human opiate addicts. In vivo evidence for opiate receptor sites on T-lymphocytes. *Journal of Immunology, 125,* 2539–2543.

Metzger, D. S., Woody, G., McLellan, T., O'Brien, C. P., Druley, P., Navaline, H., De Philippis, D., Stolley, P., & Abrutyn, E. (1993). Human immunodeficiency virus seroconversion among intravenous drug users in- and out-of-treatment: An 18-month prospective follow-up. *Journal of Acquired Immune Deficiency Syndrome, 6,* 1049–1056.

Michaels, J., Price, R. W., & Rosenblum, M. K. (1988). Microglia in the human immunodeficiency virus encephalitis of acquired immune deficiency syndrome: Proliferation, infection and fusion. *Acta Neuropathologic, 76,* 373–382.

Mili, F., Flanders, D., Boring, J. R., Annest, J. L., & DeStefano, F. (1992). The association of alcohol drinking and drinking cessation to measures of the immune system in middle-aged men. *Alcoholism: Clinical and Experimental Research, 16,* 688–694.

Murphy, D. L. (1988). Heterosexual contacts of intravenous drug abusers: Implications for the next spread of the AIDS epidemic. *Advances in Alcohol and Substance Abuse, 7,* 89–97.

Navia, B. A., Jordon, B. D., Price, R. W. (1986). The AIDS dementia complex: I. Clinical features. *Annals of Neurology, 19,* 517–524.

Ochshorn-Andelson, M., Bodner, G., Toraker, P., Albeck, H., Ho, A., & Kreek, M. J. (1994). Effects of ethanol on human natural killer cell activity: In vitro and acute, low-dose in vivo studies. *Alcoholism: Clinical and Experimental Research, 18,* 1361–1367.

Paauw, D. S., Wenrich, M. D., Curtis, J. R., Carline, J. D., & Ramsey, P. G. (1995). Ability of primary care physicians to recognize physical findings Associated with HIV infection. *Journal of the America Medical Association, 274,* 1380–1382.

Pakesh, G., Loimer, N., Grunberger, J., Pfersmann, D., Linzmayer, L., & Mayerhofer, S. (1992). Neuropsychological findings and psychiatric symptoms in HIV-1 infected and noninfected drug users. *Psychiatry Research, 41,* 163–177.

Pantaleo, G., Graziosi, C., & Fauci, A. S. (1993). The immunopathogenesis of human immunodeficiency virus infection. *New England Journal of Medicine, 328,* 327–335.

Pascal, C. B. (1987). Selected legal issues about AIDS for drug abuse treatment Programs. *Journal of Psychoactive Drugs, 19,* 1–12.

Penkower, L., Dew, M. A., Kingsley, L., Becker, J. T., Satz, P., Schaerf, F. W., & Sheridan, K. (1991). Behavioral, health and psychosocial factors and risk for HIV infection among sexually active homosexual men: The multicenter AIDS cohort study. *American Journal of Public Health, 81,* 194–196.

Perelson, A. S., Neuman, A. U., Markowitz, M., Leonard, J. M., & Ho, D. D. (1996). HIV-1 dynamics in vivo: Virion clearance rate, infected cell life-span, and viral generation time. *Science, 271,* 1582–1585.

Perry, S., Fishman, B., Jacobsberg, L., Young, J., & Frances, A. (1991). Effectiveness of psychoeducational interventions in decreasing emotional distress after HIV antibody testing. *Archives of General Psychiatry, 48,* 143–147.

Peudenier, S., Hery, C., Montagnier, L., & Tardieu, M. (1991). Human microglial cells: Characterization in cerebral tissue and in primary culture, and study of their susceptibility to HIV-1 infection. *Annals of Neurology, 29,* 152–157.

Pol, S., Artru, P., Thepot, V., Berthelot, P., & Nalpas, B. (1996). Improvement of the CD4 cell count after alcohol withdrawal in HIV-positive alcoholic patients [Letter]. *AIDS, 10,* 1293–1294.

Poole, W. K., Fulkerson, W., Lou, Y., Kvale, P., Hopewell, P. C., Hirchtick, R., Glassroth, J., Rosen, M., Mangura, B., Wallace, J., Markowitz, N., & Pulmonary Complications Group of the Human Immunodeficiency Virus Infection Study Group. (1996). Overall and cause-specific mortality in a cohort of homo/bisexual men, injecting drug users, and female partners of HIV-infected men. *AIDS, 10,* 1257–1264.

Portegies, P., de Gans, J., Lange, J. M., Derix, M. M., Speelman, H., Bakker, M., Danner, S. A., & Goudsmit, J. (1989). Declining incidence of AIDS dementia complex after introduction of zidovudine treatment. *British Medical Journal, 299,* 819–821.

Price, R. W., Sidtis, J. J., & Brew, B. J. (1991). AIDS dementia complex and HIV-1 infection: A view from the clinic. *Brain Pathology, 1,* 155–160.

Price, R. W., & Worley, J. M. (1992). Management of the neurologic complications of HIV-1 infection and AIDS. In M. A. Sande & P. A. Volberding (Eds.), *The medical management of AIDS* (3rd ed., pp. 193–217). Philadelphia: Saunders.

Remick, S. C., Diamond, C., Migliozzi, J. A., Solis, O., Wagner, J. R., Haase, R. F., & Ruckderschel, J. C. (1990). Primary central nervous system lymphoma in patients with and without the acquired immune deficiency syndrome: A retrospective analysis and review of the literature. *Medicine, 69,* 345–360.

Ristow, S. S., Starkey, J. R., & Hass, G. M. (1982). Inhibition of natural killer cell activity in vitro By alcohols. *Biochemical and Biophysical Research Communications, 105,* 1315–1521.

Rosenberg, E., & Cotton, D. (1997). Primary HIV infection and the acute retroviral syndrome: The urgent need for recognition. *AIDS Clinical Care, 9*(1), 23–25.

Rothenberg, R., & Woefel, B. A. (1987). Survival with the Acquired Immunodeficiency Syndrome. *New England Journal of Medicine, 317,* 1297–1302.

Rotheram-Borus, M. J., Luna, G. C., Marotta, T., & Kelly, H. (1994). Going nowhere fast: Methamphetamine use and HIV infection. In R. J. Battjes, Z. Sloboda, & W. C. Grace (Eds.), *The context of HIV risk among drug users and their sexual partners* (NIDA Research Monograph No. 143, pp. 155–181). Washington, DC: U.S. Government Printing Office.

Rotheram-Borus, M. J., Rosario, M., Reid, H., & Koopman, C. (1995). Predicting patterns of sexual acts among homosexual and bisexual youths. *American Journal of Psychiatry, 152,* 588–595.

Scheidegger, C., & Zimmerli, W. (1996). Incidence and spectrum of severe medical complications among HIV-seronegative and HIV-seropositive narcotic drug users. *AIDS, 10,* 1407–1414.

Schleifer, S. J., Keller, S. E., Shiflett, S., & Eckholdt, H. M. (1995). *Immune changes in healthy inner city alcoholics: Role of alcoholism and co-morbid factors.* Paper presented at the third annual symposium on AIDS, Drugs of Abuse, and the Neuroimmune Axis, San Diego.

Scott, G., Fischl, M., Klimas, N., Fletcher, M., Dickinson, G., Levine, J., & Parks, W. (1985). Mothers of infants with the acquired immunodeficiency syndrome. *Journal of the American Medical Association, 253,* 363–366.

Schuckit, M., & Bogard, B. (1986). Intravenous drug use in alcoholics. *Journal of Clinical Psychiatry, 47,* 11–16.

Selwyn, P. A., Alcabes, P., Hartel, D., Buono, D., Schoenbaum, E. E., Klein, R. S., Davenny, K., & Friedland, G. H. (1992). Clinical manifestations and predictors of disease progression in drug users with human immunodeficiency virus infection. *New England Journal of Medicine, 327,* 1697–1703.

Selwyn, P., Carter, R., Schoenbaum, E., Robertson, V., Klewin, R., & Rogers, M. (1989). Knowledge of HIV antibody status and decisions to continue or terminate pregnancy among intravenous drug users. *Journal of the American Medical Association, 216,* 3567–3571.

Selwyn, P. A., & Cox, C. P. (1985). *Knowledge about AIDS and High Risk Behavior among intravenous drug abusers in New York City.* Paper presented at the annual meeting of the American Public Health Association, Washington, DC.

Selwyn, P. A., Feingold, A. R., Hartel, D., Shoenbaum, E. E., Alderman, M. H., Klein, R. S., & Friedland, G. H. (1988). Increased risk of bacterial pneumonia in HIV-infected intravenous drug users without AIDS. *AIDS, 2,* 267–272.

Selwyn, P. A., Hartel, D., Lewis, V. A., Shoenbaum, E. E., Vermund, S. H., Klein, R. S., Walker, A. T., & Friedland, G. H. (1989). A prospective study of the risk of tuberculosis among intravenous drug users with human immunodeficiency virus infection. *New England Journal of Medicine, 320,* 545–550.

Shapshak, P., Sun, N. C., Resnick, L., Thornwaite, J. T., Schiller, P., Yoshioka, M., Svenningsson, A., Tourtellotte, W. W., & Imagawa, D. T. (1991). HIV-1 propagates in human neuroblastoma cells. *Journal of AIDS, 4,* 228–232.

Silberstein, C. H., O'Dowd, M. A., Chartock, P., Shoenbaum, E. E., Friedland, G. H., Hartel, D., & McKegney, F. P. (1993). A prospective four-year follow-up of neuropsychological function in HIV seropositive and seronegative methadone-maintained patients. *General Hospital Psychiatry, 15,* 351–359.

Singh, G. K., Kochaneck, K. D., & MacDorman, M. F. (1996). Advance report of final mortality statistics, 1994. *Monthly vital statistics report; 45, 3, S* (pp. 1–13). Hyattsville, MD: National Center for Health Statistics.

Skurnick, J. H., Abrams, J., Kennedy, C. A., Valentin, S., & Cordell, J. (in press). Maintenance of safe sex behavior by serodiscordant heterosexual couples. *AIDS Education and Prevention.*

Skurnick, J. H., Kennedy, C. A., Perez, G., Abrams, J., Vermund, S. H., Denny, T., Wright, T., Quinones, M. A., & Louria, D. B. (1998). Behavioral and demograpohic risk factors for transmission of human immunodeficiency virus type 1 in heterosexual couples: Report from the heterosexual HIV transmission study. *Clinical Infectious Diseases, 26,* 855–864.

Smith, F. E., & Palmer, D. L. (1976). Alcoholism, infection and altered host defenses: A review of clinical and experimental observations. *Journal of Chronic Diseases, 29,* 35–49.

Spiegel, D., Bloom, J. R., Kraemer, H. C. & Gottheil, E. (1989). Effects of psychosocial treatment on survival of patients with metastatic breast cancer. *Lancet, 3,* 888–891.

Stahle, L., Martin, C., Svensson, J., & Sonnerborg, A. (1997). Indinavir in cerebrospinal fluid of HIV-1-infected patients. *Lancet, 350,* 1823.

Stall, R., McKusick, R., Wiley, J., Coates, T. J., & Ostrow, D. G. (1986). Alcohol and drug use during sexual activity and compliance with safe sex guidelines for AIDS. The AIDS Behavior Research Project. *Health Education Quarterly, 13,* 359–371.

Stimmel, B. (1988). To test or not to test: The value of routine testing for antibodies to the human immunodeficiency virus (HIV). *Advances in Alcohol and Substance Abuse, 7,* 2.

Stoneburner, R. L., Des Jarlais, D. C., Benezra, D., Gorelkin, L., Sotheran, J. L., Friedman, S. R., Shiltz, S., Marmor, M., Mildvan, D., & Maslansky, R. (1988). A larger spectrum of severe HIV-1 related disease in intravenous drug users in New York City. *Science, 242,* 916–919.

Tabakoff, B. (1994). Alcohol and AIDS—Is the relationship all in our heads? *Alcoholism: Clinical and Experimental Research, 18,* 415–416.

Tindall, B., & Cooper, D. A. (1991). Primary HIV infection: Host responses and intervention strategies. *AIDS, 5,* 1–7.

U.S. Department of Health and Human Services. (1987). *Alcohol and health: Sixth special report to the U. S. Congress.* Washington, DC: U.S. Government Printing Office.

Vazeux, R., Brousse, N., Jarry, A., Henin, D., Marche, C., Vedrenne, C., Mikol, J., Wolff, M., Michon, C., & Rozenbaum, W. (1987). AIDS subacute encephalitis: Identification of HIV-infected cells. *American Journal of Pathology, 126,* 403–407.

Watkins, B. A., Dorn, H. H., Kelly, W. B., Armstrong, R. C., Potts, B. J., Michaels, F., Kufta, C. V., & Dubois-Daley, M. (1990). Specific tropism of HIV-1 for microglial cells in primary human brain cultures. *Science, 249,* 549–553.

Watkins, K. E., Metzger, D., Woody, G., & McLellan, A. T. (1993). Determinants of condom use among intravenous drug users. *AIDS, 7,* 719–723.

Watters, J. K., Estilo, M. J., Clark, G. L., & Lorvick, J. (1994). Syringe and needle exchange as HIV/AIDS prevention for injection drug users. *Journal of the American Medical Association, 271,* 115–120.

Weber, R. J., Ikejiri, B., Rice, K. C., Pert, A., & Hagan, A. (1987). *Opiate receptors mediated regulation of the immune response in vivo* (NIDA Research Monograph No. 76, pp. 431–348). Washington, DC: U.S. Government Printing Office.

Wellman, M. C. (1992). Neuropsychological impairment among intravenous drug users in pre-AIDS stages of HIV infection. *International Journal of Neuroscience, 64,* 183–194.

Yazdanian, M., Ratigan, S., Joseph, D., Silverstein, H., Riska, P., Johnstone, J. N., Richter, I., Norris, S., Hattox, S., & Boeghringer Ingelheim Pharmaceuticals. (1997). *Nevirapine, a non-nucleoside reverse transcriptase inhibitor, readily permeates the blood–brain barrier.* Fourth conference on Retroviruses and Opportunistic Infections, Washington, DC.

Zenilman, J. M., Hook, E. W., Shepherd, M., Smith, P., Rompalo, A. M., & Celentano, D. D. (1994). Alcohol and other substance use in STD clinic patients: Relationships with STDs and prevalent HIV infection. *Sexually Transmitted Diseases, 21,* 220–225.

14

Adolescent Substance Abuse

YIFRAH KAMINER
OSCAR G. BUKSTEIN

INTRODUCTION

There is mounting concern for adolescents' physical and mental health due to continued increases in the prevalence of substance use (Johnston, O'Malley, & Bachman, 1995), the decrease in age of initiation (Reich, Cloninger, Van Eerdevegh, Rice, & Mullaney, 1988), and the role of drugs in the leading causes of adolescent morbidity and mortality in the United States: motor vehicle accidents, suicidal behavior, violence, drowning, and unprotected sexual behavior (Kaminer, 1994). Adolescent substance use disorders (SUDs) which include substance abuse and substance dependence as defined in the fourth edition of the *Diagnostic and Statistical Manual of Mental Disorders* (DSM-IV; American Psychiatric Association, 1994), are also associated with drug-related chronic problems in several life domains including psychiatric status, school or employment performance, family function, peer social relationships, legal status, and recreational activities.

The clinical research of adolescent SUDs has historically lagged behind both the research of adult substance abuse and the study of child and adolescent psychiatric disorders. Most research on adolescents with SUDs has focused on descriptive features, diagnosis, psychiatric comorbidity, and assessment. Treatment studies of adolescents with SUDs began to emerge in the late 1970s. Most studies, however, have been characterized by only limited empirical research (Kaminer, 1994).

The objectives of this chapter are to review the latest figures and trends in adolescent substance use, nosological considerations, etiology and pathogenesis of substance use and its transition to adolescent SUDs, psychiatric comorbidity, prevention, assessment, and treatment/aftercare continuum. As a point of clarification, the generic term "substance use" refers here to nonpathological use of any licit drug (tobacco, alcohol, and inhalants) or illicit drug (controlled substances, both those that are essentially proscribed for everyone and those that are available by prescription). The term "substance abuse" is used generically indicating pathological use. Terms such as "substance abuse," "substance dependence," and "substance use disorders" are specifically mentioned as part of a formal classification system (e.g., DSM-IV).

EPIDEMIOLOGY

Cross-sectional and longitudinal surveys of youth drawn from representative national and regional samples document use patterns. The main consistent source of information on adolescent substance use has been the Monitoring the Future surveys, which have covered nationally representative samples of high school seniors annually since 1975 (Johnston et al., 1995). The 1995 survey of approximately 50,000 students including 8th- and 10th-graders, and high school seniors indicated an upswing in the use of drugs for the fourth consecutive year. The slope of the use curve shows an accelerating trend (i.e., each year since 1992, the rate of increase has been higher than the year before).

Specifically (see Table 14.1), the investigators report a sharp increase in marijuana use throughout the country at all three grade levels, as well as a gradual and less prominent increase in the use of cigarettes, stimulants (including cocaine and crack), lysergic acid diethylamide (LSD), barbiturates, and inhalants. The use of alcohol, steroids, and heroin has not changed significantly. These findings signify an alarming turnaround from the general downward trend in the prevalence of drug use that characterized the 1980s. The researchers indicated that some important attitudes and beliefs about drugs which play a critical role in deterring use began to change in all three grades, specifically, the dangers believed to be associated with the use of these drugs, as well as personal disapproval of using them.

Age of Initiation

Based on retrospective reports of grade of first use, the data provided by eighth-graders indicated that three substances were initiated by more than 50% of users in sixth grade or earlier. These "gateway drugs" were alcohol, tobacco, and inhalants (O'Malley, Johnston, & Bachman, 1995).

Gender

In general, male students use substances of all kinds more than female students; however, the differences are much smaller, and the direction sometimes reversed, for younger adolescents (Johnston et al., 1995). O'Malley et al. (1995) suggested that this tendency for younger females may be closer to

TABLE 14.1 Drug Use among 8th-, 10th-, and 12th-Graders

	8th-graders			10th-graders			12th-graders		
	1993	1994	1995	1993	1994	1995	1993	1994	1995
Marijuana/hashhish									
Lifetime	12.6%	16.7%	19.9%	24.4%	30.4%	34.1%	35.3%	38.2%	41.7%
Annual	9.2	13.0	15.8	19.2	25.2	28.7	26.0	30.7	34.7
30-day	5.1	7.8	9.1	10.9	15.8	17.2	15.5	19.0	21.2
Daily	0.4	0.7	0.8	1.0	2.2	2.8	2.4	3.6	4.6
Inhalants									
Lifetime	19.4	19.9	21.6	17.5	18.0	19.0	17.4	17.7	17.4
Annual	11.0	11.7	12.8	8.4	9.1	9.6	7.0	7.7	8.0
30-day	5.4	5.6	6.1	3.3	3.6	3.5	2.5	2.7	3.2
Daily	0.3	0.2	0.2	0.2	0.1	0.1	0.1	0.1	0.1
Hallucinogens									
Lifetime	3.9	4.3	5.2	6.8	8.1	9.3	10.9	11.4	12.7
Annual	2.6	2.7	3.6	4.7	5.8	7.2	7.4	7.6	9.3
30-day	1.2	1.3	1.7	1.9	2.4	3.3	2.7	3.1	4.4
Daily	0.1	0.1	0.1	0.1	0.1	*	0.1	0.1	0.1
Cocaine									
Lifetime	2.9	3.6	4.2	3.6	4.3	5.0	6.1	5.9	6.0
Annual	1.7	2.1	2.6	2.1	2.8	3.5	3.3	3.6	4.0
30-day	0.7	1.0	1.2	0.9	1.2	1.7	1.3	1.5	1.8
Daily	0.1	0.1	0.1	0.1	0.1	0.1	0.1	0.1	0.2
Crack cocaine									
Lifetime	1.7	2.4	2.7	1.8	2.1	2.8	2.6	3.0	3.0
Annual	1.0	1.3	1.6	1.1	1.4	1.8	1.5	1.9	2.1
30-day	0.4	0.7	0.7	0.5	0.6	0.9	0.7	0.8	1.0
Daily	0.1	*	*	*	*	*	0.1	0.1	0.1
Heroin									
Lifetime	1.4	2.0	2.3	1.3	1.5	1.7	1.1	1.2	1.6
Annual	0.7	1.2	1.4	0.7	0.9	1.1	0.5	0.6	1.1
30-day	0.4	0.6	0.6	0.3	0.4	0.6	0.2	0.3	0.6
Daily	*	0.1	*	*	*	*	*	*	0.1
Stimulants									
Lifetime	11.8	12.3	13.1	14.9	15.1	17.4	15.1	15.7	15.3
Annual	7.2	7.9	8.7	9.6	10.2	11.9	8.4	9.4	9.3
30-day	3.6	3.6	4.2	4.3	4.5	5.3	3.7	4.0	4.0
Daily	0.1	0.1	0.2	0.3	0.1	0.2	0.2	0.2	0.3
Alcohol[a]									
Lifetime	55.7	55.8	54.5	71.6	71.1	70.5	80.0	80.4	80.7
Annual	45.4	46.8	45.3	63.4	63.9	63.5	72.7	73.0	73.7
30-day	24.3	25.5	24.6	38.2	39.2	38.8	48.6	50.1	51.3
Daily	1.0	1.0	0.7	1.8	1.7	1.7	3.4	2.9	3.5
Cigarettes (any use)									
Lifetime	45.3	46.1	46.4	56.3	56.9	57.6	61.9	62.0	64.2
30-day	16.7	18.6	19.1	24.7	25.4	27.9	29.9	31.2	33.5
Daily	8.3	8.8	9.3	14.2	14.6	16.3	19.0	19.4	21.6
½ pack + per day	3.5	3.6	3.4	7.0	7.6	8.3	10.9	11.2	12.4
Steroids									
Lifetime	1.6	2.0	2.0	1.7	1.8	2.0	2.0	2.4	2.3
Annual	0.9	1.2	1.0	1.0	1.1	1.2	1.2	1.3	1.5
30-day	0.5	0.5	0.6	0.5	0.6	0.6	0.7	0.9	0.7
Daily	0.1	*	*	*	0.1	0.1	0.1	0.4	0.2

Note. Data from the National Institute on Drug Abuse's 1995 Monitoring the Future study show the percentage of 8th-, 10th-, and 12th-graders who used drugs, including alcohol and tobacco, in the past 3 years. The University of Michigan's Institute for Social Research has conducted the survey each year since 1975 among a representative sample of 12th-graders; 8th- and 10th-graders were surveyed for the first time in 1991.

* < 0.05%.

[a] Starting in 1993, the question text was changed slightly to indicate that a "drink" meant "more than a few sips."

males in rates of substance use and may have to do with slightly earlier female maturation and with their tendency to associate with older male students.

Racial or Ethnic Group

African American students tend to report lower rates of psychoactive drug use than other racial or ethnic groups at all three grades, Caucasian students are the highest for most drugs at 12th grade, and Hispanic students are highest at 8th grade for all illicit drug classes and for alcohol. At 12th grade, Hispanics are highest only for cocaine, heroin, and steroids (Bachman et al., 1991). It has been reported that Native American seniors are ranked at the top with Caucasian seniors whereas Asian American seniors show the opposite trend (Bachman et al., 1991).

The prevalence rates derived from the survey fail to reflect adequately the magnitude of high-risk behaviors, clinical significance, and adolescent health problems. They may serve at best as a periodic "snapshot" of adolescent substance use. Surveys of regional communities have placed lifetime prevalence figures for substance abuse/dependence during adolescence between approximately 3% and 10% (Babor et al., 1991; Kashani et al., 1987; Lewinsohn et al., 1993; Reinharz, Giaconia, Lefkowitz, Pakiz, & Frost, 1993). The disturbing data regarding the present trend of adolescent substance use need to be addressed by reexamining our prevention efforts, public policy, and treatment strategies.

NOSOLOGY

The ideal diagnostic label indicates the cause of a disorder, its natural history, the most likely prognosis, and the best available treatment (Schuckit, Zisook, & Mortola, 1985). Substance use and abuse occurs on a continuum (Clayton, 1992), and the cutoff point for making a diagnosis of abuse/dependence is somewhat arbitrary particularly in adolescents (Rohde, Lewinsohn, & Seeley 1996). Clinical psychiatry traditionally followed the dichotomous paradigm of the DSM nosology regardless of its limitation providing information in terms of pathogenesis and treatment response (Bukstein & Kaminer, 1994). In addition, the serious negative impact of drugs on adolescents or adults who experience subdiagnostic levels of problematic substance use has been recognized but has not been addressed by the DSM system (Lewinsohn, Rohde, & Seeley 1996; Sobell & Sobell, 1993). In DSM-III-R (American Psychiatric Association, 1987) psychoactive substance abuse was a residual category. This disorder was considered a less maladaptive disorder than psychoactive substance dependence and could be applied to a majority of adolescents identified with a pathological pattern of substance use. However, its residual category status could jeopardize the availability of treatment for adolescents with substance abuse because it implied that this disorder was not severe enough to justify treatment, particularly in comparison with the substance dependence category.

The same DSM-IV diagnostic criteria are utilized for the diagnosis of substance abuse and dependence for adolescents as for that of adults. Empirical data generally support the utility of DSM-IV criteria for alcohol dependence among adolescents (Martin, Kaczynski, Maisto, Bukstein, & Moss, 1995). Lewinsohn et al. (1996) reported on a strong similarity between adolescents and adults in the frequency of 8 out of the 11 symptoms of DSM-IV criteria for abuse and dependence. Among adolescents with a diagnosis, the most frequently reported symptoms were "reduced activities, tolerance, consuming more than intended, and desire to cut down" (Stewart & Brown, 1995; Lewinsohn et al., 1996).

Professionals working with adolescents may find the conceptual framework of DSM-IV more favorable in its terminology related to adolescent substance abuse. Substance dependence in DSM-IV is based on the presence of three or more criteria out of seven, and none of the classic, restrictive symptoms of tolerance, withdrawal, or withdrawal avoidance is necessary for diagnosis. Subtypes for physiological dependence have been added to allow clinicians to note the presence of tolerance or withdrawal. Substance abuse in DSM-IV has been reinstated as a specific category. The set of criteria has been expanded from two to four items by the addition of "recurrent legal problems" and "failure to fulfill major role obligations" to the DSM-III-R criteria.

The implications in differentiating treatment of either substance abuse or dependence have gained a cardinal importance due to empirical evidence provided by Hasin, Grant, and Endicott (1990). They concluded that a majority of adults diagnosed as abusers had never progressed to dependence. Abuse and dependence are distinct. Abuse is not a prodrome and it may be developmentally limited in many adolescents.

Research on alcoholic typologies in adults has generated support for two distinct multivariate subtypes of alcoholism (Babor, 1994) and inspired clinical trials in patient–treatment matching (Kadden, Cooney, Getter, & Litt, 1989; Litt, Babor, DelBoca, Kadden, & Cooney, 1992). Two recent classification systems—type 1–type 2 (Cloninger, 1987; Sigvardsson, Bohman, & Cloninger, 1996), and type A–type B (Babor, Hoffman, DelBoca, Hesselbrock, & Kaplan, 1992)—represent the two basic types of alcoholism proposed in the literature and have an important common theme pertinent to adolescence, namely, early age of onset of type 2 and type B. These typologies, or any other age-of-onset-based subtyping, may have significant implications for recognition of adolescent substance abuse heterogeneity, improving knowledge regarding the pathogenesis of the disorder, effective psychosocial and/or biologically based treatment matching strategies, and guidance public health personnel in planning for the allocation of treatment resources.

A recent trend in the research for subtypes of substance abuse has been the study of temperament. Temperament deviations are associated with an increased risk for psychopathology and substance abuse (Reich, Earls, Frankel, & Shayka, 1993). For example, children with a "difficult temperament" more commonly manifest externalizing and internalizing behavior problems by middle childhood (Earls & Jung, 1987) and in adolescence (Maziade, Caron,

Cote, Boutin, & Thivierge, 1990) compared to children whose temperament is normative. Increased behavioral activity level is noted in both youth at high risk for substance abuse and those having a substance use disorder (Tarter, Laird, & Moss, 1990; Tarter, Laird, Mostefa, Bukstein, & Kaminer, 1990). Other temperamental trait deviations found in high-risk youth include reduced attention-span persistence (Schaeffer, Parson, & Yohman, 1984), increased impulsivity (Noll, Zucker, Fitzgerald, & Curtis, 1992; Shedler & Block, 1990), and such negative affect states as irritability (Brook, Whiteman, Gordon, & Brook, 1990) and emotional reactivity (Blackson, 1994). Tarter, Kirisci, Hegedeus, Mezzich, and Yanyukov (1994) developed a difficult temperament index to classify adolescent alcoholics. These clusters are similar to the adult subtyping of (Cloninger, 1987; Babor et al., 1992). A small cohort of adolescent inpatients with behavioral dyscontrol and hypophoria were included in cluster 2 and those with primarily negative affect were included in cluster 1. Cluster 2 patients had an earlier onset of first substance use, first substance abuse diagnosis, and first psychiatric diagnosis as compared to cluster 1. Those adolescents with a difficult temperament displayed a high conditional probability to develop psychiatric disorders such as conduct disorder, attention-deficit/hyperactivity disorder, anxiety disorders, and mood disorders (Tarter et al., 1994).

The search for subtyping of adolescent substance abuse is complex; therefore, it is important to identify promising avenues of investigation. Cross-sectional and longitudinal studies of adolescents should include large cohorts of subjects from the general population and from high-risk and clinical samples.

ETIOLOGY AND PATHOGENESIS

Genetic and biological factors as well as environmental variables have been extensively researched to address questions regarding the etiology of SUDs. Most researchers acknowledge a multifactorial consensus as presented in the biopsychosocial paradigm for the etiology and pathogenesis of these disorders.

Genetic and Biological Factors

Most of the data regarding the genetic and biological contribution to the development of substance abuse are being derived from alcoholism research. It has been suggested that individuals may enter life with a certain level of a genetic predisposition toward alcoholism or other SUDs. Convergent evidence from twin, adoption, and biological response studies suggests that genetic factors may indeed play a role in the etiology of alcoholism (Bohman, Sigvardsson, & Cloninger, 1981; Cloninger, Bohman, & Sigvardsson, 1981). Investigations of neuropsychological and physiological precursors or markers of alcoholism, conducted with sons of alcoholics and nonalcoholics, suggest some possible biological differences that may increase vulnerability to alcoholism. Goodwin (1985) suggested that children of alcoholics may be deficient in serotonin or may have an increased level of serotonin in the presence of alcohol. The "addictive cycle"—a pattern in which a person initially drinks to feel good and then later has to resume drinking after an abstinence period to stop feeling bad—may result from such a problem with serotonin. Children of alcoholics are also suspected to have increased tolerance to alcohol. Kumpfer and Demarsh (1986) reviewed 10 more differences.

There are indications that adolescent substance abuse may be part of a broader genetic constellation. Some theorists suggest that polydrug abuse (abuse of a wide variety of substances) constitutes evidence against a genetic interpretation of addiction. Cadoret, Troughton, O'Gorman, and Heywood (1986) suggest instead that some underlying biochemical route may be involved both in substance abuse and in problem or deviant behavior, especially delinquency. They summarized their findings of an adoption study as follows: "There appear to be two genetic pathways to drug abuse: one through antisocial personality (and indirectly from biologic parents with antisocial behavior) and the second from biologic parents with alcohol problems to individuals who themselves are not antisocial" (p. 1136).

Environmental Theories

The evidence supporting a genetic factor in alcoholism and substance abuse is paralleled by evidence supporting the role of psychosocial, familial, peer, and other environmental and interactional variables. Lettieri (1985) listed more than 40 articles covering a wide range of mainly psychosocial hypotheses about initiation and continuation of substance use and eventual transition from use to abuse. Two of the most influential theories have been postulated by the Jessor and Jessor (1977) and by Kandel (1978).

The Jessors have formulated the problem behavior theory, which explains substance use as a component of a "deviance syndrome" or "proneness" to problem behavior (Jessor, 1987). This model extends beyond genetic and biological considerations. The primary focus of the theory is on three systems of psychosocial influence: the personality system, the perceived environment system, and the behavior system. Together, these three systems generate a dynamic state called "proneness," which specified the likelihood of occurrence of normative development or problem behavior that departs from the social and legal norms.

Also, longitudinal studies have documented that personality characteristics such as aggressiveness and rebelliousness are predictive factors that precede the use of substances and can be identified in preschoolers. Kandel (1982) made two pivotal contributions. She formulated four broad classes of predictors: (1) parental influences, (2) peer influences, (3) adolescent beliefs and values, and (4) adolescent involvement in various shared activities. Kandel also conceptualized the "gateway" theory to adolescent substance use and abuse. According to Kandel (1982), alcohol and marijuana are pivotal "gateway" substances, and she formulated several distinct developmental stages in the initiation and progression of substance use by adolescents, including (1) beer or wine, (2) cigarettes or hard liquor, (3) marijuana, and (4) other illicit substances. Participation in each stage is necessary but not a sufficient condition for progression into a latter stage. Problem drinking may take place between marijuana and other illicit drug use and therefore represents an additional stage in the transition of substance use (Donovan & Jessor, 1983).

Parental Influences

Three different types of parental characteristics predict initiation of substance use: parental substance use/abuse behaviors, parental attitudes toward substances, and parental–child interactions. Studies suggest that exposing a child (particularly a young child) to substance abuse behavior by the caretaker and to the nonfulfillment of parental responsibilities that follows affects the child by providing models and by reinforcement of related behaviors. Ahmed, Bush, Davidson, and Iannotti (1984) reported on a measure of "salience," defined as the number of household users of a substance and the degree of children's involvement in parental substance-taking behavior; this measure was found to be the best predictor of both expectations of use and actual abuse of alcohol. Salience was also a strong predictor of children's cigarette and marijuana use. Among the environmental characteristics of these families, the following factors were noted: high stress, poor and inconsistent family management skills, increased separation, divorce, death, prison terms, and decreased family activities.

Chemically dependent families are often socially isolated from the community, partly because of their need for secrecy and partly because of community rejection. Parents in substance-abusing families have fewer friends and are less involved in recreational, social, religious, and cultural activities (Kumpfer & Demarsh, 1986). Because of such families' social isolation, the children have fewer opportunities to interact with other children, have fewer friends, and express a desire to have more friends but doubt their abilities to make friends. Emotional neglect is frequently reported; substance-abusing parents have only a limited to involve themselves meaningfully and emotionally with their children and also have been found to spend less time in planned and structured activities with their children (Kumpfer & Demarsh, 1986). In addition, more psychopathology and significantly more depression have been detected in substance-abusing parents. The emotional impact on children from these families results in the children's having difficulty with identifying and expressing positive feelings. Parents who are substance abusers are also characterized by difficulty in coping with everyday realities and responsibilities. Lack of energy for better parenting, because of the drain on the family's time, finances, and emotional/social resources created by the substance abuse, has been noted (Kumpfer & Demarsh, 1986).

Resentment, embarrassment, anger, fear, loneliness, depression, and insecurity are often identified or reported among these children. Intense fear of separation and abandonment is very common. Because psychopathology and emotional disturbances often precede substance abuse, these children are at high risk for the development of substance abuse and dependence. Kumpfer and Demarsh (1986) also found that children of alcoholic parents scored lower than children of nonalcoholics on measures of intelligence and cognitive performance and on two measures of self-concept.

Peer Influences

Peer influences play a crucial role in the process of involvement in the use and abuse of all substances—tobacco, alcohol, and illicit substances (especially marijuana). Because only a small fraction of adolescent substance users may progress to substance abuse, it is of a significant clinical importance to differentiate between the causes for substance use and substance abuse. Most substance use occurs due to social influences and can be attributed to the adolescent immediate subculture and lifestyle. Substance abuse is more strongly tied to a developmental process involving biobehavioral factors (Glantz & Pickens 1992), and it occurs as a part of a cluster of behaviors that form a syndrome of problem behavior (Jessor & Jessor, 1977) or general deviance (Newcomb, 1995).

Peer relationships have a significant effect on the initiation, development, and maintenance of substance abuse. The most consistent and reproducible finding in substance abuse research is the strong relationship between an individual's substance behavior and the concurrent substance use of his or her friends (Jessor & Jessor, 1977). Such an association may result from socialization, as well as from a process of interpersonal selection (assortative pairing), in which adolescents with similar values and behaviors seek each other out as friends (Kandel, 1982). Susceptibility to peer influence is related to involvement in peer-related activities and to a degree of attachment and reliance on peers rather than parents (Kandel, 1978).

Regarding values and attitudes in adolescent substance abusers, substance abuse is correlated negatively with conventional behaviors and beliefs, such as church attendance, good scholastic performance, value of academic achievement, and beliefs in the generalized expectations, norms, and values of society (Jessor, 1987). Substance abuse is correlated positively with risk-taking behavior, sensation-seeking behavior, early sexual activity, higher value of independence, and greater involvement in delinquent behavior (Jessor, 1987).

Delinquency may reach a point at which adolescent gangs, groups, and cults engage in one or more of the following shared activities: using the same drugs of choice, Satanism and related rituals, drug trafficking, and violence. Such activities are deeply rooted in the identity-creating process of these groups and are inseparable components of their code of values. Although a relatively small number of adolescents are reporting or are reported to be engaged in such activities, they constitute a growing reason for concern.

PSYCHIATRIC COMORBIDITY

The presence of one or more comorbid psychiatric disorders, both internalizing and/or externalizing types, is often noted in populations of adolescents with SUDs (Bukstein, Glancy, & Kaminer, 1992, Riggs, Baker, Mikulich, Young, & Crowley, 1995). Psychiatric disorders in childhood, featured by disruptive behavior disorders as well as mood or anxiety disorders, confer an increased risk for the development of SUDs in a majority of the cases in adolescence (Loeber, 1988; Christie et al., 1988; Bukstein, Brent, & Kaminer, 1989). The etiological mechanisms have not been systematically researched. However, a number of possible relationships exist between SUDs and psychopathology. Psychopathology may precede SUDs, may develop as a consequence of preexisting SUDs, may influence the severity of SUDs, may not be related, or may originate from a common vulnerability (Hovens, Cantwell, & Kiriakos, 1994; Meyer, 1986).

A number of psychiatric disorders are commonly associated with SUDs in youth (Bukstein et al., 1989). Conduct disorder and constituent criteria such as aggression usually precede and accompany adolescent SUDs (Huizinga & Elliot, 1981; Loeber, 1988; Milin, Halikas, Meller, & Morse, 1991). Clinical populations of adolescents with SUDs show rates of conduct disorder regularly ranging from 50% to almost 80%. Although attention-deficit/hyperactivity disorder (ADHD) is commonly noted in substance-using and -abusing youth, the observed association is likely due to the high level of comorbidity between conduct disorder and ADHD (Barkley, Fischer, Edelbrock, & Smallish, 1990; Kaminer, 1992a; Levin & Kleber, 1995, Wilens, Biederman, Spencer, & Frances, 1994). An earlier onset of conduct problems and aggressive behavior, in addition to the presence of ADHD, may increase the risk for later substance abuse (Loeber, 1988). A most recent prospective follow-up study by Biederman et al. (1997) found that adolescents with and without ADHD had a similar risk for SUDs that was mediated by conduct and bipolar disorders. Because the risk for SUDs has been shown to be elevated in adults with ADHD, it remains to be seen whether a sharp increase in SUDs rate will occur in the grown-up ADHD children included in this cohort during the transition from adolescence to adulthood.

Aggressive behaviors are present in many adolescents who have SUDs (Milin et al., 1991). Consumption of such substances as alcohol, amphetamines, phencyclidine may increase the likelihood of subsequent aggressive behavior (Moss & Tarter, 1993; Tuchfield, Clayton, & Logan, 1982). The direct pharmacological effects resulting in aggression may be further exacerbated by the presence of preexisting psychopathology, the use of multiple agents simultaneously, and the frequent relative inexperience of the adolescent substance user. Gambling behavior and pathological gambling are common among adolescents with SUDs; unfortunately, the study of the relationship between these disorders is in its infancy (Griffiths, 1995).

Mood disorders, especially depression, frequently have onsets both preceding and consequent to the onset of substance use and SUDs in adolescents

(Bukstein et al., 1992; Deykin, Levy, & Wells, 1987; Deykin, Buka, & Zeena, 1992; Hovens et al., 1994). The prevalence of depressive disorders in these studies ranged from 24% to more than 50%.

The literature supports SUDs among adolescents as a risk factor for suicidal behavior, including ideation, attempts, and completed suicide (Bukstein et al., 1993; Crumley, 1990; Kaminer, 1996). Possible mechanisms for this relationships include acute and chronic effects of psychoactive substances. Adolescent suicide victims are frequently using alcohol or other drugs at the time of suicide (Brent, Perper, & Allman, 1987). The acute substance use may produce transient but intense dysphoric states, disinhibition, impaired judgment, and increased level of impulsivity or may exacerbate preexisting psychopathology, including depression or anxiety disorders (Schuckit, 1986).

A number of studies of clinical populations show high rates of anxiety disorders among youth with SUDs (Clark et al., 1995; Clark & Sayette, 1993). In clinical populations of adolescents with SUDs, the prevalence of anxiety disorder ranged from 7% to over 40% (Clark et al., 1995; DeMilio, 1989; Stowell, 1991). The order of appearance of comorbid anxiety and SUDs appears to be variable, depending on the specific anxiety disorder. Social phobia usually precedes abuse whereas panic and generalized anxiety disorder more often follow the onset of SUDs (Kushner, Sher, & Beitman, 1990). Adolescents with SUDs often have a history of posttraumatic stress disorder (PTSD) following acute or chronic physical and sexual abuse (Clark et al., 1995; Van Hasselt, Null, Kempton, & Bukstein, 1993). Bulimia nervosa is also commonly associated with adolescents having substance use disorders (Bulik, 1987). SUDs are very common among individuals who are diagnosed with schizophrenia (Kutcher, Kachur, & Marton, 1992; Regier et al., 1990). Personality disorders (cluster B in particular) among adolescents with SUDs are highly prevalent (Grilo et al., 1995). Finally as suggested by studies showing language deficits in youth at affected or at high risk for SUDs, learning disabilities or disorders may also show an increased incidence of comorbidity (Moss, Kirisci, Gordon, & Tarter, 1994). Patients with comorbid psychiatric disorders continue to be a challenge for clinicians and researchers in the assessment and treatment domains.

PREVENTION

Efforts to curtail substance abuse concentrate on activities designed for supply-and-demand reduction. Coate and Grossman (1987) reported that use of alcohol by youths declines when either the price of alcoholic beverages or the legal drinking age increases. O'Malley and Wagenaar (1991) reported on a reduction in car accidents among youth as a result of the increase of the minimum drinking age to 21.

The goal of primary prevention among children and adolescents is to defer or preclude initiation of gateway substances such as cigarettes, alcohol, and marijuana. The traditional education program is a prevention strategy used to increase knowledge of the consequences of drug use. Investigators (Schinke, Botvin, & Orlani, 1991) found the assumption that increased knowledge decreases drug use to be invalid. Affective education, which increases self-esteem and enhances responsible decision making, and alternative activities programs for adolescents were found to be ineffective in the prevention of drug use based on meta-analysis of the literature (Tobler, 1986; Bangert-Drowns, 1988). Furthermore, all the prevention strategies noted previously were reported to increase the interest in drugs among some of the participants (Schinke et al., 1991). A more advanced prevention strategy is based on a psychosocial approach. These prevention programs are aimed at enhancing self-esteem (Schaps, Moskowitz, & Malvin, 1986), social skills, and assertive skills resisting to substance use (Botvin, Baker, Filazzola, & Botvin, 1990). However, these techniques failed to be successful in enhancing secondary prevention (Pentz, Dwyer, & MacKinnon, 1989; Elickson & Bell, 1990).

A recent study by Botvin, Baker, Dusenbury, Botvin and Diaz (1995) implemented curriculum covering a life skills and skills for resisting social influences to use drugs. This curriculum included booster sessions during 2 years after completion of the intervention. The investigators reported a significant and durable reduction in drug use 6 years later.

Recommendations

The challenge for health care providers is to identify individuals at high risk before or shortly after initiation of substance use and to intervene to reduce transitional risk. One of the largest subpopulations of children at risk are those with at least one biological parent diagnosed with alcohol dependence or substance dependence. These individuals are at greater risk of developing the same disorder, fourfold and tenfold, respectively (Goodwin, 1985; Tarter, 1992). Children of opioid dependence parents were reported to have high rates of psychopathology and significant dysfunction in the academic, family, and legal life domains (Kolar, Brown, Haertzen, & Michaelson, 1994; Wilens, Biederman, Kiely, Bredin, & Spencer, 1995). Contrary to public perception, there is a need for a more balanced view regarding the natural history of children of alcoholics (COAs) primarily because (1) regardless of popular models of dysfunctional COAs, the majority of offspring raised with a dysfunctional alcoholic parent do not develop alcoholism (Wilson & Crowe, 1991) and (2) the negative labeling of adolescent COAs regardless of their current behavior was reported to be robust and potentially harmful (Burk & Sher, 1990).

The interaction between risk and protective factors may influence the development or arrest of substance abuse in the vulnerable child. The study of resilience among youth growing up in substance-abusing families is presently undergoing further exploration (Wolin & Wolin, 1996).

It appears that to achieve realistic outcome for prevention efforts, the heterogeneity of adolescent subpopulations needs to be recognized to better understand substance use and its transition to substance abuse and dependence. This recognition is followed by determining the level of intervention required—whether it is primary, secondary, or tertiary prevention. The prevention effort must also address the adolescent needs in all domains of life, including attitudes, expectations, and interactions with the community.

Implications for policy-related initiatives have to do with supply reduction. Ethnically sensitive and appropriate prevention programs should be explored given preliminary findings regarding the merits of such programs (Catalano et al., 1993). The reduction of drinking-related car accidents should encourage community efforts to maintain the minimum drinking age at 21, especially given the recent ominous reduction of drinking age in Louisiana to 18 years of age.

ASSESSMENT

A significant step toward addressing the need for better therapeutic interventions for adolescents with SUDs has been the recognition of the assessment and treatment of SUDs as a multiphasic task. The expert committee of the Institute of Medicine report (1990) of the Adolescent Assessment/Referral System developed by the National Institute on Drug Abuse (Rahdert, 1991; Tarter, 1990) recommend a three-phase process. The initial screening phase involves identification of health disorders, psychiatric problems, and psychosocial maladjustment. Based on the screening phase, a minority of adolescents are required to go through the second phase, which includes an extensive assessment necessary for initiating integrated, problem-focused, and comprehensive treatment. This assessment provides a diagnostic summary which identifies the adolescent's treatment needs within specific life domains, such as substance use, psychiatric status, physical health status, school adjustment, vocational status, family function, peer relationship, leisure and recreation activity, and legal situation. The third phase involves the preparation and implementation of an integrative treatment plan. Determining which patients respond best to what treatments (i.e., patient–treatment matching) may increase treatment effectiveness (Tarter, 1990).

Substance use and use disorders are multidimensional behaviors that demand a thorough assessment of several dimensions of substance use behavior in addition to quantity and frequency of use (Babor et al., 1991; White & Labouvie, 1989). Within the domain of substance use behavior, important dimensions include the pattern of use (quantity, frequency, onset, and types of agents used), negative consequences (school/vocational, social/peer/family, emotional/behavioral, legal and physical), context of use (time/place, peer use/attitudes, mood antecedents, consequences, expectancies, and overall social milieu), and control of use (view of use as a problem, attempts to stop or limit use, other DSM-IV dependence criteria).

The clinician may question whether any self-report by an adolescent about substance use is accurate. Although self-reports appear to be reliable in some populations, specific populations such as extremely antisocial youth may report less use than drug clinic samples (Winters, 1992). The clinician may attempt to substantiate suspected use by reports from third parties or through the use of urine or blood toxicology. Some adolescents may also exaggerate their substance use patterns. Unfortunately, there is no known examination on the use of toxicology methods as a screen for SUDs or as a predictor of outcome.

A variety of instruments are available and others are being developed to assist the screening and detailed assessment of substance use and related behaviors and problems. The common use of instruments developed for adults or without standardization and validation may be inappropriate for adolescents (Winters, 1990). Although readers are referred elsewhere for a more detailed discussion of individual instruments (Leccese & Waldron, 1994; Winters, 1990; Winters & Stinchfield, 1995), we provide several examples of types of instruments here.

Screening instruments are used to identify the potential presence of SUDs as a preliminary step toward a more detailed, comprehensive assessment. Although many substance use/abuse screening instruments are designed to measure the substance use domain only (Cut Down; Annoyed; Guilty; Eye Opener [CAGE]; Ewing, 1984), other instruments screen other domains for psychosocial functioning (Problem-Oriented Screening Instrument for Teenagers [POSIT]; Rahdert, 1991; Drug Use Screening Inventory [DUSI]; Tarter, 1990; Personal Experience Screening Questionnaire [PESQ]; Winters, 1992). Comprehensive assessment instruments usually provide more detailed information about substance use behavior as well as other domains of functioning. The format for comprehensive instruments vary, with some being self-report questionnaires (e.g., Personal Experience Inventory [PEI]; Winters & Henly, 1988), others being structured interviews (e.g., Adolescent Drug Abuse Diagnosis [ADAD]; Friedman & Utada, 1989), and others semistructured interviews (e.g., Adolescent Problem Severity Index [APSI]; Metzger, Kushner, & McLellan, 1991, Teen-Addiction Severity Index [T-ASI]; Kaminer, Bukstein, & Tarter, 1991; Kaminer, Wagner, Plummer, & Seifer, 1993).

A SUGGESTED MODEL FOR EVALUATION AND TREATMENT OF SUDS

To develop a referral system for a treatment program, the community needs to be aware of the following: (1) the goals of the treatment program, (2) the population to be served, and (3) how to communicate with the referral system. Other questions can be answered once communication channels have been established. On the other end, the treatment service is obligated to assess the needs of the community to ensure a successful program. Needs assessment surveys, certificate of need procedures, and marketing strategies are beyond the scope of this chapter. However, it is important to get acquainted with the following services: school systems, Drug and Alcohol agencies (private, county, municipal, state, etc.), children and youth services, the juvenile justice system, mental health services, pediatricians, and private practitioners.

The referral may start by having an intake coordinator accept phone calls for screening. An intake questionnaire is recommended even for phone calls (15–20 minutes of administration preferred). Substance use patterns, psychiatric status, family function, school performance, and legal problems are the pivotal domains addressed. A scheduled outpatient multidisciplinary evaluation should follow, based on the urgency and severity of the case involved. Dispositional options (triage) involve a variety of possibilities, which may also depend on service availability.

Adolescents with SUDs, seen on an urgent basis in an emergency room or according to the previously noted procedures, can subsequently be admitted directly to an inpatient unit. Appropriate referrals to an inpatient unit may include (1) adolescents with SUDs who have failed or do not qualify for outpatient treatment; (2) dually diagnosed adolescents with moderate or severe psychiatric disorders; (3) adolescents who display a potentially morbid or mortal behavior toward themselves or others (e.g., suicidal behavior, self-injurious behavior); (4) adolescents who are intravenous drug abusers, drug dependent, or need to be detoxified; (5) patients with accompanying moderate to severe medical problems; (6) adolescents who need to be isolated from their community to ensure treatment without interruptions; and (7) pregnant adolescents who manifest SUDs that endanger the fetus.

Enrollment criteria in a drug-free outpatient or partial hospitalization setting include (1) severity of SUDs and other psychiatric disorders that do not require inpatient treatment (i.e., psychiatric disorder severity less than moderate); (2) previous successful outpatient treatment follow-up after completion of inpatient treatment; and (3) agreement for a contingency contract that will delineate frequency of visits, compliance with curriculum including random urine screening, consequences of noncompliance and relapse, and participation in the community network including self-help groups. Similar placement criteria for adolescents with SUDs, such as the American Society for Addiction Medicine criteria tailored from the Cleveland criteria (Hoffmann, Halikas, & Mee-Lee, 1987), have some level of face validity; however, no research supports them.

In conclusion, the careful assessment, triage, and treatment plan formulation are necessary to improve patient treatment matching that may result in better treatment outcome.

TREATMENT

Research into the outcomes of adolescent substance abuse treatment has lagged behind that for research into the predictors, the course, and correlates of treatment outcome among adults. Unfortunately, data indicate that most adolescents return to some level of alcohol or other drug abuse following treatment (Brown, Vik, & Creamer, 1989; Brown et al., 1990). Despite these outcomes, studies have identified specific predictors of treatment outcome, including patient or adolescent characteristics, social support system variables, and program characteristics. Adolescents in substance abuse treatment begin substance use at an earlier age and progress rapidly to the use of multiple drugs followed by the development of SUDs (Brown et al., 1989; Brown, Mott, & Stewart, 1992; Myers & Brown, 1990). Other clinical features of adolescents entering treatment include often high levels of coexisting psychopathology or early personality difficulties, deviant behavior, school difficulties including high levels of truancy, and family disruption and substance abuse (Brown et al., 1992; Bukstein et al., 1992; Doyle, Delaney, & Trobin, 1994). Several pretreatment characteristics predict completion of treatment by adolescents. They include greater severity of alcohol problems; greater use of drugs other than alcohol, marijuana, and tobacco; a higher level of internalizing problems, and lower self-esteem (Blood & Cornwall, 1994; Doyle et al., 1994, Kaminer, 1992a). Premorbid psychopathology (e.g., conduct disorder) is negatively correlated with treatment completion and with future abstinence (Myers, Brown, & Mott, 1995). Although such factors as severity of substance use may predict short-term treatment outcomes, most longer-term outcomes may depend on social/environmental factors. This is consistent with studies of relapse among adolescent populations, which suggest that relapse in adolescents is more often associated with social pressures to use rather than situations involving negative affect, as is usually found in adult relapse (Brown, Myers, Mott, & Vik, 1994; Vik, Grisel, & Brown, 1992). Attendance at self-support or aftercare groups is associated with higher rates of abstinence and other measure of improved outcome when compared with those adolescents who did not attend such groups (Brown, 1993; Harrison & Hoffmann, 1989).

Despite a higher level of return to substance use among adolescents after treatment, abstinent teens may expect decreased interpersonal conflict, improved academic functioning, and increased involvement in social and occupational activities (Brown et al., 1994). Patterns of substance abuse among adolescents appear to become more stable between 6 and 12 months after treatment (Brown et al., 1994). An extensive review of treatment outcome studies conducted in the 1970s and 1980s concluded that treatment can be effective and is better than no treatment (Catalano, Hawkins, Wells, Miller, & Brewer, 1990–1991). However, an unequivocal superiority of specific treatment modalities or components has not been demonstrated.

A number of treatment program characteristics are associated with improved abstinence and lower levels of relapse. These program characteristics include longer duration of treatment, available follow-up or aftercare treatment, involvement of family, and the availability of social support services (Fleisch, 1991; Friedman & Beschner, 1985).

Recently, there has been a shift from the conservative treatment approach that emphasized type of treatment setting, length of stay, and Twelve-Step–dominated approach to patient–treatment matching approach.

The type, frequency, dosage, and appropriateness of treatment components to patients' needs have been established as pivotal for a successful treatment outcome (Kaminer, 1994). Individualized treatment contract is a pivotal treatment component regardless of the treatment setting (Kaminer, Tarter, Bukstei, & Kabene, 1992). This treatment component is based on a contract developed from a problem list conjointly prepared by the patient and the therapist during the evaluation phase. The contract specifies long-term goals according to the T-ASI (Kaminer et al., 1991). The goals are sensible, achievable, and measurable and are divided into weekly objectives according to the following domains: substance abuse, psychiatric symptomatology, family issues, legal status, peersocial relationships, and school or vocational problems. Individual treatment is provided by a team led by a psychiatrist who supervises the primary therapists who contract with the patients. Progress on the multilevel system depends on the periodic presentation of the contract.

Continued staff development and increased awareness regarding the importance of negotiating treatment goals and developing a contract with patients is of great importance (Kaminer, 1992b). Tackling violations of contract and regulations in the treatment program is of considerable importance. The treatment team is responsible for communicating with the caretakers frequently, especially when a patient has been disciplined. A clear protocol on how to handle such situations with minors may prevent clinical difficulties and legal hazards.

Several investigators have demonstrated the effectiveness of family-based approaches, even in comparison with non–family-based interventions, in treating adolescent SUDs (Friedman & Utada, 1989; Szapocznik, Kurtines, Foote, Perez-Vidal, & Hervis, 1983; Szapocznik et al., 1988). Liddle and Dakof (1995) suggest an integrative approach for a successful family treatment model. Similarly, Multisystemic therapy (MST) represents a family–ecological systems approach with interventions targeting family functioning and communication, school and peer functioning, and community functioning (Henggeler, Melton, & Smith 1992). In addressing the frequently multidimensional nature of adolescent SUDs and associated problems, MST focuses on multiple targets and using many treatment techniques including family therapy and behavioral therapies. MST is integrative and comprehensive but targets specific, identified areas of dysfunction.

A number of cognitive-behavioral treatments, including many previously used with adults (e.g., relapse prevention), may show promise as treatment modalities for adolescents with SUDs (Marlatt & Gordon, 1985). Manual guided therapy has been found helpful with this population and the development of drug refusal skills, problem solving, and social skills training appears to be effective (Kaminer, 1994).

Many treatment programs for adolescents continue to be based on the 12 steps of Alcoholics or Narcotics Anonymous (AA or NA). Attendance at self-support groups appears to predict abstinence and other measures of improved treatment outcome (Alford, Koehler, & Leonard, 1991; Brown,

1993). Many programs augment group therapy and the attendance at self-support groups with self-paced work using structured booklets (Jaffe, 1990).

Pharmacotherapy or medication treatment potentially targets several areas, including treatment of withdrawal, use to counteract or decrease the subjective reinforcing effects of illicit substance use, and treatment of comorbid psychopathology. Unfortunately, no systematic research evaluates the efficacy and safety of any psychotropic medication in the treatment of adolescents with SUDs (Kaminer, 1995). Although clinically significant withdrawal symptoms appear to be rare in adolescents (Martin et al., 1995), there is little rationale for using different detoxification protocols than those for adults. The use of agents to block the reinforcing effects of various substances, as aversive agents (e.g., disulfiram) or to relieve craving during and after acute withdrawal, has been studied in adults but has received scant attention for adolescents. Kaminer (1992b) described the use of desipramine in an adolescent with cocaine dependence. Aversive pharmacological treatment with agents such as disulfiram is rare in adolescents. In discussing two case studies, Myers, Donaue, and Goldstein (1994) express caution in using disulfiram in adolescents. The opiate antagonist naltrexone, used safely and effectively in adults to reduce cravings for alcohol, may hold promise for the treatment of adolescents with alcohol use disorder according to a case study reported by Wold and Kaminer (1997).

The high prevalence of coexisting psychiatric disorders in adolescents with SUDs presents additional targets for pharmacological agents (Bukstein et al., 1989). Potential targets for pharmacological treatment include depression and other mood problems, ADHD, severe levels of aggressive behavior, and anxiety disorders. Unfortunately, few data in the literature demonstrate the efficacy of pharmacological agents prescribed for adolescents with SUDs and comorbid psychiatric disorders. Preliminary data suggest that selective serotonergic reuptake inhibitors may reduce problem drinking in adult drinkers (Naranjo, Kadlec, Sanheuza, Woodley-Remus, & Sellars, 1990) and both depression and drinking behavior in depressed adult alcoholics (Cornelius et al., 1993). However, a recent study indicates that these agents have a limited clinical utility (Kranzler et al., 1995). In general, clinicians should use the same caution in considering pharmacological treatment for adolescents with comorbid SUDs and psychiatric disorders as they do with youth with psychiatric symptoms alone.

SUDs may increase the potential for intentional or unintentional overdose. Some pharmacological agents may have inherent abuse potential. Critical issues in the use of pharmacotherapy include avoiding the precipitation or exacerbation of psychiatric symptoms by the abused substances and the need to achieve some level of abstinence or control of substance use before a more optimal assessment of symptoms and starting pharmacological treatment, the potential of acute drug effects resulting in intentional or unintentional overdose, and the potential abuse of the pharmacotherapeutic agents themselves. The treatment of ADHD among populations with SUDs remains problematic due to the abuse potential of central nervous system stimulants by the patient, family, and peers (Kaminer, 1995). In addition to close supervision of medication compliance, clinicians should consider the use of effective agents with much lower abuse potential such as tricyclic antidepressants, bupropion, and pemoline.

Although not specifically studied, the multiple areas of possible dysfunction in adolescents with SUDs and the many available treatment modalities suggest a multimodal approach. Treatment matching, or matching adolescents with specific characteristics with appropriate levels of care and types of treatment modalities is a concept that has received much attention in the adult literature (McLellan & Alterman, 1991). Psychiatric severity may be the best identified guide to matching (McLellan, Luborsky, Woody, O'Brien, & Druley, 1983). Friedman, Granick, Kreisher, and Terras (1993) found a trend toward better outcome for adolescents with more severe psychiatric problems.

Despite two decades of specific treatment for adolescents with SUDs, we know little about the "dose" of treatment necessary for successful outcomes, nor do we know much about the specific effects of such characteristics as gender, race and comorbid psychopathology on outcome. Research into adolescent treatment lags considerably behind adult treatment research. As the focus of treatment for adolescents with SUDs shifts from inpatient and residential settings to outpatient, partial hospitalization, and home-/family-based treatments, the need for research into treatment effectiveness is critical.

DISCHARGE AND AFTERCARE

It is generally agreed that aftercare is necessary to solidify and maximize treatment gains and to minimize relapse. Aftercare also ensures the transfer and generalization of treatment results to the patient's community. Lack of follow-up services may essentially nullify the positive effects of treatment. It would appear worthy to explore the hypothesis that adolescents who drop out of treatment and especially those with a comorbid diagnosis of conduct disorder could be better served in a facility other than a psychiatric hospital. Also, because no therapeutic intervention appears yet to be superior to another in the treatment of SUD, specialized interventions may be necessary to increase retention in treatment of this high-risk population for dropout.

Most patients return to school; therefore, school-based tertiary prevention in the form of counseling and support group for "recovered" adolescents is warranted. Adolescents enrolled in these programs may also be instrumental as role models in school-based primary and secondary prevention groups for high-risk youth. Also, continued participation in self-help groups, follow-up with an outpatient clinic, and rigorous maintenance of a contingency discharge contract are helpful for relapse prevention.

Parents/caretakers should be encouraged to support the recovery process and to maintain a risk-free lifestyle for the adolescent (e.g., be aware of ominous signs of relapse, keep curfew hours, and avoid enabling behavior).

In accord with the adult aftercare guidelines, the difference between lapse and relapse and how to initiate therapeutic contact in stressful situations should be clarified to the youngster and the family.

CONCLUSION

Despite numerous advancements in the understanding of SUDs in adolescents, the field lags considerably behind the adult literature describing the phenomenology of substance use problems and effective treatments. More research is needed to advance the field to adequately deal with this public health problem. Among the areas for further research are an incorporation of a developmental psychopathology perspective in subtyping adolescents with SUDs and related problems, describing the phenomenology of these problems and developing an age-appropriate nosology. Based on this research and a developmental perspective, clinicians should develop comprehensive intervention programs that include family, peer, educational, and community components and match specific adolescents to appropriate intervention/treatment settings and modalities.

REFERENCES

Ahmed, S. W., Bush, P. J., Davidson, F. R., & Iannotti, R. J. (1984). *Predicting children's use and intentions to use abusable substances*. Paper presented at the annual meeting of the American Public Health Association, Anaheim, CA.

Alford, G. S., Koehler, R. A. & Leonard, J. (1991). Alcoholic Anonymous–Narcotics Anonymous model inpatient treatment of chemically dependent adolescents: A 2-year outcome study. *Journal of Study on Alcohol, 52,* 118–126.

American Psychiatric Association. (1987). *Diagnostic and statistical manual of mental disorders* (3rd ed., rev.). Washington, DC: Author.

American Psychiatric Association. (1994). *Diagnostic and statistical manual of mental disorders* (4th ed.). Washington, DC: Author.

Babor, T. F. (1994). Method and theory in the classification of alcoholics. In T. A.Babor, V. Hesselbrock, R. E. Meyer, & W. Shoemaker (Eds.), *Types of alcoholics: Evidence from clinical, experimental and genetic research* (pp. 1–6). New York: Annals of the New York Academy of Science.

Babor, T. F., DelBoca, F., McLaney, M. A., Jacobi, B., Higgins-Biddle, J., & Hass, W. (1991). Just say Y. E. S.: Matching adolescents to appropriate interventions for alcohol and other drug-related problems. *Alcohol Health and Research World, 15,* 77–86.

Babor, T. F., Hoffman, M., DelBoca, F., Hesselbrock, V., & Kaplan, R. F. (1992). Types of alcoholics I: Evidence for an empirically-derived typology based on indicators of vulnerability and severity. *Archives of General Psychiatry, 49,* 599–608.

Bachman, J. G., Wallace, J. M., O'Malley, P. M., Johnston, L. D., Kurth, C. L., & Neighbors, H. W. (1991). Racial/ethnic differences in smoking, drinking and illicit drug use among American high school seniors 1976–1989. *American Journal of Public Health, 81,* 372–377.

Bangert-Drowns, R. L. (1988). The effects of school-based substance abuse education: A meta-analysis. *Journal of Drug Education, 18,* 243–264.

Barkley, R. A., Fischer, M., Edelbrock, C. S., & Smallish, L. (1990). The adolescent outcome of hyperactive children diagnosed by research criteria: I. An 8-year prospective follow-up study. *Journal of the American Academy of Child and Adolescent Psychiatry, 29,* 546–557.

Biederman, J., Wilens, T., Mick, E., Farone, S., Weber, W., Curtis, S., Thornell, A., Pfister, K., Jetton, J. G., & Soriano, J. (1997). Is ADHD a risk factor for psychoactive substance use disorders?: Findings from a four-year prospective follow-up study. *Journal of the American Academy of Child and Adolescent Psychiatry, 36,* 21–29.

Blackson, T. C. (1994). Temperament: A salient correlate of risk factors for alcohol and drug abuse. *Drug and Alcohol Dependence, 36,* 205–214.

Blood, L., & Cornwall, A. (1994). Pretreatment variables that predict completion of an adolescent substance abuse treatment program. *Journal of Nervous and Mental Disease, 182,* 14–19.

Bohman, M., Sigvardsson, S., & Cloninger, C. R. (1981). Maternal inheritance of alcohol abuse. *Archives of General Psychiatry, 38,* 965–969.

Botvin, G. J., Baker, E., Dusenbury, L., Botvin, E. M., & Diaz, T. (1995). Long-term follow-up results of a randomized drug abuse prevention trial in a white middle class population. *Journal of the American Medical Association, 273,* 1106–1112.

Botvin, G. J., Baker, E., Filazola, A., & Botvin, E. M. (1990). A cognitive behavioral approach to substance abuse prevention: One year follow-up. *Addiction Behaviors, 15,* 47–63.

Brent, D. A., Perper, J. A., & Allman, C. (1987). Alcohol, firearms and suicide among youth: Temporal trends in Allegheny County, Pennsylvania, 1960 to 1983. *Journal of the American Medical Association, 257,* 3369–3372.

Brook, J. S., Whiteman, M., Gordon, A. S., & Brook, D. W. (1990). The psychosocial etiology of adolescent drug use: A family interactional approach. *Genetic, Social, and General Psychology Monographs, 116,* 2.

Brown, S. A. (1993). Recovery patterns in adolescent substance abuse. In J. S. Baer, G. A. Marlatt, & R. J. McMahon (Eds.), *Addictive behaviors across the life span* (pp. 161–183). Newbury Park, CA: Sage.

Brown, S. A., Mott, M. A., & Stewart, M. A. (1992). Adolescent alcohol and drug abuse. In C. E. Walter (Ed.), *Handbook of clinical child psychology* (pp. 677–693). New York: Wiley.

Brown, S. A., Myers, M. G., Mott, M. A., & Vik, P. W. (1994). Correlates of success following treatment for adolescent substance abuse. *Applied and Preventive Psychology, 3,* 61–73.

Brown, S. A., Vik, P. N., & Creamer, V. (1989). Characteristics of relapse following adolescent substance abuse treatment. *Addictive Behaviors, 14,* 291–300.

Brown, S. A., Vik, P. W., McQuaid, J. R., Patterson, T., Irwin, M. R., & Grant, I. (1990). Severity of psychosocial stress and outcome of alcoholism treatment. *Journal of Abnormal Psychology, 99,* 344–348.

Bukstein, O. G., Brent, D. A., & Kaminer, Y. (1989). Comorbidity of substance abuse and other psychiatric disorders in adolescents. *American Journal of Psychiatry, 146,* 1131–1141.

Bukstein, O. G., Brent, D. B., Perper, J. A., Mortiz, G., Schweers, J., Roth, C., & Balach, L. (1993). Risk factors for completed suicide among adolescents with a lifetime history of substance abuse: A case control study. *Acta Psychiatrica Scandinavica, 88,* 403–408.

Bukstein, O. G., Glancy, L. J., & Kaminer, Y. (1992). Patterns of affective comorbidity in a clinical population of dually-diagnosed substance abusers. *Journal of American Academy of Child and Adolescent Psychiatry, 31,* 1041–1045.

Bukstein, O. G., & Kaminer, Y. (1994). The nosology of adolescent substance abuse. *American Journal of Addictions, 3,* 1–13.

Bulik, C. M. (1987). Drug and alcohol abuse by bulimic women and their families. *American Journal of Psychiatry, 144,* 1604–1606.

Burk, J. P., & Sher, K. J. (1990). Labeling the child of an alcoholic: Negative stereotyping by mental health professionals and peers. *Journal of Studies on Alcohol, 51,* 156–163.

Cadoret, R. J., Troughton, E., O'Gorman, T. W., & Heywood, E. (1986). An adoption study of genetic and environmental factor in drug abuse. *Archives of General Psychiatry, 43,* 1131–1136.

Catalano, R. F., Hawkins, D., Kreuz, C., Gillmore, M., Morrison, D., Wells, E., & Abbott, R. (1993). Using research to guide culturally appropriate drug abuse prevention. *Journal of Consulting and Clinical Psychology, 61,* 804–811.

Catalano, R. F., Hawkins, J. D., Wells, E. A., Miller, J., & Brewer, D. (1990–1991). Evaluation of the effectiveness of adolescent drug abuse treatment, assessment of risks for relapse, and promising approaches for relapse prevention. *International Journal of Addiction, 25,* 1085–1140.

Christie, K. A., Burke, J. D., Regier, D. A., Rae, D. S., Boyd, J. H., & Locke, B. Z. (1988). Epidemiologic evidence for early onset of mental disorders and higher risk of drug abuse in young adults. *American Journal of Psychiatry, 145,* 971–975.

Clark, D. B., Bukstein, O. G., Smith, M. G., Kaczynski, N. A., Mezzich, A. C., & Donovan, J. E. (1995). Identifying anxiety disorders in adolescents hospitalized for alcohol abuse or dependence. *Psychiatric Service, 46,* 618–620.

Clark, D. B., & Sayette, M. A. (1993). *Anxiety and the development of alcoholism. American Journal of Addiction, 2,* 56–76.

Clayton, R. R. (1992). Transitions in drug use: Risk and protective factors. In M. Glantz & R. Pickens (Eds.), *Vulnerability to drug abuse* (pp. 78–101). Washington, DC: American Psychiatric Press.

Cloninger, C. R. (1987). Neurogenetic adaptive mechanisms in alcoholism. *Science, 236,* 410–415.

Cloninger, C. R., Bohman, M., & Sigvardsson, S. (1981). Inheritance of alcohol abuse. *Archives of General Psychiatry, 38,* 861–871.

Coate, D., & Grossman, N. (1987, Fall). Change in alcoholic beverage prices and legal drinking age. *Alcohol Health and Research World,* 22–25.

Cornelius, J. R., Salloum, I. M., Cornelius, M. D., Perel, J. M., Thase, M. E., Ehler, J. G., & Marm, J. (1993). Fluoxetine trial in suicidal depressed alcoholics. *Psychopharmacology Bulletin, 29,* 195–199.

Crumley, F. E. (1990). Substance abuse and adolescent suicidal behavior. *Journal of the American Medical Association, 263,* 3051–3056.

DeMilio, L. (1989). Psychiatric syndromes in adolescent substance abusers. *American Journal of Psychiatry, 146,* 1212–1214.

Deykin, E. Y., Buka, S. L., & Zeena, T. H. (1992). Depressive illness among chemically dependent adolescents. *American Journal of Psychiatry, 149,* 1341–1347.

Deykin, E. Y., Levy, J. C., & Wells, V. (1987). Adolescent depression alcohol and drug abuse. *American Journal of Public Health, 77,* 178–182.

Donovan, J. E., & Jessor, R. (1983). Problem drinking and the dimension of involvement with drugs: A Guttman scalogram analysis of adolescent drug use. *American Journal of Public Health, 73,* 5433–5452.

Doyle, H., Delaney, W., & Trobin, J. (1994). Follow-up study of young attendees at an alcohol unit. *Addiction, 89,* 183–189.

Earls, F., & Jung, K. (1987). Temperament and home environment characteristics in the early development of child psychopathology. *Journal of American Academy and Child Psychiatry, 26,* 491–498.

Ellickson, P. L., & Bell, R. M. (1990). Drug prevention in junior high: A multi-site longitudinal test. *Science, 16,* 1299–1305.

Ewing, J. A. (1984). Detecting alcoholism: The CAGE questionnaire. *Journal of the American Medical Association, 252,* 1905–1907.

Fleisch, B. (1991). *Approaches in the treatment of adolescents with emotional and substance abuse problems* (DHSS Publication No. ADM 91-1744). Washington, DC: U.S. Government Printing Office.

Friedman, A. S., & Beschner, G. M. (Eds.). (1985). *Treatment services for adolescent substance abusers* (DHSS Publication No. ADM 85-1342). Washington, DC: U.S. Government Printing Office.

Friedman, A. S., Granick, S., Kreisher, C., & Terras, A. (1993). Matching adolescents who abuse drugs to treatment. *American Journal of Addiction, 2,* 232–237.

Friedman, A. S., & Utada, A. (1989). A method for diagnosing and planning the treatment of adolescent drug abusers (The Adolescent Drug Abuse Diagnosis [ADAD] Instrument). *Journal of Drug Education, 19,* 285–312.

Glantz, M., & Pickens, R. (Eds.). (1992). *Vulnerability to drug abuse.* Washington DC: American Psychological Association.

Goodwin, D. W. (1985). Alcoholism and genetics: The sins of the fathers. *Archives of General Psychiatry, 42,* 171–174.

Griffiths, M. (1995). *Adolescent gambling.* London, Routledge.

Grilo, C. M., Becker, D. F., Walker, M. L., Levy, K. N., Edell, W. S., & McGlashan, T. H. (1995). Psychiatric comorbidity in adolescent inpatients with substance use disorders. *Journal of the American Academy of Child and Adolescent Psychiatry, 34,* 1085–1091.

Harrison, P. A., & Hoffmann, N. (1989). *CATOR report: Adolescent treatment completers one year later.* St. Paul, MN: Chemical Abuse/Addiction Treatment Outcome Registry.

Hasin, D. S., Grant, B., & Endicott, J. (1990). The natural history of alcohol abuse implications for definitions of alcohol use disorders. *American Journal of Psychiatry, 147,* 337–341.

Henggeler, S. W., Melton, G. B., & Smith, L. A. (1992). Family preservation using multi-systemic therapy: An effective alternative to incarcerating serious juvenile offenders. *Journal of Consulting and Clinical Psychology, 66,* 953–961.

Hoffman, N. G., Halikas, J. A., & Mee-Lee, D. (1987). *The Cleveland admission, discharge, and transfer criteria: Model for chemical dependency treatment programs.* Cleveland: Chemical Dependency Directors Association.

Hovens, J., Cantwell, D. P., & Kiriakos, R. (1994). Psychiatric comorbidity in hospitalized adolescent substance abusers. *Journal of American Academy of Child Adolescent Psychiatry, 33,* 476–483.

Huizinga, D., & Elliot, D. S. (1981). *A longitudinal study of drug use and delinquency in a national sample of youth: An assessment of causal order* (Project Report No. 16, A National Youth Study). Boulder, CO: Behavioral Research Institute.

Institute of Medicine. (1990). *Broadening the base of treatment for alcohol problems.* Washington, DC: National Academy Press.

Jaffe, S. (1990). *Step workbook for adolescent chemical dependency recovery.* Washington, DC: American Academy of Child and Adolescent Psychiatry.

Jessor, R. (1987). Problem-behavior theory, psychosocial development and adolescent problem drinking. *British Journal of Addiction, 82,* 331–342.

Jessor, R., & Jessor, S. L. (1977). *Problem behavior and psychosocial development: A longitudinal study of youth.* New York: Academic Press.

Johnston, L. D., O'Malley, I. M., & Bachman, J. G., (1995, December 11). *News and information.* Ann Arbor: University of Michigan Press.

Kadden, R. M., Cooney, N. L., Getter, H., & Litt, M. B. (1989). Matching alcoholics to coping skills or interactional therapies: Posttreatment results. *Journal of Consulting and Clinical Psychology, 57,* 698–704.

Kaminer, Y. (1992a). Clinical implications of the relationship between attention-deficit/hyperactivity disorder and psychoactive substance use disorders. *American Journal of Addiction, 1,* 257–264.

Kaminer, Y. (1992b). Desipramine facilitation of cocaine abstinence in an adolescent *Journal of American Academy of Child And Adolescent Psychiatry, 31,* 312–317.

Kaminer, Y. (1994). *Adolescent substance abuse: A comprehensive guide to theory and practice.* New York: Plenum.

Kaminer, Y. (1995). Issues in the pharmacological treatment of adolescent substance abuse. *Journal of Child and Adolescent Psychopharmacology, 5,* 93–106.

Kaminer, Y. (1996). Adolescent substance abuse and suicidal behavior. In S. L. Jaffe (Ed.), *Adolescent substance abuse and dual disorders. Child adolescent psychiatry clinics in North America* (pp. 59–72). Philadelphia: Saunders.

Kaminer, Y., Bukstein, O. G., & Tarter, R. E. (1991). The Teen-Addiction Severity Index: Rationale and reliability. *International Journal of Addiction, 26,* 219–226.

Kaminer, Y., Tarter, R. E., Bukstein, O. G., & Kabene, M. (1992). Staff treatment completers' and noncompleters' perception of the value of treatment variables. *American Journal of Addictions, 1,* 115–120.

Kaminer, Y., Wagner, E., Plummer, B., & Seifer, R. (1993). Validation of the Teen-Addiction Severity Index (T-ASI). *American Journal of Addiction, 2,* 250–254.

Kandel, D. B. (1978). *Longitudinal research on drug use: Empirical findings and methodological issues.* New York: Hemisphere-Wiley.

Kandel, D. B. (1982). Epidemiological and psychosocial perspective on adolescent drug use. *Journal of American Academy of Child Psychiatry, 20,* 328–347.

Kashani, J. H., Beck, N. C., Hoeper, E. W., Fallahi, C., Corcoran, C. M., McAllister, J. A., Rosenberg, T. K., & Reid, J. C., (1987). Psychiatric disorders in a community sample of adolescents. *American Journal of Psychiatry, 144,* 584–589.

Kolar, A. F., Brown, B. S., Haertzen, C. A., & Michaelson, B. S. (1994). Children of substance abusers: The life experiences of children of opiate addicts in methadone maintenance. *American Journal of Drug and Alcohol Abuse, 20,* 159–171.

Kranzler, H. R., Burleson, J. A., Korner, P., Del Boca, F. K., Bohn, M. J., Brown, J., & Liebowitz, N. (1995). Placebo-controlled trial of fluoxetine as an adjunct to relapse prevention in alcoholics. *American Journal of Psychiatry, 152,* 391–397.

Kumpfer, K. L., & Demarsh, J. (1986). Future issues and promising directions in the prevention of substance abuse among youth. *Journal of Children in Contemporary Society, 18,* 49–91.

Kushner, M. G., Sher, K. J., & Beitman, B. D. (1990). The relation between alcohol problems and anxiety disorders. *American Journal of Psychiatry, 147,* 685–695.

Kutcher, S., Kachur, E., & Marton, P. (1992). Substance use among adolescents with chronic mental illnesses: A pilot study of descriptive and differentiating features. *Canadian Journal of Psychiatry, 37,* 428–431.

Leccese, M., & Waldron, H. B. (1994). Assessing adolescent substance use: A critique of current measurement instruments. *Journal of Substance Abuse Treatment, 11,* 553–563.

Lettieri, D. J. (1985). Drug abuse: A review of explanations and models of explanation. *Advances in Substance Abuse, 4,* 9–40.

Levin, F. R., & Kleber, H. D. (1995). Attention-deficit/hyperactivity disorder and substance abuse: Relationships and implications for treatment. *Harvard Review of Psychiatry, 2,* 246–258.

Lewinsohn, P. M., Rohde, P., & Seeley, J. R. (1993). Adolescent Psychopathology: III. The Clinical Consequences of comorbidity. *Journal of the American Academy of Child and Adolescent Psychiatry, 34,* 510–519.

Lewinsohn, P. M., Rohde, P., & Seeley, J. (1996). Alcohol consumption in high school adolescents: Frequency of use and dimensional structure of associated problems. *Addiction, 91,* 375–390.

Liddle, H. A., & Dakof, G. A. (1995). Family-based treatment for adolescent drug use: State of the science. In E. Rahdert & D. Czechowicz (Eds.), *Adolescent drug abuse: Clinical assessment and therapeutic interventions* (pp. 218–254). Rockville, MD: National Institute on Drug Abuse.

Litt, M. B., Babor, T. F., DelBoca, F., Kadden, R. M., & Cooney, N. L. (1992). Types of Alcoholics, II: Application of empirically derived typology to treatment matching. *Archives of General Psychiatry, 49,* 609–614.

Loeber, R. (1988). Natural histories of conduct problems, delinquency and associated substance use. In B. B. Lahey & A. E. Kazdin (Eds.), *Advances in clinical child psychology* (Vol. 11, pp. 73–124), New York: Plenum.

Marlatt, G. A., & Gordon, J. R. (Eds.). (1985). *Relapse prevention.* New York: Guilford Press.

Martin, C. S., Kaczynski, N. A., Maisto, S. A., Bukstein, O. G., & Moss, H. B. (1995). Patterns of DSM-IV alcohol abuse and dependence symptoms in adolescent drinkers. *Journal of Studies on Alcohol, 56,* 672–680.

Maziade, M., Caron, C., Cote, P., Boutin, P., & Thivierge, J. (1990). Extreme temperament and diagnosis. A study in a psychiatric sample of consecutive children. *Archives of General Psychiatry, 47,* 477–484.

McLellan, A. T., & Alterman, A. I. (1991). *Patient–treatment matching: A conceptual and methodological view with suggestions for future research in national institute on drug abuse, improving drug abuse treatment* (pp. 114–135). Washington, DC: U.S. Department of Health and Human Services.

McLellan, A. T., Luborsky, L., Woody, G. E., O'Brien, C. P., & Druley, K. A. (1983). Predicting response to alcohol and drug abuse treatment: Role of psychiatric severity. *Archives of General Psychiatry, 40,* 620–628.

Metzger, D. S., Kushner, H., & McLellan, A. T. (1991). *Adolescent Problem Severity Index. Administration manual.* Philadelphia: Biomedical Computer Research Institute.

Meyer, R. E. (1986). How to understand the relationship between psychopathology and addictive disorders: Another example of the chicken and the egg. In R. Meyer (Ed.), *Psychopathology and addictive disorders* (pp. 284–291). New York: Guilford Press.

Milin, R., Halikas, J. A., Meller, J. E., & Morse, C. (1991). Psychopathology among substance abusing juvenile offenders. *Journal of the American Academy of Child and Adolescent Psychiatry, 30,* 569–574.

Moss, H. B., Kirisci, L., Gordon, H. W., & Tarter, R. E. (1994). A neuropsychological profile of adolescent alcoholics. *Alcoholism: Clinical and Experimental Research, 18,* 159–163.

Moss, H. B., & Tarter, R. E. (1993). Substance abuse, aggression and violence: What are the connections? *American Journal of Addiction, 2,* 149–160.

Myers, M. G., & Brown, S. A. (1990). Coping responses and relapse among adolescent substance abusers. *Journal of Substance Abuse, 2,* 177–190.

Myers, M. G., Brown, S. A., & Mott, M. A. (1995). Preadolescent conduct disorder behaviors predict relapse and progression of addiction for adolescent alcohol and drug abusers. *Alcoholism: Clinical and Experimental Research, 19,* 1528–1536.

Myers, W. C., Donaue, J. E., & Goldstein, M. R. (1994). Disulfiram for alcohol use disorders in adolescents. *Journal of the American Academy of Child and Adolescent Psychiatry, 33,* 484–489.

Naranjo, C. A., Kadlec, K. E., Sanheuza, P., Woodley-Remus, D., & Sellars, E. M. (1990). Fluoxetine differentially alters alcohol intake and other consummatory behavior in problem drinkers. *Clinical Pharmacology Therapy, 47,* 490–498.

Newcomb, M. D. (1995). Identifying high-risk youth: Prevalence and patterns of adolescent drug abuse. In E. Rahdert & D. Czechowicz (Eds.), *Adolescent drug abuse: Clinical assessment and therapeutic interventions* (NIH Publication No. 95-3908, pp. 7–38). Rockville, MD: National Institute on Drug Abuse.

Noll, R. B., Zucker, R. A., Fitzgerald, H. E., & Curtis, W. J. (1992). Cognitive and motoric functioning of sons of alcoholic fathers and controls: The early childhood years. *Developmental Psychology, 28,* 665–675.

O'Malley, P. M., Johnston, L. D., & Bachman, J. G. (1995). Adolescent substance use: Epidemiology and implications for public policy. In P. D. Rogers & M. J. Werner (Eds.), *Substance abuse, pediatric clinical North America* (pp. 241–260). Philadelphia: Saunders.

O'Malley, P. M., & Wagenaar, A. C. (1991). Effects of minimum drinking age laws on alcohol use, related behaviors and traffic crash involvement among American youth: 1976–1987. *Journal of Studies on Alcohol, 52,* 478–491.

Pentz, M. A., Dwyer, J. H., & MacKinnon, D. P. (1989). A multicommunity trial for primary prevention of adolescent drug abuse. *Journal of the American Medical Association, 261,* 3259–3266.

Rahdert, E. (Ed.). (1991). *The adolescent assessment and referral system manual* (DHHS Publication No. ADM 91-1735). Rockville, MD: National Institute on Drug Abuse.

Regier, D. A., Farmer, M. E., Rae, D. S., Locke, B. Z., Keith, S. J., Judd, L. L., & Goodwin, F. R. (1990). Comorbidity of mental disorders with alcohol and other drug abuse. *Journal of the American Medical Association, 264,* 2511–2518.

Reich, T., Cloninger, P., Van Eerdevegh, J. P., Rice, J. R., & Mullaney, J. (1988). Secular trends in the familial transmission of alcoholism. *Alcoholism: Clinical and Experimental Research, 12,* 458–464.

Reich, W., Earls, F., Frankel, O., & Shayka, J. (1993). Psychopathology in children of alcoholics. *Journal of the American Academy of Child and Adolescent Psychiatry, 32,* 995–1002.

Reinherz, H. Z., Giaconia, R. M., Lefkowitz, E. S., Pakiz, B., & Frost, A. K. (1993). Prevalence of psychiatric disorders in a community population of older adolescents. *Journal of the American Academy of Child and Adolescent Psychiatry, 32,* 369–377.

Riggs, P. D., Baker S., Mikulich, S. K., Young, S. E., & Crowley, T. J. (1995). Depression in substance-dependent delinquents. *Journal of the American Academy of Child and Adolescent Psychiatry, 34,* 764–771.

Rohde, P., Lewinsohn, P. M., & Seeley, J. R. (1996). Psychiatric comorbidity with problematic alcohol use in high school students. *Journal of the American Academy of Child and Adolescent Psychiatry, 35,* 101–109.

Schaeffer, K., Parson, O., & Yohman, J. (1984). Neuropsychological differences between male familial alcoholics and nonalcoholics. *Alcoholism: Clinical and Experimental Research, 8,* 347–351.

Schaps, E., Moskowitz, J., & Malvin, J. (1986). Evaluation of seven school based prevention programs: A final report of the Napa report. *International Journal of Addictions, 21,* 1081–1112.

Schinke, S. P., Botvin, G. J., & Orlani, M. A. (1991). *Substance abuse in children and adolescent: Evaluation and intervention.* Newbury Park, CA: Sage.

Schuckit, M. A. (1986). Genetic and clinical implications of alcoholism and affective disorder. *American Journal of Psychiatry, 143,* 140–147.

Schuckit, M. A., Zisook, S., & Mortola, J. (1985). Clinical implications of DSM-III diagnosis of alcohol abuse and alcohol dependence. *American Journal of Psychiatry, 142,* 1403–1408.

Shedler, J., & Block, J. (1990). Adolescent drug use and psychological health: A longitudinal inquiry. *American Psychology, 45,* 612–630.

Sigvardsson, S., Bohman, M., & Cloninger, C. R. (1996). Replication of the Stockholm adoption study of alcoholism: Confirmatory cross-fostering analysis. *Archives of General Psychiatry, 53,* 681–688.

Sobell, M. B., & Sobell, L. C. (1993). Treatment for problem drinkers. In J. S. Baer, G. A. Marlatt, & R. J. McMahon (Eds.), *Addictive behaviors across the life span* (pp. 138–152). Newbury Park, CA: Sage.

Stewart, D. G., & Brown, S. A. (1995). Withdrawal and dependency symptoms among adolescent alcohol and drug abusers. *Addiction, 90,* 627–635.

Stowell, R. J. (1991). Dual diagnosis issues. *Psychiatry Annals, 21,* 98–104.

Szapocznik, J., Kurtines, W. M., Foote, F. H., Perez-Vidal, A., & Hervis, O. (1983). Conjoint versus one-person family therapy: Some evidence for the effectiveness of conducing family therapy through one person. *Journal of Consulting and Clinical Psychology, 51,* 889–899.

Szapocznik, J., Perez-Vidal, A., Briskman, A. L., Foote, F. H., Santisteban, D., & Hervis, O. (1988). Engaging adolescent drug abusers and their families in treatment. *Journal of Consulting and Clinical Psychology, 56,* 552–557.

Tarter, R. E. (1990). Evaluation and treatment of adolescent substance abuse: A decision tree method. *American Journal of Drug and Alcohol Abuse, 16,* 1–46.

Tarter, R. E. (1992). Prevention of drug abuse: Theory and application. *American Journal of Addiction, 1,* 2–20.

Tarter, R. E., Kirisci, L., Hegedus, A., Mezich, A., & Yanyukov, M. (1994). Heterogeneity of adolescent alcoholism. In T. F. Babor, V. Hesselbrock, R. E. Meyer, & W. Shoemaker (Eds.), *Types of alcoholics: Evidence from clinical, experimental and genetic research* (pp. 172–180). New York: Annals of the New York Academy of Science.

Tarter, R. E., Laird, S. B., & Moss, H. B. (1990). Neuropsychological and neurophysiological characteristics of children of alcoholics. In M. Windle & J. S. Searles (Eds.), *Children of alcoholics: critical perspectives* (pp. 73–98). New York: Guilford Press.

Tarter, R. E., Laird, S. B., Mostefa, K., Bukstein, O. G., & Kaminer, Y. (1990). Drug abuse severity in adolescents is associated with magnitude of deviation in temperamental traits. *British Journal of Addiction, 85,* 1501–1504.

Tobler, N. S. (1986). Meta-analysis of 143 adolescent drug prevention programs: Quantitative outcome results of program participants compared to a control or comparison group. *Journal of Drug Issues, 16,* 537–567.

Tuchfeld, B. S., Clayton, R. R., & Logan, J. A. (1982). Alcohol, drug use and delinquent and criminal behaviors among male adolescents and young adults. *Journal of Drug Issues, 2,* 185–198.

Van Hasselt, V. B., Null, J. A., Kempton, T., & Bukstein, O. G. (1993). Social skills and depression in adolescent substance abusers. *Addictive Behaviors, 18,* 9–18.

Vik, P. W., Grisel, K., & Brown, S. A. (1992). Social resource characteristics and adolescent substance abuse relapse. *Journal of Adolescent Chemical Dependency, 2,* 59–74.

White, H. R., & Labouvie, E. W. (1989). Towards the assessment of adolescent problem drinking. *Journal of Studies on Alcohol, 50,* 30–37.

Wilens, T. E., Biederman, J., Kiely, K., Bredin, E., & Spencer, T. J. (1995). Pilot study of behavioral and emotional disturbances in the high-risk children of parents with opioid dependence. *Journal of the American Academy of Child and Adolescent Psychiatry, 34,* 779–785.

Wilens, T. E., Biederman, J., Spencer, T. J., & Frances, R. J. (1994). Comorbidity of attention-deficit disorder and psychoactive substance use disorders. *Hospital and Community Psychiatry, 45,* 421–435.

Wilson, J. R., & Crowe, L. (1991). Genetics of alcoholism: Can and should youth at risk be identified? *Alcohol Health World Report, 15,* 11–17.

Winters, K. C. (1990). The need for improved assessment of adolescent substance involvement. *Journal of Drug Issues, 20,* 487–502.

Winters, K. C. (1992). Development of an adolescent alcohol and drug abuse screening scale: Personal Experience Screening Questionnaire. *Addictive Behavior, 17,* 479–490.

Winters, K. C., & Henly, G. (1988). *Personal Experience Inventory (PEI).* Los Angeles: Western Psychological Services.

Winters, K. C., & Stinchfield, R. D. (1995). Current issues and future needs in the assessment if adolescent drug abuse. In E. Rahdert & D. Czechowicz (Eds.), *Adolescent drug abuse: Clinical assessment and therapeutic interventions* (NIDA Research Monograph No. 156, pp. 146–171). Rockville, MD: National Institute on Drug Abuse.

Wold, M., & Kaminer, Y. (1997). Naltrexone for adolescent alcohol use disorders. *Journal of the American Academy of Child and Adolescent Psychiatry 36,* 6–7.

Wolin, S., & Wolin, S. J. (1996). The challenge model: Working with strengths in children of substance-abusing parents. In S. L. Jaffe (Ed.), *Adolescent substance abuse and dual disorders: Child and adolescent psychiatry clinics of North America* (pp. 243–255). Philadelphia: Saunders.

15

Geriatric Addictions

ROBERT C. ABRAMS
GEORGE S. ALEXOPOULOS

INTRODUCTION

The scope and extent of geriatric alcoholism are poorly appreciated by the general public and also by many medical practitioners. In part this reflects the newness of geriatric alcoholism as a topic of investigation (Atkinson, 1984; Blixen, McDougall, & Suen, 1997; Glynn, Bouchard, LoCastro, & Laird, 1985). Lack of disseminated knowledge is compounded by unique difficulties in the detection of alcoholism in the geriatric population. At the same time, the medical and psychiatric consequences of alcohol consumption are probably greatest for older persons. The pervasiveness of alcohol in contemporary society, coupled with the demographic and political importance of the elderly population, ensures an increasing focus on geriatric alcoholism—if not an increasing prevalence—in the future.

That greater attention will be paid to the abuse and misuse of prescription and nonprescription drugs by the elderly can also be predicted. Persons over 65 years of age account for a majority of *all* medications used in the United States, especially drugs targeted for the management of chronic conditions. Thus, the addictions that appear in geriatric patients differ from those of younger groups, both in the selection of drugs and in their clinical course. As is required for older alcoholics, treatment of geriatric patients with addiction to prescription or over-the-counter drugs requires sensitivity to the life circumstances, physiological changes, and concurrent medical and psychiatric disorders of this population. Following the discussion of geriatric alcoholism, this chapter separately considers geriatric addictions in prescription and nonprescription drugs, reviewing current knowledge and treatment approaches in each area.

GERIATRIC ALCOHOLISM

Epidemiology

General Age Trends

Cross-sectional data suggest that heavy drinking is most frequent in early middle age. In a classic study based on national survey data, Cahalan, Cisin, and Crossley (1969) found that heavy drinking peaked in the 40- to 49-year age group and declined thereafter. In the same study, the authors reported a sharp decline in the percentage of heavy drinkers among men from the 60- to 64-year age group to the over-65-year age group (from 20% to 7%). A corresponding reduction in the percentage of heavy drinkers among women was also shown but occurred earlier, at age 50. Abstinence rates for both men and women tend to increase steadily by decade (Barnes, 1979; Cahalan et al., 1969; Christopherson, Escher, & Bainton, 1984).

Closer examination of the over-60 age group reveals small but potentially meaningful deviations from the trends outlined previously. For example, some investigators suggested the possibility of an increase in alcohol abuse after 70 years of age (McCourt, Williams, & Schneider, 1971; Barnes, 1979). In Barnes's data, based on a general population survey in western New York State, heavy drinkers accounted for 24% of males ages 60–69 and 6% of males ages 70–96; among women in the study, heavy drinkers were not represented at all in the 60–69 age group yet comprised 2% of those ages 70–79. Thus, cross-sectional evidence suggests the existence of a subpopulation of alcoholics whose problem drinking begins in advanced age, distinct both from younger alcoholics and from same-age alcoholics having earlier onset. This subgroup may involve women to a greater extent than men, a possibility supported by the Framingham study, which reported a significant overall 20-year rise in alcohol consumption based largely on increases attributable to women (Gordon & Kannel, 1983). Within the over-60 population, higher-income subgroups consume more alcohol overall than lower-income subgroups (Herd, 1990), but according to data from the Epidemiologic Catchment Area (ECA) study, higher-income elderly men have a lower rate of alcoholism than lower-income elderly men (Helzer, Burnam, & McEvoy, 1991). No clear relationship has yet emerged between ethnic origin or geographic area of residence and alcoholism among the elderly, although higher rates of light drinking among whites than nonwhites have been reported (Liberto, Oslin, & Ruskin, 1992).

It has been suggested that cross-sectional prevalence data may be biased because subjects with the most severe alcoholism may have died from the medical consequences of alcoholism or been institutionalized (Caracci & Miller, 1991). Also, the failure of many cross-sectional studies to assess lifetime as well as point prevalence may lead to underestimation of geriatric alcoholism, as lifetime prevalences tend to be higher (Holzer, Robbins, & Myers, 1984). Finally, data from one of the few longitudinal studies in this area suggest that despite the lower rates of alcohol dependence and abuse in successively older cohorts, individuals may not necessarily reduce their alcohol consumption as they age (Glynn et al., 1985). Stability of individual drinking patterns, together with the less restrictive attitudes toward drinking in recent generations, may provide the basis for a future increase in geriatric alcoholism.

Prevalence of Geriatric Alcoholism in the Community

The prevalence of geriatric alcoholism among elderly living in the community still cannot be asserted with precision. Estimates of problem drinking, loosely defined as patterns of abuse or dependence leading to significant social or health consequences, have produced prevalence rates ranging from 4% to 20% in community surveys of geriatric populations in Britain and the United States (Atkinson, Ganzini, & Bernstein, 1992; Bridgewater, Leigh, James, & Potter, 1987; Calahan et al., 1969; Meyers, Hingson, Mucatel, & Goldman, 1982); these are lower than cross-sectional prevalence estimates for younger cohorts. Data from the ECA Study, representing the largest community sample assessed to date as well as the first national survey to use criteria, according to the *Diagnostic and Statistical Manual of Mental Disorders* (DSM), for alcoholism rather than estimates of alcohol consumption, suggest that alcoholism is the third most frequent disorder in the geriatric population, with rates of 1.9% to 4.6% in elderly men (Myers et al., 1984); the male predominance persists from younger ages despite the overall decline in cross-sectional prevalence.

However, differences in reported community prevalence rates of alcoholism among the elderly appear to be related to the specific site of the investigation as well as the definitions of alcohol abuse or dependence, both of which vary from study to study. For instance, it has been estimated that from 10% to 15% of all elderly persons seeking medical help are found to have an alcohol-related problem (Blixen, 1988). Alcohol abuse is probably more frequent in the community than alcohol dependence; however, there is no consensus on the specific amounts of alcohol intake that comprise "problem" or "heavy" drinking, except that because of age-associated changes in metabolism leading to decreased tolerance, these amounts are generally acknowledged to be smaller in older compared to younger adults. Another caution in the interpretation of community prevalence data in the elderly is that geriatric populations over age 60 or 65 are not homogeneous; within the "elderly" population, subgroups of patients in their mid-70s and older can have dramatically lower cross-sectional rates of alcoholism than those closer to age 60 (Barnes, 1979). The relatively low percentage of abstainers in retirement communities (21.5%, compared to 45% in the general population) (Alexander & Duff, 1988) may reflect the specifically middle- and upper-middle-class orientation of retirement communities and the important role of alcohol in their social structure. The cocktail hour remains a focal event in the daily life of many retirement communities.

Prevalence of Alcoholism in the Institutionalized Elderly

Community studies have been criticized for failing to include the most severe alcoholics, specifically those who have been institutionalized, in some cases as a result of their drinking (Caracci & Miller, 1991). For this reason, separate surveys of alcohol abuse and dependence among the institutionalized or hospitalized elderly have been undertaken. In general, the frequency of alcoholism diagnoses in the institutionalized geriatric population appears to be substantially higher than in the community at large. In an early study of 279 state and county mental hospitals, Kramer (1969) found a rate of 30% among new admissions ages 55 to 64 who were reported to be suffering from alcoholism, but a rate of only 9% in the population ages 65 to 74. Studies using clinical a diagnosis of alcoholism (vs. the amount consumed) in elderly medical and psychiatric inpatients have produced prevalence estimates of 18% and 44%, respectively (Schuckit & Miller, 1976; Gaitz & Baer, 1971). Lifetime comorbidity rates for mental illness and substance abuse in prison populations, including elderly subjects, have been reported to be as high as 94% (Abram & Teplin, 1991). High rates of lifetime alcohol abuse have been found in the elderly deinstitutionalized homeless (Caton, Shrout, Eagle, Opler, & Felix, 1994) and also on admission in nursing-home populations (Caracci & Miller, 1991); for example, a 53% lifetime prevalence of alcohol abuse was recently reported for elderly subjects residing in a veterans' long-term care facility (Herrmann & Erlyavec, 1996). The prevalence of alcohol-related hospitalizations in the over-65 population in the United States, based on Medicare claims data, has been estimated to be 54.7% for men and 14.8% for women, comparable to rates for myocardial infarction in the same age group (Adams, Zhong, Barboriak, & Rimm, 1993).

Data on Dual Diagnoses

Although the co-occurence of alcohol and substance abuse disorders with other psychiatric disorders among younger adult patients has become a topic of interest in recent years, relatively little is known about the prevalence of these "dual diagnoses" in the elderly. In younger adults, dual diagnosis patients often present with histories of polysubstance abuse, antisocial behavior, and homelessness (Mulvey, 1994). In older populations, dual-diagnosis patients tend to have mood or personality disorders and may represent as many as one-third of geriatric inpatient psychiatry admissions (Blixen et al., 1997; Mears & Spice, 1993; Speer, 1990). Geriatric dual-diagnosis patients frequently also present with complex medical conditions which may be etiologically or temporally related to either the mood or substance abuse disorder; thus, in the elderly, "dual" diagnosis might be more accurately termed "treble" diagnosis. However they are styled, elderly patients with a combined picture of alcohol abuse, depression, and significant medical illness probably comprise the group at highest risk for suicide in the general population (Conwell & Brent, 1995; Moscicki, 1995).

Additional Methodological Issues

Precision of the prevalence estimates summarized previously is to some degree compromised by methodological problems. First, most of these data are derived from self-report methods, which rely on the truthfulness, or accuracy of memory, of subjects in describing their drinking behavior. The elderly, perhaps for reasons of shame, may be even more reluctant to acknowledge their drinking than are younger subjects and, because of cognitive impairment, less likely to recall it (Saunders et al., 1991). True binge drinkers may have experienced amnestic episodes. Also, the definition of alcohol abuse in terms of quantity and frequency may need to be tailored specifically to elderly subjects, for whom the medical, functional, and social consequences of alcohol are likely to be more serious at smaller amounts of intake than for younger adults. Mears and Spice (1993) suggested that 14 "units" of alcohol ingestion per week may be a critical threshold, above which the adverse medical and social consequences of alcoholism become clinically important; however, as already noted, no such definition has been universally accepted. A wide range of conventional structured and unstructured instruments has been used to assess the extent of alcohol use, but like the CAGE questionnaire (Bernadt, Mumford, Taylor, Smith, & Murray, 1982), they lack validation in the elderly. The specificity and sensitivity of biochemical tests are low (Penn & Worthington, 1983).

Essentially only the DSM-IV (American Psychiatric Association, 1994) criteria emphasize the multiple social, health, and functional consequences of drinking behavior; however, even clinicians may confuse them with age-related cognitive or physical changes. Constellations of particular symptoms, although in themselves not unique to the elderly, have been proposed as useful in screening for alcohol abuse in this population (Mears & Spice, 1993). Such symptoms include blackouts, accidents, incontinence, and obvious neglect of hygiene and self-care. Another useful "geriatric" marker may be decline in overall functioning (Axis V of DSM-III, DSM-III-R, and DSM-IV), particularly if broadened in definition to include activities of daily living (ADL); Blow, Loveland Cook, Booth, Falcon, and Friedman (1992) showed that severely impaired functioning in elderly alcoholic veterans was associated with severity of alcoholism and with comorbid psychiatric diagnosis. Again, however, there is no consensus on the usefulness of any of these factors in screening, clinical diagnosis or epidemiological studies. Difficulties in the interpretation of prevalence estimates owing to the exclusive use of cross-sectional data are described in the section "General Age Trends."

Clinical Features

Age of Onset

The division of geriatric alcoholics into clinical subgroups according to age of onset has become generally accepted (Atkinson, 1984; Mishara & Kastenbaum, 1980). The late-onset classification in some studies refers to onset of illness after

60 (Simon, Epstein, & Reynolds, 1968; Rosin & Glatt, 1971) and represents a category of patients who begin to abuse alcohol late in life. In other studies, the age of 40 is used as the demarcation between early- and late-onset alcoholism (Schuckit & Miller, 1976; Atkinson, Turner, Kofoed, & Tolson, 1985). The early-onset classification represents the category of patients who have established a pattern of continuous abuse in early adulthood. Among patients over the age of 60 who have been hospitalized or come to psychiatric attention for alcoholism, approximately one-third will have become alcoholic after the age of 60 (late onset), whereas two-thirds will have had a long history of alcohol abuse (early onset) (Rosin & Glatt, 1971). As a rule, the early-onset patients have social and medical histories that reflect the disruption of chronic alcohol abuse and have more family alcoholism and less current psychological stability than do late-onset patients (Atkinson et al., 1985).

Irrespective of the arbitrarily defined cutoff age for late-onset alcoholism, research suggests that many actively drinking older alcoholics first developed clinically significant abuse or dependence in their 40s or 50s (Schuckit, 1982). This hypothesis is supported by the greater chance of early death among individuals whose alcoholism begins in late adolescence or early adulthood. A corollary finding is that elderly alcoholics as a group (i.e., including both early- and late-onset individuals) tend to have had less criminality, fewer contacts with the mental health system, and more overall stability early in life than younger alcoholics (Schuckit, 1982).

Although late-onset alcoholism has been conceptualized as a maladaptive response to age-related life events rather than the product of long-standing psychosocial problems (Dupree, Broskowski, & Schonfeld, 1984), the relationship between recent stressors and the development of late-onset alcoholism remains conjectural (Caracci & Miller, 1991), with no consistent evidence of association, at least in nonclinical populations, between life events and the development of alcohol abuse in old age (Borgatta, Montgomery, & Borgata, 1982; LaGreca, Akers, & Dwyer, 1988). For example, in a survey of 1,410 noninstitutionalized adults over age 60 living in both retirement and age-integrated communities, LaGreca et al. (1988) found that the majority of respondents (73.6%) had experienced at least one significantly stressful life event in the past year, including most frequently the death of a family member or close friend, personal health problems, or family members with health problems. The authors found no association between the occurrence of life events and the frequency, quantity, or negative consequences of drinking. In addition, social supports appeared to have little modifying impact with respect to drinking behavior. These findings tend to challenge the conventional view of late-onset alcoholism as having a direct relationship to recent negative life events (Dupree et al., 1984).

Course

Largely because of a dearth of longitudinal data, the course of geriatric alcoholism has not been firmly established. However, several key findings have become accepted in recent years. First, later age of onset is associated with a better prognosis (Schuckit, 1982). Second, there is greater heterogeneity in the lifetime drinking patterns of the elderly than the previous discussion of late- and early-onset alcoholism would seem to suggest. For example, Dunham (1981) described a range of distinct lifetime patterns of alcohol abuse. These patterns include "rise and sustained," involving long-standing heavy drinking, which continues into old age; "light and late rise," involving moderate drinking throughout most of adult life, which continues with variable increases into old age; "late starter," the true late-onset alcoholism; and "highly variable," involving an erratic pattern of drinking from early adulthood to old age. Another pattern is the "inactive," involving a history of significant alcoholism but not in the recent past; more often than not, these individuals remain symptom free in old age. However, longitudinal data describing *the elderly population as a whole* (i.e., not confined to known alcoholics) support the *overall* persistence of individual drinking patterns over time (Adams, Garry, Rhyne, Hunt, & Goodwin, 1990; Glynn et al., 1985). Complete abstainers are likely to remain abstinent, and light drinkers are likely to remain light drinkers. Only the heaviest drinkers within the larger geriatric population may significantly decrease alcohol consumption over long periods (Caracci & Miller, 1991).

Consequences of Geriatric Alcoholism

Overview

The deleterious consequences of alcohol abuse in the elderly have been extensively described in the literature (Liberto et al., 1992; Atkinson, 1984; Mishara & Kastenbaum, 1980). However, the range of alcohol-related prob- lems in the nonalcoholic geriatric population is less well-known. General metabolic changes of aging, including decreased activity of hepatic enzymes and reduction of lean body mass, result in slowed metabolic breakdown and elimination of all drugs. Alcohol, because it is water soluble, is distributed through a relatively small mass of lean tissue and therefore is found in higher concentrations within organs. Blood alcohol levels persist for longer periods. Moreover, aging is associated with increased sensitivity to all central nervous system (CNS)-depressing agents, including alcohol (Gambert, 1997; Raskind & Eisdorfer, 1976). These factors influence tolerance of alcohol, which is usually described as decreasing with age (Gambert, 1997; Bosmann, 1984). Thus, nonalcoholic elderly patients with pulmonary disease may experience potentially dangerous acute effects on respiration secondary to CNS responses to alcohol, cardiovascular patients may experience a masking of anginal pain without reduction in the potential for myocardial damage, and in all elderly individuals, relatively small amounts of alcohol are more likely to produce acute confusional states with associated risk falls, auto accidents, fractures, hematomas, and a host of other adverse consequences.

Alcohol affects virtually every organ system and physiological process.

For example, habitual heavy alcohol consumption can lead to erectile and ejaculatory impotence in the male. Although alcohol does not appear to affect total sleep time and may actually aid in sleep onset by reducing latency, rebound wakefulness and anxiety often occur later in the night in response to falling blood alcohol levels; also, REM (rapid eye movement) and delta sleep are markedly reduced, resulting in irritability, impaired concentration, and fatigue (Gambert, 1997).

Effects on Chronic Illnesses

Because elderly persons are already likely to have more than one chronic illness, chronic alcohol ingestion results in exacerbation of preexisting conditions, as well as new chronic illnesses. To cite only a few, chronic alcohol abuse is known to be associated with exacerbation of already impaired cardiac functioning in arteriosclerotic cardiovascular disease by increasing cardiac fibrosis and microvascular infarcts and swelling (Alexander, 1975; Factor, 1976), and chronic alcohol use may also be a primary cause of chronic cardiac disease via direct associations with hyperlipidemia, hypertension, and cardiomyopathy (Pintar, Wolanskyj, & Buggay, 1965). Against these factors, the putative cardioprotective effects of moderate drinking are minimal. Similarly, a range of liver toxicity, from early fatty changes to frank cirrhosis, can be both caused and accelerated by chronic alcoholism. The chronic gastritis commonly found in elderly alcoholics is itself associated with anemia, as are folate and vitamin B12 deficiencies. As noted later in the chapter, alcohol abuse is associated with suicide in the elderly and probably with other adverse effects on the outcomes of geriatric major depressive disorder. In addition, the course of many other chronic illnesses can be affected indirectly by the nutritional deficiencies that occur frequently in elderly alcoholics, particularly protein-calorie malnutrition as well as other factors associated with the alcoholic lifestyle, including negligent hygiene, poor medical care, and homelessness. It is not surprising, therefore, that alcoholism in the elderly is associated with an increased overall mortality (Olsen-Noll & Bosworth, 1989).

Drug Interactions

The potential for adverse drug interactions involving alcohol is also greater in the elderly, who are likely to be taking multiple prescription or over-the-counter medications at any given time. Alcohol-induced potentiation of CNS depressants such as barbiturates and benzodiazepines occurs more readily and at lower doses than in younger persons and can cause respiratory depression and death. Alcohol-induced inhibition of the metabolism of many other agents, including commonly prescribed psychiatric medications such as antipsychotics and antidepressants, can lead to toxic states; in the elderly, toxicity associated with antidepressant and mood-stabilizing medications can occur even when measured blood levels are in the standard "therapeutic" range.

Associations with Dementia and Depression

Cognitive impairment is among the most clinically important consequences of alcoholism. Among elderly alcoholics, the prevalence of dementia has been estimated to be between 25% and 60% (Bienenfeld, 1990). The alcohol-related dementia syndrome usually appears after 10 years or more of alcohol abuse, but unlike dementia of other etiologies, it is not necessarily progressive if the patient abstains from alcohol after the onset of cognitive compromise; however, it is probably not reversible either (Saunders et al., 1991). The alcohol dementia syndrome is characterized by intact registration (immediate repetition of a list), impaired recent memory (free recall of a list after a 5-minute delay), retrieval deficit syndrome (free recall is impaired, but performance can be corrected with clueing), frontal lobe dysfunction (e.g., set shifting and adherence to a complex task), constructional disturbance, and intact language function (e.g., naming) (Reichman, 1994). Some of the dementias found among elderly alcoholics are attributable to thiamine deficiency leading to Wernicke's encephalopathy, a subacute condition which can present initially with isolated memory impairment and is therefore not strictly a dementia syndrome at that stage. If the thiamine deficiency is severe or prolonged, a Wernicke–Korsakoff syndrome may result, producing an amnestic syndrome with impaired registration and free recall as well as absence of improvement in recall by cluing. In general, the clinical characteristics of the alcohol-related dementia, the degree of response to treatment with thiamine, and serial mental status testing following a period of abstinence may all help to distinguish alcohol-related dementias from degenerative, vascular, or other dementing disorders. Nevertheless, exacerbation by alcohol of primary degenerative or vascular (multi-infarct) dementia and direct CNS alcohol toxicity are each more common than the alcohol dementias just described. The clinician must learn to distinguish true dementia syndromes—chronic and involving multiple cognitive functions—from the acute-onset confusional states that can be brought on by alcohol intoxication or withdrawal and from the subacute disorders associated with alcoholics' nutritional deficiencies (Schuckit, 1982).

Depression symptoms of varying intensity are nearly universal in alcohol abuse and are usually regarded as being secondary to the abrupt drop in blood alcohol levels following an episode of heavy drinking (Schuckit, 1983) as well as to general CNS depressant effects of alcohol or the exacerbating effects of alcohol on an underlying depressive syndrome. Also, preliminary data suggest an association between alcohol abuse in early or mid-adulthood and the subsequent development of depressive symptoms later in life, an association not explained by current drinking patterns (Saunders et al., 1991), but detailed information on the implications of alcoholism for the frequency, severity, and chronicity of depressive episodes in the elderly is lacking. Depression itself may be a risk factor for the development of late-onset alcoholism; similarly, an association between the severity of combat stress and alcohol use in old age has been reported in a sample of World War II veterans (Hermann &

Eryavec, 1996). The terms "primary" and "secondary," frequently applied to either depression/anxiety symptoms or to alcoholism, may somewhat oversimplify the complex relationships between disorders. However, alcoholism is well established as a risk factor for suicide in the elderly, particularly in the context of comorbid major depression. Research estimates that alcohol is associated with 25–50% of suicides in this age group (Blumenthal, 1988).

Detection and Treatment

Detection

Alcoholism is less likely to be detected and treated in the geriatric population. Several reasons for this phenomenon have been proposed (Caracci & Miller, 1991). First, the impairments in social and occupational functioning attributed to alcoholism in younger adults are not as obvious, or simply not relevant, in the elderly. Losses of jobs, driver's licenses, and active roles in society are inevitable experiences for aging persons, alcoholics or not. Further, the medical and social correlates of alcoholism can be difficult to distinguish from those of aging itself. As described in the preceding section, the effects of chronic alcohol abuse on cognitive functioning in the elderly may be confused with the deficits associated with primary degenerative or vascular dementia; preexisting medical conditions can defy differentiation from those that are etiologically linked to chronic alcoholism; and, again, life events causing disruption of social supports, such as loss of job or spouse, are essentially normative milestones for older persons and thus of little use in detection of alcohol abuse.

In addition, elderly alcoholics are unlikely to have a primary care physician (Holroyd, Currie, Thompson-Heisterman, & Abraham, 1997), thus depriving them of an obvious route of detection, that is, consecutive longitudinal follow-up by a physician who can observe changes instead of being limited to cross-sectional observations, as occurs when emergency room visits are the primary source of medical care. Of course, some physicians are themselves "enablers," either encouraging or passively permitting the alcoholic to persist in drinking. When physicians are involved, this relaxation of the usual professional vigilance may represent an insidious age bias, which, in turn, reflects that of the larger society. Another possibility is that the physician may be alcoholic himself or herself.

Age has been identified as a general risk factor for inadequate medical treatment by health care personnel (Wetle, 1987). In a much-quoted study of medical inpatients at Johns Hopkins Hospital, only 37% of elderly individuals identified as alcoholics by standard screening tests were identified as such by their house officers; in contrast, 60% of screen-positive younger patients were identified as alcoholics by their house officers. Even when correctly diagnosed by their physicians, elderly patients were less likely than younger patients to receive treatment for their alcoholism.

Gender may also influence detection in geriatric alcoholism. Although geriatric alcoholism has a male predominance, evidence suggests that, at least in a rural setting, elderly female alcoholics may more frequently engage in solitary, secret, or "hidden" drinking and also shun treatment settings (Holroyd et al., 1997); thus, elderly females may more readily escape detection of alcoholism. Typically, the use of collateral sources of information, particularly family members, is required to uncover the "hidden" elderly drinkers.

Regardless of the degree of access to medical care, alcohol dependence or abuse is unlikely to be the chief complaint; this is true for all age groups. In an older person, unexpected or unwarranted reaction to a prescription or over-the-counter drug may be the first indication of alcohol abuse or dependence. Acute or subacute changes in sensorium or cognitive functioning, as well as florid psychotic symptoms such as delusions and hallucinations, particularly in patients without prior history of such symptoms, provide additional clues to possible alcoholism. An "inclusive" approach is generally recommended (i.e., not ruling out the possibility of alcoholism because of potentially confounding comorbid disorders). Neither should denial of symptoms be taken completely at face value; this is a nearly universal phenomenon in alcoholic patients, at least in the early phases of the illness, and can take on a seemingly impenetrable aspect in older persons. The index of suspicion should be high in all cases.

Treatment

Treatment usually begins with detoxification, which in all but the mildest cases should take place in a hospital setting. Hospitalization is recommended because of the need for careful medical monitoring and the high frequency of concurrent medical problems. The use of short-acting benzodiazepines, such as lorazepam, is generally preferred (Bienenfeld, 1990) to avoid potentially toxic accumulations of drug, although some clinicians prescribe the intermediate-acting chlordiazepoxide, which may result in a "smoother" detoxification, producing neither toxic buildup with prolonged sedation nor the drug-seeking behavior associated with other benzodiazepines (Miller, Belkin, & Gold, 1991). In setting the pace of the detoxification, clinicians should be mindful that geriatric patients are sensitive to relatively small-dose increments of all pharmacological agents, and elderly patients may require only one-third to one-half of the doses of benzodiazepines needed to protect against withdrawal symptoms in younger adults. Detoxification may unavoidably be a lengthier procedure for these patients; although anxiety and most depressive symptoms may resolve within days, full withdrawal using tapering schedules of short-acting benzodiazepines may require 1 or 2 weeks.

It is also recommended that debilitated elderly patients be given thiamine in three daily intramuscular doses of 100 mg, followed by oral thiamine and a multivitamin to avert the potential for Wernicke's encephalopathy. Initiation of pharmacological treatment for coexisting psychiatric disorders should be postponed, if possible, during the earliest stages of detoxification to avoid the hazards of polypharmacy but also because some depressive signs and symptoms are associated with the detoxification itself and may persist for varying periods; however, the details of this protocol must be determined by the needs of the individual patient.

Rehabilitation, those aspects of the treatment directed to addressing the addiction and the lifestyle that supports it, begins as soon as possible. In the hospital rehabilitation program setting, a wide range of therapeutic approaches, including behavioral, supportive, and dynamic psychotherapies, as well as Alcoholics Anonymous (AA) (Schuckit, 1977; Trice, 1959; Zimberg, 1974), is used. Of these, AA is probably the dominant model. AA stresses complete abstinence from alcohol and other nonprescribed psychoactive drugs and requires the individual's acceptance of his or her addiction and of recovery as an ongoing process. Key elements of therapy include self-disclosure (fostered by a technical anonymity), the support of peers, and attention to the maladaptive attitudes and behaviors that permitted the addiction. In inpatient settings using an AA model, individual and group therapies reinforce the AA values.

Both age-segregated and mixed-age treatment settings have their proponents (Mishara & Kastenbaum, 1980). Mixed-age settings have the potential advantage for both older and younger patients of the intergenerational perspective encouraged by the age mix. Other clinicians prefer the easier atmosphere of similar-age peer groups and cite the fear and alarm engendered in older people by the harshly confrontational styles adopted in some inpatient settings. Also, geriatric patients on mixed-age units may need to be shielded from threatening or violent behaviors of younger substance abuse and antisocial patients. Many geriatric patients, particularly women, have well-justified fears about their physical safety in such environments.

Whatever the predominant treatment model and age profile of the inpatient service, the critical factors in the treatment milieu appear to be creativity, flexibility, and sensitivity to the needs of the elderly patient. As an example, disulfiram (Antabuse), a frequently used pharmacological adjunct in the treatment of younger patients, is less often prescribed in the geriatric population because of the greater possibility of serious medical consequences from adverse reactions. Individual psychotherapies are generally practical and oriented to the "here and now," even those of a psychodynamic bent, as the more undirected, diffuse "uncovering" approaches do not seem to be well accepted by the current generation of elderly patients. Working with elderly patients in psychotherapy requires sensitivity to the experiences, lifestyle, and outlook of elderly persons, in particular to the depth and extent of losses they may have suffered.

A point of some controversy in the management of elderly alcoholics is the requirement for strict abstinence, as required by AA. Mishara and Kastenbaum (1980) have argued that abstinence may not be necessary for all geriatric problem drinkers and have accordingly proposed a broader range of criteria for successful treatment outcome—criteria that emphasize improvement in overall functioning rather than duration or completeness of abstinence. This approach can be criticized for deemphasizing the individual's adjustment to a life not organized around drinking. Abstinence is in fact a central tenet of most alcoholism treatment. In our view, care must be taken to avoid the error of minimizing patients' capacity for abstinence because of age or disability.

The need remains for well-designed clinical research on the outcomes of the various treatment approaches of geriatric alcoholism. The relevance of risk factors, such as family history and socioeconomic status, as predictors of outcomes also requires further elucidation. Older alcoholics in general appear to be as likely as younger adults to respond to treatment (Fitzgerald & Mulford, 1992). There is evidence to suggest that rates of recovery in older alcoholics (defined as abstinence) are higher when they are treated in age-segregated settings (Kashner, Rodell, Ogden, Guggenheim, & Karson, 1992). Secondary alcoholism as defined by Schuckit (1982) may have a more favorable outlook than primary alcoholism, provided that appropriate treatment is directed toward the underlying disorder. Also, late onset alcoholism probably has a better prognosis than early-onset geriatric alcoholism (Atkinson et al., 1985; Schuckit, 1982). However, differences in the age at which alcoholism is deemed to be "late onset," questions about the validity and reliability of making such determinations given the frequent difficulty of obtaining accurate histories, and the lack of consensus on the requirements for recovery all make such conclusions premature.

Summary

Geriatric alcoholism is a growing public health problem which will require increasing efforts at prevention, recognition, and treatment. In all three areas, techniques must be developed that are relevant to the special needs and experiences of the elderly population. These will be the expected rewards of the next generation of research efforts.

PRESCRIPTION DRUG ABUSE AND MISUSE IN THE ELDERLY

The elderly are the largest users of legal drugs in the U.S. population, accounting for approximately 30% of all prescriptions (Koch & Knapp, 1987). At least one drug is prescribed or administered in more than 68% of office visits by patients 65 years of age or older (Baum, Kennedy, & Forbes, 1985), with cardiovascular drugs, sedatives/hypnotics and antianxiety medications, and analgesics given most frequently. It has been estimated that 25% of all persons of geriatric age use psychoactive drugs (Finlayson, 1984), among which benzodiazepines appear to be overrepresented; probably more than one-third of daily users of benzodiazepines are in the geriatric age group (Mellinger, Balter, & Uhlenhuth, 1984). One study, for example, found that benzodiazepines were prescribed to 41% of all hospitalized elderly patients (Zisselman, Rovner, Kelly, & Woods, 1994).

The consequences of prescription drug problems among the elderly are beginning to receive greater attention. The vast distribution of such drugs, the tendency of older people to be taking multiple medications, and the increased sensitivity of the elderly to toxic effects all enhance the possibility of mishap. In the study just cited, for example, benzodiazepine use in hospitalized elderly patients was associated with increases in severity of illness, length of stay, and cost of the hospitalization (Zisselman, Rovner, Yuen, & Louis, 1996).

The extent of prescription drug problems among the elderly is still not clear. Whitcup and Miller (1987) reported that more than 20% of patients over 65 years old admitted to a psychiatric hospital in one year could be regarded as dependent on prescription drugs; of these, half were neither recognized nor detoxified, and some went on to have significant medical complications. In this same study, female benzodiazepine abusers were somewhat less likely to be identified than male alcoholics. Other studies in more representative geriatric populations have produced lower frequencies of drug abuse and dependency. Stephens, Haney, and Underwood 1981), for instance, found that of a sample of 1,101 noninstitutionalized residents of Houston over 55 years old, only about 7% could be described as misusers of prescribed psychoactive drugs. However, because 40% of the same sample used such drugs, some on a chronic basis, the overall potential for misuse appears to be considerable. Among elderly alcoholics, the frequency of prescription drug abuse or dependency is likely to be much higher (Miller et al., 1991).

Problems with prescription drugs may involve intentional abuse (either by erratic (Saunders et al., 1991) use, overuse, or contraindicated use) or unintentional misuse (usually by erroneous underdosing or overdosing). In either case, the prescribing physician must assume responsibility for considering a patient's potential to abuse medications intentionally and for recognizing a patient's capacity to follow instructions accurately. A thorough medication inventory is essential, as is a sense of the patient's character and cognitive capacity. Problems exist in institutional settings also; there is evidence that some elderly nursing home residents are receiving unnecessary or inappropriate doses of psychoactive drugs, in the case of benzodiazepines in doses sufficient to cause dependency (Beers, Dang, Hasegawa, & Tamai, 1989). However, some states (e.g., New York) have recently begun to regulate the administration of antipsychotic medications and to limit the use of the as-needed (prn) format for all psychotropic drugs.

For the elderly living independently, analgesics and anxiolytics/sedatives/hypnotics appear to be the groups of prescription drugs having the highest potential for abuse and misuse. A trend toward avoidance of stimulants has also been described (Finlayson, 1984). Benzodiazepines, as suggested earlier, comprise the most widely used prescription drug among the elderly, in rates far out of proportion to the prevalence of anxiety disorders in the geriatric population (Blazer, 1989). This appears to stem from their relative safety, cross-tolerance with alcohol (hence frequently used by elderly alcoholics), and the aggressive marketing by their manufacturers. Benzodiazepine anxiolytics are the medications most frequently prescribed for the elderly by primary care physicians; in contrast, psychiatrists most frequently prescribe antidepressants (Beardsley, Gardocki, Larson, & Hidalgo, 1988). Because primary physicians account for a higher percentage of patient visits and prescriptions in this age group, their prescribing patterns have a greater impact than those of psychiatrists and may encourage the tendency of patients to request that their depression symptoms be medicated with benzodiazepines. Possibly also involved in the extent of geriatric use and misuse of benzodiazepines is the ubiquity of sleep disturbances, even among healthy older people.

Treatment and Prevention

Hospitalization may be indicated for detoxification or gradual withdrawal from a chronically used prescription drug. Schweizer, Case, and Rickels (1989) found that a regimen of gradual tapering of benzodiazepines followed by complete discontinuation of the drugs was at least as well tolerated by hospitalized geriatric patients as by younger patients; older patients appear to able to achieve complete abstinence from benzodiazepines with comfort and safety.

The rehabilitation aspects of treatment are predicated on an understanding of the lifestyle and circumstances of the patient that support the addictive behavior. In the specific case of prescription drugs, the chief enabler is likely to be a physician, who, more than likely, is unaware to the problem to which he or she is contributing.

The physician can aid in *prevention* by prescribing analgesics conservatively for mild pain and by stressing sleep hygiene (later to bed, no daytime napping) as a first-line approach to early (sleep-onset) insomnia rather than medications. When sleep medication is indicated, the preferential selection of benzodiazepines with short half-lives will reduce the potential for toxic accumulation of metabolites. Finally, in the absence or transient presentation of mood symptoms, pain and insomnia may represent the most clinically apparent features of a depression syndrome, for which specific treatment is available.

OVER-THE-COUNTER AND ILLICIT DRUG ABUSE IN THE ELDERLY

Over-the-Counter Drug Use and Misuse

The prevalence of over-the-counter drug abuse in the geriatric population has not been clearly established, mostly because of difficulties in detecting these behaviors. However, it is known that over-the-counter drug use generally increases with age, especially in women, and that approximately two-thirds of all persons ages 60 and older consume at least one nonprescription drug daily (Whitcup & Miller, 1987). These nonprescription drugs include analgesics, cold remedies containing pseudephedrine, anticholinergics, antihistamines, laxatives, and vitamin supplements, among others. A range of medical, social, and economic factors all place the elderly at risk for abuse of, dependence on, or other misuse of over-the-counter medications. For example, many age-related conditions, such as arthritis, constipation, gastric hyperacidity, and insomnia, can be treated with over-the-counter preparations. The inappropriate substitution of over-the counter drugs for medically prescribed therapies tends to be reinforced by economic and social factors such as reduced income (nonprescription drugs tend to be less expensive than those requiring prescriptions) and limited access to physicians. Other factors that may contribute to abuse or dependence on these products are impairments in memory and judgment, failure of the elderly consumer to take into account physiological changes of aging in dosing the over-the-counter medication (abetted by absence in some package inserts of warnings to elderly users about the potential need to reduce doses), and also the misconception that over-the-counter medications are "weak" or harmless. Some elderly persons take medications belonging to other family members. Finally, a number of preparations contain substances in sufficient amounts to contribute to addiction, such as antitussive products with alcohol or stimulants with caffeine.

The consequences of misuse of over-the-counter drugs by the elderly appear to be of greater significance than was previously acknowledged. In addition to overall frailty and the potential for adverse interactions with other medications and alcohol, there is also a greater sensitivity to toxic effects. The pharmacokinetic changes associated with aging that tend to increase sensitivity are relevant to over-the-counter drugs as well. Reduced plasma protein binding, reduced activity of major metabolic pathways (particularly hepatic microsomal enzymes), slowed renal excretion, and increased CNS receptor sensitivities together have the net effect of increasing concentrations of active drugs. For many over-the-counter drugs, such as salicylates, signs and symptoms of toxicity appear at lower doses in older patients.

Moreover, older patients take nonprescription drugs over longer periods than do younger ones because the conditions they are medicating tend to be chronic. For example, elderly patients with chronic arthritis, backaches, or headaches comprise the group at greatest risk for adverse consequences of long-term aspirin or acetaminophen administration (Lamy, 1980). Iron deficiency anemia secondary to gastric bleeding is reported in chronic aspirin takers (Lamy & Kitler, 1971). As another example, peptic ulcer patients or those with chronic "acid indigestion" who are long-time users of over-the-counter antacids containing calcium carbonate are at risk to develop intractable constipation or a paradoxical gastric hypersecretion syndrome (Barreras, 1973). When used chronically, over-the-counter cold preparations containing atropine are associated with anticholinergic toxicity and exacerbation of preexisting glaucoma. Stimulant laxatives, when taken on a regular basis (as they are by as many as 30% of individuals over 60), can induce a dependent state. Of this group, a conservative estimate is that 3% significantly overuse stimulant laxatives and can be said to be dependent on them (Cummings,

1974). Long-term complications of stimulant laxative dependency or overuse include colonic mucosal changes with diminished tone and motility, sometimes affecting the absorption of other drugs, and electrolyte disturbances. Reversible inhibitors of histamine at the histamine H2-receptor, such as nizadine (Axid) or ranitidine (Zantac), are now available over the counter for "acid indigestion" and have been associated with hepatocellular injury in patients who use them chronically.

Adverse drug interactions involving over-the-counter medications are frequent in the geriatric population (Table 15.1). The potential is enormous: 80% of elderly patients taking an over-the-counter drug daily also use alcohol, prescription medications, or both (Whitcup & Miller, 1987). Many of these adverse drug interactions involve over-the-counter analgesics. For example, aspirin and acetaminophen both potentiate anticoagulants; aspirin also potentiates methotrexate and oral hypoglycemics while decreasing the effects of uricosuric agents. Nonsteroidal antiinflammatory agents (NSAIDS) may produce a reduction in renal clearance of lithium and an elevation of plasma lithium levels, resulting in signs and symptoms of lithium toxicity. Over-the-counter medications having peripheral antihistaminic and anticholinergeic properties, such as allergy, sleep, or nasal decongestant products, may compound the anticholinergic effects of antipsychotic or tricyclic antidepressant medications, with adverse consequences ranging from oversedation to delirium or central anticholinergic syndrome. As a rule, sympathomimetic amines and stimulant drugs are abused less frequently by older than by younger individuals but are sometimes used to self-medicate depression; they can induce hypertensive crises when combined with monoamine oxidase inhibitors or

TABLE 15.1. Some Common Adverse Interactions Involving Over-the-Counter Medications

Over-the-counter drug	Common adverse interactions
Aspirin	Potentiates anticoagulants, methotrexate, and oral hypoglycemics; decreases effect of uricosuric agents
Acetaminophen	Potentiates anticoagulants; may increase alcohol-related hepatoxicity
Peripheral antihistaminics (allergy and nasal decongestant preparations)	May cause anticholinergic toxicity with concurrent use of antipsychotics or tricyclic antidepressants
Pseudoephedrine and caffeine-containing stimulants	May induce hypertensive crises when used with monoamine oxidase inhibitors or tricyclic antidepressants; decreases effects of antihypertensive, antiarrhythmic, and antianxiety medications
Laxatives	Associated with digitalis toxicity when used chronically
Alcohol-containing produces (e.g., cough medications)	Can produce oversedation when used with antihistamines, benzodiazepines, barbiturates, phenothiazines, or tricyclic antidepressants
NSAIDS	Can produce elevation of plasma lithium levels and symptoms/signs of lithium toxicity

tricyclic antidepressants. Caffeine-containing stimulants can reduce the therapeutic effects of antihypertensive, antiarrhythmic, or antianxiety medications (Lamy, 1980). Finally—this list is by no means complete—digitalis toxicity has been associated with prolonged laxative use.

Over-the-counter medications should be included in every mediation inventory taken from elderly patients, many of whom will not volunteer this information because they do not necessarily believe these preparations to be medications. As always, it is helpful to be able to question collateral sources, such as family members or caregivers. Perusal of home medicine cabinets often reveals direct evidence of gross misuse of over-the-counter products; this is often an indication for greater supervision of an elderly person. For those with well-established patterns of abuse or clinically significant toxicity, there may be no alternative to hospitalization and gradual withdrawal of the over-the-counter medication.

Illicit Drug Use

Illicit drug use, especially involving substances such as marijuana, heroin, or cocaine, is relatively rare in elderly populations. Even older narcotic addicts typically rely on prescription drugs such as codeine, morphine, or meperidine (Demerol), obtained legally from physicians. Winick (1962) formulated the classic "maturing out" hypothesis to explain the disappearance of many narcotics addicts from federal records between the ages of 36 and 45. Possible explanations offered by Winick to explain this phenomenon included reduction of life stresses by this age; selection processes occurring because of death, debilitation, or incarceration, of the most severely addicted individuals; and a "burning out of the addiction." Also, some addicts are able to maintain a stable opiate habit for many years without coming to medical or legal attention or turn as they became older to more readily available substitutes, such as alcohol. Pascarelli and Fisher (1974) suggested that the older narcotic addict population may consist mainly of a subset of persons who have survived into middle or old age without coming into contact with treatment settings—a group of individuals characterized by their ability to "successfully" manage their addiction on the outside.

Elderly alcoholics comprise the subgroup for whom illicit drug use is likely to be concentrated within the geriatric population. Miller et al. (1991) make this argument based on ECA data showing that 60% of adult alcoholics were dependent on illicit drugs, compared to 17% in the general population. However, most of the information in this area is derived from clinical case reports; there is little data from surveys that address the issue directly.

CONCLUSION

Alcoholism and addictions to prescription drugs and over-the-counter medications are not uncommon disorders in the geriatric population, although their overall public health significance has only recently begun to be grasped. The Denial of the addiction on the part of elderly patients contributes to low rates of detection, as do the attitudes of family members and health care professionals who may minimize the problem. This is particularly true for substance disorders having onset in old age. In all three areas of addictive behavior discussed in this chapter, the affected elderly patient typically receives medical intervention only after a calamitous event, such as a drug- or alcohol-related accident or a major adverse drug interaction. It necessary for health care personnel to retain the same index of suspicion regarding substance abuse in an older patient as they would in a younger patient. However, age-related differences in the presentation and course of substance abuse must also be borne in mind.

Insofar as it is possible to generalize about treatment, it can be said that (1) detoxification is generally a safe procedure in the elderly but usually requires hospitalization, (2) abstinence should be the primary goal of treatment, and (3) rehabilitation can be achieved in mixed-age settings, but sensitivity to age differences is crucial.

Finally, although this chapter attempted to summarize and generalize, ideally the next generation of clinical research in this area will take into account the complexity of substance abuse disorders and the heterogeneity of the geriatric population.

REFERENCES

Abram, K. M., & Teplin, L. A. (1991). Co-occurring disorders among mentally ill jail detainees. *American Psychologist, 46*, 1036–1045.

Adams, W. L., Garry, P. J., Rhyne, R., Hunt, W. C., Goodwin, J. S. (1990). Alcohol intake in the healthy elderly: Changes with age in a cross-sectional and longitudinal study. *Journal of the American Geriatrics Society, 38*, 211–216.

Adams, W. L., Zhong, Y., Barboriak, J. J., & Rimm, A. A. (1993). Alcohol-related hospitalizations of elderly people: Prevalence and geographic variation in the United States. *Journal of the American Medical Association, 270*, 1222–1225.

Alexander, C. S. (1975). Alcoholic cardiomyopathy. *Postgraduate Medicine, 58*, 127–131.

Alexander, F., & Duff, R. W. (1988). Social interaction and alcohol use in retirement communities. *Gerontologist, 28*, 632–636.

American Psychiatric Assoviation. (1994). *Diagnostic and statistical msnusl of mental disorders* (4th ed.). Washington, DC: Author.

Atkinson, R. M. (Ed.). (1984). *Alcohol and drug abuse in old age*. Washington, DC: American Psychiatric Press.

Atkinson, R. M., Ganzini, L., & Bernstein, M. J. (1992). Alcohol and substance-use disorders in the elderly. In J. Birren, R. Sloane, & G. Cohen (Eds.), *Handbook of mental health and aging* (pp. 515–555). San Diego: Academic Press.

Atkinson, R. M., Turner, J. A. Kofoed, L. L., & Tolson, R. L. (1985). Early versus late onset alcoholism in older persons. *Alcoholism: Clinical and Experimental Research, 9*, 513–515.

Barnes, G. M. (1979). Alcohol use among older persons: Findings from a western New York State general population survey. *Journal of the American Geriatrics Society, 27,* 244–250.

Barreras, R. F. (1973). Calcium and gastric secretion. *Gastroenterology, 64,* 1168.

Baum, C., Kennedy, D. L., & Forbes, M. B. (1985). Drug utilization in the geriatric age group. In S. R. Moore & T. W. Teal (Eds.), *Geriatric drug use: Clinical and social perspectives* (pp. 63–69). New York: Pergamon Press.

Bearsley, R. S., Gardocki, G. J., Larson, D. B., & Hidalgo, J. (1988). Prescribing of psychotropic medication by primary care physicians and psychiatrists. *Archives of General Pschiatry, 45,* 1117–1119.

Beers, M. H., Dang, J., Hasegawa, J., & Tamai, I.Y. (1989). Influence of hospitalization on drug therapy in the elderly. *Journal of the American Geriatrics Society, 37,* 679–683.

Bernadt, M. W., Mumford, J., Taylor, C., Smith, B., & Murray, R.M. (1982, February). Comparison of questionnaire and laboratory tests in the detection of excessive drinking and alcoholism. *Lancet, 1,* 325–328.

Bienenfeld, D. (1990). Substance abuse in the elderly. In D. Bienenfeld (Ed.), *Vervoerdt's clinical geropsychiatry* (3rd ed.). Baltimore: Williams & Wilkins.

Blazer, D. G. (1981, January 9–10). *Epidemiology and clinical interace.* Paper presented ay the Harvard NIMH Conference on Anxiety in the Elderly, Boston.

Blixen, C. E. (1988). Aging and mental health care. *Journal of Gerontological Nursing, 14,* 11–15.

Blixen, C. E., McDougall, G. J., & Suen, L.-J. (1997). Dual diagnosis in elders discharged from a psychiatric hospital. *International Journal of Geriatric Psychiatry, 12,* 307–313.

Blow, F. C., Loveland Cook, C. A., Booth, B. M., Falcon, S. P., & Friedman, M. J. (1992). Age-related psychiatric comorbidities and level of functioning in alcoholic veterans seeking outpatient treatment. *Hospital and Community Psychiatry, 43,* 990–995.

Blumenthal, S. J. (1988). Suicide: A guide to risk factors, assessment, and treatment of suicidal patients. *Medical Clinics of North America, 72,* 937–971.

Borgatta, E. F., Montgomery, R. J. V., & Borgatta, M. L. (1982). Alcohol use and abuse: Life crisis events and the elderly. *Research in Aging, 4,* 378–408.

Bosmann, H. B. (1984). Pharmacology of alcoholism and aging. In J. T. Hartford & T. Samorajski (Eds.), *Alcoholism in the elderly: Social and biomedical issues* (pp. 161–174). New York: Raven Press.

Bridgewater, R., Leigh, S., James, O. F. W., & Potter, J. F. (1987). Alcohol consumption and dependence in elderly patients in an urban community. *British Medical Journal, 295,* 884–885.

Cahalan, D., Cisin, J. H., & Crossley, H. M. (1969). *American drinking practices.* New Brunswick, NJ: Rutgers Center of Alcohol Studies.

Caracci, G., & Miller, N. S. (1991). Epidemiology and diagnosis of alcoholism in the elderly [A review]. *International Journal of Geriatric Psychiatry, 6,* 511–515.

Caton, C. M., Shrout, P. E., Eagle, P. F., Opler, L.D., & Felix, A. (1994). Correlates of codisorders in homeless and never homeless indigent schizophrenic men. *Psychological Medicine, 24,* 681–688.

Christopherson, V. A., Escher, M. C., & Bainton, B. R. (1984). Reasons for drinking among the elderly in rural Arizona. *Journal of Studies on Alcohol, 45,* 417–423.

Conwell, Y., & Brent, D. (1995). Suicide and aging: I. *International Psychogeriatrics, 7,* 149–164.

Cummings, J. H. (1974). Progress report: Laxative abuse. *Gut, 15*, 758–766.

Dunham, R. G. (1981). Aging and changing patterns of alcohol use. *Journal of Psychoactive Drugs, 13*, 143–151.

Dupree, L. W., Broskowski, H., & Schonfeld, L. (1984). The Gerontology Alcohol Project: A behavioral treatment program for elderly alcohol abusers. *Gerontologist, 24*, 510–516.

Factor, S. M. (1976). Intramyocardial small vessel disease in chronic alcoholism. *American Heart Journal, 92*, 561–575.

Finlayson, R. E. (1984). Prescription drug abuse in older persons. In R. M. Atkinson (Ed.), *Alcohol and drug abuse in old age* (pp. 62–69). Washington, DC: American Psychiatric Press.

Fitzgerald, J. L., & Mulford, H. A. (1992). Elderly vs. younger problem drinker "treatment" and recovery experiences. *British Journal of Addiction, 87*, 1281–1291.

Gaitz, C. M., & Baer, P. E. (1971). Characteristics of elderly patients with alcoholism. *Archives of General Psychiatry, 24*, 829–836.

Gambert, S. R. (1997). The elderly. In J. H. Lowinson, P. Ruiz, R. B. Millman, & J. G. Langrod (Eds.), *Substance abuse: A comprehensive textbook*. Baltimore: Williams & Wilkins.

Glynn, R. J., Bouchard, G. R., LoCastro, J. S., & Laird, N. M. (1985). Aging and generational effects on drinking behaviors in men: Results from the Normative Aging Study. *American Journal of Public Health, 75*, 1413–1419.

Gordon, T., & Kannel, W. B. (1983). Drinking and its relation to smoking, blood pressure, blood lipids, and uric acid. *Archives of Internal Medicine, 143*, 1366–1374.

Helzer, J. E., Burnam, A., & McEvoy, L. T. (1991). Alcohol abuse and dependence. In L. N. Robins & D. A. Regier (Eds.), *Psychiatric disorders in America: The Epidemiologic Catchment Area study*. New York: Free Press.

Herd D. (1990). Subgroup differences in drinking patterns among black and white men: Results from a national survey. *Journal of Studies on Alcohol, 51*, 221–232.

Herrmann, N., & Eryavec, G. (1996). Lifetime alcohol abuse in institutionalized World War II veterans. *American Journal of Geriatric Psychiatry, 4*, 39–45.

Holroyd, S., Currie, L., Thompson-Heisterman, A., & Abraham, I. (1997). A descriptive study of elderly community-dwelling alcoholic patients in the rural south. *American Journal of Geriatric Psychiatry, 5*, 221–228.

Holzer III, C. E., Robins, L. N., & Myers, J. K. (1984). Antecedents and correlates of alcohol abuse and dependence in the elderly. In G. Maddox, L. N. Robins, & N. Rosenberg (Eds.), *Nature and extent of alcohol problems in the elderly* (NIDA Research Monograph No. 14). Washington, DC: U.S. Government Printing Office.

Kashner, T. M., Rodell, D. E., Ogden, S. R. Guggenheim, F. G., & Karson, C. N. (1992). Outcomes and costs of two VA inpatient treatment programs for older alcoholic patients. *Hospital and Community Psychiatry, 43*, 985–989.

Koch, H., & Knapp, D. E. (1987). *Highlights of drug utilization in office practice, National Ambulatory Medical Survey, 1985: Advance data from Vital and Health Statistics No. 134* (DHHS Publication No. PHS 87-1250). Washington, DC: U.S. Government Printing Office.

Kramer, M. (1969). *Patients in state and county mental hospitals* (Public Health Service Publication No. 1921). Chevy Chase, MD: National Institute of Mental Health.

LaGreca, A. J., Akers, R. L., & Dwyer, J. W. (1988). Life events and alcohol behavior among older adults. *Gerontologist, 28*, 552–558.

Lamy, P. P. (1980). *Prescribing for the elderly.* Littleton, MA: PSG.

Lamy, P. P., & Kitler, M. E. (1971). Untoward effects of drugs, part II (including nonprescription drugs). *Diseases of the Nervous System, 32,* 105–114.

Liberto, J. G., Oslin, D. W., & Ruskin, P. E. (1992). Alcoholism in older persons: A review of the literature. *Hospital and Community Psychiatry, 43,* 975–984.

McCourt, W. F., Williams, A. F., & Schneider, L. (1971). Incidence of alcoholism in a state mental hospital population. *Quarterly Journal of Studies on Alcohol, 32,* 1085.

Mears, H. J., & Spice, C. (1993). Screening for problem drinking in the elderly: A study in the elderly mentally ill. *International Journal of Geriatric Psychiatry, 8,* 319–326.

Mellinger G. D., Balter, M. B., & Uhlenhuth, E. H. (1984). Prevalence and correlates of the long-term regular use of anxiolytics. *Journal of the American Medical Association, 251,* 375–379.

Meyers, A., Hingson, R., Mucatel, M., & Goldman, E. (1982). Social and psychological correlates of problem drinking in old age. *Journal of the American Geriatrics Society, 30,* 452–456.

Miller, N. S., Belkin, B. M., & Gold, M. S. (1991). Alcohol and drug dependence among the elderly: Epidemiology, diagnosis and treatment. *Comprehensive Psychiatry, 32,* 153–165.

Mishara, B. L., & Kastenbaum, R. (1980). *Alcohol and old age.* New York: Grune & Stratton.

Moscicki, E. K. (1995). Epidemiology of suicide. *International Psychogeriatrics, 7,* 137–148.

Mulvey, E. P. (1994). Assessing the evidence of a link between mental illness and violence. *Hospital and Community Psychiatry, 45,* 663–668.

Myers, J. K., Weissman, M. M., Tischler, G. L., Holzer, C.E., Leaf, P. J., Orvaschel, H., Anthony, J. C., Boyd, J. H., Burke, J. D., Kramer, M., & Stoltzman, R. (1984). Six-month prevalence of psychiatric disorders in three communities. *Archives of General Psychiatry, 41,* 959–967.

Olsen-Noll, C. G., & Bosworth, M. F. (1989). Alcohol abuse in the elderly. *American Family Physician, 39,* 173–179.

Pascarelli, E. F., & Fisher, W. (1974). Drug dependence in the elderly. *International Journal of Aging and Human Development, 5,* 347–356.

Penn, R., & Worthington, D. J. (1983). Is serum GGT a misleading test? *British Medical Journal, 286,* 531–535.

Pintar, K. Wlanskyj, B. M., & Buggay, E. R. (1965). Alcoholic cardiomyopathy. *Canadian Medical Association Journal, 93,* 103–194.

Raskind, M. A., & Eisdorfer, C. (1976). Psychopharmacology of the aged. In L. L. Simpson (Ed.), *Drug treatment of mental disorders* (pp. 237–266). New York: Raven Press.

Reichman, W.E. (1994). Nondegenerative dementing disorders. In C.E. Coffey & J. L. Cummings, (Eds.), *Textbook of geriatric neuropsychiatry* (pp. 369–388). Washington, DC: American Psychiatric Press.

Rosin, A. J., & Glatt, M. M. (1971). Alcohol excess in the elderly. *Quarterly Journal of Studies on Alcohol, 32,* 53–59.

Saunders, P. A., Copeland, J. R. M., Dewey, M. E., Davidson, I. A., McWilliam, C., Sharma, et al. (1991). Heavy drinking as a risk factor for depression and dementia in elderly men: Findings from the Liverpool Longitudinal Community Study. *British Journal of Psychiatry, 159,* 213–216.

Schuckit, M. A. (1977). Geriatric alcoholism and drug abuse. *Gerontologist, 17,* 168–174.

Schuckit, M. A. (1982). A clinical review of alcohol, alcoholism, and the elderly patient. *Journal of Clinical Psychiatry, 43,* 396–399.

Schuckit, M. A. (1983). Alcoholism and other psychiatric disorders. *Hospital and Community Psychiatry, 34,* 1022–1027.

Schuckit, M. A., & Miller, P. (1976). Alcoholism in elderly men: Survey of a general medical ward. *Annals of the New York Academy of Sciences, 273,* 558–571.

Schweizer, E., Case, W. G., & Rickels, K. (1989). Benzodiazepine dependence and withdrawal in elderly patients. *American Journal of Psychiatry, 146,* 529–531.

Simon, A., Epstein, L.J., & Reynolds, L. (1968). Alcoholism in the geriatric mentally ill. *Geriatrics, 23,* 125–131.

Speer, D. C. (1990). Comorbid mental and substance disorders among the elderly: Conceptual issues and propositions. *Behavior Health and Aging, 1,* 163–170.

Stephens, R. C., Haney, C. A., & Underwood, S. (1981). Psychoactive drug use and potential misuse among persons aged 55 years and older. *Journal of Psychoactive Drugs, 13,* 185–193.

Trice, H. M. (1959). The affiliation motive and readiness to join Alcoholics Anonymous. *Quarterly Journal of Studies on Alcohol, 20,* 313–320.

Wetle, T. (1987). Age as a risk factor for inadequate treatment. *Journal of the American Medical Association, 258,* 516.

Whitcup, S. M., & Miller, F. (1987). Unrecognized drug dependence in psychiatrically hospitalized elderly patients. *Journal of Nervous and Mental Disease, 126,* 341–481.

Winick, C. (1962). Maturing out of narcotic addiction. *Bulletin on Narcotics, 14,* 1–7.

Zimberg, S. (1974). The two types of problem drinkers: Both can be managed. *Geriatrics, 29,* 135–138.

Zisselman, M. H., Rovner, B. W., Kelly K. G., & Woods, C. (1994). Benzodiazepine utilization in a university hospital. *American Journal of Medical Quality, 9,* 138–140.

Zisselman, M. H., Rovner, B. W., Yuen, E. J., & Louis. D.Z. (1996). Sedative-hypnotic use and increased hospitalization stay and costs in the elderly. *Journal of the American Geriatrics Society, 44,* 1371–1374.

Zisselman, M. H., Rovner, B. W., Yuen, E. J., & Sholevar, D. (1997). Physician rationale for benzodiazepine prescriptions to elderly hospitalized patients. *American Journal of Geriatric Psychiatry, 5,* 167–171.

16

Substance Abuse in Minority Populations

MARYLINN MARKARIAN
JOHN FRANKLIN

INTRODUCTION

This chapter highlights issues in the treatment of addictive disorders in African Americans, Hispanic Americans, Asian Americans, and Native Americans. It is important to consider the available data on these U.S. populations as much of our knowledge of substance abuse is based on research conducted primarily on white males. The growing ethnic diversity of the United States makes the significance of these issues even greater. This trend is likely to continue with new census rules that will allow individuals to indicate more than one racial category. This chapter reviews the data on addictive disorders in minority populations. Substantial knowledge gaps exist in minority substance abuse and continued research in this area is needed.

A major consideration regarding any discussion of ethnic differences is that the divisions along ethnic lines can be obtuse. Within each ethnic group are variations in country of origin, religious and spiritual orientation, and political and economic conditions. These differences may influence the clinical presentation and therapeutic needs of the patient. Other variables within any given ethnic group include socioeconomic status, educational level, occupational stability, dwelling situation, marital status, family of origin, and age.

This chapter posits that racial and ethnic differences are important, but so are the biological, social, economic, and psychological underpinnings to the addictive process. For example, environmental and family dysfunction drive more variables toward substance abuse than do arbitrary racial lines. Level of education, employment potential, housing neighborhood, and access to health care are largely determined by family economics. Most African Americans who live in crime- and drug-infested areas do so because living elsewhere is unaffordable. There is a fundamental difference between the Native American and African American experience versus the political and economic condition experienced by other ethnic immigrants. For many immigrants, the sole purpose of migrating to the United States is the pursuit of economic stability. This pursuit can profoundly drive the gains made even within one generation, and often does. The willful immigrant experience is different than the forced migration and institutionalization that the Africans experienced. The Native American experience also cannot be compared to the traditional immigrant experience for obvious reasons. It is not within the scope of this chapter to explore the deep and far-reaching consequences of these various experiences. It is, however, important to bear in mind the complexity of an often oversimplified and convenient use of racial and ethnic divisions.

The problem with racial divisions is demonstrated by the following example. A middle-class African American woman with a college degree, stable employment, dwelling in a reasonably safe neighborhood may share a daily world and outlook toward the future more similar to a European American woman of a similar background than to a single, unemployed African American mother dwelling in an inner city. Their experiences within ethnic groups can be vastly different. There is scant data about differences in biological vulnerability for substance abuse between ethnic groups (Chan et al., 1994; Goldman et al., 1993; Berrettini & Persico, 1996). Thus, this chapter highlights the socioeconomic and political differences in presentation and treatment.

ADDICTION TRENDS AND ETHNICITY IN WOMEN

Fewer women than men in all ethnic groups drink and they drink less. However, drinking patterns of women in the United States have changed in the last 50 years in that more women drink and more drink problematically (Blume, 1986). Population surveys have also confirmed the popular notion that the first age of use of the "gateway" drugs—tobacco and alcohol—is converging in a one-sided fashion. The median age of onset has been stable across a wide range of birth years for men. However, for women, the age of first use decreased by 2 years in a 30-year span. The convergence is two sided with smoking in this country, with an increase age of onset in males and a decrease in females. There is no significant difference between the sexes of first marijuana use, and this has historically been the case. The majority of prescription drug abusers are women with the exception of the 12–17 age range, wherein more boys are abusing than girls. Women are more likely to obtain them through medical channels whereas men obtain them through other means (Ray & Braude, 1986). Alcohol and substance abuse among women are reviewed more fully in another chapter.

Ethnic differences among women have received some attention. In terms of alcohol, African American families produce more abstainers than do European and Hispanic American families. African American women have rates of heavy drinking comparable to European American rates; however, they report fewer social and personal problems related to drinking. African American women may be more insulated from alcohol-related social problems by their families, communities, and churches. A larger proportion of African American women experience alcohol-related health problems than do European American cohorts (Herd, 1989). African American women exhibit higher rates of fetal alcohol syndrome. These findings may be attributed to issues such as nutrition and access to health care. Concurrent illicit drug use may also be a contributing factor. Currently and for the first time, a larger percentage of African American women are using illicit drugs than are their European American cohorts (Substance Abuse and Mental Health Administration, 1995).

Hispanic American women are more likely to abstain than European American women, though there is a one-sided convergence with increasing acculturation. For example, in one study, 75% of Mexican immigrant women abstained from alcohol whereas 38% of third-generation Mexican American women were abstainers (Gilbert, 1991). Furthermore, a larger proportion of Hispanic than European American women are heavy drinkers. Younger American-born Hispanic women are more likely to report moderate to heavy drinking than are their immigrant cohorts.

TREATMENT ISSUES

A greater proportion of alcoholic women than alcoholic men have a history of psychological problems and psychiatric treatment, especially depression and various anxiety disorders. Psychiatric disorders more common in alcoholic men than women are antisocial personality and compulsive gambling. Alcoholic women are more likely to attempt suicide than is the female population at large. Furthermore, Adelstein and Graham-White (1977) published data based on death certificates indicating that alcoholic females die by suicide 23 times the female population rate. Alcoholic women are also more likely to be polyaddicted than are alcoholic men, particularly to prescription drugs. It is in part these complexities that led to the impression that women have poorer outcome to treatment than do men; however, some recent outcome studies contradict this wisdom.

The course of alcoholism in women appears to have more negative psychological and interpersonal consequences than outwardly social ones (Robbins, 1989). These include feelings of guilt, shame, and depression, leading to further isolation and secret drinking. Alcoholic women are more likely than alcoholic men to be divorced when they enter treatment. Those who stay married are more likely than men to be married to alcoholic spouses, which enhances the marital discord. Brown, Seragaman, Kokin, and Shields (1995) found that in comparison to female spouses of substance abusers male spouses show (1) more symptoms of substance abuse and depression, (2) less overall physical well-being, and (3) less inclination to help others or be involved with their children. Child care has traditionally been a major obstacle to substance abuse treatment. However, this is not unique to ethnic minorities. Addictive disorders tend to require a higher intensity of treatment than do many other conditions, often requiring patients to attend multiple weekly treatments and sometimes residential treatment. Women with children often turn to family members for help, but it may not be there. Spouses, if present, may be impaired or simply not supportive. Female alcoholics are more vulnerable to arguments with family and friends related to their drinking, leading to greater isolation. Many treatment centers have developed ways to address child-care issues. For example, facilities like Women's Treatment Center in Chicago provide residential settings that accommodate small children and infants. The children are cared for by professional staff and, more important, by other recovering mothers. This is an important intervention, not only in treating but in teaching parenting skills.

Supportive networks are important to substance abuse recovery irrespective of child-care needs. A strong focus on the development of supports is indicated in the treatment of addicted women. Isolation among addicted women occurs for multiple reasons, including feelings of shame, guilt, and depression. Again, such feelings are not unique to ethnic women but may be in part gender specific, given the stereotypical association of sexual promiscuity that is attached to addicted women. Women isolate also because of the added vulnerability to violent sexual crimes that may take place particularly while they are intoxicated. For instance, Fillmore (1985) found that women who drink in bars are more likely to be victims of crime than are men who do the same. A study by Miller and Downs (1986) found that alcoholic women were significantly more likely to be victims of violent crimes than were controls. Contributing to a lack of supports is the high incidence of addictive disorders among the addict's family member. This is particularly important in the case of women addicted to cocaine and heroin. Boyd et al. (1994) found in their study that 65% of women using at least $100 weekly of crack cocaine had at least one parent with a drug or alcohol problem. Sibling use was equally high. The participants were most often initiated to crack by male relatives, and many lived with partners who abused substances. Women are very likely to enter treatment because of family and relationship problems. Creative networks should be a strong focus of recovery of addicted minority women. It may be necessary to utilize extended family as well as supports outside the family who serve as positive maternal figures.

Financial restriction is a fundamental barrier to treatment for women with added hardship for more women belonging to ethnic minority groups. Denier, Thevos, Latham, amd Randall (1991) found that among 100 inpatient cocaine abusers, women were more likely to be unemployed and when employed were more likely to hold lower-paying jobs. This was the case despite equivalent formal education attainment for both groups and not related to a larger percentage of women describing themselves as homemakers. A similar finding by Griffin, Weiss, Mirin, and Lang (1989) showed that female cocaine abusers were more likely to be unemployed, to hold lower-status jobs, and to be less able to support themselves. Among drug injectors and crack smokers Booth, Koester, and Pinto (1995) found that men were more likely than women to be employed, have an income, be involved with illegal activity, and have greater earnings in the 30 days prior to the interview. Women reported income from welfare, a spouse, or from prostitution more often than did men. Underemployment and higher rates of spousal impairment are major barriers to medical insurance access. Such barriers can grossly limit the type of treatment available to women. However, the privatization of public insurance seems to narrow the choices, at least in some regions of the country. Women's Treatment Center in Chicago has a strong focus on vocational rehabilitation. The women earn increasing community privileges and are assisted in finding gainful employment. Unfortunately, most programs are not sufficiently lengthy or comprehensive to include this feature. Other features that may be lacking noticeably are bilingual counselors and programs. Many programs do not have enough of a bilingual client base to justify, for instance, only Spanish-speaking groups. Community-based services that provide for a particular ethnic group may be best suited to provide non-English-based programs (e.g., Pilsen–Little Village Community Mental Health Center located in a Mexican American community in Chicago).

AFRICAN AMERICANS

A pattern has emerged in the literature regarding the differences in age of onset of heavy alcohol use between black and white men. Heavy alcohol use peaks in the 20s then declines in white men. Heavy use among black men is relatively low in the early years but peaks in the middle years before declining (Herd 1990). Etiological contributing factors to this pattern have yet to be determined. Heavy use may also contribute to the higher rate of alcohol-related health problems seen in black men. Herd (1994) suggests that this finding may represent a longer duration of heavy use as opposed to more discrete phases of heavy alcohol use seen in some white men. The body, it is hypothesized, is less resilient to the alcohol toxicity at older ages. The factors involved in the later onset of heavy alcohol use in African Americans and the subsequent rise in alcohol use need further research. One hypothesis may be that issues of racism and limited opportunities become more evident in young adulthood.

In addition, the prevalence of alcohol-related problems in black men shows significant differences in psychosocial distress compared to that of white men (Herd, 1994). The greatest differences between the groups are found in scores for loss of control, symptomatic drinking, binge drinking, health problems, and problems with friends and relatives. The two groups had similar drinking patterns as measured by frequency and maximum amounts consumed. Black men were significantly less permissive in attitudes toward alcohol use in particular situations such as driving a car or spending time with small children in a parental role. Further analyses showed that the higher rates of alcohol-related problems were not fully accounted for by differences in social and demographic differences between black and white men. Ziedonis, Rayford, Bryant, and Rounsaville (1994) have reported on differential rates of lifetime psychiatric comorbidity in black and white cocaine addicts. Whites had significantly higher rates of lifetime depression, alcohol dependence, and attention-deficit and conduct disorder.

An earlier study by Herd (1990), reporting on data from a 1984 national survey, showed similar findings of greater alcohol-related problems among black men than white men in the past year. The exception was drunk driving, in which white men scored higher. Black men scored higher on symptoms of physical dependence and health problems. Here the rates of frequent heavy drinking were lower, not higher, for black men. Limited financial resources and access to health care likely also contribute to the higher prevalence of alcohol-related health problems in black men. Blacks have reported to have higher rates of liver cirrhosis than do whites. Legal consequences to drinking and drug use among African Americans may be related to higher police surveillance in African American communities.

A study by Jones-Webb, Hsiao, and Hannan (1995) looked at the effect of affluence on drinking patterns of black and white men. It showed that less affluent black men when compared to less affluent white men reported greater numbers of negative consequences related to drinking and total problems. The reverse was true for affluent men, with whites reporting greater number of consequences and total problems. Lower socioeconomic class seems to have a more profound influence on alcohol-related problems for black men than for white men according to this study as well as others (Barr, Farrell, Barnes, & Welte, 1993, Herd, 1994, Jones, 1989). Jones-Webb et al. (1995) speculate that black men of lower socioeconomic status may experience more overt forms of discrimination and may be more likely to reside in communities in which there is more police surveillance. Health care and social services may also be limited. Affluence appears to be protective against alcohol-related problems for black men. Herd's (1994) analysis of a national survey demonstrated that high income among blacks is associated with lower rates of heavy drinking. This factor alone has very little effect on heavy drinking among whites.

Illicit Drugs

Historically, a greater proportion of African Americans abstain from illicit drug use than do whites. This difference is especially pronounced in the 12-to-25 age group. However, public databases such as the Client Data Acquisition Process and Drug Abuse Warning Network (DAWN) suggest that African Americans and Hispanics are overrepresented in categories of heroin and cocaine use (Hanson, 1985). In addition, a larger proportion of African Americans develop complications related to heavy use.

The increase in the public's awareness of the harmful effects of drugs led to a drop in drug use between 1985 and 1988 among all groups including African Americans (National Institute on Drug Abuse, 1990). Since the 1980s we have seen up-and-down patterns of perceived harm among high school students. However, data published by the National Institute on Drug Abuse (NIDA) in 1993 showed a worrisome finding that there was an increase in past-month illicit drug use among African Americans between 1988 and 1991; Whites and Hispanics demonstrated a decrease during the same period. Also, emerging from epidemiology studies is the higher concentration of heroin use among African Americans as compared to whites. The National Household Survey on Drug Abuse (Substance Abuse and Mental Health Administration, 1995) shows that past-month use of any illicit drug is highest for whites between the ages of 12 and 25 and highest for African Americans from the age of 26 and up. Hispanics showed the lowest rates of past-month use across all age groups. A course reading of this literature might imply that there is some intrinsic nature to the ethnic groups that accounts for the differences. Lillie-Blanton, Anthony, and Schuster (1993) conducted a study in which she regrouped participants according to neighborhood rather than race or ethnicity. She held constant social and environmental risk factors that likely influence the racial comparisons and applied this design to the apparent differences in crack cocaine use among whites, Hispanics, and African Americans. This interesting analysis revealed that the odds ratios did not vary significantly among the ethnic groups. Being African American did not place individuals at higher risk for crack use. Though this analysis does not refute the epidemiological findings of the study, it does suggest that the apparent differences may be more a product of social conditions, including availability of drugs, than are issues intrinsic to ethnicity. It is well-known that as a result of the "war on drugs" and other pressures, prisons and jails are over represented by Africans Americans arrested for drug-related charges. Inequalities in sentencing factors may belie subtle racism. For example, the differential sentencing for crack cocaine use, which is more prevalent in black communities, and powder cocaine has recently been a matter of national debate.

As with alcohol, illicit drug use appears to take a greater toll on African Americans' health as measured by emergency department data. African Americans are overrepresented in the major cities included in the DAWN survey conducted by NIDA (1990). In 1988, African Americans accounted for 39% of the drug-abuse related emergency room cases reported to DAWN. Although DAWN data are derived from large cities where African American populations are proportionally high, this is still an overrepresentation. African Americans were more likely to be treated and released rather than hospitalized as compared to whites. The 1988 survey showed cocaine was the primary drug leading to the emergency room visit. African Americans are also overrepresented in the medical examiner's data. They accounted for 30% of drug-related deaths while making up 23% of the population of the cities surveyed in DAWN. Cocaine was the most frequently listed drug followed by heroin and morphine. Much of the data about hard core drug use comes from similar data derived from public facilities. These data may seriously underestimate the persons who obtain alternative treatment for medical and psychosocial problems.

Literature reviewed by Brown, Alterman, Rutherford, Cacciola, and Zaballero (1993) suggest that correlates of heroin abuse may be educational impairment, poor employment history, history of legal problems including incarceration, and possibly psychiatric problems. A study of a national sample of youth cocaine use by Kandel and Davies (1991) implicates several correlates. Early sexual intercourse was associated with elevated lifetime cocaine use across all three ethnic groups. Recent cocaine use increased among females across all ethnic groups and males across white and Hispanic groups. Early sexual intercourse is defined as age 13 for boys and 14 for girls. The other correlate to cocaine use was daily marijuana use as defined by use at least 20 times in the last 30 days. Nobles and Goddard (1989) put forth three major processes that give rise to drug abuse among African Americans: (1) economic deprivation, racism, and environmental stress; (2) general availability of drugs and alcohol in the community; and (3) media and advertising heavily targeting the African American communities.

Prevention and Treatment Issues

Some argue that prevention and treatment of substance abuse in the African American community must recognize and address institutional racism and sociopolitical exploitation. Conversely, many in the African American community stress the issues of self-help and community empowerment to combat divisive elements leading to drug and alcohol use. For example, network therapy may have a particular role in more distressed communities. In addition to highlighting the high-risk factors, many researchers are focusing on the protective factors against substance abuse in minorities. Pro blackness and awareness of racial oppression have been associated with negative substance use attitudes (Gary & Berry, 1985). Several treatment questions are still largely unanswered in terms of the differences in treatment approaches to African Americans. There is no question that standard treatment approaches highlighted in the rest of this book can readily be applied to all ethnic groups. The course features of loss of control and compulsivity that make a drug abuser or alcoholic are not dissimilar between ethnic groups. However, as we continue to tailor treatment to individuals, race and cultural factors have to be considered important variables and in certain incidences especially addressed.

Should programs in primarily African American communities be especially designed to promote cultural sensitivity? In some sense this goes on naturally as the feel, look, and language of an Alcohol Anonymous (AA) meeting in an African American community is different from a white self-help group. AA had its beginnings in the Oxford movement and was initially white and middle class. However, the church and spiritual dimensions of black life are an integral aspect of black culture, and it is not surprising that AA has been successfully transplanted to the black community. There have been attempts to develop and describe culturally sensitive mental health facilities (Deitch & Solit, 1993; Rowe & Grills, 1993). These attempts often are trapped in a quagmire of definitions of culture, race, and what is crucial to a culturally relevant program. Culturally relevant programs might promote positive racial and cultural identity, enhance self-esteem, increase self-determination, and appreciate traditional African American values. However, other cultural tendencies, such as "Colored People" (CP) time or the tendency to start late, may reflect an unhurried approach to life that conflicts with the larger European culture. Afrocentric values stress relationships, verbal fluidity, emotional expressiveness, and spirituality.

Research questions with a hypothesis that especially addresses ethnic concerns are needed. Too often, knowledge of treatment issues in minorities is extrapolated from larger data sets. There may be dimensions to an all-black treatment program that go beyond variables currently thought to be important. Ethnic biological differences, if any exist, of African Americans need further work. Differences in health outcome and possibly medication responses need further consideration. The issue of matching or nonmatching of therapist or patients along racial and ethnic dimensions has been a subject of considerable discussion in mental health and has a role in the substance abuse field. Empathy and respect of others' cultural norms are an essential component to any discussion of cultural sensitivity. Matching of racial and cultural attributes between therapist and client may enhance empathy or in some cases result in an overidentification with the client on the part of the therapist.

HISPANIC AMERICANS

According to census data, Hispanic Americans make up 9% of the U.S. population. However, that number is expected to rise considerably in the next half century. This is a heterogeneous group. Mexican Americans make up 60%; Puerto Ricans, 12%; Cuban Americans, 5%; and other Hispanic Americans the remaining 23% (U.S. Bureau of the Census, 1996). As with other ethnic groups, a greater number of Hispanic men drink alcohol and use drugs than do Hispanic women. Mexican American men were more likely to abstain than other Hispanic men. However, they drank more heavily and reported more alcohol-related problems. Cuban men had fewer abstainers, a smaller proportion of heavy drinkers, and fewer alcohol-related problems. Drinking increased with education and income for both sexes (Caetano, 1989).

According to the 1995 National Household Survey on Drug Abuse for all age groups except 12–17, Hispanics had the fewest members in the "ever used any illicit drug" category as compared to whites and African Americans. Fewer African Americans in the 12–17 age range report ever using illicit drugs. All age groups of the African Americans remain lower than whites except for the 35-years-or-older group, where they are nearly equal to whites.

An important relationship exists between acculturation and alcohol use for Hispanics. Black and Markides's (1993) examination of data from the Hispanic Health and Nutrition Examination Survey showed a positive correlation between acculturation and probability of using alcohol and also with frequency of consumption. This finding applies to Mexican, Cuban, and Puerto Rican Americans. Acculturation involves the extent of adoption of the language and anglo traditions and values into the family system. Caetano and Medina-Mora (1990) looked at the drinking patterns of Mexican Americans as compared with Mexicans living in Mexico. A more permissive attitude about alcohol use is associated with acculturation. Alcohol use increased with acculturation in both Mexican men and woman. However, Mexican Americans report fewer alcohol-related problems than do Mexican men living in Mexico. For Mexican women born in the United States, abstention rates steadily decreased and rates of infrequent drinking steadily increased with acculturation. This pattern is not seen in Mexican-born women living in the United States (Caetano & Medina-Mora, 1990). Inhalant use has been reported to be high among Hispanic youth in southwestern border states.

Ruiz, Langrod, and Alksne (1981) delineate special cultural factors of the Puerto Rican population. Puerto Ricans are U.S. citizens. Puerto Ricans serve in the U.S. military. However, those living on the island are not allowed to vote in presidential and other federal elections nor do they have full representation in Congress. Puerto Rico is not a state, yet it is not an independent country. There is ambivalence in the way the United States views Puerto Rico that creates an identity confusion in the Puerto Rican culture. The culture was stressed by rapid and mandatory industrialization/urbanization and estranged from its agricultural and farming roots. Mexican Americans and Puerto Ricans have in common the misfortune of being seen by the mainstream United States as a burden on its economy and resources. Recent, more restrictive U.S. immigration laws may further stress Hispanic family ties, which creates a less than hospitable environment for people living in this country. The more recent and/or less assimilated also must deal with the language barrier. Mainstream America's relationship to Cuban immigrants is very different as motivated by the political regime in Cuba. The dynamic is more protective and patriarchal, creating less alienation for immigrants and their families.

Treatment Issues

Language can be the most concrete barrier to adequate treatment for Hispanics in communities without adequate Spanish-speaking facilities. However, cultural sensitivity is not guaranteed by just speaking the language. For example, Spanish-speaking male staff must be able to treat female clients with respect and sensitivity to sexual, family, and childrearing issues. A number of authors (e.g., Szapocznik & Fein, 1995) identify family issues as being perhaps the most important component of addiction treatment of the Hispanic client.

Gfroerer and De La Rosa (1993) found that parents' attitudes and use of drugs, licit or illicit, played an important role on the drug use behavior of 12- to 17-year-old Hispanic youth. Parents need to be informed clearly and honestly about their influence. Also, the role of family should be well understood by treatment staff. Each family member has a function within the family. If properly educated, the family members can each provide support using their already established role. Some of the traditional roles according to Ruiz et al. (1981) are the elderly esteemed for their wisdom, the father for his authority, mother for her devotion, and children for their future promise. Denial of alcoholism may be extensive in Hispanic fathers who drink only on the weekend and fulfill work obligations. Szapocznik and Fein (1995) include the cultural tradition of interdependence with extended family made up of uncles, aunts, cousins, and lifelong friends. Basically, the functional family does include any person who has day-to-day contact with and a role in the family. The family is an important resource and must be integrated into the treatment.

ASIAN AMERICANS

People of Asian heritage make up nearly 3% of the U.S. population according to U.S. Bureau of the Census (1996). Chinese Americans are the largest group, making up 24%; Filipinos, 20%, Asian Indians, 12%; Koreans, 12%; Japanese, 12%; and Vietnamese, 9%. Other countries of Asian immigration include Mongolia, Pakistan, Nepal, Bangladesh, Burma, Thailand, Cambodia, Maylasia, Singapore, and others. Many languages, cultures, and political systems are represented. Most of the world's major religions are represented, including Buddhism, Hinduism, Judaism, Christianity, and Islam. These religions have varying views regarding alcohol use. Alcohol use is prohibited in the Moslem teachings. Hinduism and Buddhism suggest avoidance of alcohol and other mind-altering substances. The Judeo-Christian perspective is more lenient and incorporates alcohol use into some religious ceremonies. These views affect the way society, family, and the problem drinker deal with the concept and acceptance of alcoholism. The acceptance and availability of treatment for individuals also have an impact.

The well-described "flushing " reaction seen in some Asian people has been linked to variations of aldehyde dehydrogenase isoenzymes. The reaction occurs because of a limited ability to degrade acetaldehyde to acetic acid. The toxic acetaldehyde is responsible for the flushing, headache, nausea, and other symptoms with alcohol use; estimated to occur in 47–85% of Asians (U.S. Department of Health and Human Services, 1993). This was thought to explain the lower rates of alcohol abuse among Asians. However, recent studies have shown that sociocultural factors play a substantial role in alcohol use (Johnson & Nagoski, 1990; Newlin, 1989).

Some major databases on alcoholism in ethnic minority populations do not include information on Asian Americans. The Epidemiologic Catchment Area Study, the National Household Survey on Drug Abuse, and DAWN have placed Asian Americans in the "other" category. The only national study that surveyed Asians as a specific category is the National Drug and Alcoholism Treatment Unit Survey in which Asian Americans accounted for 0.6% of the population in treatment. This is not an estimation of the extent of the problem in the nontreatment population. The available research literature is mostly community based or pertaining to a specific subgroup within the Asian American community, such as students. Zane and Saszo (1992), in their literature review, found problems such as small sample size, exclusion of high-risk populations such as recent immigrants and adolescents, inadequate translations, and lack of controls for socioeconomic and cultural factors. Given these limitations, a number of studies show that there is significant variation in drinking patterns among the different Asian groups. There is some evidence that rates of heavy drinking are higher for Filipino Americans and Japanese Americans followed by Korean Americans and Chinese Americans: 29%, 28.9%, 25.8%, and 14.2%, respectively (Kitano & Chi, 1989). The breakdown by sex found heavy drinking in 11.7% of Japanese women, 3.5% of Filipino women, and 0.8% of Korean women, whereas Chinese women registered zero.

Potential treatment problems in the Asian American community begin with the lack of acceptance of alcoholism and drug addictions as treatable illnesses. Ja and Aoki (1993) write about the typical chain of events in the life of an intact Asian family when substance abuse begins to appear. Often substance abuse problems are ignored or denied with the hope that they will disappear. Also, the family will make efforts to conceal it from the community to avoid embarrassment and shame. Prevention or early treatment is unlikely in this family and community dynamic. When denial is overwhelming, the family breaks down and may resort to shaming and other attempts at punishment. The family may also turn to extended family members and elders, basically moving gradually outward from nuclear family to external community. There is a deep sense of failure on the part of the family by the time members resort to outside professional help. It is not uncommon at this point to have the family members completely turn over the alcoholic or addict and resist participation themselves. The client is often still in denial and resistant to treatment until an alliance with staff is facilitated.

Treatment barriers begin with ignorance to the actual extent of drug and alcohol problems in the Asian American community. Asians are thought of by many as model immigrants. The 1960s brought in a large wave of educated and skilled Asian professionals. Migration since the 1970s has resulted in people with less education and fewer language and work skills immigrating to the United States (Varma & Siris, 1996). Many of them entered as refugees from war- ravaged countries. Poverty, overcrowded domiciles, discrimination, and other social problems are present in the lives of Asian Americans; however, documentation of these problems is sparse. This notion of "model" immigrant may be hurting the Asian American community from outside and within. It also lends itself to the denial within the community and amplifies the elements of shame and embarrassment felt by the family.

Better documentation of the extent of drug and alcohol abuse in the Asian American population would ideally, enhance the funding for culturally sensitive education and treatment. Education at the community level is needed to foster awareness and acceptance and assist in prevention. Treatment programs that target Asian American might consider the insular and private style of the Asian American family. Also essential is the recognition of the dominance of the family and community over the psychological and social needs of the individual. An acceptance of these differences would decrease conflict between family and treatment. This show of respect for their values may facilitate the family's participation in the treatment. A treatment goal for all individuals should be the reintegration back into their family and community if at all possible.

NATIVE AMERICANS

Alcohol abuse is recognized as a significant problem among Native Americans. In the past, arrest rates secondary to alcohol use for Native Americans have been reported to be 12 times the national average (Stewart, 1964). Although the alcohol mortality rate for Native Americans was three- to fourfold the national average, recent evidence indicates that there has been a decrease in mortality since 1969 (Burns, 1995). This drop seems to be in concert with the doubling of alcohol treatment services by the Indian Health Service in the 1980s.

Illicit drug use among Native Americans is less clear as there are poor data available. Further, the use of hallucinogens has a role in some Native American religious rituals. The heterogeneity of Native American cultures is plainly evident and further discourages simplistic discussions of Indian culture.

The "firewater" myth states that alcohol introduced to Native Americans by white settlers produced exaggerated biological effects in such persons. Garcia-Andrade, Wall, and Ehlers (1997), however, recently found less subjective intoxication among nonalcoholic mission Indian men with greater Native American heritage. The same researchers implicate alcohol expectancy and metabolism rates as possible differential effects among this tribe (Wall, Garcia-Anrade, Thomasson, Cole, & Ehlers, 1996; Garcia-Andrade et al., 1997).

Native Americans share a belief in the unity and sacredness of all nature. An individual or ethnic group may be more or less familiar with their own culture. Confrontation approaches, successful to many Anglo programs, cause Native Americans to shy away. Risk factors for alcohol and drug use in Native Americans parallel many of the same issues of other disenfranchised groups. Attempts at assimilation of Native American culture, in the context of isolation from mainstream opportunities, contributed to further cultural stress.

The recent increase in Indian-owned casinos has offered monetary opportunities but also the possibilities of increased gambling and substance abuse. The breakdown of Native American culture, a factor that allowed alcohol to take a foothold, has been reversing in recent years. Self-determination and a return to traditional spiritual and healing beliefs have helped springboard alternative indigenous models of alcohol and drug recovery.

REFERENCES

Adelstein, A., & Graham-White. (1977). Alcoholism and mortality. *Population Trends, 7.*

Anthony, J. C., Tien, A. Y., & Petronis, K. R. (1990). Epidemiologic evidence on cocaine use and panic attacks. *American Journal of Epidemiology, 129,* 543–549.

Barr, K. E. M., Farrell, M. P., Barnes, G. M., & Welte, J. W. (1993). Race, class and gender differences in substance abuse: Evidence of a middle-class/under-class polarization among black males. *Social Problems, 403,* 314–327.

Berrettini, W. H., & Persico, A. M. (1996). Dopamine D2 receptor gene polymorphisms and vulnerability to substance abuse in African Americans. *Journal of Biological Psychiatry, 40,* 144–147.

Black, S., & Markides, K. S. (1993). Acculturation and alcohol consumption in Puerto Rican, Cuban-American, and Mexican-American women in the United States. *American Journal of Public Health, 83*(6), 890–893.

Blume, S. B. (1986). Women and alcohol: A review. *Journal of the American Medical Association, 256*(11), 1467–1470.

Booth, R., Koester, S., & Pinto, F. (1995). Gender differences in sex-risk behaviors, economic livelihood, and self-concept among drug injectors and crack smokers. *American Journal on Addictions, 4*(5), 313–320.

Boyd, C., Guthrie, B., Pohl, J., Whitmarsh, J., & Henderson, D. (1994). African American women who smoke crack cocaine: Sexual trauma and the mother–daughter relationship. *Journal of Psychoactive Drugs, 26*(3), 243–247.

Brown, L. S., Jr., Alterman, A. I., Rutherford, M. J., Cacciola, J. W., Zaballero, A. R. (1963). Addiction Severity Index Scores of Four racial/ethnic and gender groups of methadone maintenance patients. *Journal of Substance Abuse, 5*(3), 269–279.

Brown, T. G., Seragaman, P., Kokin, M., & Shields, N. (1995). The role of spouses of substance abusers in treatment: Gender differences. *Journal of Psychoactive Drugs, 27,* 223–229.

Burns, T. R. (1995). How does IHS relate administratively to the high alcoholism mortality rate? *American Indian and Alaska Native Mental Health Research, 6*(3), 31–45.

Caetano, R. (1989). Drinking patterns and alcohol problems in a national sample of U.S. Hispanics. In D. L. Spiegler, D. A. Tate, S. S. Aitken, & C. M. Christian (Eds.), *Alcohol use among U.S. ethnic minorities: Proceedings of a conference on the epidemiology of alcohol use and abuse among ethnic minority groups* (NIAAA Research Monograph No. 18, DHHS Publication No. ADM 89-1435, pp. 147–162). Washington, DC: U.S. Government Printing Office.

Caetano, R., & Medina-Mora, M. E. (1990). Reasons and attitudes toward drinking and abstaining: A comparison of Mexicans and Mexican-Americans. In *Epidemiologic trends in drug use: Community epidemiology work group proceedings, June, 1990* (pp. 173–191). Rockville, MD: National Institute of Drug Abuse.

Chan, R. J., McBride, A. W., Thomasson, H. R. Ykenney, A., & Crabb, D. W. (1994). Allele frequencies of the preproenkephalin A (PENK) gene CA repeat in Asians, African-Americans, and Caucasians: Lack of evidence for different allele frequencies in alcoholics. *Alcoholism: Clinical and Experimental Research, 18*(3), 533–535.

Deitch, D., & Solit, R. (1993). International training for drug abuse treatment and the issue of cultural relevance. *Journal of Psychoactive Drugs, 25*(1), 87–95.

Denier, C., Thevos, A., Latham, P., & Randall, C. (1991). Psychosocial and psychopathology differences in hospitalized male and female cocaine abusers: A retrospective chart review. *Addictive Behaviors, 16,* 489–496.

Fillmore, K. M. (1985). The social victims of drinking. *British Journal of Addictions, 80,* 307–314.

Garcia-Andrade, C., Wall, T. L., & Ehlers, C. L. (1997, July). The firewater myth and response to alcohol in mission Indians. *American Journal of Psychiatry, 154*(7), 983–988.

Gary, L., & Berry, G. (1985). Predicting attitudes toward substance use in a black community. *Community Mental Health Journal, 21,* 45–51.

Gfroerer, J., & De La Rosa, M. (1993). Protective and risk factors associated with drug use among Hispanic youth. *Journal of Addictive Disease, 12*(2), 87–107.

Gilbert, M. J. (1991). Acculturation and changes in drinking patterns among Mexican-American women. *Alcohol Health and Research World, 15*(3), 234–238.

Goldman, D., Brown, G. L., Albaugh, B., Robin, R., Goodson, S. , Trunzo, M., Akhtar, L., Lucas-Derse, S., Long, J., Linnoila, M., & Dean, M. (1993). DRD2 dopamine receptor genotype, linkage disequilibrium, and alcoholism in American Indians and other populations. *Alcoholism: Clinical and Experimental Research, 17*(2), 199–204.

Griffin, M. L., Weiss, R. D., Mirin, S. M., & Lang, U. (1989). A comparison of male and female cocaine abusers. *Archives of General Psychiatry, 46,* 122–126.

Hanson, B. (1985). Drug treatment effectiveness: The case of racial and ethnic minorities in America—Some research questions and proposals. *International Journal of the Addictions, 20*(1), 99–137.

Herd, D. (1990). Subgroup differences in drinking patterns among black and white men: Results from a national survey. *Journal of Studies on Alcohol, 51*(3), 221–232.

Herd, D. (1994). Predicting drinking problems among black and white men: Results from a national survey. *Journal of Studies on Alcohol, 55,* 61–71.

Herd, D. (1989). The epidemiology of drinking patterns and alcohol-related problems among U.S. blacks. In D. Spiegler, D. Tate, D. S. Aitkens, & C. Christian (Eds.), *Alcohol use among U. S. ethnic minorities* (NIAAA Research Monograph No. 18, DHHS Publication No. ADM 89-1435, pp. 3–50). Washington, DC: U.S. Government Printing Office.

Ja, D., & Aoki, B. (1993). Substance abuse treatment: Cultural barriers in the Asian-American community. *Journal of Psychoactive Drugs, 25*(1), 61–71.

Johnson, R. C., & Nagoski, C. T. (1990). Asians, Asian-Americans, and alcohol. *Journal of Psychoactive Drugs, 22*(1), 45–52.

Jones, R. J. (1989). *The socio-economic context of alcohol use and depression: Results from a national survey of black and white adults.* Fifteenth annual Ketil Bruun Alcohol Epidemiology Symposium, Maastricht, Netherlands.

Jones-Webb, R., Hsiao, C., & Hannan, P. (1995). Relationships between socioeconomic status and drinking problems among black and white men. *Alcoholism: Clinical and Experimental Research, 19*(3), 623–627.

Kandel, D. B., & Davies, M. (1991). Cocaine use in a national sample of U.S. youth (NLSY): Epidemiology, predictors, and ethnic patterns. In C. Schade & S. Schober (Eds.), *The epidemiology of cocaine use and abuse* (NIDA Research Monograph No. 110, pp. 151–188). Washington, DC: U.S. Government Printing Office.

Kitano, H. H. L., & Chi, I. (1989). Asian Americans and alcohol: The Chinese, Japanese, Koreans, and Filipinos in Los Angeles. In D. Spiegler, D. Tate, S. Aitkens, & C. Christian (Eds.), *Alcohol use among U.S. ethnic minorities* (NIAAA Research

Monograph No. 18, DHHS Publication No. ADM 89-1435, pp. 373–382). Washington, DC: U.S. Government Printing Office.

Lillie-Blanton, M., Anthony, J., & Schuster, C. R. (1993, February 24). Probing the meaning of racial/ethnic group comparisons in crack cocaine smoking. *Journal of the American Medical Association, 296*(8), 993–997.

Miller, B. A., & Downs, W. R. (1986). *Conflict and violence among alcoholic women as compared to a random household sample.* Paper presented at the 38th annual meeting of the American Society of Criminology, Atlanta.

National Institute on Drug Abuse. (1990). *National Household Survey on Drug Abuse.* Rockville, MD: Author.

Newlin, D. B. (1989). The skin-flushing response: Autonomic, self-report and conditioned responses to repeated administrations of alcohol in Asian men. *Journal of Abnormal Psychology, 98,* 421–425.

Nobles, W. W., & Goddard, L. (1989). Drugs in the African-American community: A clear and present danger. In J. Dewart (Ed.), *The state of black America.* New York: The National Urban League.

Ray, B. A. & Braude, M. C. (1986). *Women and drugs: A new era for research* (NIDA Research Monograph No. 65, DHHS Publication No. ADM 90-1447). Washington, DC: U.S. Government Printing Office.

Robbins, C. (1989, March). Sex differences in psychosocial consequences of alcohol and drug abuse. *Journal of Health and Behavior, 30,* 117–130.

Rowe, D., & Grills, C. (1993). African-centered drug treatment: An alternative conceptual paradigm for drug counseling with African-American clients. *Journal of Psychoactive Drugs, 25*(1), 21–33.

Ruiz, P., Langrod, J., & Alksne, L. (1981). Rehabilitation of the Puerto Rican addict: A cultural perspective. *International Journal of the Addictions, 16*(5), 841–847.

Stewart, O. (1964). Questions regarding American Indian criminality. *Human Organ, 23,* 61–66.

Substance Abuse and Mental Health Services Administration. (1995). *National Household Survey on Drug Abuse: Population estimates* (DHHS Publication No. SMA 96-3095). Washington, DC: U.S. Government Printing Office.

Szapocznik, J., & Fein, S. (1995). *Issues in preventing alcohol and other drug abuse among Hispanic/Latino families* (CSAP Cultural Competence Series 2, DHHS Publication No. SMA 95-3034). Washington, DC: U.S. Government Printing Office.

U.S. Bureau of the Census. (1996). *Current Population Reports.* Washington, DC: U.S. Government Printing Office.

U.S. Department of Health and Human Services. (1993, September). *Alcohol and health.* Alexandria, VA: EEI.

Varma, S., & Siris, S. (1996, Spring). Alcohol abuse in Asian Americans. *American Journal on Addiction, 5*(2), 136–143.

Wall, T. L., Garcia-Andrade, C., Thomasson, H. R., Cole, M., & Ehlers, C. L. (1996). Alcohol elimination in Native American mission Indians: An investigation of interindividual variation. *Alcoholism: Clinical and Experimental Research, 20*(7), 1159–1164.

Zane, N., & Sasso, T. (1992). Research on drug abuse among Asian Pacific Americans. *Drugs and Society , 6*(3–4), 181–209.

Ziedonis, D., Rayford, B., Bryant, K. J., & Rounsaville, B. (1994, January). Psychiatric comorbidity in white and African-American cocaine addicts seeking substance abuse treatment. *Hospital and Community Psychiatry, 45*(1), 43–49.

17

❏ _____

Addictive Disorders in Women

SHEILA B. BLUME

INTRODUCTION

Why write a chapter on women? Alcoholism and other addictions have traditionally been considered problems of men. The classical studies that have shaped our understanding of the nature and course of these diseases, from Jellinek's (1952) research on phases of alcoholism to Vaillant's (1995) 45-year longitudinal study of alcohol abuse in an inner-city and college cohort, limit themselves to male subjects. The earliest screening tools were developed for men. (The first version of the Michigan Alcohol Screening Test contained a question about the subject's wife, only later changed to "spouse.") Treatment methods and programs were also initially designed for male patients, and it was not unusual for women suffering from addictive disorders to be housed on general psychiatric wards while men were in special units. Male-oriented treatment models, like the so-called boot camps for addicts in the criminal justice system, were "adapted" for women simply by subjecting them to the same program, including masculine clothing and haircuts. Early studies that included information about women often failed to analyze or report these data (Blume, 1980). Although there has been improvement, gender bias in addiction research remains evident in the 1990s (Brett, Graham, & Smythe, 1995).

In spite of these limitations, a growing body of research has identified male–female differences in the way addictions develop and in treatment needs. This chapter summarizes some of the more clinically relevant features of addictive disorders in women. A number of recent reviews are available (Blume, 1997a; Center on Addiction and Substance Abuse, 1996; Miller &

Doot, 1994), as are several federal publications on the treatment of women (U.S. Department of Health and Human Services, 1993, 1994).

EPIDEMIOLOGY

In general, men are more likely to report any use of psychoactive substances, including alcohol and nicotine. However, changes in use differ by gender. For example, over the last 30 years the proportion of U.S. men who smoke has fallen at a much greater rate (52% to 28%) than the corresponding decrease among women (34% to 22%) (Center on Addiction and Substance Abuse, 1996).

Table 17.1 summarizes data on rates of substance use disorders. These rates were estimated for noninstitutionalized U.S. adults ages 15–54, from a diagnostic interview based on criteria according to the revised third edition of *Diagnostic and Statistical Manual of Mental Disorders* (DSM-III-R; American Psychiatric Association, 1987), administered to more than 8,000 subjects in the early 1990s as part of the National Comorbidity Study (Kessler et al., 1994; Warner, Kessler, Hughes, Anthony, & Nelson, 1995). The overall higher prevalence in men masks subgroup gender differences. Women ages 45–54 reported a higher lifetime prevalence of drug dependence (other than alcohol or nicotine) than did men (3.8% compared to 2.1% for men), whereas the 12-month prevalence is similar between the sexes at this age (0.8% for women, 0.6% for men). This finding reflects the higher prevalence of prescription drug dependence in women, whereas men have higher rates of dependence on illicit drugs (Warner et al., 1995).

Among young people, ages 15–24, the male rate of 12-month drug dependence (4.5%) is about twice the female rate (2.1%). However, among young people who have used a drug within the past 12 months, the rates are almost equal (males 13.6%, females 10.6%).

Demographic risk factors for alcohol problems in women have been

TABLE 17.1. Relative Prevalence of Addictive Disorders in the United States, Ages 15–54

Disorder	Males (%)	Females (%)	Male:female ratio
Lifetime abuse/dependence			
Any substance	35.4	17.9	2.0:1
Alcohol	32.6	14.62	2.2:1
Other drug[a]	14.6	9.4	1.6:1
12-month abuse/dependence			
Any substance	16.1	6.6	2.4:1
Alcohol	14.1	5.3	2.7:1
Other drug[a]	5.1	2.2	2.3:1

Note. From the National Comorbidity Study (Warner et al., 1995).
[a]Excludes nicotine; includes nonmedical use of prescription psychotropics

found age dependent in a large general population sample (Wilsnack & Cheloha, 1987). Women ages 21–34 years reported the highest problem rates. Among them, those who were never married, childless, and not employed ("role-less") were at highest risk. For women ages 35–49, those who were divorced or separated, had children not living with them, and were unemployed ("lost role"), and for women ages 50–64, those who were married, had children not living with them, and were not working outside the home ("role entrapment") had the highest problem rates. The last group is reminiscent of the so-called empty nest syndrome described among older women.

A prominent risk factor for both alcohol and other drug abuse/dependence in women is a history of physical and/or sexual abuse (Center on Addiction and Substance Abuse, 1996, Windle, Scheidt, & Miller, 1995). In data derived from the Epidemiologic Catchment Area (ECA) study in the early 1980s, Winfield, George, Swartz, and Blazer (1990) found the lifetime prevalence of alcohol abuse/dependence increased threefold and that of other drug abuse/dependence increased fourfold in women who reported a history of sexual assault.

Several researchers documented the influence of male "significant others" on the substance use patterns of women (e.g., Amaro & Hardy-Fosta, 1995). Men are likely to introduce women to the use of drugs and to supply drugs to their female partners.

Rates of both alcohol and other drug abuse/dependence are thought to be particularly high among lesbian women (McKirnan & Peterson, 1989) and women in the criminal justice system (Center on Addiction and Substance Abuse, 1996; Teplin, Abram, & McLellan, 1996). Among women convicted of homicide, rates of alcohol abuse/dependence were increased nearly fiftyfold above rates in the general population (Eronen, 1995).

PHYSIOLOGICAL FACTORS

Pharmacology

Early research on the pharmacology of alcohol and other drugs was performed on male subjects and thought to apply to both sexes. More recently, however, it has been found that given equal doses of alcohol (even if corrected for body weight), women reach higher blood alcohol levels than men (Frezza et al., 1990). This fact is partly related to alcohol's distribution in total body water, because women have a greater proportion of fat and less body water than do men. In addition, men have higher levels of the enzyme alcohol dehydrogenase (ADH) in the gastric mucosa, leading to increased metabolism in the stomach (first-pass metabolism) and less absorption into the male bloodstream.

Gender differences in the pharmacology of other drugs are less well studied. The differences in body composition noted previously produce longer half-lives in lipid-soluble drugs such as diazepam and oxazepam in women (Barry, 1987).

Health Effects

Chronic heavy alcohol use has been linked to many serious medical complications in both sexes (Miller & Doot, 1994). However, many of these complications develop more rapidly in women, with a lower level of alcohol intake. Included are hepatic steatosis and cirrhosis, hypertension, anemia, malnutrition, gastrointestinal hemorrhage, peptic ulcer (Ashley et al., 1977), and both peripheral myopathy and cardiomyopathy (Urbano-Marquez et al., 1995). Both human immunodeficiency virus (HIV) infection and other sexually transmitted diseases are linked to substance use disorders in women (Center on Addiction and Substance Abuse, 1996). Seventy percent of currently HIV-infected women acquired the virus either through injection drug use or during sexual relations with a drug-injecting partner, compared to less than half of HIV-infected men. Addicted women, particularly those dependent on crack cocaine or heroin, often become infected by exchanging sex for drugs or by engaging in prostitution to obtain money for drugs.

Alcohol and other drug use is closely linked to smoking in women. Mortality for lung cancer in U.S. women surpassed breast cancer mortality in 1986 to become the leading cause of cancer death. The risks for coronary artery disease, obstructive lung disease, peptic ulcer, and early menopause as well as cancers of the mouth, larynx, esophagus, stomach bladder, and cervix are increased in female smokers (Cyr & Moulton, 1990), as is the risk for breast cancer in female drinkers (Longnecker, Berlin, Orza, & Chalmers, 1988).

Effects on Reproductive Functioning

Whereas single doses of alcohol have little effect on sex hormone levels in women, chronic heavy drinking leads to inhibition of ovulation, infertility, and a variety of reproductive and sexual dysfunctions (Gavaler, 1985).

Consumption of alcohol by women suppresses both sexual arousal (Wilson & Lawson, 1976) and orgasmic function (Malatesta, Pollack, Crotty, & Peacock, 1982) in a dose–response fashion. The physiological reality is contrary to the widely held cultural belief that alcohol is an aphrodisiac for women (Blume, 1991). This belief often leads alcoholic women to expect that they need alcohol to perform and enjoy the sexual act, in spite of their alcohol-related sexual problems. The clinician can help such women by explaining that their drinking has depressed rather than enhanced their sexual responsiveness, and that in the presence of a loving relationship, they will find sex more enjoyable in recovery than they did while drinking (Gavaler, Rizzo, & Rossaro, 1993).

Cocaine and amphetamines are widely believed to be sexual stimulants, whereas chronic use is often associated with loss of sexual desire and inhibited orgasm. Heroin use has been reported to suppress both ovulation and sexual desire (Gaulden, Littlefield, & Putoff, 1964), as has abuse of sedative drugs.

Fetal Alcohol and Drug Effects

Fetal alcohol syndrome (FAS), a combination of birth defects producing lifelong disability, is currently estimated to affect about 1 to 3 infants for every 1,000 live births in the United States (Institute of Medicine, 1995). FAS is thus among the three most frequent birth defects resulting in mental retardation, with a prevalence similar to Down syndrome and spina bifida. A diagnosis of FAS is based on the co-occurrence of pre- and postnatal growth deficiency, structural facial abnormalities, and central nervous system dysfunctions, including poor coordination, mental retardation, and/or behavioral dyscontrol. In addition, a wide variety of other birth defects affecting vision, hearing, and other body systems are often seen in these children. Although the full FAS syndrome is seen almost exclusively in the offspring of alcoholic women who drink heavily (average six or more drinks per day) during pregnancy, women who drink at lower levels are at risk for such fetal alcohol effects as miscarriage, low birth weight, birth defects, and behavioral abnormalities (Institute of Medicine, 1995). The prevalence of fetal alcohol effects is thought to be many times greater than that of FAS.

Fetal damage is also associated with other drug use and abuse (Hoegerman, Wilson, Thurmond, & Schnoll, 1990; Center on Addiction and Substance Abuse, 1996). Cigarette smoking during pregnancy is implicated as an important factor in miscarriage, low birth weight, and sudden infant death syndrome. Unfortunately, many young women believe that cocaine facilitates a quick and less painful delivery, whereas it actually produces obstetric complications that cause damage to the newborn, as well as birth defects secondary to its deleterious effects on fetal circulation. Pregnant heroin addicts are customarily treated with methadone as a maintenance drug rather than detoxification to abstinence, as a safer regimen for the fetus. With good prenatal care, such patients can be brought to term and experience normal deliveries. However, these infants require treatment for neonatal opiate withdrawal (U.S. Department of Health and Human Services, 1993).

Whether or not birth defects occur, untreated substance abuse/dependence in a new mother will interfere with maternal–infant bonding, parenting, and family life. Thus, pregnancy is a critical time for case finding and intervention. Among the approximately 4 million pregnancies in the United States annually, approximately 20% of women smoke, 19% use alcoholic beverages, and 13% use other substances (Center on Addiction and Substance Abuse, 1996).

GENETIC INFLUENCES

A great deal of research has been devoted to the effort to differentiate genetic from environmental factors in the etiology of alcoholism (Sigvardsson, Bohman, & Cloninger, 1996) as well as other drug dependencies (Ripple & Luthar, 1996). Almost all implicate a combination of nature and nurture

(Kendler, Walters, & Neale, 1995). Of interest here is that some studies show different patterns of alcoholism heredity for men and women, with evidence for stronger environmental influence in females (Sigvardsson et al., 1996; Cloninger, Christiansen, Reich, & Gottesman, 1978).

Studies of possible genetic markers in children of alcoholics have largely been confined to males, although Lex, Lukus, amd Greenwald (1988) replicated this work in a small number of women. Daughters of alcoholic parents have also been found to have more positive and pleasant mood reactions to a single dose of alprazolam, suggesting that they may be at greater risk for abuse of this drug (Ciraulo et al., 1996).

In addition, some research suggests that there is a genetic link between alcoholism in male relatives and major depressive disease in women, in a combination of genetic and environmental causation (Cadoret et al., 1996). A study in female twin pairs suggests separate heredity but common environmental risk factors for comorbid alcoholism and major depression in women (Kendler, Heath, Neale, Kessler, & Eaves, 1993).

PSYCHOLOGICAL FACTORS

The role of psychological factors in the etiology of substance use disorders has been a subject of uncertainty for many years. Long-term longitudinal studies of male alcoholics have found that psychiatric disorders and symptoms are more likely to be the result of alcoholism than of predisposing factors (Vaillant, 1995). However, the lack of similar studies in women leaves the question open. The strong association between childhood physical and sexual abuse and later addictive disease in women, alluded to in the section "Epidemiology," suggests mediation through such psychological symptoms as low self-esteem, depression, shame, guilt, and feelings of sexual inadequacy. One of the few longitudinal studies that did include women, a 27-year follow-up of a college drinking study (Fillmore, Bacon, & Hyman, 1979) looked at risk factors for later drinking problems. These factors were different for males and females. Although women who had alcohol-related problems in college had a higher prevalence of later problems than did their female classmates, the women at highest risk for problems later in life were those who reported in college that they drank to relieve shyness, to feel gay, to get along better on dates, and to get high. This pattern suggests psychological dependence as a risk factor for women.

Another approach to the study of psychological factors is to examine gender differences in the patterns of comorbid psychiatric disorders in identified alcoholics and other drug addicts. Both in general population studies (Helzer & Pryzbek, 1988) and in clinical populations (Hesselbrock, Meyer, & Keener, 1985; Rounsaville et al., 1991; Ross, Glaser, & Stiasny, 1988), female alcoholics and addicts have higher rates of comorbid psychiatric disorders in general, and higher rates of depressive and anxiety disorders in particular, compared to males. In fact, the only comorbid diagnoses found more frequently in addicted males are residual attention-deficit disorder, antisocial personality disorder, and pathological gambling (Lesieur, Blume, & Zoppa, 1986). Eating disorders (Walfish, Stenmark, Sarco, Shealy, & Krone, 1992) and posttraumatic stress disorder (commonly related in women to sexual abuse) (Kessler, Sonnega, Bromet, Hughes, & Nelson, 1995) are seen frequently in women with addictions.

Of particular interest from the point of view of etiology is the question concerning which disorders occur first (primary) and which develop subsequently (secondary). As mentioned earlier, Vaillant (1995) found that alcoholism was usually primary in men. However, in the general population ECA study, Helzer and Pryzbek (1988) found that among adults with lifetime diagnoses of both alcohol abuse/dependence and major depression, depression was primary in 66% of the women, compared to only 22% of men. Likewise, in an inpatient alcoholism treatment population, Hesselbrock et al. (1985) found depression primary in 66% of the women with comorbid major depression, compared to 41% of men. Similar findings were reported for alcoholic research volunteers (Roy et al., 1991) and dual-diagnosed adolescents (Deykin, Buka, & Zeena, 1992). Longitudinal survey evidence (Hartka, Johnstone, & Lieno, 1991; Wilsnack, Klassen, & Schur, 1991) also tends to support a relationship between earlier reports of depression and later increases in alcohol use or chronicity of alcohol problems. Interestingly, alcohol use at time one in these longitudinal studies in women also predicted later depression.

Taken together, the previous discussion suggests some link between primary depression and alcoholism in women. Because alcohol is not an effective antidepressant (Vaillant, 1995), the link is probably not simple self-medication. Further research is needed to elucidate this relationship. However, the relationship highlights the need to take careful psychiatric histories in all women suffering from addictive disorders, with special emphasis on the temporal development of comorbid disorders. Patients whose depression preceded their addiction or occurred during a prolonged period of abstinence are likely to have a primary depressive disorder requiring specific treatment, whereas depression secondary to addiction is more likely to improve spontaneously with recovery from the addiction. In addition, patients with primary depression should be warned about the possibility of recurrence and carefully educated to recognize early symptoms of a recurrent major depressive episode. Vigorous treatment of such an episode during remission of the patient's addiction can avoid alcohol/drug relapse and promote further progress in the patient's recovery.

SOCIOCULTURAL FACTORS

As pointed out in the section "Genetic Influences," environmental factors are particularly important in the etiology of addictive disorders in women (e.g., Cloninger et al., 1978). Sociocultural influences include general cultural and subcultural norms for alcohol, tobacco, and other drug use; culturally based attitudes and beliefs about such use (including popular media stereotypes of users and abusers); peer pressure; prescription practices; laws regulating availability and use; and the economics of supply, demand, price, and disposable income. In all societies that allow alcohol and/or drug use, these norms, attitudes, stereotypes, peer pressures, and even laws (dating as far back as the Code of Hammurabi in 2000 B.C.) differ for males and females.

Social attitudes act as a double-edged sword for women. On the one hand, the expectation that women will drink lower quantities of alcoholic beverages and drink less frequently is protective (Klee & Ames, 1987, Kubicka, Csemy, & Kozeny, 1995). On the other hand, the intense stigma linked to stereotypes of alcoholic and addicted women creates serious problems for women who drink and/or use other drugs (Blume, 1991). Behavior tolerated in men is considered scandalous for women. Compare the expression "drunk as a lord" with its feminine equivalent, "drunk as a lady." In addition, the drinking/drugging woman is considered promiscuous. Society believes, contrary to fact, that alcohol is a sexual stimulant for women, so that a woman under the influence who says no really means yes. Although a general population survey of nearly 1,000 women failed to find evidence that women who drink become less particular in their choice of sexual partner, even if drinking heavily (Klassen & Wilsnack, 1986), women's drinking is a frequent rationalization for sexual assault, including date rape (Blume, 1991). In a study of beliefs about rape, young adults considered a rapist who is intoxicated less responsible for the crime, whereas they considered a victim who has been drinking more to blame (Richardson & Campbell, 1982). It is not surprising, then, that alcoholic women are much more likely to be victims of violent crime than are matched controls, including rape (Miller & Downs, 1986). These women are also more likely to report spousal violence than are control women. Society's view of alcohol/drug-abusing women is one of moral and sexual degradation, making them acceptable targets for sexual aggression (Blume, 1991).

Another result of this stigma is denial, on the personal, family and societal levels. A woman in the early stage of alcohol/drug dependence, accepting the cultural stereotype, denies that she may have a problem ("I'm not like that!"). Families also deny that the difficulty with their mother, daughter, sister, or wife could be alcoholism or addiction ("She's not like that!"). Physicians and other health professionals often fail to diagnose alcoholism in patients who do not resemble social stereotypes. Alcoholic patients least likely to be correctly identified in a large general hospital study were those with higher incomes and educational levels, those with private insurance, and those who were female (Moore, Bone, Geller, & Mamon, 1989).

As the disease progresses in the addicted woman, intense guilt and shame often drive the sufferer into hiding, so that the alcoholic woman is far more likely to drink alone than is the alcoholic man. If she lives alone or is a single parent with small children, there may be no significant others in her social network able to recognize her problem and intervene. Although alcoholic women frequently seek medical help for a variety of complaints ranging from infertility, depression, anxiety, or insomnia to hypertension and peptic ulcer, their guilt, shame, and denial require that the interviewing professional screen actively for alcohol/drug problems. Undetected alcohol/drug use disorders can lead to inappropriate symptomatic treatment, with the danger of adding dependence on prescription sedatives, analgesics, or tranquilizers to the patient's problems. Failure in diagnosis in women of childbearing age may lead to the appearance of preventable birth defects in their offspring. Finally, delay in diagnosis allows the development of late-stage physical, psychological, and social complications, making eventual treatment more costly, more difficult, and less successful. Early diagnosis and adequate treatment of substance use disorders in women is also an important component in the prevention of teen pregnancy, acquired immune deficiency syndrome, hepatitis, suicide, and other negative outcomes.

CLINICAL FEATURES OF ADDICTIVE DISORDERS IN WOMEN

Table 17.2 summarizes the more important features that have been described in the literature as differentiating addictive disorders in women from their occurrence in men. In general, alcoholic women are less likely to report "acting out" behaviors such as breaking the law, problems with the criminal justice system, or feeling "out of control." Women more commonly report problems with health and family and psychological symptoms such as depression and low self-esteem (Ames, Schmidt, Klee, & Saltz, 1996). Because of the differences in self-identified problems and clinical manifestations, investigators developed several screening tools designed specially to identify alcoholism in women. These include the T-ACE (Sokol, Martier, & Ager, 1989), TWEAK (Russell, Martier, & Sokol, 1991), SWAG (Spak & Hallstrom, 1996) and Health Questionnaire (Blume & Russell, 1993). Laboratory testing has also been found helpful in

TABLE 17.2. Features of Addictive Disorders in Women, Compared to Men

- Start substance use later (A).
- Disease progresses more rapidly (A, C).
- Drink significantly less than males (A, C, O).
- "Significant other" more likely to be substance abuser (A, C, O).
- Higher rates of comorbid psychiatric disorders (A, C).
- Higher rates of comorbid prescription drug dependence (A).
- More likely to make suicide attempts (A).
- More likely to have a history of physical and sexual abuse (A, C, O).
- More often date the onset of pathological alcohol/drug use to a specific stressful event (A, C).
- More likely to report previous psychiatric treatment (A).
- Higher mortality rate (A).

Note. See Blume (1997a); White, Brady, and Sonne (1996); Lewis, Bucholz, Spitznagel, and Shayka (1996); and Griffin, Weiss, and Mirin (1989). A, reported for alcoholism; C, reported for cocaine; O, reported for other drugs.

screening for alcoholism in women. In a cohort of 100 early-stage alcoholic women, Hollstedt and Dahlgren (1987) found that a screening criterion of either an elevated γ-glutamyl transferase (GGT) or an increased mean corpuscular volume (MCV) correctly identified two-thirds of the women. The same two laboratory tests were found useful in screening an obstetric population and predicting birth defects (Ylikorkala, Stenman, & Halmesmaki, 1987).

Although the clinical presentation of any individual patient depends on a combination of physical, psychological, and social factors, sex differences in symptoms and problems are themselves subject to social and cultural influences. Thus, sex differences may be expected to change over time as society itself changes (Fillmore et al., 1995; Kubicka et al., 1995).

Mortality rates for alcoholic women are high (Smith, Lewis, Kercher, & Spitznagel, 1994), compared to both the general population of women and alcoholic men (Klatsky, Armstrong, & Friedman, 1992; Hill, 1986). In a longitudinal study of 5,000 treated alcoholics, the mortality rate for men was three times the expected rate, whereas for women it was 5.2 times the comparable rate in the general public (Lindberg & Agren, 1988).

TREATMENT OF ADDICTIVE DISORDERS IN WOMEN

Although utilization of treatment resources for alcoholism has increased during recent years, women remain underrepresented in treatment (Weisner, Greenfield, & Room, 1995). In the year 1989, less than 14% of all women in need of addiction treatment received it. Among pregnant women in need, only 12% received help (Center on Addiction and Substance Abuse, 1996). When women do look for help, they are more likely to use mental health services and other facilities not specific to addiction (Weisner & Schmidt, 1992). The reasons for this, including social stigma, denial, and the frequent failure to diagnose women, have been mentioned. In addition, however, the most common current organized case-finding methods (e.g., drinking driver programs, drug courts, and employee assistance programs) are primarily useful for identifying male alcoholics/addicts. Appropriate settings for identifying women in need of treatment would be medical settings of all kinds (including mental health facilities) and family counseling services. Unfortunately, organized screening in health facilities is the exception rather than the rule, and women identified in these settings are usually in late stages of addiction.

Once women reach addiction treatment, there is little research to guide us in choosing the most effective treatment. In general, adult women and men treated together in the same specialized programs do about equally well (Vannicelli, 1986; McLellan, Luborsky, & O'Brien, 1986). Few studies have looked at treatment designed specifically for women. One such study found a superior outcome in a 2-year follow-up of 100 alcoholic women randomly assigned to a specialized women's clinic compared to 100 assigned to a mixed-sex clinic (Dahlgren & Willander, 1989). Another found superior retention in treatment of cocaine-dependent women in a day program specifically designed to meet their needs, when compared to retention in standard outpatient or residential treatment (Roberts & Nishimoto, 1996). Although these results are suggestive, a great deal more research is needed, including investigation of the role of psychotropics in treating female addicts with comorbid disorders and the relative efficacy of group, individual, family, and self-help approaches, as well as women-only versus mixed-sex treatment. A women-only self-help program, Women for Sobriety, is thriving in some parts of the country (Kaskutas, 1996), while the number of women utilizing Alcoholics Anonymous is also growing (Weisner et al., 1995) and women-only Alcoholics Anonymous groups are available in some areas. Based on what is known about the characteristics of addicted women, Table 17.3 summarizes the special emphases that have been found helpful in treating these women.

PREVENTION

Effective primary prevention of alcohol, tobacco, and other drug dependence in women has received little research attention, with the exception of specific public education campaigns to prevent FAS. Such efforts have proven more effective in dissuading light and moderate drinkers to abstain during pregnancy than the heaviest alcohol consumers. Thus, screening in medical and obstetric practice remains essential.

In designing educational approaches in the schools and for the general public, it is important to remember the double-edged-sword quality of societal attitudes. The goal of reducing the social stigma attached to the female addict must be balanced against that of preserving the cultural expectation that women will practice abstinence or moderation. Straightforward information should be

TABLE 17.3. Special Considerations in Women's Treatment

- Psychiatric assessment for comorbid disorders; date of onset for each (primary/secondary).
- Attention to past history and present risk of physical and sexual assault.
- Assessment of prescription drug abuse/dependence.
- Comprehensive physical examination for physical complications and comorbid disorders.
- Need for access to health care (including obstetric care).
- Psychoeducation to include information on substance use in pregnancy.
- Child-care services for women in treatment.
- Parenting education and assistance.
- Evaluation and treatment of significant others and children.
- Positive female role models (among treatment staff; self-help).
- Attention to guilt, shame, and self-esteem issues.
- Assessment and treatment of sexual dysfunction.
- Attention to the effects of sexism in the previous experience of the patient (e.g., underemployment, lack of opportunity, and rigid sex roles).
- Avoidance of iatrogenic drug dependence.
- Special attention to the needs of minority women, lesbian women, and those in the criminal justice system.

provided about women's sensitivity to alcohol; principles for the safe use of prescribed psychoactive drugs; the health effects of tobacco, alcohol, and other drugs particular to women (e.g., breast cancer, birth defects, and obstetric complications); the dangers of using substances to "medicate" feelings of inadequacy or sexual problems; and the special risks of women from alcoholic families. These general education efforts are particularly important because the alcoholic beverage industry has targeted women as a "growth market," linking drinking in their advertisements with youth, beauty, sexual attractiveness, and success. Such advertising sends messages that can alter the cultural norms that protect women. Likewise, cigarette advertising aimed at women stressing slimness and "liberation" (e.g., the slogan "You've come a long way baby") tend to make smoking more socially acceptable for women and adolescent girls. Because smoking is more strongly associated with the use of illegal drugs in girls than boys (Center on Addiction and Substance Abuse, 1996), smoking among adolescent girls should be a priority prevention target.

In addition to general population efforts, specific alcohol/drug prevention techniques should be aimed at high-risk groups such as adolescent and adult daughters of alcoholics/ addicts, victims of physical and sexual abuse, women entering new social groups with different drinking customs (e.g., college freshmen and women entering the military), women undergoing stressful life transitions (e.g., divorce, widowhood, childbirth, and reentry into the labor force), and women acting as caretaker for a chronically ill relative. Such risk groups can be helped to develop self-esteem and coping skills that do not involve substance use.

Laws and their applications also exert an important influence on substance use disorders in women. Recently, the resources of the criminal justice system have been used to initiate prosecution of women who use alcohol and other drugs during pregnancy. Such women have been charged with "prenatal child abuse" or "delivery of controlled substances to a minor" (via the umbilical cord). Although many cases have been thrown out of court and many convictions have been reversed on appeal, the result of these policies has been less often prevention of substance use than deterring pregnant substance users from seeking either prenatal or addiction treatment (Blume, 1997b).

In summarizing this overview of use and abuse of psychoactive substances by girls and women in the United States, it is clear that our society has strong feelings about such use but has not translated those feelings into an adequate investment in prevention, treatment, and research. Let us hope that a renewed focus on the problems of women will stimulate medical and social policymakers to rethink the priority devoted to this issue.

REFERENCES

Amaro, H., & Hardy-Fosta, C. (1995). Gender relations in addiction and recovery. *Journal of Psychoactive Drugs, 27,* 325–333.

Ames, G., Schmidt, C., Klee, L., & Saltz, R. (1996). Combining methods to identify new measures of women's drinking problems. Part I: The ethnographic stage. *Addiction, 91*(6), 829–844.

Ashley, M. J., Olin, J. S., LeRiche, W. H., Kornaczewski, A., Schmidt, W., & Rankin, J. G. (1977). Morbidity in alcoholics: Evidence for accelerated development of physical disease in women. *Archives of Internal Medicine, 137*, 883–887.

Barry, P. P. (1987). Gender as a factor in treating the elderly. In R. A. Ray & M. C. Braude (Eds.), *Women and drugs: A new era for research* (NIDA Research Monograph No. 16, pp. 65–69). Rockville, MD: National Institute on Drug Abuse.

Blume, S. B. (1980). Researches on women and alcohol. In *Alcohol and women* (Research Monograph No. 1, DHEW Publication No. ADM 80-835, pp. 121–151). Washington, DC: U.S. Department of Health, Education and Welfare.

Blume, S. B. (1991). Sexuality and stigma: The alcoholic woman. *Alcohol Health and Research World, 15*(2), 139–146.

Blume, S. B. (1997a). Alcohol and other drug problems in women. In J. H. Lowinson, P. Ruiz, & R. B. Millman (Eds.), *Comprehensive textbook of substance abuse* (pp. 645–653). New York: Williams & Wilkins.

Blume, S. B. (1997b). Women and alcohol: Issues in social policy. In R. Wilsnack & S. Wilsnack (Eds.), *Gender and alcohol: Individual and social perspectives.* New Brunswick, NJ: Rutgers Center of Alcohol Studies.

Blume, S. B., & Russell, M. (1993). Alcohol and substance abuse in the practice of obstetrics and gynecology. In D. E. Stewart, & N. L. Stotland (Eds.), *Psychological aspects of women's health care: The interface between psychiatry and obstetrics and gynecology* (pp. 391–409). Washington, DC: American Psychiatric Press.

Brett, P. J., Graham, K., & Smythe, C. (1995). An analysis of specialty journals on alcohol, drugs and addictive behaviors for sex bias in research methods and reporting. *Journal of Studies on Alcohol, 56*, 24–34.

Cadoret, R. J., Winokur, G., Langbehn, D., Troughton, E., Yates, W. R., & Stewart, M. A. (1996). Depression spectrum disease: I. The role of gene–environment interaction. *American Journal of Psychiatry, 153*, 892–899.

Center on Addiction and Substance Abuse. (1996). *Substance abuse and American women.* New York: Author.

Ciraulo, D. A., Sarid-Segal, O., Knapp, C., Ciraulo, A. M., Greenblatt, D. J., & Shader, R. I. (1996). Liability to alprazolam abuse in daughters of alcoholics. *American Journal of Psychiatry, 153*, 956–958.

Cloninger, C. R., Christiansen, K. O., Reich, T., & Gottesman, I. I. (1978). Implications of sex differences in the prevalences of antisocial personality, alcoholism, and criminality for familial transmission. *Archives of General Psychiatry, 35*, 941–951.

Cyr, M. G., & Moulton, A. N. (1990). Substance abuse in women. *Obstetric and Gynecologic Clinics of North America, 17*(4), 905–925.

Dahlgren, L., & Willander, A. (1989). Are special treatment facilities for female alcoholics needed? A controlled 2-year follow-up study from a specialized female unit (EWA) versus a mixed male/female treatment facility. *Alcoholism: Clinical and Experimental Research, 13*(4), 499–504.

Deykin, E. Y., Buka, S. L., & Zeena, T. H. (1992). Depressive illness among chemically dependent adolescents. *American Journal of Psychiatry, 149*(10), 1341–1347.

Eronen, M. (1995). Mental disorders and homicidal behavior in female subjects. *American Journal of Psychiatry, 152*(8), 1216–1218.

Fillmore, K. M., Bacon, S. D., & Hyman, M. (1979). *The 27-year longitudinal panel study of drinking by students in college* (Report 1979 to National Institute of

Alcoholism and Alcohol Abuse, Contract No. ADM 281-76-0015). Washington, DC: U.S. Government Printing Office.

Fillmore, K. M., Golding, J. M., Kniep, S., Leino, E. V., Shoemaker, C., Ager, C. R., & Ferrer, H. P. (1995). Gender differences for the risk of alcohol-related problems in multiple national contexts: A research synthesis from the collaborative alcohol-related longitudinal project. In M. Galanter (Ed.), *Recent developments in alcoholism: Women and alcoholism* (Vol. 12, pp. 409–436). New York: Plenum.

Frezza, M., diPodava, C., Pozzato, G., Terpin, M., Baraona, E., & Lieber, C. S. (1990). High blood alcohol levels in women: The role of decreased gastric alcohol dehydrogenase activity and first-pass metabolism. *New England Journal of Medicine, 322*(2), 95–99.

Gavaler, J. S. (1985). Effects of alcohol on endocrine function in postmenopausal women: A review. *Journal of Studies on Alcohol, 46*, 495–516.

Gavaler, J. S., Rizzo, A., & Rossaro, L. (1993). Sexuality of alcoholic women with menstrual cycle function: Effects of duration of alcohol abstinence. *Alcoholism: Clinical and Experimental Research, 17*, 778–781.

Gaulden, E. C., Littlefield, D. C., & Putoff, O. E. (1964). Menstrual abnormalities associated with heroin addiction. *American Journal of Obstetrics and Gynecology, 90*, 155–160.

Griffin, M. L., Weiss, R. L., & Mirin, S. M. (1989). A comparison of male and female cocaine abusers. *Archives of General Psychiatry, 46*, 122–126.

Hartka, E., Johnstone, B., Lieno, E. V., (1991). A meta-analysis of expressive symptomatology and alcohol consumption over time. *British Journal of Addiction, 86*, 1283–1298.

Helzer, J. F., & Pryzbeck, T. R. (1988). The co-occurrence of alcoholism with other psychiatric disorders in the general population and its impact on treatment. *Journal of Studies on Alcohol, 49*, 219–224.

Hesselbrock, M. N., Meyer, R. E., & Keener, J. J. (1985). Psychopathology in hospitalized alcoholics. *Archives of General Psychiatry, 42*, 1050–1055.

Hill, S. Y. (1986). Physiological effects of alcohol in women. In *Women and alcohol: Health-related issues* (Research Monograph No. 16, Publication No. ADM 86-1139). Washington, DC: Department of Health and Human Services.

Hoegerman, G., Wilson, C. A., Thurmond, E., & Schnoll, S. H. (1990). Drug-exposed neonates [Special Issue on Addiction Medicine]. *Western Journal of Medicine, 152*, 559–564.

Hollstedt, C., & Dahlgren, L. (1987). Peripheral markers in the female "hidden alcoholic." *Acta Psychiatric Scandinavia, 75*, 591–596.

Institute of Medicine. (1995). *Fetal alcohol syndrome: Research base for diagnostic criteria, epidemiology, prevention, and treatment.* Washington, DC: National Academy Press.

Jellinek, E. M. (1952). Phases of alcohol addiction. *Quarterly Journal of Studies on Alcohol, 13*, 673–684.

Kaskutas, L. A. (1996). Pathways to self-help among women for sobriety. *American Journal of Drug and Alcohol Abuse, 22*(2), 259–280.

Kendler, K. S., Heath, A. C., Neale, M. C., Kessler, R. C., & Eaves, L. J. (1993). Alcoholism and major depression in women: A twin study of the causes of comorbidity. *Archives of General Psychiatry, 50*(9), 690–698.

Kendler, K. S., Walters, M. S., & Neale, M. C. (1995). The structure of the genetic and environmental risk factors for six major psychiatric disorders in women. *Archives of General Psychiatry, 52*, 374–383.

Kessler, R. C., McGonagle, K. A., Shanyang, Z., Nelson, C. B., Hughes, M., Eshleman, S., Wittchen, H. U., & Kendler, K. S. (1994). Lifetime and 12-month prevalence of 14 DSM-III-R psychiatric disorders in the United States: Results from the national comorbidity survey. *Archives of General Psychiatry, 51*(1), 8–19.

Kessler, R. C., Sonnega, A., Bromet, E., Hughes, M., & Nelson, C. B. (1995). Posttraumatic stress disorder in the national comorbidity survey. *Archives of General Psychiatry, 52*(12), 1048–1060.

Klassen, A. D., & Wilsnack, S. C. (1986). Sexual experience and drinking among women in a U.S. national survey. *Archives of Sexual Behavior, 15*, 363–392.

Klatsky, A. L., Armstrong, M. A., & Friedman, G. D. (1992). Alcohol and mortality. *Annals of Internal Medicine, 117*, 646–654.

Klee, L., & Ames, G. (1987). Reevaluating risk factors for women's drinking: A study of blue collar wives. *American Journal of Preventive Medicine, 3*, 31–41.

Kubicka, L., Csemy, L., & Kozeny, J. (1995). Prague women's drinking before and after the "velvet revolution" of 1989: A longitudinal study. *Addiction, 90*, 1471–1478.

Lesieur, H. R., Blume, S. B., & Zoppa, R. M. (1986). Alcoholism, drug abuse, and gambling. *Alcohol: Clinical and Experimental Research, 10*(1), 33–38.

Lewis, C. E., Bucholz, K. K., Spitznagel, E., & Shayka, J. J. (1996). Effects of gender and comorbidity on problem drinking in a community sample. *Alcoholism: Clinical and Experimental Research, 20*(3), 466–476.

Lex, B. W., Lukas, S. E., & Greenwald, N. E. (1988). Alcohol-induced changes in body sway in women at risk for alcoholism: A pilot study. *Journal of Studies on Alcohol, 49*, 346–356.

Lindberg, S., & Agren G. (1988). Mortality among male and female hospitalized alcoholics in Stockholm 1962–1983. *British Journal of Addiction, 83*, 1193–1200.

Longnecker, M. P., Berlin, J. A., Orza, M. J., & Chalmers, T. C. (1988). A meta-analysis of alcohol consumption in relation to breast cancer. *Journal of the American Medical Association, 260*(5), 652–656.

Malatesta, V. J., Pollack, R. H., Crotty, T. D., & Peacock, L. J. (1982). Acute alcohol intoxication and female orgasmic response. *Journal of Sex Research, 18*, 1–17.

McKirnan, D. J., & Peterson, P. L. (1989). Alcohol and drug use among homosexual men and women: Epidemiology and population characteristics. *Addictive Behaviors, 14*, 545–553.

McLellan, A. T., Luborsky, L., & O'Brien, C. P. (1986). Alcohol and drug abuse treatment in three different populations: Is there improvement and is it predictable? *American Journal of Drug and Alcohol Abuse, 12*, 101–120.

Miller, B. A., & Downs, W. R. (1986). *Conflict and violence among alcoholic women as compared to a random household sample.* Paper presented at the 38th annual meeting of the American Society of Criminology, Atlanta.

Miller, N. S., & Doot, M. C. (Eds.). (1994). *Principles of addiction medicine: Section XVI. Women, children and addiction.* Chevy Chase, MD: American Society of Addiction Medicine.

Moore, R. D., Bone, L. R., Geller, G., & Mamon, J. A. (1989). Prevalence, detection and treatment of alcoholism in hospitalized patients. *Journal of the American Medical Association, 261*, 403–408.

Richardson, D., & Campbell, J. (1982). The effect of alcohol on attributions of blame for rape. *Personality and Social Psychology Bulletin, 8*, 468–476.

Ripple, C. H., & Luthar, S. S. (1996). Familial factors in illicit drug abuse: An interdisciplinary perspective. *American Journal of Drug and Alcohol Abuse, 22*(2), 147–172.

Roberts, A. C., & Nishimoto, R. H. (1996). Predicting treatment retention of women dependent on cocaine. *American Journal of Drug and Alcohol Abuse, 22*(3), 313–333.

Ross, H. E., Glaser, F. B., & Stiasny, S. (1988). Sex differences in the prevalence of psychiatric disorder in patients with alcohol and drug problems. *British Journal of Addiction, 83,* 1179–1192.

Rounsaville, B. J., Anton, S. F., Carroll, K., Budde, D., Prusoff, B. A., & Gawin, F. (1991). Psychiatric diagnoses of treatment-seeking cocaine abusers. *Archives of General Psychiatry, 48,* 43–51.

Roy, A., DeJong, J., Lamparski, D., Adinoff, B., George, T., Moore, V., Garnett, D., Kerich, M., & Linnoila, M. (1991). Mental disorders among alcoholics. *Archives of General Psychiatry, 48,* 423–427.

Russell, M., Martier, S. S., & Sokol, R. J. (1991). Screening for pregnancy risk-drinking: Tweaking the tests. *Alcohol: Clinical and Experimental Research, 15,* 268.

Sigvardsson, S., Bohman, M., & Cloninger, C. R. (1996). Replication of the Stockholm adoption study of alcoholism: Confirmatory cross-fostering analysis. *Archives of General Psychiatry, 53*(8), 681–687.

Smith, E. M., Lewis, C. E., Kercher, C., & Spitznagel, E. (1994). Predictors of mortality in alcoholic women: A 20-year follow-up study. *Alcoholism: Clinical and Experimental Research, 18*(5), 1177–1186.

Sokol, R. J., Martier, S. S., & Ager, J. W. (1989). The T-ACE questions: Practical prenatal detection of risk-drinking. *American Journal of Obstetrics and Gynecology, 160,* 863–870.

Spak, F., & Hallstrom, T. (1996). Screening for alcohol dependence and abuse in women: Description, validation, and psychometric properties of a new screening instrument, SWAG, in a population study. *Alcoholism: Clinical and Experimental Research, 20*(4), 723–731.

Teplin, L. A., Abram, K. M., & McClellan, G. M. (1996). Prevalence of psychiatric disorders among incarcerated women. *Archives of General Psychiatry, 53*(6), 505–512.

Urbano-Marquez, A., Ramon, E., Fernandez-Sola, J., Nicolas, J. M., Pare, J. C., & Rubin, E. (1995). The greater risk of alcoholic cardiomyopathy and myopathy in women compared with men. *Journal of the American Medical Association, 274*(2), 149–154.

U.S. Department of Health and Human Services. (1993). *Pregnant, substance-using women.* DHSS Publication No. SMA 93-1998. Rockville, MD: Author.

U.S. Department of Health and Human Services. (1994). *Practical approaches in the treatment of women who abuse alcohol and other drugs* (DHSS Publication No. SMA 94-3006). Rockville, MD: Author.

Vaillant, G. E. (1995). *The natural history of alcoholism revisited.* Cambridge, MA: Harvard University Press.

Vannicelli, M. (1986). Treatment considerations. In *Women and alcohol: Health-related issues* (Research Monograph No. 16, Publication No. ADM 86-1139, pp. 130–153). Washington, DC: U.S. Department of Health and Human Services.

Walfish, S., Stenmark, D. E., Sarco, D., Shealy, J. S., & Krone, A. M. (1992). Incidence of bulimia in substance misusing women in residential treatment. *International Journal of the Addictions, 27*(4), 425–433.

Warner, L. A., Kessler, R. C., Hughes, M., Anthony, J. C., & Nelson, C. B. (1995).

Prevalence and correlates of drug use and dependence in the United States. *Archives of General Psychiatry, 52*(3), 219–228.

Weisner, C., Greenfield, T., & Room, R. (1995). Trends in the treatment of alcohol problems in the US general population, 1979 through 1990. *American Journal of Public Health, 85*(1), 55–60.

Weisner, C., & Schmidt, L. (1992). Gender disparities in treatment for alcohol problems. *Journal of the American Medical Association, 268*(14), 1872–1876.

White, K. A., Brady, K. T., & Sonne, S. (1996). Gender differences in patterns of cocaine use. *American Journal on Addictions, 5*(3), 259–261.

Wilsnack, R. W., & Cheloha, R. (1987). Women's roles and problem drinking across the life span. *Social Problems, 34,* 231–248.

Wilsnack, S. C., Klassen, A. D., & Schur, B. E. (1991). Predicting onset and chronicity of women's problem drinking: A 5-year longitudinal analysis. *American Journal of Public Health, 81,* 305–318.

Wilson, G. T., & Lawson, D. M. (1976). Effects of alcohol on sexual arousal in women. *Journal of Abnormal Psychology, 85,* 489–497.

Windle, M., Windle, R. C., Scheidt, D. M., & Miller, G. B. (1995). Physical and sexual abuse and associated mental disorders among alcoholic inpatients. *American Journal of Psychiatry, 152*(9), 1322–1328.

Winfield, I., George, L. K., Swartz, M., & Blazer, D. G. (1990). Sexual assault and psychiatric disorders among a community sample of women. *American Journal of Psychiatry, 147,* 335–341.

Ylikorkala, O., Stenman, U., & Halmesmaki, E. (1987). Gammaglutamyl transferase and mean cell volume reveal maternal alcohol abuse and fetal alcohol effects. *American Journal of Obstetrics and Gynecology, 157,* 344–348.

18

❑ _____

Addiction Psychiatry
and the Law

ALEXANDER E. OBOLSKY
SHELDON I. MILLER

INTRODUCTION

Physicians' involvement in legal proceedings is increasing (Group for Advancement of Psychiatry, 1991). The public turns to and expects the legal system to resolve conflicts to an ever-increasing degree (Pfander, 1994; Goldstein, 1988). The legal system solves ever more complex and difficult questions often involving highly technical questions. When technical issues beyond laymen's knowledge arise, the courts require the assistance of those who develop and use such knowledge and are able to apply this knowledge to the litigation in question, including the education of the judge and the jury as to their expert opinion (Harrel, 1993). Psychiatrists have a long history of involvement with the courts as expert witnesses (Louisell, 1996; Mohr, 1993; Ray, 1838). The American Board of Psychiatry and Neurology (ABPN) is now giving an examination leading to a Certificate of Added Qualifications in Forensic Psychiatry. The psychiatry Residency Review Committee has approved requirements for forensic fifth-year residency training.

Although the ABPN established forensic psychiatry as a separate subspecialty, it did not intend to keep others from providing expert opinions to the courts and attorneys. Psychiatrists with clinical and research expertise in addictions have the specialized knowledge needed by the legal system and should provide such expertise. This chapter briefly reviews the U.S. legal system, standards of admissibility of scientific expert testimony, and basic general aspects of working with attorneys and the courts, as well as some areas in which addiction psychiatrists have unique, specialized knowledge and skills that can be useful to the courts.

REVIEW OF THE U.S. LEGAL SYSTEM

The law is a body of rules by which we govern ourselves. The starting point for all laws in the United States is the Constitution. No law can be contrary to what the Constitution mandates. There are four primary sources of law in the United States: the U.S. Constitution and constitutions of various states, statutes, regulations, and case law (Group for Advancement of Psychiatry, 1991; Weiner & Wettstein, 1993). The U.S. legal system today is a combination of common law and a codified system of laws. "Common law" is the law of English customs that the colonists brought with them to America. Common law has its origin early in English history, when parties to a dispute would go to court to have a judge decide the disagreement. The judge relied on community customs and fairness in resolving the dispute.

Codified laws include "statutes" enacted by the legislative branch of the United States or a particular state; "ordinances" and "codes," which are passed by cities and counties; and rules and regulations made by governmental agencies in accordance with the authority given them by the legislative bodies that created the agencies (Belli & Wilkinson, 1986).

Finally, "case law" is a body of opinion written and developed by judges in the course of deciding particular cases (Weiner & Wettstein, 1993). Similar cases are decided similarly based on "precedent"—prior cases which are close in facts or legal principals to the case under consideration (Black, 1983).

There are two separate judicial systems in the United States—the federal system and the state systems (Belli & Wilkinson, 1986). The federal court system consists of three levels. Cases are actually tried in the lowest level, and if litigants are not satisfied with the results of trial, each has a right to appeal to a higher court. The second level of federal court consists of the intermediate appellate court: the U.S. circuit courts of appeals. If a litigant loses his or her case in district court and the court of appeals "affirms" the decision, the litigant can ask the U.S. Supreme Court to hear his or her appeal. The Supreme Court will only agree to hear those cases that will affect many more people than merely the parties in dispute.

Most states have a tripartite court system similar to the federal system: the lowest level of courts is where cases are tried, a second level consists of intermediate appellate courts, and the third level is made up of a supreme court. As in the federal system, litigants can appeal their case to a higher court.

STANDARDS OF ADMISSIBILITY
OF SCIENTIFIC EXPERT TESTIMONY

In *Daubert v. Merrell Dow Pharmaceuticals, Inc.* (1993), the U.S. Supreme Court was asked to decide what standard of admissibility courts should apply to scientific expert testimony offered to assist the trier of fact (i.e., the judge and jury) and whether trial courts may screen scientific expert testimony under any real test. The Supreme Court answered these questions by citing four factors to be used as a "test" by the trial judge in screening scientific expert testimony.

At the outset, the trial judge must determine whether the proposed expert will "testify to scientific knowledge that will assist the trier of fact to understand or determine a fact in issue." This "helpfulness" standard, which goes primarily to relevance, requires as a precondition of admissibility a "valid scientific connection to the pertinent inquiry"—a concept the Court characterized as one of fit. "Fit" requires an assessment of whether the proffered expert testimony is capable of assisting the jury in resolving the specific factual issues in the case. The Court addresses two concepts: (1) whether the expert testimony relates to a factual issue in the case and (2) whether the expert testimony is derived from a principle that is scientifically valid for the expert's particular purpose. A court must make a "preliminary assessment of whether the reasoning or methodology underlying the testimony is scientifically valid and of whether that reasoning or methodology properly can be applied to the facts in issue" (*Daubert*, 1993). The mere willingness of a qualified expert to testify to a proposition that may only marginally be called "scientific knowledge" is insufficient to meet this foundational requirement.

Although not providing a specific test for determining admissibility of expert testimony, the Court stated "some general observations" and four factors trial judges might consider:

1. *Whether the theory or technique can be or has been tested.* Opinions based on untested reasoning should be excluded. Courts must measure the evidentiary reliability of the expert's opinion by the severity, diversity, and number of tests that corroborate the theory behind the expert's opinion.

2. *Whether the theory or technique has been subjected to peer review and publication.* The fact of publication, or lack thereof, in a peer-reviewed journal is a relevant though not controlling consideration in assessing the scientific validity of a particular technique or methodology on which an opinion is premised.

3. *The known or potential rate of error, and the existence and maintenance of standards controlling the technique's operation.* The failure to duplicate actual conditions, to use sufficient samples, or to employ properly trained personnel may discredit the results of an otherwise valid technique. The foundational requirement of operating standards requires consideration not just whether the expert is using a valid technique but whether he or she is properly employing the technique. To ensure reliable results, the technique should be performed under conditions that rule out as many confounding factors as possible. When confounding factors cannot be entirely eliminated, the court must determine whether those factors so infect the protocols of the technique as to make the results unreliable.

4. *The "general acceptance" of the theory.* General acceptance applies not to the conclusion but to the reasoning or methodology that leads to the conclusion. Expert testimony based on an established scientific theory uniformly recognized as valid among experts most likely to be familiar with it

could be admissible on that basis alone. When a theory is too novel to be either generally accepted or rejected, the courts must closely scrutinize the plausibility of the expert's claim.

Besides the factors mentioned previously, the Court in *Daubert* indicated that other criteria might be relevant to the "scientific knowledge" inquiry. In a footnote, the Court referred to various factors for determining the evidentiary reliability of expert testimony: (1) the qualifications and professional stature of the testifying expert, (2) the nature and breadth of the inference adduced, (3) the strengths of opposing views and the standing of experts who express them, (4) the nonjudicial uses to which the scientific technique has been put, (5) the extent to which the expert is prepared to discuss uncertainties in the conclusions and in the techniques used to prepare the evidence, (6) the extent to which expert testimony has been offered in earlier cases to support or dispute the merits of a particular scientific procedure, (7) the "novelty" of the technique and its relationship to more established modes of scientific analysis, (8) the clarity and simplicity with which the technique can de described and its results explained, (9) the extent to which the basic data are verifiable by the court and jury, (10) the availability of other experts to test and evaluate the technique, and (11) the probative significance of the evidence in the circumstances of the case.

Daubert (1993) shows that scientific expert testimony must be carefully scrutinized by the trial court. Expert opinions are no longer admissible solely based on expert credentials and minimal relevance. The court must look for scientific expert testimony whose theories have empirical and consensual support in the scientific community and which is relevant to the specific facts of the case.

BASIC ASPECTS OF WORKING WITH ATTORNEYS AND THE COURTS

The first contact with an attorney typically begins with a phone call (Gardner, 1986; Poynter, 1997). The psychiatrist should first find out the names of the parties involved in the suit. This will prevent involvement when real or perceived conflict of interests may exist (Cohn, 1990). No opinion will be useful in a court if serious doubt is raised in the minds of a judge and/or a jury as to the doctor's impartiality. It is important to disclose any existing and/or potential conflict of interest to the attorney immediately. The attorney will then decide whether the conflict actually exists and whether it is of consequence. Of course, if the physician thinks he or she is unable to provide an impartial opinion he should not accept a case. Asking for the names of the litigants at the beginning of a conversation also prevents an embarrassing situation when experts find themselves discussing a case only to belatedly recognize they have already been hired by the opposing side.

Next the potential expert needs to hear the facts of the case. This will allow the psychiatrist to understand the context within which his or her expertise will be required (Shuman, 1996). It is also the time to ask attorneys for their theory of the case. The theory of the case refers to the legal foundation of the lawsuit or criminal case. The law may require expert opinion to prove negligence as in a malpractice case. To prove negligence, the attorney needs an expert opinion that a defendant physician's practice fell below the standard of care. In a different lawsuit an expert's opinion may be required to prove damages, such as in a car accident case where liability (i.e., guilt) does not require the physician's opinion but the damages (i.e., the existence of a mental illness caused by the accident) will require expert testimony.

After the potential expert has heard the facts of the case it, is time to ask what questions the attorney needs answered. Not uncommonly, the attorney may not know which questions to ask, and this will have to wait until the psychiatrist has reviewed the written case record (Cohn, 1990).

The expert must now answer the question, "Do I have the expertise required to handle this case?" What is the expertise required? The judges evaluate expert testimony for admissibility under the *Daubert* (1993) criteria discussed earlier. The questions for the psychiatric expert to ask in addition to the ones paused by *Daubert* are as follows (Philipsborn, 1994):

1. "Do I have sufficient clinical experience in dealing with similar cases, including the diagnosis and treatment of this type of patients." This question is of great importance in medical malpractice litigation having to do with standards of practice. It is difficult to claim expertise in standards of care without knowledge and experience in diagnosing and treating the disorder in question. Other types of legal cases where diagnosis only is required may require less direct experience in treatment on the part of the expert (Feder, 1993).

2. "Do I have access to the necessary literature to answer the questions asked?" This is another question potential expert witnesses must ask themselves. Review of pertinent literature is an important function of an expert. Opinions based on education, experience, and general knowledge of the field are acceptable, yet a thorough preparation requires review of recent literature to ensure that the opinions given are based on the most current and accepted psychiatric knowledge (Simon, 1995). It is critical to ensure that new research findings are viewed by the profession to be valid and reliable before being used in a case.

3. "Will I be able to be impartial? Will I be able to answer the question truthfully regardless of the consequences to the parties of the litigation. If my opinion that a claimant is not disabled will leave this claimant with no income, will I be able to deliver such an opinion truthfully knowing the consequences to the claimant?" If such doubts exist, this is a time to honestly share them with the attorney.

Many other factors are also measures of expertise, as the Supreme Court acknowledged in *Daubert*'s footnote. For psychiatrists, some of these include

board certification status, hospital affiliations, professional society member-
ships, publications, research involvement, depositions, and court testimony
experience (Clawar, 1988; Feder, 1985; Goldberg & Treger Shelton, 1993).
The potential expert must be ready to discuss these issues with the inquiring
attorney during this first phone call. The psychiatrist expert needs to have an
updated curriculum vitae (Poynter, 1997) and a list, for the attorney's review,
of all the legal cases in which he or she has served as an expert during the
past 4 years (Poynter, 1997). The list should include only cases in which the
psychiatrist either testified or gave a deposition.

It is imperative during this first phone call to discuss the time constraints
under which the attorney is working. Lawyers work on schedules they control
only to a degree because the court dictates much of what and when things
will happen. Should an agreed-on schedule need to be changed, the attorney
needs to be notified immediately. Missing deadlines may cause an attorney to
lose the case.

It is common for attorneys to cancel depositions and court testimonies
scheduled with a physician. It is customary practice for physicians to be
reimbursed for lost time, and these details need to be discussed before the final
agreement on physician involvement as an expert is reached. Once these issues
have been discussed, a psychiatrist and an attorney are able to make informed
decisions regarding working together on a case.

The psychiatrist provides expertise to evaluate a legal case and advise the
attorney. The expert is not hired for or paid for giving "the right" opinion.
The expert opinion that the physician reaches is a product of the application
of medical knowledge and experience to the particulars of the legal dispute.
Often what the psychiatrist thinks is a correct analysis of a case is not what
the attorney necessarily wants as an opinion.

Every case requires careful analysis, and off-the-cuff opinions should be
avoided. Such rushed opinions risk overlooking unique details of a case, thus
wasting the attorney's and the client's time and money. During the first
conversation, an expert decides whether he or she has a conflict of interest
and the necessary expertise to evaluate the case, and whether his or her
schedule can accommodate the legal timetable. Once these questions are
answered and the expert is retained, further involvement on the part of the
expert must be reimbursed. It is important again to emphasize that the
reimbursement is for the time spent and not for the opinion delivered.

An unfavorable opinion is clearly not what an attorney wants. Attorneys
may try to influence an expert by pointing out facts they feel prove their view.
It is a legitimate discussion for an expert and an attorney to have. At the end
it is the responsibility of the expert to educate the attorney and to maintain
an opinion based on a careful medical psychiatric appraisal of the facts of the
case (Zobel & Rous, 1993). Attorneys need to realistically appraise their
client's case. Considering the experts' opinions, the plaintiff attorneys drop their
lawsuits and the defense attorneys settle claims. A solid and well-reasoned
opinion goes a long way in speeding up the resolution of legal disputes.

Negotiating a working agreement with an attorney is an essential part of the first conversation. The expert should receive the agreement in writing. A typical agreement should preferably be written by the psychiatrist and specify that he or she has been hired as an expert witness on a particular case. The agreement needs to identify the anticipated activities and the fees. Cancellation charges need to be addressed in writing. It is advisable for the psychiatrist who anticipates recurring forensic work to retain the services of an attorney to draft a general letter of agreement that can be used in future cases (Holtz, 1993).

It is wise to have one's own attorney available for consultations. The attorney who hires a psychiatrist works for his or her client and does not represent the interests of the expert.

Payments (a retainer is preferred) or deadlines for particular activities such as review of records or literature research must be stated in writing. Any financial constraints should also be discussed ahead of time. The duration and the outcome of any particular lawsuit are unpredictable. A clearly written contract prepared and signed before the expert physician starts the work helps to ensure that the expert gets reimbursed for the work done on the case.

As a word of caution, emotions must not be allowed to cloud the impartial judgment of the expert. It is not the expert's case to win or lose. The job of the expert is to provide expertise in response to specific questions, to provide a solid rationale for expert opinions, to answer questions of the opposing attorney fully and truthfully, and to be a strong advocate for his or her expert opinion.

In the court of law, a medical degree provides its possessor with baseline legitimacy, not the supposition of infallibility. Others will disagree with the expert's opinion. It is not personal. It is imperative to critique the opinions of experts on the opposing side, to help analyze the opposing expert's credentials, experience, and publications without imputing base motivations. It is not professional and most importantly it detracts from the case by drawing attention to the bickering experts instead of focusing attention on the bases of the differing opinions.

Opposing attorneys question, doubt, and devalue experts' opinions (Greenwald, 1990; Keenan, 1990) It is imperative for an expert not only to provide a solid opinion but also to learn the techniques of persuasion to counteract the tactics of the opposition and to convince the judge and jury to accept his or her opinion (Brodsky, 1991; Feder, 1993; Poynter, 1997).

Some in medicine and in the general public express an opinion that experts are "hired guns" and the whole system is somehow corrupt (Ziskin, 1995; Hagen, 1997). There are dishonest experts. Yet, the presence of dishonest medical experts is no more an argument against expert witnesses than the existence of corrupt politicians an argument against a republican form of government. The legal system is adversarial, truth is evasive, and no individual scientist or physician provides an irrefutable path to truth. Authors believe that on reflection, reasonable people will agree that physician experts provide an extremely valuable service (Bartol & Bartol, 1994; Bull & Carson, 1995; Weinstock, Leong, & Silva, 1994a).

Once the expert has agreed with the attorney on the working rules of engagement and the contract has been signed, it is time to proceed with the work. Typically, experts are asked to review records and provide a verbal report. The verbal report is an opportunity to discuss and explain their findings. This is also a time to offer suggestions for a further course of action that may include an evaluation of a litigant, literature research, or a need to obtain further records.

Issuing a verbal report ensures that if the expert's opinion is not useful to the hiring attorney, the attorney does not have to pay the expert to have it written up. The work of the expert may not end at that point. The expert may still be useful in helping the attorney cope with unfavorable findings. Under these circumstances, the expert becomes a consultant whose work typically cannot be discovered by the opposing side (Bloom, 1985; Weinstock & Garrick, 1994).

In the event the psychiatrist reaches an opinion useful to the hiring attorney, the hiring attorney may request a written report. The report must include such information as to who hired the expert, what questions were asked of the physician, and what work was done by the physician. An accounting of the work might include a list of records reviewed, arranged in a chronological order, and interviews conducted with dates and durations noted (Weinstock, Leong, & Silva, 1994b).

Next the expert summarizes the interviews he or she has conducted. The arrangement of the data gained from the interview is guided by the nature of the legal case and the questions asked by the attorney. The classic psychiatric report format is therefore not automatically the format of choice. The written report must include the review of psychological test results if such testing has been performed. A review of the pertinent literature may also be included and either a bibliography or copies of the reviewed articles should be attached to the report.

The opinion section is the raison d'être for the written report. It starts with the question asked, which is then followed by a succinct answer. The answer must specify the degree of certainty the psychiatrist has in his or her opinion. Then the answer is followed by a reasoning section. In this section, the expert explains logically and supports the opinion with the data recorded in the body of the report. No new data may be referred to in this section (Weinstock et al., 1994b).

A well-reasoned opinion that is impartial, objective, and thorough helps settle cases. Both parties to the suit are better able to appraise the relative strengths and weaknesses of their stated positions and the ultimate chances when they have a report with a solid reasoning section. Occasionally an attorney will ask the expert to forgo a detailed reasoning section in the report. Instead, the attorney may ask for a brief letter stating only the expert's opinion. The attorney has the ultimate responsibility for winning a case for his or her client. The hiring attorney thus has the prerogative to choose the ultimate strategy to pursue in obtaining the best possible outcome for the client. Once an expert witness is disclosed and the report is generated, it is discoverable by the other side (Cohn, 1990).

Deposition (Poynter, 1997; Feder, 1993) is a process by which the opposing side finds out or discovers what the opposing side's expert will testify and the basis for his or her opinions. A complete preparation for the deposition is essential (Langerman, 1992) and includes a thorough review of the facts of the case, familiarity with the records reviewed, literature reviewed, and any interview-generated materials. An essential part of this preparation is a conference with the attorney before the deposition (Cohn, 1990).

Deposition is a process during which the opposing attorney discovers the expert's opinion and its basis, as well as discovering the expert's credentials and experience. It is also a time when attorneys evaluate the expert's skills as a witness. Is the expert's demeanor, speech, and ability to relate complex medical information to laypersons sufficient to be an effective witness? During the deposition, the opposing attorney asks questions of the expert in the presence of the attorney who hired the expert. A court reporter is also present. The court reporter produces a written record of the deposition. Occasionally the deposition may be videotaped.

The opposing attorney does not win the case at the deposition. The deposition is the time for an opposing attorney to attempt to lay the foundation for the impeachment of the expert at trial. The attorney does this by nailing down the expert's testimony at a deposition and then bringing it up during the cross-examination at the trial if the testimony at the trial differs from the testimony at deposition.

It takes preparation, experience, reading, and discussions with the attorneys to learn the necessary skills in deposing.

Most lawsuits settle out of court. Expert witnesses often have to be prepared to provide testimony in court but rarely do so. When required, the court testimony consists of the direct examination, the cross-examination, redirect, and re-cross-examinations (Feder, 1993; Poynter, 1997). The direct examination is the time for the expert to explain clearly and fully to the judge and the jury his or her opinion and the reasons for such. The cross-examination is the opposing attorney's time to decrease the persuasive effect and strength of the expert's opinion. To become an effective expert witness requires experience gained through testifying, feedback from both hiring and opposing attorneys, reading, watching court television, or observing life trials and other experts in the courtroom.

AREAS OF EXPERTISE OF ADDICTION PSYCHIATRISTS

Addiction psychiatrists have the specialized technical knowledge that is often required by the courts in carrying out their judicial functions. Addiction psychiatrists, especially those with the Special Qualifications in Addiction Psychiatry from the ABPN, possess the demonstrated knowledge of diagnoses of addictive disorders, available treatments and their effectiveness, the natural history of various addictive disorders, the effects of intoxication by different substances on the central nervous system (CNS), and the chronic effects of addictions on the different physiological systems, with particular emphasis on the long-term consequences for the functioning of the CNS. Certified addiction psychiatrists have the knowledge of the social, vocational, and other areas of functioning affected by substance abuse.

In these and other areas, addiction psychiatrists as expert witnesses provide an important service that allows the courts to fulfill its function (Kermani & Castaneda, 1996). What are the different legal areas in which the knowledge of addiction psychiatrists is needed?

Custody evaluations in divorce require a psychiatric expert to discuss and opine on a parent's ability to parent and to suggest the best custody options and visitation parameters to the judge. Either one or both of the parents may abuse alcohol or drugs. Literature is replete with studies showing negative short- and long-term effects of parental chemical dependency on children (e.g., Bekir, McLellan, Childress, & Gariti, 1993; Woodside, 1988; Woodside, Coughey, & Cohen, 1993). Child abuse in families in which one or both parents abuse alcohol and drugs is higher than in general population. The evidence for such an abuse must be thoroughly searched for but not automatically assumed to exist. It is a mistake both legally and psychiatrically to state that in all cases a chemically addicted person is unfit to be a parent. A full and thorough evaluation must focus on a parent's ability to parent (Gardner, 1989).

The full evaluation starts with a thorough review of records, such as previous psychiatric treatment records, chemical dependency treatment records, police records of home disturbances and arrests, and work records for evidence of alcohol- or drug-induced problems. Rich sources of information are children's school records, including school nursing notes for evidence of parental alcohol- and drug-induced problems. Third-party interviews are important sources of independent information, particularly because of the potential that both parents, in their attempts to discredit, punish, and avenge the other, may provide misleading information. The addiction psychiatrist needs to evaluate people who have observed parents and children together, such as relatives, friends, teachers, and others. The addiction psychiatrist then interviews each parent and each child separately (Gardner, 1989).

Unless the addiction psychiatrist is also a child and adolescent specialist, we advise the team approach to custody evaluations involving prepubescent children (Quinn, 1995). The addiction psychiatrist provides the evaluation for the presence or absence of chemical dependency, its extent, and its effect on the parent's ability to parent. The child and adolescent psychiatrist then incorporates the findings of the addiction psychiatrist in the final opinion on the ability to parent and custody issues. Only through such an exhaustive process can alcohol and drug abuse be given its rightful weight and the civil rights of both parents and children upheld.

Adoption proceedings also bring out alcoholism and drug abuse issues. Similarly it is imperative to evaluate the actual effects of parental alcohol and drug abuse on a particular child and not to make a decision on the fact of the existence of chemical abuse alone.

Guardianship is a process through which a person may be adjudicated as incompetent and a ward of the state. A person may be adjudicated in need of guardian of a person or estate, or both. Alcohol-induced organic disorders (Schuckit, 1995) may require a psychiatrist to explain to the court the natural history of such an illness, which will help the court to decide on the necessity of the guardianship.

An interesting issue arises in the situation of a person who is alcohol or drug dependent and has access to a large family fortune through a trust that he or she indiscriminantly squanders. This behavior may effect the person's own future and the future of others dependent on or with a personal interest in safeguarding the monies. Not infrequently a family attempts to put the breaks on a person's use of such monies to pay for their own and their friends' addictions. Legal battles rage over such issues that set individual liberty against the interests of the state. The addiction psychiatrist is in a unique position to educate the court as to the presence of alcoholism and drug addiction in general, and in a particular evaluee, the addiction's natural history and prognosis.

Personal injury is a common type of a legal case that requires psychiatric expertise (Goldberg & Treger Shelton, 1993). The contribution of addiction specialists is enormous and varied. One of the most important areas of expertise is in the effects of any particular substance of abuse on mental status, including cognition, thought processes, coordination, mood, and other CNS functions (Schuckit, 1995). The role of alcohol in car and boat accidents is just one example. The addiction psychiatrist is able to evaluate the mental state of a person at the time of the accident based on the person's characteristics, such as age, sex, weight, prior experience with alcohol, history of tolerance, and blood alcohol level at the time of the accident or shortly after. There is a well-researched and -established correlation between blood alcohol levels and impairments of the higher CNS functions (Moskowitz, Burns, & Williams, 1985; Peterson, Rothfleisch, Zelazo, & Pihl, 1990; Schuckit, 1995), including motor coordination (as in walking), judgment, mood, speech, and memory.

The field of psychiatric disability includes such diverse programs as Social Security Disability Insurance (SSDI) and Supplemental Security Income (SSI), short- and long-term disability policies, workers' compensation, and Veterans Administration disability programs.

The federal programs have been in effect for a considerable time: SSDI since 1954 and SSI since 1967 (Dilley, 1987). In providing consultative services to the Social Security System, the addiction psychiatrist, in addition to expertise in addictive disorders, needs to learn the language and concepts underlying the determination of disability, particularly the concepts of impairment and disability (Krajeski & Lipsett, 1987). The psychiatrist's report is expected to document the presence of a psychiatric disorder, the impairment of identified mental functions, and a reasoning on how the identified impairment leads to the inability for work. A psychiatrist who involves himself in social security disability evaluations must consult the disability regulations published by Social Security Administration ("the Listings") (Krajeski & Lipsett, 1987). Both programs consider alcohol and drug abuse disorders alone insufficient to qualify a claimant for disability. A patient may be eligible if other mental disorders are present. The extent of the psychiatric disability and addiction disorders leads to a great economic loss for the country. The addiction psychiatrist is uniquely qualified to evaluate those claiming disability and suffering from an addiction disorder that often leads to and coexists with other psychiatric and physical disorders.

Short- and long-term disability policies vary a great deal depending on the insurance underwriter. It is imperative for a psychiatrist to be clear as to the language of a policy in the process of evaluation. Review of a policy language is a required part of performing evaluations for private disability policies.

Malpractice litigation involving chemical dependency issues includes allegations that a physician's prescription behavior has caused addiction in a patient, that excessive drug use by a patient led to suicidal attempt or prolonged recovery, and that a psychiatrist failed to disclose medication side effects. An addiction psychiatrist is required to educate judiciary in the natural course of addictive illnesses and concurrence of addictive disorders with other clinical personality disorders, as well as to the standards of care of patients with addictions. Here is a golden opportunity to help establish through the legal system the minimal standards for treatment of addictive disorders.

The corollary to this is an important role the addiction psychiatrist may choose to play by educating different governmental agencies mandated to oversee potentially fraudulent advertising. There is a never-ending stream of fraudulent and highly questionable products, therapies, and techniques offered to the often desperate people trying to deal with their own addictions or those of their loved ones.

Many crimes are committed by those either addicted to or under the influence of alcohol and drugs. Does the state of addiction or intoxication lead to the finding of diminished criminal responsibility? Generally the answer has been in the negative. An insanity defense does not apply as a rule to alcohol or drug addiction or intoxication. In a landmark case, *United States v. Lyons* (1984), a Louisiana policeman was indicted on 12 counts of fraudulently obtaining narcotics in violation of the federal criminal law. Lyons argued and had psychiatric experts testify to the facts that his addiction was caused by a physician's prescribing the narcotics for postsurgical pain alleviation. Defense experts argued that the drugs affected Lyons's brain physiologically and psychologically, leading to alterations in his personality. The trial court barred all evidence of addiction from the trial. The court of appeals reversed the ruling. When the government-requested rehearing of the case took place, the court of appeals decided that narcotic addiction does not fit the definition of mental disease or defect of the insanity statue.

An important distinction exists between general intent and specific intent crimes. General intent means that the defendant committed an intentional action. Specific intent refers to actions that require specified further purpose in mind. For example, trespass is a general-intent crime (i.e., the defendant intended to break into the building). The example of specific intent is a crime of assault with intent to kill (i.e., perpetrator hits a victim not just to hit him but to cause death) (Kadish & Schulhofer, 1989).

Voluntary intoxication or substance abuse is not a defense for a crime of general intent. Yet the expertise of an addiction specialist is necessary in the general-intent cases because the law allows for a diminished sentence if intoxication or substance abuse is shown. Intoxication can be used as a defense in the specific-intent crimes and thus courts require expert opinions to decide whether the defendant had the capacity to form the required criminal intent while in an intoxicated condition.

Addiction psychiatrists can be called on to explain laboratory results of drug testing, its limitations, and what a particular drug level means in general and in an individual in question.

Chronic pain syndromes are seen frequently in litigation (e.g., in disability cases and the workers' compensation arena). These cases require experts with knowledge of both chronic pain and addictions occurring secondary to it. A careful evaluation of history prior to the onset of pain, its immediate treatment, subsequent treatment, and its relationship to the patient's ability to work all require a thorough evaluation for a fair resolution of conflicts arising from such a situation.

CONCLUSION

Psychiatrists specializing in the treatment of addictive disorders possess the technical knowledge needed by the courts in their task of settling conflicts. It is an important civic function for a psychiatrist to be useful to the legal system, it is intellectually challenging, and it helps develop talents rarely used in the practice of psychiatry—thus allowing for varied professional activities. Working with the legal system takes the psychiatrist outside the consulting room to the wider world where men and women afflicted with mental disorders live and work. It enriches the psychiatrist's appreciation for the world we all live in and cannot but benefit our patients.

REFERENCES

Bartol, C., & Bartol A. (1994). *Psychology and the law* (2nd ed.). Pacific Grove, CA: Brooks/Cole.

Bekir, P., McLellan, T., Childress, A. R., & Gariti, P. (1993). Role reversal in families of substance misusers: A transgenerational phenomenon. *International Journal of the Addictions, 28*(7), 613–630.

Belli, M., & Wilkinson, A. P. (1986). *Everybody's guide to the law.* San Diego, CA: Harcourt Brace Jovanovich.

Black, C. H. (1983). *Black's law dictionary.* St. Paul, MN: West.

Bloom, J. I. (1985, May). Protecting expert's reports. *Los Angeles Lawyer,* pp. 22–25.

Brodsky, S. (1991). *Testifying in court: Guidelines and maxims for the expert witness.* Washington, DC: American Psychological Association.

Bull, R., & Carson, D. (1995). *Handbook of psychology in legal contexts.* Chichester, England: Wiley.

Clawar, S. (1988, Summer). Finding a mental health expert. *The Compleat Lawyer,* pp. 36–39.

Cohn, J. B. (1990). On the practicalities of being an expert witness. *American Journal of Forensic Psychiatry, 11*(2), 11–14.

Daubert v. Merrell Dow Pharmaceuticals, Inc., 113 S. Ct. 2786 (1993).

Dilley, P. (1987). Social security disability: Political philosophy and history. In A. T. Meyerson & T. Fine (Eds.), *Psychiatric disability: Clinical, legal, and administrative dimensions.* Washington, DC: American Psychiatric Press.

Feder, H. (1985, June). The care and feeding of experts. *Trial,* pp. 49–52.

Feder, H. (1993). *Succeeding as an expert witness.* Glenwood Springs, CO: Tageh Press.

Gardner, R. A. (1989). *Family evaluation in child custody mediation, arbitration, and litigation.* Cresskill, NJ: Creative Therapeutics.

Gardner, R. C. (1986, March–April). Malpractice and the medical expert. *Case and Comment,* pp. 44–47.

Goldberg, N., & Treger Shelton, J. (1993, September). Selecting and coordinating expert witnesses. *For the Defense,* pp. 24–32.

Goldstein, R. (1988). Psychiatrists in the hot seat: discrediting doctors by impeachment of their credibility. *Bulletin of American Academy of Psychiatry and the Law, 16*(3), 225–234.

Greenwald, A. (1990, May). Deposing medical experts. *Trial,* pp. 54–57.

Group for the Advancement of Psychiatry. (1991). *The mental health professional and legal system.* New York: Brunner/Mazel.

Hagen, M. (1997). *Whores of the court: The fraud of psychiatric testimony and the rape of American justice.* New York: HarperCollins.

Harrel, P. A. (1993). A new lawyer's guide to expert use. *The Practical Lawyer, 39*(2), 55–63.

Holtz, H. (1993). *How to succeed as an independent consultant* (3rd ed.). New York: Wiley.

Kadish, S. H., & Schulhofer, S. J. (1989). *Criminal law and its processes: Cases and materials* (5th ed.). Boston: Little, Brown.

Keenan, D. (1990, February). Deposing the defendant doctor: Preparation is crucial. *Trial,* pp. 69–71.

Kermani, E., & Castaneda, R. (1996). Psychoactive substance use in forensic psychiatry. *American Journal of Drug and Alcohol Abuse, 22*(1), 1–27.

Krajeski, J., & Lipsett, M. (1987). The psychiatric consultation for social security disability insurance. In A. T. Meyerson & T. Fine (Eds.), *Psychiatric disability: Clinical, legal, and administrative dimensions.* Washington, DC: American Psychiatric Press.

Langerman, A. (1992, January). Making sure your experts shine: Effective presentation of expert witnesses. *Trial,* pp. 106–110.

Louisell, D. W. (1996). *Medical malpractice.* San Francisco: Matthew Bender.

Mohr, J. C. (1993). *Doctors and the law: Medical jurisprudence in nineteenth-century America.* New York: Oxford University Press.

Moskowitz, H., Burns, M., & Williams, A. (1985). Skills performance at low blood alcohol levels. *Journal of Studies on Alcohol, 46,* 482–485.

Peterson, J., Rothfleisch, J., Zelazo, P., & Pihl, R. (1990). Acute alcohol intoxication and cognitive functioning. *Journal of Studies on Alcohol, 51*, 114–122.

Pfander, J. (1994). The 1994 Allerton House Conference on Expert Witnesses. *Illinois Bar Journal, 82*, 500–504.

Philipsborn, J. T. (1994). On firm ground?: A discussion of the current law for the expression of opinion by psychiatrists and psychologists. *American Journal of Forensic Psychiatry, 15*(1), 53–57.

Poynter, D. (1997). *The expert witness handbook: Tips and techniques for the litigation consultant.* Santa Barbara, CA: Para.

Quinn, K. M. (1995). Guidelines for the psychiatric examination of posttraumatic stress disorder in children and adolescents. In R. Simon (Ed.), *Posttraumatic stress disorder in litigation: Guidelines for forensic assessment* (pp. 85–98). Washington, DC: American Psychiatric Press.

Ray, I. (1838). *A treatise on the medical jurisprudence of insanity.* Boston: Little, Brown.

Schuckit, M. A. (1995). *Drug and alcohol abuse: A clinical guide to diagnosis and treatment.* New York: Plenum.

Shuman, D. (1996). *Psychiatric and psychological evidence.* Deerfield, IL: Clark, Boardman Callaghan.

Simon, R. (1995). Toward the development of guidelines in the forensic psychiatric examination of posttraumatic stress disorder claimants. In R. Simon (Ed.), *Posttraumatic stress disorder in litigation: Guidelines for forensic assessment* (pp. 31–84). Washington, DC: American Psychiatric Press.

United States v. Lyons, 731 F.2d 243 (5th Cir. 1984).

Weiner, B. A., & Wettstein, R. M. (1993). *Legal issues in mental health care.* New York: Plenum.

Weinstock, R., & Garrick, T. (1994). The forensic psychiatrist as consultant. In R. Rosner (Ed.), *Principles and practice of forensic psychiatry.* New York: Chapman & Hall.

Weinstock, R., Leong, G. B., & Silva, J. A. (1994a). Defining forensic psychiatry: Roles and responsibilities. In R. Rosner (Ed.), *Principles and practice of forensic psychiatry.* New York: Chapman & Hall.

Weinstock, R., Leong, G. B., & Silva, J. A. (1994b). Forensic psychiatric report writing. In R. Rosner (Ed.), *Principles and practice of forensic psychiatry.* New York: Chapman & Hall.

Woodside, M. (1988). Children of alcoholics: Helping a vulnerable group. *Public Health Reports, 103*(6), 643–648.

Woodside, M., Coughey, K., & Cohen, R. (1993). Medical costs of children of alcoholics—pay now or pay later. *Journal of Substance Abuse, 5*(3), 281–287.

Ziskin, J. (1995). *Coping with psychiatric and psychological testimony* (5th ed.). Los Angeles: Law and Psychology Press.

Zobel, H., & Rous, S. (1993). *Doctors and the law: Defendants and expert witnesses.* New York: Norton.

Part V

Treatment Selection
and Modalities

19

□

Differential Therapies and Options

ARTHUR I. ALTERMAN
A. THOMAS McLELLAN
CHARLES P. O'BRIEN
JAMES R. McKAY

INTRODUCTION

The initial chapter that appeared in the first edition of this clinical textbook approximately 7 years ago provided a systematic coverage of the settings and forms of treatment for three major substance abuse disorders: alcohol, opiate, and cocaine dependence. The primary objectives of the current chapter are not to repeat this coverage but instead to focus on the advances and changes in the nature of treatment that have taken place since that time for alcohol, cocaine, and opiate dependence. As indicated in the original chapter, although polydrug abuse has become increasingly common, it is still the case that most of the published studies focus on users of one primary agent. Thus we consider advances in each of the forms of dependency treatment separately.

ALCOHOL ABUSE/DEPENDENCE

Addictions are considered to be chronic, recurring disorders like many other medical disorders such as high blood pressure or asthma (O'Brien & McLellan, 1996). Accordingly, the treatment of alcohol abuse/dependence continues to be conceptualized in terms of a long-term three-stage recovery model consisting of detoxification, rehabilitation, and continuing care.

Detoxification

Detoxification is frequently required following alcohol withdrawal in an alcohol-dependent person. The alcohol withdrawal syndrome (AWS) consists of eating and sleep disturbances, tremor, paroxysmal sweats, clouding of the sensorium, hallucinations, agitation, temperature elevations, pulse rate changes, and convulsions (Gorelick & Wilkins, 1986; Naranjo & Sellers, 1986). In rare cases, AWS can be life threatening (Gorelick & Wilkins, 1986; Naranjo & Sellers, 1986). The revised Clinical Institute Withdrawal Assessment for Alcohol scale (CIWA–Ar; Sullivan, Sykora, Schneiderman, Naranjo, & Sellers, 1989) continues to be the primary measure used to quantify the severity and pattern of AWS.

The primary setting for alcohol detoxification is increasingly outpatient rather than inpatient. The primary impetus for this change in treatment setting appears to be the economic market pressures just cited coupled with the findings of a random assignment study (Hayashida et al., 1989) which showed that outpatient medical detoxification could be implemented almost as effectively as inpatient detoxification for patients with mild to moderate symptomatology. Costs were found to be at least 10 times greater for inpatient treatment. At the same time, a significant proportion of the presenting cases required inpatient medical attention. In unpublished work at our center, we found that patients who had three of the four following symptoms—a history of alcohol-related seizures, a history of delirium tremens, being unemployed, and coming to the initial visit intoxicated—had a 30% chance of completing outpatient detoxification, as contrasted with a 95% chance of completing outpatient detoxification if they had none of these symptoms. It is most important that these limitations of outpatient detoxification treatment be kept in mind when decisions are made about the treatment setting for detoxification.

Treatment includes the use of medication, usually consisting of a benzodiazepine, vitamin therapy, and, in some cases, measures to correct imbalances in water and electrolytes (a detailed explanation of the methods of medical alcohol detoxification are beyond the province of this chapter but can be found in the following references: Gorelick & Wilkins, 1986; Naranjo & Sellers, 1986). Although the majority of patients can be treated successfully in nonmedical, psychosocial settings with supervision (Whitfield et al., 1978), research shows that patients treated without medications are likely to have more severe withdrawal over time (Ballenger & Post, 1978), which would ultimately include seizures and associated cognitive impairment (Linnoila, Mefford, Nutt, & Adinoff, 1987). A recent study (Saitz et al., 1994) showed that the medication regime can be individualized on the basis of CIWA–Ar symptomatology, resulting in reductions in the amount of medication prescribed.

Rehabilitation and Aftercare

Rehabilitation tends to be more intensive than continuing care and concentrates on the attainment of initial abstinence. Continuing-care treatment represents a less intensive, extended treatment that is eventually designed to help the patient focus on resolution and dealing with life problems other than use. However, the distinction between rehabilitation and aftercare is often blurred in practice. Directed efforts have been made to provide guidelines for the level of treatment intensity required by a patient as exemplified in the Cleveland criteria (Hoffman, Halikas, & Mee-Lee, 1987) and the more recent placement criteria developed by the American Society of Addiction Medicine (ASAM; 1991). Recent research by McKay and colleagues (McKay, McLellan, & Alterman, 1992; McKay, Cacciola, McLellan, Alterman, & Wirtz, 1997) has, however, only provided evidence for the validity of a few of these criteria. In that study, alcohol-dependent and cocaine-dependent patients who should have been treated in an inpatient setting, according to ASAM, were actually placed in approximately equal proportions into inpatient and outpatient (day-hospital) programs. Twelve-month outcome data on these samples indicated that those patients who were "appropriately placed in the inpatient setting" by the ASAM criteria did not have superior outcomes to patients who were "inappropriately" placed in the day-hospital program. Nevertheless, clear-cut criteria that provide guidance on the intensity and range of treatment required by the patient are sorely needed in the current treatment arena as more and more decisions about the treatment a patient will receive are taken out of the hands of the patient and determined by the gatekeepers of managed behavioral health care organizations (Committee on Opportunities in Drug Abuse Research, 1996). As indicated later in the chapter, the increase of managed behavioral health care appears primarily to have resulted in reduced access to inpatient treatment for substance abuse patients (Committee on Opportunities in Drug Abuse Research, 1996; Frank & McGuire, 1997).

Consistent with the staged model of treatment, rehabilitation and aftercare treatments may theoretically extend over a number of years. Indeed, if the concept of addiction as a chronic recurring disorder is adopted, maintenance treatment in some form can extend over the lifetime. The earlier, intensive rehabilitation treatment focuses more on achievement of initial abstinence and issues related to this. Continuing-care treatment maintains this focus while also directing more attention to dealing with life problems whose nonresolution might lead to resumption of use. In addition, some forms of continuing care provide behavioral relapse prevention treatment strategies to counteract triggers to resumption of use. For largely economic reasons, the duration of rehabilitation treatment has been curtailed in recent years to 1 month or less (Edmunds et al., 1996). Although continuing care can theoretically extend for many years, economic pressures and the sagging motivations of patients to remain in treatment result in continuing-care treatment that usually consists of no more than 1 or 2 hours per week for a period of up to 1 year. Further, with reductions in the funding of substance abuse treatment, more extensive rehabilitation and aftercare treatments may be curtailed. Therefore, data are still needed on the extent of treatment retention in aftercare treatment as well as on the extent that patients achieve treatment goals during this period. Rehabilitation and continuing-care treatment are often multimodal and may consist of a number of components, including a relatively structured group therapy which focuses on everyday activities, educational therapy, recreational and vocational therapy, participation in Alcoholics Anonymous (AA), and medical preventive and maintenance treatment. Various other treatments such as individual counseling may be included. Recently, efforts to teach patients to identify triggers for craving and ways of coping with these triggers, adopted from relapse prevention methodology (Marlatt & Gordon, 1985), have been incorporated into the group therapy process in many programs. Social skills training and relaxation therapy are other behavioral treatment components that are also found in many programs. The extent to which these various elements are employed in a particular program depend on the treatment philosophy of the treatment personnel and on cost considerations. Unfortunately, work by McLellan et al. (1997) shows that alcoholic patients frequently do not receive the treatments they need (or those described in the brochure describing the program's treatments), even in inpatient settings where these services are most needed. In their study, a specialized contract was implemented in several programs to provide limited psychiatric/family/employment professional services for patients with an evaluated need for these services at baseline. Patients who were treated under the specialized contract were guaranteed at least three sessions of focused professional services in these areas. The during-treatment and posttreatment outcomes of these service-matched patients were compared with the same measures on patients treated in the same programs by the same staff—but under treatment as usual conditions. An independent evaluation showed that the service-matched patients had better treatment retention and 20–40% better outcomes than the treatment-as-usual group.

New Psychosocial Treatments

As indicated earlier, the primary setting for treatment is now outpatient, and there is no indication at this writing that this trend will change in the near future. Several new forms of outpatient treatment have been introduced in recent years. By far the most prominent and accepted in the treatment community at this writing is motivational enhancement therapy (MET; Miller, Zweben, DiClemente, & Rychtarik, 1992). This brief treatment based on motivational psychology and behavioral change principles attempts to mobilize the individual's own resources to bring about the changes needed to bring about abstinence. A major advantage for MET is that it can be provided over a limited four-session therapy format. A second AA-oriented Twelve-Step facilitation therapy (TSF; Nowinski & Baker, 1992) also has some appeal because it formalizes and incorporates the patient's engagement in the initial recovery steps of AA within the program setting. This treatment is more lengthy than MET. Both forms of treatment are structured and implemented based on manuals.

Project MATCH

An impressive body of treatment research conducted over the past decade is the work of Project MATCH (Project MATCH Research Group, 1997), funded by the National Institute on Alcohol Abuse and Alcoholism (NIAAA), which essentially defines the boundaries of current knowledge on psychosocial treatment effectiveness for alcohol dependence. This study compared the effectiveness of three manually driven treatments considered by the collaborative Project MATCH investigative team to be distinctive, feasible to implement, and accepted by the treatment community. These were MET, TSF, and cognitive-behavioral coping skills therapy, a treatment for which there is considerable evidence of effectiveness (Donovan et al., 1994). All treatments were administered on an individual basis. Alcohol-dependent patients who were currently dependent on sedative/hypnotic drugs, stimulants, cocaine, or opiates or who had used an intravenous drug in the past 6 months were excluded. Patients were randomly assigned to receive one of these treatments. Outcome evaluations extended through 15 months after the initial treatment session. Patients participated in one of two treatment arms—outpatient ($N = 952$; 72% male) or aftercare ($N = 774$; 80% male). The latter group consisted of patients who had completed inpatient or intensive day-hospital treatment, whereas the former group had only completed detoxification. The outpatients were treated in five facilities and the inpatients in five facilities throughout the United States. Treatment duration was 12 weeks for all three treatments consisting of a weekly session for TSF and cognitive-behavioral therapy (CBT) and four sessions distributed over 12 weeks for MET. Ninety-five to 98% (outpatient, aftercare) of the participants were alcohol dependent. Treatment participation was quite remarkable, with 68% completing all scheduled treatments in the outpatient arm and 66% in the aftercare arm. CBT clients attended slightly more weeks of treatment on average (9.3 weeks) than either the MET clients (8.4 weeks) or TSF clients (8.3 weeks). This difference was statistically significant for the outpatient arm. Over 90% of the follow-up evaluations were completed at all follow-up points (3, 6, 9, 12, and 15 months) for all living participants. Noteworthy, at least with respect to the two measures of outcome that have thus far been reported (i.e., percent days abstinent and drinks per drinking day during the 1 year posttreatment period), no differences were found in the effectiveness of the three treatment forms. All produced marked evidence of reductions in alcohol use. This reduction was somewhat greater for the aftercare arm—not unexpectedly, as these patients had successfully completed rehabilitation treatment prior to the study. Patients in the aftercare arm were abstinent on nearly 90% of the days over a year beyond treatment entry, whereas outpatients did not drink on about 80% of these days.

Several measures were predictive of outcome drinking behavior. Social support for drinking was associated with more drinking for both the outpatient and inpatient arms. Higher alcohol involvement, being male, greater psychiatric severity (Addiction Severity Index psychiatric composite score), and an alcoholism typology (based on more familial alcoholism, greater alcohol dependence, and impulsivity) were associated with *more drinking* in the aftercare arm. Less motivation to stop drinking, and more sociopathy, as measured by the socialization scale of the California Psychological Inventory, were associated with more drinking in the outpatient arm.

The Project MATCH study also hypothesized a number of potential, ad hoc matching effects between specific subject variables and treatment type. The primary treatment by patient matches evaluated, based on an analysis of prior findings and theory, included alcohol involvement (Alcohol Use Inventory), cognitive impairment (several cognitive measures), conceptual level (paragraph completion test), gender, meaning seeking (Purpose in Life Scale), motivation for change (subset of URICA), psychiatric severity, sociopathy, support for drinking (Important People and Activities Instrument), and Typology (composite index). Not all the matching effects/hypotheses that were articulated involved all three treatment groups. Disappointingly, there was little evidence of matching effects in the study, at least for the two primary drinking outcome measures. Future analyses will indicate whether such matches exist for other outcomes.

The study findings revealed that treatment can be effective when administered by highly trained therapists, irrespective of the nature of the treatment. In many ways, however, the findings of Project MATCH have been disappointing. There is little question that in bringing together many of the best investigators in the alcoholism treatment field, the assessment, treatment, and evaluation methodologies of the project were exemplary. Yet some of the shortcomings of the study may result from this very strength. That is, an important distinction gaining currency in the field is that between efficacy and effectiveness. Efficacy tells us about the results that can be obtained when conditions of methodological rigor apply. Effectiveness tells us about treatment outcomes that would obtain in a real-world setting where such methodological rigor is less likely. Thus, the extent to which the Project MATCH findings apply to real-world settings is an open question. That is, the specific effects of having therapy provided by highly trained therapists who provide individual treatment and follow a treatment manual and receive consistent supervision are likely to be great. However, these conditions are much less likely to exist in the real-world treatment environment. Second, because the treatments in the project were individually administered, a decision based on the greater ability to measure therapy compliance and manual adherence in individual settings, whereas most treatment is group-based, the generalization of the findings for the different treatments is restricted. A third and related point is that there is very low availability of any of the three types of treatments studied in the "real world" and there has been a marked and general reduction in the available funding for different types of alcohol treatments. Thus, the treatments and real conditions for assigning to patients to treatment have changed so markedly that the treatment × patient matching hypotheses set forward in Project MATCH, while conceptually sound, have few practical implications for the current world of alcoholism treatment, even if some of the formulated matches came out. In the current real world of alcoholism treatment, matching is accomplished in a large proportion of patients by determining first which patients have medical problems (e.g., a history of seizures) that will influence choice of treatment and venue for detoxification. Then matching is determined by assessing which patients have a coexisting treatable psychiatric disorder (e.g., major depression, bipolar disorder, phobia, or other anxiety disorder or schizophrenic disorder) that will determine a specific course of psychoactive medication. There is also the option, not available at the time of planning of Project MATCH, of selecting naltrexone, approved by the Food and Drug Administration (FDA), for reducing alcohol craving and relapse via brain mechanisms involved in alcohol reinforcement (see "Opiate Antagonists" section below) (Volpicelli, O'Brien, Alterman, & Hayashida, 1990; Volpicelli, Alterman, Hayashida, O'Brien, & Muentz, 1992; O'Malley et al., 1992). Finally, by not including patients with other substance abuse disorders such as cocaine dependence, the findings of the Project MATCH study apply to only a subgroup (albeit an important subgroup) of the alcoholics who are in treatment in this country.

Pharmacotherapies for Alcoholism

Considerable inroads have been made in recent years in the pharmacotherapy of alcoholism. Earlier controlled studies of medications such as lithium (Dorus et al., 1989) and disulfiram (Fuller et al., 1986) presented little evidence of effectiveness. However, there is evidence that disulfiram may reduce drinking in older patients who have relapsed but have good motivation and at least moderate social stability. Disulfiram may also be more effective in preventing relapse when it is used in treatment interventions with social contracts specifying that disulfiram ingestion will be monitored by a significant other (Azrin, Sisson, Meyers, & Godley, 1982; O'Farrell, Cutter, & Floyd, 1985). Because poor compliance is a major obstacle to the effectiveness of disulfiram treatment, this sort of behavioral contracting may be an important component of treatment with this agent. However, the side effects of disulfiram and potential danger of disulfiram–ethanol reactions contraindicate its use in patients for a wide array of medical and psychiatric conditions and in pregnant women (Fuller, 1995; Schuckit, 1996).

Several promising lines of investigation of medications have begun to show evidence of their effectiveness in reducing drinking in alcoholic patients. These include opiate antagonists, acamprosate, and serotonergic agents and are reviewed next.

Opiate Antagonists

The pharmacological treatment that has generated the most promising data in recent years involved naltrexone (Schuckit, 1996, p. 670). Naltrexone is a long-acting opiate antagonist that has been used effectively for the treatment of opiate dependence (O'Brien & Woody, 1986). One event that may trigger craving for alcohol is the consumption of ethanol, which has been reported to result in the release of endogenous opioids. There is some reason to believe that an opiate antagonist may block some of these effects (Blum, Futterman, Wallace, & Schwetner, 1977; Volpicelli et al., 1990, 1992). Several moderate-sized studies provide some evidence that use of naltrexone can reduce drinking in alcoholic patients. Volpicelli et al. (1990, 1992) conducted a placebo-controlled trial in which half of 70 male patients received 50 mg of naltrexone daily for 12 weeks. Patients were initially treated in an intensive 27-hour/week day-hospital program which offered multimodal treatment for 4 weeks and aftercare treatment for the remaining time. Whereas 95% of the placebo patients relapsed to heavy drinking, only 23% of the naltrexone-treated patients relapsed. Of patients consuming alcohol during the drug trial, 95% (19/20) of the placebo patients relapsed, whereas only 8 of 16 (50%) of patients on naltrexone relapsed. Thus, there was indication of less drinking and less likelihood to relapse to heavy drinking in the event of drinking in the naltrexone-prescribed group. In an attempt to replicate the Volpicelli study, O'Malley et al. (1992), conducted a study of 97 alcoholics (26% women) who were given 50 mg of naltrexone or placebo. Half the patients received coping skills/relapse prevention therapy and the remaining patients were given supportive therapy which emphasized abstinence. The rates of self-reported abstinence during the drug trial were 61% for naltrexone and 19% for placebo, respectively, for those who had received supportive therapy but only 28% and 21%, respectively, for those receiving coping skills/relapse prevention therapy. Just as in the Volpicelli et al. (1992) study, for patients returning to drinking, those on active drug drank significantly fewer drinks per drinking day. As a result of these two modest-sized, relatively short-term clinical trials the FDA approved naltrexone for use in the treatment of alcoholism. Importantly, the FDA approval of the use of naltrexone specifies that it should be used in the context of supportive treatment (much as nicotine gum or the nicotine patch has been recommended for use in the context of supportive services). Thus it will be important for future studies of this and other promising medications to evaluate the minimally effective set of behavioral or psychosocial services that will maximize medication compliance and optimize medication cost-benefit.

   A more recent, third study by Volpicelli et al. (1997) indicates that a number of patients do not comply in taking naltrexone. Naltrexone was found to be effective in reducing drinking in those who were medication compliant. Thus, just as for the use of naltrexone in opiate-dependent patients (see below), procedures to enhance compliance may be an important component of the treatment. A number of additional ongoing studies are currently in progress evaluating the effectiveness of naltrexone. It is important to emphasize the need for more long-term studies of the effectiveness of this medication as well as the need to determine its applicability to the large body of alcohol-dependent patients who are also dependent on cocaine. Another opiate antagonist, nalmefene, also led to better drinking outcomes than placebo in a double-blind pilot study (Mason et al., 1994), although these effects do not appear to be as powerful as those of naltrexone. Further investigation of the efficacy of this drug are under way.

Acamprosate

Acamprosate (calcium bisacetyl homotaurine) is another medication that has shown initial promise in improving treatment retention and decreasing drinking in alcoholics following initial detoxification in a number of studies conducted in Europe, including large-scale German and French studies (Schuckit, 1996). Although the action of acamprosate is not entirely clear, it appears the drug functions as a γ-aminobutyric acid (GABA) receptor agonist and that it may also lower neuronal excitability by reducing the postsynaptic efficacy of excitatory amino acid (EAA) neurotransmitters. This drug will undoubtedly receive increased investigative attention.

Serotonergic Agents

Serotonin appears to play an important neurochemical role in the modulation of mood and impulse control and may therefore influence the development and maintenance of alcohol use disorders (Kranzler & Anton, 1994). Because studies have suggested that individuals with alcohol use disorders may have low levels of serotonin (Gorelick, 1989; Kranzler & Anton, 1994; Roy, Virkkunen, & Linnoila, 1990), a number of serotonergic drugs have been evaluated as possible treatments for alcoholism. The agents that have received the greatest attention are selective serotonin reuptake inhibitors (SSRIs), such as fluoxetine, and buspirone, a serotonin 1A receptor partial agonist. These types of medications appear to be primarily effective for patients currently suffering from anxiety or depression. Kranzler et al. (1994), for example, found that buspirone was associated with greater retention in a 12-week treatment trial, and that it resulted in a slower return to heavy alcohol consumption and fewer drinking days in a 6-month follow-up period after treatment in anxious patients. Several recent studies suggest that tricyclic antidepressants may reduce both depression and alcohol use in patients with major depression (Mason, Kocsis, Ritvo, & Cutler, 1996; McGrath et al., 1996). The study by Mason and colleagues was particularly interesting as the drug trial extended over a 6-month period. Thus, these two studies suggest that adverse mood states contribute to abusive drinking and that SSRI treatment can reduce these psychiatric symptoms and thereby reduce the likelihood of relapse to alcohol drinking. Again, it will be important for future research to determine the effective parameters of pharmacological and psychosocial treatments in the treatment of psychiatric symptoms and their long-term cost-benefits to the treatment of alcohol dependence.

COCAINE DEPENDENCE

Lacking a drug substitution method analogous to methadone maintenance or a specific antagonist similar to naltrexone, the initial response to cocaine dependence was to adopt the abstinence-oriented, staged model of alcoholism treatment. This chapter describes the data on the effectiveness of psychosocial treatments for cocaine dependence as well as recent intensive efforts to facilitate the initiation of abstinence by pharmacological means.

Withdrawal

Although there is no clear evidence that cocaine produces a withdrawal syndrome such as that seen with alcohol, opiates, or sedatives, there is definitely a period of physical and mental instability following continuous use of cocaine, and this has been termed the "withdrawal" period. The withdrawal effects for cocaine are irritability, weakness, a marked reduction in energy, hypersomnia, depression, loss of concentration, increased appetite, and paranoid ideation (hallucinations and delusions). Paranoid effects, if they occur, usually last from 2 to 14 days but can last longer. Kleber (1995) indicates that the symptomatology following the initial barrage of unpleasant symptoms, commonly the "crash," differs for outpatients and inpatients. In cocaine inpatients, the crash appears "to be followed by gradual improvement in the cocaine-induced impairment with normalization of sleep, energy, and hedonic response" (Kleber, 1995, p. S97). By contrast, "In outpatients, where cocaine availability and craving remain high, the crash is followed by a few days of apparent normalcy. The next phase is a prolonged period of chronic dysphoria and diminished pleasurable responses to the environment" (Kleber, 1995, p. S97). Because cocaine is typically used intermittently, even heavy users experience periods of withdrawal or "crash." (O'Brien, 1996). A residual mood disorder may be seen after cocaine withdrawal in some patients (O'Brien, 1996). Because of limited bed capacities, inpatient detoxification is generally limited to cases in need of immediate psychiatric (drug-induced psychosis) or medical (pregnancy, myocardial damage) attention, as there is no effective existing treatment for the abstinence symptomatology during the withdrawal period.

Whether or not the withdrawal symptomatology following cocaine abstinence qualifies for the formal designation of a withdrawal syndrome, the dysphoric psychological state and the physiological instability associated with cocaine abstinence appears to contribute to the considerable difficulties in retaining cocaine-dependent patients in outpatient treatment (Hoffman et al., 1994). As a consequence, there has been an intensive effort to evaluate effective psychosocial and pharmacological treatments for treating cocaine abstinence symptomatology. A recent study at our center indicated that a measure of cocaine withdrawal/abstinence symptomatology, the Cocaine Selective Severity Assessment (CSSA), modeled after measures of the AWS, was successful in predicting early dropouts from treatment (Kampman et al., in press). More effective ways of dealing with this symptomatology appear to us to be essential to the increased effectiveness of treatment for cocaine dependence.

Psychosocial Treatments

High Attrition Rates

As indicated, one of the more difficult problems for the outpatient treatment of cocaine dependence is high attrition rates. As already indicated, this is an increasingly important problem as managed care pressures increase to reduce inpatient admissions and lengths of stay for substance-dependent patients (Frank & McGuire, 1997; Edmunds et al., 1996). In this regard, Kang et al. (1991) found, for a treatment program providing once-weekly psychotherapy, that nearly half the treatment candidates (47%) dropped out before the initiation of treatment and that 31% completed fewer than six sessions. In a 12-week study of once-weekly psychotherapy and/or pharmacotherapy, Carroll, Rounsaville, Nich, et al. (1994) reported that 21% of the patients failed to complete 2 weeks of treatment and that only 49/139 (35.2%) completed the full 12 weeks of treatment. In an earlier comparison of two forms of psychosocial treatment for cocaine dependence, Carroll, Rounsaville, and Gawin (1991) reported that 24% of the patients dropped out after 1 week of the projected 12-week, once-per-week course of treatment. Similarly, Higgins et al. (1993) reported that eight (42%) of the patients attending a 3.5-hour-per-week 12-step based treatment program failed to attend more than one treatment session. Hoffman et al. (1994) also found dropout rates of 56% within the first week of treatment for a treatment which provided 90 minutes of group therapy twice weekly.

Effective Psychosocial Treatments

Notwithstanding the evidence for high attrition rates, there is accumulating evidence indicating that treatment for cocaine dependence can be relatively effective, even for patients with relatively limited social resources. Higgins et al. (1991, 1993) have presented evidence that a behavioral treatment that combined contingency reinforcement for urines negative for cocaine (not for other drugs) and aspects of Azrin's community reinforcement (CRF) treatment approach-marital, job, and recreational counseling (Azrin & Besalel, 1980; Azrin, Naster, & Jones, 1973) appeared to be effective in bringing about abstinence from cocaine during the 12-week study/treatment period. Subjects were 13 consecutively admitted outpatients who received the behavioral treatment and 15 consecutively admitted outpatients offered 12-step counseling. Thus, the study participants were not randomly assigned. Urines were taken four times weekly for all subjects, with no contingencies attached for the 12-step patients. Patients who participated in the behavioral program could earn approximately $1,000 worth in points for abstinence throughout the 12 treatment weeks which could be exchanged for merchandise or services, whereas 12-step patients could earn $240 for giving 48 urines during this time period. The CRF component of treatment was implemented in twice weekly 1-hour sessions and the 12-step counseling also consisted of 2 hours of treatment weekly and encouragement to attend at least one self-help group weekly.

Eleven of 13 behavioral patients completed treatment, as contrasted with 5 of 15 12-step patients (3 patients did not initially accept the treatment). This treatment completion rate, in itself, is relatively remarkable. Ten of 13 behavioral patients achieved 4 weeks of abstinence compared with only 3/15 for the 12-step treatment, and 3/13 were abstinent all 12 weeks. None of the 12-step patients achieved even 8 weeks of abstinence. Ninety percent of 552 urines obtained in the behavioral treatment program and 78% of the 312 from the patients receiving 12-step counseling were free of cocaine.

In a second study (Higgins et al., 1993), 38 patients were randomly assigned either to the behavioral or to a drug abuse counseling treatment. The behavioral treatment was much like that in the earlier study, and the drug counseling program was similar to the 12-step program implemented in the earlier program. The counseling consisted of one 2.5-hour group and one 1-hour individual therapy session per week for 12 weeks. Both treatment programs were extended an additional 12 weeks through 24 weeks. During weeks 13–24 counseling was reduced to once weekly for both treatment groups and three times weekly urine monitoring was reduced to twice weekly. Behavioral subjects could earn approximately $1,000 exchangeable for merchandise/services during the first 12 treatment weeks and they were given a $1 state lottery ticket for each clean urine during the weeks 13–24 treatment "fading" period. Drug counseling patients continued to receive $5 for each urine independent of its status.

The results for this latter study were similar to those obtained for the earlier study. A 58% treatment completion rate was obtained for the behavioral patients for the 24 weeks of treatment versus only 11% for drug counseling patients. Whereas 68% and 42% of the behavioral patients achieved at least 8 and 16 weeks of continuous cocaine abstinence, respectively, these rates were 11% and 5% for drug abuse counseling patients. There was little evidence of a precipitous decline in functioning for the behavioral patients following the removal of the higher-intensity treatment/contingency. A subsequent study has now extended the outcome findings to 1 year posttreatment entry, showing that the gains achieved can be sustained through this period (Higgins et al., 1995).

A study of cocaine dependence treatment by Alterman et al. (1994) compared the effectiveness of 4 weeks of intensive, highly structured-day hospital (DH; 27 hours weekly) treatment with that of inpatient treatment (INP; 48 hours of weekly scheduled treatment) with the same treatment elements. The subjects were primarily inner-city, male African Americans treated at a Veterans Administration Medical Center. Fifty-six patients were randomly assigned to the DH and 55 to the INP. Group therapy was the primary treatment with an emphasis on initiation of abstinence and a drug-free lifestyle and education about substance abuse. Both programs endorsed the self-help philosophy and expected participation in self-help groups. Both cocaine- and alcohol-dependent patients were concurrently treated in both programs. Additional treatments available were individual counseling and case management, pharmacotherapy, medical treatment, and recreational and family therapies.

The INP treatment completion rate of 89% was significantly higher than for the DH treatment (54%). However, at 7 months posttreatment entry, self-reported outcomes indicated considerable improvements for both groups in drug and alcohol use and family/social, legal, employment, and psychiatric problems. The finding of reduced cocaine use was supported by urine data. Both self-report and urine data indicated 50–60% abstinence for both groups at the follow-up assessment. Costs of the DH were about 40% less than those of the INP treatment.

Several studies by Carroll and colleagues provide further indication of the effectiveness of outpatient treatment for cocaine dependence. An initial study (Carroll et al., 1991) compared the effectiveness of a once-per-week 12-week treatment course of individual relapse prevention therapy (RPT) with that of individual interpersonal therapy (IPT) for 42 randomly assigned patients. Overall, 31% of the subjects were classified as recovered at the point of treatment termination and 52% completed treatment.

In a subsequent study, Carroll and her colleagues compared the effectiveness of RPT with that of clinical management (CM—standardized form of basic administrative management and minimal clinical support) in the context of an evaluation of the effectiveness of the medication, desipramine (DMI). In that study of 139 cocaine-dependent patients (Carroll, Power, Bryant, & Rounsaville, 1993; Carroll, Rounsaville, Gordon, et al., 1994), the investigators found evidence of reduction in cocaine use and in psychosocial and medical problems over the course of treatment and that these reductions were maintained over a 1-year posttreatment follow-up period. As in their earlier work, there was indication that RPT was the more effective psychosocial treatment. One interesting aspect of that study was a delayed effect of the RPT treatment. At 6 months posttreatment, there were modest differences between the RPT and CM groups, but at the 12-month point the differences (favoring RPT) were much greater (Carroll, Rounsaville, Nich, et al., 1994).

Similar results were shown by Woody et al. (1983) in a comparison of professional psychotherapy with standard drug counseling among methadone maintained patients (Woody, McLellan, Luborsky, & O'Brien, 1995).

Finally, research by Hoffman et al. (1994) shows the contribution of more intensive treatment to increased treatment retention over a 4-month treatment period. This study compared two levels of intensity of group treatment: either 90 minutes twice weekly or 120 minutes five times weekly. Each group therapy condition was also supplemented by one of three individual therapy conditions varying in intensity: (1) no additional treatment, (2) individual psychotherapy (twice weekly in first month and weekly thereafter), and (3) individual psychotherapy plus weekly family therapy beginning in the second month. The findings revealed that the highest dropout rates were for the low-intensity group treatment without supplemental individual treatment. Fifty-six percent of the patients in this group dropped out of treatment within the first week. This is to be contrasted with an average dropout rate of about 35% for the five other groups. Similar findings obtained for the prediction of retention in treatment for 3 months or more. This was only 14% for the low-intensity treatment and about 30% for the five other treatment conditions. Thus, it appeared that any increase in intensity of treatment above that provided by the twice-weekly group therapy, whether it took the form of additional individual therapy or more intensive group therapy, resulted in notable increases in retention. Adding individual treatments to the intensive group therapy condition failed to increase treatment retention.

Summary

It is likely that the inability to treat the symptomatology associated with initial abstinence from cocaine in an outpatient setting is a significant contributor to the high early-patient-dropout rates that are found in most outpatient treatment programs for cocaine dependence. As indicated previously, higher scores on the CSSA, a measure of withdrawal/abstinence symptomatology, predicts treatment dropout. In addition, we have found in two separate studies (Alterman, McKay, Mulvaney, & McLellan, 1996; Alterman et al., 1997) that a positive initial cocaine urine toxicology, an indication of the patient's inability to achieve abstinence, as well of the severity of cocaine dependence, is highly predictive of treatment dropout. Thus, a beginning is being made in identifying individuals at "high risk" for dropout from outpatient treatment. It appears that providing incentives to patients or more intensive treatment can help to reduce the adverse influences that bring about early treatment dropout. Other forms of psychosocial treatment such as MET (Miller et al., 1992), derived from the alcoholism field, are being examined for their effectiveness. In addition, the stage-of-change measures (Prochaska & DiClemente, 1984) that have recently been used in the alcoholism treatment field (see Project MATCH findings earlier) are being introduced to the field in another effort at enhancing the effectiveness of treatment for cocaine dependence. An alternative approach would be the establishment of an effective medication.

Pharmacotherapy

Primary Medications Studied

The reinforcing effects of cocaine and cocaine analogs correlate best with their effectiveness in blocking the dopamine (DA) transporter. This reuptake blockage results in excess synaptic DA and thus increased DA stimulation at critical brain sites. Cocaine also blocks both norepinephrine and serotonin reuptake and chronic use produces changes in these systems as measured by reductions in the neurotransmitter metabolites MHPG (3-methoxy-4-hydroxy-phenylethylene glycol) and 5-HIAA (5-hydroxyindoleacetic acid). Thus, neuro-transmitters other than DA may be involved after a period of heavy cocaine use (O'Brien, 1996, p. 681). Most efforts to identify medications that would be effective in treating patients with cocaine use disorders have been directed toward finding agents that either correct alterations in neurochemical sub-strates brought on by chronic cocaine use or block the reinforcing effects of cocaine (Kleber, 1995). Although there have been a number of promising leads, no pharmacological agent has yet generated consistent evidence of effectiveness in reducing cocaine use (Kleber, 1995; O'Brien, 1996; O'Brien & McKay, 1998). Several studies have evaluated the effects of tricyclic antidepressants, SSRIs, and monoamine oxidase inhibitors (MAOIs).

The findings of Nunes et al. (1995), for a 12-week placebo-controlled trial of imipramine (IMI; 150–300 mg/day) in 113 cocaine abusers, are noteworthy. In this study, there was some indication of higher abstinence rates, defined as three consecutive confirmed urine-negative weeks, in the group on IMI (19% vs. 7%). Evidence also suggested that these effects were stronger for depressed users of IMI (26% IMI vs. 13% placebo). Other drugs that influence the DA system have also been tried. Aman-tadine, a drug that stimulates dopaminergic transmission, may have short-term efficacy as an aid in detoxification, as cocaine urines for 21 subjects on amantadine over a 10-day trial were significantly more negative over a 1-month period than those of 21 placebo subjects (Alterman et al., 1992). This study was conducted in the context of the 27-hour-per-week DH psychosocial treatment. A second study (Kampman, Volpicelli, et al., 1996) by investigators at the same center was unable to replicate these findings. It should be noted that the psychosocial treatment was much less intensive in this latter study.

Other Medications

The kindling phenomenon has been the target of studies using car-bamazepine, an anticonvulsant, but several controlled studies have failed to demonstrate any benefit (Cornish et al., 1995; O'Brien, 1996). SSRIs have also been studied. Fluoxetine has been reported to produce a significant reduction of cocaine use in methadone-maintenance patients, as measured by lower average urinary levels of the cocaine metabolite benzoylecgonine. It is not clear that the reduced levels of benzoylecognine represent a clinically significant change in patient outcome (Batki, Manfredi, Jacob, & Jones, 1993). These findings have thus far not been replicated in primary cocaine abuse patients (Grabowski et al. 1995). An interesting line of research recently described by (Kosten, 1996) involves the use of an N-methyl-D-aspartate (NMDA)-regulated neurotransmitter, lamotragine, to combat neurotoxicity resulting from chronic cocaine use. Initial findings have dem-onstrated the drug's safety during acute cocaine administration, a reduction in cocaine use of the outpatient subjects, and selective improvement in cognitive functioning. Finally, open-label pilot research conducted at our center has shown the medication propanolol to have higher retention rates (80%) over the 7-week drug trial than did nefazodone, a combination of phentermine and fenfluramine, or a multivitamin control condition (Kampman, McGinnis, et al., 1996). A trend for reduced cocaine use as measured by urine toxicologies was also revealed for propanolol. A number of potential mechanisms may underlie the effect of propanolol, including a reduction in noradrenergic activity that may ameliorate cocaine craving and in the anxiety associated with abstinence from the drug. A double-blind study is being planned to further evaluate effectiveness.

Summary

Our review of psychosocial treatments for cocaine dependence indicates that intensive outpatient treatments in various forms can be relatively effective. The major problem in outpatient treatment appears to be treatment dropout. However, given the current environment in which treatments are becoming increasingly less, rather than more, intensive (see the section "Managed Care" below), it is likely that the effectiveness of treatment will decline in the upcoming years. With regard to pharmacological treatment, several promising drugs are being evaluated that take advantage of distinctive mechanisms. Further, the National Institute of Drug Abuse is currently funding a number of centers nationally that are dedicated to evaluating the efficacy of promising medications. Thus, there is some likelihood that evidence for one or more effective drugs will be established within the upcoming 5 to 10 years. In the same sense that most opiate-dependent persons choose not to use naltrexone (see "Opioid Dependence" below), the question remains whether the majority of patients will be inclined to make use of this medication(s). Finally, an important consideration in regard to effectiveness of medications is the psychosocial treatment context within which the medication is administered. Research by Carroll and her colleagues with cocaine-dependent patients (Carroll, Rounsaville, Gordon, et al., 1994; Carroll, Rounsaville, Nich, et al., 1994) by Volpicelli and O'Malley and their colleagues (O'Malley et al., 1992; Volpicelli et al., 1992) with alcohol-dependent patients, by Rounsaville, Glazer, Wilber, Weissman, and Kleber (1983) and Woody et al. (1983) with opiate-dependent patients, and by Glassman and Covey (1995) and Hall, Munoz, Reus, and Sees (1996) working with nicotine-dependent patients uniformly suggests that not only can psychosocial interventions be combined with pharmacological interventions in the treatment of dependence disorders, but the addition of psychosocial support and services may be necessary to achieve the full potential from even clearly effective medications. Ultimately, there is a need for studies that will specify the optimal mix of medication and psychosocial interventions for these disorders. In addition, there is a need for research designed to identify methods of increasing medication compliance such that the full potential from efficacious medications can be realized in real-world settings.

OPIOID DEPENDENCE

Just as for other addicting drugs, opiate addiction is seen as being a chronic, relapsing disorder (Cooper, 1989; O'Brien & McLellan, 1996). There are four major forms of treatment for this disorder: maintenance drug treatment, antagonist drug treatment, residential therapeutic community treatment, and outpatient drug-free treatment. Managed care restrictions on funding over the past several years have restricted the availability of therapeutic community treatment (Edmunds et al., 1996).

The three-stage recovery model that has been adopted for alcoholism and cocaine dependence has not been so clearly delineated or separated for opiate dependence. Clear many addicts who relapse are in need of detoxification. Detoxification is often presented as a treatment (and reimbursed by insurance), but research continues to suggest that it should only be considered a first step in a comprehensive rehabilitation program. The distinctions between rehabilitation and "continuing care" are not clear in the treatment of opiate addiction—at least not as it pertains to agonist or antagonist (e.g., methadone, naltrexone, or other medication) maintenance models of treatment. Although the term "continuing care" (or "aftercare") has been applied to the treatment of opioid dependence, its meaning differs from that connoted for alcoholism/cocaine dependence. That is, aftercare has been used to describe a much reduced schedule of treatment for highly stabilized, methadone-maintained addicts which could be of value in opening up resources for a greater number of new patients (Cooper, 1989) rather than an emphasis on a qualitatively different form of treatment. The following section of this chapter discusses the detoxification process for opioid dependence. This section is followed by a discussion of pharmacological and psychosocial treatments for opiate dependence.

Detoxification

Opiate detoxification is generally implemented in one of two situations. If a patient has been stabilized on methadone for a number of years, appears to have the ability to be drug free, and communicates this interest, detoxification can be accomplished using a tapered methadone schedule over several months. This process can be implemented on an outpatient basis, although hospitalization is sometimes helpful at the end of detoxification when the dose is less than 20 to 25 mg. Clonidine or lofexidine are often helpful in blocking signs and symptoms of withdrawal related to autonomic hyperactivity. Cushman (1974) showed, more than two decades ago, that only a small proportion of detoxification candidates are able to remain free of opiates for an extended period. As with detoxification alone for alcohol/cocaine dependence, this treatment is not recommended as the sole approach. Detoxification is also properly used as an initial stage of treatment for opiate dependence, usually for heroin addicts who prefer not to participate in methadone maintenance and wish to enter into a drug-free outpatient treatment or narcotic antagonist (naltrexone) treatment or into drug-free therapeutic communities.

Numerous detoxification techniques have been proposed. The most commonly used method involves transferring a patient from a short-acting opiate such as heroin to a long-acting opioid such as methadone, which blocks symptoms of withdrawal by cross-tolerance. The dose of methadone can then be gradually reduced according to a predetermined schedule with adjustments as needed if the patient reports discomfort or shows signs of a withdrawal syndrome. Clonidine and lofexidine are two nonopioid medications that are able to block many of the signs and symptoms of opiate withdrawal. The effectiveness of lofexidine in this regard is currently undergoing evaluation. These drugs can be quite useful when opioids for detoxification are not available. With all detoxification methods, prompt relapse is likely unless the patient becomes engaged in a long-term aftercare program (O'Brien, 1996; O'Brien & McKay, 1998).

A relatively new form of detoxification has received considerable attention over the past several years. Twenty-four-hour detoxifications from opiates have been accomplished in office settings using a combination of a nonopiate sedative to put patients to sleep, followed by administration of increasing doses of a short-acting opiate antagonist such as naloxone to displace all opiates from receptor sites. This process can be accomplished while the patient is asleep and has been claimed to produce a drug-free state that is unaccompanied by withdrawal symptoms (benzodiazepines and clonidine are sometimes used to medicate low-level residual withdrawal). This rapid detoxification procedure has been attractive to many clients because of its speed and the claims that it avoids withdrawal symptoms. However, at this writing, this process has not been carefully evaluated for efficacy or safety and it remains controversial because it requires anesthetization. Research is needed to determine the effectiveness of this technique.

Rehabilitation

Maintenance substitution treatment with methadone, levo-α-acetylmethadol (LAAM), or buprenorphine is discussed first, followed by a consideration of antagonist treatment. The discussion is then followed by a consideration of psychosocial treatments for opioid dependence.

Maintenance Treatment

Methadone

Although some opioid addicts are able to detoxify and remain drug free, the majority relapse, even after intensive psychotherapy (Cushman, 1974; Department of Substance Abuse Services, 1996; Gerstein et al., 1994). More important, many heroin addicts will not even consider a drug-free treatment. Thus, the majority of opioid-dependent patients are treated by a form of substitution therapy. Approximately 120,000 individuals are currently receiving methadone-maintenance (MM) treatment in the United States. MM was developed in the 1960s and consists of transferring the patient from heroin, a short-acting opiate that must be taken by injection two to four times daily, to methadone, a long-acting opioid that needs to be taken only once daily by mouth. Methadone substitutes for heroin, reduces drug-seeking behavior, and blocks opiate withdrawal symptoms (O'Brien, 1996). It stabilizes physiological systems because of its long duration of action in contrast to the short action of heroin which produces ups and downs (Kreek, 1992). Typically patients continue to use some heroin during the first few weeks or months on methadone but almost always in substantially reduced amounts and frequency. Methadone does not block the effects of heroin, but it produces cross-tolerance to heroin and all similar drugs. Thus, the effects of usual doses of heroin are diminished and over time the typical patient decreases heroin use further and then stops (O'Brien & McKay, 1998).

The changes produced by transfer to a long-acting opioid are significant. Several reviews of the opioid dependence literature concluded that in-treatment performance, as measured by decreased use of narcotics and other illicit drugs, decreased criminal activity, and increased social productivity, improves in a direct linear relationship to the length of time spent in treatment (Cooper, 1989; O'Brien, 1996). With respect to length of time in treatment, 40% to 50%, on average, of newly admitted patients leave outpatient or residential drug-free treatment within the first 3 months of treatment, compared with an average 14% dropout rate in well-run MM programs (Cooper, 1989). Importantly, a large number of studies based on a variety of nonexperimental strategies have produced consistent evidence that MM is associated with lower human immunodeficiency virus (HIV) positivity rates (Metzger et al., 1993; Moss et al., 1994; Novick et al., 1990; Serpelloni et al., 1994). In this light, research such as that reported by Zanis, McLellan, Alterman, and Cnaan (1996), in which outreach efforts can be successfully employed to return discharged MM patients to treatment, takes on increased importance. Thus, there are public health-related reasons to retain patients in methadone maintenance.

As indicated, considerable evidence has been reported that well-run MM programs, which include structured counseling and other problem-oriented treatment, are highly effective (Cooper, 1989; Dole, 1989). One of the primary requirements is that a sufficient daily dose of methadone be prescribed. Dole (1989) described unpublished data by Ball which revealed an inverse relationship between the percentage who used heroin during the past month and the dose of methadone hydrochloride prescribed. Daily doses of 60 mg and above were associated with virtually no heroin use. That is, a blood level of methadone at concentrations greater than 150 ng/ml is necessary to stop illicit opiate use. However, it is not as clear that the dose levels described by Dole (1989) are as effective as they once were. Recently, heroin in the United States has become cheaper with very high purity. Thus the average street heroin addict is likely to have a higher level of physiological dependence. This has necessitated higher doses of methadone to prevent withdrawal and to produce sufficient cross-tolerance to counter the effects of very potent heroin. Although few treatment outcome studies have been done under these new circumstances, anecdotal evidence suggests that methadone treatment may be less effective or at least more difficult in the era of cheap and potent heroin (Bickel & Amass, 1995; O'Brien & McKay, 1998). Thus, a survey by the General Accounting Office (1995) found rates of recent illicit drug use ranging from 13% to 63% in a sample of MM programs. Unpublished data from our center indicate that approximately 50% of the urine toxicologies for heroin and cocaine are positive for patients in the first 6 months of treatment (Alterman, Rutherford, Cacciola, McKay, & Woody, 1996). Research by Morral, Iguchi, Belding, and Lamb (1997) reveals that only about 30% of new patients have relatively few drug-free urines by the end of 4 months of treatment. Other changes in patients treated in MM programs may also contribute to the reduced effectiveness of MM treatment. The increase in cocaine abuse in these patients is likely to exacerbate the cycle of use. In addition, the knowledge that HIV positivity can be substantially reduced by retaining users in treatment weakens the contingency-based treatment contract which has been used in MM programs whereby continued methadone use resulted in gradual detoxification and program discharge.

LAAM

Levo-α-acetyl methadol (LAAM) is a slower-acting substance with pharmacological effects similar to that of methadone. LAAM that has been studied extensively in clinical trials prior to its approval by the FDA in 1993 (O'Brien & McKay, 1998). Its long half-life and even longer-acting metabolites produce opiate effects for about 72 hours after a single daily ingestion. This makes LAAM very convenient because it requires dosing only three times per week and still provides physiological stability (O'Brien, 1996). Studies done to date show that treatment results for those who remain on LAAM compare favorably with those obtained with methadone, although LAAM's slower onset probably contributes to the higher initial dropout rate seen when LAAM is compared with methadone (Woody & O'Brien, 1986).

Buprenorphine

Buprenorphine belongs to another class of medications called partial agonists. It is currently approved for the treatment of pain and it has shown good efficacy as a maintenance medication in addiction treatment in several clinical trials among heroin addicts (Bickel & Amass, 1995). As a partial opiate agonist, operating primarily at the μ receptor, buprenorphine activates opiate receptors producing effects similar to heroin and methadone, but there is a "ceiling" such that higher doses produce no greater effect. In studies so far, overdose from buprenorphine has not been seen and if heroin or other opioids are taken, their effects are attenuated or blocked by the presence of buprenorphine (O'Brien, 1996). At the same time, buprenorphine (like all other opiate agonist medications) produces euphoria, and there are reports of buprenorphine diversion and sale on the street. A new preparation for this medication is likely to reduce buprenorphine diversion and illicit use. By combining buprenorphine with naloxone (an opiate antagonist) injection can be prevented, thus reducing one important side effect of the medication. An additional potential benefit from this medication is that even after protracted periods of maintenance with this drug, it can be terminated at the will of the patient with no need for dose reduction schedules and very few withdrawal effects—due in large part to its very long half-life (Jasinski, Pevnick, & Griffith, 1978). This medication is expected to receive FDA approval, joining methadone and LAAM as a third option for maintenance in the treatment of heroin addicts. Based on experience from clinical trials, some heroin addicts prefer methadone, others prefer LAAM, and still others feel that they are most stable and alert on buprenorphine. As with other classes of medications, it is helpful for the clinician to have a selection of medications from which to choose.

Antagonist Treatment

The discovery of specific opiate receptor antagonists in the early 1970s gave rise to hopes for the "perfect" medication for the treatment of heroin addiction. Naltrexone seemed to be the answer because it specifically blocks μ opiate receptors and to a lesser extent κ receptors (Raynor et al., 1994), but it has little or no direct or agonist effects of its own. Naltrexone and its short-acting analog naloxone have high affinity for opiate receptors and will displace such drugs as morphine or methadone (see the section "Methadone" above), resulting in the sudden onset of withdrawal symptoms when given to people who are opioid dependent. If the heroin addict is first detoxified so that opiate receptors are gradually evacuated, naltrexone will bind to the receptors and prevent subsequent injections of heroin from having an effect. Numerous clinical trials showed that naltrexone was effective in blocking opiate receptors and safe; thus, the FDA approved it in 1983. Unfortunately, naltrexone is a very underutilized medication in the treatment of heroin addiction. Unlike methadone, it has no positive psychoactive effects. Few street heroin addicts show any interest in this type of treatment, and few programs encourage patients to try it. Opioid antagonists are more complicated to prescribe than methadone and most physicians have not been trained in their use. Opioid-dependent health care workers such as physicians, pharmacists, and nurses often do well on naltrexone because it enables them to return to work with no risk of relapse even though they work in areas with high drug availability (Washton, Pottash, & Gold, 1984). There is also evidence that naltrexone is helpful in preventing relapse in probationers who have a conditional release from prison after drug-related crimes (Cornish et al., 1997).

Psychosocial Treatment

A large body of research thus far has shown that MM is most successful when coupled with a variety of services, including regular client contact and urine drug monitoring (Cooper, 1989). Particularly because many opiate-dependent patients need assistance with vocational and legal problems and many come to treatment with additional psychiatric symptomatology (Rounsaville, Weissman, Kleber, & Wilber, 1982; McLellan, 1986), there is a need for drug counseling by a certified drug counselor and sometimes a need for psychotherapy or psychotropic medication to combat coexisting psychopathology (Woody & O'Brien, 1986). Yet the amount of psychosocial treatment provided in MM programs is typically quite modest compared to that which has been provided to alcohol- and drug-dependent patients in the past. At our own center, for example, patients are usually seen weekly for several months and then are tapered to less frequent meetings (biweekly to monthly) once the patient shows evidence of stabilization. Even this amount of treatment exceeds that provided in most community methadone programs. Not surprisingly, then, little improvement in functioning is seen for these patients beyond the first 2 months of treatment (Cacciola, Alterman, Rutherford, McKay, & McLellan, 1998; also see Morral et al., 1997).

There is clear evidence that methadone patients respond well to supplemental psychosocial services, particularly professional services. For example, a study conducted at our center 15 years ago showed psychotherapy to be highly beneficial to Veterans Administration MM patients (Woody et al., 1983). A second study extended these findings to community-based MM programs (Woody et al., 1995). Nonetheless, there is a continuing effort to further reduce the amount of psychosocial treatment provided to MM patients on the justification that more patients could be pharmacologically treated with the methadone alone and that there is a public health benefit to having more patients improve somewhat than fewer patients improving more (Cooper, 1989). A recent study by McLellan, Arndt, Metzger, Woody, and O'Brien (1993) showed that increasing the amount and range of psychosocial treatments produced superior outcomes in methadone patients. An equally important finding is that the majority of methadone patients who received minimal counseling, a level of treatment below that usually provided under standard counseling conditions, did very poorly. Thus, although the need of opioid-dependent patients appears to be for a markedly greater amount of treatment, current cost considerations are leading to even greater reductions in the amount of treatment provided.

COST-EFFECTIVENESS OF TREATMENT/MANAGED CARE

Treatment Cost-Effectiveness

There is considerable evidence that alcoholism treatment is cost-effective (McCrady & Langenbucher, 1996). Cost savings include those related to return to employability, lowered health costs, and lower health care costs for family members of treated alcoholics. There is also a considerable amount of evidence that MM treatment is linked to reduced societal costs associated with increased employability, reductions in health care, including those for AIDS, and reduced criminal activity (Gerstein et al., 1994; Hubbard et al., 1989). A recent RAND study also found treatment of cocaine dependence to be far more cost-effective (Everingham & Rydell, 1994) than a range of drug-control strategies in reducing cocaine use. Similarly, field studies of "real-world treatments" have all found that the costs of treatment are repaid two to seven times over within 1 year following treatment (Everingham & Rydell, 1994; Gerstein et al., 1994; Department of Substance Abuse Services, 1996). In addition, all these studies have independently concluded that detoxification alone or other forms of very brief treatments are less cost-effective than more protracted rehabilitation treatments (Gerstein et al., 1994; Department of Substance Abuse Services, 1996).

Managed Care

Given current societal concerns regarding the incremental increases in health care costs, access to treatment, the service "mix" offered within treatment, and the duration of treatment are all being "managed" by business organizations that specialize in the reduction of health care costs through elimination of "unnecessary or ineffective services." These organizations are under contract mostly to employers and public agencies. As independent managers of the insurance funds that have been set aside for health care benefits, these managed care organizations (MCOs) guarantee to provide (either directly or through subcontracts) all the care "medically necessary" for an employer's or state's constituents. these MCOs are paid in advance with a fixed fee for each "covered life" (capitated system) and then use a variety of techniques to manage those dollars. Under optimal conditions, the MCOs use the leverage available from the large number of covered lives (potential patient population) to make favorable contracts with groups of treatment programs or individual providers, trading lower fees for higher volume. Mass purchasing power for pharmaceuticals and days of hospital stays are also traditional methods of conserving costs. More controversial and subjective methods of controlling the actual care provided include restrictions (sometimes arbitrary) on authorizing admission to care and the nature or amounts of treatment services that will be reimbursed. Carve-out vendors are fiscal and management intermediaries that typically contract with providers for the actual delivery of mental health/drug abuse services, and so on. Access to the network is controlled by a gatekeeper who determines need for service. The criteria for these determinations are unclear and appear at this point to be largely proprietary. Carve-out vendors may be part of the health management organizations (HMOs) or independent. Increasingly even HMOs are making use of carve-out vendors as are traditional fee for service medical insurance organizations (Committee on Opportunities in Drug Abuse Research, 1996). According to a recent, nationally representative survey, about 23% of the clients of drug abuse treatment providers have their treatment paid by managed care. Managed behavioral health care began to take hold, particularly due to employer pressures for cost containment and the availability of venture capital financing for new carve-out providers (Freeman & Travin, 1994). Another impetus came from studies showing that many, but not all, drug abuse patients could be treated just as cost-effectively in outpatient settings as they could in more costly inpatient settings (Alterman et al., 1994: Center for Alcohol Studies, 1993).

Despite its growth, there is a dearth of peer-reviewed research concerning the effectiveness of managed drug abuse treatment. Research has not addressed concerns about patients being denied treatment or being undertreated; the quality of care being reduced; or the cost of care being shifted to families, public health and welfare agencies, and the criminal justice system (Mechanic, Schlesinger, & McAlpine, 1995). Thus far, four naturalistic, nonexperimental studies have reported on access to drug abuse treatment, the costs of treatment, and the utilization of services (Committee on Opportunities in Drug Abuse Research, 1996). All four studies reported lower costs in managed drug abuse care relative to traditional fee-for-service (FFS) plans. Most of the savings were the result of a marked shift in the services provided from 24-hour inpatient treatment to outpatient treatment. One of these studies was the only one that compared several models (a county agency, a preferred provider organization, an HMO) of managed care with an FFS model (Asher, Friedman, Lysionek, & Peters, 1995). The county providers used a mix of managed and unmanaged care and used a case manager to assign patients to the most appropriate care, but each service was reimbursed on an FFS basis. County clients received the greatest access to services, as determined by the proportion of the individuals in the treatment network that received substance abuse services, as well as the greatest number of units of service for the lowest average cost per client. The HMO was found to provide the least amount of services for the highest cost per patient. It is important in considering the findings to recognize that patient severity was not controlled for the different provider modalities.

Few data are available on the effectiveness of managed care services for substance abuse. The study by Asher et al. (1995) found that intensive outpatient treatment, which was only provided by HMOs, was the least effective modality with regard to the outcomes measured—criminal activity, economic status, medical care, and readmission to drug and alcohol treatment—whereas 24-hour long residential treatment, a combination of case management techniques and FFS reimbursement, was the most effective modality. A second study which compared intensive managed care, traditional managed care, private pay, and state-funded treatment found no differences in recidivism among the four groups of patients. The only predictor of recidivism was patient severity at baseline (Renz, Chung, Fillman, Mee-Lee, & Sayama, 1995). Finally, in an unpublished study (McLellan, 1996), the 6-month Addiction Severity Index outcomes of Philadelphia Medicaid patients primarily treated by FFS in 1991 were compared with those of 1995 patients treated primarily by HMOs. Patients treated in 1995 received fewer services and experienced worse outcomes relative to those treated in 1991.

SUMMARY AND TREATMENT IMPLICATIONS

There is currently only limited information on the quality and effectiveness of treatment being provided by managed behavioral health care organizations. The limited evidence thus far indicates a marked tendency to use outpatient services in lieu of inpatient services. HMOs appear to provide fewer services to patients, although much more research is needed on this question. However, the funding structure of HMOs, which is based on a fixed capitation fee per enrolled person, would seem to encourage the use of least costly services by the profit-driven HMO provider. Whether those patients with more severe symptomatology are provided with more intensive inpatient treatment to the extent that this is needed is unknown. There is a great need for rigorous research to address this issue because it is possible that the cost-reduction incentive of HMOs may override issues of quality of treatment. Nonetheless, given the current environment in which there is much pressure to further reduce capitation costs, the direction of treatment appears to be that of ever-decreasing intensity and range of services.

ACKNOWLEDGMENTS

This work was supported by grants from NIDA, NIAAA, and the Department of Veterans Affairs.

REFERENCES

Alterman, A. I., Droba, M., Cornish, J., Antello, R., Sweeney, K., Parikh, G., & O'Brien, C. P. (1992). Amantadine may facilitate detoxification of cocaine addicts. *Drug and Alcohol Dependence, 31,* 19–29.

Alterman, A. I., Kampman, K., Boardman, C., Rutherford, M. J., Cacciola, J. S., McKay, J. R., & Maany, I. (1997). An initial clean cocaine urine predicts favorable outpatient treatment response. *Drug and Alcohol Dependence, 46,* 79–85.

Alterman, A. I., McKay, J. R., Mulvaney, F., & McLellan, A. T. (1996). Prediction of attrition from day hospital treatment in lower socioeconomic cocaine dependent men. *Drug and Alcohol Dependence, 40,* 227–233.

Alterman, A. I., McLellan, A. T., O'Brien, C. P., August, D. S., Snider, E . C., Droba, M., Cornish, J. W., Hall, C. P., Raphaelson, A. H., & Schrade, F. (1994). Effectiveness and costs of inpatient vs. day hospital treatment for cocaine dependence. *Journal of Nervous and Mental Disease, 182,* 157–163.

Alterman, A. I., Rutherford, M. J., Cacciola, J. S., McKay, J. R., & Woody, G. E. (1996).

Response to methadone maintenance and counseling among antisocial patients with and without major depression. *Journal of Nervous and Mental Disease, 184,* 695–702.

American Society of Addiction Medicine. (1991). *ASAM patient placement criteria for the treatment of psychoactive substance use disorders.* Chevy Chase, MD: Author.

Asher, M., Friedman, N., Lysionek, C., & Peters, C. (1995). *Evaluation of the implementation of Pennsylvania's Act 152, 1988. The quantitative findings.* Villanova, PA: Human Organization Science Institute, Villanova University.

Azrin, N. H., & Besalel, V. A. (1980). *Job club counselor's manual.* Baltimore: University Park Press.

Azrin, N. H., Naster, B. J., & Jones, R. (1973). Reciprocity counseling: A rapid learning based procedure for marital counseling. *Behaviour Research and Therapy, 11,* 364–382.

Azrin, N. H., Sisson, R. W., Meyers, R., & Godley, M. (1982). Alcoholism treatment by disulfiram and community reinforcement therapy. *Journal of Behavioral Therapy and Experimental Psychiatry, 13,* 105–112.

Ballenger, J. C., & Post, R. M. (1978). Kindling as a model for alcohol withdrawal symptoms. *British Journal of Psychiatry, 133,* 1–14.

Batki, S. L., Manfredi, L., Jacob, P. III, & Jones, R. T. (1993). Fluoxetine for cocaine dependence in methadone maintenance: Quantitative plasma and urine cocaine/benzoylecogonine concentrations. *Journal of Clinical Psychopharmacology, 13,* 243–250.

Bickel, W. K., & Amass, L. (1995). Buprenorphine treatment of opioid dependence. *Experimental and Clinical Psychopharmacology, 3,* 477–489.

Blum, K., Futterman, S., Wallace, J. E., & Schwetner, H. A. (1977). Naloxone-induced inhibition of ethanol dependence in mice. *Nature, 265,* 49–51.

Cacciola, J. S., Alterman, A., Rutherford, M., McKay, J., & McLellan, A. T. (1998). The course of change in methadone maintenance. *Addictions, 93,* 41–49.

Carroll, K. M., Power, M. D., Bryant, K., & Rounsaville, B. J. (1993). One year follow-up status of treatment-seeking cocaine abusers: Psychopathology and dependent severity as predictors of outcome. *Journal of Nervous and Mental Disease, 181,* 71–79.

Carroll, K. M., Rounsaville, B. J., & Gawin, F. H. (1991). A comparative trial of psychotherapies for ambulatory cocaine abusers: Relapse prevention and interpersonal psychotherapy. *American Journal of Drug and Alcohol Abuse, 17,* 229–247.

Carroll, K. M., Rounsaville, B. J., Gordon, L. T., Nich, C., Jatlow, P., Bisighini, R. M., & Gawin, F. H. (1994). Psychotherapy and pharmacotherapy for ambulatory cocaine abusers. *Archives of General Psychiatry, 51,* 177–187.

Carroll, K. M., Rounsaville, B. J., Nich, C., Gordon, L. T., Wirtz, P. W., & Gawin, F. H. (1994). One year follow-up of psychotherapy and pharmacotherapy for cocaine dependence: Delayed emergence of psychotherapy effects. *Archives of General Psychiatry, 51*(12), 989–997.

Center for Alcohol Studies. (1993). *Socioeconomic evaluations of addictions treatment.* Paper presented at the President's Commission on Model State Drug Laws, Piscataway, NJ.

Committee on Opportunities in Drug Abuse Research. (1996). *Pathways of addiction.* Washington, DC: National Academy Press.

Cooper, J. R. (1989). Methadone treatment and acquired immunodeficiency syndrome. *Journal of the American Medical Association, 262,* 1664–1668.

Cornish, J. W., Maany, I., Fudala, P. J., Neal, S., Poole, S. A., Volpicelli, P., & O'Brien,

C. P. (1995). Carbamazepine treatment for cocaine dependence. *Drug and Alcohol Dependence, 38*, 221–227.

Cornish, J. W., Metzger, D., Woody, G. E., Wilson, D., McLellan, A. T., Vandergrift, B., & O'Brien, C. P. (1997). Naltrexone pharmacotherapy for opioid-dependent federal probationers. *Journal of Substance Abuse Treatment, 14*(6), 529–534.

Cushman, P. (1974). Detoxification of rehabilitated methadone patients:Frequency and predictors of long-term success. *American Journal of Drug and Alcohol Abuse, 1*, 393–408.

Department of Substance Abuse Services. (1996). *Evaluation of alcohol and drug abuse treatments in the state of Oregon.* Portland: Oregon Office of Publications.

Dole, V. P. (1989). Methadone treatment and the acquired immunodeficiency syndrome epidemic. *Journal of the American Medical Association, 262*, 1681–1682.

Donovan, D. M., Kadden, R. M., DiClemente, C. C., Carroll, K. M., Longabaugh, R., Zweben, A., & Rychtarik, R. (1994). Issues in the selection and development of therapies in alcoholism treatment matching research. *Journal of Studies on Alcohol*(Suppl. 12), 138–148.

Dorus, W., Ostrow, D., Anton, R., Cushman, P., Collins, J. F., Schaefer, M., Charles, H. L., Desai, P., Hayashida, M., Malkerneker, U., Willenbring, M., Fiscella, R., & Sather, M. R. (1989). Lithium treatment of depressed and nondepressed alcoholics. *Journal of the American Medical Association, 262*, 1646–1652.

Edmunds, M., Frank, R., Hogan, M., McCarty, D., Robinson-Beale, R., & Weisner, C. (Eds.). (1996). *Managing managed care: Quality improvement in behavioral health.* Washington, DC: National Academy Press.

Everingham, S., & Rydell, C. (1994). *Controlling cocaine.* Santa Monica, CA: RAND Corporation.

Frank, R. G., & McGuire T. G. (1997). Savings from a carve-out program for mental health and substance abuse in Massachusetts Medicaid. *Psychiatric Services, 48*(9), 1147–1152.

Freeman, M. A., & Travin, T. (1994). *Managed behavioral healthcare: History, models, key issues, future course.* Paper prepared for the Center for Mental Health Services, Substance Abuse and Mental Health Services Administration.

Fuller, R. K. (1995). Antidipsotropic medications. In R. K. Hester & W. R. Miller (Eds.), *Handbook of alcoholism treatment approaches: Effective alternatives* (2nd ed.). Needham Heights, MA: Allyn & Bacon.

Fuller, R. K., Branchey, L., Brightwell, D. R., Derman, R. M., Emrick, C. D., Iber, F. L., James, K. E., Lacoursiere, R. B., Lee, K. K., Lowenstam, I., Maany, I., Neiderheiser, D., Nocks, J. J., & Shaw, S. (1986). Disulfiram treatment of alcoholism: A Veterans Administration coopersative study. *Journal of the American Medical Association, 256*, 1449–1455.

General Accounting Office. (1995). *Report on methadone treatment.* Washington, DC: U.S. Government Printing Office.

Gerstein, D. R., Johnson, R. A., Harwood, H. J., Fountain, D., Suter, N., & Malloy, K. (1994). *Evaluating recovery services: The California Drug and Alcohol Assessment (CALDATA).* Sacramento: California Department of Alcohol and Drug Programs.

Glassman, A. H., & Covey, L. S. (1995). Nicotine dependence and treatment. In R. Michels (Ed.), *Psychiatry.* Bethesda, MD: National Institute of Drug Abuse.

Gorelick, D. A. (1989). Serotonin reuptake blockers and the treatment of alcoholism. In M. Galanter (Ed.), *Recent developments in alcoholism* (pp. 267–281). New York: Plenum.

Gorelick, D. A., & Wilkins, J. N. (1986). Special aspects of human alcohol withdrawal. In M. Galanter (Ed.), *Recent developments in alcoholism* (Vol. 4). New York: Plenum.

Grabowski, J., Rhoades, H., Elk, R., Schmidtz, J., Davis, C., Creson, D., & Kirby, K. (1995). Fluoxetine is ineffective for treatment of cocaine dependence or concurrent opiate and cocaine dependence: Two placebo-controlled, double-blind trials. *Journal of Clinical Psychopharmacology, 15,* 163–174.

Hall, S. M., Munoz, R. F., Reus, V. I., & Sees, K. L. (1996). Mood management and nicotine gum in smoking treatment: A therapeutic contact and placebo-controlled study. *Journal of Consulting and Clinical Psychology, 64*(5), 1003–1009.

Hayashida, M., Alterman, A. I., McLellan, A. T., O'Brien, C. P., Purtill, J. J., Volpicelli, J. R., Raphaelson, A. H., & Hall, C. P. (1989). Comparative effectiveness of inpatient versus outpatient medical alcohol detoxification. *New England Journal of Medicine, 320,* 358–365.

Higgins, S. T., Budney, A. J., Bickel, W. K., Badger, G., Foerg, F., & Ogden, D. (1995). Outpatient behavioral treatment for cocaine dependence: One-year outcome. *Experimental and Clinical Psychopharmacology, 3,* 205–212.

Higgins, S. T., Budney, A. J., Bickel, W. K., Hughes, J. R., Foerg, F., & Badger, G. (1993). Achieving cocaine abstinence with a behavioral approach. *American Journal of Psychiatry, 150,* 763–769.

Higgins, S. T., Delaney, D. D., Budney, A. J., Bickel, W. K., Hughes, J. R., Foerg, F., & Fenwick, J. W. (1991). A behavioral approach to achieving initial cocaine abstinence. *American Journal of Psychiatry, 148,* 1218–1224.

Hoffman, J. A., Caudill, B. D., Koman, J. J., Luckey, J. W., Flynn, P. M., & Hubbard, R. L. (1994). Comparative cocaine abuse treatment strategies: Enhancing client retention and treatment exposure. *Journal of Addictive Diseases, 13,* 115–128.

Hoffman, N. G., Halikas, J. A., & Mee-Lee, D. (1987). *The Cleveland admission, discharge, and transfer criteria: Model for chemical dependency treatment programs.* Cleveland: Northern Ohio Chemical Dependency Treatment Directors Association.

Hubbard, R. L., Marsden, M. E., Rachal, J. V., Harwood, H. J., Cavanaugh, E. R., & Ginzburg, H. M. (1989). *Drug abuse treatment: A national study of effectiveness.* Chapel Hill: University of North Carolina Press.

Jasinski, D. R., Pevnick, J. S., & Griffith, J. D. (1978). Human pharmacology and abuse potential of the analgesic buprenorphine. *Archives of General Psychiatry, 35,* 501–516.

Kampman, K. M., McGinnis, D., Volpicelli, J., Ehrman, R., Robbins, S., & O'Brien, C. P. (1996). *A case series of newly abstinent cocaine-dependent outpatients treated with propranolol.* Paper presented at the annual meeting of the College on Problems of Drug Dependence, San Juan, Puerto Rico.

Kampman, K., Volpicelli, J. R., Alterman, A. I., Cornish, J., Weinrieb, R., Epperson, L., Sparkman, T., & O'Brien, C. P. (1996). Amantadine in the early treatment of cocaine dependence: A double-blind, placebo-controlled trial. *Drug and Alcohol Dependence, 41,* 25–33.

Kampman, K., Volpicelli, J. R., McGinnis, D., Alterman, A. I., Weinrieb, R., D'Angelo, L., & Epperson, L. (in press). Reliability and validity of the Cocaine Selective Severity Assessment. *Journal of Substance Abuse.*

Kang, S., Kleinman, P. H., Woody, G. E., Millman, R. B., Todd, T. C., Kemp, J., & Lipton, D. S. (1991). Outcomes for cocaine abusers after one-a-week psychosocial therapy. *American Journal of Psychiatry, 148,* 630–635.

Kleber, H. (1995). Pharmacotherapy, current and potential, for the treatment of cocaine dependence. *Clinical Neuropharmacology, 18,* S96–S109.

Koob, G. F. (1992). Neurobiological mechanisms in cocaine and opiate dependence. In C. P. O'Brien & J. Jaffe (Eds.), *Addictive states* (pp. 79–92) New York: Raven Press.

Kosten, T. R. (1996). *NMDA regulated calcium channels as targets to prevent cocaine neurotoxicity.* Paper presented at the 35th annual meeting of the American College of Neuropharmacology, San Juan, Puerto Rico.

Kranzler, H. R., & Anton, R. F. (1994). Implications of recent neuropsychopharmacologic research for understanding the etiology and development of alcoholism. *Journal of Consulting and Clinical Psychology, 62,* 1116–1126.

Kranzler, H. R., Burleson, J. A., Del Boca, F. K., Babor, T. F., Korner, P., Brown, J., & Bohn, M. J. (1994). Buspirone treatment of anxious alcoholics: A placebo-controlled trial. *Archives of General Psychiatry, 51,* 720–731.

Kreek, M. J. (1992). Rationale for maintenance pharmacotherapy of opiate dependence. In C. P. O'Brien & J. H. Jaffe (Eds.), *Addictive states* (pp. 205–330), New York: Raven Press.

Linnoila, M., Mefford, I., Nutt, D., & Adinoff, B. (1987). Alcohol withdrawal and noradrenergic function. *Annals of Internal Medicine, 107,* 875–889.

Marlatt, G. A., & Gordon, J. R. (1985). *Relapse prevention.* New York: Guilford Press.

Mason, B. J., Kocsis, J. H., Ritvo, E. C., & Cutler, R. B. (1996). A double-blind, placebo-controlled trial of desipramine for primary alcohol dependence stratified on the presence or absence of major depression. *Journal of the American Medical Association, 275,* 761–767.

Mason, B. J., Ritvo, E. C., Morgan, R. O., Salvato, F. R., Goldberg, G., Welch, B., & Mantero-Antienza, E. (1994). A double-blind, placebo-controlled pilot study to evaluate the efficacy and safety of oral nalmefene HCl for alcohol dependence. *Alcoholism: Clinical and Experimental Research, 18,* 1162–1167.

McCrady, B., & Langenbucher, J. W. (1996). Alcohol treatment and health care system reform. *Archives of General Psychiatry, 53,* 737–746.

McGrath, P. J., Nunes, E. V., Stewart, J. W., Goldman, D., Agosti, V., Ocepek-Welikson, K., & Quitkin, F. M. (1996). Imipramine treatment of alcoholics with primary depression: A placebo-controlled clinical trial. *Archives of General Psychiatry, 53,* 232–240.

McKay, J. R., Cacciola, J. S., McLellan, A. T., Alterman, A. I., & Wirtz, P. W. (1997). An initial evaluation of the psychosocial dimensions of the American Society of Addiction Medicine criteria for inpatient versus intensive outpatient substance abuse rehabilitation. *Journal Studies of Alcohol, 58,* 239–252.

McKay, J. R., McLellan, A. T., & Alterman, A. I. (1992). An evaluation of the Cleveland criteria for inpatient substance abuse treatment. *American Journal of Psychiatry, 149,* 1212–1218.

McLellan, A. T. (1986). "Psychiatric severity" as a predictor of outcome from substance abuse treatments. In R. Meyer (Ed.), *Psychopathology and addictive disorders.* (pp. 97–139). New York: Guilford Press.

McLellan, A. T. (1996). Unpublished data.

McLellan, A. T., Arndt, I. O., Metzger, D., Woody, G., & O'Brien, C. P. (1993). The effects of psychosocial services in substance abuse treatment. *Journal of the American Medical Association, 269,* 1953–1959.

McLellan, A. T., Grissom, G., Zanis, D., Randall, M., Brill, P., & O'Brien, C. P. (1997). Improved outcomes from problem-service "matching" in substance abuse patients:

A controlled study in a four program, EAP network. *Archives of General Psychiatry,* 54(8), 691–694.

Mechanic, D., Schlesinger, M., & McAlpine, D. D. (1995). Management of mental health and substance abuse services: State of the art and early results. *Millbank Quarterly,* 73, 19–55.

Metzger, D. S., Woody, G. E., McLellan, A. T., O'Brien, C. P., Druley, P., Navaline, H., DePhilippis, D., Stolley, P., & Abrutyn, E. (1993). Human immunodeficiency virus seroconversion among in- and out-of-treatment intravenous drug users: An 18-month prospective follow-up. *Journal of Acquired Immune Deficiency Syndromes,* 6, 1049–1056.

Miller, W. R., Zweben, A., DiClemente, C. C., & Rychtarik, R. G. (1992). *Motivational enhancement therapy manual: A clinical research guide for therapists treating individuals with alcohol abuse and dependence* (NIAAA Project MATCH Monograph Series, Vol. 2, DHHHS Publication No. ADM 92-1894). Washington, DC: U.S. Government Printing Office.

Morral, A. R., Iguchi, M. Y., Belding, M. A., & Lamb, R. J. (1997). Natural classes of treatment response. *Journal of Consulting and Clinical Psychology,* 65(4), 673–685.

Moss, A. R., Vranizan, K., Gorter, R., Bachetti, P., Watters, J., & Osmond, D. (1994). HIV seroconversion in intravenous drug users in San Francisco 1985–1990. *AIDS,* 8(2), 263–265.

Naranjo, C. A., & Sellers, E. M. (1986). Clinical assessment and pharmacotherapy of the alcohol withdrawal syndrome. In M. Galanter (Ed.), *Recent developments in alcoholism* (Vol. 4). New York: Plenum.

Novick, D. M., Joseph, H., Croxon, T. S., Salsitz, E. A., Wang, G., Richman, B. L., Poretsky, L., Keefe, J. B., & Whimbey, E. (1990). Absence of antibody to human immunodeficiencey virus in long term, socially rehabilitated methadone maintenance patients. *Archives of Internal Medicine,* 150, 97–99.

Nowinski, J., & Baker, S. (1992). *The Twelve-Step facilitation handbook: A systematic approach to early recovery from alcoholism and addiction.* Lexington, MA: Lexington Books.

Nunes, E. V., McGrath, P. J., Quitkin, F. M., Ocepek-Welikson, K., Stewart, J. W., Koenig, T., Wager, S., & Klein, D. F. (1995). Imipramine treatment of cocaine abuse: Possible boundaries of efficacy. *Drug and Alcohol Dependence,* 39, 185–195.

O'Brien, C. P. (1996). Recent developments in the pharmacotherapy of substance abuse. *Journal of Consulting and Clinical Psychology,* 64, 677–686.

O'Brien, C. P., & McKay, J. R. (1998). Psychopharmacological treatments of substance use disorders. In P. E. Nathan & J. M. Gorman (Eds.), *Effective treatments for DSM-IV disorders* (pp. 127–155). New York: Oxford University Press.

O'Brien, C. P., & McLellan, A. T. (1996). Myths about the treatment of addiction. *Lancet,* 347, 237–240.

O'Brien, C. P., & Woody, G. E. (1986). The role of naltrexone in the treatment of opioid dependence. In D. Cappell, F. Glaser, Y. Israel et al. (Eds.), *Research advances in alcohol and drug dependence.* New York: Plenum.

O'Farrell, J. J., Cutter, H. S. G., & Floyd, F. J. (1985). Evaluating behavioral marital therapy for male alcoholics: Effects on marital adjustment and communication from before to after therapy. *Behavior Therapy,* 16, 147–167.

O'Malley, S. S., Jaffe, A., Chang, G., Schottenfeld, R. S., Meyer, R. E., & Rounsaville, B. (1992). Naltrexone and coping skills therapy for alcohol dependence: A controlled study. *Archives of General Psychiatry,* 49, 881–887.

Prochaska, J. O., & DiClemente, C. C. (1984). *The transtheoretical approach: Crossing traditional boundaries of therapy.* Homewood, IL: Dow Jones, Irwin.

Project MATCH Research Group. (1997). Matching alcoholism treatments to client heterogeneity: Project MATCH posttreatment drinking outcomes. *Journal of Studies on Alcohol, 58,* 7–29.

Raynor, K., Kong, H., Chen, Y., Yasuda, K., Yu, L., Bell, G. I., & Reisine, T. (1994). Pharmacological characterization of the cloned k-, d-, and m-opioid receptors. *Molecular Pharmacology, 45,* 330–334.

Renz, E. A., Chung, R., Fillman, T. O., Mee-Lee, D., & Sayama, M. (1995). The effect of managed care on the treatment outcome of substance abuse disorders. *General Hospital Psychiatry, 17,* 287–292.

Rounsaville, B., Glazer, W., Wilber, C. H., Weissman, M. M., & Kleber, H. D. (1983). Short-term interpersonal psychotherapy in methadone-maintained opiate addicts. *Archives of General Psychiatry, 40,* 630–636.

Rounsaville, B., Weissman, M., Kleber, H., & Wilber, C. (1982). Heterogeneity of Psychiatric diagnosis in treated opiate addicts. *Archives of General Psychiatry, 39,* 161–166.

Roy, A., Virkkunen, M., & Linnoila, M. (1990). Serotonin in suicide, violence, and alcoholism. In E. F. Coccaro & D. L. Murphy (Eds.), *Serotonin in major psychiatric disorders* (pp. 187–208), Washington, DC: American Psychiatric Press.

Saitz, R., Mayo-Smith, M .F., Roberts, M. S., Redmond, H. A., Bernard, D. R., & Calkins, D. R. (1994). Individualized treatment for alcohol withdrawal: a randomized double-blind controlled trial. *Journal of the American Medical Association, 272,* 519–523.

Schuckit, M. (1996). Recent developments in the pharmacotherapy of alcohol dependence. *Journal of Consulting and Clinical Psychology, 64,* 669–676.

Serpelloni, G., Carriere, M. P., Rezza, G., Morganti, S., Gomma, M., & Binkin, N. (1994). Methadone treatment as a determinant of HIV risk reduction among injecting drug users: A nested case-controlled study. *AIDS Care, 6,* 215–220.

Sullivan, J. T., Sykora, K., Schneiderman, J., Naranjo, C. A., & Sellers, E. M. (1989). Assessment of alcohol withdrawal: The revised Clinical Institute Withdrawal Assessment for Alcohol scale (CIWA–Ar). *British Journal of Addiction, 84,* 1353–1357.

Volpicelli, J. R., Alterman, A. I., Hayashida, M., O'Brien, C. P., & Muentz, L. (1992). Naltrexone in the treatment of alcohol dependence: Initial findings. *Archives of General Psychiatry, 49,* 876–880.

Volpicelli, J. R., Clay, K. L., Rhines, J. S., Volpicelli, L. A., Alterman, A. I., & O'Brien, C. P. (1997). Naltrexone and alcohol dependence: Role of subject compliance. *Archives of General Psychiatry, 54,* 737–743.

Volpicelli, J. R., O'Brien, C. P., Alterman, A. I., & Hayashida, M. (1990). Naltrexone and the treatment of alcohol dependence. In L. D. Reid (Ed.), *Opioids, bulimia and alcoholism* (pp. 195–215). New York: Springer-Verlag.

Washton, A. M., Pottash, A. C., & Gold, M. S. (1984). Naltrexone in addicted business executives and physicians. *Journal of Clinical Psychiatry, 45,* 39–41.

Whitfield, C., Thompson, G., Lamb, A., Spencer, V., Pfeifer, M., & Browing-Ferrando, M. (1978). Detoxification of 1,024 alcoholic patients without psychoactive drugs. *Journal American Medical Association, 239,* 1409–1410.

Woody, G. E., Luborsky, L., McLellan, A. T., O'Brien, C. P., Beck, A. T., Blaine, J., Herman, I., & Hole, A. (1983). Psychotherapy for opiate addicts: Does it help? *Archives of General Psychiatry, 40,* 639–645.

Woody, G. E., McLellan, A. T., Luborsky, L., & O'Brien, C. P. (1995). Psychotherapy in community methadone programs: A validation study. *American Journal of Psychiatry, 152,* 1302–1308.

Woody, G. E., & O'Brien, C. P. (1986). Update on Methadone Maintenance. In D. Cappell, F. Glaser, Y. Israel et al. (Eds.), *Research advances in alcohol and drug dependence.* New York: Plenum.

Zanis, D. A., McLellan, A. T., Alterman, A. I., & Cnaan, R. A. (1996). Efficacy of enhanced outreach counseling to reenroll high-risk drug users 1 year after discharge from treatment. *American Journal of Psychiatry, 156,* 1095–1096.

20

❑ _____

Individual Psychodynamic Psychotherapy

LANCE M. DODES
EDWARD J. KHANTZIAN

INTRODUCTION

Individual psychotherapy is widely used in treatment of addicts, though it is perhaps still underappreciated in comparison with group modalities, including self-help groups. Many addicts benefit from a combination of simultaneous individual and group treatments, and some require the individual psychotherapy to be able to remain with other treatments (Khantzian, 1986). Furthermore, a significant number cannot, or choose not to, make use of other treatment and can only be treated successfully with individual psychotherapy. This chapter rearticulates and extends ideas that we and others have developed previously, based on our understanding and treatment experience with addicted individuals over many years (Brehm & Khantzian, 1997; Dodes, 1984, 1988; Dodes & Khantzian, 1991; Khantzian, 1980, 1986, 1995).

The rationale for individual psychotherapy with addicts arises from an understanding of the psychological factors that contribute to addiction. Contemporary psychodynamic formulations stress the role of conflict, the object meaning of alcohol or drugs, deficits and dysfunctions in ego functioning, and narcissistic deficits as important factors in reliance on substances (Dodes & Khantzian, 1991). These deficits and dysfunctions result in self-regulation disturbances involving affects, self-esteem maintenance, and the capacity for self-care and self–other relations. These areas of psychological vulnerability or dysfunction contribute significantly to addictions and are targeted in psychotherapy (Khantzian, 1986, 1995).

Although we believe that there are indications for referring addicts to psychotherapy, often patients themselves begin the treatment of their addiction with psychotherapy (perhaps particularly those who are more psychologically oriented). Others start individual psychotherapy after first seeking treatment through self-help groups or a more educationally based treatment program, such as that offered in many inpatient settings and outpatient clinics. In either case, via exploring their emotional issues, patients begin to understand not only their own psychology but also the place of substance abuse in their emotional lives. This understanding, then, not only addresses the reasons for their continued problems even when chemical free but also, by placing the substance problem in the context of their emotional lives, provides a strong internal basis for avoiding relapse.

Another route into individual psychotherapy for addicted patients is via repeated treatment failures in other, less introspective settings. Some of these patients repeatedly relapse, despite clear and conscious motivation to abstain, because they are unaware of the internal, largely unconscious factors that lead them to resume substance use. Failing to recognize the role of unconscious processes causes patients to attribute their behavior to lack of willpower, which contributes further to their self-devaluation. Learning about themselves in individual psychotherapy thus contributes not only to a more stable chemical-free state and to overall general improvement in emotional function but also to diminished shame concerning their addiction.

Many addicts may also successfully pursue individual psychotherapy in conjunction with other treatment (e.g., Alcoholics Anonymous [AA], Narcotics Anonymous [NA], or a professionally led group therapy). In such cases, the individual work aims for the usual goals of insight and emotional growth while the other modalities focus on supporting the patient's chemical-free state.

A number of studies substantiate the value of individual psychotherapy with addicts. Woody et al. (1983) noted that in seven investigations with methadone-treated patients, where patients were randomly assigned to psychotherapy or a different treatment (most often drug counseling), five of the studies showed better outcome in the psychotherapy group. Woody's own group also found that patients who received psychotherapy and drug counseling had better results than did patients who received drug counseling alone, when measured in terms of number of areas of improvement, less use of illicit opiates, and lower doses of methadone required. This group (Woody, McLellan, Luborsky, & O'Brien, 1986) noted further that the patients with the most disturbed global psychiatric ratings benefited particularly from psychotherapy, as compared with drug counseling. A number of investigators have documented a high correlation between psychiatric disorders, especially depression, and addiction (Rounsaville, Weissman, Kleber, & Wilber, 1982; Khantzian & Treece, 1985). These findings have been substantiated in a more recent series of studies (Carroll & Rounsaville, 1992; Halikas, Crosby, Pearson, Nugent, & Carlson, 1994; Kessler et al., 1997; Kleinman, Miller, & Millman, 1990; Penick et al., 1994; Regier, Farmer, & Rae, 1990; Rounsaville et al., 1991; Wilens, Biederman, Spencer, & Frances, 1994; Schuckit & Hesselbrock, 1994; Schuckit, Irwin, & Brown, 1990).

Brown (1985) found that 45% of a group of abstinent alcoholics in AA sought psychotherapy, and more than 90% of them found it helpful. Rounsaville, Gawin, and Kleber (1985) also reported positive results in a preliminary study treating outpatient cocaine abusers with a modified interpersonal psychotherapy along with medication trials. Woody et al. (1986) reported that when psychotherapists were integrated in the treatment team, the entire staff reduced their stress as a result of the successful management of the most psychiatrically troubled patients. More recently, Woody, Luborsky, and O'Brien (1995) validated the benefit of psychotherapy in community programs. In contrast, Carroll et al. (1994), as well as Kang et al. (1991), reported less benefit from psychotherapy in ambulatory cocaine abusers. In the latter studies, the authors underscored the importance of the severity of illness, stages of recovery, and level of care. Finally, when psychotherapy was added to paraprofessional drug counseling in an inpatient setting (Rogalski, 1984), patients improved in compliance with treatment as measured in decreased number of discharges against medical advice, disciplinary discharges, or unauthorized absences.

In addition to these studies that statistically examined effects of psychotherapy, a significant psychodynamic literature reports on the treatability of addicted patients with psychodynamic or psychoanalytically oriented psychotherapy (Brown, 1985; Dodes, 1984, 1988, 1990, 1996; Frances, Khantzian, & Tamerin, 1989; Kaufman, 1994; Khantzian, 1986, 1997a; Krystal & Raskin, 1970; Silber, 1974; Treece & Khantzian, 1986; Wurmser, 1974; Krystal, 1982; Woody, Luborsky, McLellan, & O'Brien, 1989; Walant, 1995). The experience of treating addicted individuals in psychodynamic therapy has also provided our best information about the psychology of addiction, which in turn serves as the theoretical basis for technical approaches to the therapy of these patients.

Indications for psychodynamic psychotherapy depend on the patient's capacity to benefit as well as on his or her motivation. Addicted individuals who are able to achieve and maintain sobriety with substance abuse counseling and/or self-help groups and who are untroubled by conflict, anxiety, depression, or other symptoms are unlikely to seek psychotherapy. Addicted patients who are able to develop a therapeutic alliance, who have the capacity to be at least moderately introspective, and who have emotional suffering are candidates for psychotherapy as much as are nonaddicts with similar characteristics. Some of these patients use psychotherapy to help them to achieve abstinence, others use it to help them maintain abstinence, and both groups can also use their therapy to help their overall emotional health once they achieve abstinence.

PSYCHODYNAMIC BASIS FOR PSYCHOTHERAPY OF ADDICTED PATIENTS

There have been a number of major contributions to understanding the psychology of the addictions, particularly over the past 25 years (Dodes &

Khantzian, 1991). The most frequently described function of substance use is the management of intolerable or overwhelming affects. The idea that certain substances are preferentially chosen on the basis of their specific ability to address (ameliorate, express) certain affective states is termed the "self-medication hypothesis" (Khantzian, 1985a, 1997b). Various authors described connections between certain affects and the use of alcohol or particular drugs, for example, use of narcotics to manage rage or loneliness and use of cocaine and other stimulants to manage depression, boredom, and emptiness or to provide a sense of grandeur (Khantzian, 1985a; Wurmser, 1974; Milkman & Frosch, 1973). In a more general way, Krystal and Raskin (1970) spoke of a "defective stimulus barrier" in addicts, causing them to be susceptible to flooding with intolerable affective states that are traumatic. They described a normal process of affective development in which affects are differentiated, desomatized, and verbalized and pointed to defects in this development in (at least some) addicted individuals. These defects leave some addicts with the inability to use affects as signals, a critical capacity for managing them. Without this signal capacity, drugs may be used to ward off affective flooding.

Others have noted the quality of addicts' relatedness to their alcohol or drugs as akin to human object relationships. The chemical becomes a substitute for a longed-for or needed figure—one that has omnipotent properties or is completely controllable and available (Krystal & Raskin, 1970; Wieder & Kaplan, 1969; Wurmser, 1974).

Related to these views are observations about the narcissistic pathology of addicts. Wurmser (1974) described a "narcissistic crisis" in addicts. He noted that for some addicts, collapse of a grandiose self or of an idealized object provides the impetus for substance use in an effort to resolve feelings of narcissistic frustration, shame, and rage. Kohut (1971) also referred to the narcissistic function of alcohol or drugs in addiction as a replacement for defective psychological structure, particularly that arising from an inadequate idealized self-object.

From another perspective, Khantzian (1978, 1995) and Khantzian and Mack (1983) described defective self-care functions in addicts—the group of ego functions involved with anticipation of danger, appropriate modulated response to protect oneself, and sufficient positive self-esteem to care about oneself. These defective self-care functions may be seen in many substance abusers who characteristically place themselves in danger or fail to protect their health and well-being. In turn, this problem may be related to inadequate attention to the protection of the child by his or her parent, resulting in the failure to internalize self-care functions.

In addition to this ego deficit psychology, several investigators described a generally defective capacity to be aware of affective states in certain addicts. Some addicts appear to be "alexithymic," that is, unable to name or describe emotions in words. Krystal (1982) described substance use in some of these patients as a search for an external agent to soothe them, associated with their lack of sense of ability to soothe themselves. McDougall (1984) described patients whose use of words and ideas is without affective meaning and who use alcohol or drugs to disperse emotional arousal and thus to avoid affective flooding. Although the final appearance of this affective intolerance has the quality of an ego deficit, its underlying basis is understood to be a defensive avoidance. Krystal (1982) described this defense as arising secondary to psychological trauma in either childhood or adult life.

Khantzian (1997a) recently wrote about the preverbal origins of distress found among some substance abusers. He described a case in which early experience that remained out of conscious awareness created a nameless pain that recurred in response to a current stimulus (a film), leading to an alcoholic relapse. Of equal importance, when the early experience of abandonment again recurred in the setting of a group therapy, it could be clearly interpreted, understood, and borne rather than managed through substance abuse. Along similar lines, Walant (1995) stressed infantile origins of problems with interpersonal contact and interdependence that predispose to addictive adaptations.

Finally, addiction may play a central role in seeking restoration of inner control of one's affective state (Dodes, 1990). This need for control in addicts involves a narcissistic vulnerability to being traumatized by the experience of helplessness or powerlessness. The use of substances in these instances is seen as a way to correct the experience of helplessness. That is, by taking an action (using alcohol or drugs) that can alter their internal affective state, addicts may reassert the power to control their inner experience, undoing and reversing the feeling of powerlessness. Because a sense of control of inner experience is a central aspect of narcissism, the intense aggressive drive to achieve this control when it is felt to be threatened may appropriately be considered narcissistic rage. According to this view, narcissistic rage arising from feelings of powerlessness gives addiction its most defining characteristics, namely, its insistent, compulsive, unrelenting quality and its relative unresponsiveness to realistic factors. This also offers an explanation for why, like narcissistic rage in general, the addictive drive may well overwhelm other aspects of the personality (Dodes, 1990).

More recently, Dodes (1996) expanded this view to place addictions within the category of those psychological problems currently and historically known as compulsions. He pointed out that although addictions and compulsions are clearly similar to each other in their "compulsive" quality, they have always been seen as fundamentally different because compulsions are experienced as ego dystonic—as requirements (things one must do against one's will despite their nonsensical nature), whereas addictions have been experienced as ego syntonic—as wishes (things one does because they are pleasurable to some degree, even if destructive). Further, compulsions have been viewed as compromise formations between a forbidden wish and an opposing (superego) force, whereas addictions have been viewed as the result of either ego function (e.g., self-medication) or deficit in ego function (e.g., self-care deficiencies), rather than being centrally viewed as compromises. However, addictions commonly move from being ego syntonic to ego dystonic, and compulsions likewise often shift from being ego dystonic to being ego syntonic. Beyond this, Dodes noted that in his formulation of addiction (an action driven to correct helplessness and to express the narcissistic rage engendered by this helplessness), there is an inherent compromise formation. This compromise is expressed in the defensive *displacement* of the reassertion of power and the expression of rage to the addictive behavior. For instance, Dodes (1996) described a man who had an alcoholic binge after he was unable to fire his son from his company. Because this man felt it was wrong to fire his son despite the son's embezzlement, he felt helpless. He restored an internal sense of empowerment through his compulsive drinking, and "the addictive behavior was therefore an unconscious compromise formation in which he gave up realistic action, although he consciously experienced his behavior as purely gratifying" (p. 822). Dodes concluded that addictions are fundamentally the same as compulsions and subsequently also showed how some compulsions not usually considered addictions were true addictions psychodynamically. The important implication of this finding is that addictions should be seen as treatable in traditional psychodynamic psychotherapy as much as are compulsions, which have traditionally been understood to be amenable to a psychodynamic or psychoanalytic approach.

TECHNICAL ASPECTS OF PSYCHOTHERAPY WITH ADDICTS

There are a number of special considerations in the psychodynamic psychotherapy of addicted individuals (Dodes & Khantzian, 1991). From the formulations discussed previously, it is clear that various meanings and roles of drugs or alcohol need to be considered in understanding the patient. In addition, addicts are frequently still abusing substances at the time they are first seen, which poses an immediate threat to their emotional and physical health, their relationships, and their overall capacity to function. This threat makes it necessary to address the question of abstinence from substance use first, when beginning treatment.

The first step is diagnosing substance abuse or dependence and informing the patient of the diagnosis, since the patient may fail to perceive the extent of the problem or present with overt denial or minimization. To make the diagnosis and have a basis for showing it clearly to the patient, it is necessary to take a detailed history of the problems that have been caused by the patient's use of drugs or alcohol. In taking this history, it is useful to inquire systematically about trouble in the areas of work, medical health, relationships with friends, relationships with family (adults and children), legal problems, and intrapsychic problems (depression, shame, anxiety). It is often helpful to ask specifically what the patient is like when he or she drinks or uses drugs and the details of what happens at these times as well as the effects the patient seeks from substance use. Does he or she become more belligerent, moody, withdrawn, or sad? Might the patient have had more or better relationships with friends if he or she had never had a drink or a drug? Patients often deny trouble in their marriages but when the matter is explored in detail will acknowledge that their spouses would prefer that they drink less or have asked them on more than one occasion to cut down or stop. Upon reflection, they may recognize that their use of alcohol or drugs has silently become a source of chronic tension in their relationships. Once the patient clarifies or even lists the areas of difficulties that are due to alcohol or drugs, it is often possible for him or her to acknowledge the global impact of substance abuse on his or her life.

Focusing on the diagnosis of alcoholism or other drug abuse is more than a merely cognitive process. The realization that he or she is out of control in this area of life is a significant psychological step in itself. Brown (1985), in her work with alcoholic patients, stresses loss of control as a core issue and focus of psychotherapy. It is a blow to the narcissistic potency of the patient; as such, it may be usefully investigated because it bears on the patient's important feelings and issues concerning powerlessness and mastery (Dodes, 1988). Mack (1981) also underlined that an alcoholic's recognition of failure to be in control of his or her drinking is a first step in the assumption of responsibility.

Through all this early diagnostic and at times confrontational work, as in therapy in general, the therapist's attitude must be exploratory without being judgmental. The patient's denial or minimization is often closely connected with his or her shame, and throughout this initial evaluation the patient is simultaneously evaluating the therapist—in particular, the therapist's attitude toward the patient and his or her addictive problem. To put it another way, the patient is faced with his or her own projections onto the therapist, and it is important that the therapist not accede to the role of the harsh or punitive superego that is at risk of being invisibly imposed.

Transference issues among addicts arise from a variety of sources, as with patients in general, but often include harsh superego projections. Other common transference manifestations arise from narcissistic deficits, leading to idealizing and mirroring relationships or fearful, guarded positions against being overcontrolled or overwhelmed. Countertransference difficulties frequently encountered with substance abusers revolve around frustration, anger, and guilt, as patients' failures to abstain challenge the therapeutic potency of the treatment professional. At times, these difficulties result in withdrawal, inappropriately critical attitudes, or overinvolvement fueled by the therapist's reaction formation. The severe nature of the risks facing addicts makes the work with them both particularly challenging and rewarding. It is important for the therapist to be able to view both the overt behavior and the inner psychopathology of the addict with the same combination of objectivity and compassion that he or she brings to any patient.

Developing a therapeutic alliance early in therapy is also made difficult by the patient's frequently ambivalent relationship toward abstention from drinking or drug use at the same time that the therapist is appropriately concerned with the patient's achieving abstinence. It may be ineffective and even counterproductive to be seen as requiring (vs. suggesting) something the patient does not consciously feel is in his or her best interest. Once the patient concurs with the diagnosis, he or she has a necessary, though not always sufficient, basis for an alliance with the therapist to achieve abstinence. In fact, the psychological issues in abstention are complex.

We (Dodes, 1984; Khantzian, 1980) have addressed issues in abstention with alcoholics. Patients' achievement of abstinence hinges on the place of substance use in their psychological equilibrium but also critically on the alliance with, and transference to, the therapist. Many patients quickly achieve abstinence upon beginning psychotherapy, in spite of the evident importance to them of their drugs or alcohol. But others may continue to use substances even though not in a way that is malignantly out of control or in a way that creates an immediate emergency situation. In a number of these cases we have helped patients establish abstinence over time, psychotherapeutically. When the therapist focuses on the patient's failure to perceive the danger to him- or herself that is contained in the continued abuse, the therapist's caring concern may be internalized by the patient, providing a nucleus for the introjection of a healthy "self-care" function (Dodes, 1984). However, the patient's ability to perceive the therapist in a benign way that may be internalized depends on absence or resolution of negative transference feelings at the beginning of treatment.

For some patients, early achievement of abstinence is possible because of a genuine therapeutic alliance with the therapist; in other cases abstinence may be achieved early on because of unconscious wishes to merge with, or be held by, a therapist who is idealized or because of a compliant identification with the aggressor (Dodes, 1984). When the patient does not initially abstain, subsequent confrontation may produce abstention because the patient finally perceives the confrontation as a longed-for message of caring that was absent or insufficient in his or her childhood. (Khantzian & Mack, 1983, in their discussion of the origin of self-care deficits described this kind of parental insufficiency.) From a practical standpoint, the clinical choices involved in the end must depend on the immediate risks to the patient. If patients drink only intermittently and are able to participate genuinely in the process of psychotherapy, we have found that the psychotherapy can continue. Indeed, the psychotherapy provides an opportunity to explore the issues in the continued drinking, including problems with self-care and the transference implications of the failure to abstain. However, when drinking becomes continually destructive, patients are generally unable to participate in the process, requiring early confrontation around the need to be hospitalized or to terminate therapy. Over the course of an ongoing psychotherapy, the capacity for abstinence may vary, depending in part on shifts in the therapeutic relationship (Dodes, 1984). We discuss the question of relapses in an abstinent patient later.

Once the patient achieves abstinence, the therapy may broaden to explore all areas of his or her psychological life, as in any psychotherapy. Some authors writing about alcoholism, however, recommend a kind of staging of the therapy. In this view, the first phase is directed toward helping the patient develop an identity as an alcoholic (Brown, 1985) perhaps spending up to several years focusing on the drinking, on ways to stay sober, and on mourning the losses incurred as a result of drinking (Bean-Bayog, 1985). Kaufman (1995) similarly stresses the importance of abstinence, stabilization, and relapse prevention and then, in advanced recovery, the importance of address-ing issues of intimacy and autonomy. However, it is generally unnecessary and potentially counterproductive to attempt to direct the therapeutic process according to a preconceived agenda. As with any patient, imposing one's own focus risks interfering with the free evolution of the patient's thoughts toward deeper and more meaningful understanding of the issues that are important to the patient. In our opinion, although some addicts (like some patients in general) require a more supportive rather than an exploratory approach, or special approaches based on some of the dynamic factors described earlier, this decision should be based on an individual assessment of the patient's psychology rather than on a generalization for all substance abusers. The approach in treatment may, and should, vary according to the stage of treatment and the status of the patient's abstinence.

The idea of imposing structure in psychotherapy with addicts arises in part from concerns about the ability of such patients to tolerate the process of therapy. At the heart of this thought is the worry that exploring the important issues in their lives will lead addicts to resume their substance abuse. Actually, the reverse is often the case—patients who do not deal with the issues that trouble them may be at much greater risk of continued substance use or relapse. Nonetheless, there are difficulties with pursuing psychotherapy in some instances. At times, therapists fail to attend appropriately to the life-threatening nature of continued substance abuse (Bean-Bayog, 1985) or fail to make the diagnosis (Brown, 1985), overlooking the ongoing deteriora-tion of their patients' lives. Alcoholics may also try to use therapy to aid their denial of their alcoholism. Finally, some therapists feel that alcoholics may have difficulty with the strong transference feelings of an individual psycho-therapy (Vaillant, 1981).

However, all these concerns about individual psychotherapy hinge on failures of the therapist and may be avoided by a therapist who is attentive to these issues (Dodes, 1988, 1991). For instance, as described earlier, attention must be paid initially to achieving abstinence. Likewise, if a patient misuses the treatment to rationalize continued drug or alcohol use, an appropriately responsive therapist would recognize this misuse and bring it into the treatment process to be identified and dealt with rather than allowing it to continue. The therapist should be attentive to the psychology of an addicted patient, as to any patient, and should closely monitor the transference and the patient's capacity to observe, tolerate, and understand his or her feelings in the relationship. Addicts in fact have a wide variety of charac-terological structures, strengths, and weaknesses, and it is incorrect to think of them as a group as being incapable of dealing with strong transference feelings that arise in a psychotherapy. (Vaillant's [1981] parallel concern that therapists too cannot tolerate their countertransference feelings toward their alcoholic patients also appears incorrect, both in our experience and from a reading of the literature.) Finally, Brown's (1985) concern that a psychodynamic psychotherapy may distract the alcoholic patient from his or her task of establishing an identity as an alcoholic may be taken principally as a reminder to the therapist to attend to the patient's alcoholism rather than a contraindication to psychotherapy (Dodes, 1988).

In fact, in the ongoing therapy of addicts, once the patient achieves abstinence, the therapist should always be alert to the meanings and purposes of the patients' substance use as these become clearer. Part of the advantage of psychotherapy with addicts is that it offers an ongoing opportunity for patients to take firmer control over their addiction, based on understanding and tolerating the feelings and issues that contribute to it. The therapist's continual attentiveness to improving understanding of the patient's drug use also avoids the problem of distracting the patient from his or her addiction.

Of course, any therapist can be fooled—patients who deny, minimize, or distort the facts about their substance use may render its diagnosis and treatment impossible for any therapist. This is a limitation to psychotherapy, as it is to other attempted interventions.

Having considered early issues of abstinence and allowing the focus of the therapy to broaden, we may now consider how the dynamics of addicts may necessitate a modification of approach. In the case of alexithymic patients, Krystal (1982) and Krystal and Raskin (1970) proposed a preparatory stage in which the patient's affects are identified and explained—with the goal of increasing ego function, including improving the use of affects as signals and improving affect tolerance. McDougall (1984) focused on the countertransference problems produced with such patients. She described feelings of boredom and helplessness with consequent emotional withdrawal by the therapist and pointed to the need for the therapist to provide a consistent holding environment that may last for years before patients are able to acknowledge their emotions. She also offered an understanding of this process in terms of the patient's creating a "primitive communication that is intended, in a deeply unconscious fashion, to make the analyst experience what the distressed and misunderstood infant had once felt" (p. 399).

A contemporary psychodynamic understanding of addicted patients, however, does not usually suggest this sort of modification of approach but, rather, a need to attend to one or another aspect of the meaning and role of the addiction for a patient. For instance, for some patients it is particularly important to attend to the object meanings of the alcohol or drugs. In some patients narcissistic vulnerabilities are of paramount importance, for instance, the collapse of idealized objects as described by Wurmser (1974) or the role of particular affective states in precipitating substance use, mentioned by a number of authors. With some patients, self-care deficits as described by Khantzian and Mack (1983) are of great significance. From a different perspective, the active nature of addictive behavior in seizing control against an intolerable feeling of helplessness as described by Dodes (1990) may be an important focus in the psychotherapy of addicts. In such cases, it is important to address patients' experiences of helplessness and powerlessness as major factors in precipitating substance use.

It is also important for the therapist to be especially active with patients whose affect management and self-care are seriously impaired (Khantzian, 1986, 1995). Excessive passivity with such patients can be dangerous. It is necessary in these cases to empathically draw the patients' attention to ways in which they render themselves vulnerable as a result of their self-care deficits and to point out how these self-care deficits render them susceptible to addictive behavior. As Krystal (1982) also said, it is necessary to explore with patients the details of current life situations to help them recognize their feelings and see that these feelings may serve as "guides to appropriate reactions and self-protective behavior rather than signals for impulsive action and the obliteration of feelings with drugs" (Khantzian, 1986, p. 217).

Consistent with the need to maintain an active stance, the therapist may at times need to serve as a "primary care" physician—especially at the start of treatment, when he or she must often play multiple roles to ensure that the patient receives appropriate care from a number of sources (Khantzian, 1985b, 1988). This task may include decisions about (and active involvement in arranging) hospitalization and detoxification, involvement with AA or NA, professionally led group treatments, or pharmacological treatment. However, such an active approach, although possibly life saving, may interfere with the later development of a traditional psychotherapeutic relationship because of the transference and countertransference issues it induces, particularly in regard to the patient's realistic gratitude. If this gratitude becomes a prominent factor, referral to another therapist for continued psychotherapy may be required (Khantzian, 1985b).

Another consideration in therapy with addicted individuals is relapse, or the threat of relapse. Just as with the initial attention to abstinence, the therapy must focus on relapses when they occur. One reason for this focus is, of course, to attend to the risk to the patient. But relapses (or the patient's awareness that he or she feels a greater urge to use alcohol or drugs) also provide an opportunity to learn about the factors leading to substance use. Frequently patients are unaware of these factors; their lack of awareness contributes to their feelings of frustration and helplessness and leaves them unprepared for further relapses. A careful, even microscopic, investigation of the feelings, relationships, and events that preceded the relapse are often revealing. Once these issues and affects are clarified, they frequently contribute to an understanding of the patient's psychology in general, because they center on areas felt to be intolerable by the patient. Often, patients bring up their increased thinking about drugs or alcohol when there is an impending relapse. At other times, the therapist may infer this increased risk based on what he or she knows of the patient's history and emotional life. Conveying this perception to patients is one way to help them learn to attend to their affects (as well as thoughts and behaviors) and utilize them as signals. Dreams may also provide here, as in therapy in general, knowledge of what is currently unconscious. Often, abstinent addicts have dreams about alcohol or drugs that can indicate that something current in their lives is reviving the association with alcohol or drugs, hence warning of the need to attend to the risk of relapse. Beyond this indication, dreams may shed light on the meanings of their substance use.

Finally, a word should be said about organicity. Some treatment providers view addicted patients as too impaired in brain functioning, as a result of drug or alcohol abuse ("wet brain"), to be able to utilize a dynamic psychotherapy until after a lengthy time of abstinence. Certainly some patients exhibit impaired memory and capacity for skilled cognitive functions immediately after stopping drug or alcohol use. However, in our experience this limitation is frequently mild or not significant for all but the most severely affected addicts (e.g., alcoholics with hepatic failure and elevated blood ammonia levels). In fact, as regularly observed in inpatient treatment centers, patients can do significant work to understand themselves and the dynamic issues in their families and can also return to complex tasks within the span of a few weeks immediately following detoxification. These inpatient programs are usually designed with a first phase for detoxification over 3 to 7 days, following which patients are placed in a therapeutically and educationally intensive rehabilitation phase. It is the rare patient who cannot participate in this phase, even though inpatient centers nearly always treat patients who have been heavily abusing alcohol or drugs. The implication for psychotherapy is that it is rarely necessary to wait an extended time to begin because of organic factors. Patients who are truly impaired because their drug or alcohol use is so continuous that they are always either high/drunk or withdrawing should not be in psychotherapy to begin with as they require hospitalization to break the pattern before they will be able to attend to the work of the treatment.

PSYCHOTHERAPY AND SELF-HELP GROUPS

Because psychotherapy and self-help groups are both frequently employed in the treatment of addiction, it is important to consider the issues involved in utilizing both approaches (Dodes, 1988; Dodes & Khantzian, 1991). Although psychotherapy is frequently combined with involvement in AA or NA, some authors (Brown, 1985; Bean-Bayog, 1985; Rosen, 1981; Kaufman, 1994) suggest a staging of the therapy. According to this view, AA or NA serves as the locus for attending to the patient's addiction and his or her attempts to remain chemical free while psychotherapy is either postponed or assigned an adjunctive role of looking at other areas of the person's life and issues. Rosen (1981) took a closer look at the issues involved in this sequence and focused on the specific role of the therapy in helping patients to separate from their attachment to AA, which Rosen viewed as having elements of a symbiosis. One aspect of this attachment is the striking fact that AA, unlike psychoanalytically oriented psychotherapy, provides no mechanism for termination. In Rosen's view, working through separation and termination is particularly important to many of these patients, and he saw a critical aspect of the role of psychotherapy following AA as permitting this work.

However, as we described previously, there is usually little reason to postpone psychotherapy; consequently, it is important to understand the psychology of engaging simultaneously in psychotherapy and AA or NA. Patients in such a combined treatment often engage differently with each element; that is, patients split their transference projections, expectations, and attachments, engaging the therapy and the self-help group at separate psychological levels (Dodes, 1988). Such multiple levels of engagement are always present in any psychotherapy, especially in patients who have significant narcissistic difficulties as well as other structural conflicts. That is, functions of narcissistic mirroring and valuing are always present in therapy concurrent with other transferential and intellectual engagements and concurrent with interpretive work directed toward structural conflicts. Patients' attachment to AA provides opportunity for needed internalization of self-care and self-valuing, with AA serving as a valuing, idealized object (or self-object or transitional object); in this way, important elements of the narcissistic (idealizing and mirroring) transference are assigned to AA (Dodes, 1988). The degree to which the transference is split in this way varies in different patients. It is critical for the therapist to be aware of this split because a patient's sobriety may hinge on an idealization of AA or its "Higher Power" concept, and this sobriety may be lost if the idealization is challenged (Dodes, 1988). Consequently, the therapist must first help the patient to increase his or her tolerance of affects and "await internalization of sufficient narcissistic potency" (Dodes, 1988, p. 289) before too closely examining the defenses and functions of AA.

In our opinion, the need for a nondynamic, supportive approach through AA may lessen eventually as a consequence of the patient's growth, including that achieved via internalization (either through the therapy or through AA) of a sense of adequate narcissistic potency as well as growth in ego functions in general. At this point the patient may be able to remain chemical free without AA. However, this does not always occur and may be understood as the basis for the phenomenon of interminable treatment in AA: "Those individuals who successfully internalize [a self-care] function, may stop attending AA meetings, while those who cannot internalize it must attend forever" (Dodes, 1984, p. 253). In addition to these individuals who must attend to maintain their sobriety, many long-term AA members remain involved because of the important social and interpersonal elements in AA or because of their interest in helping others, even though they may not require AA for sobriety.

Dodes (1988) suggests that the fear of disrupting the idealizing transference to AA (and consequently losing the sobriety that is dependent on this transference) underlies the fear of psychotherapy among some patients and some treatment providers. Again, although this is a realistic concern, it is only one aspect of the need for the therapist to be attentive to the technical requirements of addicted patients and does not contraindicate psychotherapeutic treatment. Overall, the combination of psychodynamic psychotherapy and AA or NA is useful for the great majority of patients (Dodes, 1988; Khantzian, 1985b, 1988).

Finally, it is appropriate to consider the "disease concept," as this concept is closely linked with the self-help groups and has traditionally been difficult to reconcile with psychoanalytically oriented psychotherapy. Mack (1981) noted that the disease concept led to "oversimplified physiological models and a territorial smugness . . . which . . . precludes a sophisticated psychodynamic understanding of the problems of the individual alcoholic" (p. 129). In addition, the term "disease" itself has not been well or clearly defined, a fact addressed by Shaffer (1985). However, it is possible to integrate the disease concept into a traditional psychoanalytic psychotherapy (Dodes, 1988). In the first place, focusing on the addictive behavior specifically as an illness is useful because it helps to avoid the kind of failure to address the problem that some have worried about with psychotherapy. Moreover, as mentioned earlier, acknowledgment of a disease or diagnosis often arouses feelings, particularly about powerlessness in the patient's life, that may be quite important to explore (Dodes, 1988, 1990).

Because an illness or disease concept can be useful, it is helpful to integrate it with a psychoanalytical psychotherapy. To do this, Dodes (1988) suggested that the "disease" (of alcoholism, for instance) be defined to the patient as having two parts: (1) the patient's history of alcoholism, and (2) the patient's being at permanent risk of repeating this behavior in the future. This definition does not impede full psychological exploration of the meanings of the patient's drinking. The first point, clarifying and emphasizing an aspect of the patient's history, certainly does not interfere with dynamic work. It is the second point we might question. The risk of repetition of drinking that is so central to the disease idea may be troublesome for dynamic exploration if it has the quality of something that is inexplicable in dynamic terms, a kind of "black box" danger of this "disease." However, as Dodes (1988) suggested, this risk is actually the same as the regressive potential of any patient in psychotherapy. Addicts, like all other individuals in psychotherapy, never totally eliminate the potential of resuming old pathological defenses and behaviors and of regressing. Their risk of resuming substance abuse is therefore just an example of this general rule.

CONCLUSION

This chapter presented a description of individual psychodynamic psychotherapy with addicts, based on a contemporary psychoanalytical understanding of their vulnerabilities and disturbances. We emphasized disturbances in ego function and narcissistic difficulties that affect addicts' capacities to regulate their feeling life, self-esteem, and relationships. A major psychotherapeutic task for addicted patients is to bring into their awareness their emotional difficulties and the way their problems predispose them to relapse into drug/alcohol use and dependence. We have reviewed implications for technique with regard to characteristic central issues for addicts and the need in certain cases for active intervention. We explored strategies for establishing abstinence, including the value of working with self-help groups such as AA and NA. Finally, we emphasized a flexible approach with regard to the timing, sequencing, and integration of psychotherapy in relation to other interventions and needs based on patient characteristics and clinical considerations.

REFERENCES

Bean-Bayog, M. (1985). Alcoholism treatment as an alternative to psychiatric hospitalization. *Psychiatric Clinics of North America, 8*, 501–512.

Brehm, N., & Khantzian, E. J.(1997). Determinants and perpetuators of substance abuse: Psychodynamics. In J. H. Lowinson, P. Ruiz, R. B. Millman, & J. G. Langrod (Eds.), *Substance abuse: A comprehensive textbook* (3rd ed., pp. 90–100). Baltimore: Williams & Wilkins.

Brown, S. (1985). *Treating the alcoholic: A developmental model of recovery.* New York: Wiley.

Carroll, K. M., & Rounsaville, B. J. (1992). Contrast of treatment seeking and untreated cocaine abusers. *Archives of General Psychiatry, 49*, 464–471.

Carroll, K. M., Rounsaville, B. J., Gordon, L. T., Nich, C., Jatlow, P., Bisighini, R. M., & Gawin, F. H. (1994). Psychotherapy and pharmacotherapy for ambulatory cocaine abusers. *Archives of General Psychiatry, 51*, 177–187.

Dodes, L. M. (1984). Abstinence from alcohol in long-term individual psychotherapy with alcoholics. *American Journal of Psychotherapy, 38*, 248–256.

Dodes, L. M. (1988). The psychology of combining dynamic psychotherapy and Alcoholics Anonymous. *Bulletin of the Menninger Clinic, 52*, 283–293.

Dodes, L. M. (1990). Addiction, helplessness, and narcissistic rage. *Psychoanalytic Quarterly, 59*, 398–419.

Dodes, L. M. (1991). Psychotherapy is useful, often essential, for alcoholics. *The Psychodynamic Letter, 1*(2), 4–7.

Dodes, L. M. (1996) Compulsion and addiction. *Journal of the American Psychoanalytic Association, 44*, 815–835.

Dodes, L. M., & Khantzian, E. J. (1991). Psychotherapy and chemical dependence. In D. Ciraulo & R. Shader (Eds.), *Clinical manual of chemical dependence.* (pp. 345–358). Washington, DC: American Psychiatric Press.

Frances, R. J., Khantzian, E. J., & Tamerin, J. S. (1989). Psychodynamic psychotherapy. In T. B. Karasu (Ed.), *Treatment of psychiatric disorders: A task force report of the American Psychiatric Association.* (pp. 1103–1111). Washington, DC: American Psychiatric Press.

Halikas, J. A., Crosby, R. D., Pearson, V. L., Nugent, S. M., & Carlson, G. A. (1994). Psychiatric comorbidity in treatment seeking cocaine abusers. *American Journal of Addiction, 3*, 25–35.

Kang, S. Y., Kleinman, P. H., Woody, G. E., Millman, R. B., Todd, T. C., Kemp, J., & Lipton, D. S. (1991). Outcome for cocaine abusers after once-a-week psychosocial therapy. *American Journal of Psychiatry, 148*, 630–635.

Kaufman, E. (1994). *Psychotherapy of addicted persons.* New York: Guilford Press.

Kessler, R. C., Crum, R. M., Warner, L. A., Nelson, C. B., Schulenberg, J., & Anthony,

J. C. (1997). Lifetime co-occurrence of DSM-III-R alcohol abuse and dependence with other psychiatric disorders in the National Comorbidity Survey. *Archives of General Psychiatry, 54,* 313–321.

Khantzian, E. J. (1978). The ego, the self and opiate addiction: Theoretical and treatment considerations. *International Review of Psychoanalysis, 5,* 189–198.

Khantzian, E. J. (1980). The alcoholic patient: An overview and perspective. *American Journal of Psychotherapy, 34,* 4–19.

Khantzian, E. J. (1985a). The self-medication hypothesis of addictive disorders: Focus on heroin and cocaine dependence. *American Journal of Psychiatry, 142,* 1259–1264.

Khantzian, E. J. (1985b). Psychotherapeutic interventions with substance abusers: The clinical context. *Journal of Substance Abuse Treatment, 2,* 83–88.

Khantzian, E. J. (1986). A contemporary psychodynamic approach to drug abuse treatment. *American Journal of Drug and Alcohol Abuse, 12,* 213–222.

Khantzian, E. J. (1988). The primary care therapist and patient needs in substance abuse treatment. *American Journal of Drug and Alcohol Abuse, 14*(2), 159–167.

Khantzian, E. J. (1995). Self-regulation vulnerabilities in substance abusers: Treatment implications. In S. Dowling (Ed.), *The psychology and treatment of addictive behavior* (pp. 17–41). New York: International Universities Press.

Khantzian, E. J. (1997a). *Preverbal origins of distress, substance use disorders and psychotherapy.* Unpublished manuscript.

Khantzian, E. J. (1997b). The self-medication hypothesis of substance use disorders: A reconsideration and recent applications. *Harvard Review of Psychiatry, 4,* 231–244.

Khantzian, E. J., & Mack, J. (1983). Self-preservation and the care of the self. *Psychoanalytic Study of the Child, 38,* 209–232.

Khantzian, E. J., & Treece, C. (1985). DSM-III psychiatric diagnosis of narcotic addicts. *Archives of General Psychiatry, 42,* 1067–1071.

Kleimman, P. K., Miller, A. B., & Millman, R. B. (1990). Psychopathology among cocaine abusers entering treatment. *Journal of Nervous and Mental Disease, 178,* 442–447.

Kohut, H. (1971). *The analysis of the self.* Madison, CT: International Universities Press.

Krystal, H. (1982). Alexithymia and the effectiveness of psychoanalytic treatment. *International Journal of Psychoanalytic Psychotherapy, 9,* 353–378.

Krystal, H., & Raskin, H. (1970). *Drug dependence: Aspects of ego function.* Detroit: Wayne State University Press.

Mack, J. (1981). Alcoholism, A.A., and the governance of the self. In M. H. Bean & N. E. Zinberg (Eds.), *Dynamic approaches to the understanding and treatment of alcoholism* (pp. 128–162). New York: Free Press.

McDougall, J. (1984). The "disaffected" patient: Reflections on affect pathology. *Psychoanalytic Quarterly, 53,* 386–409.

Milkman, H., & Frosch, W. A. (1973). On the preferential abuse of heroin and amphetamines. *Journal of Nervous and Mental Disease, 156,* 242–248.

Penick, E. C., Powell, B. J., Nickel, E. J., Bingham, S. F., Rieseenmy, K. R., Read, M. R., & Campbell, J. (1994). Co-morbidity of lifetime psychiatric disorder among male alcoholic patients. *Alcoholism: Clinical and Experimental Research, 18,* 1289–1293.

Regier, D. A., Farmer, M. E., Rae, D. S., Locke, B. Z., Keith, S. J., Judd, L. L., & Goodwin, K. K. (1990). Comorbidity of mental disorders with alcohol and other drug abuse: Results from the Epidemiologic Catchment Area (ECA) study. *Journal of the American Medical Association, 264,* 2511–2518.

Rogalski, C. J. (1984). Professional psychotherapy and its relationship to compliance intreatment. *International Journal of the Addictions, 19*, 521–539.

Rosen, A. (1981). Psychotherapy and Alcoholics Anonymous: Can they be coordinated? *Bulletin of the Menninger Clinic, 45*, 229–246.

Rounsaville, B. J., Anton, S. F., Carroll, K., Budde, D., Prusoff, B., & Gawin, F. (1991). Psychiatric diagnosis of treatment-seeking cocaine-abusers. *Archives of General Psychiatry, 48*, 43–51.

Rounsaville, B. J., Gawin, F., & Kleber, H. (1985). Interpersonal psychotherapy adapted for ambulatory cocaine abusers. *American Journal of Drug and Alcohol Abuse, 11*, 171–191.

Rounsaville, B. J., Weissman, M., Kleber, H., & Wilber, C. (1982). Heterogeneity of psychiatric diagnosis in treated opiate addicts. *Archives of General Psychiatry, 39*, 161–166.

Schuckit, M. A., & Hesselbrock, V. (1994). Alcohol dependence and anxiety disorders: What is the relationship? *American Journal of Psychiatry, 151*, 1723–1734.

Schuckit, M. A., Irwin, M., & Brown, S. A. (1990). The history of anxiety symptoms among 171 primary alcoholics. *Journal of Studies on Alcohol, 51*, 34–41.

Shaffer, H. J. (1985). The disease controversy: Of metaphors, maps and menus. *Journal of Psychoactive Drugs, 17*, 65–76.

Silber, A. (1974). Rationale for the technique of psychotherapy with alcoholics. *International Journal of Psychoanalytic Psychotherapy, 3*, 28–47.

Treece, C., & Khantzian, E. J. (1986). Psychodynamic factors in the development of drug dependence. *Psychiatric Clinics of North America, 9*, 399–412.

Vaillant, G. E. (1981). Dangers of psychotherapy in the treatment of alcoholism. In M. H. Bean & N. E. Zinberg (Eds.), *Dynamic approaches to the understanding and treatment of alcoholism* (pp. 36–54). New York: Free Press.

Walant, K. B. (1995). *Creating the capacity for attachment: Treating addictions and the alienated self.* Northvale, NJ: Jason Aronson.

Wieder, H., & Kaplan, E. (1969). Drug use in adolescents. *Psychoanalytic Study of the Child, 24*, 399–431.

Wilens, T. E., Biederman, J., Spencer, T. J., & Frances, R. J. (1994). Comorbidity of attention deficit hyperactivity and psychoactive substance use disorders. *Hospital and Community Psychiatry, 45*, 421–435.

Woody, G. E., Luborsky, L., McLellan, A. T., & O'Brien, C. P. (1989). Individual psychotherapy for substance abuse. In T. B. Karasu (Ed.), *Treatment of psychiatric disorders: A task force report of the American Psychiatric Association.* (pp. 1417–1430). Washington, DC: American Psychiatric Press.

Woody G. E., Luborsky, L., McLellan, A. T., O'Brien, C. P., Beck, A. T., Blaine, J., Herman, I., & Hole, A. (1983). Psychotherapy for opiate addicts: Does it help? *Archives of General Psychiatry, 40*, 639–645.

Woody, G. E., McLellan, A. T., Luborsky, L., & O'Brien, C. P. (1986). Psychotherapy for substance abuse. *Psychiatric Clinics of North America, 9*, 547–562.

Woody, G. E., McLellan, A. T., Luborsky, L., & O'Brien, C. P. (1995). Psychotherapy in community methadone programs. *American Journal of Psychiatry, 152*, 1302–1308.

Wurmser, L. (1974). Psychoanalytic considerations of the etiology of compulsive drug use. *Journal of the American Psychoanalytic Association, 22*, 820–843.

21

❑

Family-Based Treatment
Stages and Outcomes

ANTHONY W. HEATH
M. DUNCAN STANTON

INTRODUCTION

As we face the beginning of a new century, there is a growing cultural awareness of the interconnectedness and interdependence of living systems and levels of systems, from cells through individuals, families, and communities to the biosphere. Businesses are *global,* communities are organizing, and we are learning, for example, that acres of aspen are really one system of trees. Today it is obvious to most that no man, woman, or child is an "island" and that the rippling affects of every action yield innumerable consequences.

In this sociopolitical context, the importance of the family in the genesis, maintenance, and alleviation of substance abuse is well established. Although it is widely acknowledged that genetic and/or other biological components are important in the etiology of many alcohol and drug abuse cases, addiction generally develops within a family context, frequently reflects other family difficulties, and is usually maintained and exacerbated by family interactive processes. Many other factors can also be critical (e.g., environmental, economic, cultural), but family variables hold a position of salience in the arena of addictive symptomatology.

Not surprisingly, treatment focused on family dynamics has developed a firm footing in the substance abuse treatment field. Family therapy is part of most successful substance abuse treatment programs and considered an essential element in relapse prevention. This chapter describes the family therapy approach to substance abuse treatment and the family patterns of addiction and reviews the documented effectiveness of family therapy to date.

FOUNDATIONS OF FAMILY THERAPY

Although family therapy was foreshadowed in the work of psychoanalysts Sigmund Freud (the "Little Hans" case), Alfred Adler, and Harry Stack Sullivan, it is generally considered to have been founded in the 1950s by an eclectic group of researchers, theorists, and psychotherapists, unknown to each other at the time. These pioneers, for a variety of reasons, began to interview family members conjointly (i.e., together), usually to gain further understanding of the psychiatric problems or symptoms manifested by one member. When seen together, the families demonstrated the myriad ways that all members become involved in a problem and the families' phenomenal resources for change. Given these experiences, the early family therapists began to shift the very focus of their treatment from the intrapsychic experiences of the patient to the relational dynamics among the family members, with an eye to the betterment of all. It soon became clear to family therapists that human problems could be conceptualized as "existing" *between* (or among) people rather than *within* them, and the "patient" became the whole family.

Over the last 40 years, the family therapy field has changed with astonishing fluidity, simultaneously growing, reevaluating, regressing, and advancing in various quarters around the world. Today, family therapy is an independent behavioral health *profession* in the United States, with a separate body of scholarly literature, over a dozen family therapy theories, separate licensing in 35 U.S. states, and separate accreditation for master's-degree and doctoral programs in family therapy per se. Family therapy is also a *practice,* or an approach to treatment practiced by all branches of the behavioral health professions. Thus, in a loose sense of the term, "family therapists" include substance abuse treatment specialists, psychiatrists, psychologists, social workers, and professional counselors.

Regardless of the license of the provider, family therapy is a way of construing human problems that dictates certain actions for their alleviation. Family therapy is thus more than a modality of treatment. Depending on theoretical orientations and other more practical constraints, family therapists conduct therapy only with the person with the most apparent problem, or only the person most concerned with the problem, the nuclear family, the extended family, or a whole social network, including friends, neighbors, other therapists, and social agents. No matter who is in the treatment room, the family therapist *thinks* family, *thinks* interaction, and *acts* to change relational patterns. It is the relational, interactional focus of the family therapist's thought and action that is characteristic, not the attention to the sociopolitical unit called a family. Family therapists work with families because the family system is one of the primary systems in which human problems can be most easily understood, and because families often provide leverage for change. Stanton (1988b) puts it like this:

> Family therapy—perhaps more appropriately, systems therapy—is an approach in which a therapist (or a team of therapists), working with varying combinations and configurations of people, devises and introduces interventions designed to alter the interaction (process, workings) of the interpersonal system and context within which one or more psychiatric/behavioral/human problems are imbedded, and thereby also alters the functioning of the individuals within the system, with the goal of alleviating or eliminating the problems. (p. 9)

Family Patterns of Addiction

Addicted people are commonly in close contact with their families of origin or the people who raised them (Cervantes, Sorenson, Wermuth, Fernandez, & Menicucci, 1988). This pattern can extend even to adult alcoholics, as many male alcoholics are observed to be in regular contact with their mothers. These data indicate that addicted people are often important in their families and that their families are important to them.

Stanton et al. (1982) summarized a number of other characteristics that distinguish drug-abusing families from other seriously dysfunctional families. The distinguishing qualities include the following:

1. A higher frequency of multigenerational chemical dependency, particularly alcohol, plus a propensity for other addictive behaviors such as gambling (such practices model behavior for children and can develop into family traditions).
2. More primitive and direct expressions of conflict in addictive families.
3. More overt alliances (e.g., between addict and overinvolved parent).
4. "Conspicuously unschizophrenic" parental behavior.
5. A drug-oriented peer group to which the addict retreats following family conflict, thus gaining an illusion of independence.
6. "Symbiotic" childrearing practices on the part of addicts' mothers, lasting longer into the addicts' adulthood.
7. A preponderance of death themes and premature, unexpected, and untimely deaths of the addict's family.
8. Pseudoindividuation of the addict across several levels, from the individual–pharmacological level to that of the drug subculture.
9. More frequent acculturation problems and parent–child cultural disparity within families of addicts.

This list should be considered no more than a sketch of the addictive family. Readers are referred to Stanton et al. (1982) for references to the original studies on which the outline is based and to Steinglass, Bennett, Wolin, and Reiss (1987) for a thorough discussion of family dynamics in alcoholism.

INDICATIONS FOR THE USE OF FAMILY THERAPY

The suffering of families in which drugs and/or alcohol are abused is legendary. Parents worry whether their abusing children will come home alive. They rage at their lack of control, they suffer the guilt of the damned, and they grasp at any suggestion that offers hope. Spouses shamefully scurry to hide advancing drinking problems from their neighbors and employers, struggle to maintain their illusions that the drinking is temporary, and wonder what they have done wrong. Children of alcoholics wonder what *they* did wrong, assume the burdens of maturity at startlingly young ages, and beg their parents to come home without stopping at the tavern. Grown children of alcoholics find themselves haunted by their pasts, despairing in relationships that inflict only pain. Substance abuse affects every member of the family, certainly for decades and perhaps for generations.

Family therapy offers every member of couples and families an opportunity to resolve the problems that plague them. Family therapists believe that family treatment is indicated when any man, woman, or child has a complaint concerning alcohol or drug abuse, whether the individual is the abuser or the "abused." Because they figuratively cast such a large net, family therapists encounter and serve many clients who present themselves for other reasons but also have concerns about substance abuse in their families. These concerns include issues of abuse, addiction, and recovery for adult and adolescent substance abusers as well as parallel issues for "codependents," children of alcoholics, and adult children of alcoholics for several generations of the family.

Substance abusers themselves are not the family members most likely to seek the services of a therapist. In fact, the most characteristic feature of substance abuse may be the abuser's denial that the use of the substance is a problem at all. Similarly, it is almost universally accepted that substance abuse is often overlooked by family members; it may even be overtly or covertly encouraged. Recognizing this fact, family therapists offer their services to *anyone* who wants to discuss the substance abuse and even go so far as to inquire about such an individual's use of alcohol and drugs. Like Al-Anon and related self-help programs, family therapists generally believe that every family member can be helped to "recover" from the abuse whether the substance abuser stops drinking and/or "drugging" or not.

Family therapy is indicated when a family member, a therapist, a treatment program, or a social institution such as a court initially identifies the problem. It is indicated when the family is mustering its forces to convince the abuser of the extent of the problem and the need for change, during residential treatment for the substance abuse (when it is used), and during recovery, when the family learns new ways to go on in life without chemicals. We offer guidelines for each of these stages of treatment later in this chapter.

An absence of family-oriented services in substance abuse treatment may have calamitous consequences. Without concurrent treatment for nonabusing members, families have been known to attempt sabotage of treatment efforts when those efforts begin to succeed (Stanton, 1979). Examples of sabotage are commonly reported in the literature; they range from the spouse who gives a bottle of liquor on a holiday to a recovering alcoholic to the parents who refuse to work together in maintaining rules for their defiant adolescent. On the other hand, Steinglass et al. (1987) asserted, at least regarding alcohol treatment, that the evidence is compelling that "involvement of a nonalcoholic spouse in a treatment program significantly improves the likelihood that the alcoholic individual will participate in treatment as well" (pp. 331–332).

Problems can also occur after residential treatment is completed if families are left out of the treatment process. Sobriety for an individual often has difficult consequences for other family members, who may gain sudden awareness of their own problems or of other problems in their families. Divorce is not uncommon when adult substance abusers "dry out" or "clean up" (Stanton, 1985). The family is crucial in determining whether or not someone remains addicted, and the social context of the abuser must be changed for treatment to "take hold."

Families can prove to be a highly positive influence in recovery as well. In a fascinating observational account of substance abuse among his contemporaries, Auerswald (1980) observed that significant improvements in substance abusers' interpersonal lives often led to a reduction—without professional intervention—in their use of intoxicants. Eldred and Washington (1976) found that heroin addicts rated their families of origin or their in-laws as most likely to be helpful to them in their attempts to give up drugs; their second choice was their opposite-sex partner. Similarly, Levy (1972) found that in a five year follow-up of narcotics addicts, patients who successfully overcame drug abuse most often had family support. Family therapists enlist the inherent leverage of loving family members.

Like other treatment professionals who have worked with substance-abusing families, family therapists know the difficulty involved in treating substance abuse. Only by working together with extended families, specialists in the field of chemical dependency, physicians monitoring pharmacotherapy, and self-help programs can substance abuse and its related problems be ameliorated.

Professionals must talk to each other if therapy is to succeed. For example, outpatient family therapists must visit local treatment centers and get to know the treatment team. This effort facilitates referrals to residential treatment and subsequent referral for continued therapy upon release. It has been our experience that staff members of Twelve-Step treatment programs often suspect, as do many Alcoholics Anonymous (AA) members, that all therapists harbor hostile and ignorant beliefs about addicts. Yet many family therapists would agree with this statement by Davis (1987): "As a therapist, I operate according to the same presuppositions that operate in self-help groups: that every patient/client already has the resources or the capacity to develop the resources needed, that experts don't have all the answers, and that we are ultimately responsible for our own behaviors" (pp. 138–139).

This is not to say, however, that family therapists universally believe that attendance at AA, Al-Anon, or other self-help groups is necessary for healthy recovery in every case. In those instances in which substance abusers and their families are adamantly opposed to involvement in Twelve-Step groups, family therapy may serve as a satisfactory alternative (Heath & Atkinson, 1988).

CLINICAL INTERVENTION IN FAMILY THERAPY

Entire books have been written specifically about family therapy with substance abusers, most notably six texts focusing on the problem of alcoholism (Bepko & Krestan, 1985; Elkin, 1984; Kaufman, 1984; Wegscheider, 1981; Davis, 1987; Steinglass et al., 1987), two on drug *and* alcohol abuse (Kaufman & Kaufmann, 1979; Treadway, 1989), one on drug abuse and addiction (Stanton et al., 1982), and one on addicts and other seriously disturbed young adults (Haley, 1980). Similarly, many different modalities of family treatment have been described, including marital therapy; group therapy for parents; concurrent parent and index patient therapy, therapy with individual families, both inpatient and outpatient; sibling-oriented therapy; multiple-family therapy; social network therapy; and family therapy with one person. The purpose of this section is to introduce fundamental methods of family therapy assessment and treatment with substance abusers and their families. Readers interested in studying this area further on their own are referred to the synopses by Heath and Atkinson (1988) and Stanton (1988a), plus the other literature cited later, for a broader understanding of the full range of theoretical and clinical approaches within the overall family therapy community.

STAGES OF FAMILY THERAPY

Our purpose here is to present a selective, integrative model of the stages of family therapy that synthesizes literature on family therapy with alcoholic adults (e.g., Berenson, 1976a, 1976b, 1979, 1986; Davis, 1987; Steinglass et al., 1987) and drug-abusing adolescents and young adults (e.g., Kosten, Jalali, & Kleber, 1982–1983; Piercy & Frankel, 1989; Stanton & Landau-Stanton, 1990; Stanton & Todd, 1979; Stanton et al., 1982) and to emphasize the relatively high degree of consensus among these authors. Although detailed presentation of the techniques of family therapy is beyond the scope of this chapter, the literature cited herein comprises a veritable treasure chest of useful family therapy methods.

Stage 1: Problem Definition and Contracting

The first stage of family therapy begins when someone contacts a therapist and requests help. Family therapists work in a wide variety of treatment settings, so often they can easily be located in behavioral health centers, family service agencies, inpatient and outpatient drug and alcohol treatment centers, employee assistance programs, and private practices. Interestingly, family therapists also work in therapeutic communities, where families once were excluded. By making family therapy available, such therapeutic communities are bringing the "real world" into the center and helping families to prepare for the reunion.

The therapist's first step is to convene enough of the family to gain adequate leverage to initiate change in family interaction regarding the substance abuse. As previously discussed, this may involve 1, 2, or 30 family members, and may include other members of the substance abuser's community. Family therapists generally start by working with the most motivated family member or members, convening other family members as necessary (Berenson, cited in Stanton, 1981a).

Next, family therapists attempt to identify and define the problem. When substance abuse is suspected, many begin by asking simple questions, such as "Who drinks" or "What medications are used in your family?" We ironically refer to these as loaded questions and ask them of all our clients as a matter of course.

To assess the degree of substance abuse, particularly with adult clients, Davis (1987) suggests the use of a standardized questionnaire, such as the Michigan Alcoholism Screening Test (Selzer, 1971) or the National Council on Alcoholism's Major and Minor Criteria for Alcoholism (Criteria Committee, 1972). The history of the abuse, degree of physiological addiction, organic consequences of long-term addiction, prior treatment contacts, family perception of the abuse and its consequences, codependence, and coping behaviors are also topics that deserve careful assessment by qualified practitioners (Steinglass et al., 1987). If the therapist is not medically trained, clients are commonly referred to a physician for diagnosis and medical treatment when substance abuse has been chronic and/or when there is any indication of organic impairment due to substance abuse or disease. Family therapists often suggest that another family member accompany the substance abuser to the physician, to offer support and to inform the physician of the history of the abuse.

Information gathered during the assessment can then be used by the therapist, when appropriate, to state with confidence that—by some objective standards—the family has a serious drug or alcohol problem. Such confidence is necessary to overcome denial that a substance abuse problem exists—a defense which can be anticipated in such families (Bepko & Krestan, 1985). It is important to note that many family therapists avoid becoming personally involved in a debate over whether the substance abuse is really "addiction" or "alcoholism" (e.g., Davis, 1987). In discussing alcoholism, Davis stated: "This is not the time to fight over the presence of an 'ism.' It is enough to establish that there is a serious problem that needs treatment. The drinker and family members can make up their own minds after some success with AA and family therapy as to whether they have been dealing with alcoholism" (p. 53).

Once the problem is defined, the therapist and family identify and prioritize their goals for treatment, starting with the primary goal of helping the substance abuser become "clean and sober" and directly relating each subsequent goal to this primary one. When families bring up additional issues, the therapist may ask the family to justify them as relevant to the main goal of sobriety (Stanton & Todd, 1979). Considered together, these goals form the basis for determining whether an acceptable treatment contract can be agreed on with the family (Steinglass et al., 1987).

From the beginning, family therapists work to establish alliances with the senior sober family members. If the abuser is an adolescent or young adult, both parents are involved in these alliances whenever possible. Parents are kept working *together* and are steered away from discussing their marital difficulties, which could divide them and deter them from the primary objective of therapy (Stanton & Todd, 1979). This alliance forms the basis for establishing appropriate parental influence in families with substance-abusing adolescents (Stanton et al., 1982; Piercy & Frankel, 1989).

Family therapists' alliances with sober family members and parents of substance abusers direct their approach to motivating clients in therapy. Family members are the most effective motivators known; the most evangelistic therapist cannot do as well. Thus, by forming alliances and encouraging sober family members to step up the pressure, family therapists help to motivate the substance abuser to pursue and maintain sobriety. Similarly, other professional helpers (e.g., school counselors, teachers, police officers, and probation officers) may be enlisted to exert benevolent influence. Here the family therapist serves as coach, initially promoting the effective use of every reasonable threat, promise, and consequence to encourage abstinence and later encouraging the family to serve as the recovering addict's sponsor to help prevent relapse. For an interesting example of the motivating influence of a family member, we recommend Heard's (1982) rich description of how he used a deathbed wish of a deceased grandfather to promote the recovery of a 23-year-old heroin addict.

Family therapists consider it extremely important during this initial stage to assume a *nonblaming stance* (Stanton & Todd, 1979) toward the entire family. We find that the confronting techniques used in group therapy with substance abusers tend to fan the fires of resistance and to inspire counterattack when dealing with families. Challenges can still be offered to these families, but they must be expressed in nonpejorative ways. Many family therapists use positive interpretation in commenting on family members' behavior. Stanton and Todd (1979) referred to this as ascribing noble intentions or noble ascriptions (Stanton et al., 1982). Examples of positive interpretation include such statements as "He's defending the family like any good son would" and "You're trying your best to be a good mother." Such statements tune into both the caring and frustration that most family members experience; they seem to lessen client resistance and promote compliance.

Steinglass et al. (1987) emphasized that it is essential at this point in therapy to label the substance abuse as a *family* problem and to convince the family members that they are all essential players in the recovery process. Writing about alcoholism, these authors stated that whenever alcoholism is identified as a problem, the therapist must, in the same session, "get across to the family that there is no issue more important at this stage of the work than the cessation of drinking, and that the family and the therapist must mobilize all resources toward that goal and that goal alone" (p. 354). Family therapists characteristically invite family members to become part of the solution to problems.

In the quest for the answer to the question, "Why did this happen to me?," many families in treatment accept that genetics and/or a disease process is responsible for their substance abuse, particularly when the problem is alcoholism. At best, these theoretical explanations can reduce guilt, blame, and shame in families; facilitate entrance into therapy; and promote recovery. Genetic or disease explanations are almost always more useful than moralistic explanations. At worst, though, these explanations (1) provoke fear and enable discouraged, wallowing inaction and irresponsible behavior in the family; and (2) engender inaction in a therapist who sees no leeway for change.

Family therapists do not allow themselves or their clients to become discouraged by the disease explanation of the cause of drug and alcohol addiction; they cannot afford to wait for a pill to cure the disease. Instead, they help their client families to understand that by working together they can overcome all of the disease's symptoms, reverse the ostensible destiny, and lead happy, chemical-free lives.

Of course, there are—and probably always will be—people who reject genetic and disease explanations for addiction. Regarding the former, they may be justified, because there is still no genetic evidence in a large proportion of alcoholics. In any case, these people can learn to live responsibly and avoid blame and shame. They can work together with their loved ones to overcome their problems.

Stage 2: Establishing the Context for a Chemically Free Life

When substance abuse is identified as a problem, and a therapeutic contract is negotiated, family therapy enters a second stage in which a context for sobriety is established. Berenson (1976b) stated that this stage involves "management of an ongoing, serious drinking problem and setting up a context so that the alcoholic will stop drinking" (p. 33).

Cessation of a substance abuse is *generally* accepted by family therapists as a prerequisite for further treatment (e.g., Bepko & Krestan, 1985). Furthermore, many believe that therapists must consistently demonstrate conviction of the importance of abstinence over the course of therapy (e.g., Davis, 1987). In the words of Steinglass et al. (1987):

> Meaningful therapy with an Alcoholic Family cannot proceed if the therapist adopts a laissez-faire attitude about drinking behavior and acquiesces in a decision to allow the identified alcoholic to continue drinking. The therapist

must take a firm stand on this issue at the start of therapy, while at the same time acknowledging that it may not be an easy task and that there may be a number of slips before abstinence is achieved. (p. 343)

On the other hand, Berenson, whose innovative work with alcoholics was described by Stanton (1981a), believes that therapists should concern themselves with achieving substantial changes in drunken behavior instead of abstinence from drinking. Berenson considers it tactically unwise to take a resolute stand in favor of total abstinence, even though abstinence is usually the ultimate goal. This position on abstinence runs counter to the beliefs of several others, including Davis (1987) and Bepko and Krestan (1985). It is consistent, however, with the problem-solving models that were applied to drug problems by Haley (1976), Stanton and Todd (e.g., 1979), and others (e.g., Heath & Ayers, 1991), who often prefer to leave the decision about the importance of total abstinence to parents or others. These authors believe that therapists who assume a less adamant, less certain position on the necessity of abstinence enjoy more maneuverability (cf. Fisch, Weakland, & Segal, 1982) in therapy. For example, a therapist who states that he or she is not sure whether abstinence will prove necessary may be able to stay out of a couple's argument over the issue long enough to help them try out several new solutions to the problems brought on by the substance abuse.

Independent of the issue of abstinence, Berenson believes that early in therapy the therapist must exert a major effort to get the family system calmed down, reducing the emotionality and increasing the psychological distance between family members. Families at this stage of therapy are often overwrought and involved in intense battles and patterns of over- and underresponsibility that lock members together. (See Bepko & Krestan, 1985, for a thorough discussion of the therapeutic process of assessing and interrupting overresponsible and underresponsible behaviors.)

Family therapists often refer family members to Al-Anon, Nar-Anon, Alateen, Alatot, and related self-help programs at this stage, encouraging clients to shop around until they find groups that are "socially compatible and geographically accessible" (Davis, 1987, p. 56). According to Bepko and Krestan (1985), the goal of this involvement is to help the family members "shift their role behavior significantly both in the interest of their greatest well-being and with the expectation that a change in their part of the family interaction will eventually lead to the drinker's sobriety" (p. 104). Davis (1987) suggested that therapists must consistently assign visits to self-help groups because participation in groups enhances family therapy in several ways. Participation in self-help groups encourages detachment from substance-abusing behavior, provides validating experiences and 24-hour crisis support through sponsors, and emphasizes personal responsibility (Davis, 1987).

Many family therapists supplement the work of self-help groups by helping the spouses of substance abusers to achieve a greater degree of emotional detachment. Berenson begins by getting spouses of alcoholics into support groups, usually Al-Anon or other spouses' groups (Stanton, 1981a).

Next, he prepares spouses for the impending period of pain and depression, perhaps even noting that they may have suicidal thoughts as a part of "hitting bottom." Finally, Berenson helps spouses gain distance from their alcoholic partners, often by suggesting brief separations (e.g., a week away from home) in order to promote differentiation. Berenson warns spouses that their alcoholic partner may try to get them back by intensifying the symptom, usually by increased drinking.

At this point Berenson may involve the alcoholics more in therapy, empathizing with how isolated and alone they may feel. Concomitantly, he helps spouses stick to the plan so that the drunks have a chance to get sober. He tells spouses that they should not expect the alcoholic to improve but suggests that when they realize that the alcoholics cannot be controlled, the alcoholics may be able to make a change for the better. Berenson does not support hostile moves against the alcoholic but only supports moves the spouses make for themselves.

Berenson has suggested several helpful rules for therapists working through this stage of family therapy (Stanton, 1981a). First, therapists must have no expectations that change will occur; rather than "hoping," they must be "hopeless." Second, therapists should want family members to feel both helpless and hopeless—that is, to "hit bottom," if they have not done so already. Third, therapists must not look for a single strategic intervention to reverse the multitude of problems in these families but should work patiently in a simple, straightforward manner.

Finally, many family therapists move toward getting the substance abuser to attend AA, Narcotics Anonymous, or Cocaine Anonymous as the final step in the second stage of therapy. Bepko and Krestan (1985) suggested that it is not advisable for therapists to argue with clients about the value of AA, but they should describe AA and its purpose "in a way that is palatable to the particular client" (p. 103). Most family therapists state clearly that AA is one of the most effective treatments for addiction. We help each substance abuser find a group with which he or she feels comfortable, then encourage attendance for a while before making a decision whether to continue. For the individuals who feel uncomfortable with AA's use of the "Higher Power," we recommend the secular sobriety groups.

Stage 3: Halting Substance Abuse

In the family therapy of substance abuse there always comes a moment of truth. As a result of the changes in their family members' behavior and the probably firm position of the therapist, substance abusers suddenly become aware that they are going to have to choose between their families and their drugs. Substance abusers, when consistently confronted (or abandoned) by parents, spouses, children, friends, employers, and perhaps even recovering people in self-help groups and/or a therapist, often "hit bottom" and turn to the therapist for help in changing their ways.

At this juncture, Steinglass et al. (1987) suggest that there are basically three possible ways for therapists to proceed. First, a therapist who identifies physical dependence on alcohol or drugs should arrange safe detoxification for the addicted and refuse to continue therapy unless this option is completed, because without medical intervention the addict's independent withdrawal is unlikely and possibly dangerous. Second, the therapist can agree to let the family attempt detoxification on an outpatient basis, on the condition that if there has been no meaningful progress made toward detoxification in 2 weeks (maximum), medical treatment will be pursued. Third, the therapist can allow outpatient recovery alone, using the family as the "treatment team" if there is evidence that physical addiction is minimal or absent (Scott & Van Deusen, 1982; Stanton & Todd, 1982). Whichever course of action is selected, it is essential for the family therapist to keep all family members involved in the change process, partially so that later they can accept some responsibility for the success of the treatment (Stanton & Todd, 1979). When treatment is left to the "professionals," families often fail to realize their responsibility for change. And later, should the recovery process go awry, they blame the setback on the treatment program.

Stage 4: Managing the Crisis and Stabilizing the Family

When the substance abuser becomes "clean and sober," the family therapist should be prepared for a new set of problems. Family members, stunned by the unfamiliar behavior of the sober or clean family member and often terribly frightened, have been known to make seemingly irrational statements, such as "I liked you better when you were drinking." One woman we know actually gave a bottle of bourbon to her recently sober husband for his birthday. The potential for relapse is understandably high in this stage.

In discussing alcoholic families, Steinglass et al. (1987) named an analogous stage, "the emotional desert." In their description, families that have been organized around alcohol for many years experience a profound sense of emptiness when the drinking stops. Steinglass et al. (1987) explain that these families "have the sensation of having been cut adrift, loosened from their familiar moorings, lost in a desert without any landmarks upon which to focus to regain their bearings" (p. 344). Instead of experiencing joy over the newfound sobriety, the family members feel empty and depressed. It is not surprising that members of newly sober families tend to interact in the same way they did while one of their own was abusing drugs and/or alcohol.

Couples often experience a feeling of "walking on eggshells" at home and drift into a kind of emotional divorce. Both partners want to preserve the sobriety and the peace, so they interact sparingly and hesitantly, unwittingly reestablishing the same patterns of closeness and distance that they enacted previously. For example, a recently sober alcoholic, wanting to talk with his wife about his feelings, approached her late at night, waking her from a sound sleep, just as he did when he was drunk. She, in turn, rebuffed his awkward attempt at communication, leaving him to go off alone to sulk as once he went off to drink. Thus, when recovering couples get to know each other anew, they often find themselves bored, irrationally angry, and unable to resolve problems that were once avoided with the help of intoxicants.

In the case of addicted young people, a family crisis can be anticipated 3 or 4 weeks into this part of treatment (Stanton & Todd, 1979). Commonly, the crisis occurs in the marital relationship of the parents, who take steps toward separation. Such a crisis puts tremendous pressure on the addict to become "dirty" again to reunite his or her family.

Siblings and children of recovering substance abusers also can inadvertently exert pressure to revert to old ways. Gradually these families begin to notice other family problems, long hidden from attention by the magnitude of alcohol or other drug problems. As the blur of intoxication clears, children who were once considered helpful may suddenly be seen as withdrawn and depressed, children who were once seen as doing fine in school may be seen to be just getting by, and the marijuana smoking of adolescents may be discovered for the first time.

There is some disagreement among family therapists over how quickly to move to resolve family problems in this stage. Berenson suggested that it is usually advisable to begin this stage with a hiatus from therapy while things calm down, and thus he does not schedule regular appointments but tells clients, "Get back to me in a month or so" (Stanton, 1981a). Meanwhile, he encourages his clients to continue their self-help group activities, with the understanding that if their distress continues beyond 6 to 12 months, family therapy will resume on a more regular basis. Then, after a period of sobriety, Berenson returns to a more orthodox therapy schedule. Others (e.g., Bepko & Krestan, 1985; Steinglass et al., 1987) believe that regularly scheduled family therapy sessions can be very helpful at these times, especially if they focus on solving the series of problems that hound these families and wear them down.

Therapy in this stage should be focused on keeping a family as calm as possible (Bepko & Krestan, 1985) while helping the family establish a new form of stability that is not based on substance abuse (Steinglass et al., 1987). Toward this end, the therapist works to minimize stress and deescalate conflict, congratulates individuals for their contributions to the family's recovery and encourages them to focus on their own issues, predicts and addresses common difficulties in recovery and fears about relapse, and facilitates minor structural changes in the family to allow adequate parenting (Bepko & Krestan, 1985). Changes in parenting practices are especially vital when the recovering substance abuser is an adolescent (Fishman, Stanton, & Rosman, 1982; Piercy & Frankel, 1989; Stanton & Landau-Stanton, 1990).

Should a relapse into drinking or drug taking occur, the question of responsibility arises. Who is responsible for the relapse? Although conventional drug treatment programs and many individual therapists either thrust the responsibility on the substance abuser or accept it themselves, family therapists tend to assign the responsibility to the abuser's family. As Stanton and Todd (1979) suggested, "It should be remembered that the addicted individual was raised by, and in most cases is still being maintained by, his family of origin. It is thus with the family that responsibility rests, and the therapist should help the family either to accept it or to effectively disengage from the addict so that he must accept it on his own" (p. 62).

Similarly, the therapist must assign credit to the entire family when credit is due (Stanton, 1981b). Each member, particularly the often-neglected spouse, is praised for his or her contribution to the growing "health" of the family. By identifying and rewarding individual contributions, the family therapist spreads out the glory that is usually bestowed on the recovering abuser and promotes long-lasting changes in family interaction.

Stage 5: Family Reorganization and Recovery

Whereas in stage 4 families remain organized around substance abuse and therapy is focused on resolving difficulties with substance abuse (or the lack thereof), stage 5 is concerned with helping the families move away from interaction focused on substance abuse issues and toward fundamentally better relationships. Here the substance abuser is stabilized and "clean and sober"; the therapy now focuses on developing a better marriage, establishing more satisfactory parent–child relationships, and perhaps confronting long-standing family-of-origin and codependence issues.

Steinglass et al. (1987) called this process "family reorganization" (p. 344). Although some families restabilize before reaching this phase and remain organized around alcoholism issues ("dry alcoholic" families), we have observed that for others the previous stages of therapy culminate in a serious family crisis. This crisis then leads to disorganization and ultimately to a fundamentally different organizational pattern which is encouraged in this stage of therapy.

Bepko and Krestan (1985) enumerated four goals for their analogue of this stage, which they termed "rebalancing" (p. 135). These goals follow:

1. Shift extremes of behavior from rigid complementarity to greater symmetry or more overt complementarity ("correct" complementarity for the specific relationship).
2. Help the couple/family to resolve issues of power and control.
3. Directly address the pride structures of both partners so that new forms of role behavior are permitted without the need for alcohol.
4. Help the couple to achieve whatever level of closeness and intimacy is desirable for them. (pp. 135–136)

(See Bepko & Krestan, 1985, for a detailed discussion of therapeutic methods used to implement these goals.)

Davis (1987) also emphasized that therapists must help family members to reconsider and redefine the substance abuser's role in the family at this stage of therapy. Old expectations and old behavioral patterns, which were based on living with the addiction, must be replaced by new adaptive ones. For example, a family that has grown used to an alcoholic husband/father may continue to withdraw every time he shows a hint of anger, leave him out of family decisions, and disregard his parenting efforts. In this stage of therapy, the father must learn to deal with his anger, to participate in making responsible decisions, and to function as a father, *and* the family members must allow him to change.

In the treatment of a family with a young addict during this stage, the therapy evolves beyond stage 4 crisis management and toward other issues, such as finding gainful employment and a place to live away from home for the recovering addict (Stanton & Todd, 1979). Parents are often involved in these "launchings" so they can feel part of the addict's eventual success. Over time, it becomes increasingly possible to shift the parents' attention to other siblings, grandchildren, or retirement planning, thereby allowing both the parents and the recovering addict to let go. Should marital issues surface, as they often do, family therapists try to prevent young addicts from getting involved in their parents' marriages.

Berenson focuses his work in this stage on the couple's relationship, with the aim of decreasing the emotional distance between the couple without a return either to drinking or to discussions centered on alcohol (Stanton, 1981a). In conjoint sessions with couples and/or multiple-couple groups, Berenson and other family therapists often focus on the severe sexual problems that are common in such marriages (Stanton, 1981a) and teach new skills for dealing with stress and conflict (Bepko & Krestan, 1985). Therapy sessions with the extended family are scheduled when relatives or in-laws are disruptive (Stanton & Landau-Stanton, 1990).

Finally, it is also during this stage that a number of family therapists (e.g., Coleman, Kaplan, & Downing, 1986; Reilly, 1976; Rosenbaum & Richman, 1972; Stanton, 1977) deal with the often unexpected and unresolved losses and deaths that so many chemically dependent families have experienced. These issues may not need to be covered to effect abstinence initially, but unresolved grief can "eat away" at progress unless it is brought to terms. Some sort of family grief work seems to be indicated to maintain lasting change.

Stage 6: Ending Therapy

In the ideal course of therapy with a substance-abusing family, treatment comes to an end when the clients and therapist(s) agree to stop meeting regularly. Family therapists tend to agree to stop when they believe that serious structural and functional problems that have maintained substance abuse have been replaced with new family rules, roles, and interactional patterns. Optimally, substance abuse has not been replaced with other addictive behaviors; however, sometimes socially acceptable "addictions" (e.g., "workaholism") are tolerated by family therapists when they are tolerated by family members.

Because such abstract concepts as "rules," "roles," "interactional patterns," and even "addictive behaviors" are usually used only by therapists to describe families, this description of the ideal changes seen in therapy reflects only the therapist's perspective. The *clients'* view of successful therapy is much more difficult to articulate, partly because their descriptions of success are situation-specific and partly because of a dearth of qualitative research on the topic. For our purposes here, suffice it to say that from the clients' point of view, therapy ends satisfactorily when they believe that family relationships are acceptably harmonious and that major family problems— including substance abuse—have been resolved to the point of becoming tolerable.

The length of therapy and the specific definition of successful treatment vary widely among models of therapy and among individual families. Stanton and Todd (1979), in describing their brief therapy model for treating drug addicts, have broadly stated that therapy is appropriately concluded when "adequate change has occurred and been maintained long enough for the family to feel a sense of real accomplishment" (p. 64). Adherents of other models would not even attempt to reorganize family structure in the ways prescribed in our fifth stage. Instead, they conclude treatment when family members feel satisfied that the problems originally presented have been resolved (e.g., Heath & Ayers, 1991).

The ending of therapy, often called "termination," need not be thought of as an event or as a process with a distinct end point. Elsewhere, I (A. W. H.) suggested that such a view of termination exposes an assumption that therapy is a lot like surgery, which ideally results in a permanent "cure" of some sort (Heath, 1985). This unintentional metaphor seems terribly inaccurate to the experienced therapist, partly because many client families who have completed therapy later seek counsel from the same therapist on new and unrelated issues.

For therapists who see therapy as a problem-solving endeavor, it is helpful to use outpatient medical practice as a metaphor to guide outpatient family therapy. In other words, family therapists can be likened to physicians to whom clients ("patients") turn for assistance with a variety of concerns over the decades. Of course, in the treatment of substance abuse, therapy "visits" continue on a regularly scheduled basis until the abuse has ceased. But as significant progress occurs, therapists gradually increase the intervals between sessions. Then, when all parties agree to cease regularly scheduled sessions, occasional innoculatory follow-up sessions ("checkups") are scheduled, one at a time, at intervals of 2 to 6 months. It is made clear to clients that they are welcome to schedule future appointments at any time and to cancel sessions that seem unnecessary. Therapy clients, like medical patients, are never made permanently "healthy," and the door to the therapist's office remains open, like the physician's.

Finally, it should be noted that family therapy sometimes ends unexpectedly and prematurely, at least as seen from the therapist's perspective. No matter how skilled the therapist, and no matter what the stage of treatment, families generally stop coming to therapy when they want to. In such circumstances, responsible therapists make every reasonable effort to determine whether client families are satisfied or dissatisfied with services rendered and to respond accordingly. They offer additional services or referrals for any family member, as well as professional opinions about remaining problems and caveats when appropriate.

In conclusion, the six-stage model presented here is intentionally inclusive. We have made no effort to spell out or resolve differences among models of family therapy or to examine the differences between treating drug addicts and alcoholics. Instead, we have broadly sketched a viable course of treatment for the family with a substance-abusing member. Clinicians may wish to emphasize some stages of therapy more than others, depending on their models of treatment.

SPECIAL CONSIDERATIONS IN FAMILY THERAPY

A number of special clinical considerations concern family therapists when they work with substance abusers and their families. The most salient of these considerations are discussed next. Interested readers will find insightful discussions of many of the day-to-day issues that face family therapists in the previously referenced texts, particularly Stanton et al. (1982).

Convening Difficulties

One of the problems identified by therapists working with substance abusers and their families is the difficulty in convening the whole family for therapy (Stanton & Todd, 1981). The families of addicts are particularly difficult to engage in treatment. Fathers, in particular, often appear threatened by treatment and defensive about their contribution to the problem. Because many have drinking problems themselves, they may also fear being blamed.

Experienced family therapists, recognizing hesitancy to participate in therapy, work hard to recruit families into therapy. They do not rely on other family members to do the recruiting, because this approach often fails. Instead, they work energetically and enthusiastically to extend personal invitations to the reluctant. With less seriously disturbed families, one telephone call may enable a therapist to reassure family members that their contributions are important to the solution of the substance abuse. With more disturbed families, it may be necessary to meet on "neutral turf" (e.g., a restaurant), to write multiple letters, or to pay family members for participation in treatment. Stanton and others (Stanton & Todd, 1981; Stanton et al., 1982) described engagement procedures in substantial detail, suggesting 21 principles for getting reluctant families into therapy.

Control of the Case

To shift the responsibility for dealing with the substance abuser's problems to the family, a family therapist must have control of the case. The family therapist therefore may wish to direct the overall case management, including the treatment plan, the use of medication and drug tests, and decisions about hospitalization. The family therapist's being the primary therapist also helps to keep substance abusers from manipulating the relationships among a number of therapists.

Stanton et al. (1982) estimated that approximately half the effectiveness of treatment of drug addicts and their families depends on the efficiency and cohesiveness of the treatment system. If family members receive varied advice, they often end up arguing about the therapy rather than working toward recovery. Cohesion in the treatment system of substance abusers necessarily includes the self-help programs used by their families. It is vital for therapists to know the local self-help groups and to work with them for the sake of their clients.

Medication and Management

Family therapists who work with substance abusers and their families must have at least a basic knowledge of drug pharmacology. This information aids them during the detoxification process and reduces the tendency toward overcaution that sometimes occurs when a therapist is ignorant of drug effects.

In regard to the use of pharmacotherapy, it is vital that physicians, family therapists, and drug counselors work as a treatment team. Cooperation and open lines of communication are necessary to counteract the manipulative behaviors of many substance abusers. As a part of the team, the family therapist and physician must work together to encourage family compliance with prescribed medication and to provide each other with information on patient and family functioning (Woody, Carr, Stanton, & Hargrove, 1982).

Family therapists must have influence over the use of methadone. Families tend to believe that their recovering members are inherently helpless, fragile, handicapped people and thus they forgive the most outrageous behavior. For family therapists to effectively argue that addicts can be competent and can function adequately without drugs, they must assert that they are primarily concerned with the addicts' detoxifying and getting off all drugs, including methadone. To encourage the cessation of methadone use, family therapists and the families themselves must have significant input into how it is dispensed (Woody et al., 1982; Stanton & Todd, 1982).

Involving Parents in Decisions

When a substance abuser is an adolescent or a young adult, it is vital to involve parents in all decisions about the treatment of their youth. Thus parents should be involved in decisions about hospitalization, medication, and drug tests. Family therapists make parents part of the treatment team because it helps to get couples working together and because the responsibility for the resolution of the problem is rightly theirs. When the parents of the young person are divorced or unmarried, the same holds true.

Codependence

"Codependence" is a word often used to describe the process underlying many problems in the families of substance abusers. There is, to date, little consensus over how the term is defined, but according to Schaef (1986), one of the chemical dependency field's most respected authors, codependence is a disease that parallels the alcoholic disease process and has specific and characteristic symptoms (e.g., external referencing, caretaking, self-centeredness, control issues, dishonesty, frozen feelings, perfectionism, and fear). Codependence has replaced the concept of "enabling" and focused attention on the suffering of those who live with, or have lived with, a substance abuser.

Family therapists have learned a great deal about addiction and addiction treatment from Schaef (1986) and others (e.g., Beattie, 1987; Wegscheider, 1981) who have bridged the family therapy and chemical dependency treatment professions. We have learned, for example, to address the individual fears and difficulties of the parents, spouses, children, and grown children of alcoholics. We have learned of the many advantages of self-help groups and popular books on codependence for codependents. We have also learned to recognize addictive processes at work in families when individuals express any of the hallmark symptoms of codependence. We already know that the pain of addiction affects everyone in and around these families, often for generations.

Treatment Delivery Systems

Conceptualizing substance abuse problems within an interpersonal systems or family framework is not consonant with the medical model of substance abuse treatment. According to accepted practices, substance abuse is diagnosed and treated as are other diseases. Nevertheless, the Joint Commission on the Accreditation of Healthcare Organizations requires that treatment programs involve families in the treatment process.

Managed care organizations often will not pay for outpatient family therapy when substance abuse is suspected, preferring more specialized—and expensive—intensive outpatient treatment services. However, many family therapists and others who practice family therapy are now on the provider lists of managed care companies across the United States, making their services at least partially reimbursable. With ever-increasing pressure to keep costs low in both private and public sector, there are limits on payment for outpatient behavioral health services of all sorts. This often restricts access to psychotherapy to 10 sessions per year for all but the wealthiest families who can pay the current fee-for-service rate.

Confidentiality

If substance abuse, especially of the heavy variety, is seen as a family phenomenon, many of the existent regulations concerning confidentiality in behavioral health and medicine do not make sense. Although there may be exceptions, such as in emergencies, some of the standing regulations on confidentiality may perpetuate the problem. Shielding a person's drug or alcohol problem from his or her family may even be an exercise in self-delusion—the family members often already know about it—but at the very least, it results in "buying into" the family's denial. Thus, confidentiality provisions in law and ethical standards can give license to denial by sanctioning the identified patient as the problem and denying the importance of the family. For these reasons, we believe there is a need to change legal and ethical standards to distinguish between confidentiality within the family and confidentiality between the family and others, at least when there is evidence of substance abuse.

Therapist Support

Conducting family therapy with substance-abusing families can be grueling work. Therapists find it to be demanding and draining and occasionally find that the programs in which they work take on the characteristics of addictive family systems (e.g., "cross-generational" alliances, denial of problems, secrets, and "wet" and "dry" behaviors). It is therefore vitally important, for the sake of therapists and clients alike, to establish and maintain healthy administrative policies and procedures that support front-line therapists.

Protection from unmanageable caseloads should be included in the policies. In addition, treatment centers should make ample provision for supervision and consultation on all cases. When appropriate, consultants knowledgeable about family therapy and addiction should be retained. Similarly, continuing education should be made available to allow therapists to continue their learning while getting "out of the shop" for a while. Time away from providing services is essential in maintaining one's balance.

OUTCOMES OF FAMILY THERAPY

For more than 25 years, researchers have examined family therapy's effectiveness in treating substance abuse. Certainly since the National Institute on Alcohol Abuse and Alcoholism proclaimed that family therapy was "one of the outstanding current advances in the area of psychotherapy" for alcoholism (Keller, 1974, p. 166), researchers have measured the value of family and couple therapy with alcohol and drug problems of every sort. Fortunately for our purposes here, the extensive research has been reviewed and meta-analyses have been performed for the literature on family therapy's impact on alcoholism (Edwards & Steinglass, 1995) and drug problems (Stanton & Shadish, 1997). In the paragraphs that follow, we use this review literature to shed light on the critical question of effectiveness.

Edwards and Steinglass (1995) published the most recent review and "meta-analysis" of the outcomes of family treatment of alcoholism. For those unfamiliar with the term, meta-analysis is an accepted approach used to evaluate the quality and overall findings of a body of research studies. In meta-analysis, the results of individual studies are abstracted, quantified, coded, and assembled into a database. This database is then statistically analyzed to reveal patterns within the literature. By combining studies into a larger composite, meta-analysis enables researchers to identify the degree to which treatments are effective.

Edwards and Steinglass (1995) sought answers to three questions:

1. Is family–couple treatment effective for alcoholism?
2. Is it cost-effective?
3. What factors influence the effectiveness of family–couple treatment?

The authors reviewed and analyzed 21 outcome studies that were published between 1972 and 1993. All studies examined "family-involved" treatment for alcoholism, all had a control group, and all included objective data about subjects' drinking and drinking-related problems. The exhaustive review covers initiation of treatment, primary treatment/rehabilitation, and aftercare. The authors conclude with these answers to the three questions:

1. Family–couple therapy effectively motivates alcoholics to enter treatment and may help reduce drinking prior to treatment.
2. Once in treatment, family–couple therapy is marginally more effective than individual treatment for alcoholism. Family-involved relapse prevention programs show promise, but studies are limited to 2 years in duration.
3. Cost-effectiveness of family–couple therapy has been inadequately studied to draw any conclusions.
4. The effectiveness of family–couple therapy is mediated by the gender of the alcoholic family member, the couples' investment in their relationship with each other, and the family's commitment to abstinence.

Stanton and Shadish (1997) recently published their comprehensive review of the research into family–couple therapy with drug abusers and their families. This meta-analysis examined the 15 controlled outcome studies of family or couples treatment for the abuse of—or addiction to—one or more of the illicit drugs. Stanton and Shadish (1997) found that the design quality of the 15 studies was very good. All used random assignment to two or more treatment conditions. The results of this meta-analysis can be summarized as follows:

1. Studies that compared family or couple treatments with nonfamily treatments (e.g., individual, group, or psychoeducational treatment) found better results for family therapy. Family therapy was found to be more effective, less expensive, or both.

2. Family therapy works equally well for adolescent and adult drug abusers.
3. Comparisons between different "schools" of family therapy are not conclusive.
4. Family therapy has shown higher rates of engagement and retention in treatment than nonfamily approaches.

It should be noted that the Stanton and Shadish (1997) meta-analysis examined predominantly *family* therapy approaches—usually including the index patient's family of origin—whereas the studies in Edward and Steinglass's meta-analysis for alcoholism were primarily couple treatment. In any case, these reviews establish that involving families in the treatment of substance abuse can both (1) reduce treatment dropout and (2) improve results.

CONCLUSION

Substance abuse affects everyone in the family. Family therapy is an ecological and inclusive process that can benefit all those involved and change the multigenerational dynamics of substance abuse. In other words, family therapy is an effective and efficient approach to both treatment *and* prevention. Given society's concern about drug abuse and the incredible cost of drug abuse in our country, family therapy is making a significant contribution.

REFERENCES

Auerswald, E. (1980). Drug use and families—in the context of twentieth century science. In C. Ellis (Ed.), *Drug abuse from the family perspective: Coping is a family affair* (DHHS Publication No. ADM 80-910, pp. 117–126). Washington, DC: U.S. Government Printing Office.

Beattie, M. (1987). *Codependent no more.* Center City, MN: Hazelden.

Bepko, C., & Krestan, J. (1985). *The responsibility trap.* New York: Free Press.

Berenson, D. (1976a). A family approach to alcoholism. *Psychiatric Opinions, 13,* 33–38.

Berenson, D. (1976b). Alcohol and the family system. In P. Guerin (Ed.), *Family therapy: Theory and practice* (pp. 284–297). New York: Gardner Press.

Berenson, D. (1979). The therapist's relationship with couples with an alcoholic member. In E. Kaufman & P. Kaufmann (Eds.), *The family therapy of drug and alcohol abuse* (pp. 233–242). New York: Gardner Press.

Berenson, D. (1986). The family treatment of alcoholism. *Family Therapy Today, 1,* 1–2, 6–7.

Cervantes, O. F., Sorenson, J. L., Wermuth, L., Fernandez, L., & Menicucci, L. (1988). Family ties of drug abusers. *Psychology of Addictive Behaviors, 2*(1), 34–39.

Christopher, J. (1988). *How to stay sober: Recovery without religion.* Buffalo, NY: Prometheus Books.

Coleman, S., Kaplan, J., & Downing, R. (1986). Life cycle and loss: The spiritual vacuum of heroin addiction. *Family Process, 25*(1), 5–23.

Criteria Committee, National Council on Alcoholism. (1972). Criteria for diagnosis of alcoholism. *American Journal of Psychiatry, 128,* 129–135.

Davis, D. (1987). *Alcoholism treatment: An integrative family and individual approach.* New York: Gardner Press.

Edwards, M., & Steinglass, P. (1995). Family therapy treatment outcomes for alcoholism. *Journal of Marital and Family Therapy, 21*(4), 475–509.

Eldred, C., & Washington, M. (1976). Interpersonal relationships in heroin use by men and women and their role in treatment outcome. *International Journal of the Addictions, 11,* 117–130.

Elkin, M. (1984). *Families under the influence: Changing alcoholic patterns.* New York: Norton.

Fisch, R., Weakland, J., & Segal, L. (1982). *The tactics of change: Doing therapy briefly.* San Francisco: Jossey-Bass.

Fishman, H. C., Stanton, M. D., & Rosman, B. (1982). Treating families of adolescent drug abusers. In M. D. Stanton, T. C. Todd, & Associates (Eds.), *The family therapy of drug abuse and addiction* (pp. 335–357). New York: Guilford Press.

Haley, J. (1980). *Leaving home: The therapy of disturbed young people.* New York: McGraw-Hill.

Heard, D. (1982). Death as a motivator: Using crisis induction to break through the denial system. In M. D. Stanton, T. C. Todd, & Associates (Eds.), *The family therapy of drug abuse and addiction* (pp. 203–234). New York: Guilford Press.

Heath, A. (1985). Some new directions in ending family therapy. In D. Breunlin (Ed.), *Stages: Patterns of change over time* (pp. 33–40). Rockville, MD: Aspen.

Heath, A., & Atkinson, B. (1988). Systematic treatment of substance abuse: A graduate course. *Journal of Marital and Family Therapy, 14,* 411–418.

Heath, A., & Ayers, T. (1991). MRI brief therapy with adolescent substance abusers. In T. Todd & M. Seleckman (Eds.), *Family therapy approaches with adolescent substance abusers* (pp. 49–69). Boston: Allyn & Bacon.

Joint Commission on Accreditation for Healthcare Organizations. (1989). *Accreditation manual for hospitals.* Chicago: Author.

Kaufman, E. (Ed.). (1984). *Power to change: Family case studies in the treatment of alcoholism.* New York: Gardner Press.

Kaufman, E., & Kaufmann, P. (Eds.). (1979). *Family therapy of drug and alcohol abuse.* New York: Gardner Press.

Keller, M. (1974). Trends in the treatment of alcoholism. In M. Keller (Ed.), *Second special report to the U.S. Congress on alcohol and health* (DHEW Publication No. ADM 75-212, pp. 111–127). Washington, DC: U.S. Government Printing Office.

Kosten, T., Jalali, B., & Kleber, H. (1982–1983). Complementary marital roles of male heroin addicts: Evolution and intervention tactics. *American Journal of Drug and Alcohol Abuse, 9*(2), 155–169.

Levy, B. (1972). Five years later: A follow-up of 50 narcotic addicts. *American Journal of Psychiatry, 7,* 102–106.

Piercy, F., & Frankel, B. (1989). The evolution of an integrative family therapy for substance-abusing adolescents: Toward the mutual enhancement of research and practice. *Journal of Family Psychology, 3,* 149–171.

Reilly, D. (1976). Family factors in the etiology and treatment of youthful drug abuse. *Family Therapy, 2,* 149–171.

Rosenbaum, M., & Richman, J. (1972). Family dynamics and drug overdoses. *Suicide and Life-Threatening Behavior, 2*, 19–25.

Schaef, A. (1986). *Codependence misunderstood/mistreated.* New York: Harper & Row.

Scott, S., & Van Deusen, J. (1982). Detoxification at home: A family approach. In M. D. Stanton, T. C. Todd, & Associates (Eds.), *The family therapy of drug abuse and addiction* (pp. 310–334). New York: Guilford Press.

Selzer, M. (1971). The Michigan Alcoholism Screening Test (MAST): The quest for a diagnostic instrument. *American Journal of Psuchiatry, 127*, 89–94.

Stanton, M. D. (1977). The addict as savior: Heroin, death and the family. *Family Process, 16*, 191–197.

Stanton, M. D. (1979). Family treatment approaches to drug abuse problems: A review. *Family Process, 18*, 251–280.

Stanton, M. D. (1981a). Strategic approaches to family therapy. In A. Gurman & D. Kniskern (Eds.), *Handbook of family therapy* (pp. 361–402). New York: Brunner/Mazel.

Stanton, M. D. (1981b). Who should get credit for change which occurs in therapy? In A. S. Gurman (Ed.), *Questions and answers in the practice of family therapy* (pp. 519–522). New York: Brunner/Mazel.

Stanton, M. D. (1985). The family and drug abuse. In T. Bratter & G. Forrest (Eds.), *Alcoholism and substance abuse: Strategies for clinical intervention* (pp. 398–430). New York: Free Press.

Stanton, M. D. (1988a). Coursework and self-study in the family treatment of alcohol and drug abuse: Expanding Heath and Atkinson's curriculum. *Journal of Marital and Family Therapy, 14*(4), 419–427.

Stanton, M. D. (1988b). The lobster quadrille: Issues and dilemmas for family therapy research. In L. Wynne (Ed.), *The state of the art in family therapy research: Controversies and recommendations* (pp. 7–31). New York: Family Process Press.

Stanton, M. D., & Landau-Stanton, J. (1990). Therapy with families of adolescent substance abusers. In H. Milkman & L. Sederer (Eds.), *Treatment choices in substance abuse* (pp. 329–339). Lexington, MA: Lexington Books.

Stanton, M. D., & Shadish, W. R. (1997). Outcome, attrition, and family-couples treatment for drug abuse: A meta-analysis and review of the controlled, comparative studies. *Psychological Bulletin, 122*(2), 170–191.

Stanton, M. D., & Todd, T. C. (1979). Structural therapy with drug addicts. In E. Kaufman & P. Kaufmann (Eds.), *Family therapy of drug and alcohol abuse* (pp. 55–69). New York: Gardner Press.

Stanton, M. D., & Todd, T. C. (1981). Engaging resistant families in treatment: II. Principles and techniques in recruitment. *Family Process, 20*(3), 261–280.

Stanton, M. D., & Todd, T. C. (1982). The therapy model. In M. D. Stanton, T. C. Todd, & Associates (Eds.), *The family therapy of drug abuse and addiction* (pp. 109–153). New York: Guilford Press.

Stanton, M. D., Todd, T. C., & Associates. (Eds.). (1982). *The family therapy of drug abuse and addiction.* New York: Guilford Press.

Steinglass, P. (1976). Experimenting with family treatment approaches to alcoholism, 1950–1975: A review. *Family Process, 15*, 97–123.

Steinglass, P., Bennett, L., Wolin, S., & Reiss, D. (1987). *The alcoholic family.* New York: Basic Books.

Treadway, D. (1989). *Before it's too late: Working with substance abuse in the family.* New York: Norton.

Wegscheider, S. (1981). *Another change: Hope and health for the alcoholic family.* Palo Alto, CA: Science and Behavior Books.

Woody, G., Carr, E., Stanton, M. D., & Hargrove, H. (1982). Program flexibility and support. In M. D. Stanton, T. C. Todd, & Associates (Eds.), *The family therapy of drug abuse and addiction* (pp. 393–402). New York: Guilford Press.

22

Group Therapy, Self-Help Groups, and Network Therapy

MARC GALANTER
RICARDO CASTAÑEDA
HUGO FRANCO

INTRODUCTION

Treatment modalities that employ social networks, such as group therapy and self-help programs, are of particular importance in treating alcoholism and drug abuse. One reason is that the addictions are characterized by massive denial of illness, and rehabilitation must begin with a frank acknowledgment of the nature of the patient's addictive process. The consensual validation and influence necessary to achieve such pronounced attitude change are most effectively gained through group influence. Indeed, for this purpose, a fellow addict carries the greatest amount of credibility. Another reason for employing social networks is that they provide an avenue for maintaining ties to the patient beyond the traditional therapeutic relationship. Furthermore, therapists are not in the position to confront, cajole, support, and express feeling in a manner that can influence the abuser to return to abstinence; a group of fellow addicts or members of the patient's family can do so quite directly.

This chapter explores the impact of group treatment in a number of disparate settings. We look at therapy groups directed specifically at the treatment of addiction, at Twelve-Step programs such as Alcoholics Anonymous (AA), and Narcotics Anonymous (NA), and at institution-based self-help for substance abusers. The role of the clinician varies considerably in relation to each of these modalities; in each case, the mental health professional is provided with an unusual opportunity to step out of the traditional role of the psychodynamic therapist or the psychopharmacologist and examine the ways in which social influence is wrought through the group setting.

GROUP THERAPY FOR ALCOHOLISM AND DRUG ABUSE

A Historical Note

Group therapy constitutes the most commonly applied modality for the treatment of alcoholism and other substance abuse (Golden, Khantzian, & McAuliffe, 1994; Gwinner 1979). In fact, group therapy is frequently regarded as the psychotherapeutic treatment of choice for addicted individuals (Matano & Yalom, 1991; Cooper, 1987). The fact that it is less expensive than individual therapy is important as well (Kanas, 1982).

Numerous group therapy designs have been implemented in different treatment settings, including ambulatory clinics and such residential facilities as hospitals and therapeutic communities (Golden et al., 1994; Brandsma & Pattison, 1984). Group therapy designs include those that are professionally led (e.g., psychoeducational, cognitive, behavioral, interactional, and psychodynamic groups) as well as large groups that represent the hallmark of such self-help groups as AA and others. In general, all groups, irrespective of their theoretical approach, provide a core set of therapeutic factors, including (1) an opportunity to experience a sense of affiliation and cohesion, (2) a dosing of comfort and support which are balanced with varying styles of confrontation and identification of addictive and maladaptive behaviors, and (3) opportunities to learn or develop better coping skills and behaviors. Although a clear consensus exists among group therapists that group therapy approaches are effective and popular (Matano & Yalom, 1991), many group practices can claim neither adequate descriptions of methodology nor supportive outcome studies to document their efficacy relative to other group or individual treatment approaches (Golden et al., 1994; Cartwright, 1987; Castañeda & Galanter, 1987). Groups, nonetheless, have been reported as more efficacious than other addiction treatments such as individual, family, and couple therapy (Kang, Kleinman, & Woody, 1991; Bowers & al-Redha, 1990).

Group approaches allow for the development of a confrontational yet supportive environment in which a set of values is both jointly and individually pursued, which includes (1) abstinence from addictive substances and (2) the development of adaptive lifestyles. The opportunities afforded by the group setting for the addicted individual "to belong," following "a rite of passage" which requires the endorsement of group values and accepted behaviors, as well as a degree of "subordination" to the accepted authority of the group leader(s), eventually lead to a shared feeling of optimism about the benefits of talking to other group members about personal problems in a way that is acceptable to them. The individual's approach and definition of his or her problems in the context of the group, therefore, now fall under the monumental influence of peers who are less tolerant of denial and evasion than are individual therapists or teachers. Substance abusers, for example, are often impulsive and have a tendency to act out. These characteristics, which frequently are severely disruptive of individual treatment, are, in fact, more easily managed in the context of a group. The group structure and format, however, need to be adequately designed to attend to the specific characteristic behaviors of substance abusers. Addictive individuals may adopt uncooperative stances, monopolize group discussions, and arrive at group sessions while intoxicated; they may display low tolerance for frustration and poor attendance. Well-run groups can exercise strong peer pressure to confront such behaviors. They are effective settings to break down the denial of addictive or risky behaviors and its consequences and to encourage specific behavioral changes and abstinence.

Vannicelli (1982) points out that group treatment offers alcoholics unique opportunities to (1) share and to identify with others with similar problems, (2) understand their own attitudes toward alcoholism and their defenses against giving up alcohol by confronting similar attitudes and defenses in others, and (3) learn to communicate needs and feelings more effectively. Kanas (1982) pointed out that in general, group treatment for the addicted population is not only as effective as any other form of therapy but also much more economical than individual treatment.

How to Refer a Patient to Group Therapy

It is important to adequately match the treatment needs of an addicted individual with the most appropriate group therapy format. Psychotherapeutic groups for alcoholics, for example, generally fare better when all members are alcoholics and the focus of the group is on the characteristic behaviors and consequences of this problem. Usually each group includes from 5 to 12 members who meet from one to three times a week. Criteria for exclusion include severe sociopathy or lack of motivation for treatment, acute or poorly controlled psychotic disorders, and the presence of transient or permanent severe cognitive deficits. Those patients who, because of their dual problems—addiction and mental illness—cannot be integrated into single-problem group formats must be treated within specialized dual-diagnosis groups and treatment settings (Minkoff & Drake, 1991; Galanter, Casteñeda, & Ferman, 1988). Vannicelli (1982) observed that often patients are eventually excluded from the addiction group if they are unable to commit themselves to working toward abstinence. Polyaddicted individuals frequently are better integrated within multifocused groups. While dependent and nonsociopathic individuals are more easily engaged in interactional group models, individuals with sociopathic and other character problems are better retained in coping-skills groups (Poldrugo & Forti, 1988; Cooney, Kadden, Litt, & Getter, 1991).

Group Treatment Modalities

Group treatment for alcoholism and other addictions was developed out of general disappointment with the results of individual therapy (Cooper, 1987). In the case of opiate addicts, for example, group treatment met the need to provide treatment for patients in methadone programs. These programs were developed in the face of the overwhelming failure of the early programs for opiate addicts requiring complete detoxification and abstinence (Ben-Yehuda, 1980). Groups for substance abusers have evolved from poorly defined and passive groups with unclear focus and didactic groups in which all communication flows through the leader to a variety of more sophisticated approaches such as the following:

1. Groups with an interpersonal pattern and focus (Yalom, Bloch, Bond, Zimmerman, & Quail, 1978) whose leader is trained to interpret psychodynamic issues and is sensitive to interpersonal interactions in the here and now (Kanas, 1982; Khantzian, Halliday, Golden, & McAuliffe, 1992).
2. Interactional models (Matano & Yalom, 1991; Vanicelli, 1984) in which abstinence and the identification of maladaptive interpersonal patterns are identified through discussions of feelings and problems in the here and now. Newly endorsed adaptive behaviors, which are reinforced in the context of the interactive group process, are meant to replace addictive–acting-out behavior outside the group setting.
3. Cognitive-behavioral groups which conceptualize addictions as learned behaviors, subject to modification through various modalities of interventions, such as identification of conditioned stimuli associated with specific addictive behaviors, avoidance of such stimuli, development of enhanced contingency management strategies, and response–desensitization (McAuliffe & Ch'ien, 1986).
4. The psychoeducational group model, probably the most popular group approach, which promotes a sense of commitment to continued treatment through a process of education and raising of awareness about the behavioral, medical, and psychosocial consequences of addiction. These groups emphasize the identification, avoidance, and mastering of specific "internal" and external situations are associated with addictive behaviors. The value of this group format may very well lie in its ability to engage addicts in the beginning phases of treatment and to facilitate the transition of the addicted individual into more specific treatment strategies, including individual and psychopharmacological (Minkoff & Drake, 1991).

Table 22.1 presents brief descriptions of different group modalities for treatment of alcoholics that can be defined at this time.

The optimum style for a leader conducting a group for substance abusers appears to be one in which the focus is group rather than leader determined,

TABLE 22.1. Different Group Modalities for Treatment of Alcoholics

Category	Technique	Goals	Curative factors
Interactional	Interpretation of interactional process; promotion of self-disclosure and emotion expression	Promotion of understanding and resolution of interpersonal problems	Increased awareness of own relatedness
Modified interactional	Processing of interactional problems, but strong emphasis on ancillary supports for abstinence such as AA and Antabuse	Promotion of abstinence and improvement of interpersonal difficulties	Incorporation of specific resources to support abstinence and improvement of interpersonal relatedness
Behavioral	Reinforcement of abstinence-promoting behaviors; punishment of undesirable behaviors	Specific behavior modification	Prevention of specific responses
Insight-oriented psychotherapy	Exploration and interpretation of group and individual processes	Promotion of ability to tolerate distressing feelings without resorting to alcohol	Increased insight and improved ability to tolerate stress
Supportive	Specific support offered to individuals, to enable them to draw on their own resources	Promotion of adaptation to alcohol-free living	Improvement in self-confidence, and incorporation of specific recommendations

in which the leader not only is knowledgeable about substance abuse but also acts as a facilitator of interpersonal process, and in which the group members seek to understand each other from their own perspective.

Groups differ in their aims and the style of their leaders. Some groups allow for discussion of issues other than addiction in the hope that group members will identify the association between the addictive behavior and all other problems. Other groups focus primarily on relapse prevention through the identification and discussion of all problems, even if unrelated to the addictive behavior. Groups also vary according to the degree of support offered to members—from confrontational groups that give support only when a patient espouses the views of the group leader to supportive groups that accept and explore individual attitudes and beliefs.

Despite the obvious importance of group style and the need for clearly described group techniques, little has been written that provides group leaders with specific group strategies (Vannicelli, Canning, & Griefen, 1984). The question of the group's style (defined as the way in which the group's goals and processes are linked) is not merely one of academic importance. For example, Harticollis (1980) found that psychoanalytical groups are widely regarded as inadequate and are not recommended for active substance abusers because of the counterproductive degree of anxiety that they generate. An early study by Ends and Page (1957) demonstrated that the style of a group of alcoholics predicted treatment outcome. In this study, alcoholics were assigned to one of several groups of different designs. Group styles varied from one group described as relatively unfocused and "client centered," whose leader avoided a dominant role and instead promoted interpersonal processes among the group members, to another group based on learning theory, whose leader assumed a dominant role, offered only conditional support, and focused strongly on punishment and reward. At follow-up, those alcoholics treated in the client-centered group fared far better than those included in the confrontational group.

Exploratory and Supportive Groups

An interesting model, the modified dynamic group psychotherapy, developed by Khantzian allows for the identification of individuals' vulnerabilities and problems within a context of "safety." Abstinence is strongly endorsed, and the group, which requires an active style of leadership, promotes mutual support and outreach and constantly strives to identify and manage contingencies for relapse (Khantzian et al., 1992). According to Cooper (1987), psychotherapeutic groups based on exploration and interpretation aim at forging an increased ability in their members to tolerate higher levels of distressing feelings without resorting to mood-altering substances. In contrast, purely supportive treatment groups aim at helping addicted group members to tolerate abstinence and assist them in remaining chemical-free without necessarily understanding the determinants of their addiction.

The Interactional Group Model

Yalom et al. (1978) described an important group style in which therapy is conducted in weekly 90-minute meetings of 8 to 10 members who, under the leadership of two trained group therapists, are encouraged to explore their interpersonal relationships with the group leaders and the other members. An effort is made to create an environment of safety, cohesion, and trust, where members engage in in-depth self-disclosure and affective expression (Yalom et at., 1978). The goal of the group is not abstinence but the understanding and working through of interpersonal conflicts. (However, "improvement" without abstinence is often illusory.) In fact, groups of alcoholics are oriented away from an explicit discussion of drinking. The leaders emphasize that they do not see the group as the main instrument for achieving abstinence, and patients are encouraged to attend AA or to seek other forms of treatment for this purpose. Within this format, a group member can be described as "improved" along a series of 19 possible areas of growth, irrespective of the severity of his or her drinking (Yalom et al., 1978).

This interactional model was further developed by Vannicelli (1982, 1984), who, unlike Yalom et al. (1978), recommends that the group leaders strongly support abstinence as essential to the patient's eventual emotional stability. The group leaders firmly endorse simultaneous use of other supports, such as AA and Antabuse (disulfiram) therapy. In contrast to working with neurotics, whose anxieties provide motivation and direction for treatment, the leaders of such a group of alcoholics are forced to intervene to provide limits and focus without generation of more anxiety than necessary. The group therapists resist members' inquiries into the leaders' drinking habits by instead exploring the patients' underlying concerns about whether they will be helped and understood. Patients who miss early group sessions are actively sought out and brought back into the group. Confrontation (particularly of actively drinking members) is used sparingly and only with the aim of providing better understanding of the behavior and thus promoting growth and the necessary goal of activity changes.

Other Groups for Addicted Populations

Interpersonal Problem-Solving Skill Groups. According to Jehoda (1958), interpersonal problem-solving skill groups are based on the premise that the capacity to solve problems in life determines quality of mental health. Several empirical studies lend some support to this assumption, suggesting that there is a relation between cognitive interpersonal problem-solving skills and psychological adjustment. These groups have been implemented for alcoholics (Intagliata, 1978) and heroin addicts (Platt, Scura, & Harmon, 1960) with some degree of success. Usually problem-solving skill groups are run for a limited number of sessions (frequently 10) and are organized to teach a several-step approach to interpersonal problem solving. Most often, such steps include the following: (1) recognize that a problem exists, (2) define the problem, (3) generate several possible solutions, and (4) select the best alternative after determining the likely consequences of each of the available possible solutions to the problem. Follow-up studies determined that groups with this format were effective in generating specific skills such as anticipating and planning ahead for problems, even following discharge from the treatment programs. The value of problem-solving skill groups with respect to other primary modalities of addiction treatment, however, remains to be determined. It is unclear, for instance, whether these groups contribute to the overall rates of abstinence achieved in inpatient and outpatient treatment programs.

Educational Groups. Educational groups represent important ancillary treatment modalities in substance abuse treatment, not only for addicts but for their relatives and other social contacts. The obvious purpose of these groups is to provide information on issues relevant to specific addictions, such as the natural course and medical consequences of alcoholism, the implications of intravenous addiction for sexual contacts and the family, the availability of community resources, and so forth. Often, educational groups provide opportunities for cognitive reframing and behavioral changes along specific guidelines. These groups are often welcomed by some treatment-resistant addicts and alcoholics who cannot cooperate with other forms of therapy. More often than not, educational groups offer structured, group-specific, didactic material delivered by different means, including videotapes, audiocassettes, or lectures; these presentations are followed by discussions led by an experienced and knowledgeable leader.

Activity Groups. Like educational groups, activity groups constitute another important ancillary modality in the treatment of alcoholics and other addicts. Unlike educational groups, however, patient participation is the main goal of activity groups, which can evolve around a variety of occupational and recreational avenues. In a safe and sober context, the addict can expedite socialization, recreation, and self- and group expression. Activity groups are often the source of valuable insight into patients' deficits and assets, both of which may go undetected by treatment staff members concerned with more narrowly focused treatment interventions, such as psychotherapists and nurses. When appropriately designed, activity groups may constitute invaluable sources of self-discovery, self-esteem, and newly acquired skills that facilitate sober social interactions.

Other groups also promote the acquisition of specific skills, such as those devoted to reviewing relapse prevention techniques and those aimed at building social skills. These groups are particularly helpful in the early stages of the rehabilitation process of the alcoholic patient.

Relationship of Group Therapy to Individual Treatment

It is not a surprise that group therapists maintain that group treatment is the treatment of choice for alcoholics and other addicts (Matano & Yalom, 1991). In support of this, such group therapists as Kanas (1982) invoke not only the difficulty that these patients have in developing an "analyzable transference neurosis" in individual therapy but also the patients' tendency to display impulsive acting out—both characteristics that are better addressed in the anxiety-diffusing context of a group setting. Alcoholics, for example, are often seen as being orally fixated with resulting "narcissistic, passive–dependent, and depressive personality traits" (Feibel, 1960). Platt et al. (1960) and Feibel (1960) pointed out that individual insight-oriented psychotherapy is often said to be contraindicated in addicts because the following problems often present in these patients: intolerance of anxiety, episodes of rage and self-destructive behavior as a result of frustrated infantile needs, poor impulse control, and (probably most important) the tendency to develop a primitive transference toward the therapist.

Pfeffer, Friedland, and Wortis (1949) describe an undeniable advantage of group therapy over individual treatment—namely, the easily generated peer pressure, which can often promote behavioral changes and a reduction of denial of addiction and interpersonal difficulties. In addition, peer-generated support often satisfies narcissistic and dependency needs. Primitive, intense transferences are often avoided in the group setting because of diffusion among the other members of the group and the "relative transparency of the group leaders" (Kanas, 1982, p. 161). The tendency to leave treatment prematurely in individual therapy is often countered by the group's ability to promote a reduction of anxiety and to generate a therapeutic alliance, not only with the leader but also with the other group members. As stated previously, it is important when deciding between groups and individual therapy to assess both the patient's ability to tolerate and benefit from social interactions and his or her level of cognitive and psychological functioning. Patients with moderate cognitive deficits or paranoid or other psychotic disorders are likely to become isolated or hostile and to leave the group setting prematurely.

Following is a clinical example of the success of group therapy in a case in which individual therapy had no impact. At the time of referral, J. M. was a 45-year-old white male, employed as a middle-level administrator in a municipal institution. He had been married for more than 15 years and had three children. His chief complaints were frequent mood changes of many years' duration and unprovoked bouts of anger often directed at his wife, children, and coworkers. Although he had no history of psychiatric or medical problems, he reluctantly acknowledged that his wife thought he drank too much and that his boss had strongly demanded that he do something about his angry outbursts and poor job attendance. The patient was referred for individual therapy, but initial attempts at establishing a therapeutic relationship failed. He displayed markedly narcissistic personality traits, which resulted in an often disruptive relationship with the therapist, and he had difficulty in recognizing any interpersonal and mood problems associated with his alcohol consumption. The patient, however, acknowledged drinking more and more often than what was "healthy" for him. His motivation for treatment derived from his determination to maintain his current employment and his interest in "learning how to avoid depressive thinking."

Both the patient and the therapist felt that no progress was being made in individual therapy, and the therapist then referred the patient to alcoholism group treatment. In the group, the patient was exposed to other group members' descriptions of their problems of mood and social relations. On two occasions during the beginning phases of his involvement with the group, he came to the group while intoxicated. The threat of expulsion from the group in the face of these intoxications brought into focus the similar situation he faced at work, where his drinking was also jeopardizing his ability to remain employed. Confronted by group members and therapists alike, he eventually identified a relationship between his drinking and his angry outbursts at home and at work. From the outset, his drinking was interpreted by other group members as a reflection of his alcoholism rather than the expression of psychological conflicts. After a few months in treatment, this patient finally felt that he indeed was an alcoholic. The absence of drinking was associated with a total remission of depressive moods. He eventually made a commitment to abstinence, and he has remained in group treatment for several years.

Other Group Treatment Considerations

Group psychotherapy based on interpersonal and interpretive approaches rests in part on the self-medication hypothesis, which contends that substance abuse should be understood as the outcome of efforts at self-medication of distressing symptoms (Cooper, 1987; Khantzian, 1989). Recent challenges to this theory, however, suggest that drug abuse (particularly abuse of cocaine) may not necessarily be related to attempts at self-medication (Castañeda, Galanter, & Franco, 1989). Accordingly, it is advisable that group leaders be knowledgeable about addiction and able to anticipate that addicted group members may display drug-seeking behaviors that can best be regarded as conditioned responses (triggered by specific internal or environmental cues, such as the sight of a bottle or feelings of euphoria and celebration) rather than attempts on the part of the addict at dealing with emotional conflict (Galanter & Castañeda, 1985).

Groups with Methadone-Maintenance Patients

Groups with methadone-maintenance patients experience problems that relate more to the structure of the therapy than to the group content. Encouragement is always needed for patients to participate in these groups. Often, groups for these patients are an efficient way of coping with problems under professional guidance and peers' support (Ben-Yehuda, 1980). These groups generally go through several stages: the development of esprit de corps, the division of labor, the establishment of group cohesion, and the development of outside-the-group relations.

Drinking by some group members is to be expected in alcoholic groups. Full-blown slips or covert drinking by any group member interrupts the group process, elicits drinking-related thoughts and behaviors in other members, and requires specific and prompt intervention by the group leader. Often, however, a well-managed drinking episode represents an invaluable learning opportunity for all group members. A slip is not in itself cause for dismissal from the group. A resumption of drinking illustrates to all members the importance of prompt identification and interruption of denial and the need to constantly ensure the effectiveness of selected measures for maintaining abstinence. Responsibility for the slip should be defined to the group as resting entirely on the patient who is drinking and not on any past event or interaction between other group members.

Drinking can assume different forms, depending on whether it is acknowledged or denied by the person and whether or not, despite the drinking, the group member professes adherence to the group norms regarding abstinence and self-disclosure. Those patients who keep drinking and express no intention to stop should be asked to leave the group. Dismissal from the group is best explained to the patient and to the other group members as justified by the person's present drinking behavior. Readmission into the group once the patient is willing to accept the group norms, including a commitment to achieving abstinence, should always be offered to a patient who is leaving the group. A different approach is to be adopted with patients who express a desire to end the relapse and agree to participate in a discussion within the group of their active drinking. Initially, any information from any source (within or outside the group) that a group member is drinking should be immediately shared with all members. If the patient is intoxicated, he or she needs to be asked to leave the group and to return sober to the following session. The next meeting should serve as an occasion to explore feelings about drinking behavior and denial. At this point the group norms are reiterated; if necessary, specific contingency contracts with the drinking member are drawn up.

Another presentation of the problem is the patient who drinks yet refuses to acknowledge it. It should be part of the group contract that any important information concerning drinking behavior by a group member should be shared with the group. In the face of contrasting versions of a patient's behavior, clarification should be sought from the patient in a way that facilitates "voluntary" disclosure. Eventually, it may be necessary to confront the patient directly; if denial persists, the patient should leave the group.

Outcome Studies

Given the immense popularity of group treatment for alcoholics and other substance abusers, it is surprising to find so few controlled outcome studies (Kang et al., 1991; Poldrugo & Forti, 1988; Bowers & al-Rheda, 1990; Cooney et al., 1991; Yalom et al., 1978). Yalom et al. (1978) reported significant improvement at 8-month and 1-year follow-ups of both alcoholics and neurotics treated in weekly interactional group therapy. Improvement was measured along specific variables, however, and not according to the quality of abstinence eventually attained by the group members. In an early report, Ends and Page (1957) compared the outcome effects on alcoholics of several group therapy designs, including groups based on learning theory, client-centered (supportive) groups, psychoanalytical groups, and nonpsychotherapy discussion groups. They found that both client-centered and psychoanalytical groups yielded better outcomes than did discussion groups and groups based on learning theory, as measured by improvement in self-concept at a 1½-year follow-up. Client-centered groups also were associated with lower rates of readmission than all other groups in this and a subsequent study (Ends & Page, 1959). Mindlin and Belden (1965) studied the attitudes of hospitalized alcoholics before and after participation in group psychotherapy, occupational groups, or no-group treatment and found that group psychotherapy signifi-cantly improved motivation for treatment and attitude toward alcoholism.

THE ROLE OF TWELVE-STEP GROUPS IN THE TREATMENT OF ALCOHOLISM AND DRUG ABUSE

Self-help groups represent a widely available resource for the treatment of alcoholism as well as other forms of chemical dependency. AA and other

Twelve-Step organizations such as NA and Cocaine Anonymous (CA) have not only provided a large population of addicts with support and guidance but also contributed conceptually to the field of understanding and treating substance abuse. However, important questions for the clinician and the researcher need to be answered before the proper role of Twelve-Step programs in the treatment of addicts can be established. In what ways are such self-help programs compatible with professional care? In what ways do these groups achieve their effects? For which patients are they most useful? Familiarity with self-help groups is essential both for the clinician providing care for substance abusers and for the researcher attempting to understand psychosocial factors involved in the outcome of addictions.

History of Self-Help Programs

Self-help groups can be understood as a grassroots response to a perceived need for services and support (Tracy & Gussow, 1976; Levy, 1976). In this sense, AA is the prototypical organization; it provided a model for the other successful groups such as NA and CA, as well as for its more closely related offspring such as Al-Anon, Alateen, and Children of Alcoholics. Levy (1976) proposed a rough division of self-help groups in two types of organizations: type I groups, which are truly mutual help organizations and include all Twelve-Step programs, and type II groups, which more frequently operate as foundations and place more emphasis on promoting biomedical research, fundraising, public education, and legislative and lobbying activities (Levy, 1976). Type I and type II groups are by no means totally exclusive, as type I associations promote public education and type II groups sometimes provide direct services.

The development of AA has exerted a major influence on the self-help movement in general. The next section is concerned only with the development of AA and related Twelve-Step programs for addictions, which are clearly defined as type I associations.

Origins and Growth of Alcoholics Anonymous

AA's principal founder, "Bill W.," in accordance with the AA tradition of anonymity, was himself an alcoholic. Bill was spiritually influenced by a drinking friend, Edwin Thatcher, who belonged to the Oxford Group, an evangelical religious sect (Kurtz, 1982). Thatcher, usually referred to as Ebby, attributed his abstinence to his involvement with the Oxford Group, which displayed many of the characteristics later adopted by AA, such as open confessions and guidance from members of the group. Bill W. continued to drink despite his encounter with Ebby in 1934, but he felt that there was a kinship of common suffering among alcoholics. During his final hospital detoxification, he experienced an altered state of consciousness characterized by a strong feeling of proximity with God, which gave him a sense of mission to help other alcoholics to achieve sobriety.

Bill's initial efforts to influence other alcoholics were unsuccessful until, in May 1935, he met another member of the Oxford Group, "Dr. Bob," who a month later achieved sobriety and became the cofounder of AA. The number of alcoholics who experienced spiritual recovery and achieved sobriety in AA progressively increased; in 1939, when group membership reached 100, they published *Alcoholics Anonymous,* the book that became the bible for the movement (Galanter, 1989). AA institutionalized practices such as a 90-day induction period, sponsorship relationships, the "Twelve Steps," and recruitment for the fellowship. The expansion and stability of the organization resulted from its "Twelve Traditions," which avoid concentration of power within the organization, prevent involvement of AA with other causes, maintain the anonymity of its membership, and preserve the neutrality of the association in relation to controversial issues. Its membership continued to grow; AA is now a global organization, reported to have more than 75,000 informal groups in the United States and 114 other countries, with a membership estimated at 1.5 million. The birth and development of NA illustrate how AA provided a model to other self-help programs for addictions.

History and Approach of Narcotics Anonymous

Although the NA program was first applied to drug addiction at the U.S. Public Health Service Hospital at Lexington, Kentucky, in 1947, it was an NA group independent of any institution and formed by AA members who were addicts in Sun Valley, California, in 1953, which expanded and gave NA its current form (Peyrot, 1985). The Sun Valley NA group did not identify itself with a program organized in New York City in 1948 by Dan Carlson, an addict formerly exposed to the Lexington program, because the Sun Valley founders felt that NA should strictly adhere to AA's Twelve Steps and Twelve Traditions by not identifying itself with any specific agency and by not accepting government funds.

There are a few differences between AA and NA. NA members usually use illegal drugs, in contrast to most AA members until recently, who could be described as traditional alcoholics. Also, instead of using the term "alcoholism," NA refers to its problem as "addiction" and addresses the entire range of abusable psychoactive substances. There is, however, a clear overlap of approach and membership between the organizations, despite their complete independence of each other. Following in the footsteps of AA, NA has experienced fast-paced growth. It became an international organization, present in at least 36 countries, with a probable membership of 250,000. According to the NA World Service Office, which publishes NA literature and centralizes information within NA, the growth rate of the organization's membership has been 30–40% a year (Wells, 1987). The growth of NA and other Twelve-Step programs demonstrates the organizational strength and appeal of the AA model.

How Twelve-Step Programs Work

Participation in a Twelve-Step program can start at the moment the addict meets a member of an organization, reads its literature, or simply attends meetings (e.g., an open meeting or an institutional meeting run by AA or NA speakers) (Galanter, 1989). A desire to stop drinking and/or abusing other drugs is the only requirement for membership. Total abstinence becomes a goal from the outset of the participation in the fellowship. Initial participation turns into an induction period, which, in the case of AA, for instance, lasts 90 days and encourages daily attendance at meetings. The member is exposed to the Twelve-Step approach to recovery; the First Step consists of admitting powerlessness over the addiction, and consequently breaking with denial. Seeking sponsorship from another member who has been sober for months (preferably more than a year) is also encouraged. Sponsors are usually of the same sex if the group is large enough, so that emotional entanglements can be avoided to keep from distracting the members from the purpose of attaining and maintaining sobriety. Open meetings usually consist of talks by a leader and two or three speakers who share their experiences of how the Twelve-Step program related to their recovery.

The Twelve-Step program is an attempt to effect changes in the addicts' lives that go beyond just stopping the use of substances—changes in personal values and interpersonal behavior, as well as continued participation in the fellowship. The Twelve Steps are studied and followed with the guidance of a sponsor and participation in meetings focused on each step. Each step involves changes in behavior and attitudes that may profoundly affect the addict's life. To achieve the Ninth Step, for instance, the addict makes amends to people formerly harmed by his or her behavior. These amends may result in changes in the way in which the person relates to others and interprets the problems that have affected past and present relationships. For instance, an alcoholic man may "talk" to a deceased father whom he formerly hated and attempt a "conciliation" with his image of his dead father. The Twelfth Step encourages propagation of the group's philosophy and consequently fosters the individual's recovery by providing opportunities to others to recover and expand the fellowship.

Traditionally, Twelve-Step meetings are open to all members, but they may be directed to special-interest groups (e.g., gays, women, minority groups, and physicians). Meetings can be of different types, such as discussions, Twelve-Step study, and testimonials; some may be open to nonmembers, and others may be for members only. If the recovery progresses, the member will learn strategies to avoid relapse (e.g., "One day at a time"), will obtain help from other members, and will eventually help fellow addicts in their recovery. By helping other addicts and by sponsoring newcomers to the program, the individual is helping himself or herself by becoming more involved with the recovery process and the organization's philosophy.

Why Twelve-Step Programs Work

It is still unclear why Twelve-Step programs can help people exposed to them. From an existential perspective, AA, for instance, encourages acceptance of one's finitude and essential limitation by conveying the idea of powerlessness over alcohol. On the other hand, one can go beyond this imitation by relating to others and sharing some of the painful aspects of human existence. Kurtz (1982) emphasized that consistency in thought and action is crucial to maintaining a conscious effort to be honest with oneself and others. This effort produces an increased awareness of one's own needs for growth. AA stresses the need for consistency in thought and action in all stages of its recovery program.

From a learning theory perspective, the group selectively reinforces social and cognitive behaviors that usually are incompatible with the addictive behavior. Attendance at meetings is basically incompatible with using the same time to drink or abuse other drugs. Achievements resulting from sobriety are generously praised, and strategies of self-monitoring and self-control are constantly reinforced through constant interactions with others attempting to remain sober. Self-monitoring of emotions and behaviors is enhanced by helping the addict to detect reactions to certain internal and external stimuli (craving, distress with interpersonal problems, denial in the presence of depressive feelings, unrealistic goals when under pressure, etc.). In addition to self-monitoring, self-control is enhanced by learning a new repertoire of cognitive and social behaviors, such as attending more meetings when craving increases, using the Twelve Steps to cope with stressful life events, and obtaining group support to face painful feelings about oneself and others. Other theoretical perspectives used to understand Twelve-Step programs include operant and social learning views; however, because experimentation with the processes involved in participation in Twelve-Step programs is an almost impossible proposition, the use of learning models remains largely descriptive and speculative.

Self-Help and Treatment Outcome

AA has received more attention from investigators studying outcome variables than other Twelve-Step programs. Consequently, most of our knowledge about the impact of Twelve-Step programs on the lives of addicts is limited to the effects of AA on some samples of alcoholics. The structure of Twelve-Step organizations and their emphasis on anonymity make scientific research on these groups a very difficult task (Glaser & Osborne, 1982). Investigators have studied outcome variables related to participation in AA, such as severity of drinking, personality traits, attendance at meetings, total abstinence versus controlled drinking as a therapeutic goal, and concomitance of AA attendance with professional care (Thurstin, Alfano, & Sherer, 1986; Thurstin, Alfano, & Nerviano, 1987; Seixas, Washburn, & Eisen, 1988; Elal-Lawrence, Slade, & Dewey, 1987).

The first variable to deserve attention is that those alcoholics who join AA are not representative of the total population of alcoholics receiving treatment (Emrick, 1987). AA members tend to be, as common sense would indicate, more sociable and affiliative. Studies also suggest that AA members have more severe problems resulting from their drinking and experience more guilt regarding their behavior. Attendance to meetings has been associated in some studies (Emrick, 1987) with better outcome, although the nature of this association remains unclear. Thurstin et al. (1986) found no clear personality traits that might seem to be associated with AA membership, but they reported that success among members appears to be related to less depression, less anxiety, and better sociability. AA seems not to benefit those who can become nonproblem users and may actually be detrimental to patients who can learn to control their drinking (Emrick, 1987). AA members who receive other forms of treatment concomitantly with their participation in AA meetings probably do better.

As noted earlier, several problems make it difficult to study outcome factors related to participation in Twelve-Step programs. One is the changing composition of AA membership: more women, younger people, and multiply addicted alcoholics that have been joining the organization. The heterogeneity of addictive disorders, the anonymity of membership, the impossibility of experimentation with components of the programs, the self-selection factor in affiliation, and the lack of appropriate group controls all impose serious methodological difficulties in evaluating outcome variables. For clinical purposes, the benefit of membership in self-help groups has to be empirically evaluated for each individual patient.

Self-Help Groups and the Clinician

The relationship between professional treatment and membership in a Twelve-Step group has been less than systematically addressed. Clark (1987) proposed guidelines to orient the clinician. Clearly, acquaintance with Twelve-Step programs is essential for the clinician to orient patients regarding their needs and to respond to possible conflicts between the nature and goals of professional care and the demands of participation in self-help organizations. Clinicians treating addicts can learn about Twelve-Step programs by attending local meetings, by becoming familiar with the fellowships' literature, and by exploring their patients' experiences in the context of their membership in these organizations.

One point deserving emphasis is that physicians should be aware of the danger of prescribing habit-forming substances to addicts, not only because of the inherent dangers involved in the use of these substances but also because of the goals of programs that demand complete avoidance of chemical solutions for life's problems (Zweben, 1987). When psychotropic medication is strongly recommended, the benefits and risks involved in their use should be carefully discussed with the patient in the context of the goals of Twelve-

Step programs. An occasional sponsor may be opposed to any medication, even when a patient clearly needs pharmacological treatment to alleviate disabling behavioral or physical conditions. In this situation, the clinician has to address the nature of the conflict involved in the treatment by making the needed medical treatment compatible with the program philosophy. This desirable goal can only be achieved when the clinician is well informed about the nature of Twelve-Step programs and can help the patient to integrate the rationale for medical treatment with the general goals of his or her membership in the self-help program. Avoidance of prescribing drugs with habit-forming potential, willingness to educate patients about the nature of their problems, and a positive attitude toward Twelve-Step organizations make it easier for clinicians to integrate their interventions with the orientation of the fellowship. Candidates for controlled drinking should not be encouraged to participate in abstinence-oriented programs because the incompatibility of the goals of professional treatment with a Twelve-Step orientation may prove to be very detrimental to therapy (Emrick, 1987).

Clinicians should, in general, encourage their patients to get exposed to Twelve-Step programs, but they should remember that a large number of addicts who never participate in these organizations can make good use of professional treatment and successfully recover. Because the composition of the membership of self-help groups continually changes, it is possible for patients treated with psychotropic medication, including methadone, to benefit from participation in these groups (Obuchowsky & Zweben, 1987).

INSTITUTIONAL SELF-HELP TREATMENT GROUPS FOR SUBSTANCE ABUSE

Most ambulatory programs for substance abuse treatment are modeled after ones used in general psychiatric clinics. They rely primarily on professionally conducted individual and small-group therapy. Whether there are more cost-effective options or more potent ones has yet to be fully explored. One alternative approach to conventional institutional treatment is based on psychological influence in a self-help group context and is designed to allow for decreased staffing. Such an approach to group treatment is designed to draw on the principles of zealous group psychology observed in free-standing self-help approaches to addictive illness, such as those of AA and the drug-free therapeutic communities, but at the same time serves as the primary group-based modality employed in an institutional treatment setting. In other words, it can be employed in institutional settings such as hospitals and clinics and still capture the psychological effect of free-standing self-help groups.

In a study conducted on this treatment model (Galanter, 1982, 1983), primary therapists were social workers and paraprofessionals experienced in alcoholism treatment, supervised by attending psychiatrists. There was one social worker and one paraprofessional treating patients in the experimental self-help treatment program and two members of each of the latter disciplines treating the controls; the self-help program therefore operated at half the usual staffing level. The program included an alcohol clinic attached to an inpatient detoxification unit.

The control and the experimental self-help programs illustrate the contrast between institution-based self-help groups and conventional care. In the study (Galanter, 1982, 1983), the programs operated simultaneously and independently in the outpatient department. Therapists in each program were encouraged to perfect their respective clinical approaches, and each group of therapists received clinical supervision appropriate to their own needs and experience. Differences between the two programs are outlined here to illustrate the operation of institutionally grounded self-help group care.

The Orientation Program

In the control (traditional) group setting, two primary therapists served as co-leaders of a group for their own patients, and attendance in each session ranged between 8 and 15. In the self-help program the same format was used, but groups were led by patients of the primary therapists who had established sobriety and had demonstrated a measure of social stability over several months. These "senior patients" monitored the progress of patients in the orientation group and were supervised by the primary therapists, who attended the orientation for part of each session, participating in a limited fashion only. A patient in crisis might be invited to return to the orientation group if this invitation was seen as helpful.

Group Therapy

Weekly group meetings were oriented toward practical life issues among controls, but insight was encouraged; progress toward abstinence was a major theme. The two primary therapists served as facilitators for the group, using their own empathic manner to encourage mutual acceptance and support. When confrontation was necessary, the therapists undertook it in a forthright but supportive manner. In the self-help program, groups met with the same frequency, but senior patients assumed the leadership role. Primary therapists attended part of each session and participated intermittently; they served, however, primarily in a coordinating capacity for these groups and supervised the senior patients. Patients were encouraged to deal with unusual problems by recourse to their peers in the program, either in their therapy group or through senior patients.

Peer Therapy

Self-help program patients were made aware that the primary source of support in the clinic was the peer group. New patients were encouraged to seek out peers and senior patients who would be available to assist them through the program. Senior patients were supervised in assisting with crises when this assistance was judged clinically appropriate by the primary therapists. The senior patient program was operated in the self-help modality. Potential senior patients were screened for sobriety and social stability and assisted in patient management of the program for a time-limited period. Those who served as group leaders met weekly as a group with the primary therapists, focusing on their therapeutic functions in the unit. Under supervision of the therapists, they directed orientation, therapy, and activity groups. Their interventions in more difficult patients' problems were reviewed with the primary therapists, and they referred self-help patients to their respective primary therapists for more troublesome problems. Other senior patients had administrative functions in the program.

Meetings of the full patient complement also took place in the self-help program. A monthly evening meeting open to all patients served as a focus for group spirit and as a context for organizing recreational activities. The meetings were run collaboratively by staff and senior patients, with program-wide activities and patients' progress as the focus. Socialization at the time of these meetings focused on the status of patients' recovery.

Outcome and Comments

In two outcome studies (Galanter, 1982, 1983), we found that the experimental program, with half the staffing of the traditional modality, was quite viable in a municipal hospital alcoholism treatment program. Furthermore, retention of inpatients upon transfer to the alcohol clinic was 38% greater than in the control (non-self-help) program; rates of abstinence in outpatients were no less, and social adjustment over the course of a 12-month follow-up was enhanced. The self-help format appears, therefore, to offer a format for institutional treatment that is less expensive and potentially more effective.

The following case example illustrates the ethos of the self-help program: A 36-year-old outpatient came to the clinic intoxicated, without a scheduled visit, and asked to speak with a senior patient whom he knew well. He had been in outpatient treatment for 8 months, and had been abstinent for the last 4 months. Five days earlier, he had begun drinking subsequent to a crisis in his family and had missed his group meeting. He gave a history of falling down a staircase earlier in the day, bruising his head. The senior patient he had asked to see and another one were present, and they encouraged him to seek a medical evaluation. The case was then reviewed with the primary therapist, who saw him briefly, wrote a referral for medical assessment, and returned him to the two senior patients' care. After an hour, the senior patients prevailed on him to go with one of them to the emergency service. The other took him on the following afternoon to a meeting of an AA group he had previously attended. The patient was able to maintain abstinence until his next weekly group therapy meeting, at which time a group member offered to get together with him during the ensuing week to provide him with some encouragement.

Given a need for increased substance abuse treatment services, it is important to note that counseling staff members (social workers and counselors) comprise 66% of the staffs in all federally assisted alcoholism treatment facilities, which constitute the bulk of publicly supported programs (Vischi, Jones, Shank, & Lima, 1980). The question then arises as to whether these counseling staffers are used in the most cost-effective way. One problematic aspect of this issue is illustrated by the finding of Paredes and Gregory (1979) that in alcoholism treatment programs, the economic resources invested in alcoholism treatment are not positively correlated with outcome. They concluded that the type and quantity of therapeutic resources invested are related to the characteristics of the agencies themselves rather than to a treatment strategy conceived for optimal cost-effectiveness.

Two issues common to most small-group therapies for substance abuse in the clinic setting are relevant here. In the first place, whether behavioral, insight-oriented, or directive, they all focus on the concerns of a relatively small number of patients involved in the therapy group (typically 6 to 10), to the exclusion of other program participants. Second, it is generally agreed that such small-group therapy for alcoholics offers a better outcome when conducted in the context of a multimodality program. Such a program may integrate treatment components to implement a carefully structured plan, as described by Hunt and Azrin (1973).

These two aspects of small-group therapy may be considered in relation to a self-help–oriented treatment program such as the one described previously. With regard to group size, such a program introduces the option of the patients' strong identification with and sense of cohesion in a treatment network of many more than 6 to 10 patients. In fact, it encourages affiliative feelings among the full complement of self-help patients, providing an experience of a large, zealous group (Galanter, 1989). This cohension is promoted by therapeutic contact with a number of senior patients who are involved in the therapy groups; by programwide patient-run activities, such as the orientation groups open to patients in crisis; and in monthly large-group meetings, also open to all patients. This broader identification forms the bulwark of a self-help orientation.

THE NETWORK THERAPY TECHNIQUE

This approach can be useful in addressing a broad range of addicted patients characterized by the following clinical hallmarks of addictive illness. When they initiate consumption of their addictive agent, be it alcohol, cocaine, opiates, or depressant drugs, they frequently cannot limit that consumption to a reasonable and predictable level; this phenomenon has been termed "loss of control" by clinicians who treat alcohol- or drug-dependent persons (Jellinek, 1963). Second, they consistently demonstrate relapse to the agent of abuse, that is, they attempted to stop using the drug for varying periods of time but returned to it, despite a specific intent to avoid it.

This treatment approach is not necessary for those abusers who can, in fact, learn to set limits on their use of alcohol or drugs; their abuse may be treated as a behavioral symptom in a more traditional psychotherapeutic fashion. Nor is it directed at those patients for whom the addictive pattern is most unmanageable (e.g., addicted people with unusual destabilizing circumstances such as homelessness, severe character pathology, or psychosis). These patients may need special supportive care (e.g., inpatient detoxification or long-term residential treatment).

Key Elements

Three elements are essential to the network therapy technique. The first is a cognitive behavioral approach to relapse prevention, independently reported to be valuable in addiction treatment (Marlatt & Gordon, 1985). Emphasis in this approach is placed on triggers to relapse and behavioral techniques for avoiding them, rather than on exploring underlying psychodynamic issues.

Second, support of the patient's natural social network is engaged in treatment. Peer support in AA has long been shown to be an effective vehicle for promoting abstinence, and the idea of the therapist's intervening with family and friends in starting treatment was employed in one of the early ambulatory techniques specific to addiction (Johnson, 1986). The involvement of spouses (McCrady, Stout, Noel, Abrams, & Fisher-Nelson, 1991) has since been shown to be effective in enhancing the outcome of professional therapy.

Third, the orchestration of resources to provide community reinforcement suggests a more robust treatment intervention by providing a support for drug-free rehabilitation (Azrin, Sisson, & Meyers, 1982). In this relation, Khantzian, points to the "primary care therapist" as one who functions in direct coordinating and monitoring roles in order to combine psychotherapeutic and self-help elements (Khantzian, 1988). It is this overall management role over circumstances outside as well as inside the office session that is presented to trainees to maximize the effectiveness of the intervention.

Starting a Network

Patients should be asked to bring their spouse or a close friend to the first session. Alcoholic patients often dislike certain things they hear when they first come for treatment and may deny or rationalize even if they voluntarily sought help. Because of their denial, a significant other is essential to both history taking and implementing a viable treatment plan. A close relative or spouse can often cut through the denial in a way that an unfamiliar therapist cannot and can therefore be invaluable in setting a standard of realism in dealing with the addiction.

Once the patient comes for an appointment, establishing a network is a task undertaken with active collaboration of patient and therapist. The two, aided by those parties who join the network initially, must search for the right balance of members. The therapist must carefully promote the choice of appropriate network members, however, just as the platoon leader selects those who will go into combat.

Defining the Network's Task

As conceived here, the therapist's relationship to the network is like that of a task-oriented team leader rather than that of a family therapist oriented toward insight. The network is established to implement a straightforward task: aiding the therapist in sustaining the patient's abstinence. It must be directed with the same clarity of purpose that a task force is directed in any effective organization. Competing and alternative goals must be suppressed or at least prevented from interfering with the primary task.

Unlike family members involved in traditional family therapy, network members are not led to expect symptom relief for themselves or self-realization. This lack of expectation prevents the development of competing goals for the network's meetings. It also provides the members protection from having their own motives scrutinized and thereby supports their continuing involvement without the threat of an assault on their psychological defenses.

Adapting Individual Therapy to the Network Treatment

Of first importance is the need to address exposure to substances of abuse or to cues that might precipitate alcohol or drug use (Galanter, 1993). Both patient and therapist should be sensitive to this matter and explore these situations as they arise. Second, a stable social context in an appropriate social environment—one conducive to abstinence with minimal disruption of life circumstances—should be supported. Considerations of minor disruptions in place of residence, friends, or job need not be a primary issue for the patient with character disorder or neurosis, but they cannot go untended here. For a considerable period, the substance abuser is highly vulnerable to exacerbations of the addictive illness and in some respects must be viewed with the considerable caution with which one treats the recently compensated psychotic.

STUDY ON TRAINING NAIVE THERAPISTS

A course of training for psychiatric residents naive to addiction and ambulatory treatments was undertaken over a period of 2 academic years. Before beginning treatment, the residents were given a structured treatment manual for network therapy and participated in a 13-session seminar on application of the network therapy technique. Cocaine-abusing patients were eligible for treatment in this study if they could come for evaluation with a friend or family member who could participate in their treatment. In all, 22 patients were enrolled. The treating psychiatric residents were able to establish requisite networks for 20 of these patients (i.e., a network with at least one member). The networks had an average of 2.3 members, and the most typical configuration included family members and friends. Supervisors' evaluation of videotapes of the network sessions employing standardized instruments indicated good adherence to the manualized treatment, with effective use of network therapy techniques. The outcome of treatment (Galanter, Keller, & Dermatis, 1997) reflected retention and abstinence rates as good as, or better than, comparable ambulatory care carried out by therapists experienced in addiction treatment. The study demonstrated the feasibility of teaching the network technique to therapists naive to addiction treatment.

REFERENCES

Azrin, N. H., Sisson, R. W., & Meyers, R. (1982). Alcoholism treatment by disulfiram and community reinforcement therapy. *Journal of Behavior Therapy and Experimental Psychiatry, 13,* 105–112.

Ben-Yehuda, N. (1980). Group therapy with methadone-maintained patients: Structural problems and solutions. *International Journal of Group Psychotherapy, 30,* 331–345.

Bowers T. G., & al-Rheda, M. R. (1990) A comparison of outcome with group/marital and standard/individual therapies with alcoholics. *Journal of Studies on Alcohol, 51,* 301–309.

Brandsma, J. M., & Pattison, E. M. (1984). Group treatment methods with alcoholics. In M. Galanter & E. M. Pattison (Eds.), *Advances in the psychosocial treatment of alcoholism* (pp. 17–30). Washington, DC: American Psychiatric Press.

Cartwright, A. (1987). Group work with substance abusers: Basic issues and future research. *British Journal of Addiction, 82,* 951–953.

Castañeda, R., & Galanter, M. (1987). A review of treatment modalities for alcoholism and their outcome. *American Journal of Social Psychiatry, 7,* 237–244.

Castañeda, R., Galanter, M., & Franco, H. (1989). Self-medication among addicts with primary psychiatric disorders. *Comprehensive Psychiatry, 30,* 80–83.

Clark, H. W. (1987). On professional therapists and Alcoholics Anonymous. *Journal of Psychoactive Drugs, 19,* 233–242.

Cooney, N. L., Kadden, R. M., Litt, M. D., & Getter, H. (1991). Matching alcoholics to coping skills or interactional therapies: Two year-follow-up results. *Journal of Consultational Clinical Psychology, 59,* 598–601.

Cooper, D. E. (1987). The role of group psychotherapy in the treatment of substance abusers. *American Journal of Psychotherapy, 41,* 55–67.

Elal-Lawrence, G., Slade, P. D., & Dewey, M. E. (1987). Treatment and follow-up variables discriminating abstainers, controlled drinkers and relapsers. *Journal of Studies on Alcohol, 48,* 39–46.

Emrick, C. D. (1987). Alcoholics Anonymous: Affiliation processes and effectiveness as treatment. *Alcoholism: Clinical and Experimental Research, 11,* 416–442.

Ends, E. J., & Page, C. W. (1957). A study of three types of group psychotherapy with hospitalized male inebriates. *Quarterly Journal of Studies on Alcohol, 18,* 263–277.

Ends, E. J., & Page, C. W. (1959). Group psychotherapy and concomitant psychological changes. *Psychological Monograph, 73,* 1–31.

Feibel, C. (1960). The archaic personality structure of alcoholics and its indications for therapy. *International Journal of Group Psychotherapy, 10,* 39–45.

Galanter, M. (1982). Overview: Charismatic religious sects and psychiatry. *American Journal of Psychiatry, 139,* 1539–1548.

Galanter, M. (1983). Engaged members of the Unification Church: The impact of a charismatic group on adaptation and behavior. *Archives of General Psychiatry, 40,* 1197–1202.

Galanter, M. (1989). *Cults: Faith, healing and coercion.* New York: Oxford University Press.

Galanter, M. (1993). Network therapy for addiction: A model for office practice. *American Journal of Psychiatry, 150,* 28–36.

Galanter, M., & Castañeda, R. (1985). Self-destructive behavior in the substance abuser. *Psychiatric Clinics of North America, 8,* 251–261.

Galanter, M., Castañeda, R., & Ferman, J. (1988). Substance abuse among general psychiatric patients: Place of presentation, diagnosis and treatment. *American Journal of Substance Abuse, 14,* 211–235.

Galanter, M., Keller, D., & Dermatis, H. (1997). Network therapy for addiction: Assessment of the clinical outcome of training. *American Journal of Drug and Alcohol Abuse, 23,* 355–367.

Glaser, F. B., & Osborne, A. (1982). Does AA really work? *British Journal of Addiction, 77,* 123–129.

Golden, S. J., Khantzian, E. J., & McAuliffe, W. E. (1994). Group therapy. In M. Galanter (Ed.), *Substance abuse treatment* (pp. 303–315). New York: American Psychiatric Press.

Gwinner, P. (1979). Treatment approaches. In M. Grant & P. Gwinner (Eds.), *Alcoholism in perspective* (pp. 113–121). Baltimore: University Park Press.

Harticollis, P. (1980). Alcoholism, borderline and narcissistic disorders: A psychoanalytic overview. In W. Fann (Ed.), *Phenomenology and treatment of alcoholism* (pp. 93–110). New York: Spectrum.

Hunt, G. M., & Azrin, N. H. (1973). A community-reinforcement approach to alcoholism. *Behaviour Research and Therapy, 11,* 91–104.

Intagliata, J. C. (1978). Increasing the interpersonal problem-solving skills of an alcoholic population. *Journal of Consulting and Clinical Psychology, 46,* 489–498.

Jehoda, M. (1958). *Current concepts in positive mental health.* New York: Basic Books.

Jellinek, E. M. (1963). *The disease concept of alcoholism.* New Haven, CT: Hillhouse.

Johnson, V. E. (1986). *Intervention: How to help someone who doesn't want help.* Minneapolis: Johnson Institute.

Kanas, N. (1982). Alcoholism and group psychotherapy. In E. Kauffman & M. Pattison (Eds.), *Comprehensive textbook of alcoholism* (pp. 1011–1021). New York: Gardner Press.

Kang, S. Y., Kleinman, P. H., & Woody, G. E. (1991). Outcomes for cocaine abusers after once-a-week psychosocial therapy. *American Journal of Psychiatry, 131,* 160–164.

Khantzian, E. J. (1988). The primary care therapist and patient needs in substance abuse treatment. *American Journal of Drug and Alcohol Abuse, 14*(2), 159–167.

Khantzian, E. J. (1989). The self-medication hypothesis for substance abusers. *American Journal of Psychiatry, 30,* 81–83.

Khantzian, E. J., Halliday, K. S., Golden, S., & McAuliffe, W. E. (1992). Modified group therapy for substance abusers: A psychodynamic approach to relapse prevention. *American Journal of Addictions, 1,* 67–76.

Kurtz, E. (1982). Why AA works. *Journal of Studies on Alcohol, 43,* 38–80.

Levy, L. H. (1976). Self-help health groups: Types and psychological processes. *Journal of Applied Behavioral Science, 12,* 310–322.

Marlatt, G. A., & Gordon, J. R. (Eds.).(1985). *Relapse prevention: Maintenance strategies in the treatment of addictive behaviors.* New York: Guilford Press.

Matano R. N., & Yalom, I. D. (1991). Approaches to chemical dependency: Chemical dependency and interactive group therapy—A synthesis. *International Journal of Group Psychotherapy, 41,* 269–293.

McAuliffe, W. E., & Chi'en, J. M. N. (1986). Recovery training and self-help: Relapse prevention program for treated opiate addicts. *Journal of Substance Abuse Treatment, 3,* 9–20.

McCrady, B. S., Stout, R., Noel, N., Abrams, D., & Fisher-Nelson, H. (1991). Effectiveness of three types of spouse-involved behavioral alcoholism treatment. *British Journal of Addictions, 86,* 1415–1424.

Mindlin, D. F., & Belden, E. (1965). Attitude changes with alcoholics in group therapy. *California Mental Health Review Digest, 3,* 102–103.

Minkoff, K., & Drake, R. E. (Eds.). (1991). *Dual diagnosis of major mental illness and substance abuse disorder.* San Francisco: Jossey-Bass.

Obuchowsky, M. A., & Zweben, J. E. (1987). Bridging the gap: The methadone client in 12-step programs. *Journal of Psychoactive Drugs, 19,* 301–302.

Paredes, A., & Gregory, D. (1979). Therapeutic impact and fiscal investment in alcoholism services. In M. Galanter (Ed.), *Currents in alcoholism* (Vol. 4, pp. 441–456). New York: Grune & Stratton.

Peyrot, M. (1985). Narcotics Anonymous: Its history, structure, and approach. *International Journal of the Addictions, 20,* 1509–1522.

Pfeffer, A. Z., Friedland, P., & Wortis, S. B. (1949). Group psychotherapy with alcoholics. *Quarterly Journal of Studies on Alcohol, 10,* 198–216.

Platt, J. J., Scura, W., & Harmon, J. R. (1960). Problem-solving thinking of youthful incarcerated heroin addicts: The archaic personality structure of alcoholics and its indications for group therapy. *International Journal of Group Psychotherapy, 10,* 39–45.

Poldrugo, F., & Forti, B. (1988). Personality disorders and alcoholism treatment outcome. *Drug and Alcohol Dependence, 21,* 171–176.

Seixas, F., Washburn, S., & Eisen, S. V. (1988). Alcoholism, Alcoholics Anonymous attendance, and outcome in a prison system. *American Journal of Drug and Alcohol Abuse, 14,* 515–524.

Thurstin, A. H., Alfano, A. M., & Nerviano, V. J. (1987). The efficacy of AA attendance for aftercare of inpatient alcoholics: Some follow-up data. *International Journal of the Addictions, 22,* 1083–1090.

Thurstin, A. H., Alfano, A. M., & Sherer, M. (1986). Pretreatment MMPI profiles of AA members and non-members. *Journal of Studies on Alcohol, 47,* 468–471.

Tracy, G. S., & Gussow, Z. (1976). Self-help health groups: A grass roots response to a need for services. *Journal of Applied Behavioral Science, 12,* 381–396.

Vannicelli, M. (1982). Group psychotherapy with alcoholics: Special techniques. *Journal of Studies on Alcohol, 43,* 17–37.

Vannicelli, M., Canning, D., & Griefen, M. (1984). Group therapy with alcoholics: A group case study. *International Journal of Group Psychotherapy, 34,* 127–147.

Vischi, T. R., Jones, K. R., Shank, E. L., & Lima, L. H. (1980). *The alcohol, drug abuse and mental health national data book* (DHHS Publication No. 80-983). Washington, DC: U.S. Government Printing Office.

Wells, B. (1987). Narcotics Anonymous (NA): The phenomenal growth of an important resource [Editorial]. *British Journal of Addiction, 82,* 581–582.

Yalom, I. D., Bloch, S., Bond, G., Zimmerman, E., & Quails, B. (1978). Alcoholics in interactional group therapy. *Archives of General Psychiatry, 35,* 419–425.

Zweben, J. E. (1987). Can the patient on medication be sent to 12-step programs? *Journal of Psychoactive Drugs, 19,* 299–300.

23

Cognitive Therapy

JUDITH S. BECK
BRUCE S. LIESE

INTRODUCTION

Kim is a 32-year-old woman with a long and complex history of substance abuse that began when she was 13 years old. At various times over the past 19 years, Kim has experimented with most illicit drugs (including marijuana, heroin, LSD, Ecstasy, and cocaine) and she has been dependent on nicotine, alcohol, amphetamines, and barbiturates. She also suffers from chronic depression. She has intermittently been treated for depression since she was 15 years old and she has been in and out of drug treatment programs since age 19. Kim has never been married. She works as a night janitor at a fast-food restaurant.

At present, Kim smokes marijuana several times each day. She says, "I smoke so much, I don't even get high anymore." She reports that she smokes to deal with her feelings of depression, emptiness, and loneliness. She often views herself as helpless and hopeless but says she has no plans to kill herself because she is afraid of dying. She has gained over 50 pounds in the last few years and she says she wants to "do nothing but sit around the house all day."

Kim meets criteria for avoidant personality disorder with dependent and borderline features. She describes constant loneliness, boredom, and isolation. Nonetheless, she refuses to take social or occupational risks, claiming, "If I put myself out there I'll only get burned." To support this claim, she lists numerous failed relationships and jobs.

Eventually Kim enters a self-help group for women with depression where she admits to daily marijuana use. Another group member, Mary, explains that she, too, was a heavy marijuana smoker at one time. Mary passionately warns Kim that she will only feel better when she quits smoking marijuana. After listening to Mary, Kim is somewhat motivated to stop, but she finds it impossible to quit. After only a few days of abstinence she feels much more depressed and anxious, so she resumes smoking.

For the past several years cognitive therapy has been refined to help people like Kim who are addicted to alcohol, nicotine, cocaine, heroin, marijuana, and other psychoactive substances (A. T. Beck, Wright, Newman, & Liese, 1993; Liese & Beck, 1997; Liese, 1993, 1994a, 1994b; Liese & Franz, 1996; Wright, Beck, Newman, & Liese, 1992). We have also used cognitive therapy with people who engage in compulsive gambling, shopping, and sexual behaviors. Individuals like Kim have taught us a great deal about the development, maintenance, and treatment of addictive behaviors (Liese & Franz, 1996).

The cognitive therapy of substance abuse is quite similar to cognitive therapy for other psychological problems, including depression (A. T. Beck, Rush, Shaw, & Emery, 1979), anxiety (A. T. Beck & Emery, with Greenberg, 1985), and personality disorders (A. T. Beck, Freeman, & Associates, 1990). Each places emphasis on *collaboration, case conceptualization, structure, patient education,* and the application of standard *cognitive-behavioral techniques.* In addition, when working with substance abuse patients, cognitive therapists focus on the cognitive and behavioral sequences leading to drug use, management of cravings, avoidance of high-risk situations, case management, mood regulation (i.e., coping), and lifestyle change. The cognitive therapy of substance abuse is an integrative, collaborative endeavor. Patients are encouraged simultaneously to seek adjunct services (e.g., Twelve-Step and other programs) to reinforce their progress in cognitive therapy. When they find adjunct services to be valuable, they are helped to integrate and maintain their positive changes.

In the cognitive therapy of substance abuse, thoughts and beliefs are viewed as playing a major role in the mediation of addictive behaviors (actual drug use), negative emotions (e.g., anxiety and depression), and physiological responses (including some withdrawal symptoms). Although strategies and interventions vary somewhat from individual to individual and from drug to drug, the basic conceptualization of the patient in cognitive terms remains constant (A. T. Beck et al., 1993; see Figure 23.1 for the basic cognitive model of substance abuse).

When timely and appropriate, cognitive therapists assess the development of their patients' beliefs about themselves, their early life experiences, exposure to drugs or alcohol, the development of drug-related beliefs, and their eventual reliance on drugs (Liese & Franz, 1996; see Figure 23.2). An important assumption is that substance abuse is learned and can be modified by changing cognitive-behavioral processes.

Our model for cognitive therapy of substance abuse has been substantially influenced by other cognitive-behaviorists. For example, Marlatt and Gordon

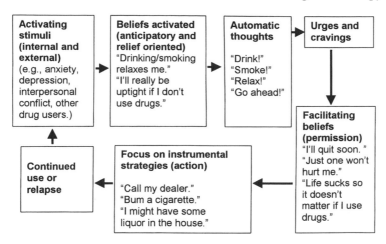

FIGURE 23.1. The cognitive model of substance abuse. Adapted from Beck et al. (1993). Copyright 1993 by The Guilford Press. Adapted by permission.

(1985, 1989) presented a profoundly important model of relapse prevention that has contributed greatly to our own work. Identifying high-risk situations, understanding the decision chain leading to drug use, modification of drug users' dysfunctional lifestyles, and learning from lapses to prevent full-fledged relapses are all integral to the relapse prevention model and the cognitive models of addiction.

There are a number of cognitive-behavioral therapies for substance abuse and dependence (see Liese & Najavits, 1997), but this chapter focuses primarily on the cognitive model defined by Aaron T. Beck and colleagues. First we demonstrate and illustrate cognitive case conceptualization; then we outline principles of treatment. Finally, we describe treatment planning, including specific cognitive and behavioral interventions. Our patient, Kim, is used as an example throughout.

THE COGNITIVE CONCEPTUALIZATION DIAGRAM

Cognitive therapy begins with a relatively structured formulation of the case, using a standardized form for structuring the case conceptualization (J. S. Beck, 1995). Kim's current difficulties are conceptualized using this form (see Figure 23.3). She holds fundamental beliefs that she is helpless and incompetent, bad, unlovable, and vulnerable. These beliefs originated in childhood (and became stronger and stronger as time went on). The next to last of eight children in a poor family, Kim was emotionally neglected, deprived, and occasionally physically abused by a depressed, alcoholic mother. Her father was cold, distant, and uninterested in Kim. He left the family when Kim was 7 and never contacted them again. Kim had few friends, felt rejected by her

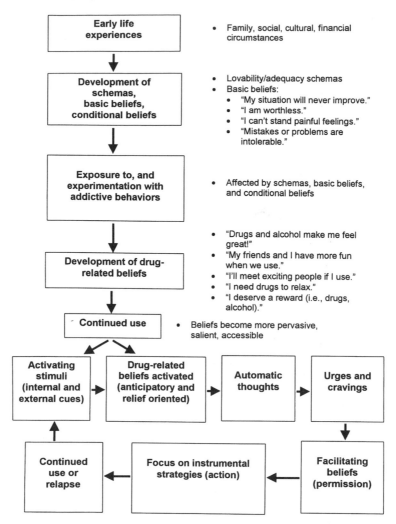

FIGURE 23.2. The cognitive developmental model of substance abuse. Adapted from Liese and Franz (1996). Copyright 1996 by The Guilford Press. Adapted by permission.

family, did poorly in school, and dropped out when she was halfway through 11th grade.

Kim's core beliefs of helplessness, badness, and vulnerability have caused her great pain, and over the years she has developed guidelines and rules (i.e., conditional assumptions) for survival. One such conditional assumption is, "If I avoid challenges (or quit challenging situations early), I won't have to face inevitable failure." Thus, time after time, situation after situation, Kim employs a characteristic compensatory strategy—she avoids applying for any but the most menial and unchallenging jobs. She then quits these jobs when the smallest problems arise (believing she is helpless to solve problems). Likewise, she tries only halfheartedly in drug treatment programs and drops out prematurely (believing she is incapable of abstaining from drugs). She also avoids conflicts with others, believing that she is undeserving or incapable of getting what she wants.

Kim's core beliefs of badness and unlovability permeate virtually all of her relationships. In addition to her conditional belief, "If I try to get what I want from a relationship, I'll fail" (which stems from a core belief of helplessness), she also believes, "If I assert myself or let others get too close, they'll reject me because nobody could possibly love me." Therefore, she employs such compensatory strategies as isolating herself, avoiding assertion, avoiding intimacy, and, perhaps most obvious, taking drugs. Most of her social contacts are with other substance abusers who manipulate and take advantage of her.

Kim also has a core belief that she is vulnerable, especially to negative emotion. Her conditional assumption is, "If I start to feel bad, my emotions will get out of control and overwhelm me." She avoids even mildly challenging situations in which she predicts she will feel sad, rejected, or helpless. Avoidance itself, however, often leads to boredom and frustration, which increases her sense of failure and helplessness.

Kim discovered at an early age that she could feel good by drinking alcohol and taking drugs. As a result, she failed to develop healthier coping strategies (e.g., learning to tolerate bad moods, solving problems, asserting herself, or looking at situations more realistically). For much of her life, she has tried to cope with a combination of avoidance and substance use.

The cognitive conceptualization diagram in Figure 23.3 demonstrates how Kim's thinking in specific situations leads to drug use. In situation #1, for example, Kim thinks about going to work. She has a mental image of her supervisor looking at her "with a mean face" and she thinks, "All he ever does is criticize me. I'll probably get fired soon." This is an *automatic thought* because it seems to pop into Kim's mind spontaneously. Prior to receiving therapy, Kim had little awareness of her automatic thoughts; she was much more aware of her subsequent negative emotions. As a result, she felt helpless and her behavioral reaction was to stay home and take drugs.

Why does Kim consistently have these types of failure, or helpless, thoughts in situation after situation? As described previously, Kim fundamentally sees herself as a helpless failure. These negative core beliefs about herself influence Kim's every perception. She *assumes* she will fail, never thinking to question such premises about herself. Given this tendency, it is no surprise that Kim avoids challenges or quits early. She thinks it is just a matter of time until her failure becomes apparent.

In situation #2 (see Figure 23.3), Kim is considering whether or not to go to a party given by neighbors. Because of her belief that she is unlovable, she automatically thinks, "I won't have a good time. I don't fit in." Accepting these thoughts as true, she feels sad and chooses to stay home and get high. Whereas many automatic thoughts have a grain of truth, they are usually

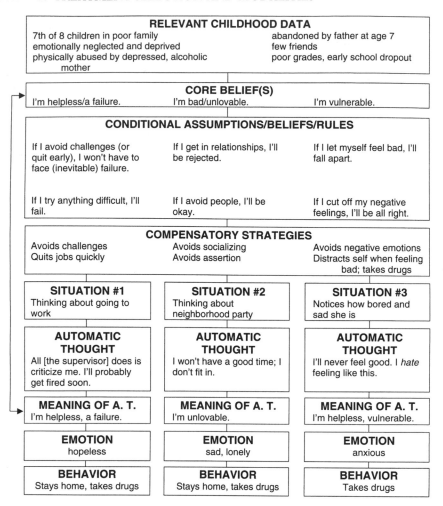

FIGURE 23.3. Cognitive conceptualization diagram. Adapted from J. S. Beck (1995). Copyright 1993 by J. S. Beck. Adapted by permission.

distorted in some way. Had Kim evaluated her thoughts critically, she would have concluded that she could not predict the future with certainty, that several neighbors had seemed pleasant to her in the past, and that the reason for the neighbors on the street to have the party in the first place was to get to know one another better. Kim's core belief of unlovability once again led her to accept negative thoughts as true and to use her characteristic dysfunctional strategies of avoidance and drug use.

In situation #3, Kim became aware of how bored and sad she felt. She thought to herself, "I'll never feel good. I *hate* feeling like this." Her negative prediction and intolerance of dysphoria were again linked to her core beliefs of helplessness and vulnerability. And, again, Kim coped with her feeling of anxiety by turning to drugs.

The cognitive conceptualization diagram can serve as an aid to identify quickly the most central beliefs and dysfunctional strategies of substance abusers, to recognize how their beliefs influence their perceptions of current situations, and to explain why they react emotionally and behaviorally in such ineffective ways. An important part of the cognitive approach is to help patients begin to question the validity of their perceptions and the accuracy of their automatic thoughts that lead to drug abuse.

An initial step in therapy is to help patients realize that their automatic thoughts are not completely valid. When they test their thinking and modify it so it more closely resembles reality, they feel better. A later step is to help them use the same kind of evaluative process with their assumptions and core beliefs, to guide them in understanding that their beliefs are ideas, not necessarily truths. Once they see themselves in a more realistic light, they begin to perceive situations differently, feel better emotionally, and can employ more functional behavioral strategies learned in therapy. When this occurs, they become less likely to "need" drugs for mood regulation because they have developed internal strategies for coping.

Cognitive therapy for substance abuse, therefore, aims to modify thoughts and beliefs associated with drug use and develop new behaviors to take the place of dysfunctional ones. (A third focus, described later in this chapter, is on practical problem solving and modifying the patient's lifestyle to decrease the likelihood of relapse.) The modification of patients' long-term negative beliefs about the self is crucial to their ability to see alternative explanations for distressing events, to use more functional coping strategies learned in therapy, and to create better lives.

At some point, cognitive therapists may explore childhood issues that relate to patients' core beliefs and addictive behaviors. Such exploration helps clinicians and patients understand how patients can have such rigid, global, and inaccurate negative ideas about themselves.

The drug-related cognitive conceptualization diagram in Figure 23.4 illustrates how Kim's core beliefs lead to specific assumptions about her ability to stop using, to employment of her compensatory strategies in treatment, and to her emotional and behavioral reactions to specific therapy situations. Her therapist helps her identify her automatic thoughts which interfere with doing therapy homework, with revealing her drug use honestly, and with taking an active role in problem solving during therapy sessions. Together they evaluate her thoughts and help her see each situation in a more realistic way, which then allows her to use therapy more effectively.

Figure 23.5, reflecting the basic cognitive model of substance abuse, presents an analysis of Kim's drug-taking behavior that emphasizes the cyclical nature of drug abuse. Kim, like most substance abusers, believed that taking drugs was an automatic process, beyond her control. This diagram helps her identify the sequence of events leading to an incident of drug use and identifies potential points of intervention in the future. In this example, Kim feels

RELVANT CHILDHOOD DATA	
7th of 8 children in poor family emotionally neglected and deprived physically abused by depressed, alcoholic mother	abandoned by father at age 7 few friends poor grades, early school dropout

CORE BELIEF(S)		
I'm helpless/a failure.	I'm bad/unlovable.	I'm vulnerable.

CONDITIONAL ASSUMPTIONS/BELIEFS/RULES		
If I try to give up drugs, I won't be able to.	If my therapist thinks badly of me, I'm a worthless person.	If I don't use drugs, I won't be able to stand it.

COMPENSATORY STRATEGIES		
Tries only half-heartedly to give up drugs Misses sessions Drops out of treatment programs prematurely	Reveals little to therapist Lies about/minimizes continued drug use	Continues drug use

SITUATION #1 Thinking about doing therapy homework	SITUATION #2 In therapy session	SITUATION #3 In therapy session
AUTOMATIC THOUGHT What's the use? I can't do this. It'll never work, anyway.	**AUTOMATIC THOUGHT** [My therapist] will think I'm bad if I tell her about my drug use.	**AUTOMATIC THOUGHT** If I talk about my work problems, it won't help, and I'll just feel worse.
MEANING OF A. T. I'm helpless, a failure.	**MEANING OF A. T.** I'm bad (and helpless to affect therapist's opinion of me).	**MEANING OF A. T.** I'm vulnerable.
EMOTION sad	**EMOTION** anxious	**EMOTION** anxious
BEHAVIOR Watches TV instead, then takes drugs	**BEHAVIOR** Lies about drug use	**BEHAVIOR** Doesn't contribute to setting of agenda in session

FIGURE 23.4. Drug-related cognitive conceptualization diagram. Adapted from J. S. Beck (1995). Copyright 1993 by J. S. Beck. Adapted by permission.

hopeless because she predicts she will lose her job. As she searches for a way to cope with her dysphoria, a basic drug-related belief emerges ("If I feel bad, I should smoke") and she thinks, "I might as well use." She then experiences urges and cravings and gives herself permission to use ("My life is crummy. I deserve to feel better"); she hunts for her marijuana stash and smokes a joint. This typical sequence of events takes place in seconds and Kim initially believes it is automatic. By breaking it down into a series of steps, Kim can learn a variety of ways to intervene at each stage along the way.

Figure 23.6 (reflecting the developmental model) again illustrates how Kim's early life experiences lead to the development of negative core beliefs

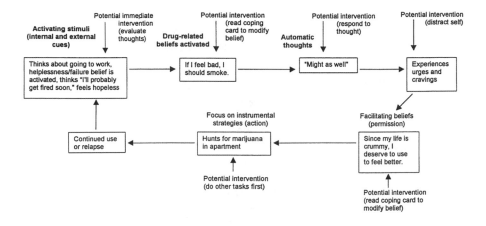

FIGURE 23.5. Cognitive model of substance abuse.

and assumptions about herself. As she reaches adolescence, she becomes influenced by a broad societal glamorization of drugs and even more compellingly by people in her immediate environment, and she develops a set of beliefs about the benefits of drug taking. These beliefs become activated in the presence of internal or external triggers (activating stimuli) and lead to her taking drugs in specific situations.

PRINCIPLES OF TREATMENT

A cognitive therapist could use hundreds of specific interventions with any given patient at any given time. In this section, we discuss the principles that apply to all patients who abuse substances. The purpose of these principles is to guide the clinician in choosing any specific intervention.

1. Cognitive therapy is based on a unique cognitive conceptualization of each patient.
2. A strong therapeutic alliance with the active collaboration of patient and therapist is essential.
3. Cognitive therapy is goal oriented and problem focused.
4. The initial focus of therapy is on the present.
5. Cognitive therapy is time sensitive.
6. Therapy sessions are structured, with active participation by both therapist and patient.
7. Patients are taught to identify, evaluate, and respond to their dysfunctional thoughts and beliefs.
8. Cognitive therapy emphasizes psychoeducation and relapse prevention.

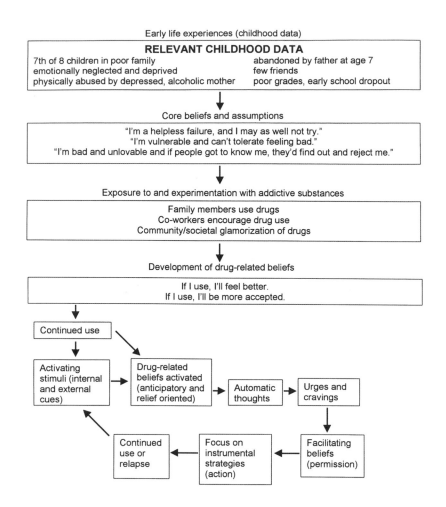

FIGURE 23.6. A cognitive–developmental model of substance abuse.

Principle 1: Cognitive Therapy Is Based on a Unique Cognitive Conceptualization of Each Patient

Conceptualization of the case includes an analysis of the current problematic situations of substance abusers and their associated thoughts and reactions (emotional, behavioral, and physiological). Therapists and patients look for themes expressed in the patients' automatic thoughts and the meaning of their thoughts to identify their most basic, dysfunctional beliefs about themselves, their worlds, and other people (e.g., "I am inadequate/worthless/weak." "The world is a hostile place." "People will take advantage of me.").

They also identify the consistent patterns of behavior that patients develop to cope with these negative ideas (e.g., taking drugs, preying on people, and distancing themselves from others). The connection between these core beliefs and compensatory strategies becomes clearer when therapists and patients identify the central conditional assumptions that guide patients' behavior and the specific drug-related assumptions as well (e.g., "If I try to resist drugs, I won't be able to" is a subset of a more central belief, "If I try to do anything difficult, I'll probably fail [because I'm so weak or incompetent]").

Therapists and patients look at patients' developmental histories to shed light on how they might have come to hold such strong, rigid, negative core beliefs yet how these beliefs might not be true today (and, in most cases, were not true, or completely true, even in childhood). They also look at patients' enduring patterns of interpretation that have caused them, throughout their lives, to process information so negatively.

In addition, therapists literally draw scenarios in which patients take drugs (Figure 23.5) to illustrate the cyclical process of drug use and the many opportunities to intervene and avert a lapse or relapse.

Principle 2: A Strong Therapeutic Alliance with the Active Collaboration of Patient and Therapist Is Essential

For successful treatment, therapists and patients must develop caring, collaborative, respectful attitudes toward one another. Effective therapists explain their therapeutic approach, encourage patients to express skepticism, help them test over time the validity of their doubts, provide explanations for their interventions, share their cognitive formulation to make sure they have an accurate understanding of the patient, and consistently ask for feedback.

Therapists who are typically very collaborative find that they can easily establish sound therapeutic relationships with most substance abuse patients, though all therapists eventually find that a strong alliance is difficult to establish with some. Even the most experienced therapist with the essential characteristics of warmth, empathy, caring, genuine regard, and competence finds it challenging to develop good relationships with occasional patients who are suspicious, manipulative, deceitful, or avoidant. Therapists are encouraged to examine relationship problems by developing conceptualization diagrams of the patient, using examples of difficulties that arise in sessions to form hypotheses about assumptions that guide the patients' behaviors during therapy sessions (e.g., Figure 23.4).

An effective therapist seeks to avoid activating patients' core beliefs through his or her own behavior in therapy and helps patients test the validity of their ideas about the therapist. For example, Kim's therapist asked her for evidence when she stated that she believed the therapist was judging her as "bad" for having a drug problem. Of course, effective therapists need to examine their own thoughts, feelings, and behaviors periodically to ensure that they are *not* viewing their patients in a negative light. When therapists maintain true nonjudgmental attitudes, they can sincerely tell patients that they are *not* negatively evaluating them. They can further explain that they view patients as using drugs to try to cope with the difficulties inherent in their lives.

At times a persistent problem in the therapeutic relationships arises from a clash of patients' and therapists' assumptions. Therapists are advised to do conceptualization diagrams of patients and of themselves to identify dysfunctional ideas they may have about interacting with difficult people.

For example, one substance-abusing patient held a broad assumption, "If I show any weakness, others will hurt me," and a subset assumption, "If I listen to my therapist, he'll see me as weak." As a result, the patient was very controlling in session, kept contradicting and criticizing the therapist, and would not do any self-help assignments suggested by the therapist. The problem persisted, at least in part, because the *therapist* had a broad assumption, "If people don't listen to me, they don't value me (and therefore don't deserve my strong efforts)." The therapist became irritated with the patient, expressing his dissatisfaction through his body language and tone of voice. The patient, already hypervigilant for possible harm from others, picked up on the therapist's negative attitude and dropped out of therapy prematurely.

Liese and Franz (1996) identify common dysfunctional beliefs of therapists that interfere with delivering therapy to substance abuse patients. Although many patients may minimize or deny their drug or alcohol use, confronting them with their falsehoods is almost certain to result in diminished therapeutic efficacy and dropping out.

When patients report no incidents of substance use during the previous week, it is often useful to inquire about times when they felt cravings or when their resolve not to use was relatively weak. In this way, therapists can obtain the relevant cognitive material (high-risk situations and associated dysfunctional core beliefs, relevant assumptions, and automatic thoughts) to help patients make or continue to make an effective response in the coming week.

Because patients with drug or alcohol problems are more likely to drop out of therapy than are patients without substance abuse (Swett & Noones, 1989; Gilbert, Fine, & Haley, 1994; MacNair & Corazzini, 1994), it is essential to build a sound therapeutic relationship. Liese and Beck (1997) describe how the use of basic cognitive therapy skills can maximize the probability that substance abusers will stay in treatment. Figure 23.7 presents their model for conceptualizing missed sessions and dropout.

Therapists increase the likelihood of successful treatment by emphasizing that they and the patient are on the same team, working toward the patient's long-term goals, and by demonstrating that therapy is not an adversarial relationship in which the patient must be on guard, defensive, or confrontive to avoid harm. The therapist and patient collaboratively make a majority of the decisions about therapy. However, therapists should be aware of a common compensatory strategy of some substance abuse patients to avoid either coming to therapy or bringing up their difficulties in abstaining from drug use. It is important, therefore, for the therapist to help the patient recognize in a nonconfrontive manner that the advantages of such avoidance are clearly and significantly overshadowed by the disadvantages.

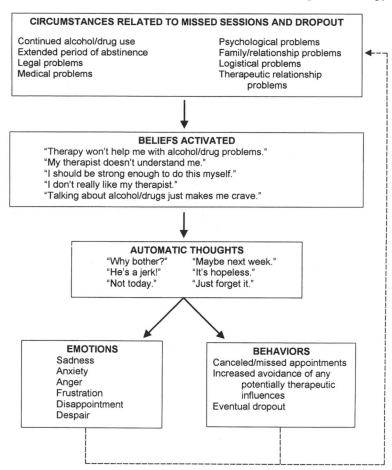

FIGURE 23.7. Cognitive conceptualization of missed sessions and dropout. From Liese and Beck (1997). Copyright 1997 by B. S. Liese. Reprinted by permission.

Principle 3: Cognitive Therapy Is Goal Oriented and Problem Focused

At an initial session and periodically after that, therapists ask patients to set goals. They guide patients to specify objectives in specific behavioral terms by asking, "How would you like to be different by the end of therapy and what would you like to be *doing* differently?" It is important for therapists to give substance abuse patients feedback about the reasonableness of their goals, as at times they have unrealistic expectations. Therapists also aid patients in identifying shorter-term goals and propose a process through which the patient can meet those goals.

For example, Kim's therapist helped her specify her longer-term goal of "being happy" in behavioral terms: getting a job she enjoyed, entering into a satisfying intimate relationship, getting along better with her family, and staying off drugs. He helped her set smaller goals along the way. A first step in getting a new job was to improve her attendance and performance at her current job so she could get a reasonable reference.

Therapists must also question patients about the degree to which they *really* want to meet their goals. A helpful technique is the advantage/disadvantage analysis (Figure 23.8) in which the therapist continually elicits from the patient and emphasizes the benefits of achieving a goal while eliciting and reframing (helping the patient develop a more functional view) the disadvantages.

For some patients, a goal of harm reduction is more acceptable, and more achievable, than complete abstinence (Des Jarlais, 1995; Marlatt, Larimer, Baer, & Quigley, 1993; Marlatt & Tapert, 1993). Occasional drug use can reinforce dysfunctional beliefs such as "I can't stop" or "Using is okay"; therefore complete abstinence is much more desirable. On the other hand, a significant decrease in drug use is obviously more desirable than early dropout from therapy, which can occur if the therapist tries too early, too soon, or too strongly to impose a total ban on taking drugs.

Principle 4: The Initial Focus of Therapy Is on the Present

Therapists initially emphasize current problems and specific situations that are distressing to the patient. When the patient has a comorbid diagnosis, it is important to address problems related to both. For example, Kim needed help in problem solving about a critical supervisor at work and in learning alternate coping strategies (instead of using drugs) when she was distressed about a work problem. She and her therapist discussed how to respond to the almost instantaneous hurt she felt when the supervisor rebuked her for lateness, how to decrease her anger by rehearsing a coping statement addressing her activated core belief, how to use anger management techniques such as controlled breathing and time out, and how to talk to the supervisor in a reasonable, effective manner (through role playing).

The therapist also elicited and helped Kim respond to automatic thoughts they predicted might interfere with her ability to use what she had learned in session. Through a combination of Socratic questioning and modeling, Kim learned to respond to a number of automatic thoughts ("I should tell him [supervisor] off" was followed by "He's just trying to do his job right; I don't have to take him so personally; I want to stay in control and keep this job; I can just say 'okay' for now and talk to [my therapist] about this problem." Toward the middle of therapy, when therapist and patient were evaluating and modifying Kim's beliefs, especially about herself and her relationship to other people, they began discussing her past as well—to see how she developed these ideas and how they related to her current difficulties.

Principle 5: Cognitive Therapy Is Time Sensitive

The course of therapy for many patients with substance abuse varies dramatically, depending on the severity and course of the substance use. Weekly

Advantages of Abstinence	Advantages of Taking Drugs (with reframe)
1. Feel better about myself. 2. Feel more in control. 3. Get to work on time. 4. More likely to keep my job. 5. Save money. 6. Better for my health. 7. Not get so criticized by my sister. 8. Not hang around other "druggies" so much. 9. Spend my time better.	1. Escape from feeling bad (**BUT** it's only a temporary escape and I don't really solve my problems). 2. Have people to hang out with (**BUT** they're druggies and I don't really like them). 3. It's hard work to quit (**BUT** I'll do it step-by-step with my therapist).
Disadvantages of Abstinence (with reframe)	**Disadvantages of Taking Drugs**
1. I may feel bored and anxious (**BUT** it's only temporary and it's good to learn to stand bad feelings). 2. I don't know what to do with my time (**BUT** I can learn in therapy how to spend time better). 3. I won't be able to hang out with my "friends" (**BUT** I do want to meet new "non-druggie" friends).	1. Seems to make me depressed. 2. Costs money. 3. Bad for my health. 4. Makes me feel like I'm not in control of my life. 5. Makes me feel unmotivated. 6. Hard to solve my real problems. 7. May make me lose my job. 8. Makes relationship with my sister worse. 9. Stops me from going out and making new friends. 10. Makes me feel like I'm wasting time. 11. Makes me feel stuck, like I'm not getting anywhere.

FIGURE 23.8. Advantages/disadvantages analysis.

sessions are recommended until symptoms are significantly reduced and substance use has diminished or stopped. With effective treatment, patients stabilize their moods, learn more tools, and gain confidence in their ability to use alternate coping strategies when in distress. At this point therapist and patient may experiment with spacing out therapy sessions. Typically they reduce the frequency of sessions from once a week to once every 2 weeks, then to once every 3 or 4 weeks, until termination (unless otherwise indicated). After termination, patients are advised to return to therapy when life stressors activate dysfunctional beliefs and they find they are tempted to resort to drug use again.

Principle 6: Therapy Sessions Are Structured, with Active Participation by Both Therapist and Patient

Typically, therapists try to adhere to a fairly fixed structure (unless such structure is interfering with the therapeutic alliance) to function efficiently during the session. Usually therapists first check their patients' mood (preferably eliciting a self-report as well as by using objective measures of depression, anxiety, and hopelessness). They inquire about patients' attributions for progress if they are improving, with the aim of reinforcing positive behaviors and thoughts that may have contributed to their improvement. At this point therapists also ask a standard question about the frequency and amount of substance use in the past week and elicit patients' feelings about coming to therapy that day.

Next the therapist and patient collaboratively set an agenda and decide which problem(s) to focus on in the session. Standard agenda items include the successes and difficulties the patient experienced during the past week in dealing with high-risk situations and cravings and upcoming situations that could lead to drug use or dropout.

The therapist then makes a bridge from the previous session or sessions, asking the patient to recall the important things they discussed and the conclusions they reached. If the patient has difficulty remembering the content, they collaboratively problem solve to make it more likely that the patient will be able to make better use of future sessions. Encouraging patients to record the most important points and to review these points during the week helps them integrate the lessons of therapy. Also, during this segment of the therapy session, the therapist reviews the therapy homework completed during the week, as well as inquiring about important events that occurred (positive and negative). When therapists suspect that patients have reacted badly to a previous session, they may ask for more feedback about the session.

Next, the therapist and patient collaboratively reprioritize topics on the agenda with a discussion of how to use the remaining time in the therapy session. Typically they decide to address drug-related and other topics of concern to the patient. As they discuss the first problem, they collect data about the problem, conceptualize how and why the problem arose, evaluate the patient's thoughts in or about the problematic situation, modify relevant dysfunctional beliefs, and do problem solving as needed. In the context of discussing this problem, the therapist teaches the patient needed skills: interpersonal skills (e.g., communication and assertion skills), mood management skills (e.g., relaxation, dysphoria tolerance, and anger management), behavioral skills (e.g., alternate behaviors when cravings start or intensify), and cognitive skills (e.g., modifying dysfunctional ideas through worksheets or reading coping cards).

Homework is collaboratively set and individually designed, based on the problem(s) discussed in sessions. Typically, it includes monitoring drug use and dysphoria, responding to automatic thoughts and beliefs, practicing skills learned in session, and following through on problem solving discussed in session.

Throughout the session, the therapist summarizes the material the patient has presented and checks on the patient's comprehension by asking what the "main message" has been in their discussion. At the end of the session the therapist or patient summarizes what occurred during the session, checking that the patient understands and is likely to do the agreed-on homework. Finally, the therapist asks for feedback about the session. Skillful, empathic questioning to elicit the patient's honest reaction to the session and nondefensive, problem-solving-oriented responses by the therapist facilitate greater progress and lessen the chance of dropout.

Adhering to this structure has many benefits: The most important issues will be discussed, there will be needed continuity between sessions, drug use will be monitored and attended to, and problems will be tackled head on. In addition, the structure facilitates patients' learning of necessary skills and increases the likelihood that they will be equipped to exercise alternative behaviors and deal with challenges in the coming week. The structure also ensures that patient and therapist share an understanding of the most important lessons of the session and that the patient is given the essential opportunity to provide feedback so therapy can be modified to make it most useful to the patient.

Principle 7: Patients Are Taught to Identify, Evaluate, and Respond to Their Dysfunctional Thoughts and Beliefs

The therapist emphasizes the cognitive model at each session—that the patients' thoughts in specific situations influence how they react emotionally, physiologically, and behaviorally and that by evaluating and correcting their dysfunctional thinking, they can feel better and behave more functionally. The therapist does not assume a priori that any given automatic thought is distorted; instead, the therapist and patient collaboratively investigate the degree to which a given thought is valid or not. When thoughts *are* accurate (e.g., "I want a fix."), they either do problem solving (discuss ways to respond to the thought and alternate courses of action) or explore the validity of the conclusion the patient has drawn (e.g., "Wanting a fix shows how weak I am and I might as well give in."). When evaluating thoughts and beliefs, the therapist primarily uses questioning rather than telling or persuading the patient, and standard tools such as the Dysfunctional Thought Record (J. S. Beck, 1995) are used whenever appropriate.

Principle 8: Cognitive Therapy Emphasizes Psychoeducation and Relapse Prevention

From the first session on, the therapist keeps in mind what is important for patients to learn in the session and how to maximize the possibility of their retaining this knowledge in the coming week and in the future. The therapist encourages patients to write down important points during or at the end of the session or does the writing for them if necessary. When patients are illiterate, the therapist must use ingenuity to create a system for helping the patients remember what they need (e.g., audiotaping the session or a brief summary of the session, illustrating important points in pictorial form, or brainstorming whom the patient might ask to read therapy notes).

The therapist not only tries a number of interventions with patients to help them change their thinking, mood, and behavior but also teaches *them* how to use these strategies themselves. For example, the therapist teaches Kim how to identify her negative thoughts when she feels dysphoric, how to test and respond to these thoughts, how to examine advantages and disadvantages of behaviors, how to use alternate coping strategies when she experiences urgings and cravings, how to communicate more effectively with people, how to plan her day to avoid high-risk situations, and many more cognitive, behavioral, mood-stabilizing, and general life skills.

Prior to termination, therapist and patient use a variety of strategies to minimize the risk of relapse. They review the important skills the patient learned; they predict upcoming difficulties and do advance problem solving; they note early warning signs of a potential lapse; they discuss how to limit a possible, and in some cases, a probable, lapse so it does not turn into a relapse. They also collaboratively agree on the point at which the patient needs to return to therapy, that is, the signs that a lapse or relapse is imminent (instead of waiting until the patient hits rock bottom). Finally, they develop a plan for patients to continue to work on their long-term goals by themselves or, preferably, with the support of friends or family.

TREATMENT PLANNING

The first step in treatment planning is completing a thorough diagnostic assessment based on criteria according to the fourth edition of the *Diagnostic and Statistical Manual of Mental Disorders* (DSM-IV; American Psychiatric Association, 1994). It is essential to ascertain the presence of comorbid Axis I and Axis II disorders as well as medical complications.

According to one study (Regier et al., 1990), over a third of patients with a substance use disorder also had a concurrent Axis I disorder. The treatment plan should address both. For example, Kim's therapist conceptualized that she was at least in part medicating her depression through the use of marijuana. In addition to treating her substance use, the therapist also initially focused treatment on the depression itself, using standard cognitive therapy to reduce her depressive symptomatology: activity monitoring and scheduling, identifying and responding to her negative cognitions (e.g., "I can't do anything right." "I'm such a failure." "What's the use [of trying to feel better,]"), and active problem solving (e.g., about work problems, about loneliness, about inactivity), among others (see A. T. Beck et al., 1979; J. S. Beck, 1995).

Kim also had an Axis II diagnosis: avoidant personality disorder with dependent and borderline features. One important implication of her personality makeup was the strong likelihood that highly dysfunctional, negative beliefs (e.g., "I am helpless; I am vulnerable; I am bad") might arise in the therapy session itself. Her therapist planned treatment to avoid intense schema activation early in therapy that might have led to early dropout.

A second important step in treatment planning is conceptualizing the patient's motivation for change. Prochaska and colleagues (Prochaska & DiClemente, 1986; Prochaska, Norcross, & DiClemente, 1994; Prochaska,

DiClemente, & Norcross, 1992) describe five stages of change. In developing a treatment plan, the therapist needs to identify whether patients are at the precontemplation stage (in which they are only minimally, if at all, distressed about their problems and have little motivation to change), the contemplation stage (in which they have sufficient motivation to consider their problems and think about change, although not necessarily enough motivation to take constructive action), the preparation stage (in which they do want help to make changes but may not feel they know what to do), the action stage (in which they actually do start to change their behavior), or the maintenance stage (in which they are motivated to continue to change).

Kim, for example, was at the contemplation stage when she entered therapy. Her therapist helped her identify the difficulties associated with her substance use, some of which she had avoided focusing on before therapy. Her therapist also helped her do an advantage/disadvantage analysis of using versus abstaining from marijuana (Figure 23.8). Her therapist helped her "reframe" or find a functional response to her dysfunctional ideas of not changing. These kinds of techniques helped move Kim from the contemplation to the preparation stage. Had her therapist started with a treatment plan that emphasized immediate change of substance use behaviors, it is likely that Kim would have resisted, tried only halfheartedly, or dropped out of therapy altogether.

Part of every treatment plan involves socializing patients to the cognitive model so that they begin to view their reactions as stemming from their (often distorted) perceptions of situations. Once her therapist taught her to ask herself what was going through her mind just before she reached for a joint or when she felt dysphoric, Kim was able to understand how her automatic thoughts influenced her emotional and behavioral reaction. Later her therapist taught her how to identify the more complex sequence (Figure 23.5) leading to drug use and helped her identify specifically how she could intervene at each stage.

An essential element in treatment planning is taking into consideration the strength of the therapeutic alliance. Substance abuse patients often enter treatment with dysfunctional beliefs about the therapist or the therapy, such as:

"My therapist may try to force me to do things I don't want to."
"This therapy may do me more harm than good."
"He probably thinks he's some expert who knows everything."
"He'll be pushy and controlling."
"He'll think I'm a failure if I ever use again."
"I'm better off without therapy."

The treatment plan should include the identification and testing of these dysfunctional beliefs. Left unaddressed, patients may prematurely drop out.

A good treatment plan also specifies patients' specific problems (or, positively framed, their goals) and the concrete steps therapist and patient will take to ameliorate them. Kim and her therapist discussed her work difficulties. They did a combination of problem solving and correcting distortions in her thinking around getting to work on time, coping with boredom on the job, receiving undue criticism, and relating better to her coworkers. Eventually, however, she did seek a new job, when it became clear that the disadvantages of the job (low pay, lack of stimulation, lack of positive reinforcement, lack of upward opportunity) still outweighed the positive aspects, and her therapist helped and encouraged her in the job search.

The work problem was one of the first difficulties they tackled because Kim was motivated to work on it, because losing this job would have put Kim at higher risk of increased substance use, because she was already turning to marijuana to cope with her dissatisfaction and dysphoria engendered by work, and because it seemed likely that she and the therapist could make a positive impact on her work difficulties in a short period. Other problems they also addressed early in therapy were associated with alleviating depression, as mentioned earlier. Later in therapy they did problem solving about situations that were more chronic and less acute in nature: getting along better with her family, meeting new friends, and developing broader interests and sources of satisfaction.

Her therapist continuously assessed Kim's stage of readiness to change her substance abuse behavior by measuring the strength of her beliefs. At the beginning of therapy she believed that her marijuana use might contribute to her difficulties at work, her general isolation from people, and her lack of motivation. However, she also believed that nothing, including therapy, could help. After several weeks, she began to see things differently, especially when she recognized that some initial behavioral activation and responding to automatic thoughts improved her mood. At this point, she was ready to conceptualize in specific instances how she came to use marijuana, to start monitoring her substance use, to learn strategies to manage her cravings, to avoid high-risk situations, to respond to her drug-related beliefs, to join a self-help group, and to make some lifestyle changes. These strategies are described next.

Teaching Patients to Observe Drug Use Sequences

Kim's therapist used a blank version of Figure 23.5, asking Kim to fill in the boxes after thinking about a typical recent episode of marijuana use. For the first time it became clear to Kim that her behavior was at least somewhat voluntary. Previously she had believed that her drug use was completely out of her control.

The therapist reviewed with Kim how a typical activating stimulus gave rise to negative thoughts, which led to feelings of hopelessness. They discussed how in the future she could learn to intervene. First, she could respond to her negative thoughts and thereby reduce her dysphoria. If she failed to do so, she could still respond to her drug-related beliefs. She could, for example, read a coping card they would develop in session. Such a coping card might contain "things to do if I want to smoke." These coping cards are not merely affirmations but jointly composed statements that the patient strongly endorses in session. They might include such practical behaviors as the following:

1. Go for a walk.
2. Call a friend on the phone.
3. Go out for coffee.
4. Watch a videotaped movie.
5. Read my Narcotics Anonymous book.

If Kim's automatic thoughts about drug use continued, she would have another opportunity to respond. Upon experiencing urges and cravings, she could instruct herself to ignore these sensations and/or she could distract herself. For example, she might create a coping card that said:

"If I feel cravings, *they are just cravings*. I don't have to pay attention to them. They'll definitely go away. I can stand them. I've stood lots of cravings in the past. I'll be *very* glad in a few minutes that I ignored them. Every time I ignore them, I get stronger!"

If she recognized her permission-giving beliefs, she could read another coping card that might say:

"Don't reach for a joint. Wait 5 minutes. You are strong enough to wait. In the meantime, do the things on my TO DO LIST."

If she found herself focusing on instrumental strategies to get drugs, she could enforce another waiting period or do other tasks, outlined in therapy. A careful analysis of the drug-taking sequence, along with potential interventions, gave Kim hope that she could conquer this problem.

Kim and her therapist collaboratively developed the coping cards over the course of several sessions. First they discussed what Kim wished she would be able to tell herself at each stage. Before writing the coping cards, the therapist asked Kim how much she believed each statement. When the strength of her belief was less than 90–100%, they reworded the statement or discussed it further to increase its validity in her mind. Her therapist conceptualized that if Kim did not believe an idea quite strongly in session, it was quite unlikely that the card could have a sufficiently strong impact on her in the presence of activating stimuli.

Monitoring Progress

Therapist and patient monitor progress in several ways. Most obvious is the patient's self-report of drug use, which the therapist elicits at each session. Urine and breathalyzer tests can be useful in motivating patients to decrease their use and to increase the veracity of their self-reports. When patients do use, they are encouraged to see such use not as an indication of outright failure but, rather, as an opportunity to learn from the experience and to make future abstinence more likely. Standardized self-report instruments such as the Timeline Followback (Sobell & Sobell, 1993) or Form 90 (Miller, 1996) are often used; the Addiction Severity Index (McLellan, Luborsky, Woody, & O'Brien, 1980; McLellan, 1992) is also a useful tool. Of course, monitoring drug use by reports from others, such as family members or probation officers, is frequently appropriate.

When a patient has a comorbid Axis I disorder, progress is also measured by standard instruments such as the Beck Depression Inventory (A. T. Beck & Steer, 1993b), Beck Anxiety Inventory (A. T. Beck & Steer, 1993a), and Beck Hopelessness Scale (A. T. Beck & Steer, 1988). Lowered test scores provide an opportunity for the therapist to reinforce the positive changes patients have made in their thinking and behavior in the past week. High test scores raise a red flag, and careful questioning about events and perceptions in the past week often reveals important agenda items that need to be discussed to prevent a possible resumption of drug use in the coming week.

It is also important for the therapist to monitor how patients have been spending their time on an ongoing basis. Kim, for example, made some important changes early in therapy: spending less time passively watching television alone and not visiting with drug-abusing friends. Had her therapist not been vigilant in checking on the maintenance of these improvements, he would not have discovered significant backsliding many weeks later, which potentially could have led to a lapse or relapse.

Another important facet of monitoring is ongoing assessment of the strength of old, dysfunctional beliefs and of the new, more functional ideas. At each session, the therapist assessed how much Kim believed such drug-related ideas as "I can't stand to feel bored" and "Smoking marijuana is the only way for me to feel better," and how much she believed the new ideas they had collaboratively developed, such as "My life will get better if I don't use"; "I can feel better by answering my negative thoughts and doing things on my Things To Do card." This ongoing monitoring again helped the therapist to intervene at an early level when Kim's dysfunctional beliefs occasionally resurfaced strongly.

Dealing with High-Risk Situations

Marlatt and Gordon (1985) observed that exposure to activating stimuli, or triggers, makes drug abuse patients more likely to use. In a high-risk situation, activating stimuli trigger drug-related beliefs and automatic thoughts, leading to urges and cravings. These stimuli are idiosyncratic to the patient; what triggers one patient may not activate dysfunctional beliefs and cravings in the next person.

Activating stimuli can be internal (within the individual) or external. Internal cues include dysphoric mood states such as depression, anxiety, loneliness, frustration, or boredom or physical factors such as pain, hunger, fatigue, or uncomfortable sensations. Although many patients use drugs to regulate their negative moods (i.e., to feel less dysphoric), many also use drugs when they already feel good to "celebrate" or feel great.

External cues occur outside the individual: people, places, or things related to drug use, such as interpersonal discord or seeing drugs or drug paraphernalia. In one study, Marlatt and colleagues (Cummings, Gordon, & Marlatt, 1980) found that 35% of relapses in their sample were precipitated by negative emotional states, 20% by social pressure, and 16% by interpersonal conflict.

The therapist helps patients identify the high-risk situations in which their drug-related beliefs and cravings are likely to occur. They are encouraged to avoid these situations and are taught interpersonal skills to handle conflict and pressure to use. These behavioral changes are insufficient, however, in significantly reducing or eliminating drug use or relapse. Modification of drug-related beliefs is essential.

Dealing with Cravings and Urges

Patients should learn both cognitive and behavioral techniques to deal with cravings. Distraction techniques are usually helpful and patients should devise a list of things they can easily arrange to do (e.g., exercise, read, and talk to a friend on the telephone). Thought stopping can reduce urges. Snapping a rubber band on her wrist and yelling "Stop!" while envisioning a stop sign helped Kim deal with her craving.

The therapist should aid patients in identifying their specific beliefs that encourage the use of drugs to deal with cravings, for example, "I can't stand it [the craving]"; "If I have cravings, I have to give in" (A. T. Beck et al., 1993; Liese & Franz, 1996). Socratic questioning, examining past experiences of resisting craving, reflecting on the relative difficulty versus impossibility of tolerating cravings, and other standard cognitive techniques help modify these dysfunctional ideas.

Case Management and Lifestyle Change

Helping patients solve their real-life problems is an essential part of cognitive therapy. Patients who abuse drugs often have complex health-related, legal, employment, housing, and/or family difficulties. Therapists should refer patients for specialized assistance when needed. Therefore, they need to be aware of community resources and available social services. Sometimes the therapist can help patients identify people in their family or social network who can help them work through their practical problems.

In some cases, however, it is desirable or necessary for the therapist to help patients directly in session to take needed steps to improve their lives. Examining employment ads in the local newspaper, for example, or completing necessary forms (for public assistance, medical or legal services, or public housing) with the patient is often an enormous help and an important part of treatment.

Some degree of lifestyle change is usually necessary for substance abuse patients to reduce or eliminate their substance use and to maintain their progress. Often the therapist needs to help the patient repair important supportive relationships and/or to develop new relationships with individuals who do not use. Many substance abusers are deficient in interpersonal skills and need to learn these skills through discussion and role playing in session. Patients often have dysfunctional beliefs about relationships as well, and modification of these beliefs is a necessary step in improving how they relate to others.

Patients sometimes need help in identifying how and where they can start building a new, nonusing network of friends. The therapist can facilitate the initiation or reestablishment of contact with nonusers in the patient's current environment as well as encouraging the patient to engage in new activities, identified in session, where he or she can meet new people.

Appropriate self-help groups can be a valuable adjunct to therapy—for meeting new nonusing people, for reinforcing more functional beliefs, and for encouraging a healthier lifestyle. Therapists should be aware of self-help groups in their area and encourage patients to attend when appropriate. Alcoholics Anonymous, Narcotics Anonymous, Rational Recovery, and Moderation Management are a few examples of groups that can be of significant benefit to patients. Therapists can help patients who are reluctant to attend self-help groups or to try new activities by eliciting their automatic thoughts and aiding them in evaluating and responding to these thoughts. Problem solving may be needed to help the patient choose appropriate groups or activities, find transportation, and manage anxiety about trying new experiences.

Reducing Dropout

Recent studies have shown that approximately 30% to 60% of substance abuse patients drop out of therapy (Wierzbicki & Pekarik, 1993). Many factors account for such a high rate, including continued substance use; legal, medical, or psychological problems; difficulties in family or other relationships; practical problems (e.g., transportation, finances, or time availability); dissatisfaction with therapy; and problems with the therapeutic alliance (Liese & Beck, 1997). Early in therapy, therapist and patient should predict potential difficulties that might interfere with regular attendance in therapy and either problem solve in advance or collaboratively develop a plan for regular contact (usually by phone) if the patient misses a session.

Kim's therapist, for example, helped her with such practical problems as a changing work schedule and difficulties with transportation, which otherwise would have impeded her coming to therapy. Both straightforward problem solving and responding to her negative thinking ("I'll be too tired to come after work"; "It's not worth taking two buses to get to therapy") were necessary to avert missed sessions.

To maximize patients' regular attendance, the therapist needs to monitor the strength of the therapeutic relationship at each session. Negative changes in patients' body language, tone of voice, and degree of openness usually signal that their dysfunctional beliefs (about themselves, therapy, or the therapist) have been activated. A list of 50 common beliefs leading to missed sessions and dropout (Liese & Beck, 1997) is a valuable guide for therapists.

Eliciting and testing the patient's negative thoughts and beliefs on the spot often prevents a negative reaction which otherwise might have resulted in the patient's not showing up for the subsequent session. Kim had many such cognitions, especially early in therapy: "I'm not smart enough for this kind of therapy." "I can't do this stuff." A therapist who still suspects a patient may miss the next session may be able to turn the tide by phoning the patient the day before or the day of the session and demonstrating care and concern.

Starting to formulate an accurate cognitive case conceptualization of the patient from the very first contact enables the therapist to plan therapy and specific interventions in such a way as to avoid inadvertent activation of dysfunctional beliefs in and between sessions. Kim's therapist, for example, soon recognized how overwhelmed Kim became when faced with even minor challenges. He therefore took special care to explain concepts simply, to limit the amount of material presented each session, to check on her level of understanding frequently, and to suggest homework assignments that she believed she was capable of carrying out. In these ways, the therapist was able to avoid undue activation of Kim's beliefs of helplessness and inadequacy and to maintain her attendance in therapy.

CONCLUSION

Cognitive therapy can be an effective treatment for substance abuse patients. It requires an accurate conceptualization of the patient, a sound treatment plan based on this case formulation, a strong therapeutic relationship, and specialized interventions. Structuring the therapy session, emphasizing problem solving of current difficulties, educating patients about the sequence of their drug use, identifying and planning for high-risk situations, ongoing monitoring of drug use, facilitating lifestyle change, and intensive case management are important facets of treatment.

Kim could easily have become an unemployed "revolving door" user and a burden to family, friends, and society. Effective treatment allowed her to engage in therapy; work through dysfunctional beliefs about herself and the therapist; develop functional, reasonable goals; and learn myriad skills to solve problems, tolerate negative emotion, persist when she felt hopeless, engage in alternative behaviors when she craved drugs, and develop a healthier lifestyle. Hard work by both the therapist and substance abuse patient can pay off handsomely.

REFERENCES

American Psychiatric Association. (1994). *Diagnostic and statistical manual of mental disorders* (4th ed.). Washington, DC: Author.

Beck, A. T., Emery, G., with Greenberg, R. L. (1985). *Anxiety disorders and phobias: A cognitive perspective.* New York: Basic Books.

Beck, A. T., Freeman, A., & Associates (1990). *Cognitive therapy of personality disorders.* New York: Guilford Press.

Beck, A. T., Rush, A. J., Shaw, B. F., & Emery, G. (1979). *Cognitive therapy of depression.* New York: Guilford Press.

Beck, A. T., & Steer, R. A. (1988). *Beck Hopelessness Scale manual.* San Antonio, TX: Psychological Corporation.

Beck, A. T., & Steer, R. A. (1993a). *Beck Anxiety Inventory manual.* San Antonio, TX: Psychological Corporation.

Beck, A. T., & Steer, R. A. (1993b). *Beck Depression Inventory manual.* San Antonio, TX: Psychological Corporation.

Beck, A. T., Wright, F. D., Newman, C. F., & Liese, B. S. (1993). *Cognitive therapy of substance abuse.* New York: Guilford Press.

Beck, J. S. (1995). *Cognitive therapy: Basics and beyond.* New York: Guilford Press.

Cummings, C., Gordon, J. R., & Marlatt, G. A. (1980). Relapse: Prevention and prediction. In W. R. Miller (Ed.), *The addictive behaviors: Treatment of alcoholism, drug abuse, smoking and obesity* (pp. 291–321). Oxford: Pergamon Press.

Des Jarlais, D. C. (1995). Editorial: Harm reduction—A framework for incorporating science into drug policy. *American Journal of Public Health, 85,* 10–12.

Gilbert, M., Fine, S., & Haley, G. (1994). Factors associated with dropout from group psychotherapy with depressed adolescents. *Canadian Journal of Psychiatry, 39,* 358–359.

Liese, B. S. (1993). The KUFP five-visit quit smoking program: An office-based smoking cessation protocol. *Kansas Medicine, 94,* 294–298.

Liese, B. S. (1994a). Psychological principles of substance abuse: A brief overview. *Comprehensive Therapy, 20,* 125–129.

Liese, B. S. (1994b). Brief therapy, crisis intervention, and the cognitive therapy of substance abuse. *Crisis Intervention, 1*(1), 11–29.

Liese, B. S., & Beck, A. T. (1997). Back to basics: Fundamental cognitive therapy skills for keeping drug-dependent individuals in treatment. In L. S. Onken, J. D. Blaine, & J. J. Boren (Eds.), *Beyond the therapeutic alliance: Keeping drug-dependent individuals in treatment* (NIDA Research Monograph No. 165, DHHS Publication No. 97-4142, pp. 207–230). Washington, DC: U.S. Government Printing Office.

Liese, B. S., & Franz, R. A. (1996). Treating substance use disorders with cognitive therapy: Lessons learned and implications for the future. In P. Salkovskis (Ed.), *Frontiers of cognitive therapy* (pp. 470–508). New York: Guilford Press.

Liese, B. S., & Najavits, L. M. (1997). Cognitive and behavioral therapies of substance abuse. In J. H. Lowinson, P. Ruiz, R. B. Millman, & J. G. Langrod (Eds.), *Substance abuse: A comprehensive textbook* (pp. 467–478). Baltimore: Williams & Wilkins.

MacNair, R. R., & Corazzini, J. G. (1994). Client factors influencing group therapy dropout. *Psychotherapy, 31,* 352–362.

Marlatt, G. A., & Gordon, J. R. (Eds.). (1985). *Relapse prevention: Maintenance strategies in the treatment of addictive behavior.* New York: Guilford Press.

Marlatt, G. A., & Gordon, J. R. (1989). Relapse prevention: Future directions. In M. Gossop (Ed.), *Relapse and addictive behavior* (pp. 279–291). London: Routledge.

Marlatt, G. A., Larimer, M. E., Baer, J. S., & Quigley, L. A. (1993). Harm reduction for alcohol problems: Moving beyond the controlled drinking controversy. *Behavior Therapy, 24,* 461–504.

Marlatt, G. A., & Tapert, S. F. (1993). Harm reduction: Reducing the risks of addictive behaviors. In J. Baer, G. Marlatt, & R. McMahon (Eds.), *Addictive behaviors across the lifespan* (pp. 243–273). Newbury Park, CA: Sage.

McLellan, A. T., Luborsky, L., Woody, G. E., & O'Brien, C. P. (1980). An improved diagnostic evaluation instrument for substance abuse patients. *Journal of Nervous and Mental Disease, 168,* 26–33.

McLellan, A. T., Kushner, H., Metzger, D., Peters, R., Smith, L., Grissom, G., Pettinati, H., & Argeriou, M. (1992). The fifth edition of the Addiction Severity Index: Historical critique and normative data. *Journal of Substance Abuse Treatment, 9,* 199–213.

Miller, W. R. (1996). *Form 90: A structured assessment interview for drinking and related behaviors* (NIAAA Project MATCH Monograph Series, Vol. 5). Washington, DC: U.S. Department of Health and Human Services.

Prochaska, J. O., & DiClemente, C. C. (1986). Toward a comprehensive model of change. In W. Miller & H. Heather (Eds.), *Treating addictive behaviors: Processes of change* (pp. 3–27). New York: Plenum Press.

Prochaska, J. O., DiClemente, C. C., & Norcross, J. C. (1992). In search of how people change: Applications to addictive behaviors. *American Psychologist, 47,* 1102–1114.

Prochaska, J. O., Norcross, J. C., & DiClemente, C. C. (1994). *Changing for good.* New York: William Morrow.

Regier, D. A., Farmer, M. E., Rae, D. S., Locke, B. Z., Keith, S. J., Judd, L. L., & Goodwin, F. K. (1990). Comorbidity of mental disorders with alcohol an other drug abuse: Results from the Epidemiologic Catchment Area (ECA) study. *Journal of the American Medical Association, 264,* 2511–2518.

Sobell, M. B., & Sobell, L. C. (1993). *Problem drinkers: Guided self-change treatment.* New York: Guilford Press.

Swett, C., & Noones, J. (1989). Factors associated with premature termination from outpatient treatment. *Hospital and Community Psychiatry, 40,* 947–951.

Wierzbicki, M., & Pekarik, G. (1993). A meta-analysis of psychotherapy dropout. *Professional Psychology: Research and Practice, 24,* 190–195.

Wright, F. D., Beck, A. T., Newman, C. F., & Liese, B. S. (1992). Cognitive therapy of substance abuse: Theoretical rationale. In L. S. Onken, J. D. Blaine, & J. J. Boren (Eds.), *Behavioral treatments for drug abuse and dependence* (NIDA Research Monograph No. 137, DHHS Publication No. 93-3684, pp. 123–146). Washington, DC: U.S. Government Printing Office.

24

Primary Care
Office Management

DAVID C. LEWIS
LESLIE CHERNEN

INTRODUCTION

Primary care physicians can play a pivotal role in the detection, management, and referral of patients with substance use problems. During this era of close medical cost management and rising specialist care costs, there has been increased interest in the early identification and intervention at the primary care level in alcohol, tobacco, and other drug problems (Lewis, 1997; Wright, 1995) because the routine involvement of primary care medical practitioners in the detection and management of substance use disorders can lead to considerable health, social, and economic gains (Aronson, 1995; Chappel, 1992; Lewis, 1997; Roche & Richard, 1991). Realizing these gains requires close attention to the needs of physicians, different types of patients, and the service delivery organizations.

Several influences from these three groups led to the recent focus on the screening, diagnosis, intervention and referral of substance use disorders in primary care settings, including the following:

- Realization that much of the social and economic costs of substance use disorders are not from dependent users but from harmful and "at risk" use, a patient population that sees primary care physicians frequently and addiction specialists rarely.

- A critical mass of data showing that brief intervention approaches are effective.
- Development of specific techniques for brief intervention and motivational (rather than confrontational) approaches to medical interviewing.
- An interest in early behavioral interventions by managed care organizations and the integration of behavioral delivery systems with primary care.
- Recognition of the enormous toll caused by undiagnosed and untreated drug and alcohol problems.
- Renewed interest in ensuring training concerning the screening, diagnosis, intervention, and referral of substance use disorders by all primary care physicians.
- Greater attention to differential and early diagnosis of dual/coexisting disorders, particularly substance abuse and coincident psychiatric disorders and infectious diseases (e.g., human immunodeficiency virus (HIV), tuberculosis, and hepatitis).

An impressive array of recently published materials backs up this attention to primary care: the *Diagnostic and Statistical Manual of Mental Disorders* (4th ed.)—*Primary Care Version* (American Psychiatric Association, 1995a); the *Physicians' Guide to Helping Patients with Alcohol Problems,* and accompanying training materials (National Institute on Alcohol Abuse and Alcoholism, 1995); *Patient Placement Criteria—PPC-2* (American Society of Addiction Medicine, 1996) and detoxification guidelines (Mayo-Smith, 1997); *Practice Guideline for the Treatment of Patients with Substance Use Disorders* (American Psychiatric Association, 1995b), *Alcoholism in the Elderly: Diagnosis, Treatment, Prevention—Guidelines for Primary Care Physicians* (American Medical Association, 1995); a Macy conference report entitled *Training about Alcohol and Substance Abuse for All Primary Care Physicians* (Sirica, 1995); a supplement to the *American Journal on Addictions* entitled "Identification and Treatment of Substance Abuse in Primary Care Settings" (American Academy of Addiction Psychiatry, 1996), and *Alcohol and Other Substance Abuse* (Samet, O'Conner, & Stein, 1997), a volume of the *Medical Clinics of North America.*

ROLE OF THE PHYSICIANS

In 1992, more than 100,000 deaths reportedly were due to alcohol abuse and 30,000 deaths to illegal drug use (McGinnis & Foege, 1993). Substance use problems also cause a significant number of traumatic accidents (Israel et al., 1996). Further, intravenous drug use, specifically needle sharing, is a major factor in HIV transmission, hepatitis B and C, and bacterial infection (Iber, 1991; Lewis, 1997). Consequently, changing these health-related behavioral problems presents an opportunity for the medical practitioner, who can address both the substance use etiology and the numerous associated medical complications. Moreover, clear demonstration of the cost benefits of early diagnosis and treatment for substance use disorders, coupled with the huge financial and social toll that undiagnosed and untreated substance use problems generate (Lewis, 1997), should help overcome barriers to the primary care physicians' full participation in this important health domain.

Studies in medical, surgical, and gynecological practices indicate that the prevalence of substance abuse among patients ranges from 20% to 50% (Fleming, Barry, Davis, Kahn, & Rivo, 1994a). The primary health care physician makes initial contact with this wide section of the population requiring services (Israel et al., 1996; Sanson-Fisher, Webb, & Reid, 1986). The physician also encounters many patients with multiple substance use problems and coincident substance use and psychiatric disorders (Helzer & Pryzbeck, 1988). The Epidemiologic Catchment Area survey further revealed that 45% of adults diagnosed as alcohol dependent had additional substance abuse diagnoses (21.5%) or mental disorders (36.6%). The most common problems are (in descending order) anxiety, antisocial personality, and affective disorders (Regier et al., 1990). The National Comorbidity Study affirmed the common overlap of diagnoses, finding that the diagnosis of alcohol dependency coexisted with anxiety disorders 36.9% of the time and with affective disorders 29.2% of the time (Kessler et al., 1996).

Defining the primary diagnosis is often a difficult clinical question, particularly with patients who meet criteria for depression and affective disorder and are alcohol dependent. Some studies demonstrated that alcoholics who met the criteria for major depressive disorder did not do so after detoxification from alcohol (Schuckit, 1988). A useful summary on the subject of dual diagnosis in primary care can be found in the recently published *The Medical Clinics of North America* (Ziedonis & Brady, 1997).

Screening for Substance Use Disorders

Studies suggest that despite the high use of primary care facilities by substance-abusing patients (Coleman & Veach, 1990), physicians frequently do not detect substance use problems (Deitz, Rohde, Bertolucci, & Dufour, 1994). This detection inadequacy appears to result from ineffective screening (Duszynski, Nieto, & Valente, 1995). Physicians are most likely to collect information about smoking, followed by alcohol consumption and over-the-counter drugs. They least often inquire about illicit drugs (Telfer & Clulow, 1990). In addition, physicians need to be alert to substance use disorders related to prescription drug misuse (Parran, 1997) and problematic pain management (Stimmel, 1997).

Detection rates for smoking are approximately 50%, for alcohol abuse/dependency about 20–50%, and for illegal drug use about 20% (Deitz et al., 1994; DeWeese, 1994; Duszynski et al., 1995). Physician reports of the number of patients actually screened remain well below national prevalence rates (Linn, Yager, & Leake, 1990). Physicians are more likely to be aware of substance abuse problems if these problems were previously diagnosed by another physician (Linn et al., 1990).

Specific guidelines coupled with training should improve the screening and diagnosis rates. One example, *A Physicians' Guide to Helping Patients with Alcohol Problems,* is available through the National Institute on Alcohol Abuse and Alcoholism (NIAAA; 1995). This work, prepared by an interdisciplinary group of researchers and health professionals, is based on a decade of research on the health risks associated with alcohol use and on the effectiveness of alcohol screening and intervention. It makes the following suggestions about how the physician should approach a patient with a potential drinking problem.

The guidelines first define moderate drinking as < 2 drinks/day for men and < 1 drink/day for women and all persons over 65. They define "at risk drinking" as > 14 drinks/week or > 4 drinks on occasion for men and > 7 drinks/week or > 3 drinks/occasion for women (National Institute on Alcohol Abuse and Alcoholism, 1995). The guidelines then suggest a four-step process for at risk drinkers (see Figure 24.1):

ASK about alcohol use.

ASSESS for alcohol-related problems.

ADVISE appropriate action (i.e., set a drinking goal, abstain, or obtain alcohol treatment).

MONITOR patient progress.

For screening, the simple four-item CAGE questionnaire is employed:

1. Have you ever felt you should Cut down on your drinking?
2. Have people Annoyed you by criticizing your drinking?
3. Have you ever felt bad or Guilty about drinking?
4. Have you ever taken a drink first thing in the morning (Eye-opener) to steady your nerves or get rid of a hangover?

One or more positive responses to the CAGE questionnaire alert the clinician to the need for a more complete diagnostic evaluation. Specifically, the sensitivity is 86–90% and specificity is 52–93% for one positive answer; the sensitivity is 74–78% and specificity is 76–96% for two positive answers (Schorling & Buchsbaum, 1997).

There may be additional difficulties in detecting substance-abusing patients due to the vague somatic symptoms or complicating chronic medical illnesses (Bridges & Goldberg, 1985; Katon, 1992). When patients report emotional symptoms, physicians are more likely to diagnose a psychiatric disorder (Katon, 1992). Moreover, patients do not typically initiate discussion of emotional concerns or substance abuse with their physicians (Ford, Kamerow, & Thompson, 1988). When medical practitioners fail to inquire about these issues, substance use problems remain unidentified. In addition,

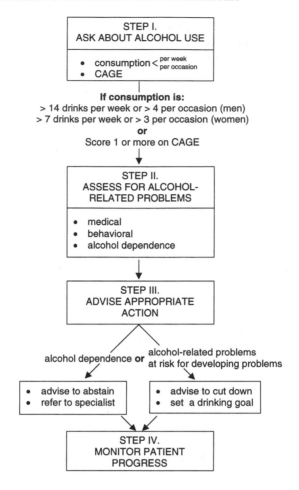

FIGURE 24.1. Approach to alcohol screening and brief intervention for physicians developed by the National Institute on Alcohol Abuse and Alcoholism.

when patients present with a substance use disorder and a medical condition, the medical condition is usually diagnosed correctly, whereas the signs and symptoms of a substance use disorder can be ignored (Deitz et al., 1994).

The frequent coexistence of substance use and psychiatric disorders and the fact that one disorder can masquerade or modify the course of the other have led to an increased and productive collaboration among primary care disciplines and psychiatry. Indicative of collaborative effort between the American Psychiatric Association (APA) and the primary care specialties is the newly issued *Diagnostic and Statistical Manual of Mental Disorders* (4th ed.)—*Primary Care Version* (American Psychiatric Association, 1995a), which proposes the following problematic substance use algorithm to be used in primary care settings.

Presenting symptoms might include the following:

- Impaired control of substance use (e.g., continued use despite knowledge of problems caused by substance).
- Guilt or regret about use, efforts to cut down, complaints or concern from others.
- Recent substance use (including medication) with resultant neurological symptoms (e.g., tremors, seizures), cardiovascular symptoms (e.g., elevated blood pressure or pulse), confusion, anxiety, sleep disturbance, depressed mood, or sexual dysfunction.
- Psychosocial dysfunction (e.g., family conflict) related to substance use.
- Tolerance (e.g., need for increasing amounts to achieve effect).

Treatment involves several steps:

Step 1. Consider the *general medical conditions and other mental disorders* that may be comorbid with a substance use disorder or that may better account for symptoms.

Step 2. If there is *impaired control of substance use* and/or *evidence of tolerance or withdrawal,* consider substance dependence.

Step 3. If there is *a problematic pattern of substance use* and the pattern of use is less severe than dependence, consider substance abuse.

Step 4. If there have been symptoms related to *recent use of a substance* (including medication), consider substance intoxication or substance-induced anxiety, mood, psychotic, sexual dysfunction, or sleep disorder.

Step 5. If there have been symptoms related to *recent cessation of (or reduction in the amount of) the use of a substance,* consider substance withdrawal or substance-induced anxiety, mood, psychotic, sexual dysfunction, or sleep disorder.

Step 6. If there are *cognitive deficits persisting after extensive use* or exposure to a substance (including medications), consider substance-induced persisting dementia or substance-induced persisting amnestic disorder.

Step 7. If the clinician *cannot determine* whether the clinically significant symptoms are related to intoxication or withdrawal or persisting effects of a substance, code other (or unknown) substance-related disorder.

Step 8. The clinician may wish to note use of a substance for which there is *no current evidence of problematic use* but for which follow-up may be appropriate including observation for suspected mental disorder.

Motivation and Behavioral Change

Interest in the effectiveness of brief interventions has drawn attention to the issue of the patients' motivational readiness to change and to the most felicitous interviewing techniques employed by physicians (Miller & Rollnick, 1991; Lipkin, Putnam, & Lazare, 1995). One model for understanding readiness for behavioral change describes a continuum of stages from a lack of awareness that behavioral change is necessary (precontemplation) through ambivalence about the need to change (contemplation) to planning the change (determination), carrying it out (action), and maintaining the new behavior (maintenance) or returning to the previous behavior (relapse) (Prochaska & DiClemente, 1983).

Motivational interviewing—a simple patient-centered technique that involves developing rapport with the patient, reviewing the results of a substance use evaluation and physical problems related to such use, determining the positive and negative aspects of the patient's substance use, setting goals, and developing an action plan—can be taught to physicians with brief clinical training and has been employed in various settings with relatively good success (Babor, Ritson, & Hodson, 1986; Clark, 1995; Rollnick, Heather, & Bell, 1992; Samet, Rollnick, & Barnes, 1996; Wallace, Cutler, & Haines, 1988). One formulation of the technique for motivational interviewing carries the acronym FRAMES (Miller & Rollnick, 1991):

F   Provide *Feedback* on drinking/drug behavior
R   Reinforce patient's *Responsibility* for changing behavior
A   State your *Advice* about changing behavior
M   Discuss a *Menu* of options to change behavior
E   Express *Empathy* for patient
S   Support patient's *Self-efficacy*

The hallmark of these interventions is that they are of low intensity, usually one or two sessions, intended primarily as an early intervention for individuals who fall short of the most severe substance use disorders and can be administered in several settings not directly within specialty services. Thus primary care practice, where people with these disorders have the most frequent contact, are a natural sight for such brief intervention approaches. The higher-intensity interventions, for example, behavioral and cognitive behavioral intervention such as cue exposure, contingency management, and coping skills treatment, can be learned and administered within the primary care setting, although they are more typically connected with specialized practices. The key, of course, is adequate training for primary care physicians.

Medical Training for Primary Care and Substance Use Disorders

Training in didactic knowledge does not appear to increase physician detection of substance use disorders (Clement, 1986; Warburg et al., 1987). However, physician substance abuse detection rates can be increased with (1) use of skills training that includes modeling, rehearsal, and feedback; (2) teaching of interactive skills such as active listening and emphatic responding; (3) provision of observation and clinical supervision in alcohol and drug treatment settings, especially with early-onset cases; and (4) training, via direct experience, with brief screening devices (Adger, McDonald, & Duggan, 1992;

Babor, 1990b; Barber & O'Brien, 1995; Dubé & Lewis, 1994; Israel et al., 1996; Fleming et al., 1994b).

A 1994 Macy conference tackled the issue of underdiagnosis and treatment. After reviewing prevalence, treatment outcome data, and current medical practices, the primary participants, consisting of leaders of the certifying boards and residency review committees from primary care and psychiatry, reached the following consensus:

> We recommend that the specialties of Family Practice, Internal Medicine, Pediatrics, and Obstetrics–Gynecology promptly respond to the need to improve the quality of care provided by physicians trained in these specialties to patients with alcohol and other drug problems.
>
> These primary care specialties should require all residents to be trained to develop and to demonstrate those skills necessary to prevent, screen for and diagnose alcohol and other drug problems; to provide initial therapeutic interventions for patients with these problems; to refer these patients for additional care when necessary; and to deliver follow-up care for these patients and their families.
>
> The certifying boards and residency review committees of these specialties should expeditiously take specific actions to strengthen their requirements so that the performance of residents in managing substance abuse patients is measurably improved. (Sirica, 1995, p. 87)

The recommendation of the Macy conference demands a threefold effort for primary care participation in addiction medicine. The first requires that all medical practitioners take on additional responsibility in the care of substance-abusing/dependent patients. The second demands that all physicians receive enhanced instruction and training in the care of substance use disorders. The third necessitates the incorporation of early detection, brief intervention, and referral strategies into the medical practitioner's repertoire of skills.

Physicians' Approach to Behavioral Change for Substance Use Disorders

Patients are receptive to physicians' suggestions and view their general practitioner as the single most important source of help and advice (Saunders & Roche, 1991). For example, when physicians suggest behavioral changes related to substance use, some patients reduce their smoking and drinking (Rollnick et al., 1992; Sanson-Fisher et al., 1986). Brief interventions also increase referrals for substance abuse treatment and lead to a reduction in consumption (Samet et al., 1996). These findings are promising because brief interventions for tobacco, alcohol, and drug use, particularly when rendered at the early stage of the problem, can be very efficacious (Babor, 1990b; Babor et al., 1986; Israel et al., 1996; Ockene et al., 1994). Keep in mind that most harm from heavy alcohol consumption in the general population occurs among nonaddicted individuals who have abusive episodes or other harmful behaviors (Babor et al., 1986; Barry & Fleming, 1994; Bien, Miller, & Tonigan, 1993).

In particular, information sessions, brief advice, self-help manuals, self-help groups, and periodic monitoring of progress by the physician have yielded modest but reliable effects on smoking and drinking behaviors (Babor, 1990a, 1990b; Buchsbaum, 1994). One recent study using 17 community-based practice sites evaluated over 700 subjects (Fleming, Barry, Manwell, Johnson, & London, 1997). After comparing intervention and control groups after 1 year, the study found that the intervention group had significant reductions from initial baseline observations in the mean number of drinks per week (19.1–11.5) and binge-drinking episodes within a 30-day period (5.7–3.1). All subjects received a health educational manual, but the intervention group consisted of structured counseling about their drinking in two visits of 15 minutes with a physician with follow-up calls from a nurse.

Referral and Treatment

Medical practitioners are more likely to assess their patients for substance abuse problems than to initiate treatment or referral (Hanna, 1991). Only a small percentage of physicians routinely intervene with their substance-abusing patients (DeWeese, 1994). However, as previously indicated, brief intervention consisting of information, advice, or counseling is often effective in the reduction of primary care patient substance use, psychosocial problems, and physician visits, particularly when other support services are available (Babor et al., 1986; Hurt et al., 1992; Fiore et al., 1990; Goldberg et al., 1994; Israel et al., 1996; Wallace et al., 1988). Recent studies found that even after 1 year, a brief (3-hour) intervention showed significant effects (Israel et al., 1996).

Despite promising results for treatment, the Epidemiologic Catchment Area study (DeWeese, 1994) found that only 24% of persons identified with substance use disorders received treatment services. Of these, 11% received treatment from a mental health or addiction specialist, 10% from general practitioners, 8% from Alcoholics or Narcotics Anonymous, and 4% from a human service professional (DeWeese, 1994). A study in Maryland indicated that only 7% of patients attending substance abuse treatment programs were referred by a physician (DeWeese, 1994). Medical practitioners are, however, more likely to refer such patients than to treat them in office (Hendryx, Doebbeling, & Kearns, 1994). Physicians are most likely to provide outside referrals for illicit drugs, followed by alcohol, over-the-counter drugs, and smoking (Gottlieb, Mullen, & McAlister, 1987), though referral and counseling percentages are low for all groups (Duszynski et al., 1995). Thus, physicians are most likely to counsel smokers and patients who abuse alcohol and are least likely to counsel over-the-counter and illicit drug abusers (Gottlieb et al., 1987). Physicians do not view referral as part of their general practice responsibilities and are not likely to refer their substance-using patients to specialized services (Rush, Powell, Crowe, & Ellis, 1995). However, they will refer when they believe that their skills are inadequate or that the patient will be noncompliant (Gottlieb et al., 1987).

When physicians do refer, they are most likely to direct alcohol abuse patients to outpatient resources, such as social workers, outpatient treatment programs, alcohol counselors, and self-help groups (Linn et al., 1990). When drug-abusing/dependent patients are referred by physicians, they are most likely to be directed to in-patient treatment facilities (Hendryx et al., 1994). Some physicians report fear of losing control over their patients subsequent to self-help group referral (Roche & Richard, 1991). This fear may partially explain why few patients who are referred are followed up for their substance use problems (Hendryx et al., 1994). Physicians would thus benefit from further guidance in using such referrals that have been so important in recovery (DuPont & McGovern, 1994; Khantzian & Mack, 1994).

Several recent articles have instructed physicians in the various treatment options for substance use disorders, providing models of local referral source directories and giving physicians tips about referral strategies using the continuum of care model (Barry & Fleming, 1994; D'Lugoff, 1994; Institute of Medicine, 1990; Nurco, Kinlock, & Hanlon, 1994). With higher levels of substance abuse medical education, clinical practicums, and continuing medical education, physicians are more confident in their ability both to manage patients with substance use disorders in the office and to refer them to outside resources (Deitz et al., 1994; Fleming et al., 1994a).

Negativity about the outcomes for these patients is not in accord with other disease management experience. In fact, care and outcomes of these patients are little different from other chronic medical conditions. For example, another practical matter familiar to the generalist is compliance with a physician's advice. By calculating compliance and relapse in selected medical disorders using the National Center for Health Statistics data, O'Brien and McLellan (1996) concluded that compliance with interventions for substance use disorders was similar to compliance for other medical conditions, such as insulin-dependent diabetes, where compliance with the medication regimen was less than 50%, and medication-dependent hypertension, where compliance with medication and diet was less than 30% for each.

One development likely to influence treatment and referral is the adoption of practice guidelines. National professional organizations such as the APA and the American Society of Addiction Medicine (ASAM) have taken this initiative. Another noteworthy development is the newly issued guideline from the NCQA (the National Committee on Quality Assurance), which reaffirms of the importance of screening and intervening of patients with these problems (Committee on Performance Measurement, 1996). This version of outcome measurement standards for organized systems of care will be implemented in 1997 (Committee on Performance Measurement, 1996). The proposed Health Plan Employer Data and Information Set (HEDIS) measurements have two components, required reporting measures and measures being evaluated for future inclusion. The HEDIS "report card" now includes a requirement for "advising smokers to quit" and pointing out the "availability of chemical dependency providers." "Screening for chemical dependency," "continuity of care for substance abusing patients," and "failure of substance abuse treatment" are being evaluated for inclusion as a future reporting requirement.

Measures under consideration concerning the effectiveness of care include several that are particularly applicable for primary care settings (e.g., "percent members reporting that their physician asked them about alcohol and drug abuse during the past year"). How much of the promulgation of guidelines serves a purely educational function and how much it may spell practice regulation is a subject of ongoing debate. Either way, in an era in which cost-effective treatments are demanded and the trend is toward evaluating outcomes, it is likely that the importance of guidelines on practice behavior will increase.

POPULATIONS

Primary care practice consists of a number of specialties and variety in patients served. In fact, the physician needs to be aware of the particular presentations of substance use disorders issues in subpopulations of patients.

Elderly

The most numerous primary care population is the elderly, but primary care physicians often fail to recognize chemical dependency problems in these patients (McMahon, 1993). Detection and management of the substance dependent elderly are constrained by physicians' views that older individuals are excessively isolated, embedded in denial, and "too old" to modify their behavior (Lipton & Lee, 1988). This is an unfortunate set of attitudes because the prevalence of alcohol problems is significant in the elderly. A study of more than 5,000 older (over 60) primary care patients revealed that 15% of men and 12% of women regularly drank in excess of the limits recommended by the NIAAA (> 14 drinks/week for men; 7 drinks/week for women). When the CAGE screening questionnaire for alcohol problems was administered to this population, 9% of men and 3% of women screened positive for alcohol abuse within the past 3 months (Adams, Barry, & Fleming, 1996).

Diagnosing elderly patients with alcohol problems can be difficult for a variety of reasons. The assessment tools are designed for younger adults in mainstream lifestyles. Moreover, the elderly may lack the obvious signs of intoxication or withdrawal. Even after cessation of prolonged high-dose alcohol intake, the elderly patient is notorious for lacking signs of alcohol withdrawal, which may obfuscate screening and diagnostic criteria. Even the common CAGE screening interview for alcohol problems relies on withdrawal symptoms for one-quarter of its validity. Further complicating the diagnosis is that it can be confused with other conditions. For example, the common signs of intoxication, such as unsteadiness or tremors, forgetfulness, and disorientation, may be mistakenly attributed to the condition of aging and increased frailty. It is also well-known that symptoms of excessive and chronic drinking can mimic clinical depression.

Also complicating this situation is the fact that the elderly with substance abuse problems have more medical problems than do their younger counterparts (Iber, 1991; McMahon, 1993). Geriatric evaluation units have indicated that for 10–15% of their patients, substance abuse/dependency is the cause of medical sequelae (Iber, 1991). A study concluded that as many as 30% of patients over age 65 who present to emergency room departments have chemical dependency issues, particularly over-the-counter and prescription drugs (Lindblom, Kostyk, Tabisz, Jacyk, & Fuchs, 1992).

Many elderly fear the "mental illness" label. Others have strong views about using Twelve-Step programs for recovery. Although true for any age group, the stigma associated with alcoholism and the shame and humiliation that accompany stigma can definitely influence recovery. Also, elders may be more likely to consider themselves "survivors" and not in need of treatment. As with people of any age, elders may differ from the physician in their cultural orientation to health care and their spiritual beliefs. Forming a supportive physician–patient relationship is critical to establishing trust and facilitating health with these patients. Nonjudgemental approaches work best (Lewis, 1997). Frequent contact with the patient helps and should continue even after a patient has been referred to care by an addiction medicine specialist.

The generation of elderly coming of age now has a different profile from alcohol abusers who are currently in their 30s and 40s. The stress factors we commonly associate with harmful drinking in the young—problems with employment, the law, or family—are not generally as prevalent now in the elderly. However, stresses that can lead to excessive drinking are certainly present in the senior population in the form of pervasive loneliness, isolation, and boredom. Other major factors also make it difficult to diagnose elderly alcohol problems.

The shame and humiliation many elders feel toward their drinking may cause them to hide their problems. But, with specific training, physicians can increase their rate of screening and documentation of elderly substance abuse (Graham, Altpeter, Emmitt-Myers, Parran, & Zyzanski, 1996). Adaptations of similar brief screening devices, as those used with younger individuals (e.g., the CAGE and the Michigan Alcohol Screening Test), also have been suggested for use with older individuals (McMahon, 1993).

Elderly persons are underrepresented in standard treatment programs (Institute of Medicine, 1990), and little has been written concerning physician referral practices in this area. Several studies indicated, however, that when elderly patients with substance use disorders are treated in standard care facilities or specialized programs to meet their needs, results are similar to or better than those for younger persons (Iber, 1991; Institute of Medicine, 1990; Lindblom et al., 1992). The American Medical Association (AMA) has prepared helpful reports and guidelines specifically directed at the diagnosis, treatment and prevention of alcoholism in the elderly (American Medical Association, 1995; Council on Scientific Affairs of the American Medical Association, 1996).

Women

Women have conventionally been underrepresented in alcohol and drug abuse treatment facilities. Yet, the frequency of at-risk drinking for men and women in primary care settings is approximately equal (Lewis, 1997). However, physicians are more likely to screen and detect substance use problems in their male patients, whereas for women, identification and referral for such problems remain low in all settings (Wilsnack, 1995). In addition, men are more likely to present in employee assistance and drinker–driver programs, which are common case-finding avenues serving alcohol and drug treatment facilities (Wilsnack, 1995). Treatment options for women historically have been severely restricted (Institute of Medicine, 1990; Wilsnack, 1995). Many chemical dependency programs deny entrance to women because they cannot accommodate women who are pregnant or have children and because they are unwilling to accept the Medicaid insurance benefits that many women patients possess (Institute of Medicine, 1990; Wilsnack, 1995). Thus, primary care physicians may be even less likely to refer their female substance-abusing patients than their male patients, despite the finding that women have equal or greater posttreatment improvement (Sanchez-Craig, Spivak, & Davila, 1991; Wilsnack, 1995).

Findings for pregnant women indicate that obstetric/gynecological (OB/GYN) medical specialists are less likely than other primary care physicians to identify or screen for substance abuse in their patients, even though 15% of all women of childbearing age are current substance abusers (Valente et al., 1992). Substance abuse in women is considered one of the most significant contemporary risks found in modern obstetrics (American College of Obstetricians and Gynecologists, 1994). Effective identification and intervention are essential elements of prenatal care (Russell, 1994; Thorp & Hiller-Sturmhofel, 1994). However, screening pregnant women for substance abuse is not routine. Laboratory tests using urine, blood, hair, and meconium assays often are administered only when alcohol and drug abuse is suspected (American College of Obstetricians and Gynecologists, 1994; Connolly & Marshall, 1991; Fox, 1994). Brief self-report screening devices (e.g., the T-ACE, Sokol, Martier, & Ager, 1989; TWEAK, Russell et al., 1991; and NET, Bottoms, Martier, & Sokol, 1989) specifically developed for pregnant women (Russell, 1994; Thorp & Hiller-Sturmhofel, 1994) have been advocated for use as routine identification measures. Unfortunately, these devices have yet to be incorporated in the OB/GYN's general practice (American College of Obstetricians and Gynecologists, 1994).

Children and Adolescents

Although substance abuse in the young has been of concern for decades (Litt & Cohen, 1970), little is known about the most efficacious means of screening and treating youth with substance use problems (Adger & Werner, 1994; Institute of Medicine, 1990). Like their adult counterparts, severely alcohol-

and drug-affected adolescents who exhibit medical sequelae are most likely to be identified by their physicians (Iber, 1991). Such youth are often remanded to costly and overcommitted inpatient residential facilities with unproven efficacy (Institute of Medicine, 1990). Pediatricians, though, are in an ideal position to assume an active role in the education of young people and their families in substance use risks and problems as well as in early identification and intervention (Adger & Werner, 1994). The *Guidelines for Adolescent Prevention Services* established by the AMA recommends that all pediatricians engage in substance abuse patient education, risk factor identification, anticipatory guidance, screening, and use of brief interventions and referrals during routine medical history taking (Adger & Werner, 1994). Recent articles describe adaptations of adult brief screens for adolescent use (Adger & Werner, 1994), brief office-based interventions geared toward youth, and available treatment alternatives (McDonald, 1989). Brief interactive skills training (Adger & Werner, 1994) and postgraduate education (Adger et al., 1992) significantly increase physician detection and management of adolescent substance use problems and lead to enhanced pediatrician leadership status in the substance use field (Gallagher, Barry, & Schoener, 1996).

SERVICE DELIVERY ISSUES

If the goal is an efficient and effective approach to major medical issues—such as high-blood pressure, cardiac arrhythmia, chronic pain, insomnia—and the disabling symptoms of major chronic diseases—such as heart disease, cancer, and AIDS—behavioral and medical approaches need to be integrated, not artificially separated.

A trend toward reintegration has been occurring. Some large purchasers of health services realize that behavioral health and primary care need to be managed and delivered in concert. The cost savings of mental health and substance abuse services in the prevention of costly medical and surgical complications are best appreciated and accounted for if services and cost management are integrated with medical/surgical/primary care core benefits. There are several advantages to integrating behavioral care within the primary care system. One is the importance of the physician's role in diagnosis and differential diagnosis. In this regard, closer alliances between primary care and mental health establishment will occur as primary care physicians take on more responsibility for the diagnosis of substance use disorders and psychiatric illnesses. The creation of a user-friendly primary care version of DSM-IV is a positive early step in this direction (Lipkin, 1996).

The integration of systems has put more value on the primary care practitioner as a member of the team and a part of networks that include formal links between primary care and specialized alcohol and drug treatment services. Much routine screening, diagnosis, and treatment of common mental illness and substance abuse can and should be handled by primary care physicians. One advantage of linking primary care services with care of patients with substance use disorders is the importance of dealing with coexisting medical disorders—counseling at-risk patients in the prevention of infection with hepatitis, HIV, and tuberculosis and providing for treatment of these conditions when necessary (O'Connor, Selwyn, & Schottenfeld, 1994).

Expansion of Primary Care to Include Care for Dependent Patients

There is a resurgence of the issue of whether more care for substance-dependent patients should and can be performed in primary care settings. One example of a policy initiative directed at expansion of addiction treatment including utilizing primary care practitioners is that proposed by the New York Academy of Medicine for the State of New York (New York Academy of Medicine, 1997). Its recommendations called for more care of addicts outside traditional treatment centers, but the intent was to increase capacity, not shift resources away from existing providers. Such recommendations are partly driven by the lack of accessible specialized treatment and partly by the AIDS epidemic. In particular, there is interest in the expansion of methadone-maintenance treatment into community-based practice settings (Institute of Medicine, 1995; Cooper, 1995; Molinari, Cooper, & Czechowicz, 1994). There the heroin-dependent patient can be maintained on methadone (Cohen et al., 1992), levo-α-acetyl methadol (LAAM; Eissenberg et al., 1997), and possibly buprenorphine (O'Connor et al., 1996). But a combination of overregulation, stigma, inadequate medical education, and high costs have combined to limit access to and expansion of this modality of care. The most comprehensive review of this situation was undertaken by the Institute of Medicine (1995).

A select but small group of "stabilized" methadone-maintenance patients have been treated successfully in general medical practice settings in New York City over several years. A first report of outcomes of this medical maintenance approach showed that 82.5% were in good standing, 5% dropped out, and 12.5% responded unfavorably and were returned to the clinics (Novick & Joseph, 1991). In a subsequent report of 100 patients maintained on methadone in general practice settings in New York City, 72% remained in good standing whereas 15% were unfavorably discharged (though only three of these for misuse of medication). The conclusion of investigators was that "carefully selected methadone maintenance patients in medical maintenance have a high retention rate and a low incidence of substance abuse and lost medication" (Novick et al., 1994).

Many countries with significant regulatory controls on the dispensation of methadone and significant problems with the stigmatization of addiction have still moved ahead to expand their opiate agonist programs in the face of the AIDS epidemic. Much of the expansion was through prescription by general practitioners. During the same period, U.S. program expansion was stagnant. A National Institute of Health consensus conference in November 1997 addressed this issue of the expansion of this form of addiction treatment to primary care settings.

The Information Revolution

The phenomenal growth of the internet, with 150 million Web pages created within 2 years, has changed the speed and efficiency of communication. The accessibility of complex knowledge will have profound implications for medical learning and practice. At least two changes are anticipated. First, the public will have greater access to health advice, including more sophisticated programs that will provide motivational guides and courses for behavioral change. A corollary development will provide expert and self-help information via electronic media directly to the people who suffer from substance use disorders. There are already several such interactive programs, and we can anticipate an acceleration of these developments. Second, the development of the Internet and other electronic technology has and will increasingly make expert consultation readily available to primary care practitioners. In the words of an advertisement in a recent *ACP Observer*: "Second Opinions a Keystroke Away" (American College of Physicians, 1996).

We already use sophisticated electronic record systems and information transfer by electronic mail. With growing Internet access, we can expect enhanced access to the Library of Medicine, the entry of on-line journals, real-time video, and distance learning via electronic networks to become a key element in continuing medical education. Not only will such readily accessible expertise change the nature of continuing medical education, but it will also change in-service training and the fundamental relationship between the generalist and specialist, making new specialized expert advice more available from the very beginning of a patient encounter. More and more the primary care physician will not simply be a gatekeeper for more costly and complicated care but, in concert with expert advice, will be the provider of care on an ongoing basis that was previously the domain of specialists.

CONCLUSION

Generalist and specialist training centers realize that they need each other to survive in this new economic climate. Natural incentives in the form of cost containment through prevention will necessitate medicine's integration of substance abuse/dependency management into its domain. The expertise of medical disciplines, including the ready access to consultation from psychiatry and addiction medicine, is part and parcel of a truly integrated system of care and training. The nature of the substance abuse/dependency field requires a multidisciplinary approach: cooperation between medical practitioners and those from other disciplines is necessary for the management of these patients (Israel et al., 1996; Lareau & Nelson, 1994; Lewis, 1996).

ACKNOWLEDGMENT

Thanks to Christopher Goodwin for his contributions to this chapter.

REFERENCES

Adams, W. L., Barry, K. L., & Fleming, M. F. (1996). Screening for problem drinking in older primary care patients. *Journal of the American Medical Association, 276,* 1964–1967.

Adger, H., McDonald, E. M., & Duggan, A. K. (1992). Evaluation of a CME workshop on alcohol and other drug use. *Substance Abuse, 13,* 129–138.

Adger, H., & Werner, M. J. (1994). The pediatrician. *Alcohol Health and Research World, 18*(2), 121–126.

American Academy of Addiction Psychiatry. (1996). Identification and treatment of substance abuse in primary care settings. *American Journal on Addictions, 5*(Suppl. 1), 4.

American College of Obstetricians and Gynocologists. (1994). Substance abuse. *International Journal of Gynecology and Obstetrics, 47,* 65–72.

American College of Physicans. (1996, July/August). [Advertisement]. *The Observer.*

American Medical Association. (1995). *Alcoholism in the elderly: Diagnosis, treatment, prevention—Guidelines for primary care physicians.* Chicago: Author.

American Psychiatric Association. (1995a). *Diagnostic and statistical manual of mental disorders* (4th ed.)—*Primary care version.* Washington, DC: Author.

American Psychiatric Association. (1995b). Practice guideline for the treatment of patients with substance use disorders: Alcohol, cocaine, opioids. *American Journal of Psychiatry, 152*(Suppl.), 5–59.

American Society of Addiction Medicine. (1996). *Patient placement criteria for the treatment of substance-related disorders* (2nd ed.). Chevy Chase, MD: Author.

Aronson, M. (1995, July/August). Alcoholism and the role of primary care physicians. *Primary Psychiatry, 64.*

Babor, T. (1990a). Alcohol and substance abuse in primary care settings. From J. Mayfield & M. Grady (Eds.), *Conference proceedings: Primary care research: An Agenda for the 90s* (DHHS Publication No. PHS 90-3460, pp. 113–115). Washington, DC: U.S. Government Printing Office.

Babor, T. F. (1990b). Brief intervention strategies for harmful drinkers. New directions for medical education. *Canadian Medical Association Journal, 143*(10), 1070–1076.

Babor, T. F., Ritson, E. B., & Hodson, R. J. (1986). Alcohol-related problems in the primary health care setting: A review of early intervention strategies. *British Journal of Addiction, 81,* 23–46.

Barber, W., & O'Brien, C. (1995). Early identification and intervention in an office setting. *Primary Psychiatry, 49–55.*

Barry, K. L., & Fleming, M. F. (1994). *The Family Physician, 18*(2), 105–109.

Bien, T. H., Miller, W. R., & Tonigan, J. S. (1993). Brief intervention for alcohol problems: A review. *Addictions, 88,* 315–336.

Bottoms, S. F., Martier, S. S., & Sokol, R. J. (1989). Refinements in screening for risk drinking in reproductive-aged women: The "net" results [Abstract]. *Alcoholism: Clinical and Experimental Research, 13*(2a), 339.

Bridges, K. W., & Goldberg, D. P. (1985). Somatic presentation of DSM-III psychiatric disorders in the primary care setting. *Journal of Psychomatic Research, 29,* 563–569.

Buchsbaum, D. (1994). Effectiveness of treatment in general medical patients with drinking problems. *Alcohol Health and Research World, 16*(2), 140–145.

Chappel, J. N. (1992). Challenges to health professional education in substance abuse in the 1990's. *Substance Abuse, 13*(4), 219–225.

Clark, W. (1995). Alcohol problems at century's end: Better strategies for physicians. *Primary Psychiatry*, 18–20.

Clement, S. (1986). The identification of alcohol-related problems by general practitioners. *British Journal of Addiction, 81*(2) 257–264.

Cohen, J., Schamroth, A., Nazareth, I., Johnson, M., Graham, S., & Thomson, D. (1992). Problem drug use in a central London general practice. *British Medical Journal, 304,* 1158–1160.

Coleman, P. R., & Veach, T. L. (1990). Substance abuse and the family physician: A survey of attitudes. *Substance Abuse, 11*(2), 84–93.

Committee on Performance Measurement. (1996). *Health plan employer data and information: HEDIS 3.0.* Bethesda, MD: National Committee for Quality Assurance.

Connolly, W. B., & Marshall, A. B. (1991). Drug addiction, pregnancy, and childbirth: Legal issues for the medical and social services community. *Clinics in Perinatology, 18*(1), 147–185.

Cooper, J. R. (1995). Including narcotic addiction treatment in an office-based practice. *Journal of the American Medical Association, 273*(20), 1619–1620.

Council on Scientific Affairs of the American Medical Association. (1996). Alcoholism in the elderly. *Journal of the American Medical Association, 275*(10), 797–801.

Deitz, D., Rohde, F., Bertolucci, D., & Dufour, M. (1994). Prevalence of screening for alcohol use by physicians during routine physical examinations. *Alcohol Health and Research World, 18*(2), 162–168.

D'Lugoff, B. C. (1994). Where to refer patients who abuse alcohol or other drugs. *Maryland Medical Journal, 43*(1), 63–70.

DeWeese, J. (1994). Substance abuse in Maryland: What physicians can do to help. *Maryland Medical Journal, 43*(10), 29–33.

Dubé, C. E., & Lewis, D. C. (1994). Medical education in alcohol and other drugs: Curriculum development for primary care. *Alcohol Health and Research World, 18*(2), 146–153.

DuPont, R. L., & McGovern, J. T. (1994). *A bridge to recovery: An introduction to 12-step programs.* Washington, DC: American Psychiatric Press.

Duszynski, K. R., Nieto, J., & Valente, C. M. (1995). Reported practices, attitudes, and confidence levels of primary care physicians regarding patients who abuse alcohol and other drugs. *Maryland Medical Journal, 44*(6), 439–446.

Eissenberg, T., Bigelow, G., Strain, E., Walsh, S., Brooner, R., Stitzer, M., & Johnson, R. (1997). Dose-related efficacy of levomethadyl acetate for treatment of opioid dependence. *Journal of the American Medical Association, 277*(24), 1945–1951.

Fiore, M. C., Novotny, T. E., & Pierce, J. P., Giovino, G. A., Hatziandreu, E. J., Newcomb, P. A., Surawicz, T. S., & Davis, R. M. (1990). Methods used to quit smoking in the United States: Do cessation programs help? *Journal of the American Medical Association, 263*(20), 2760–2765.

Fleming, M. F., Barry, K. L., Davis, A., Kahn, R., & Rivo, M. (1994a). Faculty development in addiction medicine: Project SAEFP, a one year follow-up study. *Education Research Methods, 26*(4), 221–225.

Fleming, M. F., Barry, K., Davis, A., Kropp, S., Kahn, R., & Rivo, M. (1994b). Medical education about substance abuse: Changes in curriculum and faculty between 1976 and 1992. *Academic Medicine, 69*(5), 362–369.

Fleming, M. F., Barry, K. L., Manwell, L. B., Johnson, K., & London, R. (1997). Brief physician advice for problem alcohol drinkers: A randomized controlled trial in community-based primary care practices. *Journal of the American Medical Association, 277,* 1039–1045.

Ford, D. E., Kamerow, D. B., & Thompson, J. W. (1988). Who talks to physicians about mental health and substance abuse problems? *Journal of General Internal Medicine, 3*(4), 363–369.

Fox, C. H. (1994). Cocaine use in pregnancy. *Journal of the American Board of Family Practice, 7,* 225–228.

Gallagher, R. E., Barry, L. C., & Schoener, E. P. (1996). Sociometric assessment of leadership status in substance abuse training. *Substance Abuse, 17*(3), 151–157.

Goldberg, D. N., Hoffman, A. M., & Farinha, M. F., Marder, D. C., Tinson-Mitchem, L., Burton, D., & Smith, E. G. (1994). Physician delivery of smoking cessation advice based on the stages-of-change model. *American Journal of Prevention Medicine, 10*(5), 267–274.

Gottlieb, N. H., Mullen, P. D., & McAlister, A. L. (1987). Patients' substance abuse and the primary care physician: Patterns of practice. *Addictive Behaviors, 12,* 23–32.

Graham, A. V., Altpeter, M., Emmitt-Myers, S., Parran, T. V., Zyzanski, S. (1996). Teaching faculty about substance abuse: Evaluating clinical competence and professional development. *Substance Abuse, 17*(3), 139–150.

Hanna, E. Z. (1991). Attitudes toward problem drinkers revisited: Patient–therapist factors contributing to the differential treatment of patients with alcohol problems. *Journal of Clinical and Experimental Research, 15*(6), 927–931.

Helzer, J. E., & Pryzbeck, T. R. (1988). The co-occurrence of alcoholism with other psychiatric disorders in the general population and its impact on treatment. *Journal of the Study of Alcohol, 49,* 219–224.

Hendryx, M. S., Doebbeling, B. N., & Kearns, D. L. (1994). The cost-effectiveness of treatment for alcoholism: A first approximation. *Family Practice Research Journal, 14*(2), 127–137.

Hurt, R. D., Lauger, G. G., Offord, K. P., Bruse, B. K., Dale, L. C., McClain, F. L., & Eberman, K. M. (1992). An integrated approach to the treatment of nicotine dependence. *Journal of General Internal Medicine, 7,* 114–116.

Iber, F. L. (1991). *Alcohol and drug abuse as encountered in office practice.* Boston: CRC Press.

Institute of Medicine. (1990). *Broadening the base of treatment for alcohol problems.* Washington, DC: National Academy Press.

Institute of Medicine. (1995). *Federal regulation of methadone treatment.* Washington, DC: National Academy of Medicine.

Israel, Y., Hollander, O., Sanchez-Craig, M., Booker, S., Miller, V., Gindrich, R., & Rankin, J. G. (1996). Screening for problem drinking and counseling by the primary care physician-nurse team. *Alcoholism: Clinical and Experimental Research, 20*(8), 1443–1450.

Katon, W. (1992, March 29–31). *How does primary care address mental health needs of mentally ill and substance abusing populations?* (National Primary Care Conference Proceedings, pp. 307–326). Washington, DC: U.S. Public Health Services, Health Resources and Services Administration, Department of Health and Human Services.

Kessler, R. C., Nelson, C. B., McGonagle, K. A., Edlund, M. J., Frank, R. G., & Leaf, P. J. (1996). The epidemiology of co-occurring addictive and mental disorders: Implications for prevention and service utilization. *American Journal of Orthopsychiatry, 66,* 17–31.

Khantzian, E., & Mack, J. (1994). How AA works and why it's important for clinicians to understand. *Journal of Substance Abuse Treatment, 11*(2), 77–92.

Lareau, M. W., & Nelson, E. S. (1994). The physician and licensed mental health professional team: Prevalence and feasibility. *Family Systems Medicine, 12*(1), 37–45.

Lewis, D. C. (1996). The role of internal medicine in addiction medicine. *Journal of Addictive Diseases, 15*(1), 1–17.

Lewis, D. C. (1997). The role of the generalist in the care of the substance abusing patient. *Medical Clinics of North America, 81*(4), 831–844.

Lindblom, L., Kostyk, D., Tabisz, E., Jacyk, W. R., & Fuchs, D. (1992). Chemical abuse: An intervention program for the elderly. *Journal of Gerontological Nursing, 18*(4), 6–14.

Linn, L. S., Yager, J., & Leake, B. (1990). Professional vs. personal factors related to physicians' attitudes toward drug testing. *Journal of Drug Education, 20*(2), 95–109.

Lipkin, M. (1996). Two cultures divided by a common classification. *Primary Psychiatry, 15*, 20–23.

Lipkin, M., Jr., Putnam, S. M., & Lazare, A. (Eds.). (1995). *The medical interview: Clinical care, education, and research.* New York: Springer.

Lipton, H. L., & Lee, P. R. (1988). *Drugs and the elderly: Clinical, social and policy perspectives.* Stanford, CA: Stanford University Press.

Litt, I. F., & Cohen, M. I. (1970). The drug-using adolescent as a pediatric patient. *The Journal of Pediatrics, 77*(2), 195–202.

Mayo-Smith, M. F. (1997). Pharmacological management of alcohol withdrawal. *Journal of the American Medical Association, 278*(2), 144–151.

McDonald, D. L. (1989). *Drugs, drinking, and adolescents* (2nd ed.) Chicago: Yearbook Medical Publishers.

McGinnis, J. M., & Foege, W. H. (1993). Actual causes of death in the United States. *Journal of the American Medical Association, 270*, 2202–2212.

McMahon, A. L. (1993). Substance abuse among the elderly. *Nurse Practitioner Forum, 4*(4), 231–238.

Miller, W. R., & Rollnick, S. (1991). *Motivational interviewing: Preparing people to change addictive behavior.* New York: Guilford Press.

Molinari, S. P., Cooper, J. R., & Czechowicz, D. J. (1994). Federal regulation of clinical practice in narcotic addiction treatment: Purpose, status, and alternatives. *Journal of Law, Medicine, and Ethics, 22*(3), 231–239.

National Institute on Alcohol Abuse and Alcoholism. (1995). *The physician's guide to helping patients with alcohol problems* (Publication No. 95-3769). Washington, DC: National Institutes of Health.

New York Academy of Medicine. (1997). *Addiction treatment: Promoting a medical approach to substance use.* New York: Author.

Novick, D. M., & Joseph, H. (1991). Medical maintenance: The treatment of chronic opiate dependence in general medical practice. *Journal of Substance Abuse Treatment, 8*, 233–239.

Novick, D. M., Joseph, H., Salsitz, E. A., Kalin, M. F., Keefe, J. B., Miller, E. L., & Richman, B. L. (1994). Outcomes of treatment of socially rehabilitated methadone maintenance patients in physicians' offices (medical maintenance): Follow-up at three and a half to nine and a fourth years. *Journal of General Internal Medicine, 9*, 127–130.

Nurco, D. N., Kinlock, T. W., & Hanlon, T. E. (1994). The nature and status of drug abuse treatment. *Maryland Medical Journal, 43*(1), 51–57.

O'Brien, C., & McLellan, A. (1996). Myths about the treatment of addiction. *Lancet, 347*, 237–240.

O'Connor, P. G., Oliveto, A. H., Shi, J. M., Triffleman, E., Carroll, K. M., Kosten, T. R., & Rounasaville, B. J. (1996). A pilot study of primary-care-based buprenorphine maintenance for heroin dependence. *American Journal of Drug and Alcohol Abuse, 22*(4), 523–531.

O'Connor, P. G., Selwyn, P. A., & Schottenfeld, R. S. (1994). Medical care for injection drug users with human immunodeficiency virus infection. *New England Journal of Medicine, 331,* 450–459.

Ockene, J., Kristeller, J., Pbert, L., Herbert, J. R., Luippold, R., Goldberg, R. J., Landon, J., & Kalan, K. (1994). The physician-delivered smoking intervention project: Can short-term interventions produce long-term effects for a general outpatient population? *Health Psychology, 13*(3), 278–281.

Parran, T. (1997). Prescription drug abuse: A question of balance. *Medical Clinics of North America, 81*(4), 967–978.

Prochaska, J. O., & DiClemente, C. C. (1983). Stages and processes of self-change of smoking: Toward an integrated model of change. *Journal of Clinical Consulting Psychology, 51,* 390–395.

Regier, D. A., Farmer, M. E., Rae, D. S., Locke, B. Z., Keith, S. J., Judd, L. L., & Goodwin, K. K. (1990). Comorbidity of mental disorders with alcohol and other drug abuse. *Journal of the American Medical Association, 264,* 2511–2518.

Roche, A., & Richard, G.P. (1991). Doctors' willingness to intervene in patients' drug and alcohol problems. *Social Science Medical Journal, 33,* 1053–1061.

Rollnick, S., Heather, N., & Bell, A. (1992). Negotiating behavior change in medical settings: The development of brief motivational interviewing. *Journal of Mental Health, 1,* 25–32.

Rush, B. R., Powell, L. Y., Crowe, T. G., & Ellis, K. (1995). Early intervention for alcohol use: Family physicians' motivations and perceived barriers. *Canadian Medical Association Journal, 152,* 863–869.

Russell, M. (1994). New assessment tools for risk drinking during pregnancy: T-ACE, TWEAK, and others. *Alcohol Health and Research World, 18*(1), 55–61.

Russell, M., Martier, S. S., Sokol, R. J., Jacobson, S., Jacobson, J., & Bottoms, S. (1991). Screening for pregnancy risk drinking: TWEAKing the tests [Abstract]. *Alcoholism: Clinical and Experimental Research, 15*(2), 368.

Samet, J. H., O'Connor, P. G., & Stein, M. D. (Eds.). (1997). *The medical clinics of North America: Alcohol and other substance abuse* (Vol. 81). Philadelphia: Saunders.

Samet, J. H., Rollnick, S., & Barnes, H. (1996). Beyond CAGE: A brief clinical approach after detection of substance abuse. *Archives of Internal Medicine, 156,* 2287–2293.

Sanchez-Craig, M., Spivak, K., & Davila, R. (1991). Superior outcome of females over males after brief treatment for reduction of heavy drinking: Replication and report of therapist effects. *British Journal of Addiction, 86,* 867–876.

Sanson-Fisher, R., Webb, G., & Reid, A. (1986). The role of the medical practitioner as an agent for disease prevention. *Better Health Commission: Looking Forward to Better Health, 3,* 201–212.

Saunders, J. B., & Roche, A. M. (1991). Medical education in substance use disorders. *Drug and Alcohol Review, 10,* 263–275.

Schorling, J. B., & Buchsbaum, D. (1997). Screening for alcohol and drug abuse. *Medical Clinics of North America, 81*(4), 845–866.

Schuckit, M. A. (1988). Alcoholic patients with secondary depression. *American Journal of Psychiatry, 140,* 711–714.

Sirica, C. (Ed.). (1995). *Training about alcohol and substance abuse for all primary care physicians*. New York: Josiah Macy, Jr., Foundation.

Sokol, R. J., Martier, S. S., & Ager, J. W. (1989). The T-ACE questions: Practical prenatal detention of risk-drinking. *American Journal of Obstetrics and Gynecology 160*(4), 863–870.

Stimmel, B. (1997). *Pain and its relief without addiction: Clinical issues in the use of opioids and other analgesics*. New York: Haworth Medical Press.

Telfer, L., & Clulow, C. (1990). Heroin misusers: What they think of their general practitioners. *British Journal of Addiction, 85*, 137–140.

Thorp, J. M., & Hiller-Sturmhofel, S. (1994). The obstetrician/gynecologist. *Alcohol Health and Research World, 18*(2), 117–120.

Valente, C. M., Duszynski, K. R., Smoot, R. T., Ferentz, K. S., Levine, D. M., & Troisi, A. J. (1992). Physician estimates of substance abuse in Baltimore and Cumberland: 1991. *Maryland Medical Journal, 41*(11), 973–978.

Wallace, P., Cutler, S., & Haines, A. (1988). Randomized controlled trial of general practitioner intervention in patients with excessive alcohol consumption, *British Medical Journal, 297*, 663–668.

Warburg, M. M., Cleary, P., Rohman, M., Barnes, H., Aronson, M., & Delbanco, T. (1987). Residents' attitudes, knowledge, and behavior regarding diagnosis and treatment of alcoholism. *Journal of Medical Education, 62*, 497–503.

Wilsnack, S. (1995). Alcohol use and alcohol problems in women. In A. L. Stanton & J. Gallant (Eds.), *Psychology of women's health: Progress and challenges in research and application* (pp. 381–443). Washington, DC: American Psychological Association.

Wright, C. (1995). Physician intervention in alcoholism-past and present. *Maryland Medical Journal, 44*(6), 447–452.

Ziedonis, D., & Brady, K. (1997). Dual diagnosis in primary care: Detecting and treating both the addiction and the mental illness. In J. H. Samet, P. G. O'Connor, & M. D. Stein (Eds.), *The medical clinics of North America: Alcohol and other substance abuse* (Vol. 81, pp. 1017–1036). Philadelphia: Saunders.

25

❏ _____

Psychopharmacological Treatments

ELINORE F. McCANCE-KATZ
THOMAS R. KOSTEN

INTRODUCTION

This chapter reviews pharmacotherapies for abuse of nicotine, alcohol, opioids, and cocaine. Pharmacotherapies for substance use disorders have been developed to address two broad treatment categories: (1) acute withdrawal or the initial attainment of abstinence and (2) chronic maintenance or the prevention of relapse. Agents for acute withdrawal are most relevant to dependence on opioids and alcohol. Because nicotine and cocaine withdrawal is less medically important, the emphasis of these drugs is on the initial attainment of abstinence.

Maintenance agents might directly benefit any protracted withdrawal syndrome, but the general rationale for maintenance pharmacotherapies are as either blocking or substitution agents. Blocking agents maintain drug abstinence by preventing the abused drug from producing its behavioral or physiological effects. For example, the competitive opioid antagonist naltrexone completely blocks the effects of heroin, including the subjective euphoria and the production of physiological dependence from repeated heroin use. Before administering these blocking agents, detoxification is required to prevent the precipitation of a withdrawal syndrome from the abused drug. In contrast, the substitution agents maintain the dependent state and will not precipitate withdrawal when given to drug-dependent patients. The rationale for substitution agents is to prevent illicit drug use by reducing drug hunger and withdrawal as well as by producing cross-tolerance. Cross tolerance means that tolerance, which is the diminished intensity of a drug's effects after repeated and sustained dosing, will develop not only to the precise drug that is being taken repeatedly but also to other drugs from the same pharmacological class (e.g., methadone and heroin, which are both opioids). Examples of substitution agents that produce cross-tolerance to heroin and have been shown to be effective in reducing illicit opioid use are methadone and levo-α-acetylmethadol (LAAM).

These two maintenance strategies of either blocking or substitution are not necessarily incompatible, and partial agonists provide a pharmacological tool to combine both approaches in treating drug dependence. At low dosages, these partial agonists suppress withdrawal symptoms in dependent patients and produce some subjective reinforcing properties, whereas at higher dosages these same medications block the reinforcement from full agonists that might be abused. Buprenorphine is an example of such a partial opioid agonist, which at low doses suppresses heroin withdrawal and at high doses blocks the "high" from heroin. Finally, all these agents must be administered in the context of psychosocial interventions developed to insure compliance with the medications as well as to facilitate the rehabilitation that is a necessary component to any drug abuse treatment program.

In the following sections, we review a variety of standard treatments for substance use disorders as well as several new agents. The goal is to provide an overview of current pharmacological treatments for nicotine, alcohol, opioid, and cocaine use disorders.

NICOTINE PHARMACOTHERAPIES

A variety of pharmacotherapies are available for the treatment of nicotine dependence. Pharmacotherapies for nicotine dependence which have been shown to have some efficacy for smoking cessation include the acute withdrawal medications: nicotine replacement therapy and medications that can mimic nicotine effects. An antagonist therapy for nicotine dependence is also being developed. The following sections review these treatments, which are summarized in Table 25.1.

Acute Withdrawal Medications

Nicotine polacrilex gum was approved as a prescription treatment for tobacco dependence in 1984 and is now available as an over-the-counter aid to smoking cessation. The gum contains 2 or 4 mg of nicotine; 50–90% of the nicotine is released depending on the rate of chewing and is absorbed through the buccal mucosa with peak nicotine concentrations reached in 15–30 minutes (as compared to 1–2 minutes after initiating smoking a cigarette) (Lee & D'Alonzo, 1993). Recent evidence shows that scheduled dosing (i.e., one piece of gum/hour) is more effective than using the gum as needed for craving (Sachs, 1991; Hughes, 1996). Absorption of nicotine is decreased in an acidic environment and patients should be instructed not to consume acidic bever-

TABLE 25.1. Pharmacotherapies for Nicotine Dependence

Treatment agent	Dose	Administration	Length of treatment	Outcome
Nicotine polacrilex gum	Nicotine 2 mg/piece; nicotine 4 mg/piece	1 piece/hour; oral	4–6 weeks	1-year abstinence rate: 8–29%
Nicotine patch	Nicotine 15 mg; nicotine 21–22 mg	16-hour patch; 24-hour patch	Up to 20 weeks	6-month abstinence rate: 22–42%
Nicotine spray	Nicotine 1 mg; 5–40 mg/day	Two nasal sprays/dose	3–12 months	1-year abstinence rate: 18–27%
Bupropion	300 mg/day	Oral	12 weeks	6-month abstinence rate: 59%
Clonidine	0.2–.75 mg/day	Oral	2–12 weeks	3- to 12-month follow-up abstinence rate: 14–27%

ages such as coffee, juices, and soda immediately before, during, or after use of the gum (Henningfield, Stapleton, Benowitz, Grayson, & London, 1993). Nicotine polacrilex has been shown to reduce withdrawal symptoms of anger/irritability, anxiety, depression, and decreased concentration, although craving for cigarettes is unaffected and patients should be advised of this prior to initiation of nicotine pilocrilex gum treatment (Lee & D'Alonzo, 1993). The average length of treatment is 4–6 weeks and prospective studies of longer treatment periods differ as to therapeutic benefit (Fagerstrom & Melin, 1985; Hatsukami, Huber, Callies, & Skoog, 1993). One-year follow-up studies show that quit rates for nicotine polacrilex gum range from 8–10% when given with physician advice and minimal support. This increases to 29% when combined with behavioral treatment (Hall, Hall, & Ginsberg, 1990). The 4 mg dose of nicotine polacrilex gum was shown to be more efficacious than the 2 mg nicotine dose in the treatment of highly dependent smokers who smoke in excess of 25 cigarettes daily (Sachs, 1995).

Transdermal nicotine administration represents another variation of the nicotine replacement approach to smoking cessation. Nicotine is delivered into the systemic circulation via the skin and is effective in reducing nicotine withdrawal symptoms. These systems are available in regimens that deliver nicotine over a 16- or 24-hour duration (delivering 15 mg and 21–22 mg, respectively) (Palmer, Buckley, & Faulds, 1992) and may be used for up to 20 weeks including a tapering course. Nicotine is slowly absorbed, with peak levels reached 6–10 hours after application, and nicotine levels are about half those obtained through smoking. Following 4–6 weeks of treatment at the initial nicotine dose, a tapering schedule is usually implemented with 2–4 weeks of either 10 mg/16 hours or 14 mg/24 hours. This is followed by 2–4 weeks of the lowest nicotine dose: 5 mg/16 hours or 7 mg/24 hours. Abrupt cessation of patch use has not been associated with significant withdrawal; therefore tapering may not be necessary (Fiore, Smith, Jorenby, & Baker, 1994). Transdermal nicotine systems have been generally well tolerated, with minor side effects of local irritation at the application site, mild gastric disturbances, and sleep disturbances. Nicotine patches produce end-of-treatment smoking cessation rates from 18% to 77% (about twice that of placebo-treated subjects) and 6-month abstinence rates range from 22% to 42% (compared to 5–28% for placebo-treated subjects). Although nicotine patches are an effective aid to smoking cessation, the wide range in abstinence rates may be influenced by the components (or lack thereof) of concomitant counseling (Fiore, Jorenby, Baker, & Kenford, 1992).

Nicotine nasal spray is a relatively fast delivery system for producing low levels of nicotine in venous blood (Johansson, Olsson, Bende, Carlsson, & Gunnarsson, 1991). Time to peak nicotine venous blood level was found to be 11.5 minutes, which, although slower than that associated with smoking, is faster than for nicotine polacrilex gum or the nicotine patch. This faster delivery of nicotine is expected to produce more rapid relief of withdrawal and craving and allows the patient to experience a greater sense of control. Two randomized double-blind, placebo-controlled studies examined the effectiveness of nicotine nasal spray on smoking cessation (Schneider et al., 1995; Hjalmarson, Franzon, Westin, & Wilkund, 1994). Both showed a significant increase in abstinence in groups randomized to nicotine spray treatment at all follow-ups. Side effects of nicotine nasal spray are throat irritation, coughing, sneezing, and watering eyes, reported in up to 75% of users. Nicotine nasal spray does appear to have abuse liability, as reports indicate that some patients who quit smoking with nicotine nasal spray continued to use it for long periods (Sutherland et al., 1992). Because of its significant side effects, nicotine nasal spray is not recommended as an initial treatment for smokers but may be appropriate for those who failed to stop smoking with use of the nicotine gum or patch.

Studies show that failure in smoking cessation is predicted by a past history of depression and/or dysphoria prior to or at the onset of an attempt to quit smoking (Hall, Munoz, Reus, & Sees, 1993). This led to the hypothesis that antidepressant agents might be effective medications for smoking cessation. Study results have been mixed: imipramine had no effect (Hughes, 1994) but nortriptyline was effective (Humfleet et al., 1996).

Bupropion, an antidepressant agent that decreases reuptake of dopamine, norepinephrine, and serotonin, was recently recommended for approval as a smoking cessation agent. A study in which bupropion 300 mg daily or placebo was administered for 3 months to heavy smokers (1 pack daily) with multiple failed quit attempts showed a significant difference in abstinence rates (59% [bupropion] vs. 20%). At the end of the medication treatment period, 2 of 14 who successfully quit on bupropion had relapsed and all the placebo-treated patients had relapsed. At the 6-month follow-up, the bupropion group that had successfully quit smoking had no further relapses (Ferry et al., 1992).

Nicotine can decrease anxiety related to stress, and, conversely, anxiety can be a prominent symptom of withdrawal in smokers. Buspirone is a serotonin 1A ($5\text{-}HT_{1A}$) partial agonist, which can be useful in the treatment of anxiety disorders. It has also been found to improve short-term smoking cessation rates in smokers and abstinence rates in smokers with high anxiety levels (Hughes, 1994). Buspirone is generally well tolerated and has no abuse liability. It may be useful in selected smokers as an aid to smoking cessation.

Clonidine is an noradrenergic α-2 agonist which decreases central sympathetic activity. As such, it is an effective agent in lowering blood pressure and also decreases symptoms of opioid and alcohol withdrawal, which led to its use in nicotine withdrawal (Hughes, 1994). Clonidine in doses of 0.1–0.4 mg daily administered orally or transdermally for 3 to 4 weeks has been shown to reduce withdrawal symptoms and to ameliorate craving, but side effects of sedation, postural hypotension, dizziness, and dry mouth may also occur (Gourlay & Benowitz, 1995). Clonidine may be an effective treatment for those who do not want nicotine replacement therapy or who have failed other smoking cessation methods.

Antagonist Therapy

Mecamylamine is a noncompetitive antagonist of the central nervous system and peripheral nicotine receptors which has been shown to block many of the physiological, behavioral, and reinforcing effects of nicotine (Clarke, 1991; Rose, 1996). By occupying nicotine receptors, mecamylamine has been shown to effectively attenuate smoking reward and facilitate smoking cessation (Rose, 1996). Given to smokers who are not trying to quit, mecamylamine treatment is associated with an increase in cigarette consumption in an attempt to overcome the blockade. However, it does not induce nicotine withdrawal (Clarke, 1991). Two studies suggested short-term efficacy of mecamylamine, but significant dropout rates were observed with the high doses used (Clarke, 1991; Stolerman, Goldfarb, Fink, & Jarrick, 1973). The side effect profile of mecamylamine includes abdominal cramps, headache, dry mouth, and constipation. A recent double-blind study combined mecamylamine (5 mg twice daily) with nicotine administered through a transdermal patch (Rose et al., 1994). The combination of antagonist–agonist therapy resulted in a threefold enhancement in continuous smoking abstinence over nicotine-patch-alone treatment. This effect was maintained throughout the 12-month follow-up period. Although antagonist treatment for opioid dependence has had little success due to compliance problems (Rounsaville, 1995), smokers may be a more compliant group and, in combination with a behavioral therapy, mecamylamine may be a promising treatment for smoking cessation.

ALCOHOL PHARMACOTHERAPIES

Acute Withdrawal Medications

Acute withdrawal from alcohol can precipitate a medical emergency with the evolution of delirium tremens, a condition with 15% mortality if untreated.

Because of the seriousness of this condition, treatments have been developed to reduce autonomic hyperactivity as well as to prevent seizures which can be the most serious complication. The current standard approach to alcohol detoxification uses tapering dosages of a benzodiazepine. Benzodiazepines with active metabolites such as chlordiazepoxide are effective in relieving the autonomic hyperactivity of withdrawal and will prevent seizures. Benzodiazepines are initially made available on an as-needed basis with parameters for dosing based on appearance of withdrawal symptoms including agitation, diaphoresis, tremor, hypertension, and tachycardia. Although detoxification schedules must be individualized, a benzodiazepine taper can usually be accomplished in 3 days. Patients with hepatic disease should be detoxified with lorazepam or oxazepam because these drugs have no active metabolites requiring hepatic clearance. Lorazepam is also a good choice for detoxification of the patient with severe vomiting as it is well absorbed by the intramuscular route of administration.

In the last few years some new benzodiazepines, such as clonazepam, have been developed with long durations of action enabling practical use of once-daily dosing for treatment of alcohol withdrawal. Coupled with the availability of these new agents, the earlier recommendation of Sellers et al. (1983) for using a single high-loading dose of benzodiazepine to facilitate detoxification without any subsequent benzodiazepine dosing has become more practical. Because the need for several days of benzodiazepine dosing is eliminated, the associated need for careful daily monitoring of vital signs before these later doses is also eliminated. While an outpatient detoxification might be accomplished with only one physician visit, a significant risk of overdose from using alcohol after this large loading dose has limited its practical application.

The second approach to improving the symptoms associated with alcohol withdrawal uses beta blockers, such as atenolol, to decrease autonomic arousal during alcohol withdrawal (Kraus, Gottlieb, Horwitz, & Anscher, 1985). The combination of these agents with moderate doses of benzodiazepines facilitates successful alcohol detoxification without increasing medical risk. For milder withdrawal, clonidine may be as effective as chlordiazepoxide (Baumgartner & Rowen, 1987), and lofexidine can have similar efficacy with less hypotension and sedation (Brunning, Mumford, & Keaney, 1986).

The third approach using alternative agents to benzodiazepines for alcohol detoxification examined two anticonvulsant medications most carefully: carbamazepine and valproate. In outpatient randomized clinical trials comparing carbamazepine to tapering dosages of benzodiazepines, the patients receiving carbamazepine had higher success rates and fewer withdrawal symptoms during alcohol detoxification (Agricola, 1982; Malcolm, Ballenger, Sturgis, & Anton, 1989). Several studies reported on the use of valproate, which similarly appears to show good success when used alone for alcohol detoxification (Lambie, Johnson, Vijayasen, & Whiteside, 1980; Hillbom et al., 1989; Roy-Byrne, Ward, & Donnelly, 1989). Valproate was also reported to reduce the amount of other medications needed for withdrawal (Lambie et al., 1980), but the lack of a statistical analysis of these data warrants caution in interpretation.

Maintenance Medications

Over the years, a wide range of agents have been suggested for reducing relapse to alcohol abuse following acute detoxification. The oldest drug for the treatment of alcoholism is disulfiram (Antabuse). Most recently, two classes of agents have demonstrated some efficacy. These include the opioid antagonist naltrexone and serotonergic agents such as serotonin reuptake inhibitors, odansetron, and buspirone. Acamprosate is currently being studied as a maintenance treatment for alcohol dependence but is not yet available. Table 25.2 summarizes treatments.

Disulfiram was first used in the treatment of alcoholism in 1948 when it was accidentally discovered that humans pretreated with disulfiram experienced a characteristic unpleasant reaction to alcohol in even small amounts (Hald, Jacobsen, & Larsen, 1948). Disulfiram is a relatively nonspecific irreversible inhibitor of sulfhydryl-containing enzymes (Wright & Moore, 1990). The target enzyme for the pharmacological effect of disulfiram in the treatment of alcohol addiction is aldehyde dehydrogenase. This enzyme converts acetaldehyde to acetate in alcohol metabolism. The increased concentration of acetaldehyde after alcohol ingestion in the presence of disulfiram is responsible for the disulfiram–alcohol reaction. This reaction is characterized by flushing, weakness, nausea, tachycardia, and, in some instances, hypotension (Wright & Moore, 1990). Treatment of this reaction is primarily supportive and includes fluid hydration, oxygen, and Trendelenberg posture (Elenbaas, 1977). Disulfiram must not be initiated until alcohol is completely eliminated (usually by 24 hours after the last drink). Standard dosing is 250 mg orally daily (range 125–500 mg daily). The time to onset of aldehyde dehydrogenase inhibition sufficient to result in a reaction on alcohol consumption is 12 hours, and aldehyde dehydrogenase recovery is complete within 6 days of the last disulfiram dose (Helander & Carlsson, 1990). Disulfiram has not been shown to be effective in achieving abstinence or delaying relapse

TABLE 25.2. Maintenance Medications for Alcohol Disorders

Medication	Dose	Action
Disulfiram	250 mg/day	Noxious reaction with alcohol consumption due to increased acetaldehyde levels
Naltrexone	50 mg/day	Blocks opioid receptors; decreases alcohol craving/relapse
Buspirone	15–60 mg/day	Anxiolytic with no abuse liability
Acamprosate (not available in the United States)	≤ 60 kg: 1,332 mg/day; ≤ 60 kg: 1,998 mg/day	Stimulates GABA transmission, which may reduce craving; no abuse liability

(Fuller & Roth, 1979). However, in motivated patients who are intelligent, not impulsive, with no comorbid major psychiatric disorder and in combination with psychosocial treatments, disulfiram may be effective (Fuller et al., 1986). Patients taking disulfiram must be warned to avoid alcohol containing products and foods. Disulfiram may also produce a variety of adverse effects which are rare, but the most severe are hepatotoxicity and neuropathies. This medication should be avoided in patients with moderate to severe hepatic dysfunction, peripheral neuropathies, pregnancy, renal failure, or cardiac disease.

The rationale for the use of opioid antagonists in the treatment of alcohol dependence is supported by several lines of evidence. First, there are similarities in the effects of opiates and alcohol in their sedating properties as well as the type of euphoria produced. Many opiate addicts abuse alcohol when heroin is not available or in addition to heroin. Furthermore, there is cross-tolerance between opiates and alcohol in the relief of withdrawal symptoms as well as in the production of sedation and other subjective effects. Animal studies have shown that the consumption of alcohol results in the release of beta- and met-endorphins from the hypothalamus and is of greater magnitude in animals with a high alcohol preference (Hyytia & Sinclair, 1993). Small doses of morphine have been shown to increase alcohol self-administration in animals, whereas opioid antagonists such as naltrexone decreased alcohol reinforcement (Volpicelli, Alterman, O'Brien, & Hayashida, 1992). Several animal studies indicated that opioid antagonists attenuate alcohol-induced effects and decrease overall consumption (Kornet, Goosen, & Van Ree, 1991; Le, Quan, & Chow, 1993).

Two clinical studies tested the hypothesis that opioid antagonists would decrease alcohol consumption. Volpicelli et al. (1992) conducted a double-blind, controlled study in which 35 male veterans were randomized to naltrexone (50 mg daily) and 35 to placebo. Naltrexone was found to significantly reduce alcohol craving, days of drinking per week, and the rate of relapse among those who drank. The second study done by O'Malley et al. (1992) involved 97 subjects and used a 2×2 design in which two of the groups received naltrexone 50 mg daily and two of the groups received placebo crossed with either coping skills therapy or a supportive therapy. During this 12-week trial, the rate of relapse in those patients treated with naltrexone was 45%, whereas patients on placebo had a 90% relapse rate. Naltrexone was well tolerated and appeared to reduce alcohol consumption and relapse rates. The psychotherapy also had an interesting interaction with naltrexone treatment. Although the patients in the coping skills group were more likely to initiate drinking, they were less likely to relapse than were patients treated with supportive therapy. For those subjects who drank during the study, the most success in avoiding relapse was attained by the naltrexone and coping skills group, which had a relapse rate of less than 35%. The worst outcome was in the placebo and supportive therapy group where 90% relapsed, and for this placebo group most of the relapses occurred within 30 days of initiating the study. Thus, the second study showed great promise not only for this pharmacotherapy but also in matching it to a specific psycho-therapeutic intervention.

A 6-month follow-up study recently reported on the persistence of naltrexone and psychotherapy effects following discontinuation of treatment for alcohol dependence (O'Malley et al., 1996). Subjects who received naltrex-one were less likely to drink heavily (≥ 5 drinks/day in men and ≥ 4 drinks/day in women) or meet criteria for alcohol abuse or dependence than those who received placebo. However, the effect of naltrexone on abstinence rates was observed only through the first month of follow-up. Coping skills therapy was associated with decreased drinking in those who had received placebo, although psychotherapy treatment was not predictive of an alcohol disorder at follow-up. The findings in this study suggest that some patients may benefit from a period of naltrexone treatment exceeding 12 weeks.

Another series of studies examined serotonergic agents and found that several of them show good efficacy in reducing alcohol relapse compared to placebo (Sellers, Higgins, & Sobell, 1992). Unfortunately, careful studies have not been done with the newer serotonin reuptake inhibitors in the United States: sertraline and paroxetine. Several short-term clinical trials of the serotonin reuptake inhibitors that lasted 2 to 4 weeks demonstrated the effectiveness of fluoxetine, zimeldine, citalopram, and viqualine in early-stage problem drinkers (Sellers et al., 1992). This reduction in alcohol use seems independent of antidepressant activity but is relatively modest in its efficacy. The average reduction in alcohol consumption was only 9% to 17%. Two more recent studies of fluoxetine 60 mg daily (Kranzler, Bauer, Hersh, & Klinghoffer, 1995) and citalopram 40 mg daily (Naranjo, Bremner, & Lanctot, 1995) showed no significant effect of either drug in alcohol-dependent patients, calling into question the utility of these drugs in alcoholism treatment.

Another study examined the 5-HT$_3$ antagonist ondansetron for alcohol dependence (Sellers et al., 1992). Using 71 male alcohol abusers without anxiety disorders, a 6-week trial compared ondansetron at 0.5 and 4 mg to placebo. Using daily urine alcohol determinations, the 0.5 mg ondansetron group showed increasing reduction in ethanol consumption at weeks 4 to 6 compared to pretreatment. For placebo, there was a reduction of 1.5 drinks per day on drinking days, but ondansetron reduced use by 2.3 drinks per drinking day. When the heaviest drinkers who consumed more than 10.5 drinks per day were excluded, a highly significant and clinically important effect was found with up to a 37% reduction in drinking compared to baseline. This reduction was 20% greater than found with placebo. These are the first clinical data to suggest that a 5-HT$_3$ antagonist may decrease alcohol consumption. However, the interesting dose dependence with less efficiency at a larger dose of ondansetron remains to be explained.

One of the key issues in evaluating the utility of serotonergic agents for alcoholism is whether their antianxiety properties contribute to the reduction in alcohol use because anxiety disorders are quite prevalent in substance abusers (Sellers et al., 1992). Buspirone has been shown to reduce anxiety and the desire to drink in anxious alcoholics (Bruno, 1989) and was superior to placebo in abstinent alcoholics with comorbid generalized anxiety disorder in self-reports of alcohol use, anxiety level, and treatment retention (Tollefson, Montague-Clouse, & Tollefson, 1992). A recent double-blind, placebo-controlled study evaluated buspirone in the context of relapse prevention in anxious alcoholics following 12 weeks of treatment and at 6 months post-treatment (Kranzler et al., 1994). Buspirone-treated subjects were more likely to remain in treatment and buspirone was significantly more effective as an anxiolytic in patients with high pretreatment anxiety levels. Although buspirone did not significantly reduce frequency of alcohol consumption during the treatment period, patients who received buspirone had significantly fewer drinking days in the follow-up period.

A medication not yet available in the United States shows promise in the treatment of alcohol disorders. Acamprosate (calcium acetylhomotaurinate), an analogue of homocysteic acid, has a structure similar to γ-aminobutyric acid (GABA) and, as such, has been reported to stimulate inhibitory GABA transmission and to antagonize excitatory amino acids (Zeise, Kasparov, Capogna, & Zieglgansberger, 1993). These properties have been postulated to be important to reduction in alcohol craving (Littleton, 1995). Acamprosate has no abuse potential or no hypnotic muscle relaxant or anxiolytic properties. Two placebo-controlled studies reported on acamprosate in the treatment of alcoholism. In one study, 272 patients were randomized to 48 weeks of acamprosate or placebo and then followed for an additional 48 weeks without medication. Those who received acamprosate had a higher continuous abstinence rate during treatment and were significantly more likely to remain abstinent in the follow-up period (Sass, Soyka, Mann, & Zieglgansberger, 1996). The second study reported on 455 alcohol-dependent patients randomly assigned to acamprosate or placebo for 360 days. Acamprosate was well tolerated and was associated with longer duration of abstinence relative to placebo (Whitworth et al., 1996).

OPIOID PHARMACOTHERAPIES

Acute Withdrawal Medications

Patients with opioid dependence are at risk for opioid overdose. This is a medical emergency and can be life-threatening when complications of coma and respiratory arrest occur. The opioid antagonist naloxone is an injectable drug which rapidly reverses effects of opioid overdose by displacing the opioid from receptors in the brain. Naloxone may be administered intravenously or, in those without venous access, by subcutaneous injection. A dosage of 0.4–0.8 mg should reverse most opioid overdoses. In dependent patients, lower doses (0.1–0.2 mg) may be sufficient; furthermore, it is not advisable to precipitate withdrawal in these patients. Therefore, in these cases, treatment should begin with lower naloxone doses and dosage increased as clinically indicated. Once the symptoms of overdose have abated, it is important to continue to monitor level of consciousness and respiratory status because long-acting opioids may require prolonged naloxone treatment which may be administered by intravenous infusion. Patients with opioid overdose should react within minutes to this treatment. Failure to do so should call into question the working diagnosis.

The development in 1978 of clonidine as a treatment to reduce the severity of acute opioid withdrawal was followed by a series of studies designed to reduce the duration of withdrawal (Gold, Redmond, & Kleber, 1978). Using the opioid antagonists naloxone or naltrexone to precipitate withdrawal while simultaneously treating the patient with relatively high doses of clonidine has enabled opioid-dependent patients to become drug free within as little as 3 days while minimizing the antagonist-precipitated symptoms (Charney et al., 1982; Kleber, Topazian, Gaspari, Riordan, & Kosten, 1987; Vining, Kosten, & Kleber, 1988). Furthermore, the duration of withdrawal using this approach was equivalent for methadone- or heroin-dependent patients. This equivalence was interesting because ordinarily withdrawal symptoms last nearly twice as long after abruptly stopping methadone as after stopping heroin (Kleber, 1981).

Administering an antagonist such as naltrexone precipitates withdrawal within minutes for both types of patients, and this process of precipitation appears to equalize the duration of subsequent withdrawal symptoms. The amount of clonidine needed to ameliorate these symptoms was also lessened by larger initial doses of naltrexone. Detoxification with a starting dose of 12.5 mg of naltrexone required clonidine for only 4 days, with a total dose of 1.7 mg and a peak dose of 0.6 mg on day 1 (Vining et al., 1988). Thus, a more rapid and comfortable procedure has evolved for acute detoxification. A recent study showed that clonidine or clonidine and naltrexone in combination are both efficacious regimens for the ambulatory treatment of opioid withdrawal with 70% of subjects completing detoxification (O'Connor et al., 1995). These protocols are summarized in Table 25.3. Tapering doses of methadone are often used in ambulatory detoxification, but the protracted withdrawal syndrome associated with methadone cessation has contributed to a high rate of relapse to opioid use with this method (Senay, Dorus, Goldberg, & Thornton, 1977). Khan, Mumford, Rogers, and Beckford (1997) recently showed that methadone detoxification can be successfully completed using lofexidine, an α-2 adrenergic agonist that produces less hypotension than clonidine. Lofexidine was equal to clonidine in reducing symptoms of opioid withdrawal and side effects of hypotension and lethargy were reported by substantially fewer patients in the lofexidine group.

Another recent development in opioid detoxification has been the use of buprenorphine, a partial opioid agonist (Kosten & Kleber, 1988; Lewis, 1985). Both heroin addicts and methadone-maintained patients have been switched to buprenorphine for a month of stabilization at once-daily doses ranging from 2 mg to 8 mg sublingually. Following this month, buprenorphine was abruptly stopped, and the patient given a high dose of intravenous

TABLE 25.3. Ambulatory Opioid Detoxification Medication Protocols

Clonidine detoxification (9-day protocol)								
	1	Detoxification day 2 3 4			5 6 7		8	9
Clonidine[a,b]	0.1–0.2 mg (oral) Max. dose: 1 mg on day 1	Every 4 hours as needed Max. dose: 1.2 mg on days 2–4			Taper to 0 on days 5–8			
Naltrexone[b]							25 mg	50 mg

Clonidine with naltrexone induction (5-day protocol)				
Clonidine[b]	Preload: 0.2–0.4 mg Max. dose: 1.2 mg on days 1–2		Taper to 0 on days 3–5	
Oxazepam[b]	Preload: 30–60 mg			
Naltrexone[b]	12.5 mg	25 mg	50 mg	50 mg 50 mg

Note. As needed: oxazepam 30–60 mg every 6 hours: cramps, insomnia; ibuprofen 600 mg every 6 hours: cramps; prochlorperazine 5 mg IM every 6 hours: vomiting.
[a]Hold for SBP < 90 mm Hg.
[b]Oral dosing.

naloxone (35 mg) to precipitate withdrawal from the buprenorphine (Kosten, Krystal, et al., 1989). This withdrawal syndrome is relatively mild and can be treated with clonidine if necessary. Following precipitated withdrawal, the patient may be started on naltrexone the same day. A recent randomized trial comparing this buprenorphine procedure to standard clonidine detoxification showed greater success and fewer withdrawal symptoms using buprenorphine (Shi et al., 1993).

Success rates for detoxification have generally assessed only short-term outcomes of either becoming opioid free or starting naltrexone. Longer-term positive outcomes are critical but essentially depend on strategies to maintain these patients on naltrexone because relapse to illicit opioid use is quite frequent (usually over 90%) over even a 6- to 12-month period without sustained outpatient treatment (Kleber, 1981; Kosten & Kleber, 1984).

Maintenance Medications

The two opioid maintenance pharmacotherapies most frequently used in the United States are naltrexone and methadone, but one investigational agent, LAAM, was approved in 1993 by the Food and Drug Administration, and buprenorphine should also become available in the next few years. These latter agents address some limitations of methadone and naltrexone—difficulties with detoxification from methadone maintenance to a drug-free state and poor acceptability and retention on naltrexone. Although these limitations are serious, maintenance can be quite therapeutic when several clinical guidelines are followed.

Naltrexone is an opioid antagonist that is administered orally and can be used in those patients who do not want to be maintained on opioids. Naltrexone should not be initiated until the patient is completely detoxified from opioids to avoid precipitating withdrawal. This detoxification up to 7–10 days of abstinence from short-acting opioids and 10 days of abstinence from long-acting opioids such as methadone (unless detoxification is accomplished with a naltrexone induction; see earlier). If any doubt exists as to the opioid history, a naloxone challenge may be given in which 2 ml of naloxone (0.4 mg/ml) solution is prepared and an initial dose of 0.5 ml of this solution (0.2 mg of naloxone) is administered intravenously. Symptoms of opioid withdrawal (mydriasis, dysphoria, diaphoresis, and gastrointestinal discomfort) in approximately 30 seconds indicate that the patient remains dependent. If no withdrawal is observed, the remaining naloxone solution is administered and observation continued. If intravenous access is not available, 2 ml of the naloxone solution may be administered subcutaneously with an observation period of 45 minutes (Galloway & Hayner, 1993).

Naltrexone can be administered at a dose of 50 mg daily, 100 mg every 2 days, or 150 mg every third day which will attenuate opioid effects and assist in relapse prevention. Naltrexone should be administered for at least 6 months and discontinuation carefully planned with the patient. Naltrexone side effects are few, but hepatotoxicity has been reported and hepatic function should be determined prior to treatment and monitored at 3-month intervals. The biggest problem with naltrexone has been a lack of patient compliance.

For patients who chronically relapse to opioid dependence, the treatment of choice is maintenance with a long-acting opioid. The goal of treatment with any long-acting opioid is to achieve a stable dose that reduces, or, ideally, eliminates, illicit opioid craving and use, and which facilitates the engagement of the patient in a comprehensive program that promotes rehabilitation and prevents abuse of other drugs. Because treatment with long-acting opioids results in dependence, it is important to select patients who have a history of prolonged dependence (greater than 1 year) and who demonstrate physiological dependence.

Methadone is the most widely used of these long-acting opioids. It is effective in decreasing psychosocial consequences and medical morbidity associated with opioid dependence. It is also an important tool in decreasing the spread of human immunodeficiency virus infection among injection drug users. The efficacy of methadone spans a wide range of doses and each patient's dose must be individually titrated. Methadone 40–60 mg daily will block opioid withdrawal symptoms, but doses of 70–80 mg daily are more often needed to curb craving. Generally, doses greater than 60 mg daily are associated with better retention and less illicit opioid use (Ball & Ross, 1991).

An alternative to methadone maintenance is LAAM (Blaine, Thomas, Barnett, Whysner, & Renault, 1981). LAAM has been shown to be comparable to methadone in reduction of illicit opioid use (Ling, Charuvastra, Kain, & Klett, 1976). This congener of methadone has a long terminal half-life of 48–72 hours, so that dosing can be as infrequent as every 2 to 3 days. A large clinical trial ($N = 430$) compared a fixed dose of LAAM (80 mg every other day) to two different doses of methadone (50 mg or 100 mg daily); retention was somewhat poorer with LAAM primarily due to dropout during the initial month of dosage stabilization. When heroin addicts first enter either methadone or LAAM maintenance, the dose is lower than the ultimate maintenance dose (e.g., 25 mg rather than 100 mg of methadone daily), and the dose is gradually increased over several weeks to prevent overdose. Because of its longer half-life, LAAM took longer than methadone to reach a steady state that the patients found comfortable. During this period of dose titration, patients in the LAAM group were more likely to drop out of treatment. By the 40-week time point, the LAAM group retention rate was 40%, whereas the two methadone groups retained 60% (50 mg) and 70% (100 mg) of patients. Illicit opioid use was substantially reduced in the LAAM group, however, and this reduction to about 15%, between weeks 8 and 40 of the trial, was significantly lower than the reduction to about 40% in the 50 mg methadone group and equivalent to the 100 mg methadone group. Thus, LAAM shows good potential as an alternative to methadone, with the advantage of not needing to provide take-home medication. Its limitations during the stabilization phase may be approached in various ways, including starting patients on daily methadone and then converting them to LAAM, when they become candidates for less frequent clinic attendance.

The most recent alternative opioid maintenance treatment is buprenorphine (Jasinski, Pevnick, & Griffith, 1978; Lewis, 1985). Outpatient experience with this medication is rapidly accumulating in the United States, and it has been widely available in other countries for several years. Several 6-month outpatient trials compared sublingual buprenorphine to methadone for the treatment of opioid addicts and have suggested good efficacy at 8 to 16 mg daily.

Two treatment studies were published comparing buprenorphine to methadone for opioid dependence. In the study by Johnson, Fudala, and Jaffe (1992), buprenorphine at 8 mg daily was equivalent to 65 mg daily of methadone in rates of illicit opioid use and in treatment retention during the 6-month trial. At 8 mg daily of buprenorphine, only 37% of the urines were positive for illicit opioids, whereas at 20 mg daily of methadone there was significantly higher rates of illicit opioid use. Although opioid-free urines were greater on 65 mg than 20 mg of methadone, overall about 50% of the urines were opioid positive in the methadone-treated patients.

Kosten, Schottenfeld, Ziedonis, and Falcioni (1993) reported on 125 opioid-dependent patients who were randomized to either 2 mg or 6 mg of buprenorphine daily or to 35 mg or 65 mg of methadone daily. The 6 mg dose of buprenorphine was superior to 2 mg in reducing illicit opioid use, but the higher dosage did not improve treatment retention. Treatment retention was significantly better on methadone, and the methadone patients had significantly more opioid-free urines (51% vs. 26%). Abstinence for at least 3 weeks was also more common on methadone than on buprenorphine (65% vs. 27%). Thus, methadone was superior to these two buprenorphine dosages. Other studies suggest that higher-dose buprenorphine is superior to lower dose. In two outpatient dose-ranging studies (Bickel et al., 1988; Schottenfeld, Pakes, Ziedonis, & Kosten, 1993), opioid-free urines increased almost 90% at 12 to 16 mg of buprenorphine daily.

Although the abuse potential of buprenorphine appears to be less than that of a pure agonist such as heroin or methadone, this partial agonist has been abused intravenously (Quigley, Bredemeyer, & Seow, 1984). This abuse potential suggests that any treatment program designed to use this medication needs the type of controls developed for methadone-maintenance treatment because diversion to illicit use could be a problem.

In summary, buprenorphine appears to be a very promising treatment alternative for heroin addicts, particularly at dosages of 12 to 16 mg daily, where its efficacy and acceptability to opioid addicts appears to be equivalent to methadone at standard therapeutic dosages of 65 mg daily. It is associated with good treatment retention, reduces illicit opioid abuse, and provides a rapid and relatively symptom-free detoxification to a drug-free state after sustained treatment.

COCAINE PHARMACOTHERAPIES

The widespread abuse of cocaine and the debilitating nature of the psychological dependence which often develops in frequent users in combination with the high rate of comorbid medical and psychiatric conditions that occur as a consequence of cocaine abuse have made it a target of research aimed at finding effective treatments. Cocaine has effects on multiple neurotransmitters including release and reuptake blockade of dopamine, norepinephrine, and serotonin (Koe, 1976). The most widely accepted explanation of cocaine-induced reinforcement is that of dopamine reuptake inhibition, which results in increased extracellular dopamine concentrations in the mesolimbic and mesocortical reward pathways in the brain. The development of pharmacological treatments for cocaine abuse has been based on the premise that an altered neurochemical substrate underlies the chronic, high-intensity (binge) use and "crash" which follows binge use (Kuhar, Ritz, & Boja, 1991). Many medications have been studied as potential treatments for cocaine abuse, but to date, none has emerged as an accepted effective pharmacotherapy. This section briefly reviews the medications and rationale for their use in the treatment of cocaine disorders. We also briefly review new pharmacotherapies which are currently being studied as cocaine treatments.

Dopaminergic Agents

Bromocriptine is an agonist with high affinity for the dopamine-2 (D2) receptor. Treatment with bromocriptine might reverse dopaminergic deficits induced by cocaine and ameliorate craving and withdrawal. Early studies yielded conflicting results and suffered from high dropout rates and adverse events (headaches, vertigo, and/or syncope) (Giannini & Baumgartel, 1987;

Tennant & Sagherian, 1987). The use of bromocriptine to treat acute cocaine abstinence has been revisited in a small double-blind, placebo-controlled trial (Moscovitz, Brookoff, & Nelson, 1993). Bromocriptine 1.25 mg three times daily or placebo was given to patients who presented to an emergency room for minor medical complaints but who were found to be abusing cocaine by urine toxicology screen. Bromocriptine was generally well tolerated and 5 of 14 subjects on bromocriptine completed the study. Those randomized to bromocriptine had more urine toxicology screens negative for cocaine (67%) than those randomized to placebo (31%). Novel treatments with bromocriptine are being explored and could include the use of bromocriptine in combination with other agents. For example, an open-label study of the combination of bromocriptine (≤ 7.5 mg daily) and bupropion (≤ 300 mg daily) was conducted over an 8-week study period (Montoya, Preston, Rotham, Cone, & Gorelick, 1994). There was a significant reduction in pre- and posttreatment self-reports of cocaine use ($p < .01$), but no significant change in urine toxicology screens (both qualitative and quantitative). This study provides evidence for the safety of this combination but does not support efficacy for the treatment of cocaine dependence. However, these studies indicate that bromocriptine may have some utility in the treatment of cocaine dependence and should be considered in future clinical trials.

Amantadine increases dopaminergic transmission, but whether the mechanism is dopamine release, acute effects on dopamine receptors, or dopamine reuptake blockade is unclear. One study examined the effects of acute amantadine (200 or 400 mg) and chronic amantadine (100 mg twice daily for 4 days) on cocaine 0.9 mg/kg administered by nasal insufflation (Sholar, Lukas, Kouri, & Mendelson, 1994). Acute effects of both amantadine doses on cocaine responses included attenuation of heart rate increases whereas the amantadine 200 mg dose was associated with a decrease in cocaine "high." Chronic administration of amantadine 100 mg twice daily was associated with increased "high" in male subjects after cocaine administration as compared to female subjects. Clinical trials with amantadine yielded mixed results. One controlled trial showed no difference between amantadine and placebo (Weddington et al., 1991). However, in another study amantadine was evaluated in a double-blind, placebo-controlled trial in which 42 patients in a day-treatment program were randomized to amantadine 100 mg twice daily ($N = 21$) to be taken over 10½ days or placebo ($N = 21$). Urine toxicology screens showed that those who had received amantadine were significantly more likely to be free of cocaine ($p < .05$) at the 2-week and 1-month follow-up visits, although self-reports for the two treatment groups did not differ (Alterman et al., 1992). A more recent double-blind, placebo-controlled, 4-week clinical trial showed no evidence for efficacy of amantadine 300 mg daily for treatment of cocaine dependence (Kampman et al., 1996).

Bupropion is an antidepressant that enhances dopaminergic and noradrenergic neurotransmission but has little effect on serotonergic neurotransmission. An open pilot study in six methadone-maintained cocaine abusers showed bupropion 100 mg three times daily to be a promising treatment

(Margolin, Kosten, Petrakis, Avants, & Kosten, 1991). However, the results of a large multicenter study designed to assess the effectiveness of bupropion for treatment of cocaine addiction in methadone-maintained patients showed little evidence for efficacy in this group (Margolin, Kosten, et al., 1995).

Mazindol, a catecholamine reuptake blocker, was originally developed as an appetite suppressant and has also been shown to have some efficacy in the treatment of Parkinson's disease. Mazindol showed promise in an open trial, but a brief crossover study showed no significant improvement in cocaine craving or use (Diakogiannis, Steinberg, & Kosten, 1990). A recent double-blind, placebo-controlled study showed no efficacy for mazindol 2 mg daily for treatment of cocaine dependence (Stine, Krystal, Kosten, & Charney, 1995). A recent neuroimaging study of mazindol occupancy of the dopamine transporter before and during cocaine administration showed that mazindol at a dose of 4 mg daily does not occupy enough transporters to block cocaine effects (Malison et al., 1998). These findings indicate that mazindol in doses that can be tolerated by humans is unlikely to be useful as a treatment for cocaine dependence.

Antidepressants

The rationale for the use of tricyclic antidepressants is that they reduce postsynaptic dopaminergic receptor sensitivity and thus may reverse cocaine-induced supersensitivity (Gawin & Kleber, 1986). The tricyclic antidepressants, rather than acting as a general antidepressant in cocaine abusers who do not have major affective disorders, act as specific antianhedonic agents in this population. Although the positive aspects of the use of tricyclic antidepressants for treatment of cocaine abuse include a relatively benign side effect profile, lack of abuse liability, and patient acceptance, a significant disadvantage to their use lies in the delayed onset of effect (approximately 2 weeks).

Desipramine is the tricyclic antidepressant studied most extensively as a treatment for cocaine abuse. Dosages of 200–250 mg daily administered for 4–6 weeks were initially found to be effective in cocaine use disorders (Gawin et al., 1989). Others examined desipramine with less encouraging results (Covi, Montoya, Hess, & Kreiter, 1994; Levin & Lehman, 1991; Kosten, Morgan, Falcioni, & Schottenfeld, 1992; Arndt, Dorozynsky, Woody, McLellan, & O'Brien, 1992; Weddington et al., 1991). A 12-week, placebo-controlled clinical trial which examined the efficacy of desipramine and psychotherapy, alone and in combination, as a treatment for ambulatory cocaine abusers has been reported (Carroll et al., 1994). The mean dose of desipramine was 200 mg daily. All groups showed significant improvement in treatment retention and a reduction in cocaine use at 12 weeks, but there were no significant main effects for psychotherapy, pharmacotherapy, or the combination. Lower-severity patients (cocaine use 1–2.5 g/week) had improved abstinence initiation when treated with desipramine. Desipramine was significantly more effective than placebo in reducing cocaine use during the first 6 weeks of treatment. Depressed subjects had a greater reduction in cocaine use than did nondepressed subjects and had a better response to relapse prevention therapy. The findings of this study underscore the heterogeneity among cocaine abusers and the need to develop specialized treatments for distinct subgroups of cocaine abusers.

Serotonin dysregulation may be one consequence of chronic cocaine administration (Ritz, Cohen, & Kuhar, 1990). Serotonergic agents such as the reuptake inhibitor fluoxetine have been found to reduce cocaine self-administration in animal studies (Richardson & Roberts, 1991; Carroll, Lac, Asencio, & Kragh, 1990). Fluoxetine has also been shown to decrease subjective ratings of cocaine's positive mood effects in human subjects (Walsh, Preston, Sullivan, Fromme, & Bigelow, 1994).

Several recent double-blind, placebo-controlled clinical trials of fluoxetine for the treatment of cocaine dependence have been reported. Grabowski et al. (1995) found no evidence for efficacy of fluoxetine in patients with primary cocaine dependence (dose range 0–40 mg daily) or in a sample of methadone-maintained patients with cocaine dependence (fluoxetine dose range 0–20 mg daily). A study by Batki, Washburn, Delucchi, and Jones (1996) in crack-dependent patients treated for 12 weeks with fluoxetine 40 mg daily showed significantly longer treatment retention in the fluoxetine group but no decrease in cocaine craving or use. A 9-week open trial of sertraline, a potent and specific inhibitor of serotonin uptake, in 11 outpatient cocaine abusers showed reduced cocaine craving and abstinence for at least 3 weeks in five subjects (Kosten, Kosten, et al., 1992). A 12-week pilot study of gepirone (mean dose of 16.25 mg daily) compared to placebo in 41 cocaine abusers did not provide any evidence for efficacy in the treatment of cocaine abuse (Jenkins et al., 1992).

Miscellaneous Agents

Disulfiram is currently being investigated in clinical settings as a treatment for cocaine–alcohol abuse because it prevents the ingestion of alcohol with cocaine, a common practice of cocaine abusers who want to potentiate euphoria or alleviate dysphoric and stimulant effects of binge cocaine use. A small, open pilot study comparing disulfiram 250 mg daily to naltrexone 50 mg daily found that disulfiram treatment reduced both cocaine and alcohol use and lengthened periods of abstinence (Carroll, Ziedonis, O'Malley, McCance-Katz, & Rounsaville, 1993). Higgins et al. (1993) and Van Etten et al. (1994) also reported that disulfiram 250 mg daily decreased cocaine and alcohol use in their patient sample. Disulfiram has been shown to have significant interactions with cocaine (McCance-Katz, Kosten, & Jatlow, in press). In a study in which cocaine-dependent, alcohol-abusing volunteers were randomly assigned to chronic disulfiram treatment (0, 250, or 500 mg daily) and then insufflated cocaine, disulfiram treatment substantially increased systemic exposure and plasma cocaine concentrations. Cardiovascular responses were greater during disulfiram treatment. Disulfiram treatment blunted peak "high" for the low cocaine (1 mg/kg) dose but increased "high" for the cocaine 2 mg/kg dose. Disulfiram treatment increased anxiety following cocaine administration, and these responses were greatest for disulfiram 250 mg daily teatment. Recently, an outpatient, randomized clinical trial in which disulfiram 250 mg daily was administered in combination with psychotherapies in cocaine-dependent, alcohol abusing patients showed disulfiram administration to be beneficial with significant reductions in cocaine and alcohol use observed. Importantly, few adverse events were observed in this study (Carroll, Nich, Ball, McCance, & Rounsaville, 1998). Disulfiram appears to be a promising treatment for selected, motivated patients who abuse cocaine and alcohol.

Carbamazepine is an anticonvulsant medication hypothesized to have potential as a treatment for cocaine abuse because of its ability to reverse cocaine-induced "kindling" (Post & Kopanda, 1976), which was proposed to mediate cocaine craving (Halikas, Kemp, Kuhn, Carlson, & Crea, 1989). Several studies exploring the efficacy of carbamazepine for cocaine dependence showed no evidence for efficacy (Cornish et al., 1995; Kranzler et al., 1995; Montoya et al., 1994).

Cocaine abuse is a major public health problem among methadone-maintained outpatients, and several medications were studied for their ability to reduce cocaine use in this population. Bupropion 300 mg daily was compared to placebo treatment for cocaine dependence in methadone-maintained patients at three sites over a 12-week period. There was no significant effect of bupropion on cocaine use, depression, or level of psychosocial function, although exploratory analysis suggested a medication effect for those with depression at baseline (Margolin, Kosten, et al., 1995). Mazindol at a dose of 2 mg daily was not different from placebo in its effect on cocaine abuse in methadone-maintained patients (Kosten, Steinberg, & Diakogiannis, 1993). Another double-blind, placebo-controlled study of mazindol 1 mg daily for cocaine-abusing, methadone-maintained patients was also negative (Margolin, Avants, & Kosten, 1995).

Buprenorphine is a partial opioid antagonist whose relatively lower opiate agonist action was postulated to have the ability to decrease the "speedball" interaction with cocaine. Thus, buprenorphine appeared to have promise as an opioid pharmacotherapy that might be associated with decreased cocaine abuse. An early open trial in which 41 opioid-dependent patients self-selected for a 1-month trial of buprenorphine (mean dose 3.2 mg daily, maximum dose 8 mg daily) showed substantially less cocaine abuse than in patients maintained on methadone (mean dose 43 mg daily during month 1 and 54 mg daily during month 2) (Kosten, Kleber, & Morgan, 1989). Subsequent controlled trials found no efficacy for buprenorphine at 8 mg daily compared to methadone in reducing cocaine abuse (Fudala, Johnson, & Jaffe, 1991; Oliveto, Kosten, Schottenfeld, Ziedonis, & Falcioni, 1994). Another study comparing the efficacy of buprenorphine (up to 16 mg daily) and methadone (up to 90 mg daily) for decreasing cocaine use in cocaine- and opioid-dependent patients found no differences in cocaine use in the two samples (Strain, Stitzer, Liebson, & Bigelow, 1994).

Future Directions for Cocaine Pharmacotherapy

A variety of medications continue to be pursued to determine their efficacy for treatment of cocaine dependence, but two new areas appear to be promising. Self, Barnhart, Lehman, and Nestler (1996) showed that activation of the mesolimbic dopamine system which triggers relapse to cocaine-seeking behavior in animals is selectively induced by D2-like receptor agonists. Conversely, D1-like agonists prevented cocaine-seeking behavior induced by cocaine administration. These results suggest that D1 agonists should be further pursued as potential cocaine pharmacotherapies. Anti-cocaine antibodies have been developed that have been shown in animal studies to inhibit self-administration. The presence of antibody has also been shown to reduce brain cocaine levels following intravenous or intranasal cocaine administration (Fox, Kantak, & Edwards, 1996). The cocaine antibody could also be developed as an emergency treatment for cocaine toxicity. Thus, development of cocaine antibody therapy may be a promising new treatment modality which remains to be tested in humans.

PSYCHIATRIC COMORBIDITY

Drug and alcohol use disorders are associated with high rates of comorbid psychiatric disorders (American Psychiatric Association, 1995). The comorbid occurrence of substance use and psychiatric disorders is multifaceted but can be reduced to a function that either (1) the psychopathological condition predisposes to substance abuse or (2) the substance abuse predisposes to psychopathological conditions (Meyer, 1986). The diagnosis of comorbid psychiatric disorders in substance abusers is often challenging because the onset of many such disorders occurs in adolescence or early adulthood; the same period as for the onset of drug use disorders. This makes determination of primary versus secondary diagnosis difficult. However, careful developmental and family histories and attention to the presence or absence of psychiatric symptoms during periods of sobriety can be helpful adjuncts and may assist in diagnostic accuracy. Worsening psychiatric symptoms in the face of unchanging substance abuse may also indicate a comorbid psychiatric disorder that needs treatment in addition to the substance use disorder(s). Psychiatric symptoms observed during acute intoxication and withdrawal syndromes that fail to remit with sobriety are often harbingers of comorbidity.

Conversely, symptoms associated with substance use disorders including acute intoxication and withdrawal syndromes are sometimes mistaken for exacerbation of an underlying psychiatric illness resulting in misdiagnosis and inappropriate treatment. The correct diagnosis depends on an adequate observation period and careful attention to the nature and temporal sequence of psychiatric symptoms. This process may require several weeks after the last drug or alcohol use but is worth the effort because the implications for comorbid conditions and the consequences to the patient of additional psychiatric diagnoses are substantial. Inappropriate diagnosis of a psychiatric condition can foster denial in patients with primary substance use disorders and result in ineffective treatment of the substance use disorder. The pervasive nature of substance use disorders requires increased emphasis on substance abuse education for mental health providers, attention to substance abuse in the history taking and ongoing treatment, and urine toxicology screens and breathalyzers as a routine part of evaluation and treatment.

Psychotropic medication treatment of dually diagnosed patients is similar to that of psychiatric patients without substance use disorders with several caveats. Patients with psychotic disorders treated with medications that block dopamine receptors may develop postsynaptic dopaminergic supersensitivity. As a result, such patients may experience enhanced cocaine effects. These patients may benefit from treatment with the newer atypical antipsychotics which lack strong dopaminergic antagonist action. Patients with psychotic disorders who are also alcoholic should be carefully evaluated before being treated with disulfiram. Disulfiram is a dopamine β-hydroxylase inhibitor and could exacerbate psychosis in such patients. Attention-deficit/hyperactivity disorder (ADHD) is not an infrequent comorbid condition in cocaine abusers who may self-medicate with this stimulant. Such patients require a careful evaluation and, when possible, corroborating history from family and/or school records. Treatment with standard agents used for ADHD, including stimulant medications, may result in cessation of cocaine use. Depressive disorders are common in those with cocaine and alcohol use disorders. The serotonin reuptake inhibitors may be a better choice for these patients because there is some evidence that this class of drug may also reduce alcohol use. In addition, these drugs are less likely to have significant cardiovascular interactions with cocaine and are less likely to be lethal in overdose. Monoamine oxidase inhibitors should never be used in cocaine abusers because of the risk of hypertensive crisis. Benzodiazepines should be used with caution in alcoholic patients with comorbid psychiatric disorders because of cross-tolerance with alcohol and additive effects if combined with alcohol. Benzodiazepines may be required to initially stabilize patients with exacerbation of psychosis or extreme agitation but should be tapered as antipsychotics and/or mood stabilizers become therapeutic. Alcoholic patients with anxiety disorders can usually be effectively treated with serotonergic agents (serotonin reuptake inhibitors or partial agonists) or tricyclic antidepressants.

ACKNOWLEDGMENTS

This work was supported by NIDA Grant Nos. K02-DA00112 (TRK) and K20-DA00216 (EMK) and University of California at San Francisco Treatment Research Center (P50-DA09253).

REFERENCES

Agricola, R. (1982). Treatment of acute alcohol withdrawal syndrome with car-bamazepine: A double-blind comparison with tiapride. *Journal of International Medical Research, 10,* 160–165.

Alterman, A. I., Droba, M., Antelo, R. E., Cornish, J. W., Sweeney, K. K., Paarikh, G. A., & O'Brien, C. P. (1992). Amantadine may facilitate detoxification of cocaine addicts. *Drug and Alcohol Dependence, 31,* 19–29.

American Psychiatric Association. (1995). Practice guideline for the treatment of patients with substance use disorders: Alcohol, cocaine, opioids. *American Journal of Psychiatry, 152*(Suppl.), 5–59.

Arndt, I. O., Dorozynsky, L., Woody, G. E., McLellan, A. T., & O'Brien, C. P. (1992). Desipramine treatment of cocaine dependence in methadone-maintained patients. *Archives of General Psychiatry, 49,* 888–893.

Ball, J., & Ross, A. (Eds.). (1991). *The effectiveness of methadone maintenance treatment.* New York: Springer-Verlag.

Batki, S. L., Washburn, A. M., Delucchi, K., & Jones, R. T. (1996). A controlled trial of fluoxetine in crack cocaine dependence. *Drug and Alcohol Dependence, 41,* 137–142.

Baumgartner, G. R., & Rowen, R. C. (1987). Clonidine versus chlordiazepoxide in the management of acute alcohol withdrawal syndrome. *Archives of Internal Medicine, 107,* 880–884.

Bickel, W. K., Stitzer, M. L., Bigelow, G. E., Liebson, I. A., Jasinski, D. R., & Johnson, R. E. (1988). Buprenorphine: Dose-related blockade of opioid challenge effects in opioid-dependent humans. *Journal of Pharmacology and Experimental Therapeutics, 247,* 47–53.

Blaine, J. D., Thomas, D. B., Barnett, G., Whysner, J. A., & Renault, P. F. (1981). Levo-alpha-acetylmethadol (LAAM): Clinical utility and pharmaceutical development. In J. H. Lowinson & P. Ruiz (Eds.), *Substance abuse: Clinical problems and perspectives* (pp. 360–388) Baltimore: Williams & Wilkins.

Brunning, J., Mumford, J. P., & Keaney, F. P. (1986). Lofexidine in alcohol withdrawal states. *Alcohol, 21,* 167.

Bruno, F. (1989). Buspirone in the treatment of alcoholic patients. *Psychopathology, 22*(Suppl.), 49–59.

Carroll, K. M., Nich, C., Ball, S. A., McCance, E., & Rounsaville, B. J. (1998). Treatment of cocaine and alcohol dependence with psychotherapy and disulfiram. *Addictions, 93,* 713–728.

Carroll, K. M., Rounsaville, B. J., Gordon, L. T., Nich, C., Jatlow, P., Bisighini, R. M., & Gawin, F. H. (1994). Psychotherapy and pharmacotherapy for ambulatory cocaine abusers. *Archives of General Psychiatry, 51,* 177–187.

Carroll, K. M., Ziedonis, D., O'Malley, S. S., McCance-Katz, E. F., & Rounsaville, B. R. (1993). Pharmacologic interventions for abusers of alcohol and cocaine: Disulfiram versus naltrexone. *American Journal on Addictions, 2,* 77–79.

Carroll, M. E., Lac, S., Asencio, M., & Kragh, R. (1990). Fluoxetine reduces intravenous cocaine self-administration in the rat. *Pharmacology, Biochemistry and Behavior, 35,* 237–244.

Charney, D. S., Riordan, C. E., Kleber, H. D., Murburg, M., Braverman, P., Sternberg, D. E., Heninger, G. R., & Redmond, D. E. (1982). Clonidine and naltrexone: A safe, effective and rapid treatment of abrupt withdrawal from methadone therapy. *Archives of General Psychiatry, 39,* 1327–1332.

Clarke, P. B. S. (1991). Nicotinic receptor blockade therapy and smoking cessation. *British Journal of Addictions, 86,* 501–505.

Cornish, J. W., Maany, I., Fudala, P. J., Neal, S., Poole, S. A., Volpicelli, P., & O'Brien, C. P. (1995). Carbamazepine treatment for cocaine dependence. *Drug and Alcohol Dependence, 38,* 221–227.

Covi, L., Montoya, I. D., Hess, J., & Kreiter, N. (1994). Double-blind comparison of desipramine and placebo for treatment of cocaine dependence. *Clinical Pharmacology and Therapeutics, 55,* 132–138.

Diakogiannis, I. A., Steinberg, M., & Kosten, T. R. (1990). Mazindol treatment of cocaine abuse: A double-blind investigation. In L. S. Onken, J. D. Blaine, & J. J. Boren (Eds.), *Integrating behavior with medication in the treatment of drug dependence* (NIDA Research Monograph No. 105, p. 514). Washington, DC: U.S. Government Printing Office.

Elenbaas, R. M. (1977). Drug therapy reviews: Management of the disulfiram–alcohol reaction. *American Journal of Hospital Pharmacy, 34,* 827–831.

Fagerstrom, K. O., & Melin, B. (1985). Nicotine chewing gum in smoking cessation: Efficacy, nicotine dependence, therapy duration, and clinical recommendations. In J. Grabowski & S. M. Hall (Eds.), *Pharmacological adjuncts in smoking cesssation* (NIDA Research Monograph No. 53, pp. 102–109). Washington, DC: U.S. Government Printing Office.

Ferry, L. H., Robbins, A. S., Scariati, P. D., Masterson, A., Abbey, D. E., & Burchette, R. J. (1992). Enhancement of smoking cessation using the antidepressant bupropion hydrochloride [Abstract]. *Circulation, 86,* 671.

Fiore, M. C., Jorenby, D. E., Baker, T. B., & Kenford, S. L. (1992). Tobacco dependence and the nicotine patch: Clinical guidelines for effective use. *Journal of the American Medical Association, 268,* 2687–2694.

Fiore, M. C., Smith, S. S., Jorenby, D. E., & Baker, T. B. (1994). The effectiveness of the nicotine patch for smoking cessation: A meta analysis. *Journal of the American Medical Association, 271,* 1940–1946.

Fox, B. S., Kantak, K. M., & Edwards, M. A. (1996). Efficacy of a therapeutic cocaine vaccine in rodent models. *Nature Medicine, 2,* 1129–1132.

Fudala, P. J., Johnson, R. E., & Jaffe, J. H. (1991). Outpatient comparison of buprenorphine and methadone maintenance: II. Effects on cocaine usage, retention time in study and missed clinic visits. In L. S. Onken, J. D. Blaine, & J. J. Boren (Eds.), *Integrating behavior with medication in the treatment of drug dependence* (NIDA Research Monograph No. 105, pp. 587–588). Washington, DC: U.S. Government Printing Office.

Fuller, R. F., Branchey, L., Brightwell, D. R., Derman, R. M., Emrick, C. D., Iber, F. L., James, K. E., Lacoursiere, R. B., Lee, K. K., Lowenstein, I., Maany, I., Neiderhiser D., Nocks J. J., & Shaw S. (1986). Disulfiram treatment of alcoholism: A Veteran's Administration cooperative study. *Journal of the American Medical Association, 256,* 1449–1455.

Fuller, R. F., & Roth, H. P. (1979). Disulfiram for the treatment of alcoholism: An evaluation in 128 men. *Annals of Internal Medicine, 90,* 901–904.

Galloway, G., & Hayner, G. (1993). Haight-Ashbury Free Clinics' drug detoxification protocols. Part 2: Opioid blockade. *Journal of Psychoactive Drugs, 25,* 251–252.

Gawin, F. H., & Kleber, H. D. (1986). Pharmacological treatment of cocaine abuse. *Psychiatric Clinics of North America, 9,* 573–583.

Gawin, F. H., Kleber, H. D., Byck, R., Rounsaville, B. J., Kosten, T. R., Jatlow, P. I., &

Morgan, C. (1989). Desipramine facilitation of initial cocaine abstinence. *Archives of General Psychiatry, 46,* 117–121.

Giannini, A. J., & Baumgartel, P. (1987). Bromocriptine in cocaine withdrawal. *Journal of Clinical Pharmacology, 27,* 267–270.

Gold, M. S., Redmond, D. E., & Kleber, H. D. (1978). Clonidine for opiate withdrawal. *Lancet, 1,* 929–930.

Gourlay, S. G., & Benowitz, N. L. (1995). Is clonidine an effective smoking cessation therapy? *Drugs, 50,* 197–207.

Grabowski, J., Rhoades, H., Elk, R., Schitz, J., Davis, C., Creson, D., & Kirby, K. (1995). Fluoxetine is ineffective for treatment of cocaine dependence or concurrent opiate and cocaine dependence: Two placebo-controlled, double-blind trials. *Journal of Clinical Psychopharmacology, 15,* 163–174.

Hald, J., Jacobsen, E., & Larsen, V. (1948). The sensitizing effect of tetraethylthiuram disulfide (Antabuse) to ethyl alcohol. *Acta Pharmacologica Toxicologica, 4,* 285–296.

Halikas, J., Kemp, K., Kuhn, K., Carlson, G., & Crea, F. (1989). Carbamazepine for cocaine addiction? *Lancet, 1,* 623–624.

Hall, S. M., Hall, R. G., & Ginsberg, D. (1990). Pharmacology and behavioral treatment for cigarette smoking. In M. Hersen, R. M. Eisler, & P. M. Miller (Eds.), *Progress in behavior modification* (pp. 86–118). Newbury Park, CA: Sage.

Hall, S. M., Munoz, R. F., Reus, V., & Sees, K. (1993). Nicotine, negative affect, and depression. *Journal of Consulting and Clinical Psychology, 61,* 761–767.

Hatsukami, D. K., Huber, M., Callies, A., & Skoog, K. (1993). Physical dependence on nicotine gum: Effect of duration of use. *Psychopharmacology, 111,* 449–456.

Helander, A., & Carlsson, S. (1990). Use of leukocyte aldehyde dehydrogenase activity to monitor inhibitory effect of disulfiram treatment in alcoholism. *Alcoholism: Clinical and Experimental Research, 14,* 48–52.

Henningfield, J. E., Stapleton, J. M., Benowitz, N. L., Grayson, R. F., & London, E. D. (1993). Higher levels of nicotine in arterial than in venous blood after cigarette smoking. *Drug and Alcohol Dependence, 33,* 23–29.

Hillbom, M., Tokola, R., Kuusela, V., Karkkainen, P., Kalli-Lemma, L., Pilke, A., & Kaste, M. (1989). Prevention of alcohol withdrawal seizures with carbamazepine and valproic acid. *Alcohol, 6,* 223–226.

Hjalmarson, A., Franzon, M., Westin, A., & Wilkund, O. (1994). Effect of nicotine nasal spray on smoking cessation. *Archives of Internal Medicine, 154,* 2567–2572.

Hughes, J. R. (1994). Non-nicotine pharmacotherapies for smoking cessation. *Journal of Drug Development, 9,* 197–203.

Hughes, J. R. (1996). Treatment of nicotine dependence. In C. R. Schuster, S. W. Gust, & M. J. Kuhar (Eds.), *Pharmacological aspects of drug dependence: Toward an integrative neurobehavioral approach* (pp. 599–618). New York: Springer-Verlag.

Humfleet, G., Hall, S., Reus, V., Sees, K., Munoz, R., & Triffleman, E. (1996). *The efficacy of nortriptyline as an adjunct to psychological treatment for smokers with and without depressive histories* (NIDA Research Monograph No. 162, p. 334). Washington, DC: U.S. Government Printing Office.

Hyytia, P., & Sinclair, S. D. (1993). Responding for oral ethanol after naloxone treatment by alcohol-preferring AA rats. *Alcoholism: Clinical and Experimental Research, 17,* 631–636.

Jasinski, D. R., Pevnick, J. S., & Griffith, J. D. (1978). Human pharmacology and abuse potential of the analgesic buprenorphine. *Archives of General Psychiatry, 35,* 510–516.

Jenkins, S. W., Warfield, N. A., Blaine, J. D., Cornish, J., Ling, W., Rosen, M. I., Urschel, H. III, Wesson, D., & Ziedonis, D. (1992). A pilot trial of gepirone vs. placebo in the treatment of cocaine dependency. *Psychopharmacology Bulletin, 28,* 21–26.

Johansson, C. J., Olsson, P., Bende, M., Carlsson, T., & Gunnarsson, P. O. (1991). Absolute bioavailability of nicotine applied to different nasal regions. *European Journal of Clinical Pharmacology, 41,* 585–588.

Johnson, R. E., Fudala, P. J., & Jaffe, J. H. (1992). A controlled trial of buprenorphine for opioid dependence. *Journal of the American Medical Association, 267,* 2750–2755.

Kampman, K., Volpicelli, J. R., Alterman, A., Cornish, J., Weinrieb, R., Epperson, L., Sparkman, T., & O'Brien, C. P. (1996). Amantadine in the early treatment of cocaine dependence: A double-blind, placebo-controlled trial. *Drug and Alcohol Dependence, 41,* 25–33.

Khan, A., Mumford, J. P., Rogers, G. A., & Beckford, H. (1997). Double-blind study of lofexidine and clonidine in the detoxification of opiate addicts in hospital. *Drug and Alcohol Dependence, 44,* 57–61.

Kleber, H. D. (1981). Detoxification from narcotics. In J. H. Lowinson & P. Ruiz (Eds.), *Substance abuse: Clinical problems and perspectives* (pp. 317–338). Baltimore: William & Wilkins.

Kleber, H. D., Topazian, M., Gaspari, J., Riordan, C. E., & Kosten, T. (1987). Clonidine and naltrexone in the outpatient treatment of heroin withdrawal. *American Journal of Drug and Alcohol Abuse, 13,* 1–17.

Koe, B. K. (1976). Molecular geometry of inhibitors of the uptake of catecholamines and serotonin in synaptosomal preparations of rat brain. *Journal of Pharmacology and Experimental Therapeutics, 199,* 649–661.

Kornet, M., Goosen, C., & Van Ree, J. M. (1991). Effect of naltrexone on alcohol consumption during chronic alcohol drinking and after a period of imposed abstinence in free choice drinking rhesus monkeys. *Psychopharmacology, 104,* 367–376.

Kosten, T. A., Kosten, T. R., Gawin, F. H., Gordon, L. T., Hogan, I. F., & Kleber, H. D. (1992). An open trial of sertraline for cocaine abuse. *American Journal on Addictions, 1,* 349–353.

Kosten, T. R., & Kleber, H. D. (1984). Strategies to improve compliance with narcotic antagonists. *American Journal of Drug and Alcohol Abuse, 10,* 249–266.

Kosten, T. R., & Kleber, H. D. (1988). Buprenorphine detoxification from opioid dependence: A pilot study. *Life Sciences, 42,* 635–641.

Kosten, T. R., Kleber, H. D., & Morgan, C. H. (1989). Treatment of cocaine abuse using buprenorphine. *Biological Psychiatry, 26,* 637–639.

Kosten, T. R., Krystal, J. H., Charney, D. S., Price, L. H., Morgan, C. H., & Kleber, H. D. (1989). Rapid from opioid dependence. *American Journal of Psychiatry, 146,* 1349.

Kosten, T. R., Morgan, C. M., Falcioni, J., & Schottenfeld, R. S. (1992). Pharmacotherapy for cocaine-abusing methadone-maintained patients using amantadine or desipramine. *Archives of General Psychiatry, 49,* 894–898.

Kosten, T. R., Schottenfeld, R. S., Ziedonis, D., & Falcioni, J. (1993). Buprenorphine vs. methadone maintenance for opioid dependence. *Journal of Nervous and Mental Disease, 181,* 358–364.

Kosten, T. R., Steinberg, M., & Diakogiannis, I. (1993). Crossover trial of mazindol for cocaine dependence. *American Journal on Addictions, 2,* 161–164.

Kranzler, H. R., Bauer, L. O., Hersh, D., & Klinghoffer, V. (1995). Carbamazepine treatment of cocaine dependence: A placebo-controlled trial. *Drug and Alcohol Dependence, 38,* 203–211.

Kranzler, H. R., Burleson, J. A., Del Boca, F. K., Babor, T. F., Korner, P., Brown, J., & Bohn M. (1994). Bupsirone treatment of anxious alcoholics. *Archives of General Psychiatry, 51,* 720–731.

Kraus, M. L., Gottlieb, L. D., Horwitz, R. L., & Anscher, M. (1985). Randomized clinical trial of atenolol in patients with alcohol withdrawal. *New England Journal of Medicine, 313,* 905–909.

Kuhar, M. J., Ritz, M. C., & Boja, J. W. (1991). The dopamine hypothesis of the reinforcing properties of cocaine. *Trends in Neurosciences, 14,* 299–302.

Lambie, D. G., Johnson, R. H., Vijayasen, M. E., & Whiteside, E. A. (1980). Sodium valproate in the treatment of the alcohol withdrawal syndrome. *Australian and New Zealand Journal of Psychiatry, 14,* 213–215.

Le, A. D., Quan, B., & Chow, S. (1993). Maintenance of naltrexone (N)-induced reduction in ethanol (E) intake by DGAVP. *Alcoholism: Clinical and Experimental Research, 17,* 481.

Lee, E. W., & D'Alonzo, G. E. (1993). Cigarette smoking, nicotine addiction, and its pharmacologic treatment. *Archives of Internal Medicine, 153,* 34–48.

Levin, F. R., & Lehman, A. F. (1991). Meta-analysis of desipramine as an adjunct in the treatment of cocaine addiction. *Journal of Clinical Psychopharmacology, 11,* 374–378.

Lewis, J. W. (1985). Buprenorphine. *Drug and Alcohol Dependence, 14,* 363–372.

Ling, W., Charuvastra, V. C., Kain, S. C., & Klett, C. J. (1976). Methadyl acetate and methadone as maintenance treatment for heroin addicts. *Archives of General Psychiatry, 33,* 709–712.

Littleton, J. (1995). Acamprosate in alcohol dependence: How does it work? *Addiction, 90,* 1179–1188.

Malcolm, R., Ballenger, J. C., Sturgis, E. T., & Anton, R. (1989). Double-blind controlled trial comparing carbamazepine to oxazepam treatment of alcohol withdrawal. *American Journal of Psychiatry, 146,* 617–621.

Malison, R. T., McCance, E. F., Carpenter, L. L., Baldwin, R. M., Seibyl J. P., Price, L. H., Kosten. T. R., & Innis, R. B. (1998). [123I]β-CIT SPECT imaging of dopamine transporter availability after mazindol administration in human cocaine addicts. *Psychopharmacology, 137,* 321–325.

Margolin, A., Avants, S. K., & Kosten, T. R. (1995). Mazindol for relapse prevention to cocaine abuse in methadone-maintained patients. *American Journal of Drug and Alcohol Abuse, 2,* 469–481.

Margolin, A., Kosten, T. R., Avants, S. K., Wilkins, J., Ling, W., Beckson, M., Arndt, I. O., Cornish, J., Ascher, J. A., & Li, S. H. (1995). A multicenter trial of bupropion for cocaine dependence in methadone-maintained patients. *Drug and Alcohol Dependence, 40,* 125–131.

Margolin, A., Kosten, T., Petrakis, I., Avants, S. K., & Kosten, T. (1991). Bupropion reduces cocaine abuse in methadone-maintained patients. *Archives of General Psychiatry, 48,* 87.

McCance-Katz, E. F., Kosten, T. R., & Jatlow, P. I. (in press). Disulfiram effects on acute cocaine administration. *Drug and Alcohol Dependence.*

Meyer, R. E. (1986). How to understand the relationship between psychopathology and addictive disorders: Another example of the chicken and the egg. In R. E. Meyer (Ed.), *Psychopathology and addictive disorders* (pp. 3–16). New York: Guilford Press.

Montoya, I. D., Preston, K., Rotham, R., Cone, E., & Gorelick, D. A. (1994). Safety and efficacy of bupropion in combination with bromocriptine for treatment of cocaine dependence. In *Problems of drug dependence, 1995. Proceedings of the 57th annual scientific meeting of the College on Problems of Drug Dependence* (NIDA Research Monograph No. 153, p. 304). Washington, DC: U.S. Government Printing Office.

Moscovitz, H., Brookoff, D., & Nelson, L. (1993). A randomized trial of bromocriptine for cocaine users presenting to the emergency department. *Journal of General Internal Medicine, 8,* 1–4.

Naranjo, C. A., Bremner, K. E., & Lanctot, K. L. (1995). Effects of citalopram and a brief psychosocial intervention on alcohol intake, dependence and problems. *Addiction, 90,* 87–99.

O'Connor, P. G., Waugh, M. E., Carroll, K. M., Rounsaville, B. J., Diakogiannis, I. A., & Schottenfeld, R. S. (1995). Primary care-based ambulatory opioid detoxification: The results of a clinical trial. *Journal of General Internal Medicine, 10,* 255–260.

Oliveto, A. H., Kosten, T. R., Schottenfeld, R., Ziedonis, D., & Falcioni, J. (1994) A comparison of cocaine use in buprenorphine- and methadone-maintained cocaine users. *American Journal on Addictions, 3,* 43–48.

O'Malley, S. S., Jaffe, A. J., Chang, G., Rode, S., Schottenfeld, R. S., Meyer, R. E., & Rounsaville, B. J. (1996). Six-month follow-up of naltrexone and psychotherapy for alcohol dependence. *Archives of General Psychiatry, 53,* 217–224.

O'Malley, S. S., Jaffe, A. J., Chang, G., Schottenfeld, R. S., Meyer, R. E., & Rounsaville, B. J. (1992). Naltrexone and coping skills therapy for alcohol dependence: A controlled study. *Archives of General Psychiatry, 49,* 881–887.

Palmer, K. J., Buckley, M. M., & Faulds, D. (1992). Transdermal nicotine: A review of its pharmacodynamic and pharmacokinetic properties, and therapeutic efficacy as an aid to smoking cessation. *Drugs, 44,* 498–529.

Post, R. M., & Kopanda, R. T. (1976). Cocaine kindling and psychosis. *American Journal of Psychiatry, 133,* 627–634.

Quigley, A. J., Bredemeyer, D. E., & Seow, S. S. (1984). A case of buprenorphine abuse. *Medical Journal of Australia, 142,* 425–426.

Richardson, N., & Roberts, D. (1991). Fluoxetine pretreatment reduces breaking points on a progressive ratio schedule reinforced by intravenous cocaine self-administration in the rat. *Life Sciences, 49,* 833–840.

Ritz, M. C., Cohen, E., & Kuhar, M. (1990). Cocaine inhibition of ligand binding at dopamine, norepinephrine and serotonin transporters: A structure-activity study. *Life Sciences, 46,* 635–645.

Rose, J. E. (1996). Nicotine addiction and its treatment. *Annual Review of Medicine, 47,* 493–507.

Rose, J. E., Behm, F. M., Westman, E. C., Levin, E. D., Stein, R. M., & Ripka, G. V. (1994). Mecamylamine combined with nicotine skin patch facilitates smoking cessation beyond nicotine patch treatment alone. *Clinical Pharmacology and Therapeutics, 56,* 86–99.

Rounsaville, B. J. (1995). Can psychotherapy rescue naltrexone treatment of opioid addiction? In L. S. Onken, J. D. Blaine, & J. J. Boren (Eds.), *Integrating behavior therapies with medication in the treatment of drug dependence* (NIDA Research

Monograph No. 150, pp. 37–52). Washington, DC: U.S. Government Printing Office.

Roy-Byrne, P. P., Ward, N. G., & Donnelly, P. J. (1989). Valproate in anxiety and withdrawal syndromes. *Journal of Clinical Psychiatry, 50*(Suppl.), 44–48.

Sachs, D. P. L. (1991). Advances in smoking cessation treatment. *Current Pulmonology, 12,* 139–198.

Sachs, D. P. L. (1995). Effectiveness of the 4-mg dose of nicotine polacrilex for the initial treatment of high-dependent smokers. *Archives of Internal Medicine, 155,* 1973–1980.

Sass, H., Soyka, M., Mann, K., & Zieglgansberger, W. (1996). Relapse prevention by acamprosate. *Archives of General Psychiatry, 53,* 673–680.

Schneider, N. G., Olmstead, R., Mody, F. R., Doan, K., Franzon, M., & Steinberg, C. (1995). Efficacy of a nicotine nasal spray in smoking cessation: A placebo-controlled, double-blind trial. *Addiction, 90,* 1671–1682.

Schottenfeld, R. S., Pakes, J., Ziedonis, D. M., & Kosten, T. (1993). Buprenorphine: Dose related effects on cocaine and opiate use in cocaine-abusing opioid-dependent humans. *Biological Psychiatry, 34,* 66–74.

Self, D. W., Barnhart, W. J., Lehman, D. A., & Nestler, E. J. (1996). Opposite modulation of cocaine-seeking behavior by D1 and D2-like dopamine receptor agonists. *Science, 271,* 1586–1589.

Sellers, E. M., Higgins, G. A., & Sobell, M. B. (1992). 5-HT and alcohol abuse. *Trends in Pharmacological Sciences, 13,* 69–75.

Sellers, E. M., Naranjo, C. A., Harrison, M., Devenyi, P., Roach, C., & Sykora, K. (1983). Diazepam loading: Simplified treatment of alcohol withdrawal. *Clinical Pharmacology and Therapeutics, 34,* 822–826.

Senay, E. C., Dorus, W., Goldberg, F., & Thornton, W. (1977). Withdrawal from methadone maintenance: Rate of withdrawal and expectation. *Archives of General Psychiatry, 34,* 361–367.

Shi, J. M., O'Connor, P. G., Constantino, J. A., Carroll, K. M., Schottenfeld, R. S., & Rounsaville, B. J. (1993). *Three methods of ambulatory opiate detoxification: Preliminary results of a randomized clinical trial* (NIDA Research Monograph No. 132, p. 309). Washington, DC: U.S. Government Printing Office.

Sholar, M. B., Lukas, S. E., Kouri, K. M., & Mendelson, J. H. (1994). Acute and chronic amantadine pre-treatment attenuates some of cocaine's effect in human subjects. In L. S. Harris (Ed.), *Problems of drug dependence, 1993. Proceedings of the 55th annual scientific meeting of the College on Problems of Drug Dependence* (NIDA Research Monograph No. 141, p. 431). Washington, DC: U.S. Government Printing Office.

Stine, S. M., Krystal, J. H., Kosten, T. R., & Charney, D. S. (1995). Mazindol treatment for cocaine dependence. *Drug and Alcohol Dependence, 39,* 245–252.

Stolerman, I. P., Goldfarb, T., Fink, R., & Jarrick, M. E. (1973). Influencing cigarette smoking with nicotine antagonists. *Psychopharmacologia, 28,* 247–259.

Strain, E. C., Stitzer, M. L., Liebson, I. A., & Bigelow, G. E. (1994). Buprenorphine versus methadone in the treatment of opioid-dependent cocaine users. *Psychopharmacology, 116,* 401–406.

Sutherland, G., Stapleton, J. A., Russell, M. A. H., Jarvis, M. J., Hajek, P., Belcher, M., & Feyerabend, C. (1992). Randomized controlled trial of nasal nicotine spray in smoking cessation. *Lancet, 340,* 324–329.

Tennant, F. S., & Sagherian, A. A. (1987). Double-blind comparison of amantadine and bromocriptine for ambulatory withdrawal from cocaine dependence. *Archives of Internal Medicine, 147,* 109–112.

Tollefson, G. D., Montague-Clouse, J., & Tollefson, S. L. (1992). Treatment of comorbid generalized anxiety in a recently detoxified alcohol population with a selective serotonergic drug (buspirone). *Journal of Clinical Psychopharmacology, 12,* 19–26.

Van Etten, M. L., Higgins, S. T., Budney, A. J., Bickel, W. K., Hughes, J. R., & Foerg, F. (1994). Disulfiram therapy in patients abusing cocaine and alcohol. In L. S. Harris (Ed.), *Problems of drug dependence, 1993. Proceedings of the 55th annual scientific meeting of the College on Problems of Drug Dependence* (NIDA Research Monograph No. 141, p. 443). Washington, DC: U.S. Government Printing Office.

Vining, E., Kosten, T. R., & Kleber, H. D. (1988). Clinical utility of rapid clonidine naltrexone detoxification for opioid abusers. *British Journal of Addictions, 83,* 567–575.

Volpicelli, J., Alterman, A. I., O'Brien, C. P., & Hayashida, M. (1992). Naltrexone in the treatment of alcohol dependence. *Archives of General Psychiatry, 49,* 867–880.

Walsh, S. L., Preston, K. L., Sullivan, J. T., Fromme, R., & Bigelow, G. E. (1994). Fluoxetine alters the effects of intravenous cocaine in humans. *Journal of Clinical Psychopharmacology, 14,* 396–407.

Weddington, W. W., Brown, B. S., Haertzen, C. A., Mahaffrey, J. R., Kolar, A. F., & Jaffe, J. H. (1991). Comparison of amantadine and desipramine combined with psychotherapy for treatment of cocaine dependence. *American Journal of Drug and Alcohol Abuse, 17,* 137–152.

Whitworth, A. B., Fischer, F., Lesch, O. M., Nimmerrichter, A., Oberbauer, H., Platz, T., Potgieter, A., Walter, H., & Fleischhaker, W. W. (1996). Comparison of acamprosate and placebo in long-term treatment of alcohol dependence. *Lancet, 347,* 1438–1442.

Wright, C., & Moore, R. D. (1990). Disulfiram treatment of alcoholism. *American Journal of Medicine, 88,* 647–655.

Zeise, M. L., Kasparov, S., Capogna, M., & Zieglgansberger, W. (1993). Acamprosate (calciumacetylhomotaurinate) decreases postsynaptic potentials in the rat neocortex: Possible involvement of excitatory amino acid receptors. *European Journal of Pharmacology, 231,* 47–52.

Index